FREEMAN SNOW

CASES AND OPINIONS
ON
INTERNATIONAL LAW
WITH
NOTES AND A SYLLABUS

Elibron Classics
www.elibron.com

Elibron Classics series.

ISBN 1-4021-0912-1 (paperback)
ISBN 1-4021-2408-2 (hardcover)

This Elibron Classics Replica Edition is an unabridged facsimile
of the edition published in 1893 by the Boston Book Company, Boston.

CASES AND OPINIONS

ON

INTERNATIONAL LAW

WITH

NOTES AND A SYLLABUS.

BY

FREEMAN SNOW, Ph.D., LL.B.

INSTRUCTOR IN INTERNATIONAL LAW IN HARVARD UNIVERSITY.

BOSTON:
THE BOSTON BOOK COMPANY.
1893.

PREFACE.

THE design of this work was formed some years since, while teaching the subject of International Law in the United States Naval Academy, and the greater part of the compilation was made during a subsequent residence of three years in France, Germany, and England; but other duties have, till the present time, prevented its completion.

The object has been primarily to provide a convenient collection of materials relating to International Law, for the use of students. To avoid the method of instruction by lectures alone, and the even less satisfactory method of recitation from text-books, it is believed, that the "case system," introduced into the Harvard Law School a score of years ago, by Professor Langdell, offers a happy substitute. Indeed, having employed that system for the last half dozen years, in classes in International Law, in Harvard University, I am thoroughly convinced that it is well adapted to that subject; the only drawback has been the difficulty of finding the necessary materials in a convenient form.

By this method, the student is called upon to take an active part in the exercises of the lecture room; he is to report briefly the facts and judgment in a given case, and then is to explain the principles and their application, and must maintain his position against the criticisms of the instructor, and the other members of the class. The student should thus acquire a firmer grasp of the subject than he can get from the study of text-books alone; he is, moreover, more interested in his work, as, I believe, experience has shown wherever the system has been introduced. These cases are, to a large degree, the original sources of the rules of International Law; and they furnish the opportunity of becoming familiar with the ideas of the eminent men—judges and statesmen—who have controlled the development of this law. Many of the cases, in addition to deciding the single point at issue, are admirable expositions of general principles, and give, besides, a concise history of the subject.

It is not proposed, however, to discard text-books. It is indeed the justly celebrated authors of treatises on International Law who have analyzed and systematized the subject, and who have reduced it to a science. A collection of cases and opinions, moreover, must necessarily leave many gaps, to be filled by means of text-books or lectures. And it is the purpose of the syllabus—a leading feature of this book—to make available the opinions of a number of the most eminent writers, of different countries, by grouping references to their works under specific heads. It will thus be made possible to compare their opinions, in many cases, with the sources upon which they all rely.

It is thought, further, that a collection of leading cases and opinions may prove to be a convenience for those who are called upon to deal with the practical questions of International Law, viz., Lawyers, Legislators, and Diplomatists. With this end in view, it has been the almost invariable rule to give the decisions of courts in the exact language of the judges, though necessarily leaving out, in some cases, the less pertinent parts. In this respect this volume differs radically from Mr. Pitt Cobbett's excellent work upon the same subject.

FREEMAN SNOW.

CAMBRIDGE, MASS.,
Sept. 1st, 1893.

TABLE OF CONTENTS.

CHAPTER III.

JURISDICTION ON THE HIGH SEAS.

CHAPTER IV.

NATIONALITY.

PART II.

International Relations as Modified by War.

CHAPTER I.

MEASURES SHORT OF WAR.

CHAPTER II.

EFFECTS OF WAR AS BETWEEN ENEMIES.

CHAPTER III.

RELATIONS BETWEEN BELLIGERENTS AND NEUTRALS.

APPENDIX.

TABLE OF CASES.

SYLLABUS.

[*Explanation of References.*—The references in this Syllabus to the standard modern authors, are to the following editions of their works:—

Bluntschli, 2d French Ed., translated by M. C. Lardy (1874); Calvo, 5th Ed. (1888); Creasey, "First Platform of International Law," (1876); Hall, 3d Ed. (1890); Halleck, Ed. by Sir S. Baker (1878); Heffter, 4th French Ed. by F. H. Geffcken, translated by J. Bergson (1883); Phillimore, 3d Ed. (1879-); Walker, T. A. "The Science of International Law" (1893); Wheaton, Ed. by Lawrence (1863), and by Dana (1866), referred to by title Wheaton (L) and (D); Woolsey, Ed. by T. S. Woolsey (1890); Wharton's "Digest of International Law" will be referred to as "Wharton's Digest."

This collection of Cases and Opinions will be cited as Cases and Op.]

INTRODUCTION.

1. **Definitions of International Law, or the Law of Nations.** (Halleck, I., 41; Wheaton (L), 26, (D), 23; Hall, 1; Woolsey, 2; Creasey, 1; Calvo, I., 139.)

2. **Origin of the terms "Law of Nations," and "International Law."** Compare with the terms "*Jus Gentium*," "*Jus Naturale*," "Droit des gens," "Droit international," "Völkerrecht." (Wheaton (L), 14–21 and notes, (D), 4–6, 16–21 and note 7; Woolsey, 10; Creasey, 17–21.)

3. **Is International Law a branch of true Law? Objections by Austin and his followers to the term "law" as used in "international law," on the ground that there is no superior power to enforce it: it has no "sanction." In accordance with this view see,** (Austin's Jurisprudence, abridged Ed., pp. 5-18, 59-63, 74, 85; Stephen's History of the Criminal Law, II., 32 *et seq.*; Holland's "Jurisprudence," 96–97, 291–293.)

Opposed to this view (Sir Henry Maine: "International Law," 26–53; T. J. Lawrence: "Essays on International Law", 1; Hall, 14–17; Bluntschli, 2–10; Woolsey, 26–29; Walker, 1–40, 45–56; Creasey, 70–76.)

4. **The Sources and Nature of International Law.** (Wheaton, chapter I.; Halleck, I., chapter II.; Hall, 1–14; Bluntschli, 1–19; Sir H. Maine, 1–25; Calvo, I., 139–167; Phillimore, I., chapter III.)

5. **Historical sketch of International Law.** (Halleck, chapter I., Walker, 57–112; Calvo, I., 1–137. For extended works, see Ward's Law of Nations; Wheaton's History of the Law of Nations; Laurent: L'Histoire de l'Humanité, etc.)

6. **International Law is a part of the law of States.** (Cases and Op., 1–4; Woolsey, § 29.)

7. **The leading writers on International Law.** (Calvo, I., 27–32, 45–46, 51–55, 61–63, 70–73, 101–120; Halleck, I., chapter I.)

8. **Private International Law, or the Conflict of Laws.** (Hall, 54; Woolsey, §§ 73–74; Calvo, I., 120–125.)

PART I.

INTERNATIONAL LAW IN TIME OF PEACE.

I. Sovereign States—De facto States.

(*a*) *Sovereign States.*

9. **Sovereign States are the Subjects or Persons of International Law.** (Hall, 18–19; Bluntschli, Arts. 17–27; Phillimore, I., 79; Heffter, 43; Wheat. (D), § 16.)

10. **Definition and Nature of Sovereign States.** (Wheaton (L), 31–33, 58 (D), 29–31; Hall, 18–21, 24, 25; Bluntschli, Arts. 18–21, 64; Woolsey, 34–36; Halleck, I., 58–59; Phillimore, I., 81–85; Creasey, 6, 93; Calvo, I., 168–170; Heffter, 45.)

11. **Distinction between Internal Sovereignty and External Sovereignty of States.** (Wheaton (D), 31 (L), 35 ; Bluntschli, Art. 64 ; Holland : Jurisprudence, 40, 276, 295.)

12. **Internal changes in a State do not affect its standing in International Law.** (Hall, 22, 23 ; Wheaton (L), 39, (D), 33–34 ; Bluntschli, Arts. 39–40; Creasey, 99–109 ; Woolsey, 38, 39 ; Phillimore, I., 202–212.)

13. **The fundamental Rights and Duties of States.** (Hall, 45–47 ; Halleck, I., 80–82 ; Wheaton (L), 115, (D), 89, 90.)

14. **Classification of States: "Centralized States," "Personal Union," "Real Union," (Bunderstaat), "Confederate Union," (Staatenbund), Protected State, Neutralised State.** (Hall, 25–31 ; Bluntschli, Arts. 70–76 ; Wheaton (D), 40–41, 73, 78, 82, and note 32 (L), 71–76 ; Halleck, I., 62–66 ; Phillimore, I., 94–101 ; Calvo, I., 173–179 ; Creasey, 135–142.)

15. **The Equality of States.** (Wheaton (L), 58, (D), 52 ; Halleck, I., 99–123 ; Heffter, 65–70 ; Woolsey, § 54 ; Bluntschli, Art. 81 ; T. J. Lawrence, Essays, No. 5.)

16. **Date of the commencement of States.** (Hall, 87–90 ; Wheaton (L), 46–47 ; (D), 41 ; Bluntschli, Art. 29 ; Halleck, I., 74 and note 1.)

17. **Effects of the recognition of a new State by the parent State, and by third States.** (Hall, 88–93 ; Bluntschli, Art. 30 ; Wheaton (D), 32 ; Halleck, I., 72 and note 1.)

18. **When is the recognition by third States of a new State claiming independence, proper?** (Cases and Op., 13 ; Hall, 90–93 ; Bluntschli, Arts. 31–35 ; Halleck, I., 72–74 ; Wheaton (L), 46–47 ; (D), 41–46 and note 16 ; Creasey, 677–681 ; Phillimore, II.)

19. **Methods of Recognition—The Congo State.** (Hall, 88, note 193, § 26.*)

20. **The effect of a change of Sovereignty upon public rights and obligations.** (Case of the Texan Bonds, Cases and Op., 18, and 20, n.; Opinion of Kent, *Ib.*, 21 ; Hall, 102–103 ;

Wheaton (D), 42–49; (L), 48–53; Creasey, 144–146; Phillimore, I., 211; Woolsey, § 38.)

21. **Effect of change of Sovereignty upon private rights.** (Case of U. S. v. Percheman, Cases and Op., 21; Opinion of Bayard, *Ib.*, 22.)

(*b*) *De Facto States.*

22. **What are de facto States, or Belligerent Communities?** (Hall, 31–33; Halleck, I., 68.)

23. **Recognition of Belligerency.** (Opinion of Dana, Cases and Op., 24; The *Lilla*, *Ib.*, 27; and see Wheaton (L), 40 note, (D), note 15; Hall, 35–37; Wharton's Digest, I., § 69; Woolsey, § 41.)

24. **Have Belligerent Communities any legal right to recognition by Sovereign States?** (Hall, 33–35; Bluntschli, Art. 512, n.)

25. **Forms of recognition.** (Hall, 37–39; Wheaton (D), 37, n.)

26. **Recognition of the Confederate States, 1861.** (Hall, 39–42; Woolsey, § 180; Bluntschli, in R. D. J., II., 462; Wheaton (D), 37, note.)

27. **Succession to the rights of Belligerent Communities.** (U. S. v. Prioleau, Cases and Op., 28; U. S. v. McRae, *Ib.*, 32, n.)

28. **When a Belligerent Community becomes independent, what are its relations to the contract rights and duties of the parent State, as to (1) Treaty obligations, (2) Property, (3) Debts.** (Hall, 94–102; Bluntschli, Arts., 47, 48.)

29. **Right of the United States to the British American Fisheries.** (Hall, 97–99; Wharton's Digest, III., § 302.)

II. The Territorial Property of a State.

(*a*). *Extent and Nature of Territorial Property.*

30. **In what does the territorial property of a State consist?** (Hall, 104, § 30; Wheaton (D), § 162.)

31. **What is the nature of the proprietary title of a State in (1) the land owned by individuals, (2) public lands, (3) navy yards, arsenals, etc., (4) lakes and rivers, (5) the marginal sea.** (Halleck, I., 128–131; Bluntschli, Arts. 276–277; Wheaton (D), § 164; Hall, 151.)

32. **Eminent Domain; "Absolute" and "Paramount" rights in the soil; "Property" and "Domain."** (Halleck, I., 128–130; Wheaton (D), § 163.)

(*b*). *Acquisition of Territory.*

33. **Modes of acquiring territory.** (Hall, § 31; Halleck, I., 131; Wheaton (D), § 161.)

34. **Title to territory based on discovery.** (Case of Johnson v. McIntosh, Cases and Op., 6.)

35. **Title to territory, based on prior discovery of the coast, of mouths of rivers, upon occupation, exploration, and contiguity.** (1) The Oregon Territory, Cases and Op., 9; (2) Delagoa Bay, *Ib.*, 11; (3) Texas, Hall, 111–113.)

36. **Inchoate title acquired by discovery. Occupation, to give title, requires (1) intention to occupy, (2) continuous occupation, (3) to be a State act, or one adopted by the State.** (Hall, 106–107; Bluntschli, Arts. 278–279: Phillimore, I., 329; Walker, 159, 160.)

37. **Abandonment of territory once occupied.** (Santa Lucia, Cases and Op., 12; Hall, 118.)

38. **To what extent inland does the discovery of the coast give rights? The discovery of the mouth of a river?** (Cases and Op., 12, note; Hall, 108–110, and 108, note 2; Walker, 161.)

39. **Tendency to change the law of occupation—Berlin Conference, 1885.** (Hall, § 33.*)

40. **Does prescription give a valid title to territory by the rules of International Law?** (Hall, 121–122, § 36; Philli-

more, I., 353–368; Wheaton (D), 239, and note 101 (L), 303; Creasey, 249–255.)

41. **Acquisition of territory by accretion.** (Cases: The *Anna*, Cases and Op., 393; Opinion of Attorney-General Cushing, *Ib.*, 16; Phillimore, I., 342–345; Hall, 123; Creasey, 241–249; Bluntschli, Arts. 294–295.)

42. **Acquisition of territory by conquest or cession.** (Phillimore, I., 369–387; Bluntschli, Arts., 285–286.)

(c) *Acquisition of Rights in Foreign Territory.*

43. **Servitudes in International Law.** (Phillimore, I., 388–392; Bluntschli, Arts. 353–359; Hall, 157, note 2; Creasey, 255–259.)

44. **The navigation of rivers.** (Cases: 1. Opinion of Wheaton, Cases and Op., 32; 2. Navigation of the Mississippi, *Ib.*, 33; 3. Navigation of the St. Lawrence, *Ib.*, 35; 4. European rivers, *Ib.*, 40; Hall, 131–139 and notes; Bluntschli, Arts. 311–315; Woolsey, 79–83; Halleck, I., 147–152.)

45. **Protectorates over semi-civilized peoples.** (Hall, 127, § 38.*)

(d) *Boundaries.*

46. **The Political Department of the Government, in the United States, determines what are the boundaries under treaties.** (Foster v. Neilson, Cases and Op., 14; *in re* Cooper—The Sayward Case, 143 U. S. Rep., 472.)

47. **River boundaries are how determined?** (Opinion of Attorney-General Cushing, Cases and Op., 16; Bluntschli, Arts. 298–300.)

48. **How are boundaries usually determined in the case of lakes and mountains?** (Hall, 125–126; Bluntschli, Arts., 297, 301–303.)

(e). *Territorial Waters of a State.*

49. **The history of attempts to appropriate the seas, or por-**

tions of them; the contest between mare clausum and mare liberum. (Hall, 139–151, § 40; Wheaton's History of the Law of Nations, 152–162; Calvo, I., 471–476; Phillimore, I., 247–256; Creasey, 226–231; Woolsey, § 59; Cauchy (Ed., 1862), II., 92–124; Wheaton (D), note No. 113; Walker, 163–171.)

50. **The origin of the rule limiting the territorial right of a State in the sea to a marine league from the shore. Terrae dominium finitur ubi finitur armorum vis."** (Phillimore, I., 274 *et seq.;* Hall, 151–153; Wheaton (D), § 189 and note No. 105; Creasey, 233–240; Walker, 171–175; The Case of The Queen v. Keyn, Cases and Op., 55; Woolsey, 68–70; Halleck, I., §§ 13–14; Calvo, I., 477–480; Wharton's Dig., § 32.)

51. **Bays, Gulfs, and Straits, which are more than six miles wide.** (1. The Sound Dues, Cases and Op., 41; 2. The Bosphorus and the Dardanelles, *Ib.*, 43; 3. Regina v. Cunningham, *Ib.*, 44; 4. Cable Co. v. Telegraph Co., *Ib.*, 45; 5 Manchester v. Massachusetts, *Ib.*, 47; 6. The Grange, *Ib.*, 47 n., see also: Hall, 153–156; Bluntschli, Art. 309; Perels, 42–46; Woolsey, 76–79; Halleck, I., 139–145; Calvo, I., 480–506; Wharton's Dig., § 28, 29.)

52. **Interoceanic Canals—Suez Canal neutralized.** (Calvo, I., 507–516; Boyd's Wheaton, § 205 b. & c.; T. J. Lawrence, Essays, 37.)

III. Territorial Jurisdiction.

(a) *Doctrine of Exterritoriality—Exception to the Rule of Exclusive Territorial Jurisdiction.*

53. **Sovereigns are exempt in their persons and property from the jurisdiction of foreign courts of law.** (1. Vavasseur v. Krupp, Cases and Op., 72; 2. De Haber v. Queen of Portugal, *Ib.*, 76; 3 Prioleau v. U. S. and Andrew Johnson, *Ib.*, 77; 4. U. S. v. Wagner, *Ib.*, 79; 5. other cases, *Ib.*, 82, note. And see: Hall, 162–167; Phillimore, II., 133–155; Bluntschli, Arts. 129–134.)

54. **Diplomatic Agents—Immunities from Criminal Jurisdiction.**

(1. Bishop of Ross, Cases and Op., 83; 2. Mendoza, *Ib.*, 85; 3. Da Sa. *Ib.*, 86; 4. Gyllenborg, *Ib.*, 87; 5. Cellamare, *Ib.*, 88. And see: Hall, 168–170; Halleck, I., 287 298; Phillimore, II., 199–218.)

55. **Diplomatic Agents—Immunities from Civil Jurisdiction.** (1. Ambassador of Peter the Great, Cases and Op., 89; 2. Taylor v. Best, *Ib.*, 90; 3. Wheaton's Case, *Ib.*, 94; 4. Baron de Wrech, *Ib.*, 97; 5 Dubois, *Ib.*, 98; 6 Dillon, *Ib.*, 99; 7. Other cases, *Ib.*, 102, note. See also: Hall, 170–179; Halleck, I., 285–287; Bluntschli, Arts. 135–153; Phillimore, II., 219–240; Wheaton, (D), 299–320, (L), 392–416.)

56. **Armed Forces and Ships of War in foreign territory are not subject to the local jurisdiction.** (1. Exchange v. McFaddon, Cases and Op., 103; 2. The Constitution, *Ib.*, 114 and 115, note. And see: Hall, 182–195; Wheaton (D), § 100 and notes, Nos. 61 and 63; Wharton's Dig., § 36; Halleck I., 176–190; Bluntschli, Art. 321; Phillimore, I., 476–483.)

57. **Public ships other than ships of war are not subject to civil process in foreign ports.** (The *Parlement Belge*, Cases and Op., 116 and 120, note; Hall, § 57.)

58. **Merchant vessels are not, as a general rule, exempt from the local jurisdiction, in foreign ports.** (1. The *Newton* and the *Sally*, Cases and Op., 121; 2. The *Tempest*, *Ib.*, 122; 3. *L'Anemone*, *Ib.*, 124; 4. Wildenhus, *Ib.*, 126; 5 Ellis v. Mitchell, *Ib.*, 133; 6. The Creole, *Ib.*, 136; 7. Other cases, *Ib.*, 132, note. And see Hall, 198–201; Halleck, I., 190–192; Bluntschli; Phillimore, I., 483–487.)

59. **Reasons for the fiction of Exterritoriality—The reasons usually given criticised.** (Hall, 196, 197; Wheaton (D), 303, 304, note.)

(*b*) *Right of Asylum.*

60. **Legations do not, as a rule, grant asylum to political refugees nor to fugitives from justice—Exception, in the case of Spanish American States.** (1. Duke of Ripperda, Cases and Op., 139; 2. U. S. v. Jeffers, *Ib.*, 140; 3. Opinion of Secretary Fish, *Ib.*, 142. See also: Hall, 176–179; Bluntschli, Arts. 151, 200, 201.)

61. **Whether ships of war may grant asylum to political refugees, opinions differ. It is the common practice in Spanish American waters.**—(John Brown Cases and Op., 144 and 146, note.)

62. **Merchant ships, having no immunities from foreign jurisdiction, by International Law, cannot properly grant asylum to political or other refugees.** (1. Sotelo, Cases and Op., 147 ; 2. Opinion of Lord Aberdeen, *Ib.*, 148 ; 3. Gomez, *Ib.*, 149 ; 4. Barrundia, *Ib.*, 150, note ; J. B. Moore, in the Political Science Quarterly for 1892.)

(*c*) *Other Questions of Territorial Jurisdiction.*

63. **Jurisdiction over passing vessels.** (Hall, 201–203 and notes ; The Queen v. Keyn.)

64. **Are aliens exempt from military duty?** (Hall, 204–206 ; Bluntschli, Art. 391 ; Wharton's Digest, § 202.)

65. **Are offenses committed by foreigners, beyond the limits of a State, subject to the Jurisdiction of its Courts?** (Case of Cutting, Cases and Op., 172 and 174, note ; Hall, 206–209 and notes ; Wharton's Philosophy of Crim. Law, 309 *et seq.* ; Fiore, in R. D. I., XI., 302–319.)

66. **Criminal Jurisdiction of the State Courts in the United States.** (U. S. v. Bevans, 3 Wheaton's Rep., 336 at 386.)

67. **Extradition of fugitives from Justice—1. It is not a duty under International Law, in the absence of treaty—2. In the United States it is exclusively a Federal question—3. A person extradited is to be tried for that offense only for which he was extradited.** (1. U. S. v. Rauscher, Cases and Op., 151 and 157, note ; 2. Arguelles, Moore, on Extradition, I., 33, Spear, on extradition, 13–14 ; 3. *Ex parte* Holmes, Moore I., 55–58 ; Spear, 20 ; Winslow, Moore, I., 196, 212.)

68. **As to the surrender, under extradition treaties, by a State of its own citizens.** (Case of Trimble, Cases and Op., 158 and 160, note ; Moore, on Extradition, I., 152–193.)

69. **States do not, as a rule, surrender persons charged with political or military offenses—What is a political offense?** (1. Cazo, Cases and Op., 161 ; 2. St. Albans Raid, *Ib.*, 162 ;

3. *In re* Castioni, *Ib.*, 168 and 171, note; Moore, I., 303–326; Heffter, § 63; Bluntschli, Art. 394; Walker, 236–238.)

70. **Leading works on Extradition.** (Billot: Traite de l'Extradition, 1874; S. Spear, 1879; E. Clarke, ; J. B. Moore, 1891; De Stieglitz; L. Lammasch.)

71. **Extraterritorial acts of persons by order of their Government.** (Case of McLeod, Cases and Op., 175; Hall, 213–219; Wheaton (L), 189, note.)

82. **The Extraterritorial acts by a State in self-defense.** (1. The Caroline, Cases and Op., 177; 2. Seizure of St. Marks, *Ib.*, 178; 3. The *Virginius*, *Ib.*, 179. See Hall, 265–274.)

73. **Responsibility for injury to foreigners by civil commotions and mob violence.** (The New Orleans Riot, 1851, Cases and Op., 181; New Orleans Mob, 1891, *Ib.*, 183, note; James Bryce, in the New Review for May, 1891; Calvo, 4th Ed., III., 142–156; Bluntschli, Art. 380 bis; Hall, 218–219.)

IV. Jurisdiction on the High Seas.

74. **Is the jurisdiction of a State over its citizens and property on the high seas exclusive?** (Hall, 243–244; Wheaton (D), §§ 106–107).

75. **Theory of the territoriality of merchant vessels.** (Hall, 244–251; Bluntschli, Art. 317; Heffter, § 78.)

76. **Impressment of Seamen.** (Wheaton (D), § 108–109 and note 67.)

77. **Jurisdiction over merchant vessels on the high seas.** (1. The *Atalanta*, Cases and Op., 184; 2. John Anderson, *Ib.*, 185; 3. Regina v. Leslie, *Ib.*, 187; 4. The *Belgenland*, *Ib.*, 189.)

78. **Municipal Seizures beyond the Three-mile Limit.** (Case of Church v. Hubbart, Cases and Op., 193 and 194, note; Argument of E. J. Phelps before the Behring Sea Tri-

bunal, Am. Case, 150; Act of Congress, March 2, 1797, § 27; Dana's note to Wheaton, No. 108; Boyd's Wheaton, § 179*a*, Wharton's Digest, I., pp. 105, 106, 109–112.)

79. **Piracy—Definition and character of Piracy jure gentium.** (1. Opinion of Sir L. Jenkins, Cases and Op., 195; 2. U. S. v. Smith, *Ib.*, 196; 3. Other cases in the U. S. Sup. Court are, U. S. v. Palmer, 3 Wh., 610; U. S. v. Klintock, 5 Wh., 152; U. S. v. Pirates, *Ib.*, 185; U. S. v. Holmes, *Ib.*, 412. See also: Lawrence's note to Wheaton, No. 79; Hall, 252–261; Phillimore, I., 489 *et seq.*; Bluntschli, Arts. 343–352.)

80. **May Rebels and Insurgents be regarded as Pirates? Piracy by Municipal Law.** (1. U. S. v. The *Ambrose Light*, Cases and Op., 200 and 204, note; 2. The Magellan Pirates, *Ib.*, 205; 3. The *Montezuma*, *Ib.*, 206; 4. The *Huascar*, *Ib.*, 208. See also: U. S. v. Baker, 5 Blatch., 6, and Wharton's Dig., III., 464; The *Chesapeake*, *Ib.*, I., 72; The Carthagenian Insurgents, *Ib.*, III., 466, and Hall, 261. And see: Hall, 261–264; Calvo, §§ 1146–1148; Woolsey, § 145; Wheaton (D), 196, note.)

81. **The Slave Trade is not Piracy jure gentium.** (Case of *Le Louis*, Cases and Op., 209; The *Antelope*, 10 Wheaton, 66. See also: Wheaton (D), §§ 125–133, and notes 85–89; Woolsey, § 146.)

V. Intervention.

82. **Character of Intervention—Conditions of.** (Hall, 281–283; Bluntschli, Art. 474; Wheaton (D), § 63; Wharton's Dig., I., § 45; Phillimore, I., 553–638; Heffter, 108–111; Creasey, 278–296.)

83. **Intervention, on the ground of self-preservation, for the protection of (1) institutions, (2) good order, (3) the external safety of the intervening State.** (Hall, 283–285; Pomeroy, 245; Creasey, 297–308).

84. **Intervention against illegal or immoral acts—Case of Greece, 1826; Bulgaria, 1876.** (Hall, 286.)

85. **Intervention under a treaty of guarantee—by invitation of one of the parties in a civil war—under collective authority of the body of States.** (Hall, 289–293; Bluntschli, Art. 476; the case of the Allies in 1821, in Spain and Italy; Belgium, 1830; U. S. in Peru, 1881.)

VI. *Nationality.*

86 **In what does Nationality consist? The Doctrine of Indelible Allegiance.—Expatriation.** (1. Opinion of Cockburn, Cases and Op., 213; 2. Macdonald's case, *Ib.*, 214; 3. Isaac Williams, *Ib.*, 215, note; 4. Legislation on Expatriation, *Ib.*; 5. Message of President Grant, *Ib.*, 216; 6. Alibert's case, *Ib.*, 218 and 219, note. See also: Hall, 220–232; Wheaton (L), 891 *et seq.;* Creasey, 357; Halleck, I., 348 *et seq.;* Walker, 204–218; Heffter, 136–138; Wharton's Digest, § 171; Calvo, II., 24.)

87. **Citizenship—Naturalization.** (Cases: *Ex parte* Chin King, Cases and Op., 219; Hausding's case, *Ib.*, 222; Emden's case, *Ib.*, 223; Prussian Subject, *Ib.*, 224. See also, Hall, 232–237; Phillimore, I., 443–459; Wharton's Dig., §§ 173–174; Halleck, I., 356.)

88. **If a naturalized citizen returns to his native land, what are his rights?** (Case of Wagner, Cases and Op., 225; Wharton's Dig., II., §§ 181–182.)

89. **Nationality of children born abroad; of illegitimate children; of married women.** (Hall, 224.)

90. **What is the effect of domicil, and a declaration of intention to become a citizen, upon the nationality of a foreigner?—Is he entitled to the protection of his adopted State when he goes abroad?** (Case of Koszta, Cases and Op., 226; Tousig's case, *Ib.*, 228. And see: Hall, 237–241; Halleck, I., 357; Woolsey, 502; Calvo, II., 45; Wharton's Dig., II., 397.)

91. **Persons destitute of nationality—*Heimathlosen.***—(Hall, 241; Bluntschli, Art. 369.)

92. **Status of the Chinese in the United States.—Treaty of 1880,**

and Acts of Congress of May 6, 1882, July 5, 1884, and the Geary Act of 1892.—Under the fourteenth Amendment to the Constitution, Chinese children born in the United States are citizens thereof.—It was so held in the case of Look Tin Sing, 35 Fed. Rep., 354, and in the case of Chin Sing.

93. **Status of Indians in the United States.** Indian tribes designated by MARSHALL, C. J., in 1831, as "Domestic Dependent Nations" (the Cherokee Nation v. Georgia, 5 Peters' Rep., 1.) Since 1871 no formal treaties have been made with tribes, and they have been subjected to the authority of Congress. But in 1884, the Supreme Court held that an Indian born in a tribe, though having left it, was not a citizen, and the fourteenth amendment did not apply to him. By the legislation of 1885, however, Indians even in tribes have been generally subjected to the jurisdiction of the Federal Courts; and it would seem that they should now be citizens by birth under the fourteenth amendment. (1. Elk v. Wilkins, Cases and Op., 230; 2. U. S. v. Kagama, *Ib.*, 233; and see the case of Crow Dog, 109 U. S. Rep., 556; Wharton's Dig., II., 532.)

VII. *International Agents of a State.*

94. **Persons designated by the Constitution of a State to manage its Foreign Affairs—Department of Foreign Affairs—State Department, in the United States.** (Hall, 294, 295.)

95. **Diplomatic Agents.** (1. Ambassadors, Legates, Nuncios. 2. Envoys and Ministers Plenipotentiary. 3. Ministers resident. 4. Chargés d'Affaires. The first three classes are accredited to the Sovereign, the fourth to the Minister of Foreign Affairs.)

96. **Rights of Diplomatic Agents—Refusal to receive a Minister—must be persons grata—Credentials; Letters of Credence, Letters Patent; Full powers; Instructions; Passport.** (Hall, 296–301; Bluntschli, Arts. 159–190; Wheaton (L), 273–293; Phillimore, II., 156–198, 246–264; Halleck, I., 300–304; Calvo, III., § 1312 *et seq.*; Woolsey, 126–135; Heffter, 479–484, 491–499, 507–514; Wharton's Dig., I., §§ 82–83.)

97. **Termination of Mission—Recall, and Dismissal.** (Hall, 301–305; Wheaton (D), § 250; Wharton's Dig., § 84; Heffter, 516–522; and *Ib.*, 522–545 "L'Art Diplomatique;" Bluntschli, Arts., 227–240.)

98. **Ambassadors' Rights in friendly States, on their way to or return from their posts.** (Hall, §§ 99–101; Phillimore, II., 215–218; Heffter, 488–490; Woolsey, § 97; Wheaton (D), §§ 244–247.)

99. **Consuls: Origin of office—Functions—Appointment—Dismissal—Privileges—Consuls Diplomatically accredited—"Lettre de provision"—Exequatur.** (Schuyler's "American Diplomacy," 41–104; Hall, 314–322; Wheaton (D), § 120; Phillimore, II., 265–336; Heffter, 555–566; Woolsey, 152–157; Calvo, III., § 1368–1390; Halleck, I., 310–330; Wharton's Digest, §§ 113–124.)

100. **Judicial Functions of Consuls in semi-civilized lands.** (Phillimore, II., 337–342; Halleck, I., 330–347; Wharton's Dig., § 125.)

VIII. Treaties.

101. **What Treaties are not subjects of International Law?** (Hall, 323 and note; Bluntschli, Art. 443.)

102. **Kinds of Treaties—Conditions necessary to the validity of Treaties—Authority of persons contracting—Freedom of Consent—Intimidation—Fraud, etc.** (Hall, 323–327; Heffter, 190–204; Woolsey, 159–164; Wheaton (D), §§ 252–262; Halleck, I., 234–237; Bluntschli, Arts. 402–424, 442; Phillimore, II., 68–83; Pomeroy, 340 *et seq.*)

103. **Forms—Tacit and express ratification—Refusal to ratify—Completion of ratification.** (Hall, 329–334; Pomeroy, 332; Wheaton (D), §§ 256–264.)

104. **Interpretation of Treaties. Convention of 1818 between England and the United States (Fisheries), the Clayton-Bulwer Treaty (1850.)** (Hall, 334–342; Heffter, § 95; Woolsey, 173–174; Phillimore, II., 94–125; Wheaton (D), § 287.)

105. **Conflict between different Treaties, or between different Parts of the same Treaty.** (Hall, 340–342; Phillimore II., 126–132; Calvo, §§ 720–723; Bluntschli, Art. 414.)

106. **Treaties of Guarantee.** (Hall, 342–345; Bluntschli, Arts. 437–440; Phillimore, II., 84–93; Woolsey, 166–170; Heffter, § 97.)

107. **Legislation necessary to carry treaties into effect—Is the House of Representatives in the United States under obligation to pass acts necessary to carry treaties into effect? The Jay Treaty, 1794, The Alaska Treaty, 1867.** (Wheaton (D), § 266; Halleck, I., 222–224; Calvo, III., §§ 1643–1647; Wharton's Dig., § 131*a*.)

108. **A Treaty dates from the time of Signing, not from that of Ratification.**

109. **The obligation of Treaties—Difference between a void and a voidable Treaty—Test of voidability.** (Hall, 351, 359; Creasey, 40–44; Phillimore, II., 76; M. Bernard, "Lectures on Diplomacy," 168; Heffter, § 98; Bluntschli, Arts. 415, 456–461; Pomeroy, 347; Maine: "Ancient Law," 23; Fiore, Part I., Chapter IV.; Halleck, I., 243, 244; Wharton's Dig., 137*a*.)

110. **Most favored Nation Clause in Commercial Treaties.** (Wharton's Dig., § 134.)

111. **Renewal of Treaties.** (Hall, 117.)

IX. Amicable Settlement of Disputes and Attempts to Mitigate the Evils of War.

112. **Arbitration—Mediation.** (Hall, 361–363; Bluntschli, Arts. 488–498; Calvo, § 1706 *et seq.*; Rouard de Card, "L'Arbitrage International"; Creasey, 397–399; Wharton's Dig., § 316; Sheldon Amos: "Political and Legal Remedies for War"; R. D. J., VI., 117–128, 421–452, VII., 57–69, 277, 418, 423–426, 708, VIII., 167, X., 661; Halleck, I., 413–418; Phillimore, III., 1–17.)

113. **International acts and movements with a view to mitigate the**

evils of war. (The "Declaration of Paris," Appendix B; The "Declaration of St. Petersburg," *Ib.*, C; The "Geneva Convention," *Ib.*, D; The "Brussels Congress," 1874. See on this Congress: Revue de Droit International, VII., 87, 438; Diplomatic Review, III., 9 *et seq.*; Halleck, I., 418-421 and notes; Calvo, IV., § 1898.)

114. **Acts of Individuals and Societies: Founding of the "Institute of International Law," 1871, and the "Association for the Reform and Codification of International Law," at about the same time.** (Annuaire de l'Institute, I., 27; R. D. J., VII., 307. For code of the "Institute," etc., see Appendix, F;" and for Von Moltke's criticism of it, see his letter to Bluntschli, R. D. J., XIII., 79 *et seq.*)

PART II.

INTERNATIONAL RELATIONS AS MODIFIED BY WAR.

I. MEASURES SHORT OF WAR—DEFINITION OF WAR—DECLARATION OF WAR.

115. **Reprisals—Retorsion—Pacific Blockade.** (1. Silesian Loan, Cases and Op., 243; 2. Don Pacifico, *Ib.*, 246; 3. Other Cases, *Ib.*, 248, note. And see: Hall, 364–373; Wheaton (D), §§ 290–292 and note No. 151; (L), pp. 505–510 and note No. 168; Bluntschli, Arts. 499–508; Halleck, I., 422–428; Phillimore, III., § 18–43; Calvo, III., § 1809 *et seq.*; Heffter, §§ 110–112; Woolsey, 181–187; Walker, 154–158.)

116. **Hostile Embargo.** (The *Boedus Lust*, Cases and Op., 249 and note. See also: Hall, 373; Wheaton (D), § 293 and note No. 152; Halleck, I. 433; Phillimore, III., 44-49; Calvo, III., § 1824 *et seq.*; Woolsey, 180.)

117. **Declaration of War—War without a Declaration—Civil War—Date of the beginning of a War.** (1. The *Teutonia*, Cases and Op., 250; The Prize Cases, *Ib.*, 254. And see: Hall, 374–382; Heffter, § 121; Halleck, I., 474–480; Phillimore, III., 85–113; Calvo, IV., § 1899 *et seq.*)

118. **Definition of War—Its Object—Causes of War—Kinds of War.** (Creasey, 360–392; Heffter, §§ 113, 119; Phillimore, III., 77–84; Halleck, I., 439–453, 454–473; Bluntschli, Arts. 510–528; Wheaton (D), § 296; Calvo, IV., 1–40 a resume of opinions of writers; Woolsey, 210.)

II. Effects of War as between Enemies.

(*a*) *Laws and Usages of War—Conduct of Hostilities.*

119. **Who are enemies in a war? One theory is that all citizens or subjects of one belligerent state are the enemies of all the citizens or subjects of the other. Another theory is that war is a contest between states, and that private individuals of the belligerent states are not enemies at all. The first is the old view, and is still supported by the better authority.** (Creasey, 376–388; Calvo, §§ 2035–2036; Halleck, II., 52–53; Bluntschli, Arts. 529–530; Woolsey, 550; Walker, 273.)

120. **All peaceful relations between the belligerent States and their citizens cease on the breaking out of war. But modern usage permits alien enemies to remain in the territory unmolested unless their presence becomes dangerous to the state.** (Hall, 389–393; Heffter, p. 289 and note 9; Calvo, §§ 1912–1914; Phillimore, III., 128–130; Halleck, I., 483–485.)

121. **Who are Non-Combatants?** (Hall, 394–396; Woolsey, 216–221; Halleck, II., 2–3.)

122. **Who are lawful Combatants?—Conditions—Authority—Organisation—Dress.** (Hall, 396, 514–525 and notes; Halleck, II., 6–9; Bluntschli, Arts. 569–573; Calvo, §§ 2049–2058; Walker, 249; Woolsey, 214–215.)

123. **Maritime War.—Privateers—Letters of Marque and Reprisal—Volunteer Navy.** (Hall, 525–529; Wheaton (D), § 358 and note No. 173; Wharton's Digest, §§ 383–385; Calvo, § 2297 *et seq.*; Halleck, II., 9–20; Woolsey, 201–208; Heffter, § 124; Declaration of Paris, Appendix B.)

124. **Prisoners of War.—Who may be taken prisoners?—Treatment—Parole—Exchange—Ransom.** (Hall, 403–413; Halleck, II., 3 n., 74–89; Davis, 233–237; Creasey, 452–458; Calvo, §§ 2133–2157; Bluntschli, Arts. 593–626.)

125. **Care of the sick and wounded—Geneva Convention—Red-Cross Society.** (Hall, 399–403 ; Bluntschli, Arts. 586–592 ; Calvo, § 2034 *et seq.*; Moynier : "Le Croix Rouge" ; Boyland : "Six Months under the Red Cross.")

126. **Instruments of War—Means of Destruction.** (Hall, 529–531 ; Halleck, II., 20–22 ; Woolsey, 211–213 ; Bluntschli, Arts. 557–560 ; Heffter, § 125 ; St. Petersburg Declaration, Appendix D.)

127. **Devastation.—Is it ever lawful?** (Hall, 533–534 ; Halleck, II., 117–119.)

128. **Bombardment of towns—Fortified—Open.** (Hall, 535 ; Davis, 219–222 ; Woolsey, 223–224 ; Bluntschli, Arts. 552–554, *bis;* Calvo ; §§ 2067–2095. All the important cases will be found in Calvo.)

129. **Deceit—Spies—Balloons.** (Hall, 535–539 ; Halleck, II., 22–35 ; Calvo, §§ 2106–2126 ; Bluntschli, Arts. 627–636 ; Davis, 241–244.)

(b) Effect of War upon Property, and Commercial Relations with the Enemy.

130. **When war breaks out between two states, the movable or personal property of citizens of either, found in the territory of the other, on land, was by the old and strict rule of war confiscable. Debts due to citizens of the enemy State followed the same rule. But in modern practice this rule has become nearly obsolete.** (1. Ware v. Hylton, Cases and Op., 260 ; Brown v. United States, *Ib.*, 263 ; *Ex parte* Boussmaker, *Ib.*, 267 ; Wolff v. Oxholm, *Ib.*, 268. See also : Hall, 435–440 ; Halleck, I., 485–492 ; Wheaton (D), §§ 298–308 and notes No. 156 and 157 : Phillimore, III., 128–148 ; Woolsey, 194–198 ; Heffter, § 140 ; Calvo, §§ 1915–1925.)

131. **Property of the enemy found afloat in ports, on the breaking out of war was generally confiscable as prize until a very recent time. But here, too, later practice would seem to have discarded the harsher rule. Compare with Embargo—case of Boedus Lust.** (Phillimore, III., 132 ; Wheaton (D), 389, note ; Halleck, I., 491–492 ; The *Johanna Emilie*, Cases and Op. 270, n.)

132. **Debts of a State due to the Enemy and the interest thereon are not confiscable.** (Hall, 435; Woolsey, 196; Discussion in the case of the Silesian Loan; Phillimore, III., 148.)

133. **Immovable property—lands and houses—of the enemy within the limits of the other belligerents are never confiscated.** (Phillimore, III., 148.)

134. **Property of the enemy found on the sea or in the ports of the enemy, is confiscable as prize of war—Modified by the Declaration of Paris.** (Appendix B. Hall, 435, § 143, and 442, § 146.)

135. **Contracts between enemies made before the war.—1. Executed Contracts.—2. Executory Contracts.—Statutes of Limitation.—Interest on Debts.—How affected by war?** (1. Hanger v. Abbott, Cases and Op., 270; 2. Griswold v. Waddington, *Ib.*, 274; 3. N. Y. Life Ins. Co. v. Stathem, *Ib.*, 278. See also: Gamba v. Le Mesurier, 4 East., 407; Halleck, I., 481; Walker, 276; Hall, 388; Kent, I., 68.)

136. **Effect of war upon treaties between the belligerent States previously existing.** (Wheaton (L), 460–477 (D), 352 and note; Hall, 382–387; Phillimore, III., 792–811; Bluntschli, Art. 538; Case of the Society for the Propagation of the Gospel v. New Haven, Wheaton's Rep., 494; Heffter, § 122.)

(c) *Trade with the Enemy.*

137. **Trade or Intercourse with the enemy is wholly interdicted; and is in all cases illegal, unless under a license of the State.** (1. The *Hoop*, Cases and Op., 283; 2. Potts v. Bell, *Ib.*, 287. See also: Hall, 387–388; Kent, I., 66–69; Halleck, II., 154–158; Heffter, § 123; Phillimore, III., 116–120; Calvo, §§ 1926–1929; Woolsey, 255; Wheaton (D), §§ 309–317, and note No. 158.)

138. **Licenses to trade.—They must, as a rule, be granted by the Supreme Authority of the State, and must be granted or assented to by both belligerents.** (Hall, 553–556; Halleck, II., 364–379; Woolsey, 256. Case of the *Sea Lion*,

Cases and Op., 300, gives the practice of the United States; also Cappell v. Hall, 7 Wall., 542.)

139. **After the outbreak of war, a citizen may not go or send to the enemy's country to bring away his property.** (The *Rapid*, Cases and Op., 288.)

140. **Citizens who are residing in the enemy's country, on the outbreak of war should be granted a reasonable time to return with their property to their own country.** (1. The *St. Lawrence*, Cases and Op., 290; 2. The Brig *Joseph*, *Ib.*, 292; 3. The *William Bagalay*, *Ib.*, 293; 4. Other cases, *Ib.*, 294 n.)

141. **Contracts entered into with enemies during war by citizens residing in the enemy's country.** (Kershaw v. Kelsey, Cases and Op., 295.)

142. **Bills of exchange drawn by a citizen, while a prisoner in the enemy's country, upon a person in his own country, and sold to an enemy—Is this a trading with the enemy?** (Antoine v. Morshead, Cases and Op., 308; and Kent, I., 67; Halleck, I., 481; Wheaton (D), § 317.)

143. **Agents—Right to employ agents in the enemy's country—appointed (1) before the war—(2) During the war.** (United States v. Grossmayer, Cases and Op., 298; Filor's case, 9 Wall., 45.)

144. **Insurance on ships of the enemy.** (Furtado v. Rodgers, Cases and Op., 303.)

145. **Ransom Contracts—Ransom Bill—Safe Conduct—Exception to the rule in respect to trade with the enemy.** (1. Cornu v. Blackburn, Cases and Op., 310; 2. The *Charming Nancy*, *Ib.*, 312; 3. The *Patrixent*, *Ib.*, 313; 4. Anthon v. Fisher and other cases, *Ib.*, 314, n. See also: Hall, 459–461; Halleck, II., 358–361; Wheaton (D), § 411, and note No. 199; Phillimore, III., 644–647; Woolsey, 245–247; Calvo, §§ 2422–2429.)

146. **Pacific intercourse of Belligerents—Commercia belli: Flags**

of Truce — Truces—Passports—Armistices—Cartels—Capitulations—License to Trade—Ransoms. (Hall, 540-556; Halleck, II., 340-363; Woolsey, 255-260; Bluntschli, Arts. 674-699; Calvo, §§ 2411-2452; Wheaton (D), §§ 399-408.)

(*d*) *Commercial Domicil—National Character of Property.*

147. **The National Character of property, in time of war, depends upon the domicil of the owner—French Rule.** (1. The *Indian Chief*, Cases and Op., 315; 2. The Prize cases, *Ib.*, 334; The *Venus*, *Ib.*, 319; 4. *Le Hardy*, *Ib.*, 337.)

148. **What constitutes Domicil — How determined — Animus manendi—Time.** (The *Harmony*, Cases and Op., 326. And see: Hall, 498-500; Halleck, I., 360-367; Wheaton (D), §§ 318-332; Phillimore, III., 725-734; Calvo, §§ 1936-1945.)

149. **House of Trade —It takes the National Character of the country in which it is established—Exception: House of trade in a neutral State, and the partners, or some of them, reside in an enemy country.** (Hall, 501; Wheaton (D), § 334.)

150. **The Product of the Enemy's Soil takes the National Character of the country where it is situated.** (Bentzen v. Boyle, Cases and Op., 330; Hall, 502; Wheaton (D), §§ 336-339.)

(*e*) *Ownership of Goods in transitu, on the Ocean, in time of War.*

151. **In time of war, or in contemplation of war, Goods shipped on contract are at the risk of the Consignee during transit—The French rule permits the shipper to take the risk by agreement.** (1. The Packet *de Bilboa*, Cases and Op., 339; 2. The *San Jose Indiano*, *Ib.*, 342; 3. The *Sally*, *Ib.*, 344; 4. The *Anna Catharina*, *Ib.*, 346; 5. *Les Trois Frères*, *Ib.*, 348. See also: Hall, 506, 507; Halleck, II., 128-137; Kent, I., 87; Calvo, §§ 2315-2320; Phillimore, III., 740-745.)

152. **Transfer in transitu—Stoppage in transitu—According to the**

rule of the English and American Prize Courts, property, in hostile at the time of shipment, cannot change its character during transit by sale to a neutral. (1. The *Vrow Margaretha*, Cases and Op., 350; 2. The *Jan Frederick*, *Ib.*, 352; 3. The *Ann Green*, *Ib.*, 354; 4. The *Francis and Cargo*, *Ib.*, 355, note. And see: The *San Jose Indiano*, *Ib.*, 343; Hall, 506; Halleck, II., 136–138; Duer, "On Insurance," I., 441–444; Phillimore, III., 739–740; Calvo, §§ 2321, 2322, dissents from the English and American view.)

153. **National character of merchant ships, and their transfer during war from a Belligerent to a Neutral.** (Hall, 504–505; Halleck, II., 138–144; Phillimore, III., 734–739; Calvo, §§ 2327–2338.)

154. **Proofs of the National Character of merchant ships.** (Calvo, §§ 2339–2366; Halleck, II., 145–151.)

155. **Fishing Boats generally exempt from seizure.** (Halleck, II., 151–152; Calvo, §§ 2368–2373. Does not apply to vessels employed in the Great Fisheries; Hall, 449–451; Woolsey, 303.)

156. **Freight in the case of captured vessels.** (1. The *Vrow Henrica*, Cases and Op., 356; 2. The *Fortuna*, *Ib.*, 357.)

(*f*) *Recapture—Salvage—Postliminium—Rescue.*

157. **Recapture—Salvage—When does title to recaptured property vest in the Captor?** (1. The *Santa Cruz*, Cases and Op., 358; 2. The *Carlotta*, *Ib.*, 360. And see: Hall, 493–495; Halleck, II., 524–533; Phillimore, III., 615–643; Wheaton (D), pp. 456–475; Woolsey, 247–252; Creasey, 564; Kent, I., 108–109.)

158. **Rescue by Neutrals.** (The *Emily St. Pierre*, Cases and Op., 361; The *Love*, *Ib.*, 363.)

(*g*) *Enemy Property on Land—Military Occupation.*

159. **Public Property of the Enemy—Lands, Buildings, Archives, Works of Art—Movable or personal Property.** (Mohr and

Haas v. Hatzfeld, Cases and Op., 377. See also: Hall, 416–422; Dana's Wheaton, 438, note; Halleck, II., 97, 102–108, 469–473; Calvo, §§ 2201–2214.)

160. **Private property, Real and Personal, as a rule, not confiscable, at least not by way of Booty, though personal property may be taken by way of Contributions and Requisitions--Comparison in respect to the different rule applied to enemy's property at sea and on land.** (Wheaton (D), § 335, and note No. 171; Hall, 423 *et seq.*; Creasey, 536–556; Heffter, § 133; Bluntschli, Art. 665; T. J. Lawrence, Essays, No. 1; Halleck, II., 124–128; Calvo, § 2294 *et seq.*)

161. **Requisitions and Contributions in land wars—Will they be resorted to in maritime wars?** (Hall, 425–435; Halleck, I., 265, II., 109–119; Calvo, §§ 2231–2255; Bluntschli, Arts. 653–656; Woolsey, 220; Edwards, "The Germans in France"; Sherman's "Memoirs," II., 175, 181–184, 207, 227.)

162. **The Bombardment of Towns.** (Hall, 534, 535.)

163. **Military Occupation—The general character of the Right and Jurisdiction of an Invader over the territory occupied by his armies—Old Theories—Modern View.** (Hall, 462–469; Halleck, II., 444–449; Bluntschli, Arts. 539–541; Calvo, §§ 2166–2198; Woolsey, 252; Creasey, 502–512.)

164. **Relation of the territory occupied to the Government of the Invader—To that of the State invaded.** (1. United States v. Rice, Cases and Op., 364; 2. Fleming v. Page, *Ib.*, 365; 3. Cross v. Harrison, *Ib.*, 371; 4. Jecker v. Montgomery, *Ib.*, 373; 5. Case of Guerin, *Ib.*, 375; 6. Case of Villasseque, *Ib.*, 380. See also: Halleck, II., 449–461; Hall, 497.)

165. **De facto and Constructive Occupation.**—(Hall, 480–485; Halleck, II., 446–449; Creasey, 503; Walker, 344–346.)

166. **Rights of the Occupier over the Persons of the territory occupied—"War Rebel."** (Hall, 469–476; Halleck, II., 464–468; Creasey, 516; Calvo, § 2166 *et seq.*)

167. **Rights of the invader over Incorporeal Things, as Debts, etc.** (Occupation of Naples (1495), Cases and Op., 384. See also: Hall, 418; Halleck, II., 473–479; Phillimore, III., 832–840.)

(h) *Termination of War—Conquest—Cession.*

168. **What marks the date of the end of a War?—Treaties of Peace—Proclamations in Civil Wars.** (1. The *Thetis*, Cases and Op., 399; 2. The *Protector*, *Ib.*, 391. See also: Hall, 557; Heffter, § 176; Phillimore, III., 770; Calvo, §§ 3153–3154.)

169. **Effect of Treaties of Peace in settling general rights and obligations of the parties—Effect upon acts done before the war—Upon acts done during the war—Upon acts done subsequently to the treaty of peace.** (Hall, 557–565; Phillimore, III., 770–784; Heffter, §§ 179–183; Woolsey, 263–266; Calvo, §§ 3155–3159. Cases: The *Mentor*, Cases and Op., 385; 2. The *Nymph*, *Ib.*, 386; 3. The *Swineherd*, *Ib.*, 388.)

170. **Postliminium—Uti possidetis—How do they apply to territory?** (Hall, 486, 568; Halleck, II., 512–522; Phillimore, III., 616–618; Woolsey, 248–252; Heffter, §§ 187–191; Bluntschli, Arts. 515, 727–741; Calvo, §§ 3150, 3169 *et seq.*)

171. **Conquest—Cession** (The Elector of Hesse Cassel, Cases and Op., 381; 2. U. S. v. Moreno, *Ib.*, 375; Am. Ins. Co. v. Canter, *Ib.*, 372. And see: Hall, 565–573; Halleck, II., 480 *et seq.*; Heffter, § 133; Dana's Note to Wheaton, No. 169; Calvo, §§ 2453–2490.)

III. Relations between Belligerents and Neutrals.

(a) *A General View of the Relations between Belligerents and Neutrals.*

172. **Historical Sketch of the Subject.** (Hall, 576–594; Halleck, II., 173 *et seq.*; Woolsey, 266–273; Wheaton (D), §§ 412–425; Creasey, 470–482; Heffter, §§ 145–148; Phillimore, 225.

(*b*) *Neutral Duties.*

173. **Neutrals are not to permit their Territory to be used for hostile purposes by either belligerent—Transit of troops—Fitting out hostile expeditions—Capture of vessels in neutral waters.** (1. The *Anna,* Cases and Op., 293; 2. The *General Armstrong, Ib.,* 396; 3. The *Perle, Ib.,* 398; 4. The *Ann, Ib.,* 400; Other cases, *Ib.,* 401, note. See also: Hall, 495–612; Halleck, II., 173–181; Phillimore, III., 225–236; Heffter, §§ 146–147; Calvo, § 2615 *et seq.*; Bluntschli, Art. 749 *et seq.*)

174. **Equipment of vessels of war in neutral territory.** (1. U. S. Neutrality Acts, Cases and Op., 402; 2. British Foreign Enlistment Acts, *Ib.,* 403; 3. *La Amistad de Rues, Ib.,* 406; 4. The *Santissima Trinidad, Ib.,* 408; 5. U. S. v. Quincy, *Ib.,* 412; 6. The *Meteor, Ib.,* 418; 7. The Terceira Affair, *Ib.,* 421; 8. The *Alabama,* 425; 9. The *Florida, Ib.,* 428; 10. The *Shenandoah, Ib.,* 429; 11. The *Georgia, Ib.,* 429; 12. The *Sumpter,* etc., *Ib.,* 430; 13. The Geneva Award, *Ib.,* 431. See also: Hall, 612–620; Halleck, II., 184–195; Dana's Note to Wheaton, No. 215; Walker, 458–502; Phillimore, III., 236 *et seq.*)

175. **Loans of Money to Belligerents.** (Hall, 597–599; Bluntschli, Art. 768; Halleck, II., 195; Phillimore, III., 247.)

176. **Sale of Munitions of War by a Neutral State.** (Sale of Arms to France, Cases and Op., 459; Hall, 599.)

177. **Aid to Insurgents—Loans—Munitions of War.** (1. De Wütz v. Hendricks, Cases and Op., 438; 2. Thompson v. Powles, *Ib.,* 440; 3. Kennett v. Chambers, *Ib.,* 441; 4. U. S. v. Trumbull, *Ib.,* 443; 5. The *Salvador, Ib.,* 455. And see: Phillimore, III., 247–250).

(*c*) *Contraband of War.*

178. **General Law of Contraband.** (Hall, 644; Halleck, II., 244; Woolsey, 318; Phillimore, III., 338; Wheaton (D), § 476 *et seq.*)

179. **It was formerly the custom to declare by proclamation at the**

beginning of a war what articles would be considered Contraband. (Proclamation of Charles I., Cases and Op., 462.)

180. **Classification of Contraband — Res ancipitis usus — Occasional contraband.** (1. The *Peterhoff*, Cases and Op., 465; 2. The *Commercen*, *Ib.*, 470; 3. *Il Volante*, *Ib.*, 472; 4. Other cases, *Ib.*, 471, note. And see: Hall, 658–668; Halleck, II., 251–264; Heffter, § 160; Wheaton (D), §§ 477–500; Davies, 340–350; Woolsey, 321–329.)

181. **Penalty for carrying contraband — Time when penalty attaches—Rule of English and American Courts—French Rule.** (1. The *Neutralitet*, Cases and Op., 474; 2. Seton v. Low, *Ib.*, 475; 3. *Ex parte* Chavasse, *Ib.*, 476.)

182. **Dispatches and Persons as Contraband.** (1. The *Atalanta*, Cases and Op., 477; 2. The *Rapid*, *Ib.*, 480; 3. The *Madison*, *Ib.*, 482; 4. The *Orozembo*, *Ib.*, 483; 5. The *Trent*, *Ib.*, 486. And see: Hall, 675–686; Halleck, II., 324, note; Woolsey, 335–339; Heffter, § 161 *a*.)

(*d*) *Blockade.*

183. **The purpose of Blockade—What is an effective Blockade—Notification—De facto Blockade.** (1. The *Neptunus*, Cases and Op., 490; 2. The *Betsy*, *Ib.*, 492; 3. The *Nancy*, *Ib.*, 494; 4. The *Ocean*, *Ib.*, 495; 5. Other cases, *Ib.*, 496, note. See: Hall, 696–714; Halleck, II., 211–225; Woolsey, 342–350; Heffter, §§ 154–156; Wheaton (D), §§ 511–520.)

184. **Penalty for Breach of Blockade—When does the penalty attach?—French Rule.** (The *Helen*, Cases and Op., 497. And Hall, 715; Woolsey, 350–351.)

(*e*) *Rule of the War of* 1756.

185. **Neutrals may not engage in a trade during war, from which they were excluded in time of peace.** (1. The *Immanuel*, Cases and Op., 502; 2. The *Emanuel*, *Ib.*, 504. See also: Hall, 639–642; Halleck, II., 330–339; Woolsey, 339–342; Bluntschli, Art. 800, r.; Phillimore, III., 370–386.)

(*f*) *Continuous Voyages.*

186. **Colonial Trade, and Coasting Trade—Extension in 1793.** (1. The *William*, Cases and Op., 505; Hall, 672; Woolsey, 355; Phillimore, III., 388.)

187. **Applied to the Carriage of Contraband, and the breach of blockade by American Courts.** (The *Stephen Hart*, Cases and Op., 509. See also: Hall, 673; Walker, 514, 515, 525; Phillimore, III., 391–403. Extract from the *Bermuda*, pp. 391–395, from the *Peterhoff*, pp. 395-396, from Hobbs v. Hemning, pp. 397–403; Bluntschli, Art. 835, r. 5; Calvo, §§ 2762–2766.)

(*g*) *The Right of Search and Capture.*

188. **The Right of Visit and Search is a belligerent right, to which Neutrals are subject—And resistance in any manner to this right entails condemnation.** (The *Maria*, Cases and Op., 515. And see: Hall, 725–731; Halleck, II., 267, 268, 283–296; Phillimore, III., 522, 544, 550; Woolsey, 358, 361; Calvo, §§ 2939–3003, as to whole subject of Visit and Search; Wheaton (D), §§ 525–528; Heffter, §§ 167–170.)

189. **Formalities of the Exercise of the Right of Search—Grounds of Capture—False Documents—Spoliation of Papers.** (Hall, 732–741; Halleck, II., 297–299; Phillimore, III., 536.)

190. **The Right of Visit and Search in time of peace—Impressment of Seamen—Slave Trade—Protection of Seals—Piracy.** (Halleck, II., 268–282; Phillimore, III., 525–529. And see the case of *Le Louis*, Cases and Op., § 21 c, and p. 518, note; Woolsey, 365–386; The Behring Sea Arbitration, Cases and Op., 521.)

191. **The Right to capture Enemy's goods in Neutral vessels, and Neutral goods in Enemy's vessels—"Free ships, free goods"—Declaration of Paris.** (Hall, 687–695, 717–723.)

(*h*) *Prize Courts.*

192. **The Constitution of Prize Courts in different Countries.**

(Phillimore, III., 658–665; Lawrence's Wheaton, 960–976.)

193. **The Principles and Practice of Prize Courts.** (Phillimore, III., 666–679.)

194. **Decisions of Prize Courts—They are courts of the captors' country.** (Decisions of Prize Courts, Cases and Op., 518.)

195. **Prize Courts on board ships—Practice of Captain Semmes, of the Alabama.** (Cases and Op., 519.)

CASES AND OPINIONS

ON

INTERNATIONAL LAW.

INTRODUCTION.

SECTION 1.—INTERNATIONAL LAW IS A PART OF THE MUNICIPAL LAW OF STATES.

OPINION OF BLACKSTONE.

(Blackstone's Commentaries, Book, IV. Chap. IV.)

THE law of nations is a system of rules, deducible by natural reason, and established by universal consent among the civilized inhabitants of the world; in order to decide all disputes, to regulate all ceremonies and civilities, and to insure the observance of justice and good faith, in that intercourse which must frequently occur between two or more independent states, and the individuals belonging to each.

This general law is founded upon this principle, that different nations ought in time of peace to do one another all the good they can, and in time of war as little harm as possible, without prejudice to their own real interests. And, as none of these states will allow a superiority in the other, therefore neither can dictate or prescribe the rules of this law to the rest; but such rules must necessarily result from those principles of natural justice, in which all the learned of every nation agree; or they depend upon mutual compacts or treaties between the respective communities; in the construction of which there is also no judge to resort to, but the law of nature and reason, being the only one in which all the contracting parties are equally conversant, and to which they are equally subject.

In arbitrary states this law, wherever it contradicts or is not provided for by the municipal law of the country, is enforced by the royal power; but since in England no royal power can introduce a new law, or suspend the execution of the old, therefore the law of nations (wherever any question arises which is properly the object of its jurisdiction) is here adopted in its full extent by the common law, and is held to be a part of the law of the land. And those acts of parliament, which have from time to time been made to enforce this universal law, or to facilitate the execution of its decisions, are not to be considered as introductive of any new rule, but merely as declaratory of the old fundamental constitutions of the kingdom; without which it must cease to be a part of the civilized world. Thus in mercantile questions, such as bills of exchange and the like; in all marine causes, relating to freight, average, demurrage, insurances, bottomry, and others of a similar nature; the law merchant, which is a branch of the law of nations, is regularly and constantly adhered to. So too in all disputes relating to prizes, to shipwrecks, to hostages, and ransom bills, there is no other rule of decision but this great universal law, collected from history and usage, and such writers of all nations and languages as are generally approved and allowed of.

But, though in civil transactions and questions of property between the subjects of different states, the law of nations has much scope and extent, as adopted by the law of England; yet the present branch of our inquiries will fall within a narrow compass, as offenses against the law of nations can rarely be the object of the criminal law of any particular state. For offenses against this law are principally incident to whole states or nations; in which case recourse can only be had to war; which is an appeal to the God of hosts, to punish such infractions of public faith as are committed by one independent people against another: neither state having any superior jurisdiction to resort to upon earth for justice. But where the individuals of any state violate this general law, it is then the interest as well as duty of the government, under which they live, to animadvert upon them with a becoming severity, that the peace of the world may be maintained.

For in vain would nations in their collective capacity observe these universal rules, if private subjects were at liberty to break them at their own discretion, and involve the two states in a war. It is therefore incumbent upon the nation injured, first to demand satisfaction and justice to be done on the offender, by the state to which he belongs; and, if that be refused or neglected, the sovereign then avows himself an accomplice or abettor of his subject's crime, and draws upon his community the calamities of foreign war.

THE SCOTIA.

Supreme Court of the United States, 1871.

(14 *Wallace*, 170.)

Discussion of General Principles.

Judgment by Strong, J.:—

* * * "Undoubtedly, no single nation can change the law of the sea. That law is of universal obligation, and no statute of one or two nations can create obligations for the world. Like all the laws of nations, it rests upon the common consent of civilized communities. It is of force, not because it was prescribed by any superior power, but because it has been generally accepted as a rule of conduct. Whatever may have been its origin, whether in the usages of navigation or in the ordinances of maritime states, or in both, it has become the law of the sea only by the concurrent sanction of those nations who may be said to constitute the commercial world. Many of the usages which prevail, and which have the force of law, doubtless originated in the positive prescriptions of some single state, which were at first of limited effect, but which when generally accepted became of universal obligation. The Rhodian law is supposed to have been the first system of marine rules. It was a code for Rhodians only, but it soon became of general authority because accepted and assented to as a wise and desirable system by other maritime nations. The same may be said of the Amalphitan Table, of the ordinances of the Hanseatic League, and of parts of the marine ordinances of Louis XIV. They all became the law of the sea, not on account of their origin, but by reason of their acceptance as such. And it is evident that unless general assent is efficacious to give sanction to international law, there never can be that growth and development of maritime rules which the constant changes in the instruments and necessities of navigation require. Changes in nautical rules have taken place. How have they been accomplished, if not by the concurrent assent, expressed or understood, of maritime nations?

When, therefore, we find such rules of navigation as are mentioned in the British orders in council of January 9th, 1863, and in our act of Congress of 1864, accepted as obligatory rules by more than thirty of the principal commercial states of the world, including almost all which have any shipping on the Atlantic Ocean, we are constrained to regard them as in part at least, and so far as relates to these vessels, the laws of the sea, and as having been the law at the time when the collision of which the libellants complain took place.

This is not giving to the statutes of any nation extra-territorial effect. It is not treating them as general maritime laws, but it is recognition of the historical fact that by common consent of mankind these rules have been acquiesced in as of general obligation. Of that fact we think we may take judicial notice. Foreign municipal laws must, indeed, be proved as facts, but it is not so with the law of nations." [1]

[1] In the case of the *Charming Betsy*, 2 Cranch, 64, 118, MARSHALL, C. J., said: "It has also been observed that an act of Congress ought never to be construed to violate the law of nations if any other possible construction remains, and, consequently, can never be construed to violate neutral rights, or to affect neutral commerce further than is warranted by the law of nations as understood in this country."

In the case of the *Nereid*, 9 Cranch, 388, 423, the same judge said: "Till such an act [of Congress] be passed, the court is bound by the law of nations, which is a part of the law of the land." See also *Talbot* v. *Seeman*, 1 Cranch, 1, 43, and 14 Wallace 170, 188.

In the case of *Bentzon* v. *Boyle*, 9 Cranch, 191, 198, MARSHALL, C. J., said: "The law of nations is the great source from which we derive those rules, respecting belligerent and neutral rights, which are recognized by all civilized states throughout Europe and America. This law is in part unwritten, and in part conventional. To ascertain that which is unwritten, we resort to the great principles of reason and justice; but, as these principles will be differently understood by different nations under different circumstances, we consider them as being, in some degree, fixed and rendered stable by a series of judicial decisions. The decisions of the courts of every country, so far as they are founded upon the law common to every country, will be received, not as authority, but with respect. The decisions of the courts of every country show how the law of nations, in the given case, is understood in that country, and will be considered in adopting the rule which is to prevail in this."

Bishop says (*Criminal Law*, 7th Ed., I. 60): "Doubtless if the legislature, by words admitting of no interpretation, commands a court to violate the law of nations, the judges have no alternative but to obey. Yet no statutes have ever been framed in form thus conclusive; and if a case is *prima facie* within the legislative words, still a court will not take the jurisdiction should the law of nations forbid." Again (p. 69): "All statutes are to be construed in connection with one another, with the common law, with the constitution, and with the law of nations."

PART I.

INTERNATIONAL RELATIONS IN TIME OF PEACE.

CHAPTER I.

STATES—TERRITORIAL RIGHTS.

SECTION 2.—DEFINITION AND CHARACTER OF SOVEREIGN STATES.

HALLECK'S INTERNATIONAL LAW, I. 58.

"A STATE is a body politic, or society of men united together for mutual advantage and safety. Such a society has affairs and interests peculiar to itself, and is capable of deliberation and resolution; it is therefore regarded as a kind of moral person, possessing a will and an understanding, and susceptible of rights and obligations. From the nature and design of such a society, it is necessary that there should be established in it a *public authority*, to order and direct what is to be done by each individual in relation to the end and object of the association. This political authority, whether vested in a single individual or in a number of individuals, is properly the *sovereignty* of the State.

"This term, however, in international law, is usually employed to express the external rather than the internal character of a nation, with respect to its ability or capacity to govern itself, independently of foreign powers. A sovereign State may, therefore, be defined to be any nation or people organized into a body politic and exercising the rights of self-government."

SECTION 3.—ACQUISITION OF TERRITORY.

JOHNSON v. McINTOSH.

SUPREME COURT OF THE UNITED STATES, 1823.

(8 *Wheaton*, 533.)

Discovery gives a valid title to territory occupied by uncivilized peoples.

The right of the North American Indians to the lands which they possessed was that of occupancy merely.

JUDGMENT—MARSHALL, C. J.—(Only so much of the decision is given as applies to discovery:)

"The plaintiffs in this cause claim the land, in their declaration mentioned, under two grants, purporting to be made, the first in 1773, and the last in 1775, by the chiefs of certain Indian tribes, constituting the Illinois and the Praukeshaw nations; and the question is, whether this title can be recognized in the courts of the United States.

"The facts, as stated in the case argued, show the authority of the chiefs who executed this conveyance so far as it could be given by their own people; and likewise show, that the particular tribes for whom these chiefs acted were in rightful possession of the land they sold. The inquiry, therefore, is, in a great measure, confined to the power of Indians to give, and of private individuals to receive, a title which can be sustained in the courts of this country.

"As the rights of society, to prescribe those rules by which property may be acquired and preserved is not, and cannot be, drawn into question; as the title to lands, especially, is and must be admitted to depend entirely upon the law of the nation in which they lie, it will be necessary, in pursuing this inquiry, to examine, not singly those principles of abstract justice, which the Creator of all things has impressed on the mind of His creature man, and which are admitted to regulate, in a great degree, the rights of civilized nations, whose perfect independence is acknowledged; but those principles also which our own government has adopted in the particular case, and given us as the rule for our decision.

"On the discovery of this immense continent the nations of Europe were eager to appropriate to themselves so much of it as they could respectively acquire. Its vast extent offered an ample field to the ambition and enterprise of all; and the character and religion of its inhabitants afforded an apology for considering them as a people over whom the superior genius of Europe might claim an ascendency. The potentates of the old world found no difficulty in convincing themselves that they made ample compensation to the inhabitants of the new, by bestowing on them civilization and Christianity, in exchange for unlimited independence. But, as they were all in pursuit of nearly the same object, it was necessary, in order to avoid conflicting settlements, and consequent war with each other, to establish a principle which all should acknowledge as the law by which the rights of acquisition, which they all asserted, should be regulated as between themselves. This principle was, that discovery gave title to the government by whose subjects, or by whose authority, it was made, against all other European governments, which title might be consummated by possession.

"The exclusion of all other Europeans necessarily gave to the nation making the discovery the sole right of acquiring the soil from the natives, and establishing settlements upon it. It was a right with which no Europeans could interfere.

"It was a right which all asserted for themselves, and to the assertion of which, by others, all assented.

"Those relations which were to exist between the discoverer and the natives were to be regulated by themselves. The rights thus acquired being exclusive, no other power could interpose between them.

"On the establishment of these relations, the rights of the original inhabitants were, in no instance, entirely disregarded, but were necessarily, to a considerable extent, impaired. They were admitted to be the rightful occupants of the soil, with a legal as well as just claim to retain possession of it, and to use it according to their own discretion; but their rights to complete sovereignty, as independent nations, were necessarily diminished and their power to dispose of the soil at their own will, to whomsoever they pleased, was denied by the original fundamental principle, that discovery gave exclusive title to those who made it.

"While the different nations of Europe respected the right of the natives, as occupants, they asserted the ultimate dominion to be in themselves; and claimed and exercised, as a consequence of this ultimate dominion, a power to grant the soil, while yet in possession of the natives. These grants have been understood by all to convey a title to the grantees, subject only to the Indian right of occupancy.

"The history of America, from its discovery to the present day, proves, we think, the universal recognition of these principles.

"Spain did not rest her title solely on the grant of the Pope. Her discussions respecting boundary, with France, with Great Britain, and with the United States, all show that she placed it on the rights given by discovery. Portugal sustained her claim to the Brazils by the same title.

"France, also, founded her title to the vast territories she claimed in America on discovery. However conciliatory her conduct to the natives may have been, she still asserted her right of dominion over a great extent of country not actually settled by Frenchmen, and her exclusive right to acquire and dispose of the soil which remained in the occupation of Indians. * * *

"The States of Holland also made acquisitions in America, and sustained their right on the common principle adopted by all Europe. * * *

"No one of the powers of Europe gave its full assent to this principle more unequivocally than England. The documents upon this subject are ample and complete. So early as the year 1496, her monarch granted a commission to the Cabots, to discover countries then unknown to *Christian people*, and to take possession of them in the name of the king of England. Two years afterwards, Cabot proceeded on this voyage, and discovered the continent of North America, along which he sailed as far south as Virginia. To this discovery the English trace their title.

"In this first effort made by the English government to acquire territory on the continent, we perceive a complete recognition of the principle which has been mentioned. The right of discovery given by this commission is confined to countries 'then unknown to all Christian people;' and of these countries Cabot was empowered to take possession in the name of the king of England, thus asserting a right to take possession notwithstanding the occupancy of the natives, who were heathen, and, at the same time, admitting any prior title of any Christian people who may have made a previous discovery. * * *

"Thus, all nations of Europe, who have acquired territory on this continent, have asserted in themselves and have recognized in others, the exclusive right of the discoverer to appropriate the lands occupied by the Indians. * * *

"The power now possessed by the government of the United States to grant lands, resided, while we were colonies, in the crown, or its grantees.

"The validity of the titles given by either has never been questioned in our courts. It has been exercised uniformly over territory in possession of the Indians. The existence of this power must negative the existence of any right which may conflict with, and control it. An absolute title to lands cannot exist, at the same time, in different persons, or in different governments.

"An absolute, must be an exclusive title, or at least a title which excludes all others not compatible with it. All our institutions recognize the absolute title of the crown, subject only to the Indian right of occupancy, and recognize the absolute title of the crown to extinguish that right. This is incompatible with an absolute and complete title in the Indians."

THE OREGON TERRITORY.

(*Wheaton's International Law, 8d. Ed. p. 220.*)

THE claim of the United States to the territory between the Rocky Mountains and the Pacific Ocean, and between the 42d degree and 54th degree and 40 minutes of north latitude, is rested by them upon the following grounds:—

1. The first discovery of the mouth of the river Columbia by Captain Gray, of Boston, in 1792: the first discovery of the sources of that river, and the exploration of its course to the sea by Captains Lewis and Clark, in 1805–6; and the establishment of the first posts and settlements in the territory in question by citizens of the United States.

2. The virtual recognition by the British government of the title of the United States in the restitution of the settlement of Astoria or Fort George, at the mouth of the Columbia River, which had been captured by the British during the late war between the two countries, and which was restored in virtue of the 1st article of the treaty of Ghent, 1814, stipulating that "all territory, places, and possessions whatever, taken by either party from the other during the war," etc., "shall be restored without delay." This restitution was made without any reservation or exception whatsoever, communicated at the time to the American government.

3. The acquisition by the United States of all the titles of Spain, which titles were derived from the discovery of the coasts of the region in question, by Spanish subjects, before they had been seen by the people of any other civilized nation. By the 3d article of the treaty of 1819, between the United States and Spain, the boundary line between the two countries, west of the Mississippi, was established from the mouth of the river Sabine, to

certain points on the Red River and the Arkansas, and running along the parallel of 42 degrees north to the South Sea; His Catholic Majesty ceding to the United States "all his rights, claims, and pretensions, to any territories east and north of the said line; and" renouncing "for himself, his heirs and successors, all claim to the said territories forever." The boundary thus agreed on with Spain was confirmed by the treaty of 1828, between the United States and Mexico, which had, in the meantime, become independent of Spain.

4. Upon the ground of *contiguity*, which should give to the United States a stronger right to those territories than could be advanced by any other power. "If," said Mr. Gallatin, "a few trading factories on the shores of Hudson's Bay have been considered by Great Britain as giving an exclusive right of occupancy as far as the Rocky Mountains; if the infant settlements on the more southern Atlantic shores justified a claim thence to the South Seas, and which was actually enforced to the Mississippi; that of the millions of American citizens already within reach of those seas cannot consistently be rejected. It will not be denied that the extent of contiguous country to which an actual settlement gives a prior right, must depend, in a considerable degree, on the magnitude and population of that settlement, and on the facility with which the vacant adjacent land may, within a short time, be occupied, settled, and cultivated by such population, compared with the probability of its being occupied and settled from any other quarter. This doctrine was admitted to its fullest extent by Great Britain, as appeared by all her charters, extending from the Atlantic to the Pacific, given to colonies established then only on the borders of the Atlantic. How much more natural and stronger the claim, when made by a nation whose population extended to the central parts of the continent, and whose dominions were by all acknowledged to extend to the Rocky Mountains."

The exclusive claim of the United States is opposed by Great Britain on the following grounds:—

1. That the Columbia was not discovered by Gray, who had only entered its mouth, discovered four years previously by Lieutenant Meares of the British navy; and that the exploration of the interior borders of the Columbia by Lewis and Clark could not be considered as confirming the claim of the United States, because, if not before, at least in the same and subsequent years, the British Northwest Company had, by means of their agents, already established their posts on the head waters or main branch of the river.

2. That the restitution of Astoria, in 1818, was accompanied by

express reservations of the claim of Great Britain to that territory, upon which the American settlement must be considered an encroachment.

3. That the titles to the territory in question, derived by the United States from Spain through the treaty of 1819, amounted to nothing more than the rights secured to Spain equally with Great Britain by the Nootka Sound Convention of 1790: namely, to settle on any part of those countries, to navigate and fish in their waters, and to trade with the natives.

4. That the charters granted by British sovereigns to colonies on the Atlantic coasts were nothing more than cessions to the grantees of whatever rights the grantor might consider himself to possess, and could not be considered as binding the subjects of any other nation, or as part of the law of nations, until they had been confirmed by treaties.

DELAGOA BAY, 1872.

(*Hall's International Law., 3d. Ed.*, 119.)

"A SOMEWHAT recent controversy to which title by occupation has given rise turned mainly upon the effect of a temporary cessation of the authority of the occupying state. From 1823 to 1875, when the matter was settled by arbitration, a dispute existed between England and Portugal as to some territory at Delagoa Bay, which was claimed by the former under a cession by native chiefs in the first-mentioned year, and by the latter on the grounds, amongst others, of continuous occupation. It was admitted that Portuguese territory reached to the northern bank of the Rio de Espirito Santo, or English River, which flows into a bay, and that a port and village had long been established there. The question was whether the sovereignty of Portugal extended south of the river, or whether the lands on that side had remained in the possession of their original owners. England relied upon the facts that the natives professed to be independent in 1823, that they acted as such, and that the commandant of the fort repudiated the possession of authority over them. In the memorials which were submitted on behalf of Portugal, amidst much which had no special reference to the territory in dispute, there was enough to show that posts had been maintained within it from time to time, and that authority had probably been exercised intermittently over the natives. The area of the territory being small, and all of it being within easy reach of a force in possession of the Portuguese settlement, there could be little difficulty in keeping up sufficient control to prevent a title by occupation from dying out. There was, therefore, a presumption in favor of the Portuguese claim. The French government, which acted as arbitrator, took the view that the interruption of occupation, which undoubtedly took place in 1823, was not sufficient to oust a title supported by occasional acts of sovereignty done through nearly three centuries, and adjudged the territory in question to Portugal." [The award in favor of Portugal was in substance, on the grounds of first discovery, in the 16th century, and of continued occupation and control of the territory in dispute.]

SANTA LUCIA.

(*Phillimore's International Law*, 3d *Ed.*, 368.)

"There was a dispute of long standing between France and England respecting Santa Lucia, one of the Antilles Islands. After the treaty of Aix-la-Chapelle (1748), the matter was referred to the decision of certain commissioners, and it was the subject of various State Papers in 1751 and 1754.

"The French negotiators maintained, that though the English had established themselves in 1639, they had been driven out or massacred by the Caribbees in 1640, and they had, *animo et facto* and *sine spe redeundi*, abandoned the island; that Santa Lucia being *vacant*, the French had seized it again in 1650, when it became immediately, and without the necessity of any prescriptive aid, their property.

"The English negotiators contended that their *dereliction* had been the result of violence, that they had not *abandoned* the island *sine spe redeundi*, and that it was not competent to France to profit by this act of violence, and surreptitiously obtain the territory of another state; and that by such a proceeding no *dominium* could accrue to them. The principal discussion turned, not upon the nature of the conditions of prescriptive acquisition, but upon the nature of the conditions of voluntary dereliction, by which the rights of property were lost, and the possession returned to the class of vacant and unowned territories." [1]

[1] At the present time it is generally conceded that discovery alone is not enough to give title to territory; it must be followed by actual occupation.

In regard to the extent of the interior country to which the occupation of the

SECTION 4.—RECOGNITION OF INDEPENDENCE.

J. Q. ADAMS TO PRESIDENT MONROE, AUG. 24, 1818.

(1 *Wharton's Digest*, 121.)

"THERE is a stage in such (revolutionary) contests when the party struggling for independence has, as I conceive, a right to demand its acknowledgment by neutral parties, and when the acknowledgment may be granted without departure from the obligations of neutrality. It is the stage when the independence is established as matter of fact, so as to leave the chance of the opposite party to recover their dominion utterly desperate. The neutral nation must, of course, judge for itself when this period has arrived; and as the belligerent nation has the same right to judge for itself, it is very likely to judge differently from the neutral and to make it a cause or pretext for war, as Great Britain did expressly against France in our Revolution, and substantially against Holland.

"If war thus results, in point of fact, from the measure of recognizing a contested independence, the moral right or wrong of the war depends upon the justice and sincerity and prudence with which the recognizing nation took the step. I am satisfied that the cause of the South Americans, so far as it consists in the assertion of independence against Spain, is just. But the justice of a cause, however it may enlist individual feelings in its favor, is not sufficient to justify third parties in siding with it. The fact and the right combined can alone authorize a neutral to acknowledge a new and disputed sovereignty."[1]

sea-coast gives title, the extravagant claim was put forward in some of the earlier charters, granting lands in North America, that such right extended from the Atlantic to the Pacific Ocean. A more reasonable rule was laid down by the United States commissioners, appointed to settle the boundary of Louisiana, namely, "that when any European nation takes possession of any extent of sea-coast, that possession is understood as extending into the interior country, to the sources of the rivers emptying themselves within that coast, to all their branches, and the country they cover, and to give it a right in exclusion of all other nations to the same."

[1] In *M'Ilvaine* v. *Coxe's Lessee*, 4 Cranch, 212, the Supreme Court of the United States say: "That the several states which composed this Union, so far at least as regarded their municipal regulations, became entitled, from the time when they

Section 5.—Boundaries.

FOSTER & ELAM v. NEILSON.

Supreme Court of the United States, 1829.

(2 *Peters*, 253.)

This was the case of lands in the disputed territory between the rivers Iberville and Perdido granted to the plaintiffs by the Spanish governor. The defendant alleged that by the treaty of Ildefonso, 1800, this territory was ceded by Spain to France, and in 1803, by France to the United States. And it was a question of the interpretation of the treaty of cession.

The court refused to go into the merits of the treaty, but considered itself bound by the decision of the political department of the government, whose province it was to deal with foreign relations.

Extract from the judgment, Marshall, C. J.:—

"* * * In a controversy between two nations concerning national boundary, it is scarcely possible that the courts of either should refuse to abide by the measures adopted by its own government.

"There being no common tribunal to decide between them, each determines for itself on its own rights, and if they cannot adjust their differences peaceably, the right remains with the strongest. The judiciary is not that department of the government to which the assertion of its interests against foreign powers is confided; and its duty commonly is to decide upon individual rights, according to those principles which the political departments of the nation have established. If the course of the nation has been a plain one, its courts would hesitate to pronounce it erroneous.

declared themselves independent, to all the rights and powers of sovereign states, and that they did not derive them from concessions made by the British king. The treaty of peace contains a recognition of their independence, not a grant of it. From hence it results, that the laws of the several state governments were the laws of sovereign states, and as such were obligatory upon the people of such state from the time they were enacted."

New states may be recognized conditionally. By the 43d article of the treaty of Berlin, 1878, it is stipulated that the independence of Roumania shall be recognized by the high contracting parties "on the conditions laid down in the two following articles." These conditions are, first, that no person shall be deprived of civil or political rights by reason of his creed; and, second, that Roumania shall restore to Russia certain territory detached from Russia by the treaty of Paris, 1856.

Servia was recognized upon a similar condition as to religious freedom. (Articles 34 and 35.)

"We think then, however individual judges might construe the treaty of St. Ildefonso, it is the province of the court to conform its decisions to the will of the legislature, if that will has been clearly expressed. * * *

"After these acts of sovereign power over the territory in dispute, asserting the American construction of the treaty by which the government claims it, to maintain the opposite construction in its own courts would certainly be an anomaly in the history and practice of nations. If those departments which are entrusted with the foreign intercourse of the nation, which assert and maintain its interests against foreign powers, have unequivocally asserted its right of dominion over a country of which it is in possession, and which it claims under a treaty; if the legislature has acted on the construction thus asserted, it is not in its own courts that this construction is to be denied. A question like this respecting the boundaries of nations, is, as has been truly said, more a political than a legal question; and in its discussion the courts of every country must respect the pronounced will of the legislature."[1]

HARCOURT v. GAILLARD.

SUPREME COURT OF THE UNITED STATES.

(12 *Wheaton*, 523.)

This was the case of a British grant of land within the limits of the old thirteen colonies, made during the Revolutionary war, in 1777.

Held that such grant was invalid, on the ground that the title to lands had already passed to the United States.

Extract from the opinion of the court:—

"But this is not the material fact in the case; it is this, that this limit was claimed and asserted by both of those states in the Declaration of Independence, and the right to it was established by the most solemn of all international acts, the treaty of peace. It has never been admitted by the United States, that they acquired anything by way of cession from Great Britain by that treaty. It has been viewed only as a recognition of pre-existing rights, and on that principle the soil and sovereignty, within their acknowledged limits, were as much theirs at the declaration of independence as at this

[1] To the same effect, see *In re Cooper*, 143 United States Reports, 472.

hour. By reference to the treaty, it will be found that it amounts to a simple recognition of the independence and the limits of the United States, without any language purporting a cession or relinquishment of right on the part of Great Britain. In the last article of the treaty of Ghent will be found a provision respecting grants of land made in the islands then in dispute between the two states, which affords an illustration of this doctrine. By that article, a stipulation is made in favor of grants before the war, but none for those which were made during the war. And such is unquestionably the law of nations. War is a suit prosecuted by the sword; and where the question to be decided is one of original claim to territory, grants of soil made *flagrante bello* by the party that fails can only derive validity from treaty stipulations."

OPINION OF THE ATTORNEY-GENERAL OF THE UNITED STATES, 1856.

(8 *Op. Att.-Gen.* 175.)

When a river forms the boundary between two states.

SIR,—Your note of this date, communicating a clause in the draft of the proposed report of the commissioners for determining the boundary between the Mexican Republic and the United States, presents the following question of public law:

"A portion of the boundary is formed by the Rio Bravo, which is subject to change its course in two ways: first, by gradual accretion of one of its banks, followed, in many cases, by corresponding degradation of the opposite bank; and, secondly, by the more violent action of the water, leaving its actual bed and forcing for itself a new one in another direction. In case of any such changes in the bed of the river, does the boundary line shift with them, or does that line remain constant where the main course of the river ran as represented by the maps accompanying the report of the commissioners?

"The response to this inquiry depends, in part, on the terms of the treaty between the two republics prescribing the boundary line, the material part of which, in so far as regards the present question, is to effect, that the line 'beginning in the Gulf of Mexico, three leagues from land, opposite the mouth of the Rio Grande,' shall proceed thence 'up the middle of that river' to a certain point. The treaty further provides that commissioners appointed by the two governments shall survey and mark out upon the land the stipulated line, which, as agreed upon and established by them, shall in all time be faithfully respected, without any variation therein, unless by express and free consent of both republics (Treaty of December 30, 1853, 10 Stat. at Large, p. 1032.)

"If the question here were of certain other parts of the boundary which are to run on parallels of latitude or by straight line from point to point, in that case the monuments placed by the commissioners, or the line as otherwise fixed by descriptive words referring to natural objects, or by the drawings and maps of the commissioners, would, it is plain, be conclusive, in all time, by force of the stipulations of the treaty. It would be the line agreed upon and established, even although it should afterwards prove that, by reason of error of astronomical observations or of calculation, it varied from the parallel of latitude where that was the line, or in the other part did not make exactly a straight line. So, if, in another portion of the boundary, which calls for the rivers Gila and Colorado, there were controversy concerning the identity of either as upon the northeastern boundary of the United States, as there once was in regard to the true St. Croix, then, also, by force of the treaty, the determination of that point, by the commissioners, would be conclusive in all time. But the present question is a different one, and depends in part for its solution upon other considerations.

"In this case the boundary is not an astronomical or geographical line, but a natural object, defined by the treaty. And there is no equivocation here between two distinct natural objects, each of them answering to the descriptive language of a stipulation. It is the Rio Bravo, with a course as definite, and almost as destitute of tributaries and embranchments, in its main course, as the Nile. That is a fact which cannot be modified by surveys or reports.

"However, the established principles of public law come in here to settle the question in all its relations.

"The respective territories of the United States and of the Mexican Republic are arcifinious; that is to say, territories separated not by a mathematical line, but by natural objects of indeterminate natural extension which of themselves serve to *keep off* the public enemy. Such are mountains and rivers. (Barbeyrac's Grotius, liv. ii., chap. 3, § 16 and note; Coceii Grotius Illustratus, ibid.)

"When a river is the dividing limit of arcifinious territories, the natural changes to which itself is liable, or which its action may produce on the face of the country, give rise to various questions, according to the physical events which occur, and the previous relation of the river to the respective territories. The most simple of all the original conditions of the inquiry is where the river appertains by convention equally to both countries, their rights being on either side to the *filum aquæ*, or middle of the channel of the stream. That is the present fact.

"With such conditions, whatever changes happen to either bank of the river by accretion on the one or degradation of the other; that is, by the gradual and, as it were, insensible accession or abstraction of mere particles, the river as it runs continues to be the boundary. One country may, in process of time, lose a little of its territory, and the other gain a little, but the territorial relations cannot be reversed by such imperceptible mutations in the course of the river. The general aspect of things remains unchanged. And the convenience of allowing the river to retain its previous function, notwithstanding such insensible changes in its course, or in either of its banks, outweighs the inconveniences even to the injured party; it is a detriment, which, happening gradually, is inappreciable in the successive moments of its progression.

"But, on the other hand, if, deserting its original bed, the river forces for itself a new channel in another direction, then the nation, through whose territory the river thus breaks its way, suffers injury by the loss of territory greater than the benefit of retaining the natural river boundary, and that boundary remains in the middle of the deserted river bed. For, in truth, just as a stone pillar constitutes a boundary, not because it is a stone, but because of the place in which it stands, so a river is made the limit of nations, not because it is running water bearing a certain geographical name, but because it is water flowing in a given channel, and within given banks, which are the real international boundary."

SECTION 6.—THE EFFECT OF A CHANGE OF SOVEREIGNTY.

(a) *Upon Public Rights and Obligations.*

TEXAN BONDS.

(1 *Wharton's Digest*, 20–23.)

During the period of Texan independence, that State had issued bonds to the extent of many millions of dollars, secured by the revenues of the State; and in 1845, when Texas was annexed to the United States, her custom houses and the control over customs duties passed to the federal government. Some of these bonds were held in England; and an attempt was made before the claims commis-

sion of 1853, for the adjustment of claims between England and the United States, to hold the federal government responsible for the payment of the Texan bonds.

In his opinion, Mr. Upham, commissioner said :—

" The matter of the indebtedness of Texas was a distinct subject of agreement by the terms of the union. According to those terms the vacant and unappropriated lands within the limits of Texas were to be retained by her, ' and applied to the payment of the debts and liabilities of the Republic of Texas, and the residue of the lands, after discharging these debts and liabilities, was to be disposed of as the State might direct, but in no event were the debts and liabilities to become a charge upon the Government of the United States.' (U. S. Statutes at Large, vol. 5, p. 798.)

" The lands of Texas were thus specifically set apart for the payment of the debts of Texas, by agreement of the two Governments, in addition to any separate pledge Texas had previously made of this class of property, for the payment of her debts.

" The United States subsequently, by act of Congress, on the 9th of September, 1850, on condition of the cession of large tracts of these lands, agreed to pay Texas $10,000,000, but stipulated ' that $5,000,000 of the amount should be retained in the United States treasury until creditors, holding bonds, for which duties on imports were specifically pledged, should file releases of all claims against the United States.' [U. S. Statutes at Large, vol. 9, ch. 49, p. 446.]

" It thus appears that the United States has acted, from the outset, in concert with Texas, in causing express provision to be made for the payment of these debts.

" A difficulty early arose in carrying the law, above cited, into effect, for the reason that the pledge of payment of the debts of Texas was made generally upon her revenues, and was not specific ' on imposts ' *eo nomine*, and for the further reason that doubts arose whether any portion of the debts could be paid under this contract, unless the whole could be discharged."

(Report of the commission of claims under the convention of 1853.)

Mr. Dana says of this case :—

" It certainly would not be satisfactory to say that the United States discharges its obligation to the creditors of Texas, to whom her customs were pledged, by paying only the amount of the customs received.

" The United States determines what those duties shall be, in reference to the interest and policy of the whole Republic. The condition of Texas is changed by her annexation. The new government has a large control over the material resources of the inhabitants, in the way of internal revenues, excise or direct taxation, in its demands on the services of the people, and in the debts it can impose; in fact, the entire public system of Texas has passed into other hands, and no such state of things any longer exists as that to which the creditor looked. It may be better or worse, but it is not the same; and, if the duties laid by the United States and collected in Texan ports did not in fact pay the debts, it would be unjust for the United States to limit the payment of the creditor to them. The truth is, by the annexation the United States changed the nature of the thing pledged, and is bound generally to do equity to the creditor." (Dana's Wheaton, note 18.)

Mr. Lawrence says: "The liability of the United States for the debts of Texas came before the mixed commission, under the convention with England of 1853, in the case of a British subject who had received before the annexation, bonds secured by a pledge of the faith and revenue of Texas. It was disposed of on the ground that never having been made a subject for international interposition against the United States, it did not fall within the scope of the convention; but it seemed to be admitted that the liability of the United States, if any, arose, not from the merger, but from the transfer, under the Constitution of the United States, to the Federal Government of the duties on imports. It was said by the American Commissioner, in announcing his opinion, that it was an inaccurate view of the case to regard this annexation as an entire adoption of one nation and its revenues by another. 'Texas is still a sovereign State, with all the rights and capacities of government, except that her international relations are controlled by the United States, and she has transferred to the United States her right of duties on imports.'

"And he seemed to consider any claim arising from the previous pledge of such duties to be limited to their value. The British commissioner held that the obligation of Texas to pay her debts is not in dispute, nor has it been argued that the mere act of her annexation to the United States has transferred her liabilities to the Federal Government, though certainly, as regards foreign governments, the United States is now bound to see that the obligations of Texas are fulfilled. It is the transfer of the integral revenues of Texas to the Federal Government that is relied on as creating the new liability."[1]

(Decisions of the Commission of Claims under the convention of 1853, pp. 405–420. Lawrence's Wheaton, ed. 1863, p. 54, note).

[1] When Lombardy and Venice were respectively acquired by Italy at the close of the wars of 1859 and 1866 with Austria, the Italian government assumed no part of the general debt of Austria, but only the local debts of the ceded provinces.

OPINION OF CHANCELLOR KENT.

(*Kent's Commentaries, I.* 25.)

"It is well to be understood, at a period when alterations in the constitutions of governments, and revolutions in states, are familiar, that it is a clear position of the law of nations, that treaties are not affected, nor positive obligations of any kind with other powers, or with creditors, weakened, by any such mutations. A state neither loses any of its rights, nor is discharged from any of its duties, by a change in the form of its civil government. The body politic is still the same, though it may have a different organ of communication. So, if a state should be divided in respect to territory, its rights and obligations are not impaired; and if they have not been apportioned by special agreement, those rights are to be enjoyed, and those obligations fulfilled, by all the parts in common."

(*b*) *Upon Private Rights.*

THE UNITED STATES v. PERCHEMAN.

Supreme Court of the United States, 1833.

(7 *Peters*, 51, 86.)

Juan Percheman claimed two thousand acres of land lying in the territory of Florida, by virtue of a grant of the Spanish governor of that province made in 1815. After Florida was ceded to the United States by the treaty of 1819, this claim was rejected by the United States commissioners appointed to settle claims to territory in Florida; and the question then came before the court for decision.

Held that title to private property in the soil is not affected by a cession of territory.

Marshall, C. J., delivered the opinion of the court, an extract from which is as follows:—

So, in the case of the cession of Alsace and Lorraine to Germany in 1871, no part of the French national debt was assumed by Germany on their account. (Bluntschli: Droit International, Article 48.)

On the other hand, on the seizure of Schleswig-Holstein by Prussia, in 1866, the debt of Denmark was divided between that country and Schleswig-Holstein; "and in the same year, Italy, by convention with France, took upon itself so much of the Papal debt as was proportionate to the revenues of the Papal provinces which it had appropriated." (Hall's International Law, 3d ed., 102, note.)

"It may not be unworthy of remark that it is very unusual even in cases of conquest, for the conqueror to do more than to displace the sovereign and assume dominion over the country. The modern usage of nations, which has become law, would be violated; that sense of justice and of right which is acknowledged and felt by the whole civilized world would be outraged, if private property should be generally confiscated, and private rights annulled. The people change their allegiance; their relation to their ancient sovereign is dissolved; but their relations to each other, and their rights of property, remain undisturbed. If this be the modern rule even in cases of conquest, who can doubt its application to the case of an amicable cession of territory? Had Florida changed its sovereign by an act containing no stipulation respecting the property of individuals, the right of property in all those who became subjects or citizens of the new government would have been unaffected by the change. It would have remained the same as under the ancient sovereign. * * *

"A cession of territory is never understood to be a cession of the property belonging to its inhabitants. The king cedes that only which belonged to him. Lands he had previously granted were not his to cede. Neither party could so understand the cession. Neither party could consider itself as attempting a wrong to individuals, condemned by the practice of the whole civilized world. The cession of a territory by its name from one sovereign to another, conveying the compound idea of surrendering at the same time the lands and the people who inhabit them, would be necessarily understood to pass the sovereignty only, and not to interfere with private property."[1]

OPINION OF BAYARD, SECRETARY OF STATE.

Despatch to Roberts, March 20, 1886.

(1 *Wharton's Digest*, 16.)

In the territory conquered by Chili from Peru in the war of 1879–1882, citizens of the United States had acquired certain rights from the Peruvian government which, after the conquest, the Chilian government was inclined not to respect. In Mr. Bayard's opinion, rights of individuals acquired under a former government should be respected in the case even of conquest by another government.

"The decision now made rests on an alleged rule of international law which, assumed, as it now is, by the Government of Chili,

[1] To the same effect in *Mutual Ass. Society* v. *Watts*, 1 Wheaton, 279, 282.

becomes a proper matter of discussion between ourselves and that Government. It is asserted by the Government of Chili (for, in international relations, and the maintenance of international duties, the action of the judiciary in Chili is to be treated, when assumed by the Government, as the act of the Government) that a sovereign, when occupying a conquered territory, has, by international law, the right to test titles acquired under his predecessor by applying to them his own municipal law, and not the municipal law of his predecessor under which they vested. * * *

"The Government of the United States, therefore, holds that titles derived from a duly constituted prior foreign Government to which it has succeeded are 'consecrated by the law of nations' even as against titles claimed under its own subsequent laws. The rights of a resident—neutral—having become fixed and vested by the law of the country—cannot be denied or injuriously affected by a change in the sovereignty or public control of that country by transfer to another Government. His remedies may be affected by the change of sovereignty, but his *rights* at the time of the change must be measured and determined by the law under which he acquired them. * * * The Government of the United States is therefore prepared to insist on the continued validity of such titles, as held by citizens of the United States, when attacked by foreign Governments succeeding that by which they [were] granted. Title to land and landed improvements, is, by the law of nations, a continuous right, not subject to be divested by any retroactive legislation of new Governments taking the place of that by which such title was lawfully granted. Of course it is not intended here to deny the prerogative of a conqueror to confiscate for political offenses, or to withdraw franchises which by the law of nations can be withdrawn by Governments for the time being. Such prerogatives have been conceded by the United States as well as by other members of the family of nations by which international law is constituted. What, however, is here denied, is the right of any Government to declare titles lawfully granted by its predecessor to be vacated because they could not have been lawfully granted if its own law had, at the time in question, prevailed.

"This pretension strikes at that principle of historical municipal continuity of Governments which is at the basis of international law."

SECTION 7.—DE FACTO GOVERNMENTS.

(a) *Recognition of Belligerency.*

OPINION OF DANA.

(*Dana's Edition of Wheaton, p. 34, note.*)

"THE occasion for the accordance of belligerent rights arises when a civil conflict exists within a foreign state. The reason which requires and which can alone justify this step by the government of another country, is, that its own rights and interests are so far affected as to require a definition of its own relations to the parties. Where a parent government is seeking to subdue an insurrection by municipal force, and the insurgents claim a political nationality and belligerent rights which the parent government does not concede, a recognition by a foreign state of full belligerent rights, if not justified by necessity, is a gratuitous demonstration of moral support to the rebellion, and of censure upon the parent government. But the situation of a foreign state with reference to the contest and the condition of affairs between the contending parties, may be such as to justify this act. It is important, therefore, to determine what state of affairs, and what relations of the foreign state, justify the recognition.

"It is certain that the state of things between the parent state and insurgents must amount in fact to a *war*, in the sense of international law, that is, powers and rights of war must be in actual exercise: otherwise the recognition is falsified, for the recognition is of a fact. The tests to determine the question are various, and far more decisive where there is maritime war and commercial relations with foreigners. * * *

"As to the relation of the foreign state to the contest, if it is solely on land, and the foreign state is not contiguous, it is difficult to imagine a call for the recognition. If, for instance, the United States should formally recognize belligerent rights of an insurgent community at the center of Europe, with no seaports, it would require a hardly supposable necessity to make it else than a mere demonstration of moral support. But a case may arise where a foreign state must decide whether to hold the parent state responsible for acts done by the insurgents or to deal with the insurgents as a *de facto* government. (Mr. Canning to Lord Granville on the Greek War, June 22, 1826.) If the foreign state recognizes belligerency in the insurgents, it releases the parent state from responsibility for whatever may be done by the insurgents, or not done by the parent state, where the insurgent power extends. (Mr. Adams to Mr. Seward, June 11, 1861, Dip. Con. 105.) In a contest wholly upon land, a contiguous state may be obliged to make the decision whether or not to regard it as war; but, in practice this has not been done by a general and prospective declaration, but by actual treatment of cases as they arise. Where the insurgents and the parent state are maritime, and the foreign nation has extensive commercial relations and trade at the ports of both, and the foreign nation and either or both of the contending parties have considerable naval force, and the domestic contest must extend itself over the sea, then the relations of the foreign state to this contest are far different. In such a state of things, the liability to political complications, and the questions of right and duty to be decided at once, usually away from home, by private citizens or naval officers, seem to require an authoritative and general decision as to the *status* of the three parties involved. If the contest is a war, all foreign citizens and officers, whether executive or judicial, are to follow one line of conduct. If it is not a war, they are to follow a totally different line. If it is a war, the commissioned cruisers of both sides may stop, search and capture the foreign merchant-vessel; and that vessel must make no resistance, and must submit to adjudication by a prize court. If it is not a war, the cruisers of neither party can stop or search the foreign merchant-vessel; and that vessel may resist all attempts in that direction, and the ships of war of the foreign state may attack and capture any cruiser persisting in the attempt. If it is war, foreign nations must await the adjudication of prize tribunals. If it is not war, no such tribunal can be opened. If it is a war, the parent state may institute a blockade *jure gentium* of the insurgent ports, which foreigners must respect; but, if it is not a war, foreign nations having large commercial intercourse with the country, will not respect a closing of insurgent ports by paper decrees only. If it is a war, the insurgent cruisers are to be treated by foreign citizens and officials, at sea and in port, as lawful belligerents. If it is not a war, those cruisers are pirates, and may be treated as such. If it is a war, the rules and risks respecting carrying contraband, or despatches, or military persons come into play. If it is not a war, they do not. Within foreign jurisdiction, if it is a war, acts of the insurgents in the way of preparation and equipments for hostility, may be breaches of neutrality laws; while, if it is not a war they do not come into that category, but into the category of piracy, or of crimes by municipal law.

"Now, all private citizens of a foreign state, and all its executive officers, and judicial magistrates, look to the political department of their government to prescribe the rules of their conduct, in all their possible relations with the parties to the contest. This rule is prescribed in the best and most intelligible manner for all possible contingencies by the simple declaration that the contest is, or is not, to be treated as war. If the state of things requires the decision, it must be made by the political department of the government. It is not fit that cases should be left to be decided as they may arise, by private citizens, or naval or judicial officers, at home or abroad, by sea or land. It is, therefore, the custom of nations for the political department of a foreign state to make the decision. It owes it to its own citizens, to the contending parties, and to the peace of the world, to make that decision seasonably. If it issues a formal declaration of belligerent rights prematurely, or in a contest with which it has no complexity, it is a gratuitous and unfriendly act. If the parent government complains of it, the complaint must be upon one of these grounds. To decide whether the recognition was uncalled for and premature, requires something more than a consideration of proximate facts, and the overt and formal acts, of the contending parties. The foreign state is bound and entitled to consider the preceding history of the parties; the magnitude and completeness of the political and military organization and preparations on each side; the probable extent of the conflict by sea and land; the probable extent and rapidity of its development; and, above all, the probability that its own merchant-vessels, naval officers, and consuls may be precipitated into sudden and difficult complications abroad. The best that can be said is, that the foreign state may protect itself by a seasonable decision, either upon a test case that arises, or by a general prospective decision; while, on the other hand, if it makes the recognition prematurely, it is liable to the suspicion of an unfriendly purpose to the parent state. The recognition of belligerent rights is not solely to the advantage of the insurgents. They gain the great advantage of a recognized *status*, and the opportunity to employ commissioned cruisers at sea, and to exert all the powers known to maritime warfare, with the sanction of foreign nations. They can obtain abroad loans, military, and naval materials, and enlist men, as against everything but neutrality laws; their flag and commissions are acknowledged, their revenue laws are respected, and they acquire a *quasi* political recognition.

On the other hand, the parent government is relieved from responsibility for acts done in the insurgent territory; its blockade of its own ports is respected; and it acquires a right to exert, against neutral commerce, all the powers of a party to a maritime war."

THE LILLA.

U. S. DISTRICT COURT FOR MASSACHUSETTS, 1862.

(2 *Sprague's Decisions*, 177.)

The Lilla was condemned by a Prize Court of the Confederate States, and subsequently sailed under the British flag. *Held*, that the Federal courts would not acknowledge the validity of the decisions of the prize courts of the Confederacy, although they had recognized the belligerence of that government.

This was a Maine brig called the Betsy Ames, captured by a Confederate privateer commanded by H. S. Libby, carried into Charleston, S. C., and there condemned and sold, the purchasers being John Fraser & Co. of that city. Her name was changed to the Mary Wright, and, loaded with cotton, under the command of Libby, she ran the blockade, arrived at Liverpool on the 2d of April, 1862, and disposed of her cargo. April 24th she was registered as a British vessel, called the Lilla, and in the name of R. G. B., as sole owner. A fortnight later she sailed for Nassau, N. P., under the command of A., according to her papers, but really still under command of Libby. There is evidence going to show that it was arranged that Fraser & Co. should have a steamer of theirs follow to Nassau, there take on the Lilla's cargo and proceed to Charleston.

Parts of the cargo were falsely documented in the name of R. G. B. for the purpose of deceiving the United States cruisers.

The vessel was seized by the United States gunboat Quaker City, brought in, and claimed by her original owners.

SPRAGUE, J., decided that R. G. B. lost whatever he possessed in the cargo by reason of his falsely documenting other goods as his own to deceive belligerent cruisers and that the vessel should be restored upon the authority of the Act of 1800, Chap. 14, secs. 1, 2. U. S. Stats. at Large, 16, which provides that when a merchant vessel, belonging to any person under the protection of the United States, shall have been taken by a public enemy, and shall be recaptured by a public armed vessel of the United States, such vessel not having been condemned by competent authority before the recapture, the same shall be restored to the former owners upon payment of one-eighth part of the true value, for and in lieu of salvage. The court also says:—

"The second objection to this claim is also fatal. There is no doubt that this vessel was the property of Maxwell and others, until her capture by a Confederate privateer. But it is contended that she has since been condemned and sold by a Prize Court in Charleston, S. C., and the purchasers conveyed her to the claimant Bushby. If this were so, of which there is no sufficient proof, still, such proceedings would not divest the title of the original owner. In the case of *The Amy Warwick*, this Court *held*, that treating the Confederates in some respects as belligerents was not an abandonment of sovereign rights, and by no means precluded us from treating them in other respects as rebels. Most assuredly I shall not recognize the Southern Confederates as a nation, or as having a government competent to establish Prize Courts. No proceedings of any such supposed tribunals can have any validity here, and a sale under them would convey no title to the purchaser, nor would it confer upon him any right to give a title to others. But it is argued that, under the Queen's proclamation, recognizing the Confederates as belligerents, a British court would hold a sale to be valid. What the decision of a British Court might be upon that question, we do not know, it never having been there litigated. But such a decision, if made, would be no more binding upon our courts than the political views of the British government would be upon the President or the Congress."

(*b*) *Succession to the Rights of Belligerent Communities.*

UNITED STATES OF AMERICA v. PRIOLEAU.

CHANCERY, 1866.

(25 *Law Journal*, *Chancery*, *N. S.*, 7.)

Upon the suppression of the Rebellion in 1865, the title to the public property of the Confederate government became immediately vested in the government of the United States.

Toward the end of the civil war in the United States (1861–1865), the Confederate government having got possession of 1,365 bales of cotton in Texas, had it shipped from Galveston to Havana, where it was consigned to an agent of Fraser & Co. On the 10th of

June, 1865, the cotton was shipped from Havana to Liverpool, consigned to the defendants Fraser, Trenholm & Co. (Prioleau being the English member of the firm), and was of the value of 40,000*l.* Fraser, Trenholm & Co. had made a contract with one M'Rae, general European agent of the Confederate government, to build eight steamships to be employed in transporting cotton and other produce from the Confederate States. They were to receive all consignments of said merchandise and sell the same according to the instructions they should receive for that purpose. The company were to advance the expenses of transportation, and were then to recoup themselves out of the proceeds of the consignments. They had already expended 20,000*l* for sailing expenses, to say nothing of the cost of the ships.

When this consignment of cotton arrived in Liverpool, the Confederate government had been dissolved, and the Confederate States had submitted to the authority of the United States government; and the latter government filed a bill praying to have the cotton delivered up to them, and for an injunction and receiver.

Judgment.— WOOD, V. C.: "There are one or two points which, I think, are tolerably clear in this case. The first point is with reference to the right of the United States of America, at this moment, to the cotton, subject to the agreement. I treat it first in that way. It has scarcely been disputed on the present argument, and could hardly be disputed at any further stage of the inquiry, that the right is clear and distinct, because the cotton in question is the admitted result of funds raised by a *de facto* government, exercising authority in what were called the Confederate States of America; that is to say, several of those states which, in union, formerly constituted the United States, and which now, in fact, constitute them; and that *de facto* government, exercising its powers over a considererable number of states (more than one would be quite enough), raises money—be it by voluntary contribution, or be it by taxation, is not of much importance. The defendant Prioleau, in cross-examination, admits that they exercised considerable power of taxation; and with those means, and claiming to exercise that authority, they obtained from several of the States of America funds by which they purchased this cotton for the use of the *de facto* government. That being so, and that *de facto* government being displaced, I apprehend it is quite clear that the United States of America (that is to say, the government which has been successful in displacing the *de facto* government, and whose authority was usurped or displaced, or whatever term you may choose to apply to it), the authority being restored, stand, in reference to this cotton, in the position of those who have acquired, on behalf of the citizens of the United States, a public property; because otherwise, as has been well said, there would be no body who could sue in respect of, or deal with, property that has been raised, not by contribution of any one sovereign state (which might raise a question, owing to the peculiar constitution of the Union, if it had been raised in Virginia or Texas, or in any given State), but the cotton is the product of levies, voluntary or otherwise, on the members of the several states which have united themselves into the Confederate States of America, and which are now under the control of the present plaintiffs, and are represented, for all purposes, by the present plaintiffs. That being so, the right of the present plaintiffs to this cotton, subject to this agreement is, I think, clear, because the agreement is an agreement purporting to be made on behalf of the then *de facto* existing government, and not of any other persons. That case of *The King of the Two Sicilies* and the case of *The King of Spain*, and other cases of the same kind, which it is not necessary to go through, show that whenever a government *de facto* has obtained the possession of property, as a government, and for the purposes of the government *de facto*, the government which displaces it succeeds to all the rights of the former government, and, among other things, succeeds to the property they have so acquired.

"Now I come to the second head of the question, and I confess at this moment, as at present advised, I do not feel much doubt on the subject, namely, the question whether or not, taking this property, they must or must not take it subject to the agreement. It appears to me, at present, they must take it subject to the agreement. It is an agreement entered into by a *de facto* government, treating with persons who have a perfect right to deal with them. I apprehend if they had been American subjects they might do so. One of them. Prioleau, is not an American subject; he is a naturalized British subject; he would have a perfect right to deal with a *de facto* government; and it cannot be compared with any one of those cases Mr. Gifford put, of persons taking the property of another with knowledge of the rights of that other. That is a species of argument that cannot be applied to international cases of this description, and for a very good reason; if so, there would be no possibility during the existence of a government *de facto* of any person dealing with that government in any part of the world. The courts of every country recognize a government *de facto* to this extent, for the purpose of saying—you are established *de facto*, if you are carrying on the course of government, if you are allowed by those whom you affect to govern to levy taxes on them, and they pay those taxes, and contribution is made accordingly, or you are acquiring proprety, and are at war, having the rights of belligerents, not being treated as mere rebels by persons who say they are the authorized government of the country. Other nations can have nothing to do with that matter. They say we are bound to protect our subjects who treat with the existing government; and we must give to those subjects, in our country, every right which the government *de facto* can give to them, and must not allow the succeeding government to assert any right as against the contracts which have been entered into by the government *de facto;* but, as expressed by Lord Cranworth in the case referred to, they must succeed in every respect to the property as they find it, and subject to all the conditions and liabilities to which it is subject and by which they are bound. Otherwise, I do not see any answer to Mr. James's illustration, and I do not see why there should not have been a bill filed to have the *Alabama* delivered up; * * * because on the theory of the present plaintiffs, it was their property just as much as their cotton is now. If the case had been this (and it is the only case I can consider as making any difference, but that difference would be fatal to the plaintiffs' case in another point of view): if they had been a set of marauders, a set of robbers (as was said to be the case in the kingdom of Naples, truly or untruly), devastating the country, and acquiring property in that way, and then affecting to deal with your subjects in England, it would not be the United States, but the individuals who had been robbed and suffered, who could come as plaintiffs. The United States could only come to claim this because it has been raised by public contribution; and although the United States, who are now the government *de facto* and *de jure*, claim it as public property, yet it would not be public property unless it was raised, as I have said, by exercising the rights of government, and not by means of mere robbery and violence.

"I confess, therefore, I have so little doubt, that this agreement is one that would be binding on the plaintiffs, that I cannot act against these gentlemen without securing to them the reasonable benefit of this agreement; and I cannot put them under any terms which would exclude them from the reasonable benefit of what they are entitled to, and must be held entitled to, as I think, at the hearing of the cause."

[The Vice Chancellor then proceeds to decree that the cotton was now the property of the United States Government, but that they must take it subject to the obligations entered into respecting it by the *de facto* Confederate Government.

The defendant Prioleau was appointed receiver, with power to sell the cotton, but he was required to give security for its value ultra the 20,000*l.*, the amount of the defendant's lien.[1]]

SECTION 8.—TERRITORIAL WATERS OF A STATE.

(*a*) *Rivers.*

OPINION OF WHEATON.

(*Wheaton's International Law, 3d Ed.*, 242.)

"The territory of the state includes the lakes, seas, and rivers, entirely inclosed within its limits. The rivers which flow through the territory also form a part of the domain from their sources to their mouths, or as far as they flow within the territory, including the bays or estuaries formed by their junction with the sea. * * *

"Things of which the use is inexhaustible, such as the sea and running water, cannot be so appropriated as to exclude others from using these elements in any manner which does not occasion a loss

[1] In the case of the *United States of America* v. *McRae*, 1869, *L. R.* 8 *Eq.* 69, JAMES, V. C., held, "that, upon the suppression of a rebellion, the restored legitimate government is entitled, as of right, to all moneys, goods, and treasure which were public property of the government at the time of the outbreak, such right being in no way affected by the wrongful seizure of the property by the usurping government.

"But with respect to property which has been voluntarily contributed to, or acquired by, the insurrectionary government in the exercise of its usurped authority, and has been impressed in its hands with the character of public property, the legitimate government is not, on its restoration, entitled by title paramount, but as successor only (and to that extent recognizing the authority) of the displaced usurping government; and in seeking to recover such property from an agent of the displaced government can only do so to the same extent, and subject to the same rights and obligations, as if that government had not been displaced and was itself proceeding against the agent.

"Therefore, a bill by the United States Government, after the suppression of the rebellion, against an agent of the late Confederate Government, for an account of his dealings in respect of the Confederate loan, which he was employed to raise in this country [England], was dismissed with costs, in the absence of proof that any property to which the plaintiffs were entitled in their own right, as distinguished from their right as successors of the Confederate Government, ever reached the hands of the defendant, and on the plaintiff declining to have the account taken on the same footing as if taken between the Confederate Government and the defendant as the agent of such government, and to pay what, on the footing of such account might be found due from them." (Quoted from 2 Phillimore's International Law, 154.)

or inconvenience to the proprietor. This is what is called an *innocent use*. Thus we have seen that the jurisdiction possessed by one nation over sounds, straits, and other arms of the sea, leading through its own territory to that of another, or to other seas common to all nations, does not exclude others from the right of innocent passage through these communications. The same principle is applicable to rivers flowing from one state through the territory of another into the sea, or into the territory of a third state. The right of navigating, for commercial purposes, a river which flows through the territories of different states, is common to all the nations inhabiting the different parts of its banks; but this right of innocent passage being what the text writers call an *imperfect right*, its exercise is necessarily modified by the safety and convenience of the state affected by it, and can only be effectually secured by mutual convention regulating the mode of its exercise."

THE NAVIGATION OF THE MISSISSIPPI.

(*Wheaton's International Law, 3d Ed.*, 247.)

"By the treaty of peace concluded at Paris, in 1763, between France, Spain, and Great Britain, the province of Canada was ceded to Great Britain by France, and that of Florida to the same power by Spain, and the boundary between the French and British possessions in North America was ascertained by a line drawn through the middle of the river Mississippi from its source to the Iberville, and from thence through the latter river and the lakes of Maurepas and Pontchartrain to the sea. The right of navigating the Mississippi was at the same time secured to the subjects of Great Britain from its source to the sea, and the passages in and out of its mouth, without being stopped, or visited, or subjected to the payments of any duty whatsoever. The province of Louisiana was soon afterwards ceded by France to Spain; and by the treaty of Paris, 1783, Florida was retroceded to Spain by Great Britain. The independence of the United States was acknowledged, and the right of navigating the Mississippi was secured to the citizens of the United States and the subjects of Great Britain by the separate treaty between these powers. But Spain having become thus possessed of both banks of the Mississippi at its mouth, and a considerable distance above its mouth, claimed its exclusive navigation below the point where the southern boundary of the United States struck the river. This claim was resisted, and the right to participate in the navigation of the river from its source to the sea was insisted on by the United States, under the treaties of 1763 and 1783, as well as by the law of nature and nations. The dispute was terminated by the treaty of San Lorenzo el Real, in 1795 by the 4th article of which His Catholic Majesty agreed that the navigation of the Mississippi, in its whole breadth, from its source to the ocean, should be free to the citizens of the United States; and by the 22d article, they were permitted to deposit their goods at the port of New Orleans, and to export them from thence, without paying any other duty than the hire of the warehouses. The subsequent acquisition of Louisiana and Florida by the United States having included within their territory the whole river from its source to the Gulf of Mexico, and the stipulation in the treaty of 1783, securing to British subjects a right to participate in its navigation, not having been renewed by the treaty of Ghent, in 1814, the right of navigating the Mississippi is now vested exclusively in the United States.

"The right of the United States to participate with Spain in the navigation of the river Mississippi, was rested by the American Government on the sentiment written in deep characters on the heart of man, that the ocean is free to all men, and its rivers to all its inhabitants. This natural right was found to be universally acknowledged and protected in all tracts of country, united under the same political society, by laying the navigable rivers open to all their inhabitants. When these rivers enter the limits of another society, if the right of the upper inhabitants to descend the stream was in any case obstructed, it was an act of force by a stronger society against a weaker, condemned by the judgment of mankind. * * *

"If the appeal was to the law of nature and nations, as expressed by writers on the subject, it was agreed by them, that even if the river, where it passes between Florida and Louisiana, were the exclusive right of Spain, still an innocent passage along it was a natural right in those inhabiting its borders above. It would, indeed, be what those writers call an *imperfect* right, because the modification of its exercise depends, in a considerable degree, on the conveniency of the nation through which they were to pass. But it was still a *right*, as real as any other right however well defined; and were it to be refused, or to be so shackled by regulations not necessary for the peace or safety of the inhabitants, as to render its use impracticable to us, it would then be an injury, of which we should be entitled to demand redress. The right of the upper inhabitants to use this navigation was the counterpart to that of those possessing the shores below, and founded in the same natural relations with the soil and water. * * *

"It was a principle, too, that the right to a thing gives a right to the means without which it could not be used, that is to say, that the means follow the end. Thus a right to navigate a river draws to it a right to moor vessels to its shores, to land on them in cases of distress, or for other necessary purposes, etc. This principle was founded in natural reason, was evidenced by the common sense of mankind, and declared by the writers before quoted." (Jefferson's instructions to U. S. ministers in Spain, March 18, 1792. Waite's State Papers, vol. x. pp. 135–140.)

THE NAVIGATION OF THE ST. LAWRENCE.

(*Wheaton's International Law, 3d Ed.*, 252.)

"The relative position of the United States and Great Britain in respect to the navigation of the great northern lakes and the river St. Lawrence, appears to be similar to that of the United States and Spain, previously to the cession of Louisiana and Florida, in respect to the Mississippi; the United States being in possession of the southern shores of the lakes and the river St. Lawrence to the point where their northern boundary line strikes the river, and Great Britain, of the northern shores of the lakes and the river in its whole extent to the sea, as well as of the southern banks of the river from the latitude 45° north to its mouth.

"The claim of the people of the United States, of a right to navigate the St. Lawrence to and from the sea, was, in 1826, the subject of discussion between the American and British Governments.

"On the part of the United States Government, this right is rested on the same grounds of natural right and obvious necessity which had formerly been urged in respect to the river Mississippi. The dispute between different European powers respecting the navigation of the Scheldt, in 1784, was also referred to in the correspondence on this subject, and the case of that river was distinguished from that of the St. Lawrence by its peculiar circumstances. Among others, it is known to have been alleged by the Dutch, that the whole course of the two branches of this river which passed within the dominions of Holland was entirely *artificial;* that it owed its existence to the skill and labor of Dutchmen; that its banks had been erected and maintained by them at a great expense. Hence, probably, the motive for that stipulation in the treaty of Westphalia, that the lower Scheldt, with the canals of Sas and Swin, and other mouths of the sea adjoining them, should be kept closed on the side belonging to Holland.

"But the case of the St. Lawrence was totally different, and the principles on which its free navigation was maintained by the United States had recently received an unequivocal confirmation in the solemn act of the principal States of Europe. In the treaties concluded at the Congress of Vienna, it had been stipulated that the navigation of the Rhine, the Neckar, the Mayn, the Moselle, the Maese, and the Scheldt, should be free to all nations. These stipulations, to which Great Britain was a party, might be considered as an indication of the present judgment of Europe upon the general question. The importance of the present claim might be estimated by the fact that the inhabitants of at least eight states of the American Union, besides the territory of Michigan, had an immediate interest in it, besides the prospective interests of other parts connected with this river and the inland seas through which it communicates with the ocean. The right of this great and growing population to the use of this, its only natural outlet to the ocean, was supported by the same principles and authorities which had been urged by Mr. Jefferson in the negotiation with Spain respecting the navigation of the river Mississippi.

"The present claim was also fortified by the consideration that this navigation was, before the war of the American Revolution, the common property of all the British subjects inhabiting this continent, having been acquired from France by the united exertions of the mother country and the colonies in the war of 1756. The claim of the United States to the free navigation of the St. Lawrence was of the same nature with that of Great Britain to the navigation of the Mississippi, as recognized by the 7th article of the treaty of Paris, 1763, when the north and lower shores of that river were held by another power. The claims, whilst necessary to the United States, was not injurious to Great Britain, nor could it violate any of her just rights.

"On the part of the British Government, the claim was considered as involving the question whether a *perfect* right to the free navigation of the river St. Lawrence could be maintained according to the principles and practice of the law of nations."

"The liberty of passage to be enjoyed by one nation through the dominions of another was treated by the most eminent writers on public law as a qualified, occasional exception to the paramount rights of property. They made no distinction between the right of passage by a river, flowing from the possessions of one nation through those of another, to the ocean, and the same right to be enjoyed by means of any highway, whether of land or water, generally accessible to the inhabitants of the earth. The right of passage, then, must hold good for other purposes, besides those of trade,—for objects of war as well as for objects of peace,—for all nations, no less than for any nation in particular, and be attached to artificial as well as to natural highways. The principle could not, therefore, be insisted on by the American Government, unless it was prepared to apply the same principle by reciprocity, in favor of British subjects, to the navigation of the Mississippi and the Hudson, access to which from Canada might be obtained by a few miles of land-carriage, or by the artificial communications created by the canals of New York and Ohio. Hence the necessity which has been felt by the writers on public law, of controlling the operation of a principle so extensive and dangerous, by restricting the right of transit to purposes of *innocent* utility, to be exclusively determined by the local sovereign.

"Hence the right in question is termed by them an *imperfect* right. But there was nothing in these writers, or in the stipulations of the treaties of Vienna, respecting the navigation of the great rivers of Germany, to countenance the American doctrine of an absolute, natural right. These stipulations were the result of mutual consent, founded on consideration of mutual interest growing out of the relative situation of the different states concerned in this navigation.

"The same observation would apply to the various conventional regulations, which had been, at different periods, applied to the navigation of the river Mississippi.

"As to any supposed right derived from the simultaneous acquisition of the St. Lawrence by the British and American people, it could not be allowed to have survived the treaty of 1783, by which the independence of the United States was acknowledged, and a partition of the British dominions in North America was made between the new government and that of the mother country.

"To this argument it was replied, on the part of the United States, that, if the St. Lawrence were regarded as a *strait* connecting navigable seas, as it ought properly to be, there would be less controversy. The principle on which the right to navigate straits depends, is, that they are accessorial to those seas which they unite, and the right of navigating which is not exclusive, but common to all nations; the right to navigate the seas drawing after it that of passing the straits. The United States and Great Britain have between them the exclusive right of navigating the lakes. The St. Lawrence connects them with the ocean. "The right to navigate both (the lakes and the ocean) includes that of passing from one to the other through the natural link. Was it then reasonable or just that one of the two co-proprietors of the lakes should altogether exclude his associate from the use of a common bounty of nature, necessary to the full enjoyment of them? The distinction between the right of passage, claimed by one nation through the territories of another, on land, and that on navigable water, though not always clearly marked by the writers on public law, has a manifest existence in the nature of things. In the former case, the passage can hardly ever take place, especially if it be of numerous bodies, without some detriment or inconvenience to the state whose territory is traversed. But in the case of a passage on water no such injury is sustained.

"The American government did not mean to contend for any principle the benefit of which, in analogous circumstances, it would deny to Great Britain. If, therefore, in the further progress of discovery, a connection should be developed between the Mississippi river and Upper Canada, similar to that which exists between the United States and the St. Lawrence, the American government would be always ready to apply, in respect to the Mississippi, the same principles it contended for in respect to the St. Lawrence. But the case of rivers, which rise and debouch altogether within the limits of the same nation, ought not to be confounded with those which, having their sources and navigable portions of their streams in states above, finally discharge themselves within the limits of other states below. In the former case, the question as to opening the navigation to other nations depended upon the same considerations which might influence the regulation of other commercial intercourse with foreign states, and was to be exclusively determined by the local sovereign. But in respect to the latter the free navigation of the river was a natural right in the upper inhabitants, of which they could not be entirely deprived by the arbitrary caprice of the lower state. Nor was the fact of subjecting the use of this right to treaty regulations, as was proposed at Vienna to be done in respect to the navigation of the European rivers, sufficient to prove that the origin of the right was conventional and not natural. It often happened to be highly convenient, if not sometimes indispensable, to avoid controversies by prescribing certain rules for the enjoyment of a natural right. The law of nature, though sufficiently intelligible in its great outlines and general purposes, does not always reach every minute detail which is called for by the complicated wants and varieties of modern navigation and commerce.

"Hence the right of navigating the ocean itself, in many instances, principally incident to a state of war, is subjected, by innumerable treaties, to various regulations. These regulations—the transactions of Vienna, and other analogous stipulations—should be regarded only as the spontaneous homage of man to the paramount Law-giver of the universe, by delivering his great works from the artificial shackles and selfish contrivances to which they have been arbitrarily and unjustly subjected."

[By the reciprocity treaty of 1854, the citizens and inhabitants of the United States were permitted to navigate the river St. Lawrence and the Canadian canals between the great lakes and the Atlantic Ocean; and British subjects were granted the right to navigate Lake Michigan. This treaty was abrogated in 1866.

The treaty of Washington of May 8, 1871, provides as follows:

ARTICLE XXVI.

"The navigation of the river St. Lawrence, ascending and descending, from the forty-fifth parallel of north latitude, where it ceases to form the boundary between the two countries, from, to, and into the sea, shall forever remain free and open for the purposes of commerce to the citizens of the United States, subject to any laws and regulations of Great Britain, or of the Dominion of Canada, not inconsistent with such privilege of free navigation.

"The navigation of the rivers Yukon, Porcupine, and Stikine, ascending and descending, from, to, and into the sea, shall forever remain free and open for the purposes of commerce to the subjects of Her Britannic Majesty and to the citizens of the United States, subject to any laws and regulations of either country within its own territory, not inconsistent with such privilege of navigation."

ARTICLE XXVII.

"The Government of Her Britannic Majesty engages to urge upon the Government of the Dominion of Canada to secure to the citizens of the United States the use of the Welland, St. Lawrence, and other canals in the Dominion on terms of equality with the inhabitants of the Dominion; and the Government of the United States engages that the subjects of Her Britannic Majesty shall enjoy the use of the St. Clair Flats canal on terms of equality with the inhabitants of the United States, and further engages to urge upon the state governments to secure to the subjects of Her Britannic Majesty the use of the several state canals connected with the navigation of the lakes or rivers traversed by, or contiguous to the boundary line between the possessions of the high contracting parties, on terms of equality with the inhabitants of the United States."

ARTICLE XXVIII.

"The navigation of Lake Michigan shall also, for the term of years [ten] mentioned in article XXXIII. of this treaty be free and open for the purposes of commerce to the subjects of Her Britannic Majesty, subject to any laws and regulations of the United States or of the states bordering thereon not inconsistent with such privilege of free navigation.—[F. S.]

THE NAVIGATION OF EUROPEAN RIVERS.

(*Wheaton's International Law, 3d Ed.*, 244.)

By the treaty of Westphalia, 1648, confirmed by subsequent treaties, * * * the navigation of the river Scheldt was closed to the Belgic provinces, in favor of the Dutch.

The forcible opening of this navigation by the French on the occupation of Belgium by the arms of the French Republic, in 1792, in violation of these treaties, was one of the principal ostensible causes of the war between France on one side, and Great Britain and Holland on the other. By the treaties of Vienna, the Belgic provinces were united to Holland under the same sovereign, and the navigation of the Scheldt was placed on the same footing of freedom with that of the Rhine and other great European rivers. And by the treaty of 1831, for the separation of Holland from Belgium, the free navigation of the Scheldt was, in like manner, secured, subject to certain duties, to be collected by the Dutch government.[1]

"By the treaty of Vienna, 1815, the commercial navigation of rivers which separate different states, or flow through their respective territories, was declared to be entirely free in their whole course, from the point where each river becomes navigable to its mouth; provided that regulations relating to the police of the navigation should be observed, which regulations were to be uniform, and as favorable as possible to the commerce of all nations.

"By the *Annexe* XVI. to the final act of the Congress of Vienna, the free navigation of the Rhine is confirmed 'in its whole course, from the point where it becomes navigable to the sea, ascending or descending;' and detailed regulations are provided respecting the navigation of that river, and the Neckar, the Mayn, the Moselle, the

[1] By the treaty of May 12, 1863, between Belgium and the Netherlands, the King of the Netherlands renounces the Scheldt dues for 17,141,640 florins to be paid by Belgium. See Dana's note to Wheaton, p. 276.

Meuse, and the Scheldt, which are declared in like manner to be free from the point where each of these rivers becomes navigable to its mouth. Similar regulations respecting the free navigation of the Elbe were established among the powers interested in the commerce of that river, by an act signed at Dresden the 12th December, 1821. And the stipulations between the different powers interested in the free navigation of the Vistula and other rivers of ancient Poland, contained in the treaty of the 3d May, 1815, between Austria and Russia, and of the same date between Russia and Prussia, to which last Austria subsequently acceded, are confirmed by the final act of the Congress of Vienna. The same treaty also extends the general principles adopted by the Congress relating to the navigation of rivers to that of the Po." [The Danube was declared free to commerce, under certain restrictions, by the treaty of Paris, in 1856. See further, on the navigation of rivers, Schuyler's American Diplomacy; Calvo's International Law, 4th Ed., I., 451–467; Hertslet's Map of Europe by Treaty; Englehardt, in the Revue de Droit, International, vol. XI., pp. 363–381. F. S.][1]

(*b*) *Straits.*

THE SOUND DUES.

(*Wheaton's International Law, 3d Ed.*, 231.)

"The supremacy asserted by the king of Denmark over the Sound and the two Belts which form the outlet of the Baltic Sea into the ocean, is rested by the Danish public jurists upon immemorial prescription, sanctioned by a long succession of treaties with other powers. According to these writers, the Danish claim of sovereignty has been exercised from the earliest times beneficially for the protection of commerce against pirates and other enemies by means of guard-ships, and against the perils of the sea by the establishment of lights and land-marks. The Danes continued for several centuries masters of the coasts on both sides of the Sound, the province of Scania not having been ceded to Sweden until the treaty of Roeskild, in 1658, confirmed by that of 1660, in which it was stipulated that Sweden

[1] *South American Rivers.*—The River La Plata, with its branches the Parana and the Uruguay, was opened to general commerce during the period from 1851 to 1859, and the Amazon, during that from 1858 to 1867. (Schuyler's American Diplomacy, 310–344.)

African Rivers.—By act of the conference of Berlin, 1885, the principles of free navigation were extended to the Congo and the Niger.

should never lay claim to the Sound tolls in consequence of the cession, but should content herself with a compensation for keeping up the light-houses on the coast of Scania. The exclusive right of Denmark was recognized as early as 1368, by a treaty with the Hanseatic republics, and by that of 1490, with Henry VII., of England, which forbids English vessels from passing the Great Belt as well as the Sound, unless in case of unavoidable necessity; in which case they were to pay the same duties at Wyborg, as if they had passed the Sound at Elsinore.

"The treaty concluded at Spire, in 1544, with the Emperor Charles V., which has commonly been referred to as the origin, or at least the first recognition, of the Danish claim to the Sound tolls, merely stipulates, in general terms, that the merchants of the Low Countries frequenting the ports of Denmark should pay the same duties as formerly.

"The treaty concluded at Christianople, in 1645, between Denmark and the United Provinces of the Netherlands, is the earliest convention with any foreign power by which the amount of duties to be levied on the passage of the Sound and Belts was definitely ascertained. A tariff of specific duties on certain articles therein enumerated was annexed to this treaty, and it was stipulated that, 'goods not mentioned in the list should pay according to mercantile usage, and what has been practiced from ancient times.'

"A treaty was concluded between the two countries at Copenhagen, in 1701, by which the obscurity in that of Christianople as to the non-specified articles, was meant to be cleared up. By the third article of the new treaty it was declared that as to the goods not specified in the former treaty, 'the Sound duties are to be paid *according to their value;*' that is, they are to be valued *according to the place from whence they come,* and one per centum of their value to be paid.

"These two treaties of 1645 and 1701, are consequently referred to in all subsequent treaties, as furnishing the standard by which the rates of these duties are to be measured as to *privileged* nations. Those *not privileged,* pay according to a more ancient tariff for the specified articles, and one and a quarter per centum on unspecified articles.

"By the arrangement concluded at London and Elsinore, in 1841, between Denmark and Great Britain, the tariff of duties levied on the passage of the Sound and Belts was revised, the duties on non-enumerated articles were made specific, and others reduced in amount, whilst some of the abuses which had crept into the manner of levying the duties in general were corrected. The benefit of this arrangement, which is to subsist for the term of ten years, has been extended to all other nations *privileged* by treaty."

[The Sound dues became so great a burden to commerce that active opposition to them finally arose both in Europe and America; and the right of Denmark to collect them was warmly disputed, especially in the United States. Denmark therefore, in 1855, suggested a project of capitalizing the Sound dues; and in accordance with this suggestion, a European Congress met at Copenhagen, in the winter of 1856, and concluded a treaty, March 14, 1857, by which these dues were forever abolished, in consideration of a present payment of 35,000,000 rix-dollars. The United States declined to become a party to the treaty, because, as President Pierce said, "Denmark does not offer to submit to the convention the question of her right to levy the Sound dues." And further that the proposition contemplated a political result—"the balance of power among the governments of Europe." The United States, however, concluded a separate treaty with Denmark, April 11, 1857, by which 717,829 rix-dollars were paid to Denmark, in consideration of her agreement to keep up lights, buoys, and pilot establishments, thus avoiding the recognition of the right of Denmark to collect the dues. See Schuyler's American Diplomacy, 306; H. R. Ex. Doc., No. 108, 33d Congress, 1st Sess. and Senate Ex. Doc., No., 28, 35th Cong., 1st Sess.—F. S.]

THE BOSPHORUS AND THE DARDANELLES.

(*Wheaton's International Law, 3d Ed., 230.*)

"So long as the shores of the Black Sea were exclusively possessed by Turkey, that sea might with propriety be considered a *mare clausum*; and there seems no reason to question the right of the Ottoman Porte to exclude other nations from navigating the passage which connects it with the Mediterranean, both shores of this passage being at the same time portions of the Turkish territory; but since the territorial acquisitions made by Russia, and the commercial establishments formed by her on the shores of the Euxine, both that empire and the other maritime powers have become entitled to participate in the commerce of the Black Sea, and consequently to the free navigation of the Dardanelles and the Bosphorus. This right was expressly recognized by the seventh article of the treaty of Adrianople, concluded in 1829, between

Russia and the Porte, both as to Russian vessels and those of other European States in amity with Turkey.

"The right of foreign vessels to navigate the interior waters of Turkey, which connect the Black Sea with the Mediterranean does not extend to ships of war. The ancient rule of the Ottoman Empire, established for its own security, by which the entry of foreign vessels of war into the canal of Constantinople, including the strait of the Dardanelles and that of the Black Sea, has been at all times prohibited, was expressly recognized by the treaty concluded at London the 13th July, 1841, between the five great European powers and the Ottoman Porte.

"By the second article, * * * the Sultan reserved the faculty of granting, as heretofore, firmans allowing the passage to light armed vessels employed, according to usage, in the service of the diplomatic legations of friendly powers."

["By the treaty of Paris in 1856, as modified by the treaty London in 1871, the Black Sea was thrown open to merchant vessels of all nations; but the streets are closed to ships of war, except that the Sultan has the faculty of opening them in time of peace to the war vessels of friendly and allied powers in case he deems it necessary for carrying out the stipulations of the treaty of Paris. The United States have never adhered to either of these treaties, and have always maintained that their right to send ships of war into the Black Sea cannot be legally taken from them by any arrangement concluded by European powers to which they are not parties. No attempt, however, has ever been made to exercise these rights. All American ships of war have, while reserving all question of right, asked permission of the Porte to pass the Dardanelles." Schuyler's American Diplomacy, 317.]

(c) *Bays.*

REGINA v. CUNNINGHAM.

COURT FOR CROWN CASES RESERVED, 1859.

(*Bell's Crown Cases*, 722.)

Held, that a crime, committed on a ship lying in the Bristol Channel, at a point where it is more than ten miles wide, is committed within the body of the adjoining county, and subject, therefore, to the jurisdiction of the courts of said county.

This was an action upon an indictment against the three mates of an American vessel, for feloniously wounding one of their seamen.

The offense charged took place in the Penarth Roads, ninety miles from the mouth of the Bristol Channel. The venue was Glamorganshire—the offense took place three-quarters of a mile from the coast of Glamorganshire, at a spot always covered by the tide, but a quarter of a mile from a place which is left dry by the tide.

It was ten miles to the opposite shore. The exact place was between Glamorganshire and an island called the Flat Holms, part of the county of Glamorganshire, and two miles inside that island.

Counsel for the prisoners contended that the offense was committed on the high seas—the Crown that it was in the county of Glamorgan.

The judgment of the court was delivered by COCKBURN, C. J.—"In this case we are of opinion that the conviction is right. The only question with which it becomes necessary for us to deal is whether the part of the sea on which the vessel was at the time when the offense was committed, forms part of the county of Glamorgan; and we are of opinion that it does. The sea in question is part of the Bristol Channel, both shores of which form part of England and Wales, of the county of Somerset on the one side and the county of Glamorgan on the other. We are of opinion that, looking at the local situation of this sea, it must be taken to belong to the counties respectively by the shores of which it is bounded; and the fact of the Holms, between which and the shore of the county of Glamorgan the place in question is situated, having always been treated as part of the parish of Cardiff and as part of the county of Glamorgan, is a strong illustration of the principle on which we proceed, namely, that the whole of this inland sea between the counties of Somerset and Glamorgan is to be considered as within the counties, by the shores of which its several parts are respectively bounded. We are, therefore, of opinion that the place in question is within the body of the county of Glamorgan."

THE DIRECT UNITED STATES CABLE COMPANY v. THE ANGLO-AMERICAN TELEGRAPH COMPANY.

PRIVY COUNCIL, 1877.

(Law Reports, 2 App. Cases, 394.)

Held, that Conception Bay, in Newfoundland, which is something over fifteen miles wide, and forty to fifty miles long, is a British bay, and a part of the territorial waters of Newfoundland.

This suit was one in which the Respondent Company had obtained an injunction against the Appellant Company restraining them from laying a telegraph cable in Conception Bay, Newfoundland, and thereby infringing rights granted by the legislature of that island to the Respondent Company. The Appellant Company contended that Conception Bay (which is rather more than twenty miles wide at its mouth and runs inland between forty and fifty miles) was not British territorial waters, but a part of the high seas. The buoy and cables complained of were laid within the bay at a distance of more than three miles from the shore.

The judgment was delivered by Lord BLACKBURN, who, after reviewing the cases under the Common Law of England continued: "Passing from the Common Law of England, to the general law of nations, as indicated by the text writers on international jurisprudence, we find an universal agreement that harbors, estuaries, and bays land-locked, belong to the territory of the nation which possesses the shores round them, but no agreement as to what is the rule to determine what is "a bay" for this purpose.

"It seems generally agreed that where the configuration and dimensions of the bay are such as to show that the nation occupying the adjoining coasts also occupies the bay, it is part of the territory, and with this idea, most of the writers on the subject refer to defensibility from the shore as the test of occupation; some suggesting, therefore, a width of one cannon-shot from shore to shore, or three miles; some a cannon-shot from each shore, or six miles; some an arbitrary distance of ten miles. All of these are rules which, if adopted, would exclude Conception Bay from the territory of Newfoundland, but also would have excluded from the territory of Great Britain, that part of the British Channel which in *Reg.* v. *Cunningham* was decided to be in the county of Glamorgan. On the other hand, the diplomatists of the United States in 1793 claimed a territorial jurisdiction over much more extensive bays, and Chancellor Kent, in his Commentaries, though by no means giving the weight of his authority to this claim, gives some reasons for not considering it altogether unreasonable. It does not appear to their Lordships that jurists and text-writers are agreed what are the rules as to dimensions and configuration, which, apart from other considerations, would lead to the conclusion that a bay is or is not a part of the territory of the state possessing the adjoining coasts; and it has never, that they can find, been made the ground of any judicial determination. If it was necessary in this case to lay down a rule the difficulty of the task would not deter their Lordships from attempting to fulfill it. But in their opinion it is not necessary so to do. It seems to them that, in point of fact, the British Government has for a long period exercised dominion over this bay, and that their claim has been acquiesced in by other nations, so as to show that the bay has been for a long time occupied exclusively by Great Britain, a circumstance which in the tribunals of any country would be very important. And moreover (which in a British tribunal is conclusive), the British Legislature has by acts of Parliament declared it to be part of the British territory, and part of the country made subject to the Legislature of Newfoundland.

"Their Lordships, therefore, will humbly recommend to Her Majesty that the order of the Supreme Court of Newfoundland be affirmed and that this appeal be dismissed with costs."[1]

MANCHESTER v. MASSACHUSETTS.

SUPREME COURT OF THE UNITED STATES, 1890.

(139 *United States Reports*, 240.)

Manchester, a citizen of Rhode Island was indicted in Massachusetts for taking fish (Menhaden) in Buzzard's Bay, in contravention of the laws of Massachusetts regulating the fishery in that bay. Manchester held a United States license for the Menhaden fishery; and disputed the right of Massachusetts to any jurisdiction over such fisheries.

Held that, in the absence of legislation by Congress on this subject, the States may legally make regulations for the fisheries within their territorial waters.

Arthur Manchester was charged with fishing with a seine in Buzzard's Bay, within the jurisdiction of the Commonwealth of Massachusetts. The complaint is founded upon an act of the Massachusetts' Legislature (Laws of 1886, c. 192), entitled "An act for the protection of the fisheries in Buzzard's Bay," Section I. of which is as follows:—

"No person shall draw, set, stretch or use any drag net, set net or

[1] *The Grange* (1793), 1 Op. Att.-Gen. 32. In the case of the British ship *Grange*, captured by a French privateer in Delaware Bay, in 1793, Attorney-General Randolph held that Delaware Bay formed a part of the territorial waters of the United States, and was therefore neutral ground. He rested his arguments mainly upon the fact that the United States were proprietors of the lands, on both sides of the bay. Every consideration is excluded, "how far the spot of seizure was capable of being defended by the United States. For, although it will not be conceded that this could not be done, yet will it rather appear, that the mutual rights of the States of New Jersey and Delaware, up to the middle of the river (or bay), supersede the necessity of such an investigation."

"No. The corner-stone of our claim is, that the United States are proprietors of the lands on both sides of the Delaware, from its head to its entrance into the sea."

gill net, purse or sweep seine of any kind for taking fish anywhere in the waters of Buzzard's Bay within the jurisdiction of this Commonwealth, nor in any harbor, cove or bight of said bay except as hereinafter provided."

Buzzard's Bay, at its mouth, is more than one and less than two marine leagues in width—at the point where the acts complained of took place, it is more than two leagues in width, and the nearest mainland is not over a mile and a quarter away.

The defendant requested the Court of Massachusetts for a number of rulings, the first and third of which are (1) The act complained of was on the high seas, and without the jurisdiction of Massachusetts. (3) The defendant cannot be held unless the act complained of was done and committed within the body of a county, as understood at common law.

These instructions were refused, and the court told the jury that if they found that the place where the acts were done was within a marine league of the shore, it was within the jurisdiction of the Commonwealth.

The decision being against the defendant, he appealed to the Supreme Court of the United States.

Mr. Justice BLATCHFORD, after stating the case, delivered the opinion of the court:

"The principal contentions in this court on the part of the defendant are that, although Massachusetts, if an independent nation, could have enacted a statute like the one in question, which her own courts would have enforced, and which other nations would have recognized, yet when she became one of the United States, she surrendered to the general government her right of control over the fisheries of the ocean, and transferred to it her rights over the waters adjacent to the coast and a part of the ocean; that, as by the Constitution, article 3, section 2, the judicial power of the United States is made to extend to all cases of admiralty and maritime jurisdiction, it is consistent only with that view that the rights in respect of fisheries should be regarded as national rights, and be enforced only in national courts; that the proprietary right of Massachusetts is confined to the body of the county; that the offense committed by the defendant was committed outside of that territory, in a locality where legislative control did not rest upon title in the soil and waters, but upon rights of sovereignty inseparably connected with national character, and which were intrusted exclusively to enforcement in admiralty courts, that the Commonwealth has no jurisdiction upon the ocean within three miles of the shore; that it could not, by the statute in question, oust the United States of jurisdiction; that fishing upon the high seas is in its nature an integral part of national commerce, and its control and regulation are necessarily vested in Congress and not in the individual states; that Congress has manifested its purpose to take the regulation of coast fisheries, in the particulars covered by the Massachusetts statute in question, by the joint resolution of Congress of February 9, 1871 (16 Stat. 593), establishing the Fish Commission, and by title 51 of the Revised Statutes, entitled 'Regulation of Fisheries,' and by the act of February 28, 1887, c. 288 (24 Stat. 434), relating to the Mackerel fisheries, and by acts relating to bounties, privileges, and agreements, and by granting the license under which the defendant's steamer was fishing; and that, in view of the act of Congress authorizing such license, no statute of a state could defeat the right of the defendant to fish in the high seas under it.

"By the Public Statutes of Massachusetts, part 1, title 1, c. 1, sections 1 and 2, it is enacted as follows: Section 1. 'The territorial limits of this Commonwealth extend one marine league from its seashore at low-water mark. When an inlet or arm of the sea does not exceed two marine leagues in width between its headlands, a straight line from one headland to the other is equivalent to the shore line.' Section 2. 'The sovereignty and jurisdiction of the Commonwealth extend to all places within the boundaries thereof, subject to the rights of concurrent jurisdiction granted over places ceded to the United States.' The same Public Statutes part 1, title 1, c. 22, section 1, contain the following provision: 'The boundaries of counties bordering on the sea shall extend to the line of the Commonwealth, as defined in section one of chapter one.' Section 11 of the same chapter is as follows: 'The jurisdiction of counties separated by waters within the jurisdiction of the Commonwealth shall be concurrent upon and over such waters.' By section 2 of chapter 196 of the acts of Massachusetts of 1881, it is provided as follows: 'Section 2. The harbor and land commissioners shall locate and define the courses of the boundary lines between adjacent cities and towns bordering upon the sea, and upon arms of the sea from high-water mark outward to the line of the Commonwealth, as defined in said section one [section one of chapter one of the General Statutes], so that the same shall conform as nearly as may be to the course of the boundary lines between said adjacent cities and towns on the land; and they shall file a report of their doings with suitable plans and exhibits, showing the boundary lines of any town by them located and defined, in the registry of deeds in which deeds of real estate situated in such town are required to be recorded, and also in the office of the secretary of the Commonwealth.'

"The report of the Superior Court states that the point where the defendant was using the seine was within that part of Buzzard's Bay which the harbor and land commissioners, acting under the provisions of the act of 1881, had, so far as they were capable of doing so, assigned to and made part of the town of Falmouth; that the distance between the headlands at the mouth of Buzzard's Bay 'was more than one and less than two marine leagues;' that 'the distance across said bay, at the point where the acts of the defendant were done, is more than two marine leagues, and the opposite points are in different counties;' and that 'the place where the defendant was so engaged with said seine was about, and not exceeding, one mile and a quarter from a point on the shore midway from the north line of' the town of Falmouth 'to the south line' of that town.

"Buzzard's Bay lies wholly within the territory of Massachusetts, having Barnstable county on the one side of it, and the counties of Bristol and Plymouth on the other. The defendant offered evidence that he was fishing for menhaden only, with a purse seine; that 'the bottom of the sea was not encroached upon or disturbed; that it was impossible to discern objects across from one headland to the other at the mouth of Buzzard's Bay;' and that the steamer was duly enrolled and licensed at the port of Newport, Rhode Island, under the laws of the United States, for carrying on the menhaden fishery.

"By section 1 of chapter 196 of the laws of Massachusetts of 1881, it was enacted as follows: Section 1. 'The boundaries of cities and towns bordering upon the sea shall extend to the line of the Commonwealth as the same is defined in section one of chapter one of the General Statutes.' Section 1 of chapter 1 of the General Statutes contains the provisions before recited as now contained in the Public Statutes, chapter 1, section 1, and chapter 22, sections 1 and 11. Buzzard's Bay was undoubtedly within the territory described in the charter of the Colony of New Plymouth and the Province charter. By the definitive treaty of peace of September 3, 1783, between the United States and Great Britain (8 Stat. 81), His Britannic Majesty acknowledged the United States of which Massachusetts Bay was one, to be free, sovereign and independent States, and declared that he treated with them as such, and, for himself, his heirs and successors, relinquished all claims to the government, proprietary and territorial rights of the same and every part thereof. Therefore, if Massachusetts had continued to be an independent nation, her boundaries on the sea, as defined by her statutes, would unquestionably be acknowledged by all foreign nations, and her right to control the fisheries within those boundaries would be conceded. The limits of the right of a nation to control the fisheries on its sea-coasts, and in the bays and arms of the sea within its territory, have never been placed at less than a marine league from the coast on the open sea; and bays wholly within the territory of a nation, the headlands of which are not more than two marine leagues, or six geographical miles, apart, have always been regarded as a part of the territory of the nation in which they lie. Proceedings of the Halifax Commission of 1877, under the treaty of Washington of May 8, 1871. Executive Document No. 89, 45th Congress, 2d session, Ho. Reps., pp. 120, 121, 166.

"On this branch of the subject the case of *The Queen* v. *Keyn*, 2 Ex. D. 63, is cited for the plaintiff in error; but there the question was not as to the extent of the dominion of Great Britain over the open sea adjacent to the coast, but only as to the extent of the existing jurisdiction of the Court of Admiralty in England over offenses committed on the open sea; and the decision had nothing to do with the right of control over fisheries in the open sea or in bays or arms of the sea.

"In all the cases cited in the opinions delivered in *The Queen* v. *Keyn*, wherever the question of the right of fishery is referred to, it is conceded that the control of fisheries, to the extent of at least a marine league from the shore, belongs to the nation on whose coast the fisheries are prosecuted.

"In *Direct U. S. Cable Co.* v. *Anglo-American Tel. Co.*, 2 App. Cas. 394, it became necessary for the Privy Council to determine whether a point in Conception Bay, Newfoundland, more than three miles from the shore, was a part of the territory of Newfoundland, and within the jurisdiction of its legislature. The average width of the bay was about fifteen miles, and the distance between its headlands was rather more than twenty miles; but it was held that Conception Bay was a part of the territory of Newfoundland, because the British government had exercised exclusive dominion over it, with the acquiescence of other nations, and it had been declared by act of Parliament 'to be part of the British territory, and part of the country made subject to the legislature of Newfoundland.'

"We think it must be regarded as established that, as between nations, the minimum limit of the territorial jurisdiction of a nation over tide-waters is a marine league from its coast; that bays wholly within its territory not exceeding two marine leagues in width at the mouth are within this limit; and that included in this territorial jurisdiction is the right of control over fisheries, whether the fish be migratory, free-swimming fish, or free-moving fish, or fish attached to or embedded in the soil. The open sea within this limit is, of course, subject to the common right of navigation; and all governments, for the purpose of self-protection in time of war or for the prevention of frauds on its revenue, exercise an authority beyond this limit. Gould on Waters, part 1, c. 1, §§ 1-17, and notes; *Neill* v. *Duke of Devonshire*, 8 App. Cas., 135; *Gammell* v. *Commissioners*, 3 Macq., 419; *Mowat* v. *McFee*, 5 Sup. Ct. of Canada, 66; *The Queen* v. *Cubitt*, 22 Q. B. D., 622; St. 46 and 47 Vict. C., 22.

"It is further insisted by the plaintiff in error, that control of the fisheries of Buzzard's Bay is, by the constitution of the United States, exclusively with the United States, and that the statute of Massachusetts is repugnant to that Constitution and to the laws of the United States. * * *

"Under the grant by the Constitution of judicial power to the United States in all cases of admiralty and maritime jurisdiction, and under the rightful legislation of Congress, personal suits on maritime contracts or for maritime torts can be maintained in the state courts; and the courts of the United States, merely by virtue of this grant of judicial power, and in the absence of legislation by Congress, have no criminal jurisdiction whatever. The criminal jurisdiction of the courts of the United States is wholly derived from the statutes of the United States. * * *

"In each of the cases of *United States* v. *Bevans*, 3 Wheat., 336, and of *Commonwealth* v. *Peters*, 12 Met., 387, the place where the offense was committed was in Boston Harbor; and it was held to be within the jurisdiction of Massachusetts, according to the meaning of the statutes of the United States which punished certain offenses committed upon the high seas or in any river, haven, basin or bay 'out of the jurisdiction of any particular state.' The test applied in *Commonwealth* v. *Peters*, which was decided in the year 1847, was that the place was within a bay 'not so wide but that persons and objects on the one side can be discerned by the naked eye by persons on the opposite side,' and was therefore within the body of a county. In *United States* v. *Bevans*, MARSHALL, C. J., said: 'The jurisdiction of a state is coextensive with its territory; coextensive with its legislative power. The place described is unquestionably within the original territory of Massachusetts. It is then within the jurisdiction of Massachusetts, unless that jurisdiction has been ceded to the United States.' If the place where the offense charged in this case was committed is within the general jurisdiction of Massachusetts, then, according to the principles declared in *Smith* v. *Maryland*, the statute in question is not repugnant to the constitution and laws of the United States.

"It is also contended that the jurisdiction of a state as between it and the United States must be confined to the body of counties; that counties must be defined according to the customary English usage at the time of the adoption of the Constitution of the United States; that by this usage counties were bounded by the margin of the open sea; and that, as to bays and arms of the sea extending into the land, only such or such parts were included in counties as were so narrow that objects could be distinctly seen from one shore to the other by the naked eye. But there is no indication that the customary law of England in regard to the boundaries of counties was adopted by the Constitution of the United States as a measure to determine the territorial jurisdiction of the states.

"The extent of the territorial jurisdiction of Massachusetts over the sea adjacent to its coast is that of an independent nation; and, except so far as any right of control over this territory has been granted to the United States, this control remains with the state. In *United States* v. *Bevans*, MARSHALL, C. J., in the opinion, asks the following questions: 'Can the cession of all cases of admiralty and maritime jurisdiction be construed into a cession of the waters on which those cases may arise? As the powers of the respective Governments now stand, if two citizens of Massachusetts step into shallow water where the tide flows, and fight a duel, are they not within the jurisdiction, and punishable by the laws of Massachusetts?' The statutes of the United States define and punish but few offenses on the high seas, and, unless other offenses when committed in the sea near the coast can be punished by the states, there is a large immunity from punishment for acts which ought to be punishable as criminal. Within what are generally recognized as the territorial limits of states by the law of nations, a state can define its boundaries on the sea and the boundaries of its counties; and by this test the Commonwealth of Massachusetts can include Buzzard's Bay within the limits of its counties.

"The statutes of Massachusetts, in regard to bays at least, make definite boundaries which, before the passage of the statutes, were somewhat indefinite; and Rhode Island and some other states have passed similar statutes defining their boundaries. Public Statutes of Rhode Island, 1882, c. 1, §§ 1, 2; c. 3, § 6; Gould on Waters, § 16 and note. The waters of Buzzard's Bay are, of course, navigable waters of the United States, and the jurisdiction of Massachusetts over them is necessarily limited, *Commonwealth* v. *King*, 150 Mass., 221; but there is no occasion to consider the power of the United States to regulate or control, either by treaty or legislation, the fisheries in these waters, because there are no existing treaties or acts of Congress which relate to the menhaden fisheries in such a bay.

"The rights granted to British subjects by the treaties of June 5, 1854, and May 8, 1871, to take fish upon the shores of the United States, had expired before the statute of Massachusetts (St. 1886, c. 192) was passed, which the defendant is charged with violating. The Fish Commission was instituted 'for the protection and preservation of the food fishes of the coast of the United States.'

"Title 51 of the Revised Statutes relates solely to food fisheries, and so does the Act of 1888. Nor are we referred to any decision which holds that the other acts of Congress alluded to apply to fisheries for menhaden, which is found as a fact in this case not to be a food fish, and to be only valuable for the purpose of bait and of manufacture into fish oil.

"The statute of Massachusetts which the defendant is charged with violating is, in terms, confined to waters, 'within the jurisdiction of this commonwealth;' and it was evidently passed for the preservation of the fish, and makes no discrimination in favor of citizens of Massachusetts and against citizens of other states. If there be a liberty of fishing for swimming fish in the navigable waters of the United States common to the inhabitants or the citizens of the United States, upon which we express no opinion, the statute may well be considered as an impartial and reasonable regulation of this liberty; and the subject is one which a State may well be permitted to regulate within its territory, in the absence of any regulation by the United States. The preservation of fish, even although they are not used as food for human beings, but as food for other fish which are so used, is for the common benefit; and we are of opinion that the statute is not repugnant to the constitution and the laws of the United States.

"It may be observed that § 4398 of the Revised Statutes (a re-enactment of § 4 of the joint resolution of February 9, 1871), provides as follows, in regard to the Commission of Fish and Fisheries: 'The commissioner may take or cause to be taken at all times, in the waters of the sea-coast of the United States, where the tide ebbs and flows, and also in the waters of the lakes, such fish or specimens thereof as may in his judgment, from time to time, be needful or proper for the conduct of his duties; any law, custom or usage of any state to the contrary notwithstanding.' This enactment may not improperly be construed as suggesting that, as against the law of a state, the Fish Commissioner might not otherwise have the right to take fish in places covered by the State law.

"The pertinent observation may be made that, as Congress does not assert, by legislation, a right to control pilots in the bays, inlets, rivers, harbors, and ports of the United States, but, leaves the regulation of that matter to the states, *Cooley* v. *Board of Wardens*, 12 How., 299, so if it does not assert by affirmative legislation its right or will to assume the control of menhaden fisheries in such bays, the right to control such fisheries must remain with the State which contains such bays.

" We do not consider the question whether or not Congress would have the right to control the menhaden fisheries which the statute of Massachusetts assumes to control; but we mean to say only that as the right of control exists in the State in the absence of the affirmative action of Congress taking such control, the fact that Congress has never assumed the control of such fisheries is persuasive evidence that the right to control them still remains in the State." [1]

[1] In the case of *Dunham* v. *Lamphere*, 1855, 3 Gray, 268, before the Supreme Court of Massachusetts, SHAW, C. J., said: " We suppose the rule to be that those limits extend a marine league, or three geographical miles from the shore ; and in ascertaining the line of shore this limit does not follow each narrow inlet or arm of the sea, but when the inlet is so narrow that persons and objects, can be discerned across it by the naked eye, the line of territorial jurisdiction stretches across from one headland to the other of such inlet."

(*d*) *Marginal Seas.*

THE QUEEN v. KEYN.

COURT OF CROWN CASES RESERVED, 1876.

(*L. R.*, 2 *Exchequer Division*, 63.)

History of the development of the rule fixing the limit of territorial waters at three miles.

A foreigner, sailing along the English coast, within this three-mile zone, commits an offense against an English subject. *Held*, that he was not subject to the jurisdiction of the Admiralty, nor its successor the Central Criminal Court, in the absence of an act of Parliament expressly conferring such jurisdiction.

The prisoner was indicted at the Central Criminal Court for the manslaughter of Jessie Dorcas Young on the high seas, and within the jurisdiction of the Admiralty of England. The deceased was a passenger on board the *Strathclyde*, a British steamer bound from London to Bombay. This vessel, when one and nine-tenths of a mile from Dover pier-head, and within two and a half miles from Dover beach, was run down and sunk by the *Franconia*, a German steamer. In the collision, the deceased woman was drowned, and the prisoner, the captain of the *Franconia*, is convicted of manslaughter; but a question of law is reserved.

An objection was taken on the part of the prisoner that, inasmuch as he was a foreigner, in a foreign vessel, on a foreign voyage, sailing upon the high seas, he was not subject to the jurisdiction of any court in this country.

The Crown contends that inasmuch as, at the time of the collision, both vessels were within the distance of three miles from the English shore, the offense was committed within the realm of England, and is triable by the English court.

The case was argued before Cockburn, C. J., Lord Coleridge, C. J., Kelly, C. B., Sir R. Phillimore, Bramwell, Pollock, and Amphlett, B. B., Lush, Brett, Grove, Denman, Archibald,* Field and Lindley, JJ.

COCKBURN, C. J;—"The question is, whether the accused is amenable to our law, and whether there was jurisdiction to try him?

"The legality of the conviction is contested, on the ground that the accused is a foreigner; that the *Franconia*, the ship he commanded, was a foreign vessel, sailing from a foreign port, bound on a foreign voyage; that the alleged offense was committed on the high seas. Under these circumstances, it is contended that the accused, though he may be amenable to the law of his own country, is not capable of being tried and punished by the law of England.

"The facts on which this defense is based are not capable of being disputed; but a twofold answer is given on the part of the prosecution:—1st. That, although the occurrence on which the charge is founded took place on the high seas in this sense that the place in which it happened was not within the body of a county, it occurred within three miles of the English coast; that by the law of nations, the sea, for a space of three miles from the coast, is part of the territory of the country to which the coast belongs; that, consequently, the *Franconia*, at the time the offense was committed, was in English waters, and those on board were therefore subject to English law.

"Secondly. That, although the negligence of which the accused was guilty occurred on board a foreign vessel, the death occasioned by such negligence took place on board a British vessel; and that, as a British vessel is, in point of law to be considered British territory, the offense, having been consummated by the death of the deceased in a British ship, must be considered as having been committed on British territory. * * *

"According to the general law, a foreigner who is not resid-

*Archibald, J., died after the agument and before the judgment was delivered.

ing permanently or temporarily in British territory, or on board a British ship, cannot be held responsible for an infraction of the law of this country.

"Unless, therefore, the accused, Keyn, at the time the offense of which he has been convicted was committed, was on British territory or on board a British ship, he could not be properly brought to trial under British law, in the absence of express legislation. * * *

"In the reign of Charles II., Sir Leoline Jenkins, then the judge of the Court of Admiralty, in a charge to the grand jury at an Admiralty sessions at the Old Bailey, not only asserted the king's sovereignty within the four seas, and that it was his right and province 'to keep the public peace on these seas'—that is, as Sir Leoline expounds it, 'to preserve his subjects and allies in their possessions and properties upon these seas, and in all freedom and security to pass to and fro on them, upon their lawful occasions,' but extended this authority and jurisdiction of the King. 'To preserve the public peace and to maintain the freedom and security of navigation all the world over; so that not the utmost bound of the Atlantic Ocean, nor any corner of the Mediterranean, nor any part of the South or other seas, but that if the peace of God and the King be violated upon any of his subjects, or upon his allies or their subjects, and the offender be afterwards brought up or laid hold of in any of His Majesty's ports, such breach of the peace is to be inquired of and tried in virtue of a commission of oyer and terminer as this is, in such county, liberty, or place as His Majesty shall please to direct—so long an arm hath God by the laws given to his vicegerent the King.' * * *

"Venice, in like manner, laid claim to the Adriatic, Genoa to the Ligurian Sea, Denmark to a portion of the North Sea.

"The Portuguese claimed to bar the ocean route to India and the Indian Seas to the rest of the world, while Spain made the like assertion with reference to the West.

"All these vain and extravagant pretensions have long since given way to the influence of reason and common sense.

"If, indeed, the sovereignty thus asserted had a real existence, and could now be maintained, it would of course, independently of any question as to the three-mile zone, be conclusive of the present case. But the claim to such sovereignty, at all times unfounded, has long since been abandoned. No one would now dream of asserting that the sovereign of these realms has any greater right over the surrounding seas than the sovereigns on the opposite shores; or that it is the especial duty and privilege of the Queen of Great Britain to keep the peace in these seas; or that the Court of Admiralty could try a foreigner for an offense committed in a foreign vessel in all parts of the Channel.

"No writer of our day, except Mr. Chitty in his treatise on the prerogative, has asserted the ancient doctrine. Blackstone, in his chapter on the prerogative in the Commentaries, while he asserts that the narrow seas are part of the realm, puts it only on the ground that the jurisdiction of the Admiralty extends over these seas.

"He is silent as to any jurisdiction over foreigners within them. The concensus of jurists, which has been so much insisted on as authority, is perfectly unanimous as to the non-existence of any such jurisdiction. Indeed, it is because this claim of sovereignty is admitted to be untenable that it has been found necessary to resort to the theory of the three-mile zone.

"It is in vain, therefore, that the ancient assertion of sovereignty over the narrow seas is invoked to give countenance to the rule now sought to be established, of jurisdiction over the three-mile zone.

"If this rule is to prevail, it must be on altogether different grounds. To invoke, as its foundation or in its support, an assertion of sovereignty which, for all practical purposes, is, and always has been, idle and unfounded, and the invalidity of which renders it necessary to have recourse to the new doctrine, involves an inconsistency, on which it would be superfluous to dwell. I must confess myself unable to comprehend how, when the ancient doctrine as to sovereignty over the narrow seas is adduced, its operation can be confined to the three-mile zone. If the argument is good for anything, it must apply to the whole of the surrounding seas. But the counsel for the Crown evidently shrank from applying it to this extent. Such a pretension would not be admitted or endured by foreign nations. That it is out of this extravagant assertion of sovereignty that the doctrine of the three-mile jurisdiction, asserted on the part of the Crown, and which, the older claim being necessarily abandoned, we are now called upon to consider, has sprung up, I readily admit. * * *

"With the celebrated work of Grotius, published in 1609, began the great contest of the jurists as to the freedom of the seas. "The controversy ended, as controversies often do, in a species of compromise. While maintaining the freedom of the seas, Grotius, in his work *De Jure Belli et Pacis*, had expressed an opinion that, while no right could be acquired to the exclusive possession of the ocean, an exclusive right or jurisdiction might be acquired in respect of particular portions of the sea adjoining the territory of individual states. * * *

"Other writers adopted a similar principle, but with very varying views as to the extent to which the right might be exercised. Albericus Gentiles extended it to 100 miles; Baldus and Bodinus to sixty.

"Loccenius (*De Jure Maritimo*, ch. iv., s. 6) puts it at two days' sail; another writer makes it extend as far as could be seen from the shore. Valin, in his Commentary on the French Ordinances of 1681 (ch. v.), would have it reach as far as bottom could be found with the lead line. * * *

"Differing altogether from these writers as to the extent of maritime sovereignty, Bynkershoek, an advocate, like Grotius, for the *mare liberum*, and who entered the lists against Selden as to the dominion of England in the so-called English Sea, in his treatise *De Dominio Maris*, published in 1702, follows up the idea of Grotius as to a limited dominion of the sea from the shore. * * *

"After combating the doctrine of a *mare clausum* as regards the sea at large, and enumerating these inconsistent opinions, which he seems little disposed to respect, Bynkershoek continues: 'Hinc videas priscos juris magistros, qui dominium in mare proximum ausi sunt agnoscere, in regundis ejus finibus admodum vagari incertos.' 'Quare omnino videtur rectius,' he adds, after disposing of the foregoing opinions, 'Eo potestatem terræ extendi, quousque tormenta exploduntur; eatenus quippe, cum imperare, tum possidere videmur. Loquor autem de his temporibus; quibus illis machinis utimur; alioquin generaliter decendum esset, potestatem terræ finiri, ubi finitur armorum vis; etenim haec, ut diximus, possessionem tuetur.'

"We have here, for the first time, so far as I am aware, a suggestion as to a territorial dominion over the sea, extending as far as cannon-shot would reach—a distance which succeeding writers fixed at a marine league, or three miles. Prior to this, no one had suggested such a limit.

"The jurisdiction, assumed in the Admiralty commissions, or exercised by the Court of King's Bench in the time of the Edwards, was founded on the King's alleged sovereignty over the whole of the narrow seas; it had no reference whatever to any notion of a territorial sea. To English lawyers the idea of this limited jurisdiction was utterly unknown.

"With Selden and Hale, they stood up stoutly for the King's undivided dominion over the four seas. No English author makes any distinction, as regards the dominion of the Crown, between the narrow seas as a whole and any portion of them as adjacent to the shore. The doctrine was equally unknown to the Scotch lawyers. * * *

"Even to our times the doctrine of the three-mile zone has never been adopted by the writers on English law. To Blackstone who, in his Commentaries, treats of the sea with reference to the prerogative, as also to his modern editor, Mr. Stephen, it is unknown; equally so to Mr. Chitty, whose work on the prerogative is of the present century. It was not till the beginning of this century that any mention of such a doctrine occurs in the courts of this country. But to the continental jurists, the suggestion of Bynkershoek seemed a happy solution of the great controversy as to the freedom of the sea; and the formula, *potestas finitur ubi finitur armorum vis*, was a taking one; and succeeding publicists adopted and repeated the rule which their predecessor had laid down, without much troubling themselves to ascertain or inquire whether that rule had been recognized and adopted by the maritime nations who were to be affected by it. * * *

"But to what, after all, do these ancient authorities amount? Of what avail are they towards establishing that the soil in the three-mile zone is part of the territorial domain of the Crown? These assertions of sovereignty were manifestly based on the doctrine that the narrow seas are part of the realm of England. But that doctrine is now exploded. Who at this day would venture to affirm that the sovereignty thus asserted in those times now exists? What English lawyer is there who would not shrink from maintaining—what foreign jurist who would not deny—what foreign government which would not repel such a pretension? I listened carefully to see whether such an assertion would be made; but none was made. No one has gone the length of suggesting, much less of openly asserting, that the jurisdiction still exists. It seems to me, that when the sovereignty and jurisdiction from which the property in the soil of the sea was inferred is gone, the territorial property which was suggested to be consequent upon it, must necessarily go with it. * * *

"It thus appearing, as it seems to me that the littoral sea beyond low-water mark did not, as distinguished from the rest of the high seas, originally form part of the territory of the realm, the question again presents itself, when and how did it become so? Can a portion of that which was before high sea have been converted into British territory, without any action on the part of the British government or legislature—by the mere assertions of writers on public law—or even by the assent of other nations?

"And when in support of this position, or of the theory of the three-mile zone in general, the statements of the writers on international law are relied on, the question may well be asked, upon what authority are these statements founded?

"When and in what manner have the nations, who are to be affected by such a rule as these writers, following one another, have laid down, signified their assent to it? to say nothing of the difficulty which might be found in saying to which of these conflicting opinions such assent had been given.

"For, even if entire unanimity had existed in respect of the important particulars to which I have referred, in place of so much discrepancy of opinion, the question would still remain, how far the law as stated by the publicists had received the assent of the civilized nations of the world.

"For writers on international law, however valuable their labors may be in elucidating and ascertaining the principles and rules of law, cannot make the law. To be binding, the law must have received the assent of the nations who are to be bound by it. This assent may be express, as by treaty or the acknowledged concurrence of governments, or may be implied from established usage,—an instance of which is to be found in the fact that merchant vessels on the high seas are held to be subject only to the law of the nation under whose flag they sail, while in the ports of a foreign state they are subject to the local law as well as to that of their own country. In the absence of proof of assent, as derived from one or other of these sources, no unanimity on the part of theoretical writers would warrant the judicial application of the law on the sole authority of their views or statements. Nor, in my opinion, would the clearest proof of unanimous assent on the part of other nations be sufficient to authorize the tribunals of this country to apply, without an Act of Parliament, what would practically amount to a new law. In so doing we should be unjustifiably usurping the province of the legislature. The assent of nations is doubtless sufficient to give the power of parliamentary legislation in a matter otherwise within the sphere of international law, but it would be powerless to confer without such legislation a jurisdiction beyond and unknown to the law, such as that now insisted on, a jurisdiction over foreigners in foreign ships on a portion of the high seas.

"When I am told that all other nations have assented to such an absolute dominion on the part of the littoral state, over this portion of the sea, as that their ships may be excluded from it, and that, without any open legislation, or notice to them or their subjects, the latter may be held liable to the local law, I ask first what proof there is of such assent as here asserted; and, secondly, to what extent has such assent been carried; a question of infinite importance, when undirected by legislation, we are called upon to apply the law on the strength of such assent. It is said that we are to take the statements of the publicists as conclusive proof of the assent in question, and much has been said to impress on us the respect which is due to their authority, and that they are to be looked upon as witnesses of the facts to which they speak, witnesses whose statements, or the foundation on which those statements rest, we are scarcely at liberty to question. I demur altogether to this position. I entertain a profound respect for the opinion of jurists when dealing with the matters of judicial principle and opinion, but we are here dealing with a question not of opinion but of fact, and I must assert my entire liberty to examine the evidence and see upon what foundation these statements are based.

"The question is not one of theoretical opinion, but of fact, and, fortunately, the writers upon whose statements we are called upon to act have afforded us the means of testing those statements by reference to facts. They refer us to two things, and to these alone—treaties and usage.

"Let us look a little more closely into both.

"First, then, let us see how the matter stands, as regards treaties. It may be asserted, without fear of contradiction, that the rule that the sea surrounding the coast is to be treated as a part of the adjacent territory, so that the state shall have exclusive dominion over it, and that the law of the latter shall be generally applicable to those passing over it in the ships of other nations, has never been made the subject matter of any treaty, or, as matter of acknowledged right, has formed the basis of any treaty, or has ever been the subject of diplomatic discussion. It has been entirely the creation of the writers on international law. It is true that the writers who have been cited, constantly refer to treaties in support of the doctrine they assert. But when the treaties they refer to are looked at, they will be found to relate to two subjects only—the observance of the rights and obligations of neutrality, and the exclusive right of fishing. In fixing the limits to which these rights should extend, nations have so far followed the writers on international law as to adopt the three miles range as a convenient distance. There are several treaties by which nations have engaged, in the event of either of them being at war with a third, to treat the sea within three miles of each other's coasts as neutral territory, within which no warlike operations should be carried on; instances of which will be found in the various treatises on international law. Thus for instance, in the treaties of commerce, between Great Britain and France, of September, 1786; between France and Russia of January, 1787; between Great Britain and the United States, of October, 1794, each contracting party engages, if at war with any other nation, not to carry on hostilities within cannon shot of the coast of the other contracting party; or, if the other should be at war, not to allow its vessels to be captured within the like distance. There are many other treaties of the like tenor, a list of which is given by Azuni (vol., II p. 78); and various ordinances and laws have been made by the different states in order to give effect to them.

"Again, nations, possessing opposite or neighboring coasts, bordering on a common sea, have sometimes found it expedient to agree that the subjects of each shall exercise an exclusive right of fishing to a given distance from their own shores, and here also have accepted the three miles as a convenient distance. Such, for instance, are the treaties made between this country and the United States, in relation to the fishery off the coast of Newfoundland, and those between this country and France, in relation to the fishery on their respective shores; and local laws have been passed to give effect to these engagements.

"But in all these treaties this distance is adopted, not as matter of existing right established by the general law of nations, but as matter of mutual concession and convention. Instead of upholding the doctrine contended for, the fact of these treaties having been entered into has rather the opposite tendency; for it is obvious that, if the territorial right of a nation bordering on the sea to this portion of the adjacent waters had been established by the common assent of nations, these treaty arrangements would have been wholly superfluous.

"Each nation would have been bound, independently of treaty engagement, to respect the neutrality of the other in these waters as much as in its inland waters. The foreigner invading the rights of the local fisherman would have been amenable, consistently with international law, to local legislation prohibiting such infringement, without any stipulation to that effect by treaty. For what object, then, have treaties been resorted to? Manifestly in order to obviate all questions as to concurrent or conflicting rights arising under the law of nations.

"Possibly, after these precedents and all that has been written on this subject, it may not be too much to say that, independently of treaty, the three-mile belt of sea might at this day be taken as belonging for these purposes, to the local state.

"But it is scarcely logical to infer, from such treaties alone, that, because nations have agreed to treat the littoral sea as belonging to the country it adjoins, for certain specified objects, they have therefore assented to forego all other rights previously enjoyed in common, and have submitted themselves, even to the extent of the right of navigation on a portion of the high seas, and the liability of their subjects therein to the criminal law, to the will of the local sovereign, and the jurisdiction of the local state. Equally illogical is it, as it seems to me, from the adoption of the three-mile distance in these particular instances, to assume, independently of everything else, a recognition, by the common assent of nations, of the principle that the subjects of one state passing in ships within three miles of the coast of another, shall be in all respects subject to the law of the latter. It may be that the maritime nations of the world are prepared to acquiesce in the appropriation of the littoral sea; but I cannot think that these treaties help us much towards arriving at the conclusion that this appropriation has actually taken place. At all events, the question remains, whether judicially we can infer that the nations who have been parties to these treaties, and, still further, those who have not, have thereby assented to the application of the criminal law of other nations to their subjects on the waters in question, and on the strength of such inference so apply the criminal law of this country.

"The uncertainty in which we are left, so far as judicial knowledge is concerned, as to the extent of such assent, likewise presents, I think, a very serious obstacle to our assuming the jurisdiction we are called upon to exercise, independently of the, to my mind, still more serious difficulty, that we should be assuming it without legislative warrant.

"So much for treaties. Then how stands the matter as to usage, to which reference is so frequently made by the publicists in support of their doctrine?

"When the matter is looked into, the only usage found to exist is such as is connected with navigation, or with revenue, local fisheries, or neutrality, and it is to these alone that the usage relied on is confined. Usage as to the application of the general law of the local state to foreigners on the littoral sea, there is actually none. No nation has arrogated to itself the right of excluding foreign vessels from the use of its external littoral waters for the purpose of navigation, or has assumed the power of making foreigners in foreign ships passing through these waters subject to its law, otherwise than in respect of the matters to which I have just referred. Nor have the tribunals of any nation held foreigners in these waters amenable generally to the local criminal law in respect of offenses. It is for the first time in the annals of jurisprudence that a court of justice is now called upon to apply the criminal law of the country to such a case as the present.

"It may well be, I say again, that—after all that has been said and done in this respect—after the instances which have been mentioned of the adoption of the three-mile distance, and the repeated assertion of this doctrine by the writers on public law, a nation which should now deal with this portion of the sea as its own, so as to make foreigners within it subject to its law, for the prevention and punishment of offenses, would not be considered as infringing the rights of other nations. But I apprehend that as the ability so to deal with these waters would result, not from any original or inherent right, but, from the acquiescence of other states, some outward manifestation of the national will, in the shape of open practice or municipal legislation, so as to amount, at least constructively, to an occupation of that which was before unappropriated, would be necessary to render the foreigner, not previously amenable to our general law, subject to its control.

"That such legislation, whether consistent with the general law of nations or not, would be binding on the tribunals of this country—leaving the question of its consistency with international law to be determined between the governments of the respective nations—can of course admit of no doubt. The question is whether such legislation would not, at all events, be necessary to justify our courts in applying the law of this country to foreigners under entirely novel circumstances in which it has never been applied before. * * *

"It is unnecessary to the defense, and equally so to the decision of the case, to determine whether Parliament has the right to treat the three-mile zone as part of the realm consistently with international law.

"That is a matter on which it is for Parliament itself to decide. It is enough for us that it has, so far as to be binding upon us, the power to do so. The question is whether, acting judicially, we can treat the power of Parliament to legislate as making up for the absence of actual legislation.

"I am clearly of opinion that we cannot, and that it is only in the instance in which foreigners on the sea have been made specifically liable to our law by statutory enactment that that law can be applied to them.* * *

"Hitherto, legislation, so far as relates to foreigners in foreign ships in this part of the sea, has been confined to the maintenance of neutral rights and obligations, the prevention of breaches of the revenue and fishery laws, and, under particular circumstances, to cases of collision.

"In the two first the legislation is altogether irrespective of the three-mile distance, being founded on a totally different principle, namely, the right of a state to take all necessary measures for the protection of its territory and rights, and the prevention of any breach of its revenue laws. * * *

"It is apparent that, with the exception of the penalties imposed for violation of neutral duties or breaches of the revenue or fishery laws, there has been no assertion of legislative authority in the general application of the penal law to foreigners within the three-mile zone. The legislature has omitted to adopt the alleged sovereignty over the littoral sea, to the extent of making our penal law applicable generally to foreigners passing through it for the purpose of navigation. Can a court of justice take upon itself, in such a matter, to do what the legislature has not thought fit to do—that is, make the whole body of our penal law applicable to foreign vessels within three miles of our coast?

"It is further apparent from these instances of specific legislation that, when ascertaining its power to legislate with reference to the foreigner within the three-mile zone, Parliament has deemed it necessary, wherever it was thought right to subject him to our law, expressly to enact that he should be so. We must take this, I think, as an exposition of the opinion of Parliament that specific legislation is here necessary, and consequently, that without it the foreigner in a foreign vessel will not come within the general law of this country in respect of matters arising on the sea.

"Legislation, in relation to foreign ships coming into British ports and waters, rests on a totally different principle, as was well explained by Dr. Lushington, in the case of *The Annapolis*.[1]

"'The Parliament of Great Britain it is true,' says Dr. Lushington, 'has not, according to the principles of public law, any authority to legislate for foreign vessels on the high seas, or for foreigners out of the limits of British jurisdiction; though, if Parliament thought fit so to do, this court, in its instance jurisdiction at least, would be bound to obey. In cases admitting of doubt, the presumption would be that Parliament intended to legislate without violating any rule of international law, and the construction has been accordingly.

"'Within, however, British jurisdiction, namely, within British territory, and at sea within three miles from the coast, and within all British rivers *intra fauces*, and over foreigners in British ships, I apprehend that the British Parliament has an undoubted right to legislate. I am further of opinion that Parliament has a perfect right

[1] Lush. Adm. 295.

to say to foreign ships that they shall not, without complying with British law, enter into British ports, and that if they do enter they shall be subject to penalties, unless they have previously complied with the requisitions ordained by the British Parliament whether those requisitions be, as in former times, certificates of origin, or clearance of any description from a foreign port, or clean bills of health, or the taking on board a pilot at any place in or out of British jurisdiction before entering British waters.

" 'Whether the Parliament has so legislated is now the question to be considered.' * * *

"In the result, looking to the fact that all pretension to sovereignty or jurisdiction over foreign ships in the narrow seas has long since been wholly abandoned—to the uncertainty which attaches to the doctrine of the publicists as to the degree of sovereignty and jurisdiction which may be exercised on the so-called territorial sea—to the fact that the right of absolute sovereignty therein, and of penal jurisdiction over the subjects of other states, has never been expressly asserted or conceded among independent nations, or, in practice, exercised, and acquiesced in, except for violation of neutrality or breach of revenue or fishery laws, which, as has been pointed out, stand on a different footing as well as to the fact that, neither in legislating with reference to shipping, nor in respect of the criminal law, has Parliament thought proper to assume territorial sovereignty over the three-mile zone, so as to enact that all offenses committed upon it, by foreigners in foreign ships, should be within the criminal law of this country, but, on the contrary, wherever it was thought right to make the foreigner amenable to our law, has done so by express and specific legislation. I cannot think that, in the absence of all precedent, and of any judicial decision or authority applicable to the present purpose, we should be justified in holding an offense, committed under such circumstances, to be punishable by the law of England, especially as in so holding we must declare the whole body of our penal law to be applicable to the foreigner passing our shores in a foreign vessel on his way to a foreign port. * * *

"Having arrived at this conclusion, it becomes necessary to consider the second point taken on the part of the Crown, namely, that though the negligence of which the accused was guilty occurred on board a foreign ship, yet, the death having taken place on board a British ship, the offense was committed within the jurisdiction of a British court of justice. * * *

"The question is—and this appears to me to have been lost sight of in the argument—not whether the death of the deceased, which no doubt took place in a British ship, was the act of the defendant in such ship, but whether the defendant, at the time the act was done, was himself within British jurisdiction.

"But in point of fact, the defendant was, at the time of the occurrence, not on board the British ship, the *Strathclyde*, but on a foreign ship, the *Franconia*. * * *

"But in order to render a foreigner liable to the local law, he must, at the time the offense was committed, have been within British territory if on land, or in a British ship if at sea. I cannot think that if two ships of different nations met on the ocean, and a person on board of one of them were killed or wounded by a shot fired from the other, the person firing it would be amenable to the law of the ship in which the shot took effect."

Lush, J., said, in part: "In the reign of Richard II., the realm consisted of the land within the body of the counties. All beyond low-water mark was part of the high seas.

"At that period the three-mile radius had not been thought of. International law, which, upon this subject at least, has grown up since that period, cannot enlarge the area of our muncipal law, nor could treaties with all the nations of the world have that effect. That can only be done by Act of Parliament. As no such act has been passed, it follows that what was out of the realm then is out of the realm now, and what was part of the high seas then is part of the high seas now; and upon the high seas the Admiralty jurisdiction was confined to British ships. Therefore, although, as between nation and nation, these waters are British territory, as being under the exclusive dominion of Great Britain, in judicial language they are out of the realm, and any exercise of criminal jurisdiction over a foreign ship in these waters must in my judgment be authorized by an Act of Parliament."

Lord Coleridge, C. J., dissenting from the opinion of the majority, said, in part * * * "But, first, I think the offense was committed within the realm of England; and if so, there was jurisdiction to try it. * * *

"Now the offense was committed much nearer to the line of low-water mark than three miles; and therefore, in my opinion, upon English territory. I pass by for the moment the question of the exact limit of the realm of England beyond low-water mark, I am of opinion that it does go beyond low-water mark; and if it does, no limit has ever been suggested which would exclude from the realm the place where this offense was committed. But for the difference of opinion of the Bench, and for the great deference which is due to those who differ from me, I should have said it was impossible to hold that England ended with low-water mark.

I do not of course forget that it is freely admitted to be within the competency of Parliament to extend the realm how far soever it pleases to extend it by enactments, at least so as to bind the tribunals of the country; and I admit equally freely that no statute has in plain terms, or by definite limits, so extended it.

"But, in my judgment, no Act of Parliament was required. The proposition contended for, as I understand, is that for any act of violence committed by a foreigner upon an English subject within a few feet of low-water mark, unless it happens on board a British ship, the foreigner cannot be tried, and is dispunishable. * * *

"By a consensus of writers, without one single authority to the contrary, some portion of the coast-waters of a country is considered for some purposes to belong to the country the coasts of which they wash. * * *

"This is established as solidly, as, by the very nature of the case, any proposition of international law can be. Strictly speaking, international law is an inexact expression and it is apt to mislead if its inexactness is not kept in mind. Law implies a law-giver, and a tribunal capable of enforcing it and coercing its transgressors.

"But there is no common law-giver to sovereign states and no tribunal has the power to bind them by decrees or coerce them if they transgress. The law of nations is that collection of usages which civilized states have agreed to observe in their dealings with one another. What these usages are, whether a particular one has or has not been agreed to, must be matter of evidence. Treaties and acts of state are but evidence of the agreement of nations, and do not in this county at least *per se* bind the tribunals. Neither, certainly does a consensus of jurists; but it is evidence of the agreement of nations on international points; and on such points, when they arise, the English courts give effect, as part of English law, to such agreement. * * *

"We find a number of men of education, of many different nations, most of them uninterested in maintaining any particular thesis as to the matter now in question, agreeing generally for nearly three centuries in the proposition that the territory of a maritime country extends beyond low-water mark.

"I can hardly myself conceive stronger evidence to show that, as far as it depends on the agreement of nations, the territory of maritime countries does so extend. * * *

"If the matter were to be determined for the first time, I should not hesitate to hold that civilized nations had agreed to this prolongation of the territory of maritime states, upon the authority of the writers who have been cited in this argument as laying down the affirmative of this proposition. * * *

"Furthermore, it has been shown that English judges have held repeatedly that these coast waters are portions of the realm. It is true that this particular point does not seem ever distinctly to have arisen. But Lord Coke, Lord Stowell, Dr. Lushington, Lord Hatherley, L. C., Erle, C. J., and Lord Wensleydale (and the catalogue might be largely extended) have all, not hastily, but in writing, in prepared and deliberate judgments, as part of the reasoning necessary to support their conclusions, used language, some of them repeatedly, which I am unable to construe, except as asserting, on the part of these eminent persons, that the realm of England, the territory of England, the property of the state and Crown of England over the water and the land beneath it, extends at least so far beyond the line of low water on the English coast, as to include the place where this offense was committed. * * * The English and American text writers, and two at least of the most eminent American judges, Marshall and Story, have held the same thing.

"Further—at least in one remarkable instance—the British Parliament has declared and enacted this to be the law. In the present reign two questions arose between Her Majesty and the Prince of Wales as to the property in minerals below high-water mark around the coast of Cornwall. The first question was as to the property in minerals between high and low-water mark around the coasts of that county; and as to the property in minerals below low-water mark won by an extension of workings begun above low-water mark.

"The whole argument on the part of the Crown was founded on the proposition that the *fundus maris* below low-water mark, and therefore beyond the limits of the county of Cornwall, belonged in property to the Crown. The Prince was in possession of the disputed mines; he had worked them from land undoubtedly his own; and, therefore, unless the Crown had a right of property in the bed of the sea, not as first occupier—for the Prince was first occupier, and was in occupation—the Crown must have failed. * * * Sir John Patterson * * * thus expressed himself.—'I am of opinion, and so decide, that the right to the minerals below low-water mark remains and is vested in the Crown, although those minerals may be won by workings commenced above low-water mark and extended below it,' and he recommended the passing of an Act of Parliament to give practical effect to his decision, so far as it was in favor of the crown. The Act of Parliament accordingly was passed, the 21 & 22 Vict. c. 109.

"We have therefore, it seems, the express and definite authority of

Parliament for the proposition that the realm does not end with low-water mark, but that the open sea and the bed of it are part of the realm and of the territory of the sovereign. If so, it follows that British law is supreme over it, and that the law must be administered by some tribunal. It cannot, for the reasons assigned by my Brother Brett, be administered by the judges of oyer and terminer; it can be, and always could be, by the Admiralty, and if by the Admiralty, then by the Central Criminal Court."

The Court quashed the conviction.

The majority of the Court was composed of Cockburn, C. J., Kelly, C. B., Bramwell, J. A., Lush and Field, JJ., Sir R. Phillimore and Pollock, B.—Lord Coleridge, C. J., Brett, and Amphlett, J. A., Grove, Denman and Lindley, JJ., dissenting.[1]

[1] On account of the extreme length of the opinion of the Lord Chief Justice, a considerable part of it—and a part interesting and valuable—has been necessarily omitted. This is true notably of that portion consisting of the analysis of cases, and of the abstract of the opinions of text writers. It is regretted, too, that the opinions of the other judges cannot be given.

For criticisms of the judgment in this case, see Stephen's History of the Criminal Law, II., 29–42; Maine's International Law, p. 38; Judge Foster, in the Am. Law Rev., July, 1877; Walker's Science of International Law, p. 173.

In consequence of the decision in this case, an act was passed in the session of 1878 (41 and 42 Vict. c. 73), which would seem to adopt the view of the minority of the court. The preamble declares that "the rightful jurisdiction of her Majesty, her heirs and successors extends and has always extended over the open seas adjacent to the coasts of the United Kingdom, and of all other parts of her Majesty's dominions to such a distance as is necessary for the defense and security of such dominions," and that "it is expedient that all offenses committed in the open sea within a certain distance of the coasts of the United Kingdom and of all other parts of her Majesty's dominions, by whomsoever committed, should be dealt with according to law."

The act is entitled the Territorial Waters Jurisdiction Act, 1878; and enacts that, "An offense committed by a person, whether he is or is not a subject of her Majesty, on the open sea within the territorial waters of her Majesty's dominions, is an offense within the jurisdiction of the Admiral, although it may have been committed on board or by means of a foreign ship, and the person who committed such offense may be arrested, tried and punished accordingly.

"But no proceedings under this act are to be instituted against a foreigner, without the consent and certificate of a Secretary of State, or in the case of a colony, the certificate of the Governor.

"The Territorial waters of her Majesty's dominions, in reference to the sea, means such part of the sea adjacent to the coast of the United Kingdom, or the coast of some other part of her Majesty's dominions, as is deemed by international law to be within the territorial sovereignty of her Majesty; and for the purpose of any offense declared by this act to be within the jurisdiction of the Admiral, any part of the open sea within one marine league of the coast measured from low-water mark shall be deemed to be open sea within the territorial waters of her Majesty's dominions."

CHAPTER II.

TERRITORIAL JURISDICTION.

SECTION 9.—IMMUNITIES OF FOREIGN SOVEREIGNS.

VAVASSEUR v. KRUPP.

CHANCERY, 1878.

(*L. R.*, 9 *Chancery Div.*, 351.)

A foreign sovereign cannot be sued for the infringement of a patent.

Where a foreign sovereign has his name added as defendant, in a suit against his agents, in order to be in a position to thus claim his property, he does not thereby subject himself to the jurisdiction of the court.

Josiah Vavasseur, the plaintiff in this case, had brought an action against F. Krupp, of Essen, in Germany, Alfred Longsden, his agent in England, and Ahrens & Co., described as agents for the Government of Japan, claiming an injunction and damages for the infringement of the plaintiff's patent for making shells and other projectiles. The shells in question had been made at Essen, in Germany, had been there bought for the Government of Japan, had been brought to this country and landed here in order to be put on board three ships of war which were being built here for the Government of Japan, to be used as ammunition for the guns of those ships. On the 18th of January, 1878, an injunction was, without prejudice to any question, granted, restraining the defendants and the owners of the wharf where the shells lay from selling or delivering the shells to the Government of Japan, or to any person on their behalf, or otherwise from parting with, selling, or disposing of the shells and projectiles.

On the 11th of May an application to the court was made on behalf of the Mikado of Japan and his Envoy Extraordinary in this country, that, notwithstanding the injunction, the Mikado and his agents might be at liberty to remove the shells, and that if, and so far as might be necessary, the Mikado and his Envoy should for the purpose of making and being heard upon such application be added as defendants in the suit.

Upon this application an order was made by the Master of the Rolls that on the Mikado by his counsel submitting to the jurisdiction of this court and desiring to be made a defendant, and on payment into court by the Mikado of £100 as security for costs the name of the Mikado be added as a party defendant in the action.

Notice of motion was then given on the part of the Mikado that the injunction might be dissolved, and that the Mikado might be at liberty to take possession, and remove, out of the jurisdiction of the court, the shells in question, the property of his Imperial Majesty.

James, L. J., Brett, L. J., and Cotton, L. J., concurred, each delivering an opinion.

The following is that of Brett, L. J.:—"It does not seem to me that in this case there is any fact whatever in dispute.

"These shells were made by Krupp at Essen. That was no infringement of the plaintiff's patent. In Germany they were sold to the Mikado and paid for by the agents of the Mikado. None of these facts are in dispute; and this purchase and sale was a perfectly lawful purchase and sale. The Mikado had three ships of war building in this country, and he desired that these shells should be sent to this country and put on board these ships. They were sent to this country by the order and by the authority of the Mikado, through Ahrens & Co. They were brought into this country, and they were deposited on a wharf. The plaintiff then finding these shells in this country, and finding, as he alleges, that they were made according to the process of his patent, asserts that the bringing them into this country by Ahrens & Co. is an infringement of his patent by them; and thereupon he brings an action against Ahrens & Co., for the infringement. In that action he claims an injunction against Ahrens & Co., and it may be that he claims an order from the court to destroy those shells because he says they are an infringement of his patent. In the course of that suit an injunction is obtained against Ahrens & Co., and against others, which injunction in terms forbids them from delivering these shells, which with other things are in their possession, to the ships of the Mikado, and in fact forbids them from sending the shells to Japan. To this action the Mikado was no party, but he or his agents here come forward and claim to have the delivery and possession of these shells. The defendants in the action are not unwilling to give the shells to the Mikado, but they say, 'If we do so, it may be said that we have broken the injunction, and we may therefore be liable to certain penalties.' It seems to me beyond dispute that this was the purpose for which the Mikado came in and desired to be made a party to the suit, and the Master of the Rolls thus describes the purpose. [His Lordship then read the judgment of the Master of the Rolls.] Now it is said that in the first place there is a dispute whether these shells are the property of the Mikado. It is argued that if he were a private individual, then, although he has purchased these shells and paid for them, yet, inasmuch as there has been an infringement of the patent, the property is not in him, because the court may order the shells to be destroyed. Is that argument good or not? To my mind it is utterly fallacious. The patent law has nothing to do with the property. The facts here are undisputed that Krupp made them with his own materials in Germany, where he had a right to make them; that he entered into a contract to sell specific shells to the Mikado; that that contract was performed, and that the shells were paid for, and that they were delivered in Germany to the Mikado's agent. Well, unless the patent law prevents the property from passing, nobody can doubt that the property passed to the Mikado. Therefore the dispute is not upon facts, but upon a false theory of law, that the patent law prevented the property from passing. I am clearly of opinion that the patent law did not prevent the property from passing. The goods were the property of the Mikado. They were his property as a sovereign; they were the property of his country; and therefore he is in the position of a foreign sovereign having property here.

"Whether the fact of Ahrens & Co. bringing these goods into England under these circumstances, and with this intention, was an infringement of the patent, I decline to consider. I shall assume for this purpose that it was an infringement, and that we have in this country property of the Mikado which infringes the patent. If it is an infringement of the patent by the Mikado you cannot sue him for that infringement. If it is an infringement by the agents, you may sue the agents for that infringement, but then it is the agents whom you sue. The injunction is against the agents, the Mikado being then no party to the action, and not being forbidden to do anything. He then comes here as a sovereign, and requires the delivery of his own goods. His only difficulty is the injunction against the agents, and for the purpose of enabling the court to make an order, he what is called 'submits himself to the jurisdiction of the court.' I think the interpretation put by the Master of the Rolls upon the order then made is right, and that it was only an order that the Mikado might be made a defendant for the purpose of enabling the court to make the order which the court has made. He now says 'I know not, and I care not, whether my agents have infringed your patent law.

I have property in the country, which property is my own. I demand that it shall be delivered to me, and I make myself a defendant in your court merely for the purpose of your modifying the order which you have made, so that my agents may not be injured in consequence of their delivering to me my own property.'

"And the only order that the Master of the Rolls has made is that these goods may be delivered up to the Mikado; the meaning of which is that the mere fact of the Mikado taking these shells away shall not be considered as against Ahrens & Co. an infringement of the injunction. That is the whole effect of this order. The Mikado has a perfect right to have these goods; no court in this country can properly prevent him from having goods which are the public property of his own country. Therefore it seems to me that this order which is really made for the benefit of Ahrens & Co., was an order rightly made, and that this appeal cannot be sustained."

In regard to the point of submission to the jurisdiction, COTTON, L. J., said:—"It is said that although under ordinary circumstances there is no jurisdiction as against a foreign sovereign, yet that in this particular case there is jurisdiction in consequence of the Mikado having come in and obtained the order of the 11th of May. It is said that a sovereign suing submits himself to the court as an ordinary plaintiff, and that the Mikado, in consequence of having obtained this order and acted upon it, puts himself in the position of an ordinary plaintiff. In the first place, there is this fallacy: the Mikado is not now in any way suing in the ordinary sense of the word, nor has he come to the court to establish as against an adverse claim his title to the property, which is really what is meant by a foreign sovereign coming here to sue to establish his rights. He is simply coming, and saying, 'The order of the court, possibly inadvertently, interferes with my sovereign rights. To prevent any question as to the defendants' committing a breach of the injunction by allowing me to remove the property, make an order that they be at liberty, notwithstanding the injunction, to hand them over to me!

"So that, in my opinion, the very foundation for the suggestion fails.

"But again, even if the Mikado had brought himself into court as an ordinary defendant, that, in my opinion, would not give the court jurisdiction as against the subject-matter, namely, jurisdiction to interfere with the public property of Japan, which is represented here by the Mikado. But when one comes to look at the form of the order, the Mikado does not by it come in as an ordinary defendant. By it he simply says 'I wish to bring before the court the facts: that these are my property, that the defendants were not constructing them under a contract for me, or using them under a contract with me. I wish to show that they are my property. I wish to apply for liberty to remove them as the public property of the state of Japan, and for that purpose, if necessary, I ask to come in.'

"In my opinion, the order taken fairly must be read with reference to the purpose for which the Mikado applied, and that being so, although possibly the form is not very happy, it is like a conditional appearance entered where a defendant who considers himself improperly served with any proceeding, has entered a conditional appearance, in order to contest the questions, which he could not do without an appearance of some sort. It cannot, in my opinion, be said that the order puts the Mikado in the position of a plaintiff or of a person who is made *simpliciter* a defendant. He came in for the particular purpose of raising this question, and the form of the order, in my opinion, ought not in any way to prejudice the rights which he would have had independently of that order."

JAMES, L. J.:—"This appeal is dismissed with costs."

DE HABER v. QUEEN OF PORTUGAL.

QUEEN'S BENCH, 1851.

(17 *Queen's Bench*, 196.)

A suit cannot be maintained against a foreign sovereign.

If such a suit be instituted, the non-appearance of the defendant sovereign does not prejudice his rights.

The plaintiff commenced an action of debt in the court of the Lord Mayor of London against the Queen of Portugal. It appears that he brought action for 12,136*l* sterling which he had left in the hands of Ferreiri, a Lisbon banker and which Ferreiri paid over to the Portuguese Government. The plaintiff, proceeding according to the custom of foreign attachment in London, sent out a summons for the defendant to appear. The defendant being called and not appearing, the plaintiff alleged that Senhor *Guilherne Candida Xavier De Brito*, of London, the garnishee had money and effects of the defendant in his hands, and prayed to attach the defendant by that money. The judge awarded an attachment as prayed.

The judgment of the court was delivered by CAMPBELL, C. J.:—

* * * "Notwithstanding the dictum of *Bynkershoek*, and the outlawry of the King of Spain, supposed to be related by Selden, we cannot doubt that the awarding of the attachment in the present case by

the Lord Mayor's Court was an excess of jurisdiction, on the ground that the defendant is sued as a foreign potentate. * * * We have now to consider whether we can grant the prohibition on the application of the Queen of Portugal before she appears in the Lord Mayor's Court. The plaintiff's counsel argue that, before she can be heard, she must appear and be put in bail, in the alternative, to pay or to render. It would be very much to be lamented if, before doing justice to her, we were obliged to impose a condition upon her which would be a further indignity, and a further violation of the law of nations. If the rule were that the application for a prohibition can only be by the defendant after appearance, we should have had little scruple in making this an exception to the rule. But we find it laid down in books of the highest authority that, where the court to which the prohibition is to go has no jurisdiction, a prohibition may be granted upon the request of a *stranger*, as well as of the defendant himself.

"Therefore this court, vested with the power of preventing all inferior courts from exceeding their jurisdiction to the prejudice of the Queen or her subjects, is bound to interfere when duly informed of such an excess of jurisdiction. What has been done in this case by the Lord Mayor's Court must be considered as peculiarly in contempt of the Crown, it being an insult to an independent sovereign, giving that sovereign just cause of complaint to the British Government, and having a tendency to bring about a misunderstanding between our gracious Sovereign and her ally the Queen of Portugal.

"Therefore, upon the information and complaint of the Queen of Portugal, either as the party grieved, or as a *stranger*, we think we are bound to correct the excess of jurisdiction brought to our notice, and to prohibit the Lord Mayor's Court from proceeding further in this suit.

"Rule absolute for a prohibition."

PRIOLEAU v. UNITED STATES AND ANDREW JOHNSON.

IN EQUITY, 1866.

(*L. R.*, 2 *Equity*, 659.)

Where the United States are plaintiffs in a suit, and the defendants bring a cross-bill for discovery, and add the name of the President of the United States as defendant : *Held* that it was wrong to make the President defendant, as he cannot be compelled to answer ; but the proceedings in the original suit were stayed until the answer of the United States was put in.

This was a cross-bill to a suit of *United States* v. *Prioleau.* (*Supra*, § 7, b.)

The original suit was instituted by the United States of America suing in their corporate capacity to establish their rights to cotton shipped at Galveston, Texas, during the rebellion and consigned to the defendants, for sale in England for the benefit of the *de facto* Confederate Government. The United States, as plaintiffs, moved for an injunction to restrain the defendants from obtaining possession of the cotton from the Dock and Harbor Board, and from dealing with it otherwise than under the direction of the plaintiffs, who claimed it as State property to which they had succeeded on the dissolution of the so-called Confederate Government.

The Vice-Chancellor made an order appointing Mr. Prioleau receiver of the cotton under bond of £20,000. Messrs. Prioleau filed this cross-bill against the United State of America and President Andrew Johnson, for the purpose of obtaining discovery in reference to the matters in question in the suit.

No answer having been put in by President Johnson, the plaintiffs in the cross-suit moved that the time for closing the evidence in the first suit might be enlarged until one month after the defendants to the cross-bill had put in their answer, and that, failing such answer, the receivership of Prioleau might be discharged and his recognizances vacated.

Extracts from the opinion of the Vice-Chancellor are as follows:—

"The question in this case is one in some degree novel, but the general principles applicable to it are sufficiently established. The only difficulty in the present case is the particular mode selected by the plaintiffs in the cross-suit for arriving at the object they have in view. A bill being filed by the United States of America, under that description, against the defendants, a cross-bill is filed by the defendants for the purpose of obtaining discovery. They cannot, of course, obtain discovery upon oath from a body which is corporate —it is difficult to know how to express its position. It is not a corporation, strictly speaking, but it is a body so far corporate as not to present to the court as a suitor any one individual. Where the suitor is an individual, although he may be the sovereign of a foreign country, and may of himself in reality represent the whole country of which he is sovereign, this court has refused to acknowledge him when he comes here as a suitor in any other capacity than as a private individual. It has been determined by the highest authority that he must conform to the practice and regulations for administration of justice of the tribunals to which he resorts for relief; and among other things * * * he is obliged to answer upon oath. It is also established * * * that all persons sued in this country as a body corporate are amenable to the process of the court, and must answer by one or other of their officers upon oath, inasmuch as it is considered essential to justice that answers shall be made upon oath. * * * Now it is quite impossible, on any principle of analogy, to say that the President has been properly selected, or that he is the person for whose answer upon oath the United States must wait before they proceed in their original suit. * * * Now the selection of the President of the United States is open at once to this objection, that the court cannot take judicial notice—nor do I suppose it is a matter of fact—that the United States Government have control over their President or can compel him to produce papers or the like, and therefore I cannot make any order that the proceedings in the original suit be stayed until the President has put in his answer. * * *

"I can do no more than make an order staying proceedings until the answer of the United States is put in."

UNITED STATES OF AMERICA v. WAGNER.

COURT OF APPEALS IN CHANCERY, 1867.

(*L. R.*, 2 *Chancery Appeals*, 582.)

A Republic may sue in its own name; and it need not have or create an officer to maintain a suit on its behalf.

The bill in this suit was filed by "The United States of America" against agents of the Confederacy, doing business at Liverpool.

The bill alleges that the defendants had large quantities of cotton consigned to them—that in 1865 the rebellion was suppressed and that all the property held by the government of the so-called Confederate States, including all moneys, goods and ships in the power of the defendants, had vested in the plaintiffs. The bill prayed for an account, and for an order of payment of the money in the hands of the defendants, and a delivery of the goods and cotton in their hands. The defendants demurred generally, objecting that the bill should put forward the President of the United States or some state officer, upon whom process might be served, and who might answer a cross-bill.

The demurrer was allowed and now the plaintiffs appeal.

The opinion of Lord CAIRNS, L. J., is as follows:—

"It is admitted that, upon the statements in the bill, it must be taken that the property claimed in the suit belongs to the United States of America, a foreign sovereign State, adopting the republican form of government, and recognized and treated with as such, and under that style, by Her Majesty; but it is contended that this foreign State, being a republic, cannot sue in its own name, and must either associate with it as plaintiff, or proceed in the name of the President of the Republic, or some other officer of state.

"A proposition so startling, so grave in its consequences, and in such apparent antagonism to the rules, that the proper plaintiff is to be sought in the owner of the subject matter of the suit, and that a foreign State is at liberty to sue in any of our courts, would seem to require some argument and authority to support it. It was contended then, that when a monarch sues in our courts, he sues as the representative of the State of which he is the sovereign; that the property claimed is looked upon as the property of the people or State and that he is permitted to sue, not as for his own property, but as the head of the executive government of the State to which the property belongs: and it was contended, in like manner, that when the property belongs to a republic, the head of the executive, or in other words the President, ought to sue for it.

"This argument, in my opinion, is founded on a fallacy. The sovereign, in a monarchical form of government, may, as between himself and his subjects, be a trustee for the latter, more or less limited in his powers over the property which he seeks to recover. But in the courts of Her Majesty, as in diplomatic intercourse with the government of Her Majesty, it is the sovereign, and not the State, or the subjects of the sovereign, that is recognized. From him, and as representing him individually, and not his State or kingdom, is an ambassador received. In him individually, and not in a representative capacity is the public property assumed by all other States, and by the courts of other States, to be vested. In a republic, on the other hand, the sovereign power, and with it the public property, is held to remain and to reside in the State itself, and not in any officer of the State. It is from the State that an ambassador is accredited, and it is with the State that the diplomatic intercourse is conducted.

"It was then contended that the republic of the United States as a body politic, being plaintiff, no effectual discovery could be had from it, or relief against it, on a cross-bill; that it is a condition of obtaining relief in equity, that discovery may be had against the plaintiff on a cross-bill filed by the defendant; and that in the case of a corporation, this right is preserved by the rule that its officers may be made co-defendants for discovery.

"It is to be observed, however, with regard to the case of a corporation, where the court making an exception from its general rules allows persons who are merely witnesses to be made co-defendants for discovery, that the exception does not depend on any reasons springing out of the nature of bills and cross-bills; for the officers of a corporation may be sued with the corporation, even where no litigation has been commenced by the corporation; nor does the liability of the officers to discovery affect the question who is to be plaintiff; for the corporation sues for the corporate property without joining any officer of the corporation as a co-plaintiff.

"The rule of the court as to corporations, if it proves anything, would seem to show that in a cross-bill against the United States, there would be a right to join some officer of the United States for the purpose of discovery.

"The Vice-Chancellor appears to have thought that the President of the United States was not an officer who could thus be joined as a defendant, and I do not desire to express an opinion differing in that respect from the opinion of his Honor. But if the reference to suits against corporations does not establish a right to make some officer of the United States a co-defendant to a cross bill, it is, as I think, altogether irrelevant. It is, however, in my opinion, an error to suppose that the right of a plaintiff to sue depends in any way on the effectiveness of the discovery which on a cross-bill can be exacted from him. From an infant, a lunatic, a representative, trustee, or executor, wholly ignorant of the occurrences which are the subjects of the suit, no practical discovery can be obtained, and yet they can maintain a suit.

"I apprehend that the only rule is, that the person, State, or corporation which has the interest must be the plaintiff, and the court will do the best the law admits of to secure to the defendant such defensive discovery and relief as he may be entitled to. The court can in all cases suspend relief on the original bill until justice is in this respect done to the defendant.

"The case of the *Columbian Government* v. *Rothschild*, 1 Sim., 94, however, was said to be, and the Vice-Chancellor appears to have considered that it was, a binding authority against a suit in this form. I cannot so view that case. The bill was filed in the name of the State of Columbia, and if this bill had been filed in the name of the Government of the United States, the case would have been analagous. Dealing with the words before him, Sir John Leach appears to have held, and to have most properly held, that an unknown and undefined body, such as the government of a State, could not sue by that quasi-corporate name, and the expressions in his judgment seem to me to intimate no more than that if the persons so described could sue at all they must come forward as individuals, and show that they were entitled to represent their State.

"Nothing could be more unreasonable than to suppose that by observations of this kind Sir John Leach meant to decide for the first time, that a republic could not sue in its own name, but must have, or must create, some officer to maintain a suit on its behalf.

"I think the demurrer in this case must be overruled." [1]

1 Other cases bearing upon the subject of this section are: *The King of Spain* v. *Hullet and Widder*, 1 Clarke and Finnelly, 348 (1833):—Don Justo José de Machado was appointed by the Spanish government to receive money for that government due from France. Upon receiving it, Machado brought the money to England and deposited a considerable portion of it with the defendants. The King of Spain applied to Machado for the money, but this demand was refused, whereupon the King brought a bill for discovery and for payment of the money into court, against Machado (who was out of the jurisdiction). The bill was demurred to for lack of parties, etc., but the demurrer was overruled, and the defendants appealed, mainly on the ground that it had never been held that a foreign sovereign could sue in courts of equity in England, and on principle such suit should not be allowed. This appeal was dismissed. Fifteen days later, the defendants filed a cross-bill in Chancery, the rules of which court compel the identical plaintiff in the original bill to himself swear to his answer to a cross-bill. The plaintiff asked to put in an answer either by his agent, or without oath or signature.

The House of Lords refused to deviate from the practice of the court.

Rothschild v. *Queen of Portugal*, 3 Younge and Collyer 594, (1839):—The bill was brought for discovery from the Queen of Portugal, as to matters stated in the bill, and for a commission to examine witnesses in Portugal, and for an injunction to restrain an action commenced against the plaintiff by the Queen of Portugal. This action was in contract, the Queen suing Messrs. Rothschild on some bonds deposited with them. The present plaintiffs now seek by this bill for discovery of certain correspondence and other matters to aid them in their defence.

The Queen demurs to the bill on two grounds, (1) that as a sovereign, the suit was not maintainable against her—(2) that the plaintiffs had made no case for discovery.

The first point only is considered.

The court overruled the demurrer, and, in the course of its decision, Baron Alderson said: "I am therefore of opinion that Her Most Faithful Majesty being a suitor voluntarily in a court of English law, becomes subject, as to all matters connected with that suit, to the jurisdiction of the Court of Equity."

SECTION 10.—IMMUNITIES OF DIPLOMATIC AGENTS.

(a) *Criminal Jurisdiction.*

CASE OF LESLIE, BISHOP OF ROSS, 1571.

(*Ward's Law of Nations*, II., 486.)

Is the ambassador of a deposed sovereign entitled to the immunites accorded to diplomatic agents?

In the year 1567, Leslie, Bishop of Ross came to the court of England, in behalf of Mary Queen of Scots; who, although she was detained prisoner in England, was allowed to send him to plead before the commissioners appointed to examine into her cause. Nothing was determined by the commission: but Leslie continued at court, and exercised the office of ambassador of Mary for the space of one yeár, when, being concerned in raising a rebellion against the English Government, he was committed to the custody of the Bishop of London. From this he was soon liberated, and returning to his function of ambassador, continued to preserve it near two years longer. At that time, being detected in the attempt to raise a serious conspiracy in favor of Mary, against Elizabeth, he was once more committed; and the following questions concerning him were propounded to David Lewis, Valentine Dale, William Drury, William Aubrey, and Henry Jones, learned civil lawyers: 1. Whether an ambassador, procuring an insurrection in the Prince's country towards whom he is ambassador, is to enjoy the privilege of an ambassador?

2. Whether he may not, *jure gentium et civili Romanorum*, be punished as an enemy, traitor, or conspirator against that Prince, notwithstanding he be an ambassador?

To these two questions they answered: "Touching these two questions, we are of opinion, that an ambassador procuring an insurrection or rebellion in the Prince's country towards whom he is ambassador, ought not, *jure gentium et civili Romanorum*, to enjoy the privileges otherwise due to an ambassador: but that he may, notwithstanding, be punished for the same.

3. Whether, if the Prince be deposed by the common authority of the realm, and another elected and invested of that crown, the solic-

itor or doer of his causes, and for his aid (although the other Prince do suffer such one to be in his realm), is to be accounted an ambassador, or to enjoy the privilege of an ambassador?

To this they answered: "We do think that the solicitor of a Prince lawfully deposed, and another being invested in his place, cannot have the privilege of an ambassador; for that none but Princes, and such other as have sovereignty, may have ambassadors."

4. Whether a Prince, coming into another realm, and remaining there under custody and guard, ought, or may have there his solicitor of his causes, and if he have, whether he is to be accounted an ambassador?

To this they answered: "We do think that a Prince coming into another Prince's realm, and being there under guard and custody, and remaining still a Prince, may have a solicitor there; but whether he is to be accounted an ambassador, that dependeth on the nature of his commission."

5. Whether, if such a solicitor be so appointed by a Prince so flying, or coming into another Prince's realm—if the Prince in whose realm the Prince so in guard, and his solicitor is, shall denounce, or cause to be denounced, to such a solicitor or to such a Prince under custody, that his said solicitor—shall hereafter be taken for no ambassador—whether then such solicitor or agent can justly claim the privilege of ambassador?

To this they answered: "We do think that the Prince to whom any person is sent in message of ambassador, may for causes forbid him to enter into his lands, or when he hath received him, command him to depart; yet so long as he doth remain in the realm, and not exceed the bounds of an ambassador, he may claim his privilege as ambassador, or solicitor, according to the quality of his commission."

6. Whether, if an ambassador be confederate, or aider, or comforter of any traitor, knowing his treason toward that prince, toward whom, and in whose realm he pretendeth to be ambassador, is not punishable by the Prince in whose realm and against whom such treason is committed, or confederacy for treason conspired?

And to this they answered: "We do think that an ambassador aiding and comforting any traitor in his treason toward the Prince with whom he pretendeth to be ambassador in his realm, knowing the same treason, is punishable by the same Prince against whom such treason is committed."

These answers of the civilians were supposed to be so decisive in favor of the intentions of the court, that the Bishop was sent for from his confinement in the Isle of Ely, and after being sharply rebuked, was told he should no longer be considered as an ambassador, but severely punished as one who well deserved it. He, however, answered with much firmness and apparent knowledge of the law of nations, "that he was the ambassador of an absolute Queen, and of one who was unjustly deposed, and had, according to his duty, carefully endeavored to effectuate the delivery of his Princess, and the safety of both kingdoms; that he came into England with the full authority of an ambassador, upon public warrandise, or safe conduct which he had produced; and that the sacred privileges of ambassadors were by no means to be violated."

Burleigh, in return, observed "that no privilege or public warrandise could protect ambassadors that offend against the public majesty of a Prince, but they are liable to *penal actions* for the same; otherwise lewd ambassadors might attempt the life of Princes without any punishment." The bishop persisted in his positions, and maintained that the privileges of ambassadors had never been violated *via juris sed via facti*, not by regular form of trial, but by violence; his boldness, or the true view which he seems to have taken of this nice subject, appears so far to have weighed with the Ministers of Elizabeth, that they did not dare to put him to death, with the Duke of Norfolk and other conspirators, but after detaining him for some time in prison, banished him the country in 1573.

MENDOZA'S CASE, 1584.

(*Ward's Law of Nations*, II., 522.)

An ambassador cannot be punished, but may be sent out of the country.

In the year, 1584, Mendoza, the Spanish ambassador in England, having conspired to introduce foreign troops, and dethrone the Queen, it was a matter of difficulty how he should be punished. Had the council thought the opinions of Lewis Dale and the other civilians good law, they probably would have acted upon them; for here was a case precisely similar to that on which they had been consulted. They however took the opinions of the celebrated Albericus Gentilis, then in England, and of Hottoman in France, who both asserted that an ambassador, though a conspirator, could not be put to death, but should be referred to his principal for punishment; or, (according to Hottoman) sent away by force out of the country. In consequence of this, Mendoza was simply ordered to depart the realm, and a commissioner sent to Spain to prefer a complaint against him. (Camden, 296.)

CASE OF DA SA, 1653.

(*Ward's Law of Nations*, II., 537.)

The brother of an ambassador and a member of his suite, was executed, for sedition and murder.

"In 1653, Don Pantaleon Sa, brother to the Portuguese ambassador in England, quarrelled with an Englishman, Colonel Gerhard, about some matter in the new exchange; a scuffle ensued, in which Gerhard was severely wounded. The quarrel was renewed the next day, at the same place; but this time Sa came with fifty followers, all armed to the teeth, with the deliberate intention of destroying his adversary. The result was, that many English were wounded, and one person (a Mr. Greenway), accidentally present, killed; that the Guards were called in, and fired upon by the Portuguese, several of whom they took to prison; the rest, with Sa, took refuge in the hotel of the Portuguese ambassador. The ambassador was afterwards required to deliver up others, of the delinquents, which request he complied with, and his brother was among them. He interceded for his brother; but Cromwell resolved, if he could, to try him by the law of the land. He, therefore, consulted the most eminent of the professors of the civil law to settle *how* such a barbarous murder might be punished. But these disagreeing among themselves, he left the decision of the affair to a court of delegates, consisting of the Chief Justice and two other judges, three noblemen, and three doctors of the civil law. Before these Sa was examined.

"At first he was supposed to be a colleague in the embassy, and he vaunted himself that he was the king's ambassador, 'and subject to the jurisdiction of no one else.' He was made, however, to produce his credentials, by which all that could be proved was that the king intended in a little time to recall his brother, and to give him a commission to manage his affairs in England. This being judged insufficient to prove him an ambassador, he was, without any further regard to the privilege of that character, ordered, as well as all the rest, to plead to the indictment.

"Such is the accurate statement of the affair till it came to a jury, as it appears from the account of Zouch, a civilian of eminence and himself a delegate in the cause.

"It is evident, from this account of the matter, and one of more authority can hardly be met with, that had Sa been actually *ambassador*, instead of forming a part of the *suite*, the proceedings against him would have been the same with those in the cases cited above. All, therefore, that can fairly be drawn from this precedent, *as to the decision of the then existing law of England*, is that the *suite* of an ambassador, if they committed murder, were liable to be tried for it by the courts of the country. Zouch asserts expressly, that his own opinion upon the main question agreed with that of Grotius and the best authors, as to the exemption of ambassadors themselves; and it should appear from his *Solutio Quæstionis*, that if Sa could have proved that he was an actual ambassador, his plea before the delegates would have been allowed."

GYLLENBORG'S CASE, 1717.

(*Ward's Law of Nations*, II., 548.)

It was held in this case, that if an ambassador conspires to overthrow the government to which he is accredited, he may be arrested; and that his papers may be seized.

On the 29th of January, 1717, the government of England having certain information of a conspiracy to invade the country and dethrone the King, contrived by Gyllenborg, the ambassador of Sweden, at that time at peace with Great Britain; they ordered the arrest of that minister, which was accordingly effected. General Wade and Colonel Blakeney to whom the charge was entrusted, found him making up dispatches, which they told him they had orders to seize; and they even insisted upon searching his cabinet, which, upon the refusal of his lady to deliver the keys, they actually broke open. Gyllenborg complained of these proceedings, as a direct breach of the law of nations, and some of the foreign ministers at the court of London expressed themselves to the same effect; upon which the secretaries of state, Methuen and Stanhope, wrote circular letters to them, to assign reasons for the arrest, which satisfied them all except Montleone, the Spanish ambassador, who in his answer observed, that he was sorry *no other way* could be fallen upon for preserving the peace of the kingdom, than that of the arrest of a public minister, and the seizure of his papers, which are the repositories of his secrets, two facts which seemed sensibly to wound the law of nations. The observation, however, answers itself; since the confession that there was *no other way*, proves that this extremity was the simple consequence of those universal laws, which ever will

and must overcome all other; I mean legitimate necessity, and self-defence.

PRINCE CELLAMARE'S CASE, 1718.

(*Marten's Causes Célèbres*, I., 149.)

For conspiring against the state, an ambassador was arrested and conducted across the frontier into his own country.

Prince Cellamare, the ambassador of Spain at Paris, was the instrument of Alberoni's hostile intrigues against the regent.

He was in close correspondence with many of the malcontent French nobility, but his chief confidants were the Duke and Duchess of Maine, who had never forgiven the Duke's removal from the posts of authority assigned to him by the will of Louis XIV.

A plot was organized (though it seems doubtful how far the design was seriously entertained) for carrying off the regent into Spain, and placing Philip V. at the head of the French Government. Assistance was expected from Brittany, which was just then in agitation in consequence of an attempt against the ancient privileges of the province; and a fleet was actually dispatched from Spain to support the insurrection. The confederates, however, were betrayed to Dubois; an agent of Cellamare was seized at Poitiers on his way to Madrid; and dispatches of which he was the bearer fully compromised all the principal parties to the scheme.

A detachment of troops was sent to guard the hotel of the ambassador, while the Minister of War, Le Blanc, and the Minister of Foreign Affairs, Dubois, made an examination of his papers.

Cellamare appealed to the other ambassadors resident in Paris, but regarding such a conspiracy as depriving him of all privileges, they refused to interfere.

On the other hand, to justify these extreme measures, the regent published a circular letter to the foreign ministers setting forth the facts of the conspiracy, and the imminent danger to the state.

Some days later, letters of Cellamare were made public, which proved conclusively his part in the conspiracy.

Cellamare was then confined in the château De Blois, with orders to detain him there till the French ambassador at Madrid should arrive in France.

On the news of the arrival of the French ambassador at Bayonne, the order was given to conduct Cellamare to the Spanish frontier, and this order was carried out on the 6th of March, 1719.

(b) *Civil Jurisdiction.*

THE AMBASSADOR OF PETER THE GREAT, 1708.

(*Blackstone's Commentaries, Book I., Chap. VII.*)

Neither an ambassador nor any of his suite can be prosecuted for any debt or contract in the courts of the country in which they reside.

"In respect to civil suits, all the foreign jurists agree, that neither an ambassador, nor any of his train or *comites*, can be prosecuted for any debt or contract in the courts of that kingdom wherein he is sent to reside. Yet Sir Edward Coke maintains, that, if an ambassador make a contract which is good *jure gentium*, he shall answer for it here. But the truth is, so few cases, if any, had arisen, wherein the privilege was either claimed or disputed, even with regard to civil suits that our law-books are, in general, quite silent upon it previous to the reign of Queen Anne; when an ambassador from Peter the Great, Czar of Muscovy, was actually arrested and taken out of his coach in London, for a debt of fifty pounds which he had there contracted. Instead of applying to be discharged upon his privilege, he gave bail to the action, and the next day complained to the Queen. The persons who were concerned in the arrest were examined before the privy council, of which the Lord Chief Justice Holt was at the same time sworn a member, and seventeen were committed to prison: most of them were prosecuted by information in the Court of Queen's Bench at the suit of the attorney-general, and at their trial before the Lord Chief Justice were convicted of the facts by the jury, reserving the question of law, how far those facts were criminal, to be afterwards argued before the judges; which question was never determined. In the meantime the Czar resented this affront very highly, and demanded that the sheriff of Middlesex and all others concerned in the arrest should be punished with instant death. But the Queen, to the amazement of that despotic court, directed her secretary to inform him 'that she could inflict no punishment upon any, the meanest of her subjects, unless warranted by the law of the land; and therefore was persuaded that he would not insist upon impossibilities.' To satisfy, however, the clamors of the foreign ministers, who made it a common cause, as well as to appease the wrath of Peter, a bill was brought into parliament, and afterwards passed into a law, to prevent and punish such outrageous insolence for the future. And with a copy of this act, elegantly engrossed and illuminated, accompanied by a letter from the Queen, an ambassador extraordinary was commissioned to appear at Moscow, who declared 'that though her majesty could not inflict such a punishment as was required, because of the defect in that particular of the former established constitutions of her kingdom, yet, with the unanimous consent of the parliament, she had caused a new act to be passed, to serve as a law for the future.' This humiliating step was accepted as a full satisfaction by the Czar; and the offenders, at his request, were discharged from all farther prosecution.

"This statute recites the arrest which had been made in 'contempt of the protection granted by her majesty, contrary to the law of nations, and in prejudice of the rights and privileges, which ambassadors and other public ministers have at all times been thereby possessed of, and ought to be kept sacred and inviolable:' wherefore it enacts that for the future all process whereby the person of any ambassador, or of his domestic or domestic servant may be arrested, or his goods distrained or seized, shall be utterly null and void; and the persons prosecuting, soliciting, or executing such process shall be deemed violaters of the law of nations, and disturbers of the public repose; and shall suffer such penalties and corporal punishment as the lord chancellor and the two chief justices, or any two of them, shall think fit. But it is expressly provided, that no trader within the description of the bankrupt laws, who shall be in the service of any ambassador, shall be privileged or protected by this act; nor shall any one be punished for arresting an ambassador's servant, unless his name be registered with the secretary of state, and by him transmitted to the sheriffs of London and Middlesex. Exceptions that are strictly conformable to the rights of ambassadors as observed in the most civilized countries. And, in consequence of this statute, thus declaring and enforcing the law of nations, these privileges are now held to be part of the law of the land, and are constantly allowed in the courts of common law."

TAYLOR v. BEST.

COMMON PLEAS, 1854.

(14 *Common Bench*, 487.)

A public minister who engages in trade, in the country to which he is accredited, does not thereby forfeit the privileges and immunities accorded to diplomatic agents. But when he voluntarily appears, in compliance with a writ, and submits himself to the jurisdiction, the court will not interfere for his relief.

This was an action brought by the plaintiff against the four defendants, to recover 250*l* deposited in their hands for shares in an intended Sulphate company, of which they were directors.

A writ being issued, the plaintiff's attorney wrote to the defendant Drouet, asking the name of his solicitor to whom he should send the process for an undertaking to appear.—M. Drouet instructs his attorney to write to the plaintiff's attorney, requesting that the process be sent to him. The cause came to an issue, notice of trial was given, appearance duly entered and Drouet obtained a rule for a special jury.

Two days later Drouet took out a summons on the other parties to the suit to show why all proceedings should not be stayed, or why his name should not be struck out of the proceedings on the ground that he was protected from such a suit by reason of his being a public minister, first secretary of the Belgian legation at the court of St. James.

The defendant Drouet obtained a rule *nisi*.

JERVIS, C. J. :—"This case was very elaborately argued yesterday, and the importance of the subject induced the court to take time to look into the various authorities which were referred to. I am of opinion that the rule should be discharged. There is no doubt that the defendant Drouet fills the character of a public minister to which the privilege contended for is applicable: and I think it is equally clear, that, if the privilege does attach, it is not, in the case of an ambassador or public minister, forfeited by the party's engaging in trade, as it would, by virtue of the proviso in the 7 Anne, c. 12, s. 5, in the case of an ambassador's servant. If an ambassador or public minister, during his residence in this country, violates the character in which he is accredited to our court, by engaging in commercial transactions, that may raise a question between the government of this country and that of the country by which he is sent; but he does not thereby lose the general privilege which the law of nations has conferred upon persons filling that high character,—the proviso in the statute of Anne limiting the privilege in cases of trading applying only to the servants of the embassy.

"For this, Barbuit's Case, Cas. Temp. Talbot, 281, is an authority.

"Admitting, then, that M. Drouet is a person entitled to the privileges and immunities which the law of England accords to ambassadors from foreign friendly courts, and that he does not forfeit them by engaging in commercial ventures,—the question is whether he is, under all the circumstances disclosed by the affidavit before us, entitled to the privilege which he claims.

"Although it is admitted that no process can be available against the person or the goods of a foreign ambassador or minister, no case has been cited to show that an application in the present form, to stay all proceedings, is available in the courts of this country. On the contrary, in the case of ambassadors' servants, it appears that the practice has been, not to stay the proceedings altogether, but to discharge the party from custody, on entering a common appearance. The case of *Crosse* v. *Talbot*, 8 Mod. 288, recognizes that as the true principle. The motion on the part of the defendant there was to set aside the bail-bond given upon his arrest, on his filing common bail; and the rule was discharged, on the ground that the party did not bring himself strictly within the privilege allowed to the servant of an ambassador; the court holding that, to entitle him to the privilege, he ought to be a *domestic* servant, and really to exercise the duties of the office, and that his being a mere nominal servant is not enough. And the reporter adds,—'A great many cases have since been determined upon the same principle; but it was in these cases held, that the idea of a *domestic* servant was not confined to his living in a foreign minister's house, provided he was a real servant, and actually performed the service.' The course, therefore, seems to have been in these cases, not to move to stay all proceedings, but to move to set aside or cancel the bail-bond, upon the defendant's filing common bail. No case has been cited of a motion to stay the proceedings, where the personal liberty of the applicant has not been interfered with. Further, I am aware of no case in which, where there are several defendants, and the action has been allowed to go on to the verge of trial, the proceedings have been stayed upon the application of one of the defendants.

"Such a course would be obviously unjust to the other defendants, seeing that the expense they had already incurred would thereby be rendered useless. Without, however, dwelling upon that, it seems to me that this motion must fail, upon the merits.

"The action is brought against four defendants,—the writ being sued out against M. Drouet and the three others as joint-contractors. No doubt, the plaintiff was bound, at the peril of a plea in abatement, to sue all. The writ being issued, nothing is done upon it which can at all interfere with the exercise by M. Drouet of his diplomatic functions, or with his personal comfort or dignity. But, knowing that a writ has issued, or having reason to believe that it is about to issue, he causes his attorney to write to the plaintiff's attorney, desiring that the process may be sent to him for an undertaking to appear. He, therefore, voluntarily attorns and submits himself to the jurisdiction of the court. Under these circumstances, I think he cannot be permitted now to complain that the suit has been improperly instituted against him. On the contrary, I think, that, by analogy to the doctrine cited from the learned jurists whose works have been so laboriously consulted, the action may well be maintained.

"It is said,—and perhaps truly said,—that an ambassador or foreign minister is privileged from suit in the courts of the country to which he is accredited, or, at all events, from being proceeded against in a manner which may ultimately result in the coercion of his person, or the seizure of his personal effects necessary to his comfort and dignity; and that he cannot be compelled, *in invitum*, or against his will, to engage in any litigation in the courts of the country to which he is sent. But all the foreign jurists hold, that, if the suit can be founded without attacking the personal liberty of the ambassador, or interfering with his dignity or personal comfort, it may proceed. Various passages have been cited to show, that, in countries, where the Civil law prevails, and where jurisdiction can be founded by a proceeding *in rem* in the first instance, where there are houses or lands, which are immovable, that may be taken to found the jurisdiction, the suit may proceed. Movable goods, too, which are unconnected with the personal comfort and dignity of the ambassador, may be taken for the same purpose.

"And when we consider the effect of the proceeding, and what may be done by the party sued, there seems to be no substantial distinction between the two modes: because, although it is true, that, in countries where the Civil law prevails, the proceeding is *in rem*, and the means of litigation between the parties incidentally established without any molestation or interference with the person of the defendant; yet if the defendant chooses to appear, for the purpose of protecting his goods and investigating the matter in dispute, he may convert that which was originally a proceeding *in rem* into a proceeding *in personam*. And such is commonly the course in the Scotch courts. If, therefore, as in Holland, and in some other countries, where goods may be taken for the purpose of founding jurisdiction, the defendant may come in and convert the proceeding *in rem* into a proceeding *in personam*, and so attorn or submit himself to the jurisdiction, it seems to me that there is no distinction between that case and the present, where there has been no attempt on the part of the plaintiff to disturb the comfort or interfere with the personal liberty of the foreign minister; but where there has been the mere issuing of a writ to which he has voluntarily appeared, and thus submitted himself to the jurisdiction, I do not feel myself at all pressed by the argument urged by Mr. Willes, that the privilege in question, being the privilege of the sovereign, cannot be abandoned or waived by the ambassador; for, when the authorities upon which that argument is sought to be sustained, come to be examined, they do not shew that the ambassador may not submit himself to the jurisdiction for the purpose of having the matter in difference investigated and ascertained; but only that the sacred character of the person of the ambassador cannot be affected by any act or consent on his part; and that, by interfering with the person of the ambassador, or with the goods which are essential to the personal comfort and dignity of his position, you are in effect attacking the privilege of his master.

That, however, is not the case here; for anything that appears, M. Drouet is sued,—he being a joint-contractor and so a necessary party to the action,—merely for the purpose of ascertaining the liability of the other defendants. If he had not thought fit to attorn to the jurisdiction, but had allowed judgment to go against him by default, *non constat* that anything would have been done upon the judgment, otherwise than by enforcing it against the other defendants. If any *ca. sa. or fi. fa.* were issued against him upon the judgment, the statute of Anne would have applied, and the court might have been called upon to interfere to prevent its being put in force against him. It seems to me that M. Drouet here has courted the jurisdiction, and that we ought not to interfere."

Cresswell, J., and Williams, J., concurred.

Pearson, for the plaintiff, asked for costs.

Per Curiam.—We say nothing about costs.

Rule discharged.

WHEATON'S CASE.

(*Wheaton's International Law, 3d Ed.*)

Where the laws of a state give to a landlord the right to detain the personal effects of a tenant, for non-payment of rent or for damages to the premises, may this right be enforced against the ambassador of a foreign state?

The Prussian Civil Code declares, that "the lessor is entitled, as a security for the rent and other demands arising under the contract, to the rights of a *Pfandgläubiger*, upon the goods brought by the tenant upon the premises, and there remaining at the expiration of the lease."

The same code defines the nature of the right of a creditor whose debt is thus secured. "A real right, as to a thing belonging to another, assigned to any person as security for a debt, and in virtue of which he may demand to be satisfied out of the substance of the thing itself, is called *Unterpfandsrecht*."

Under this law, the proprietor of the house in which the minister of the United States accredited at the court of Berlin resided, claimed the right of detaining the goods of the minister found on the premises at the expiration of the lease, in order to secure the payment of damages alleged to be due, on account of injuries done to the house during the contract. The Prussian government decided that the general exemption, under the law of nations, of the personal property, of foreign ministers from the local jurisdiction, did not extend to this case, where, it was contended, the right of detention was created by the contract itself, and by the legal effect given to it by the local law. In thus granting to the proprietor the rights of a creditor whose debt is secured by hypothecation (Pfandgläubiger,) not only in respect to the rent, but as to all other demands arising under the contract, the Prussian Civil Code confers upon him a *real right* as to all the effects of the tenant, which may be found on the premises at the expiration of the lease, by means of which he may retain them, as a security for all his claims derived from the contract.

It was stated, by the American minister, that this decision placed the members of the *corps diplomatique*, accredited at the Prussian court, on the same footing with the subjects of the country, as to the right which the Prussian Code confers upon the lessor of distraining the goods of the tenant, to enforce the performance of the contract. The only reason alleged to justify such an exception to the general principle of exemption was, that the right in question was constituted by the contract itself. It was not pretended that such an exception had been laid down by any writer of authority on the law of nations; and this consideration alone presented a strong objection against its validity, it being notorious that all the exceptions to the principle were carefully enumerated by the most esteemed public jurists. Not only is such an exception not confirmed by them, but it is expressly repelled by these writers. Nor could it be pretended that the practice of a single government, in a single case, was sufficient to create an exception to a principle which all nations regarded as sacred and inviolable.

Doubtless, by the Prussian Code, and that of most other nations, the contract of hiring gives to the proprietor the right of seizing, or detaining the goods of the tenant, for the non-payment of rent, or damages incurred by injuries done to the premises. But the question here was, not what are the rights conferred by the municipal laws of the country upon the proprietor, in respect to the tenant who is a subject of that country; but what are those rights in respect to a foreign minister, whose dwelling is a sacred asylum; whose person and property are entirely exempt from the local jurisdiction; and who can only be compelled to perform his contracts by an appeal to his own government. Here the contract of hiring constitutes, *per se*, the right in question, in this sense only, that the law furnishes to one of the parties a special remedy to compel the other to perform its stipulations. Instead of compelling the lessor to resort to a personal action against the tenant, it gives him a lien upon the goods found on the premises. This lien may be enforced against the subject of the country, because their goods are subject to its laws and its tribunals of justice; but it cannot be enforced against foreign ministers resident in the country, because they are subject neither to the one nor to the other.

To deprive a minister of his privilege in this case would be to deprive him of that independence and security which are indispensably necessary to enable him to fulfill the duties he owes to his own government. If a single article of furniture may be seized, it may all be seized, and the minister, with his family, thus be deprived of the means of subsistence. If the sanctity of his dwelling may be violated for this purpose, it may be violated for any other. If his private property may be taken upon this pretext, the property of his government, and even the archives of the legation, may be taken upon the same pretext.

In reply to these arguments it was urged, on behalf of the Prussian government, that if, in the present case any Prussian authority had pretended to exercise a right of jurisdiction, either over the person of the minister or his property, the solution of the question would doubtless appertain to the law of nations, and it must be determined according to the precepts of that law. But the only question in the present case could be, what are the legal rights established by the contract of hiring, between the proprietor and the tenant. To determine this question, there could be no other rule than the civil law of the country where the contract was made, and where it was to be executed, that is, in the present case, the civil code of Prussia.

The controversy having been terminated, as between the parties, by the proprietor of the house restoring the effects which had been detained, on the payment of a reasonable compensation for the injury done to the premises, the Prussian government proposed to the American government the following question:

"If a foreign diplomatic agent, accredited near the United States, enters, of his own accord, and in the prescribed forms, into a contract with an American citizen; and if, under such contract, the laws of the country give to such citizen, in a given case, a *real right* (*droit réel,*) over personal property (*biens mobiliers,*) belonging to such agent: does the American government assume the right of depriving the American citizen of his *real right*, at the simple instance of the diplomatic agent relying upon his extra-territoriality?"

This question was answered on the part of the American government, by assuming the instance contemplated by the Prussian government to be that of an *implied* contract, growing out of the relation of landlord and tenant, by which the former had secured to him under the municipal laws of the country, a tacit *hypothek* or lien upon the furniture of the latter. It was taken for granted that there was no express hypothecation, still less any giving in *pledge*, which implies a transfer of possession by way of security for a debt. There could be no doubt that, in this last case, the pawnee has a complete right, a *real right*, as it was called by the Prussian government, or *jus in re*, not in the least affected by diplomatic immunities.

With these distinctions and qualifications, the American government had no doubt that the view taken by its minister (Wheaton) of this question of privilege was entirely correct. The sense of that government had been clearly expressed in the act of Congress, 1790, which includes the very case of distress for rent, among other legal remedies denied to the creditors of a foreign minister.

The Prussian government adhered to its view of the case, and the question, therefore remained unsettled, as between the two governments.

CASE OF BARON DE WRECH, 1772.

(*Marten's Causes Célèbres.*)

Is it an infringement of a minister's diplomatic privileges to withhold his passports, until his debts are paid?

In 1772, the Baron de Wrech, Minister Plenipotentiary of the Landgrave of Hesse-Cassel at the court of Paris, was recalled from his embassy. He was about to quit Paris without paying the debts which he had contracted there. His creditors, especially a Marquis de Bezons, besought the Minister of Foreign Affairs not to grant the Baron his passport. It was accordingly refused. All the *corps diplomatique* at Paris remonstrated against this act as a violation of International Law.

The French Minister, *le Duc d'Aiguillon*, replied in an elaborate memoir drawn up by M. Pfeffel, upon the Rights of Ambassadors; defended, upon the authority of Grotius and Bynkershoek, the right of using that species of constraint against an ambassador which did not interfere with the exercise of his functions. He further appealed to the practice of other States, as warranting the step which had been taken, and especially to that of Hesse-Cassel itself, which had imprisoned a Dutch ambassador, in order to compel him to render an account of a charitable institution of which he had been the administrator. It was admitted that this attack on the person of an ambassador was indefensible, but it was added that Holland had not denied the jurisdiction of Hesse-Cassel in the matter.

The Landgrave was compelled to make an arrangement with the creditors of the Baron de Wrech, before that minister could obtain his passport.

CASE OF DUBOIS, 1856.

(Sen. Ex. Doc. No. 21, 34th Cong., 3d Sess.)

A foreign minister cannot be compelled to appear before a court as a witness.

A case of homicide having occurred at Washington, in 1856, in the presence of the Dutch minister, whose testimony was deemed altogether material for the trial, "and inasmuch as he was exempt from the ordinary process to compel the attendance of witnesses," an application was made by the district attorney, through the Secretary of State, to Mr. Dubois to appear and testify. The minister having refused, by the unanimous advice of his colleagues, in a note of the 11th of May, 1856, to the Secretary of State, to appear as a witness, Mr. Marcy, Secretary of State, instructed, May 15, 1856, Mr. Belmont, minister of the United States at the Hague, to bring the matter to the attention of the Netherlands Government.

Mr. Marcy says, that "it is not doubted that both by the usage of nations and the laws of the United States, Mr. Dubois has the legal right to decline to give his testimony; but he is at perfect liberty to exercise the privilege to the extent requested, and by doing so he does not subject himself to the jurisdiction of the country. The circumstances of this case are such as to appeal strongly to the universal sense of justice.

"In the event of M. Van Hall's suggesting that M. Dubois might give his deposition out of court in the case, you will not omit to state that by our constitution, in all criminal prosecutions, the accused has the right to be confronted with the witnesses against him, and hence, in order that the testimony should be legal, it must be given before the court." M. Van Hall, June 9, 1856, in a note to Mr. Belmont, declined authorizing the minister to appear in court. He said that, "availing himself of a prerogative generally conceded to the members of the diplomatic body, and recognized also by the laws of the Republic, as adverted to by Mr. Marcy, M. Dubois refused to appear before a court of justice; but being desirous to at once reconcile that prerogative with the requirements of justice, he suggested a middle course of action, and proposed to Mr. Marcy to give his declaration under oath, should he be authorized to that effect by the Government of the Netherlands. After taking the King's orders on the subject, I did not hesitate to give such authority to M. Dubois, approving at the same time, and formally, the line of conduct which he pursued on that occasion." M. Dubois addressed a note to Mr. Marcy, on the 21st of June, stating that he was authorized to make his declaration under oath at the Department of State, adding, "it is understood that, on such an occasion, no mention is to be made of a cross-examination, to which I could not subject myself." The declaration was not taken, as the district attorney stated that it would not be admitted as evidence.

DILLON'S CASE, 1854.

(1 *Wharton's Digest*, 665.)

The clause in the Constitution of the United States which gives a person accused of a criminal offense before the Federal courts the right of compulsory process to procure the presence of witnesses in his favor, and to be confronted by the witnesses against him, prevails over a treaty which exempts the consuls of a foreign State from appearing before the courts as witnesses.

In 1854 Mr. Dillon, then consul of France at San Francisco, was brought into the United States District Court, then sitting, on an attachment for refusing to obey a subpœna *duces tecum* issued from that court to compel his attendance at a criminal trial then and there pending. Mr. Dillon protested against the process on two grounds: (1) Immunity from such process by international law; (2) immunity under the French-American treaty. The second point was merged in argument in the first, since it was agreed by counsel that the treaty privilege could not stand in the way of a party's constitutional right to meet the witness against him face to face, unless that privilege was in accordance with public international law.

On this question the court (HOFFMAN, J.,) spoke as follows:

"If the accused, by virtue of the constitutional provision in this case, can compel the attendance of the consul of France, it seems necessarily to follow the attendance of an ambassador could in like manner be enforced.

"The immunity afforded to and personal inviolability of ambassadors, now universally recognized by the law of nations, has been deemed one of the most striking instances of the advance of civilization and the progress of enlightened and liberal ideas. Though resident in a foreign country to which they are deputed (1 Kent. Com., 45), their persons have, by the consent of all nations, been deemed inviolable; nor can they, says the same high authority, be made amenable to the civil or criminal jurisdiction of the country. By fiction of law, the ambassador is considered as if he were out of the territory of the foreign power, and, though he resides within the foreign state, he is considered a member of his own country, retaining his original domicile, and the Government he represents has exclusive cognizance of his conduct and control over his person. (1 Kent's Com., 46.)

"Does, then, the Constitution of the United States, by the provision in favor of persons accused of crime, intend to subject these high functionaries to the process of the courts, and does it authorize and require the courts in case of disobedience to violate their persons and disregard immunities universally conceded to them by the law of nations, by imprisoning them? If, as is the received doctrine, the ambassador cannot, even in the case of a high crime committed by himself, be proceeded against, it is obvious that for a lesser offense of a contempt or disobedience to an order of a court, he would *a fortiori* not be amenable to the law. The only ground upon which the right of a court to compel the attendance of an ambassador by its process, and to punish him if he disobey it, can be placed, is that the Constitution is in this case in conflict with and paramount to the law of nations, and the immunity usually conceded to ambassadors is, by the provision in favor of the accused in criminal cases, taken away.

"But the privilege of ambassadors from arrest, under any circumstances, has been declared by congress by special legislation. By the twenty-fifth section of the act of congress of April 30, 1790, it is enacted that, 'if any writ or process sue out of any courts of the United States, or of a particular State, or by any judge or justice therein respectively, whereby the person of an ambassador may be arrested or imprisoned, or his goods distrained, seized, or attached, such writ and process shall be deemed and adjudged to be utterly null and void to all intents, construction, and purposes whatever.'"

When the attachment was served on Mr. Dillon, he hauled down the consular flag; and the case was taken up by the French minister at Washington, as involving a gross disrespect to France. A long and animated controversy between Mr. Marcy, then Secretary of State, and the French Government ensued. The fact that an attachment had issued under which Mr. Dillon was brought into court was regarded by the French Government as not merely a contravention of the treaty, but an offense by international law; and it was argued that the disrespect was not purged by the subsequent discharge of Mr. Dillon from arrest. It was urged, also, that the fact that the subpœna contained the clause *duces tecum* involved a violation of the consular archives. Mr. Marcy, in a letter of September 11, 1854, to Mr. Mason, then minister at Paris, discusses these questions at great length. He maintains that the provision in the Federal Constitution giving defendants opportunity to meet witnesses produced against them face to face, overrides conflicting treaties, unless in cases where such treaties embody exceptions to this right recognized as such when the Constitution was framed. One of these exceptions relates to the case of diplomatic representatives. "As the law of evidence stood when the Constitution went into effect," says Mr. Marcy, "ambassadors and ministers could not be served with compulsory process to appear as witnesses, and the clause in the Constitution referred to did not give the defendant the right in criminal prosecutions to compel their attendance in court." This privilege, however, Mr. Marcy maintained, did not extend to consuls, and consuls, therefore, could only procure the privilege when given to them by treaty which, in criminal cases, was subject to the limitations of the Constitution of the United States. Mr. Marcy, however, finding that the French Government continued to regard the attachment, with the subpœna *duces tecum*, as an attack on its honor, offered, in a letter to Mr. Mason, dated January 18, 1855, to compromise the matter by a salute to the French flag upon a French man-of-war, stopping at San Francisco. Count de Sartejes, the French minister at Washington, asked in addition that when the consular flag at San Francisco was rehoisted, it should receive a salute. This was declined by Mr. Marcy.

In August, 1855, after a long and protracted controversy, the French Government agreed to accept as a sufficient satisfaction an expression of regret by the Government of the United States, coupled with the provision that "when a French national ship or squadron shall appear in the harbor of San Francisco the United States authorities there, military or naval, will salute the national flag borne by such ship or squadron with a national salute, at an hour to be specified and agreed on with the French naval commanding officer present, and the French ship or squadron whose flag is thus saluted will return the salute gun for gun."

In a dispatch to Mason, American minister to France, Mr. Marcy said: "The Constitution is to prevail over a treaty where the provisions of the one come in conflict with the other. It would be difficult to find a reputable lawyer in this country who would not yield a ready assent to this proposition. Mr. Dillon's counsel admitted it in his argument for the consul's privilege before the court in California.

"The sixth amendment to the United States Constitution gives, in general and comprehensive language, the right to a defendant in criminal prosecutions to have compulsory process to procure the attendance of witnesses in his favor. Neither Congress nor the treaty-making power are competent to put any restriction on this constitutional provision. There was, however, at the time of its adoption, some limit to the range of its operation. It did not give to such a defendant the right to have compulsory process against all persons whatever but only against such as were subject to subpœna at that time, such as might by existing law be witnesses.

"There were then persons and classes of persons who were not thus subject to that process, who, by privileges and mental disqualifications, could not be made witnesses, and this constitutional provision did not confer the right on the defendant to have compulsory process against them. As the law of evidence stood when the Constitution went into effect, ambassadors and ministers could not be served with compulsory process to appear as witnesses, and the clause in the Constitution referred to did not give to the defendant in criminal prosecutions the right to compel their attendance in court. But what was the case in this respect as to consuls? They had not the diplomatic privileges of ambassadors and ministers. After the adoption of the Constitution the defendant in a criminal prosecution had the right to compulsory process to bring into court as a witness in his behalf any foreign consul whatsoever.

"If he then had it, and has it now, when and how has this constitutional right been taken from him? Congress could not take it away, neither could the treaty-making power, for it is not within the competence of either to modify, or restrict the operation of any provision of the Constitution of the United States."[1]

[1] Other cases bearing upon this subject are :—

The Magdalina Steam Navigation Company v. *Martin*, 28 L. J., Q. B., N. S., 310, (1859), Lord CAMPBELL, C. J., said: "The question raised by this record is whether the public minister of a foreign state, accredited to and received by Her Majesty, having no real property in England, and having done nothing to disentitle him to

SECTION 11.— IMMUNITIES OF PUBLIC SHIPS.

(a) *Ships of War.*

THE SCHOONER "EXCHANGE" v. M'FADDON.

SUPREME COURT OF THE UNITED STATES, 1812.

(7 *Cranch*, 116.)

It is a principle of public law, that national ships of war, entering the port of a friendly power open to their reception, are to be considered as exempted by the consent of that power from its jurisdiction.

Appeal from the sentence of the circuit court of the United States for the district of Pennsylvania.

The schooner *Exchange*, owned by John M'Faddon and William

the privileges generally belonging to such public minister, may be sued, against his will, in the courts of this country for a debt, neither his person nor his goods being touched by the suit, while he remains such public minister." *Held*, that he could not be so sued.

Nitchencoff's Case, 10 Solic. Law Journal, 56 : "The French Court of Cassation has quashed the appeal of Nitchencoff, the Russian sentenced to imprisonment for life for a murderous attack upon M. de Balsh, in the house of the Russian Ambassador in Paris. It will be remembered that this case gave rise to a diplomatic correspondence, the Russian Government having disputed the right of the French courts to try the murderer, and claimed a right to have him given up for trial in Russia. The court laid down the law that "the fiction of the law of nations, according to which the house of an ambassador is reputed to be a continuation of the territory of his sovereign, only protects diplomatic agents and their servants, and does not exclude the jurisdiction of French courts, in case of a crime committed in such a locality by a person not belonging to the embassy, even although he is a subject of the nation from which the ambassador is accredited."

The Guiteau Trial (1881), 1 Wharton's Digest, 669 :—On the trial of Guiteau, Señor Camacho, minister from Venezuela, who was present at President Garfield's assassination, was called as a witness for the prosecution.

Before he was sworn the following statement was made by the district attorney :

"If your honor please, before the gentleman is sworn, I desire to state, or rather I think it due to the witness to state that he is the minister from Venezuela to this

Greetham, sailed from Baltimore, October 27, 1809, for St. Sebastians, in Spain. On the 30th of December, 1810, she was seized by the order of Napoleon Bonaparte; and was then armed and commissioned as a public vessel of the French government, under the name of *Balaou*. On a voyage to the West Indies, she put into the port of Philadelphia, in July, 1811, and on the 24th of August was libelled by the original owners. As no claimant appeared, Mr. Dallas, the attorney of the United States for the district of Pennsylvania filed (at the suggestion of the executive department of the United States, it is believed) a suggestion that inasmuch as there was peace between France and the United States, the public vessels of the former may enter into the ports and harbors of the latter and depart at will without seizure or detention in any way.

The district judge dismissed the libel, on the ground that a public armed vessel of a foreign power, at peace with the United States, is not subject to the ordinary judicial tribunals of the country, so far as regards the question of title, by which the foreign sovereign claims to hold her.

The libellants appealed to the circuit court, where the sentence was reversed—from the sentence of reversal, the district attorney appealed to this court.

MARSHALL, C. J.:—"This case involves the very delicate and important inquiry, whether an American citizen can assert, in an American court, a title to an armed national vessel, found within the waters of the United States.

"The question has been considered with an earnest solicitude,

Government, and entitled under the law governing diplomatic relations to be relieved from service by subpœna or sworn as a witness in any case.

"Under the instructions of his Government, owing to the friendship of that Government for the United States, and the great respect for the memory of the man who was assassinated, they have instructed him to waive his rights and appear as a witness in the case, the same as any witness who is a citizen of this country."

Respublica v. *DeLongchamps*, 1 Dallas, 110 (1784):—The defendant threatened to assault the Secretary of the French Legation, the threats being made in the house of the French minister. The defendant was fined $500 and imprisoned two years.

United States v. *Liddle*, 2 Wash. Circ. Ct., 205 (1808):—Indictment for assault and battery on a member of the Spanish Legation. The law is the same whether the attacked is a private party or an ambassador, viz., if the ambassador was the prior assaulting party, the defendant is excused for his subsequent assault.

United States v. *Ortega*, 4 Wash. Circ. Ct., 531 (1825):—Indictment for an assault on the Spanish Chargé d'Affaires. Cites Liddle's case and affirms it: "A foreign minister, by committing the first assault, so far loses his privilege, that he cannot complain of an infraction of the law of nations; if in his turn, he should be assaulted by the party aggrieved."

that the decision may conform to those principles of national and municipal law by which it ought to be regulated.

"In exploring an unbeaten path, with few, if any aids, from precedents or written law, the court has found it necessary to rely much on general principles, and on a train of reasoning, founded on cases in some degree analogous to this.

"The jurisdiction of courts is a branch of that which is possessed by the nation as an independent sovereign power.

"The jurisdiction of the nation within its own territory is necessarily exclusive and absolute. It is susceptible of no limitation not imposed by itself. Any restriction upon it, deriving validity from an external source, would imply a diminution of its own sovereignty to the extent of the restriction, and an investment of that sovereignty to the same extent in that power which could impose such restrictions.

"All exceptions, therefore, to the full and complete power of a nation within its own territories, must be traced up to the consent of the nation itself. They can flow from no other legitimate source.

"This consent may be either express or implied. In the latter case, it is less determinate, exposed more to the uncertainties of construction; but, if understood, not less obligatory.

"The world being composed of distinct sovereignties, possessing equal rights and equal independence, whose mutual benefit is promoted by intercourse with each other, and by an interchange of those good offices which humanity dictates and its wants require, all sovereigns have consented to a relaxation in practice, in cases under certain peculiar circumstances, of that absolute and complete jurisdiction within their respective territories which sovereignty confers.

"This consent may, in some instances, be tested by common usage, and by common opinion, growing out of that usage.

"A nation would justly be considered as violating its faith, although that faith might not be expressly plighted, which should suddenly and without previous notice, exercise its territorial powers in a manner not consonant to the usages and received obligations of the civilized world.

"This full and absolute territorial jurisdiction being alike the attribute of every sovereign, and being incapable of conferring extraterritorial power, would not seem to contemplate foreign sovereigns nor their sovereign rights as its objects. One sovereign being in no respect amenable to another, and being bound by obligations of the highest character not to degrade the dignity of his nation, by placing himself or its sovereign rights within the jurisdiction of another, can be supposed to enter a foreign territory only under an express license, or in the confidence that the immunities belonging to his independent sovereign station, will be extended to him.

"This perfect equality and absolute independence of sovereigns, and this common interest impelling them to mutual intercourse, and an interchange of good offices with each other, have given rise to a class of cases in which every sovereign is understood to waive the exercise of a part of that complete exclusive territorial jurisdiction, which has been stated to be the attribute of every nation.

"1st. One of these is admitted to be the exemption of the person of the sovereign from arrest or detention within a foreign territory.

"If he enters that territory with the knowledge and license of its sovereign, that license, although containing no stipulation exempting his person from arrest, is universally understood to imply such stipulation.

"Why has the whole civilized world concurred in this construction? The answer cannot be mistaken. A foreign sovereign is not understood as intending to subject himself to a jurisdiction incompatible with his dignity and the dignity of his nation, and it is to avoid this subjection that the license has been obtained. The character to whom it is given, and the object for which it is granted, equally require that it should be construed to impart full security to the person who has obtained it. This security, however, need not be expressed; it is implied from the circumstances of the case. Should one sovereign enter the territory of another, without the consent of that other, expressed or implied, it would present a question which does not appear to be perfectly settled, a decision of which is not necessary to any conclusion to which the court may come in the cause under consideration. If he did not thereby expose himself to the territorial jurisdiction of the sovereign, whose dominions he had entered, it would seem to be because all sovereigns impliedly engage not to avail themselves of a power over their equal, which a romantic confidence in their magnanimity has placed in their hands.

"2d. A second case, standing on the same principles with the first, is the immunity which all civilized nations allow to foreign ministers.

"Whatever may be the principle on which this immunity is established, whether we consider him as in the place of the sovereign he represents, or by a political fiction suppose him to be extraterritorial, and therefore, in point of law, not within the jurisdiction of the sovereign at whose court he resides; still the immunity itself is granted by the governing power of the nation to which the minister is deputed, his fiction of extra-territoriality could not be erected and supported against the will of the sovereign of the territory. He is supposed to assent to it.

"This consent is not expressed. It is true that in some countries, and in this among others, a special law is enacted for the case. But the law obviously proceeds on the idea of prescribing the punishment of an act previously unlawful, not of granting to a foreign minister a privilege which he would not otherwise possess.

"The assent of the sovereign to the very important and extensive exemptions from territorial jurisdiction which are admitted to attach to foreign ministers, is implied from the considerations that, without such exemption, every sovereign would hazard his own dignity by employing a public minister abroad. His minister would owe temporary and local allegiance to a foreign prince, and would be less competent to the objects of his mission. A sovereign committing the interests of his nation with a foreign power, to the care of a person whom he has selected for that purpose, cannot intend to subject his minister in any degree to that power; and therefore a consent to receive him, implies a consent that he shall possess those privileges which his principal intended he should retain, privileges which are essential to the dignity of his sovereign, and to the duties he is bound to perform.

"In what cases a minister, by infracting the laws of the country in which he resides, may subject himself to other punishment than will be inflicted by his own sovereign, is an inquiry foreign to the present purpose. If his crimes be such as to render him amenable to the local jurisdiction, it must be because they forfeit the privileges annexed to his character; and the minister, by violating the conditions under which he was received as the representative of a foreign sovereign, has surrendered the immunities granted on those conditions; or, according to the true meaning of the original assent, has ceased to be entitled to them.

"3d. A third case in which a sovereign is understood to cede a portion of his territorial jurisdiction is, where he allows the troops of a foreign prince to pass through his dominions.

"In such case, without any express declaration waiving jurisdiction over the army to which this right of passage has been granted, the sovereign who should attempt to exercise it would certainly be considered as violating his faith. By exercising it, the purpose for which the free passage was granted would be defeated, and a portion of the military force of a foreign independent nation would be diverted from those national objects and duties to which it was applicable, and would be withdrawn from the control of the sovereign whose power and whose safety might greatly depend on retaining the exclusive command and disposition of this force. The grant of a free passage, therefore, implies a waiver of all jurisdiction over the troops during their passage, and permits the foreign general to use that discipline, and to inflict those punishments which the government of his army may require.

"But if, without such express permit, an army should be led through the territories of a foreign prince, might the jurisdiction of the territory be rightfully exercised over the individuals composing this army?

"Without doubt a military force can never gain immunities of any other description than those which war gives, by entering a foreign territory against the will of its sovereign. But if his consent, instead of being expressed by a particular license, be expressed by a general declaration that foreign troops may pass through a specified tract of country, a distinction between such general permit and a particular license is not perceived. It would seem reasonable that every immunity which would be conferred by a special license, would be, in like manner conferred by such general permit. We have seen that a license to pass through a territory implies immunities not expressed, and it is material to inquire why the license itself may not be presumed?

"It is obvious that the passage of an army through a foreign territory will probably be at all times inconvenient and injurious, and would often be imminently dangerous to the sovereign through whose dominion it passed. Such a practice would break down some of the most decisive distinctions between peace and war, and would reduce a nation to the necessity of resisting by war an act not absolutely hostile in its character, or of exposing itself to the stratagems and frauds of a power whose integrity might be doubted, and who might enter the country under deceitful pretexts. It is for reasons like these that the general license to foreigners to enter the dominions of a friendly power, is never understood to extend to a military force; and an army marching into the dominions of another sovereign, may justly be considered as committing an act of hostility; and if not opposed by force, acquires no privileges by its irregular and improper conduct. It may, however, well be questioned whether any other than the sovereign power of the state be capable of deciding that such military commander is without a license.

"But the rule which is applicable to armies, does not appear to be equally applicable to ships of war entering the ports of a friendly power. The injury inseparable from the march of an army through an inhabited country and the dangers often, indeed generally, attending it, do not ensue from admitting a ship of war, without a special license, into a friendly port. A different rule, therefore, with respect to this species of military force has been generally adopted. If, for reasons of state, the ports of a nation generally, or any particular ports be closed against vessels of war generally, or the vessels of any particular nation, notice is usually given of such determination. If there be no prohibition, the ports of a friendly nation are considered as open to the public ships of all powers with whom it is at peace, and they are supposed to enter such ports and to remain in them while allowed to remain, under the protection of the government of the place.

"In almost every instance, the treaties between civilized nations contain a stipulation to this effect in favor of vessels driven in by stress of weather or other urgent necessity. In such cases the sovereign is bound by compact to authorize foreign vessels to enter his ports. The treaty bids him to allow vessels in distress to find refuge and asylum in his ports, and this is a license which he is not at liberty to retract. If would be difficult to assign a reason for withholding from a license thus granted, any immunity from local jurisdiction which would be implied in a special license.

"If there be no treaty applicable to the case, and the sovereign, from motives deemed adequate by himself, permits his ports to remain open to the public ships of foreign friendly powers, the conclusion seems irresistible, that they enter by his assent. And if they enter by his assent necessarily implied, no just reason is perceived by the court for distinguishing their case from that of vessels which enter by express assent. In all the cases of exemption which have been reviewed, much has been implied; but the obligation of what was implied has been found equal to the obligation of that which was expressed. Are there reasons for denying the application of this principle to ships of war?

"In this part of the subject a difficulty is to be encountered, the seriousness of which is acknowledged, but which the court will not attempt to evade.

"These treaties which provide for the admission and safe departure of public vessels entering a port from stress of weather, or other urgent cause, provide in like manner for the private vessels of the nation; and where public vessels enter a port under the general license which is implied merely from the absence of a prohibition, they are, it may be urged, in the same condition with merchant vessels entering the same port for the purposes of trade who cannot thereby claim any exemption from the jurisdiction of the country. It may be contended, certainly with much plausibility if not correctness, that the same rule, and same principle are applicable to public and private ships; and since it is admitted that private ships, entering without special license become subject to the local jurisdiction, it is demanded on what authority an exception is made in favor of ships of war.

"It is by no means conceded, that a private vessel really availing herself of an asylum provided by treaty, and not attempting to trade, would become amenable to the local jurisdiction unless she committed some act forfeiting the protection she claims under compact. On the contrary, motives may be assigned for stipulating and according immunities to vessels in cases of distress, which would not be demanded for, or allowed to those which enter voluntarily, and for ordinary purposes. On this part of the subject, however, the court does not mean to indicate any opinion. The case itself may possibly occur, and ought not to be prejudiced.

"Without deciding how far such stipulations in favor of distressed vessels, as are usual in treaties, may exempt private ships from the jurisdiction of the place, it may safely be asserted that the whole reasoning upon which such exemption has been implied in other cases, applies with full force to the exemption of ships of war in this.

"'It is impossible to conceive,' says Vattel, 'that a prince who sends an ambassador or any other minister can have any intention of subjecting him to the authority of a foreign power, and this consideration furnishes an additional argument, which completely establishes the independency of a public minister. If it cannot be reasonably presumed that his sovereign means to subject him to the authority of the prince to whom he is sent, the latter, in receiving the minister, consents to admit him on the footing of independency; and thus there exists between the two princes a tacit convention, which gives a new force to the natural obligation.'

"Equally impossible is it to conceive, whatever may be the construction as to private ships, that a prince who stipulates a passage for his troops, or an asylum for his ships of war in distress, should mean to subject his army or his navy to the jurisdiction of a foreign sovereign. And if this cannot be presumed, the sovereign of the port must be considered as having conceded the privilege to the extent in which it must have been understood to be asked.

"To the court, it appears, that where, without treaty, the ports of a nation are open to the private and public ships of a friendly power, whose subjects have also liberty without special license, to enter the country for business or amusement, a clear distinction is to be drawn between the rights accorded to private individuals or trading vessels, and those accorded to public armed ships which constitute a part of the military force of the nation.

"The preceding reasoning, has maintained the propositions that all exemptions from territorial jurisdiction must be derived from the consent of the sovereign of the territory; that this consent may be implied or expressed; and that, when implied, its extent must be regulated by the nature of the case and the views under which the parties requiring and conceding it must be supposed to act.

"When private individuals of one nation spread themselves through another as business or caprice may direct, mingling indiscriminately with the inhabitants of that other, or when merchant vessels enter for the purposes of trade, it would be obviously inconvenient and dangerous to society, and would subject the laws to continual infraction, and the government to degradation, if such individuals or merchants did not owe temporary and local allegiance, and were not amenable to the jurisdiction of the country. Nor can the foreign sovereign have any motive for wishing such exemption. His subjects thus passing into foreign countries, are not employed by him, nor are they engaged in national pursuits. Consequently there are powerful motives for not exempting persons of this description from the jurisdiction of the country in which they are found, and no one motive for requiring it. The implied license, therefore, under which they enter, can never be construed to grant such exemption. But in all respects different is the situation of a public armed ship. She constitutes a part of the military force of her nation; acts under the immediate and direct command of the sovereign; is employed by him in national objects. He has many and powerful motives for preventing those objects from being defeated by the interference of a foreign state. Such interference cannot take place without affecting his power and his dignity. The implied license, therefore, under which such vessel enters a friendly port, may reasonably be construed, and, it seems to the court, ought to be construed, as containing an exemption from the jurisdiction of the sovereign, within whose territory she claims the rites of hospitality.

"Upon these principles, by the unanimous consent of nations, a foreigner is amenable to the laws of the place; but certainly in practice, nations have not yet asserted their jurisdiction over the public armed ships of a foreign sovereign, entering a port open for their reception.

"Bynkershoek, a jurist of great reputation, has indeed maintained that the property of a foreign sovereign is not distinguishable by any legal exemption from the property of an ordinary individual, and has quoted several cases in which courts have exercised jurisdiction over causes in which a foreign sovereign was made a party defendant.

"Without indicating any opinion on this question, it may safely be affirmed, that there is a manifest distinction between the private property of the person who happens to be a prince, and that military force which supports the sovereign power, and maintains the dignity and the independence of a nation. A prince, by acquiring private property in a foreign country, may possibly be considered as subjecting that property to the territorial jurisdiction; he may be considered as so far laying down the prince, and assuming the character of a private individual; but this he cannot be presumed to do with respect to any portion of that armed force, which upholds his crown, and the nation he is intrusted to govern.

"The only applicable case cited by Bynkershoek, is that of the Spanish ships of war, seized in Flushing for a debt due from the King of Spain. In that case the states generally interposed; and there is reason to believe, from the manner in which the transaction is stated, that, either by the interference of government, or the decision of the court, the vessels were released. This case of the Spanish vessels is, it is believed, the only case furnished by the history of the world, of an attempt made by an individual to assert a claim against a foreign prince, by seizing the armed vessels of the nation. That this proceeding was at once arrested by the government, in a nation which appears to have asserted the power of proceeding in the same manner against the private property of the prince, would seem to furnish no feeble argument in support of the universality of the opinion in favor of the exemption claimed for ships of war. The distinction made in our own laws between public and private ships would appear to proceed from the same opinion.

"It seems, then, to the court, to be a principle of public law, that national ships of war, entering the port of a friendly power open for their reception, are to be considered as exempted by the consent of that power from its jurisdiction.

"Without doubt, the sovereign of the place is capable of destroying this implication. He may claim and exercise jurisdiction, either by employing force, or by subjecting such vessels to the ordinary tribunals. But, until such power be exerted in a manner not to be misunderstood, the sovereign cannot be considered as having imparted to the ordinary tribunals a jurisdiction, which it would be a breach of faith to exercise. Those general statutory provisions, therefore, which are descriptive of the ordinary jurisdiction of the judicial tribunals, which give an individual whose property has been wrested from him, a right to claim that property in the courts of the country in which it is found, ought not, in the opinion of this court, to be so construed as to give them jurisdiction in a case in which the sovereign power has impliedly consented to waive its jurisdiction.

"The arguments in favor of this opinion which have been drawn from the general inability of the judicial power to enforce its decisions in cases of this description, from the consideration that the sovereign power of the nation is alone competent to avenge wrongs committed by a sovereign, that the questions to which such wrongs give birth are rather questions of policy than of law, that they are for diplomatic, rather than legal discussion, are of great weight, and merit serious attention. But the argument has already been drawn to a length which forbids a particular examination of these points.

"The principles which have been stated will now be applied to the case at bar.

"In the present state of the evidence and proceedings, the *Exchange* must be considered as a vessel which was the property of the libellants, whose claim is repelled by the fact, that she is now a national armed vessel, commissioned by, and in the service of the Emperor of France. The evidence of this fact is not controverted. But it is contended that it constitutes no bar to an inquiry into the validity of the title, by which the emperor holds this vessel. Every person, it is alleged, who is entitled to property brought within the jurisdiction of our courts, has a right to assert his title in those courts, unless there be some law taking his case out of the general rule. It is therefore said to be the right, and if it be the right, it is the duty of the court, to inquire whether this title has been extinguished by an act, the validity of which is recognized by national or municipal law.

"If the preceding reasoning be correct, the *Exchange*, being a public armed ship, in the service of a foreign sovereign, with whom the government of the United States is at peace, and having entered an American port open for her reception, on the terms on which ships of war are generally permitted to enter the ports of a friendly power, must be considered as having come into the American territory, under an implied promise, that while necessarily within it, and demeaning herself in a friendly manner, she should be exempt from the jurisdiction of the country."

THE "CONSTITUTION."

HIGH COURT OF ADMIRALTY, 1879.

(48 *Law Journal*, *P. D. & A.*, 13.)

A ship of war of a foreign state cannot be proceeded against in a suit for salvage.

The facts are sufficiently stated in the opinion.

Sir Robert PHILLIMORE:—"In this case an application was made to the court to allow a warrant to issue of a peculiar character—a warrant which was to be served upon a ship of war belonging to an independent state at amity with Her Majesty. The court directed the case to stand over, and suggested that it would be proper that notice should be given to his Excellency, the American Minister in London, and to Lord Salisbury, as Secretary for Foreign Affairs. The court has reason to congratulate itself that it took that step, for the result has been that it has had the advantage of hearing the opinion of counsel on behalf of the United States and of the learned gentleman representing the Crown. It appears from telegrams which have passed in the case that a claim has been made by the owner of the tug for 1,500*l.*, but that the American Consul at Portsmouth has forwarded simply a cheque for 200*l.*, in recognition of the services which the tug has rendered. The owner of the tug was dissatisfied with that amount; and consequently made an application to this court for an order to issue a warrant to arrest the *Constitution* and her cargo.

"The question, therefore, which is raised under these proceedings is whether I have any jurisdiction to permit the arrest of a foreign ship of war belonging to an independent state in amity with our sovereign, and I hardly think that it can be denied that if I were to exercise the jurisdiction which is craved in the present case, I should be doing that for which there exists no direct precedent. On the contrary, I have no doubt as to this general proposition—that ships of war belonging to another nation with whom we are at peace are exempt from the civil jurisdiction of the courts of this country; and I have listened in vain for any peculiar circumstances which would take this case out of that general proposition. It has happened to me more than once to have been requested by foreign states to sit as arbitrator, and to make awards in differences which had arisen between them and British subjects. Had such an application been made in the present instance I would have gladly undertaken the duty sought to be imposed upon me; but that is not the state of matters I have now to consider. All that I have now to determine is the simple question of jurisdiction. Various cases have been cited before me in argument, all of which, with one exception, were discussed in the case of the *Charkieh*, but that was a wholly different case because the Khedive of Egypt was not an independent sovereign, and the *Charkieh* herself formed one of a fleet of merchantmen. I may in the lengthy judgment which I delivered in that cause, have let drop some expression which may have given rise to an impression that a foreign ship of war is liable to arrest, but, in that case this question, as it is here raised, had not to be decided. Now that it comes before me in this plain and simple form, I feel no doubt that it would be improper for me to accede to the request of the owner of the steam-tug, nor do I think, as I have said above, that the *Constitution* is liable to the process of this court. In regard to the question of the liability of the cargo, I must say I see no distinction between the issue of a warrant in the case of the ship and in the case of this cargo; it is on board a foreign vessel of war, and is under the charge of a foreign government for public purposes.

So that, having no authority to issue either of the warrants prayed for, and as no precedent exists for such a course, I must dismiss this motion with costs.[1]"

[1]Mr. Cobbett (Cases on International Law, 35,) says: "Before the decision in the case of the *Constitution*, some doubt seems to have existed as to whether salvage proceedings might not be instituted in the English Court of Admiralty against a public vessel. In the case of the *Charkieh*, Sir R. Phillimore had said, 'It is by no means clear that a ship of war to which salvage services have been rendered, may not, *jure gentium*, be liable to be proceeded against in the Court of Admiralty for the remuneration due for such services.'

"In a much earlier case, of the *Prins Frederik* (2 Dods., 451), a Dutch man-of-war, whilst on a voyage from Batavia to the Texel, was partially disabled by stress of weather off the Scilly Isles, and was brought into Mount's Bay with the assistance of the master and crew of a British brig, belonging to the port of Penzance. The *Prins Frederik* was at the time employed in bringing home a cargo of spice belonging to the Dutch Government, and for this purpose some of her guns had been removed. The salvors instituted salvage proceedings against the vessel, on the ground that she had for the time being, at least, lost the character and privileges of a public vessel, and also on the further ground that such proceedings being *in rem*, and not against the King of the Netherlands personally, were under any circumstances admissible. According to Lord Campbell, who quoted this case, in 1851 (17 Q. B., 212), Lord Stowell took a strong view against the asserted jurisdiction. To avoid difficulty, Lord Stowell caused a representation to be made to the Dutch government, who consented to his disposing of the matter as arbitrator. Acting under this authority, Lord Stowell awarded the sum of £800 and costs to the salvors."

Mr. Dana, in his note, No. 63, says: "It may be considered as established law,

(b) *Other Public Ships.*

THE "PARLEMENT BELGE."

COURT OF APPEALS, 1878.

(*L. R.*, 5 *Probate Div.*, 197.)

A public vessel of a foreign state—not a ship of war—carrying the mails, and also carrying merchandise, is nevertheless exempt from the jurisdiction of the admiralty courts, in England.

This was an appeal on behalf of the Crown from a decision of Sir R. J. Phillimore.

The judgment of the court (James, Baggallay, and Brett, L. JJ.) was delivered by Brett, L. J. "In this case proceedings *in rem* on behalf of the owners of the *Daring* were instituted in the Admiralty Division, in accordance with the forms prescribed by the Judicature Act, against the *Parlement Belge*, to recover redress in respect of a collision. A writ was served in the usual and prescribed manner on board the *Parlement Belge.* No appearance was entered, but the Attorney-General, in answer to a motion to direct that judgment with costs should be entered for the plaintiffs, and that a warrant should be issued for the *Parlement Belge*, filed an information and protest, asserting that the court had no jurisdiction to entertain the suit. Upon the hearing of the motion and protest the learned judge of the Admiralty Division overruled the protest and allowed the warrant of arrest to issue. The Attorney-General appealed. The protest alleged that the *Parlement Belge* was a mail packet running between Ostend and Dover, and one of the packets mentioned in article 6 of the convention of the 17th of February, 1876, made between the sovereigns of Great Britain and Belgium; that she was and is the property of his Majesty the King of the Belgians, and in his possession, control and employ as reigning sovereign of the state, and was and is a public vessel of the sovereign and state, carrying

now, that the public vessels of a foreign state, coming within the jurisdiction of a friendly state, are exempt from all forms of process in private suits. Nor will such ships be seized, or in any way interfered with, by judicial proceedings in the name and by the authority of the state, to punish violations of public laws. In such cases, the offended state will appeal directly to the other sovereign. Any proceedings against a foreign public ship would be regarded as an unfriendly if not hostile act, in the present state of the law of nations."

his Majesty's royal pennon, and was navigated and employed by and in the possession of such government, and was officered by officers of the Royal Belgian navy, holding commissions, etc. In answer it was averred on affidavits, which were not contradicted, that the packet boat, besides carrying letters, carried merchandise and passengers and their luggage for hire. * * *

"The proposition raised by the first question seems to be as follows: Has the Admiralty Division jurisdiction in respect of a collision to proceed *in rem* against, and in case of non-appearance or omission to find bail, to seize and sell, a ship present in this country, which ship is at the time of the proceedings the property of a foreign sovereign, is in his possession, control, and employ as sovereign by means of his commissioned officers, and is a public vessel of his state, in the sense of its being used for purposes treated by such sovereign and his advisers as public national services, it being admitted that such ship, though commissioned, is not an armed ship of war or employed as a part of the military force of his country? * * *

"It is admitted that neither the sovereign of Great Britain nor any friendly sovereign can be adversely personally impleaded in any court of this country. It is admitted that no armed ship of war of the sovereign of Great Britain, or of a foreign sovereign can be seized by any process whatever, exercised for any purpose by any court of this country. But it is said that this vessel, though it is the property of a friendly sovereign in his public capacity and is used for purposes treated by him as public national services, can be seized and sold under the process of the Admiralty Court of this country, because it will, if so seized and sold, be so treated, not in a suit brought against the sovereign personally, but in a suit *in rem* against the vessel itself. This contention raises two questions; first, supposing that an action *in rem* is an action against the property only, meaning thereby that it is not a legal proceeding at all against the owner of the property, yet can the property in question be subject to the jurisdiction of the court?

"Secondly, is it true to say that an action *in rem* is only and solely a legal procedure against the property, or is it not rather a procedure indirectly, if not directly, impleading the owner of the property to answer to the judgment of the court to the extent of his interest in the property? * * *

"Having carefully considered the case of the *Charkieh*, we are of opinion that the proposition deduced from the earlier cases in an earlier part of this judgment is the correct exposition of the law of nations, viz., that as a consequence of the absolute independence of every sovereign authority and of the international comity which induces every sovereign state to respect the independence of every other sovereign state, each and every one declines to exercise by means of any of its courts, any of its territorial jurisdiction over the person of any sovereign or ambassador of any other state, or over the public property of any state which is destined to its public use, or over the property of any ambassador, though such sovereign, ambassador or property be within its territory, and therefore, but for the common agreement, subject to its jurisdiction.

"This proposition would determine the first question in the present case in favor of the protest, even if an action *in rem* were held to be a proceeding solely against property, and not a procedure directly or indirectly impleading the owner of the property to answer to the judgment of the court. But we cannot allow it to be supposed that in our opinion the owner of the property is not indirectly impleaded. The course of proceeding, undoubtedly, is first to seize the property. It is undoubtedly, not necessary, in order to enable the court to proceed further, that the owner should be personally served with any process. In the majority of cases, brought under the cognizance of an Admiralty Court, no such personal service could be effected. Another course was therefore taken from the earliest times. The seizure of the property was made by means of a formality which was as public as could be devised. That formality of necessity gave notice of the suit to the agents of the owner of the property, and so, in substance, to him. Besides which, by the regular course of the admiralty, the owner was cited or had notice to appear to show cause why his property should not be liable to answer to the complainant. The owner has a right to appear and show cause, a right which cannot be denied. It is not necessary, it is true, that the notice or citation should be personally served. But unless it were considered that, either by means of the publicity of the manner of arresting the property, or by means of the publicity of the notice or citation, the owner had an opportunity of protecting his property from a final decree by the court, the judgment *in rem* of a court would be manifestly contrary to natural justice. In a claim made in respect of a collision the property is not treated as the delinquent *per se*. Though the ship has been in collision, and has caused injury by reason of the negligence or want of skill of those in charge of her, yet she cannot be made the means of compensation if those in charge of her were not the servants of her then owner, as if she was in charge of a compulsory pilot. This is conclusive to show that the liability to compensate must be fixed not merely on the property, but also on the owner through the property.

"If so, the owner is at least indirectly impleaded to answer to, that is to say, to be affected by, the judgment of the court. It is no answer to say that if the property be sold after the maritime lien has accrued, the property may be seized and sold as against the new owner.

"This is a severe law, probably arising from the difficulty of otherwise enforcing any remedy in favor of an injured suitor. But the property cannot be sold as against the new owner, if it could not have been sold as against the owner at the time when the alleged lien accrued. This doctrine of the Courts of Admiralty goes only to the extent, that the innocent purchaser takes the property subject to the inchoate maritime lien which attached to it as against him who was the owner at the time the lien attached. The new owner has the same public notice of the suit and the same opportunity and right of appearance as the former owner would have had. He is impleaded in the same way as the former owner would have been. Either is affected in his interests by the judgment of a court which is bound to give him the means of knowing that it is about to proceed to affect those interests, and that it is bound to hear him if he objects. That is, in our opinion, an impleading.

"The case of *The Bold Buccleugh* does not decide to the contrary of this. It decides that an action *in rem* is a different action from one *in personam* and has a different result. But it does not decide that a court which seizes and sells a man's property does not assume to make that man subject to its jurisdiction. To implead an independent sovereign in such a way is to call upon him to sacrifice either his property or his independence. To place him in that position is a breach of the principle upon which his immunity from jurisdiction rests. We think that he cannot be so indirectly impleaded any more than he could be directly impleaded. The case is, upon this consideration of it, brought within the general rule that a sovereign authority cannot be personally impleaded in any court.

"But it is said that the immunity is lost by reason of the ship having been used for trading purposes. As to this, it must be maintained either that the ship has been so used as to have been employed substantially as a mere trading ship and not substantially for national purposes, or that a use of her in part for trading purposes takes away the immunity, although she is in possession of the sovereign authority by the hands of commissioned officers, and is substantially in use for national purposes. Both these propositions raise the question of how the ship must be considered to have been employed.

"As to the first, the ship has been by the sovereign of Belgium, by the usual means, declared to be in his possession as sovereign, and to be a public vessel of the state. It seems very difficult to say that any court can inquire by contentious testimony whether that declaration is or is not correct. To submit to such an inquiry before the court is to submit to its jurisdiction. It has been held that if the ship be declared by the sovereign authority by the usual means to be a ship of war, that declaration cannot be inquired into. That was expressly decided under very trying circumstances in the case of the *Exchange*. Whether the ship is a public ship used for national purposes seems to come within the same rule. But if such an inquiry could properly be instituted it seems clear that in the present case the ship has been mainly used for the purpose of carrying the mails, and only subserviently to that main object for the purposes of trade. The carrying of passengers and merchandise has been subordinated to the duty of carrying the mails. The ship is not, in fact, brought within the first proposition. As to the second, it has been frequently stated that an independent sovereign cannot be personally sued, although he has carried on a private trading adventure. It has been held that an ambassador cannot be personally sued, although he has traded; and in both cases because such a suit would be inconsistent with the independence and equality of the state which he represents. If the remedy sought by an action *in rem* against public property is, as we think it is, an indirect mode of exercising the authority of the court against the owner of the property, then the attempt to exercise such an authority is an attempt inconsistent with the independence and equality of the state which is represented by such owner. The property cannot, upon the hypothesis, be denied to be public property; the case is within the terms of the rule; it is within the spirit of the rule; therefore, we are of opinion that the mere fact of the ship being used subordinately and partially for trading purposes does not take away the general immunity. For all these reasons, we are unable to agree with the learned judge, and have come to the conclusion that the judgment must be reversed." [1]

[1] In the case of *Briggs* v. *Light-Boats* in the Supreme Court of Massachusetts, 1865 (11 Allen, 157), the plaintiff had built some floating lights, for the United States government, and had delivered them and received the contract price; and the title to them had vested in the United States, subject to the builder's lien. The plaintiff now sought to enforce his lien.

GRAY, J., says, in the course of his judgment, "wherever the question has been raised, courts of admiralty have generally declined to take jurisdiction of a libel *in rem* against a public ship, without the consent of the government. In every aspect in which we can look at these suits, in the light of principle or of authority, we cannot escape the conclusion that the state courts have no jurisdiction or right to entertain them."

SECTION 12.—MERCHANT VESSELS.

THE "NEWTON," AND THE "SALLY."

CONSEIL D'ETAT, 1806.

(*Ortolan : Diplomatie de la Mer*, I., 450.)

This is one of the earliest cases tending to establish what is sometimes called the "French Rule," as regards the jurisdiction over foreign merchant vessels, by the local courts of the country whose ports they visit. According to this practice the French courts do not take jurisdiction in the case of acts which affect only the foreign vessel and its crew; unless the acts are such as disturb the peace of the port.

In 1806, while the *Newton*, an American merchant ship, was in the port of Antwerp, a quarrel took place between two sailors in a boat belonging to the ship. About the same time, when the *Sally*, also an American merchant ship, was in the port of Marseilles, the mate dangerously wounded one of the crew on the ship. The American consul claimed exclusive jurisdiction in each case. This claim was upheld by the Conseil d'Etat, in the following judgment:

"Le Conseil d'Etat qui, d'après le renvoi à lui fait par Sa Majesté, a entendu le rapport de la section de législation sur celui du grand juge, ministre de la justice, tendant à régler les limites de la juridiction que les consuls des Etats-Unis d' Amérique, aux ports de Marseille et d'Anvers, réclament par rapport aux délits commis à bord des vaisseux de leur nation étant dans les ports et les rades de France ;

"Considérant qu'un vaisseau neutre ne peut être indéfiniment considéré comme lieu neutre, et que la protection qui lui est accordée dans les ports français, ne saurait dessaisir la juridiction territoriale pour tout ce qui touche aux intérêts de l'Etat ;

"Qu'ainsi, le vaisseau neutre admis dans un port de l'Etat est de plein droit soumis aux lois de police qui régissent le lieu où il est reçu ;

"Que les gens de son équipage sont également justiciables des tribunaux du pays pour les délits qu'ils y commettraient, même à bord, envers des personnes étrangères à l'équipage, ainsi que pour les conventions civiles qu'ils pourraient faire avec elles ;

"Mais que si jusque là la juridiction territoriale est hors de doute, il n'en est pas ainsi à l' égard des délits qui se commetent à bord du vaisseau neutre de la part d'un homme de l' équipage neutre envers un autre homme du même équipage;

"Qu'en ce cas, les droits de la puissance neutre doivent être respectés, comme s'agissant de la discipline interieure du vaisseau, dans laquelle l'autorité locale ne doit pas s'ingérer toutes les fois que son secours n'est pas réclamé ou que la tranquillité du port n'est pas compromise;

"Est d'avis que cette distinction, indiquée par le rapport du grand juge et conforme à l'usage, est la seule règle qu'il convienne de suivre en cette matière;

"Et, appliquant cette doctrine aux deux espèces particulières pour lesquelles ont réclamé les consuls des Etats-Unis;

"Considérant que dans l'une de ces affaires, il s'agit d'une rixe passée dans le canot du navire Américan, le *Newton*, entre deux matelots du même navire, et dans l'autre d'une blessure grave faite par le capitaine en second du navire la *Sally* à un de ses matelots pour avoir disposé du canot sans son ordre;

"Est d'avis qu'il y a lieu d'accueillir la réclamation et d'interdire aux tribunaux français la connaisance des deux affaires précitées."

THE "TEMPEST."

COURT OF CASSATION, 1859.

(*Ortolan: Diplomatie de la Mer,* I., 455.)

The French courts take jurisdiction in the case of a murder committed on board a foreign merchant vessel lying in a French port, on the ground that such a grave crime amounts to a disturbance of the peace of the port.

In the cases of the *Sally* and the *Newton*, by a decree of the Council of State, representing the political department of the government, the French courts were prevented from exercising jurisdiction. But afterwards, in 1859, in the case of Sally, the mate of an American merchantman, the *Tempest*, who had killed one of the crew and severely wounded another on board the ship in the port of Havre, the Court of Cassation, the highest judicial tribunal of France, upon full consideration held, while the convention of 1853 was in force, that the French courts had rightful jurisdiction, for reasons which sufficiently appear in the following extract from its judgment:

"Considering that it is a principle of the law of nations that every state has sovereign jurisdiction throughout its territory;

"Considering that by the terms of article 3 of the Code Napoleon the laws of police and safety bind all those who inhabit French territory, and that consequently foreigners, even *transeuntes*, find themselves subject to those laws;

"Considering that merchant vessels entering the port of a nation other than that to which they belong cannot be withdrawn from the territorial jurisdiction, in any case in which the interest of the state of which that port forms part finds itself concerned, without danger to good order and to the dignity of the government;

"Considering that every state is interested in the repression of crimes and offenses that may be committed in the ports of its territory, not only by the men of the ship's company of a foreign merchant vessel toward men not forming part of that company, but even by men of the ship's company among themselves, whenever the act is of a nature to compromise the tranquillity of the port, or the intervention of the local authority is invoked, or the act constitutes a crime by common law, (*droit commun*, the law common to all civilized nations,) the gravity of which does not permit any nation to leave it unpunished, without impugning its rights of jurisdictional and territorial sovereignty, because that crime is in itself the most manifest as well as the most flagrant violation of the laws which it is the duty of every nation to cause to be respected in all parts of its territory."

[Article VIII. of the Treaty of 1853, referred to, stipulates that, "the respective Consuls-General, Consuls, Vice-Consuls, or Consular Agents, shall have exclusive charge of the internal order of the merchant-vessels of their nation, and shall alone take cognizance of differences which may arise, either at sea or in port, between the captain, officers and crew, without exception, particularly in reference to the adjustment of wages and the execution of contracts. The local authorities shall not, on any pretext, interfere in these differences, but shall lend forcible aid to the Consuls, when they may ask it, to arrest and imprison all persons composing the crew whom they may deem it necessary to confine. Those persons shall be arrested at the sole request of the Consuls, addressed in writing to the local authority, and supported by an official extract from the register of the ship or the list of the crew, and shall be held, during the whole time of their stay in the port, at the disposal of the Consuls. Their release shall be granted at the mere request of the Consuls made in writing. The expenses of the arrest and detention of those persons shall be paid by the Consuls."]

"L'ANEMONE."

SUPREME COURT OF MEXICO, 1875.

(*Journal de Droit International Privé*, 1876, *p*. 413.)

Where murder is committed by one Frenchman upon another, on board a French merchant vessel, at anchor in a Mexican port; *held*, that it is not necessarily a disturbance of the peace of the port, and therefore the Mexican courts will not assume jurisdiction of the case.

"Vu l'enquête relative à l'homicide commis le 3 octobre 1875 au soir, sur la personne du matelot Auguste Durand, par M. Eugène Antoni, capitaine du batîment français l'*Anémone*, mouillé à l'île de Carmen, juridiction de Campêche, et faite en conséquence du recours en supplique formé par ledit capitaine contre la décision du tribunal de circuit de Yucatan, Campêche, Tabasco et Chiapas, déclarant que les tribunaux fédéraux mexicains sont compétents pour connaître du susdit homicide; vu les réquisitions du citoyen Fiscal et la défense du licencié Sanchez Azcona, conseil d'Antoni;

"Considérant qu'il n'est pas établi que le délit en question ait troublé la tranquillité des habitants du port de l'île de Carmen, ni que les marins et autres personnes qui se trouvaient à bord dudit bâtiment aient demandé protection aux autorités mexicaines, ni formé une accusation d'homicide, mais qu'ils ont simplement porté à terre le cadavre de Durand, afin de rendre compte à l'autorité;

"Qui'l n'existe point de traités entre la République mexicaine et la France, qu'en conséquence le présent cas doit être régi par le droit de réciprocité;

"Qu' Antoni comme Durand sont de nationalité française et que le batiment l'*Anêmone* est couvert par le pavillon français; que la victime n'est point une personne étrangère à l'équipage;

"D'ou il résulte qu'on ne se trouve en présence d'aucune des circonstances qui, d'après le paragraphe 3 de l'article 189 du Code pénal et conformément au droit de réciprocité peuvent donner compétence à la juridiction mexicaine;

"Par ces motifs et conformément aux réquisitions du citoyen Fiscal de cette Cour suprême,

"Réformons la décision du tribunal de circuit de Yucatan, Campêche, Tabasco et Chiapas, en date du 12 novembre 1875, infirmant celle du tribunal de district de Campêche, du 26 octobre précédent, et décidons que cette dernière sentence sortira son plein et entier effet; en conséquence déclarons les autorités mexicaines incompétentes pour connaître des faits qui se sont passés à bord du bâtiment français l'*Anémone*, mouillé dans le port de Carmen, le 3 octobre dernier au soir; et ordonnons la mise immédiate en liberté des personnes qui ont été arrêtées par suite des susdits faits ;

"Ainsi résolu à la majorité des voix par les citoyens président et conseillers composant la première chambre de la Cour suprême de justice des Etats-Unis mexicains.

"Signé : Iglesias.—Altamirano.—Anza.—Echeverria.—Guzman.—Aguilar, secrétaire!"[1]

[1] Paragraph 3 of article 189 of the Mexican Penal Code referred to in the decision is as follows :

"Sont considérés comme exécutés sur le territoire de la République: 18 . . . 28 . . . 38 . . . les délits commis à bord d'un navire marchand étranger mouillé dans un port national ou dans les eaux territoriales de la République, si le délinquant ou l'offensé ne font pas partie de l'equipage ou s'il y a eu perturbation de la tranquillité du port. Dans le cas contraire, on suivra le droit de réciprocité."

The Circuit Court had assumed jurisdiction of the case on grounds very similar to those upon which the Supreme Court of the United States decided the case of Wildenhus :

"Le tribunal de circuit fondait son infirmation sur les motifs suivants :

"Tous les marins de l'équipage, au nombre de sept, avaient retiré de l'eau le cadavre de la victime et l'avaient porté à terre ; là, ils avaient rendu compte à l'autorité et fait leurs déclarations.

"Lorsqu'un crime ou délit de droit commun commis à bord d'un navire marchand étranger a troublé la tranquillité du port, les autorités du pays sont compétentes pour en connaître.

"Ces autorités sont également compétentes lorsque les intéressés ont réclamé leur protection.

"L'homicide est un délit public qui, même commis sur des particuliers, menace la sécurité de tous.

"Par le seul fait de s'être adressés à l'autorité locale en lui présentant le cadavre de Durand, pour lui permettre de faire une enquête et de châtier le coupable, les marins ont demandé aide et protection à l'autorité du port et se sont soumis à sa juridiction."

In comparing this case with that of the *Tempest*, the counsel for the defense said: "Ce n'est pas comme pour le crime commis au Havre en 1859 à bord du navire américain le *Tempest* ; là, les autorités françaises durent intervenir (tant l'émotion était grande!) pour protéger le coupable contre les marins du port et les habitants de la ville qui lui eussent inévitablement fait application de la loi de Lynch."

CASE OF WILDENHUS.

SUPREME COURT OF THE UNITED STATES, 1886.

(120 *U. S. Reports*, 1.)

Where a merchant vessel is found in a foreign port, it is generally understood that all matters of discipline and all things done on board which affect only the vessel or those belonging to her, or which do not involve the peace or dignity of the country, or the tranquillity of the port, should be left by the local government to be dealt with by the authorities of the nation to which the vessel belongs.

But if crimes are committed on board of a character to disturb the tranquillity of the port, the courts of the country should take jurisdiction. And murder is held to be such a crime.

While the Belgian steamer "Noordland" was moored to a dock in Jersey City, New Jersey, an affray arose between decks in which Joseph Wildenhus killed one Fijeus. Wildenhus was arrested by the Jersey City authorities; whereupon the Belgian consul applied to the U. S. circuit court for New Jersey, for his release upon a writ of *habeas corpus.*

The court refused to deliver the prisoner, and to reverse that decision. An appeal is taken to this court.

WAITE, C. J., delivered the opinion of the court, from which the following are extracts.

"The courts of the United States have power to issue writs of *habeas corpus* which shall extend to prisoners in jail when they are in 'custody in violation of the Constitution or a law or treaty of the United States,' and the question we have to consider is, whether these prisoners are held in violation of the provisions of the existing treaty between the United States and Belgium.

"It is part of the law of civilized nations that when a merchant vessel of one country enters the ports of another for the purposes of trade, it subjects itself to the law of the place to which it goes, unless by treaty or otherwise the two countries have come to some different understanding or agreement. * * * And the English judges have uniformly recognized the rights of the courts of the country of which the port is part to punish crimes committed by one foreigner on another in a foreign merchant ship. * * * As the owner has voluntarily taken his vessel for his own private purposes to a place within the dominion of a government other than his own, and from which he seeks protection during his stay, he owes that government such allegiance for the time being as is due for the protection to which he becomes entitled.

"From experience, however, it was found long ago that it would be beneficial to commerce if the local government would abstain from interfering with the internal discipline of the ship, and the general regulation of the rights and duties of the officers and crew towards the vessel or among themselves. And so by comity it came to be generally understood among civilized nations that all matters of discipline and all things done on board which affected only the vessel or those belonging to her, and did not involve the peace or dignity of the country, or the tranquillity of the port, should be left by the local government to be dealt with by the authorities of the nation to which the vessel belonged as the laws of that nation or the interest of its commerce should require. But if crimes are committed on board of a character to disturb the peace and tranquillity of the country to which the vessel has been brought, the offenders have never by comity or usage been entitled to any exemption from the operation of the local laws for their punishment, if the local tribunals see fit to assert their authority.

"Such being the general public law on this subject, treaties and conventions have been entered into by nations having commercial intercourse, the purpose of which was to settle and define the rights and duties of the contracting parties with respect to each other in these particulars, and thus prevent the inconvenience that might arise from attempts to exercise conflicting jurisdictions. * * *

"It * * * appears that at first provision was made only for giving consuls police authority over the interior of the ship and jurisdiction in civil matters arising out of disputes or differences on board, that is to say, between those belonging to the vessel. Under this police authority the duties of the consuls were evidently confined to the maintenance of order and discipline on board. This gave them no power to punish for crimes against the peace of the country. In fact, they were expressly prohibited from interfering with the local police in matters of that kind. The cases of the *Sally* and the *Newton* are illustrative of this position. That of the *Sally* related to the discipline of the ship and that of the *Newton* to the maintenance of order on board. In neither case was the disturbance of a character to affect the peace or the dignity of the country.

"In the next conventions, consuls were simply made judges and arbitrators to settle and adjust differences between those on board, This clearly related to such differences between those belonging to the vessel as are capable of adjustment and settlement by judicial decision or by arbitration, for it simply made the consuls judges or arbitrators in such matters. That would of itself exclude all idea of punishment for crimes against the state which affected the peace and tranquillity of the port; but, to prevent all doubt on this subject, it was expressly provided that it should not apply to differences of that character.

"Next came a form of convention which in terms gave the consuls authority to cause proper order to be maintained on board and to decide disputes between the officers and crew, but allowed the local authorities to interfere if the disorders taking place on board were of such a nature as to disturb the public tranquillity, and that is substantially all there is in the convention with Belgium which we have now to consider. This treaty is the law which now governs the conduct of the United States and Belgium towards each other in this particular. Each nation has granted to the other such local jurisdiction within its own dominion as may be necessary to maintain order on board a merchant vessel, but has reserved to itself the right to interfere if the disorder on board is of a nature to disturb the public tranquillity.

"The treaty is part of the supreme law of the United States, and has the same force and effect in New Jersey that it is entitled to elsewhere. If it gives the consul of Belgium exclusive jurisdiction over the offense which it is alleged has been committed, within the territory of New Jersey, we see no reason why he may not enforce his rights under the treaty by writ of *habeas corpus* in any proper court of the United States. This being the case, the only important question left for our determination is whether the thing which has been done—the disorder that has arisen—on board this vessel is of a nature to disturb the public peace, or, as some writers term it, the 'public repose' of the people who look to the State of New Jersey for their protection. If the thing done—'the disorder,' as it is called in the treaty—is of a character to affect those on shore or in the port when it becomes known, the fact that only those on the ship saw it when it was done is a matter of no moment. Those who are not on the vessel pay no special attention to the mere disputes or quarrels of the seamen while on board, whether they occur under deck or above. Neither do they as a rule care for anything done on board which relates only to the discipline of the ship, or to the preservation of order and authority. Not so, however, with crimes which from their gravity awaken a public interest as soon as they become known, and especially those of a character which every civilized nation considers itself bound to provide a severe punishment for when committed within its own jurisdiction. In such cases inquiry is certain to be instituted at once to ascertain how or why the thing was done, and the popular excitement rises or falls as the news spreads and the facts become known. It is not alone the publicity of the act, or the noise and clamor which attends it, that fixes the nature of the crime, but the act itself. If that is of a character to awaken public interest when it becomes known, it is a disorder, the nature of which is to affect the community at large, and consequently to invoke the power of the local government whose people have been disturbed by what was done. The very nature of such an act is to disturb the quiet of a peaceful community, and to create, in the language of the treaty a 'disorder' which will 'disturb tranquillity and public order on shore or in port.' The principle which governs the whole matter is this: Disorders which disturb only the peace of the ship or those on board are to be dealt with exclusively by the sovereignty of the home of the ship, but those which disturb the public peace may be suppressed, and, if need be, the offenders punished by the proper authorities of the local jurisdiction. It may not be easy at all times to determine to which of the two jurisdictions a particular act of disorder belongs. Much will undoubtedly depend on the attending circumstances of the particular case, but all must concede that felonious homicide is a subject for the local jurisdiction, and that if the proper authorities are proceeding with the case in a regular way, the consul has no right to interfere to prevent it. That, according to the petition for the *habeas corpus*, is this case."

THE "RELIANCE."

U. S. CIRCUIT COURT FOR SO. DIST. OF N. Y., 1848.

(1 *Abbott's Adm. Rep.*, 317.)

The *Reliance*, a British vessel, rescued goods from the wreck of another British vessel; and afterwards arrived in the port of New York, and instituted proceedings for salvage. Jurisdiction was refused.

This was a libel *in rem* filed by the owner, master and crew of the bark *Reliance* against One Hundred and Ninety-four shawls salved by the libellants from the wreck of the *Lady Kenneway* to recover salvage compensation.

The *Reliance* was a British vessel which left Liverpool bound to New York. Near the coast of England, she fell in with the *Lady Kenneway* and boarded her, finding no person on board.

The *Lady Kenneway* was a British East Indiaman, owned in

London, on her way to London from Bombay. The master of the *Reliance* ordered several cases containing shawls to be taken from her, and then abandoned her. The *Reliance* pursued her way to New York, where she arrived December 1, 1847.

A libel was filed against the chief part of the articles brought from the *Lady Kenneway*. The British consul, by leave of the court, intervened in behalf of the unknown British owners, praying the court to order restitution for their benefit of the property attached, after allowing the libellants a reasonable salvage, if, in the judgment of the court, "they proved a case of derelict, and their consequent right to salvage."

The individual claimants, as well as the consul, set up defenses against the award of salvage, charging waste, damage, and destruction of the apparel and stores of the vessel.

It is insisted that the court should decline jurisdiction in the case, because the *Lady Kenneway* was an English vessel, then on a homeward voyage, with her cargo for an English market, and the *Reliance* at the time, was an English vessel, with a British crew on board, who had signed British articles and that accordingly both vessels and libellants were bound to return to terminate the voyage at a British port.

BETTS, J.— " * * * As a general principle, the citizens or subjects of the same nation have no right to invoke a foreign tribunal to adjudicate between them, as to matters of tort or contract solely affecting themselves. It rests in the discretion of the court, whose authority is invoked, to determine whether it will take cognizance of such matters or not. * * *

"As maritime courts proceed upon a common rule of right and compensation in salvage cases, the question of jurisdiction in that class of actions will seldom be raised or regarded before them.

"The courts will take cognizance of those cases as matters of course, if either party is territorially within the jurisdiction of the court; and the property being brought within their jurisdiction, although the salvors and claimants may be citizens or subjects of different nations, the court will unhesitatingly dispose of the subject, if satisfied that the whole right is before it,—salvage being essentially a question of the *jus gentium*. * * *

"I find no authority of weight which imposes on the courts of our country the necessity of determining controversies between foreigners resident abroad, either in common-law actions, transitory in their nature, or maritime proceedings when the remedy is *in rem*.

"If the doctrine were peremptory, imparting to suitors the right to such aid, and imposing on courts the obligation to afford it, actions for supplies and materials, on charter-parties and bills of lading, or by mechanics for labor, would be comprehended within the class, equally with suits for wages on bottomry bonds or for salvage compensation.

"I am satisfied the law is not so. In my judgment it would be lamentable if courts were compelled to defer the business of the citizens of the country to bestow their time in litigation between parties owing no allegiance to its laws, and contributing in no way to its support. Should it transpire, in the progress of the litigation, that the law of the domicile of the parties must be ascertained in order to adjudge rightly on their claims, or that witnesses must be examined there to fix the facts in controversy, the court might be compelled to suspend its movement and wait until these cardinal particulars could be supplied from abroad. Every tribunal experiences the inconvenience and unsatisfactoriness of so settling controversies between those even who can have no other means of redress, and will recognize the value of the principle which enables them, in regard to foreigners, to remit their controversies to their home tribunals, where the law is known, and the facts can be more surely determined. This court has, in repeated instances, acted upon this acceptation of the law; and believing it to be the sound and safe rule, I shall adhere to it in all cases authorizing that exercise of discretion.

"The question to be considered is, whether, in this case, the rights of parties would be best promoted by retaining the case and disposing of the subject here, or by remitting it to the home courts of the salvors and claimants.

"The answer advances many grave imputations against the conduct of the master and seamen on board the wreck and after the property came into their possession, and these charges are not without color of proof to support them. Their case does not, accordingly, come before the court with the most persuasive claims to its interposition and favor. When salvage services are eminently meritorious, and the only inquiry to be made is the rate of award to be allotted, Admiralty Courts would be solicitous to give every practicable despatch to suits by the salvors, and relieve them both from delay and expense in obtaining their just reward. It would scarcely occur that any court would withhold its aid from such suitors. It is quite different when the foreign owner of the property charges his fellow-subject with embezzlement and spoliation, and other wanton misconduct in respect to it, and prays the privilege to contest his claim to compensation before the authorities of their common country. * * *

"The termination of the voyage of the *Reliance* was in England, where it is to be presumed she would arrive within a short period after leaving this port, and it is most fitting that the question of the obligations and privileges of her master and crew, in respect to services rendered a British vessel, a wreck or in distress on the English coast, should be determined in the courts of that nation. * * *

"As the libellants may not reclaim the property attached in their behalf, the decree will make provision enabling the claimants who have intervened in their own right, and the British Consul in behalf of unknown owners, to take the goods out of court and ship them to their port of destination." [1]

[1] In the case of *Aertsen* v. *Ship Aurora* (1800), Bee's Adm. Reports, 161, the suit was brought for seamen's wages and to obtain a discharge on account of the captain's ill treatment. In the course of the judgment the judge said: "From this evidence I do not find sufficient evidence to entitle these three men to their discharge (from the completion of the voyage).

"(1) Because no unlawful weapon was used.

"(2) Sufficient provocation for the captain's acts.

"This is the case of a neutral vessel, the crew of which are bound by their articles to return to Hamburgh, before they are entitled to receive their wages, and the 12th of those articles stipulates that everything *not* specified therein shall be regulated according to the marine law of Hamburgh for regulating the conduct of officers and seamen aboard vessels belonging to that place."

The suit was dismissed with costs.

In *Willendson* v. *The Forsöket*, 1 Peter's Adm., 197, the plaintiff, a sailor on a Danish ship, cited his captain on a claim for wages. The judge, in the course of his opinion, says that his general rule has been not to take cognizance of disputes between masters and crews of foreign ships.

"I have," said he, "* * * in peculiar cases * * * compelled the payment of wages * * * assisted in recovering deserters * * * (and in) reducing to obedience perverse and rebellious mariners.

"In the case now before me I see no cause to warrant my taking cognizance. It is the duty of the master to return the seaman to his own country. This he offers to do. * * * He must give the sailor a certificate of forgiveness of past offenses, to avail him in his own country. * * * If * * * there shall appear no deception in the present offer (to carry the seaman home) I shall not further interfere, but dismiss the suit."

Mr. Hamilton Fish, Secretary of State, in a dispatch to General Schenck, United States Minister in London (November 8, 1873), said: "Referring to the case of Albert Allen Gardner, master of the American ship *Anna Camp*, tried in the County Court at Liverpool, in May last, copies of certain papers relating to which were forwarded to you by General Badeau, I desire to call your attention to the claim of jurisdiction put forth by the local common-law courts of Great Britain in this and other similar cases.

"It seems to be claimed by the courts in question that their jurisdiction extends to the hearing and determining of causes arising upon complaints between masters and mariners of vessels of the United States, not only where the occurrences upon which the complaint may be founded took place within British ports or waters,

ELLIS v. MITCHELL.

SUPREME COURT OF HONG KONG, 1874.

(*U. S. Foreign Relations*, 1875, 600.)

This was the case of a controversy between a seaman and the master of an American ship in regard to wages, and some other matters in the port of Hong Kong. The American consul at that place undertook to decide the dispute. *Held*, that, in the absence of express authority under treaty, he could not exercise jurisdiction in such matters.

Judgment, SMALL, C. J.:—

"Our decision in this appeal having been for some time come to, we handed to the registrar our concluded judgment and by our direction he gave it out on the 7th of November last. That decision was in the following terms: 'We have fully considered all the facts in this case and the very able arguments which, on the part of the appellant, Mr. Kingsmill submitted to us. The respondent did not appear. We are of opinion that the appellant has failed to show that the decision in the summary branch of this court is wrong. It is our duty, therefore, to dismiss this appeal.' The respondent has incurred no costs; we say nothing as to costs. Some questions as to the duties and jurisdiction of consuls have arisen in this case to which we should wish to advert, but as these questions arise out of this case, rather than lead up to our decision, we purpose at a more convenient opportunity to refer to them. It seems to us that a somewhat exaggerated notion as to the duties and jurisdiction of consuls in this colony is prevalent.

"The grounds and reasons for the decision in this case were very carefully considered and conferred on between us. We were agreed in the conclusion that the appeal must be dismissed. In order that the parties might not be kept longer in suspense, we directed the decision which I have just read to be given out by the registrar on the

but also when the offense which is made the ground of action was committed on board the vessel on the high seas.

"The exercise of this jurisdiction by the common-law courts at Liverpool has already been the cause of much annoyance and in some instances serious inconvenience to masters and owners of American vessels, and if persisted in may affect injuriously the interests of American shipping."

Mr. Fish proceeds to quote from the decision of Judge BETTS, in the case of the *Reliance*, and to commend the principles there set forth as the only proper rule to be followed.

7th day of November, as I have already said. There seems to have been a grave misapprehension that this case came before Mr. Justice Snowden as an appeal from the decision of the consul of the United States.

"It was not so. From the first it was treated by the learned judge as being untouched by decision, and, indeed, as a matter entirely *ultra vires* the consul of the United States. True it is that a discharge of the plaintiff from the ship, and an account taken in the presence of the consul of wages earned, were produced and relied on by the defendant, the master of the ship, as an answer to the plaintiff's claim; but it was held in the summary branch of this court, upon the evidence before it, that in no way was the consul acting or intervening judicially, either as to the discharge, or as to the account. No claim for unlawful dismissal had been raised before the consul. It might have been properly raised before the proper judicial tribunal of and within the United States; but no evidence was adduced to show that that authority was vested by the law of the United States in the consul here. Even if it had been so vested by any such law of the Union, it required the force of a treaty, and an act of Parliament, or local ordinance, to enable the consul to exercise any extra-territorial judicial power within British territory. Although some instructions to the consuls were produced to the court, no act of Congress was produced, nor was there any evidence that there was any such act, or common-law power in a consul. According to Chancellor Kent's Commentaries, vol. I., p. 50, *et seq.*, 'consuls are commercial agents. * * * In some places they have been invested with judicial powers over disputes between their own merchants in foreign ports; but in the commercial treaties made by Great Britain there is rarely any stipulation for clothing them with judicial authority, except in treaties with the Barbary powers. And in England it has been held that a consul is not strictly a judicial officer, and they have there no judicial power.' He cites *Waldron* v. *Combe*, 3 Taunton, 162. The words of the Chief-Justice MANSFIELD there are, 'The vice consul is no judicial officer.' At page 51 the very learned chancellor proceeds: 'No government can invest its consuls with judicial power over their own subjects in a foreign country without the consent of the foreign government, founded on treaty.' At page 52, he says: 'It is likewise made their duty (*i. e.* of consuls), where the laws of the country permit, to administer on the personal estates of American citizens dying within their consulates,' etc. And in note (6) he says, 'American consuls cannot take cognizance of the offenses of seamen in foreign ports, nor exempt the master from his own responsibility.' He cites Ware's Reports (American), 367. And to conclude all, he says at page

53: 'The consular convention between France and this country (*i. e.* the United States) in 1778 allowed consuls to exercise police over all vessels of their respective nations within the interior of the vessels, and to exercise a species of civil jurisdiction by determining disputes concerning wages, and between the master and crews of vessels belonging to their own country. The jurisdiction claimed under the consular convention with France was merely voluntary, and although exclusive of any coercive authority, and we (*i. e.* the United States) have no treaty at present which concedes even such consular functions.' We quote the 9th edition of Kent's Commentaries (1858). We have before us the valuable work of Judge Bouvier, the law-dictionary, the 4th edition of 1872, and in it we find nothing to vary all that Chancellor Kent asserts. Parsons' Law of Shipping, published in 1869, is to the same effect. One quotation from Parsons, vol. II., p. 56.

"He there says, 'a discharge (*i. e.* of a seaman,) when made in a foreign port, is required to be made before the consul; but the payment of wages already due is not.' And this to such an extent that the learned author adds, 'and the consul has no right to charge a commission for witnessing the settlement,' in other words, he has nothing to do with the settlement of the wages due; *a fortiori* he has no authority in reference to damages for breach of contract, or otherwise, between the master and the seaman. Now, if the consul has no such authority, the authority must be somewhere, and it cannot be contended, upon any grounds of which we are aware, that this court has not the fullest authority over all such disputes. It is quite clear that the legislature of this country can, by statute or ordinance, give extra-territorial powers to consuls, but as all such powers are in derogation of the royal prerogative all such laws must be construed strictly. It appears to us that ordinance No. 4, of 1850, has no bearing on the question before us. It relates to cases of desertion from ships, and to nothing else. Ordinance No. 6, of 1862, is prohibitory. It says that no British seaman shall be discharged elsewhere than at the harbor-master's office, and that every seaman discharged from a foreign ship, represented by a consul here, 'shall, within twenty-four hours of being discharged at the office of his consul, or vice-consul, produce at the harbor-master's office a certificate of his discharge.' Now, this is not an enabling statute, and it gives no power to any consul which he had not before. All it does is to assume that every discharge of a foreign seaman will have been given at the office of the consulate of his country. But for legislation the discharge of a seaman is a matter between master and seaman only.

No treaty has been produced, no act of Parliament or ordinance other than those above cited, has been brought to the notice of this court. In the absence of any such we are driven back to the international law, as laid down by Chancellor Kent, page 51, that the consul of the United States is not a judicial officer, 'that they have no judicial power' and, page 53, that there is no treaty with the United States which authorizes consuls to exercise a species of jurisdiction by determining disputes concerning wages between masters and crews belonging to their own country in this colony. We conclude, therefore, that the consul of the United States has no judicial powers or authority whatever in this colony as to wages or damages for wrongs, between United States masters and seamen, which the judicial authorities here can recognize, but that this court must decide such questions when brought before it.

"What we have said as to the consul of the United States applies to consuls from all other foreign states. No such claim is, we believe, set up in any other part of the British dominions. In China, every consul of every foreign power has judicial authority over its own subjects; but this extra-territorial jurisdiction is the result of express treaty, and is conferred on them by the enactments of the legislative authority of each foreign state. The exaggerated notion as to consular authority here has probably arisen from the powers conceded to them in China, but which are not conceded here.

"In a colony so distant as Hong-Kong is from London, convenience has rendered direct communication between the colonial government and consuls here on many subjects properly diplomatic, convenient for all parties. This has probably tended to induce an overestimate of the position of consuls here in reference to judicial authority. We feel great respect for the consuls in this colony, both officially and personally, but we must see that the authority of this court is not curtailed beyond what the law permits. If circumstances render it proper or convenient that judicial authority should in this colony vest in consuls, it must be obtained by treaty and legislation. This court has no power to concede it."

THE "CREOLE," 1841.

(*Wheaton's International Law, 8th Ed.*, 165, *Note.*)

"The brig *Creole*, an American merchant vessel, sailed from a port in Virginia in 1841, bound to New Orleans, having on board one hundred and thirty-five slaves. A portion of the slaves rose against the officers and got complete possession of the vessel, killing one passenger and severely wounding the captain and others of the crew, in the struggle. They compelled the mate, under threat of death, to navigate the vessel to Nassau, where she arrived and came to anchor. At the request of the United States consul at Nassau, nineteen of the slaves, who were identified as having taken part in the acts of violence, were arrested by the local authorities, and held to await the decision of the British Government. As to the rest of the slaves, there was a question whether they got on shore and gained their liberty by their own act, or through the positive and officious interference of the colonial authorities, while the vessel was under the control of the consul and master. Mr. Webster, Secretary of State, addressed a letter to Lord Ashburton on this subject. His position is, that 'if a vessel of the United States, pursuing lawful voyages from port to port along their own shore, are driven by stress of weather, or carried by unlawful force, into British ports, the government of the United States cannot consent that the local authorities in those ports shall take advantage of such misfortunes, and enter them for the purpose of interfering with the condition of persons or things on board, as established by their own laws. If slaves, the property of citizens of the United States, escape into British territories, it is not expected that they will be restored. In that case, the territorial jurisdiction of England will have become exclusive over them, and must decide their condition. But slaves on board of American vessels lying in British waters are not within the exclusive jurisdiction of England, or under the exclusive operation of English law; and this founds the broad distinction between the cases. * * * In the opinion of the government of the United States, such vessels, so driven and so detained by necessity in a friendly port, ought to be regarded as still pursuing their original voyage, and turned out of their direct course by disaster or by wrongful violence; that they ought to receive all assistance necessary to enable them to resume that direct course, etc. * * *'

"The United States Government demanded the restoration of the slaves, which was refused by the British Government, on the ground, that, being in fact at liberty within the British dominions, they could not be seized there when charged with no crime against British law, and while there was no treaty of extradition. This case was then submitted, as a private claim for pecuniary indemnity, to the commission under the convention of Feb. 8, 1853. The commissioners being unable to agree, it was by the terms of the convention, referred to an umpire, Mr. Joshua Bates, of London.

"In deciding the case, Mr. Bates stated two propositions of law:—

"1. That, as the slaves were perfectly quiet, and on board an American ship under the command of the captain, the authorities should have seen that the captain was protected in his rights over them.

"2. That, 'the municipal law of England cannot authorize a magistrate to violate the law of nations, by invading with an armed force the vessel of a friendly nation that has committed no offense, and forcibly dissolving the relations which, by the laws of his country, the master is bound to preserve and enforce on board.'"[1]

[1] Mr. Dana criticises the decision of Mr. Bates in this case. "It may be conceded, as a general statement," he says, "that local authorities ought to give active aid to a master in defending and enforcing, against the inmates of his vessel, the rights with which his own nation has intrusted him, if these rights are of a character generally recognized among all nations, and not prohibited by the law of the place. But it may well admit of doubt, whether the local authorities must give active aid to the master against persons on board his vessel who are doing no more than peacefully and quietly dissolving, or refusing to recognize a relation which exists only by force of the law of the nation to which the vessel belongs, if the law is peculiar to that nation, and one which the law of the other country regards as against common right and public morals. The local authorities might not interfere to dissolve such relations, where the peace of the port or the public morals are not put in peril; but they might, it would seem, decline to lend force to compel their continuance. *See* also the adverse criticism of Hall (Int. Law., 3d Ed., p. 199).

In the case of the *Fortuna*, 1803 (5 C. Rob., 27), the ship was proceeded against for a violation of the blockade of the Weser. The master of the captured vessel gave as an excuse for entering the blockaded place, the want of provisions, and a strong westerly wind. Sir W. Scott held that "want of provisions" was not such an "imperative and over-ruling compulsion" as to excuse a breach of blockade. But on the other ground, after further proof, the vessel was restored.

In the case of *United States* v. *Dickelman*, 1875, 92 U. S., 520, the Supreme Court emphatically affirmed the rule that merchant vessels are subject to the local jurisdiction when in foreign ports.

WAITE, C. J., in giving the opinion of the court said: "As to the general law of nations, the merchant vessels of one country visiting the ports of another for the purposes of trade subject themselves to the laws which govern the port they visit, so long as they remain; and this as well in war as in peace, unless it is otherwise provided by treaty."

SECTION 13.—RIGHT OF ASYLUM.

(a) *In Legations.*

DUKE OF RIPPERDA'S CASE, 1726.

(*Martens: Causes Célèbres*, I., 178.)

Right of asylum in the British legation in Madrid denied by the government of Spain.

Baron Ripperda had been a colonel in the service of the States-General of the United Provinces, and had been sent by them as minister plenipotentiary to the court of Madrid. After two years of residence at this court, he had so captivated the mind of Philip V., that that monarch took him into his service, made him minister of finance and of foreign affairs, and conferred upon him the title of Duke. Accused by the Imperial Ambassador at Madrid of secretly favoring the interests of Holland and England, he was finally deprived of his offices, though granted a pension by the King. Fearing, as he said, the enmity of the populace, he took refuge in the hotel of the English Ambassador, Lord Stanhope. The Spanish government would seem at first to have acquiesced in this arrangement, but learning that the Duke had important state papers in his possession, it demanded his delivery. Not meeting with a compliance to this demand, the question was referred to the Council of Castile, whether, without violating the law of nations, the Duke of Ripperda could be forcibly taken from the house of the English Ambassador. The Council replied in the affirmative: "To act otherwise would be to employ a system which had been adopted to facilitate the intercourse of sovereigns, for the destruction and ruin of their authority. To extend the privileges accorded to the hotels of ambassadors in favor of merely ordinary offenses to persons intrusted with the finances, the powers, and the secrets of a state, when they have betrayed the duties of their office, would be to introduce into the world a principle most injurious to all nations. If this maxim were to become the rule, sovereigns would be obliged to see maintained at their own courts those persons most actively engaged in machinations for their ruin."

Lord Stanhope's house had already been under strict surveillance; and, on the receipt of the opinion of the council, the Spanish government, without further notice to the ambassador, forced an entrance and arrested the Duke of Ripperda. The English government protested vigorously, and particularly as to the manner of the proceedings; and the incident aggravating the already strained relations between the two countries, finally resulted in war the next year.[1]

UNITED STATES *v.* JEFFERS.

U. S. Circuit Court for Dist. of Washington, 1836.

(4 *Cranch, C. C. Rep.*, 704.)

A slave who had escaped from his master, had taken service in the house of the Secretary of the British Legation in Washington.

An officer of the District of Columbia, who removed the slave and restored him to his master, was, by order of the Court, dismissed from office.

Francis S. Key, Attorney of the United States for the District of Columbia, having laid before the court a letter to him from the Secretary of State, wherein it appeared that a constable, Madison Jeffers, had removed from the house of Mr. Bankhead, the British Secretary of Legation, a colored lad employed for hire in his family in order to restore the said lad to his master; it was, on the motion of said attorney of the United States, ordered, that the said Madison Jeffers be removed from the office of constable of the County of Washington, unless he show cause to the contrary on the thirty-first day of May instant, provided, etc. "By order of the court, May 30th, 1836."

The rule having been duly served, the said Madison Jeffers appeared on the 31st of May and, by way of showing cause, filed his affidavit admitting the facts, but alleging his ignorance of the diplomatic

[1] Vattel, writing thirty years later, says of the opinion of the Council of Castile, "On ne peut rien dire de plus vrai et de plus judicieux sur cette matière."

Merlin said, "On voit par ces détails, que le droit d'asyle est, à l'égard des hôtels des ambassadeurs, une source perpêtuelle de dissensions et de querelles. Le bien des nations demanderait, sans doute, qu'on l'abolit tout-à-fait : et cela paraît d'autant plus raisonable, qu'il y a plusieurs états dans lesquels il n'est point connu."

In 1747, a Swedish merchant of the name of Springer, accused of high-treason, took refuge in the hotel of the English Ambassador, Colonel Guideckens, at Stockholm. The ambassador refused to surrender him; the Swedish government surrounded his house with troops, searched everybody who entered it, and caused the carriage of the ambassador, when he left the hotel, to be followed by a guard. Guideckens surrendered Springer under a protest as to the violence done to his ambassadorial privilege. England demanded reparation, and Sweden steadily refused to give it, and the ambassadors from the two courts were mutually withdrawn.

privileges, and his belief that he was executing his duty lawfully, in arresting a fugitive slave, and disclaiming all intentional disrespect to Mr. Bankhead.

His counsel, Mr. W. L. Brent, contended that Jeffers, as the agent of the owner of the slave, had a right to take him anywhere; and also that, as a constable, he had a right to take up a runaway, that the diplomatic privilege extends only to foreign ministers and upon certains terms; and not to servants of a secretary of legation.

That the servant had not been registered according to the Act of Congress of 30th of April, 1790, § 26 (Stat. at Large, 112), and therefore Jeffers had a right to arrest him; because the act of Congress for punishing the violation of privilege does not extend to those who may arrest a servant not registered. By not registering his servant, the minister has waived his privilege, *Seacourt* v. *Bowlney*, 1 Wils., 20.

The court stopped Mr. Key in reply. THURSTON, J., said he wished no further time or argument. He was of opinion that Jeffers should be dismissed from office.

MORSELL, J., concurred.

CRANCH, C. J., would have taken time to consider; but said that his present opinion coincided with that of the court.

Whereupon the court passed the following order:

"Madison Jeffers, upon whom a rule was laid on the 30th of May last, to show cause why he should not be removed from the office of constable for the county of Washington, upon the grounds therein stated, appeared and filed his affidavit, and the same was read and heard, and he was further heard by his counsel whereupon

"It is considered by the court, that the said Madison Jeffers was guilty of a violation of the privileges of His Britannic Majesty's Envoy Extraordinary and Minister Plenipotentiary, as stated, in his letter to the Secretary of State referred to in the said rule; and the said Madison Jeffers, having shown no sufficient cause to the contrary, it is thereupon considered by the Court, this 7th day of June, 1836, that the said Madison Jeffers be, and he is hereby, removed from his said office of constable for the county aforesaid."

OPINION OF MR. FISH, SECRETARY OF STATE.

LETTER TO MR. PRESTON, DEC. 11, 1875.

(*U. S. Foreign Relations*, 1875, p., 343.)

A criticism of the practice of granting asylum to political refugees, by foreign legations, in the Spanish American States.

"The right to grant asylum to fugitives is one of the still open questions of public law. The practice, however, has been to tolerate the exercise of that right, not only in American countries of Spanish origin, but in Spain itself, as well as in Hayti. This practice, however, has never addressed itself to the full favor of this Government. In withholding approval of it, we have been actuated by respect for consistency.

"It is not probable that the practice would ever be attempted in this country, or, if attempted, could be tolerated, and the discountenance which the United States extends to the practice is upon the principle of doing to others as we would they should do unto us, so that when we acknowledge the sovereignty of a foreign state by concluding treaties with and by accrediting diplomatic officers to its Government, we impliedly, at least, acknowledge it as a political equal, and we claim to extend to all the political prerogatives and immunities which we may claim for ourselves.

"We sincerely desire that it may be universally recognized that foreign legations shall nowhere be made a harbor for persons either charged with crimes or who may fear that such a charge may be made.

"Prominent among the reasons for objection on our part to giving asylum in a legation, especially in the Governments to the south of us, is that such a practice obviously tends to the encouragement of offenses for which asylum may be desired.

"There is cause to believe that the instability of the Governments in countries where the practice has been tolerated may in a great degree be imputed to such toleration. For this reason, if for none other, the Government of the United States, which is one of law and order and of constitutional observance, desires to extend no encouragement to a practice which it believes to be calculated to promote and encourage revolutionary movements and ambitious plottings.

"Instances, too, have occurred where asylum having been granted with impunity, has been grossly abused to the defeat of justice, not only against political offenders, but also against persons charged with infamous crimes. Such abuses are plainly incompatible with the stability and the welfare of Governments, and of society itself.

"Temptations sufficient to lead to an abuse of the practice cannot fail to abound in most persons who may exercise it. Such temptations are incident to human nature, and in countries where political revolutions are of frequent occurrence one must be gifted with uncommon self-denial to be wholly free from their influences.

"It is believed, however, to be sound policy not to expose a minister in a foreign country to the embarrassments attendant upon the practice. Still, this Government is not, by itself, and independently of all others, disposed to absolutely prohibit its diplomatic representatives abroad from granting asylum in every case in which application therefor may be made.

"We do not, however, withhold from them our views of the practice, and will expect that, if they do exercise the prerogative, it will be done under their own responsibility to their own Government. We would prefer, therefore, not formally to assent to the propositions contained in the memorandum above referred to without ascertaining the views of the other Governments concerned in regard to them.

"Some, at least, of those propositions appear to be fair enough; but as the circumstances of cases in which asylum may be granted greatly vary, it would, in the opinion of the undersigned, be preferable, until an understanding and an approach to accord of views as to the future practice in this regard can be had by the other powers, that every such case should be treated according to its merits, rather than that we should be fettered in advance by rules which may be found not to be practically applicable or useful."[1]

[1] The printed personal instructions of the government of the United States to its diplomatic agents of date of 1885, contains the following clause :—

"In some countries, where frequent insurrections occur and consequently instability of government exists, the practice of exterritorial asylum has become so firmly established, that it is often invoked by unsuccessful insurgents, and is practically recognized by the local government to the extent even of respecting the premises of a consulate in which such fugitives may take refuge. This Government does not sanction the usage, and enjoins upon its representatives in such countries the avoidance of all pretexts for its exercise. While indisposed to direct its agents to deny temporary shelter to any person whose life may be threatened by mob violence, it deems it proper to instruct its representatives that it will not countenance them in any attempt to knowingly harbor offenders against the laws from the pursuit of the legitimate agents of justice."

(*b*) *On Board Ships of War.*

CASE OF JOHN BROWN.

Opinion of Sir William Scott, 1820.

(*Halleck's International Law*, I., 185.)

In the opinion of Sir William Scott, the right of asylum as regards political refugees does not properly belong to ships of war.

In 1820, John Brown, a British subject, commanded a vessel engaged in the revolt against the Spanish Colonies. He was taken prisoner by the Spaniards, but escaped from prison, and took refuge on board H. M. S. "Tyne," lying in the port of Lima. Sir William Scott, being requested by the Admiralty, gave his opinion on the question, as follows :—"Sir,—I have to acknowledge the receipt of your letter dated the 25th ult., enclosing copies of a letter, and its enclosures from Captain Falcon, of H. M. S. 'Tyne,' and of the case and opinion of the King's Advocate, relative to Mr. John Brown, a native of Ireland, who, being a prisoner, in the hands of the Spaniards, effected his escape and came on board the 'Tyne' at Callao, and has since arrived on board the same within the realm of England (having claimed the protection of the flag), and acquainting me that their Lordships conceiving that they had no authority to detain him, and being supported in that opinion by the concurrence of the King's Advocate, had allowed him to depart without restraint. Upon this statement I have no observation to make, not being desired by their Lordships to make any; but if my opinion had been required, it would have coincided with what has been advised and done. A more extensive and important question is proposed to me, viz.: 'Whether any British subject coming on board any of H. M.'s ships of war, in a foreign port and from the judicature of the State within whose territory such port may be situated, is entitled to the protection of the British flag, and to be deemed as within the Kingdom of Great Britain and Ireland?' Upon this question proposed generally I feel no hesitation in declaring that I know of no such right of protection belonging to the British flag, and that I think such a pretension is unfounded in point of principle, is injurious to the rights of other countries, and is inconsistent with those of our own. The rights of territories are local and are fixed by known and determined limits. Ships are mere movables and are treated as such in the general purchase of nations. It is true that armed neutralities have attempted to give them a territorial character, but the attempt when made has been always most perseveringly, and at all hazards, resisted and defeated by the arms of our country, as inconsistent with the rights of hostility and capture. No such character is allowed to protect ships of war, when offending against the laws of neutrality upon the high seas, where no local authority whatever exists; still less can it be claimed where there is a visible and acknowledged authority, belonging to an independent State in amity with the nation of which the ships of war belong. Such a claim can lead to nothing but to the confusion and hostility which wait upon conflicting rights. The common convenience of nations has for certain reasons, and to a certain extent, established in favor of foreign ships of war, that they themselves shall not be liable to the civil process of the country in whose ports they are lying, though even the immunity has been occasionally questioned. But that individuals, merely belonging to the same country with the ships of war, are exempt from the civil and criminal process of the country in its ordinary administration of justice by getting on board such ship, and claiming what is called the protection of the flag, is a pretension which, however heard of in practice occasionally, has no existence whatever in principle. If the British flag converts a man-of-war into a British territory, the flag of other nations must be allowed to possess the same property in their marine; for there is no principle whatever that can be appropriated exclusively to the British flag.

"It therefore must be allowed reciprocally that a Spaniard getting on board a Spanish ship of war lying in Portsmouth harbor shall be protected from British justice. I believe the administration of that justice would return a very speedy and decisive negative to any such pretension on behalf of Spaniards charged with being amenable to British law.

"But the inconvenient effects of considering such a ship a Spanish territory would go much further—to the extent of protecting a British criminal who found his way into her. For no process of British justice can be executed on a British subject in a Foreign territory. When I give this as my decided persuasion upon this subject generally, I do not mean to say that in the infinite possibility of events cases may not arise in which such a protection might be indulged.

"But such cases are justified only by their own peculiar and extraordinary circumstances, which extend no further than to those immediate cases themselves, and furnish no rule of general practice in such as are ordinary. How far the case of Mr. Brown comes within such a description I am not enabled to state confidently by any exact knowledge of the facts, and particularly of the nature and validity of that authority under which the acts charged upon him by the Spaniards are said to have been committed. It would be improper in me to define what the British Government had not thought proper to define. Holding the opinion that before any Act of Parliament or proclamation issued, it was unlawful for a British subject to accept a hostile commission from any persons either in war or rebellion against a State in amity with the Crown of Great Britain, I am led to think that the Spaniards would not have been chargeable with illegal violence if they had thought proper to employ force in taking this person out of the vessel (British), and I add that it was certainly very undesirable to furnish occasions for the lawful use of force in the intercourse of friendly nations. Taking the authority under which Brown acted to be clearly invalid (which I do not mean to assert), I think it might possibly appear that Captain Falcon's conduct was more to be commended for its humanity and spirit than for its strict legality. —William Scott, Grafton Street, 28th November, 1820."[1]

[1] On the receipt of this opinion a copy thereof was forwarded to the Foreign Office, and Lord Castlereagh, in a letter dated the 29th of December, 1820, addressed to the British minister at the Court of Spain, thus expressed himself :—

"Your Excellency will find it easy from these papers, to give such an explanation of the circumstances which attended the liberation in England of this individual, as will be satisfactory to the Spanish minister. You will at the same time, on the part of your Court, disavow Captain Falcon's conduct in rescuing Brown on board his ship within a Spanish port, and not delivering him up, upon the requisition of the local authorities. The officer, no doubt, acted upon a good motive, but in assuming that the British flag could protect him against the legal process of the territorial jurisdiction within which the parties then were, was to maintain a principle, which the British Government desires distinctly to disclaim as not consistent with their uniform practice, or with the Law of Nations." (Report of Royal Commission on Fugitive Slaves, p. LXXVII).

On the other hand, a directly opposite view was expressed by Lord Palmerston, in 1849. Mr. Addington, writing to the Secretary of the Admiralty, August 4th, said :—

"Viscount Palmerston directs me to request that you will acquaint the Board of Admiralty that his Lordship is of the opinion that it would not be right to receive and harbor on board a British ship of war any person flying from justice on a criminal charge, or who was escaping from the sentence of a court of law. But a British man-of-war has always and everywhere been considered a safe place of refuge for persons of whatever country or party who had sought shelter under the British flag from persecution on account of their political conduct or opinions ;

(c) *On Board Merchant Ships.*

SOTELO'S CASE, 1840.

(*Calvo: Droit International, 4th Ed.*, I, 569.)

The right of granting asylum to political refugees does not belong to merchant vessels, in the ports of such refugees' country.

"En 1840 le paquebot à vapeur français l'*Océan*, qui faisait des voyages réguliers entre Marseille, la côte d'Espagne et Gibraltar reçut à son bord, au mouillage de Grao (Valence), M. Sotelo, ex-ministre espagnol, poursuivi pour cause politique. Ayant remis en mer sans qu'on se fût immédiatement aperçu du nombre et de la personnalité des passagers qu'il avait embarqués, le navire se rendit à Alicante; mais là, au moment même de la visite de douane et de police, M. Sotelo fut reconnu, saisi, emmené à terre, puis emprisonné. Le

and this protection has been equally offered, whether the refugee was escaping from the arbitrary acts of a monarchical government, or from the lawless violence of a revolutionary committee. * * *

"Although the commander of a ship of war should not seek out or invite political refugees, yet he ought not to turn away or give up any who may reach his ship and have obtained admittance on board. Such officer must of course take care that such refugees shall not carry on from on board his ship any political correspondence with their partisans on shore, and he ought to avail himself of the earliest opportunity to send them to some place of safety elsewhere." (Rep. of Royal Comm. on Fug. Slaves, p. 155).

For a full discussion of the question of the exterritoriality of ships of war, see the separate reports of Lord Chief Justice Cockburn, and Mr. Rothery, in the "Report of the Royal Commission on Fugitive Slaves," 1876. Mr. Rothery takes strong ground against the right of asylum on such ships.

Sir James Fitzjames Stephen, another member of the commission, takes similar ground. (Stephen's History of the Criminal Law, II., 57).

As to American practice, Attorney-General Bradford held, in 1794, that a "writ of *habeas corpus* may be awarded to bring up an American subject unlawfully detained on board a foreign ship of war, the commander being amenable to the usual jurisdiction of the state where he happens to be, and not entitled to claim the extraterritoriality which is annexed to a foreign minister and his domicil." (Wharton's Digest, I., 138.)

But in 1855, Attorney-General Cushing—a high authority—held, that a "prisoner of war on board a foreign ship of war, or of her prize, cannot be released by *habeas corpus* issuing from courts of the United States or of a particular State." And again, in 1856, "ships of war enjoy the full rights of extraterritoriality in foreign ports and territorial waters." (Wharton's Digest, I., 138.) It would seem to follow, therefore, that right of asylum could be granted on American ships of war. In South American ports it has frequently been done.

capitaine de l'*Océan* protesta contre ce qu'il qualifiait de violation de pavillon, et réclama vainement la mise en liberté de son passager, en invoquant à la fois le droit d'asile et le principe d'exterritorialité,

"Ses communications diplomatiques échangées au sujet de cette affaire entre le gouvernement de France et celui d'Espagne établirent de la manière la plus péremptoire que la conduite des autorités d'Alicante était à l'abri de tout reproche; que nulle atteinte n'avait été portée au respect du pavillon, puisqu'il s'agissait d'un navire marchand ordinaire et d'une mesure de haute police exécutée dans l'intérieur du port; que M. Sotelo, embarqué subrepticement à Valence, port espagnol, avait pu régulièrement être saisi et arrêté à bord de l'*Océan* dans un autre port du même pays; enfin que la circonstance d'avoir navigué en pleine mer pendant un certain temps, avant d'atteindre Alicante ne pouvait altérer la nature du fait délictueux accompli au point de départ et constaté au point d'arrivée sous l'empire des mêmes lois de la même législation territoriale."

OPINION OF LORD ABERDEEN, 1844.

(*Rep. of Royal Comm. on Fugitive Slaves*, 154.)

Merchant vessels possess no right of asylum.

Viscount Canning writes to the Secretary of the Admiralty, March 20, 1844, as follows:—

"Sir,—I have laid before the Earl of Aberdeen Sir J. Barrow's letter of the 9th instant, from which it appears that the Lords Commissioners of the Admiralty wish to know what line of conduct should be pursued by the commanders of the hired vessels which convey the mails between this country and the Peninsula, if it should happen that the authorities of Vigo should attempt to remove from any of these vessels a Spanish subject who may have embarked at Lisbon, being provided with a Portuguese passport, countersigned by the British, French, and Belgian Legations at Lisbon.

"In answer to the above inquiry, I am directed by Lord Aberdeen to acquaint you, for the information of the Lords Commissioners of the Admiralty, that there is no stipulation in the existing treaties between this country and Spain which can be deemed sufficient to debar the Spanish Government from exercising the right which, in his Lordship's opinion, appertains to that government of claiming its own subjects when they may be found in a Spanish port as passengers on board vessels hired to convey the mails between this country and the Peninsula."

CASE OF GOMEZ.

BAYARD, SEC. OF ST., TO HALL, MARCH 12, 1884.

(*U. S. Foreign Relations*, 1885, *p.* 82).

Merchant vessels possess no right of asylum.

"Sir,—I have to acknowledge the receipt of your No. 316, of the 10th ultimo, in which you enclose copies of the correspondence between the legation at Guatemala and Mr. Leavitt, the United States consul at Managua, respecting the case of José Dolores Gomez, and request more definite instructions for such cases.

"It appears that Mr. Gomez, who is said to be a political fugitive from Nicaragua, voluntarily took passage at San José de Guatemala for Punta Arenas, Costa Rica, on board the Pacific Mail steamship Honduras with the knowledge that the vessel would enter *en route* the port of San Juan del Sur, Nicaragua.

"The government of Nicaragua upon learning of this fact ordered the commandant of the port of San Juan del Sur, to arrest Gomez upon the arrival of the Honduras at that port.

"The minister for foreign affairs of Nicaragua informed Mr. Leavitt, United States consul at Managua, of the action of the government by a telegram, as follows:

"'Government has ordered the commander of port San Juan del Sur to arrest José Dolores Gomez, a fugitive prisoner, who is on board of the steamer Honduras, now *en route* to that port. I suppose the captain will not interfere with the action of the commander, but to avoid whatever difficulties likely to arise I suggest you to send a telegraphic message to the captain of the Honduras, at San Juan del Sur, stating that the order has been issued by the government and recommending him to support the commander as there is no ground on the part of the captain to hinder the execution of the government order.'

"It appears that, before Mr. Leavitt had an opportunity to act upon this request, you telegraphed him as follows:

"'Reported here arrest of a transit passenger bound to Panama on board steamer Honduras at San Juan del Sur. Say respectfully to Nicaraguan minister of foreign affairs that our government never has consented and never will consent to the arrest and removal from an American vessel in a foreign port, of any passenger in transit, much less if offense is political.'

"It appears that Mr. Leavitt declined to comply with the request of the minister of foreign affairs, and followed your instructions by submitting a copy in writing to the minister.

"From the brief outline given by the consul of the subsequent proceedings, it appears that the government authorities at San Juan del Sur, upon the arrival of the Honduras at that port, requested the captain to deliver up Mr. Gomez. This he declined to do, and set sail without proper clearance papers.

"The consul reports that for these offenses the captain has been tried by the Nicaraguan government and found guilty, and although he has not been able to learn the nature of the sentence, he is convinced, from the present attitude of the government, that the sentence will be executed in case of the return of the captain or the vessel within the jurisdiction of the Government of Nicaragua.

"As the nature and character of the proceedings against the captain of the Honduras are not known to this Department, a full and detailed report should be made as early as practicable. It is clear that Mr. Gomez voluntarily entered the jurisdiction of a country whose laws he had violated. * * *

"It may be safely affirmed that when a merchant vessel of one country visits the ports of another for the purposes of trade, it owes temporary allegiance and is amenable to the jurisdiction of that country, and is subject to the laws which govern the port it visits so long as it remains, unless it is otherwise provided by treaty.

"Any exemption or immunity from local jurisdiction must be derived from the consent of that country. No such exemption is made in the treaty of commerce and navigation concluded between this country and Nicaragua on the 21st day of June, 1867." [1]

[1] In the similar case of Barrundia, 1890, the government of the United States set up a different rule. Barrundia was a political refugee from Guatemala who took passage, at a Mexican port, on the Pacific Mail Steamship *Acapulco* (American) for Salvador. The steamer was to call on the way at several ports of Guatemala; and on learning of the movements of Barrundia, the government of Guatemala proposed to arrest him. That it could legally do so was the opinion of the American Minister, Mizner, and the American Consul-General, Hosmer, and they so advised the captain of the *Acapulco*, and the authorities of Guatemala. In the attempt to arrest Barrundia on board the steamship, he resisted and was killed.

For his part in the affair, Mr. Mizner was severely censured, and recalled from his post. Commander Reiter of the U. S. ship of war, *Ranger*, who was present in the port at the time, was also sent into disgrace for not interfering to prevent the arrest.

In his dispatch to Mr. Mizner of November 18, 1890, Mr. Blaine reviews the facts and the law of the case; much of his argument has no bearing on the case, and many of his citations go to disprove his own view of it. It is hardly too much to say that there is no foundation in International Law for the position of the

Section 14.—Extradition.

UNITED STATES v. RAUSCHER.

Supreme Court of the United States, 1886.

(119 *United States Reports*, 407.)

There is no rule of international law requiring States to deliver up fugitives from justice from other States.

In the United States, extradition is exclusively a Federal question.

A person extradited under treaty can be tried for that offense only for which he was extradited.

Judgment.—Miller, J.:—

"This case comes before us on a certificate of division of opinion between the judges holding the Circuit Court of the United States for the Southern District of New York arising after verdict of guilty, and before judgment, on a motion in arrest of judgment.

"The prisoner, William Rauscher, was indicted by a grand jury, for that on the 9th day of October, 1884, on the high seas, out of the jurisdiction of any particular state of the United States, and within the admiralty and maritime jurisdiction thereof, he, the said William Rauscher, being then and there second mate of the ship J. F. Chapman, unlawfully made an assault upon Janssen, one of the crew of the vessel of which he was an officer, and unlawfully inflicted upon said Janssen cruel and unusual punishment. This indictment was found under § 5347 of the Revised Statutes of the United States. * * *

"The prisoner having been extradited upon a charge of murder on the high seas of one Janssen, under § 5339 Rev. Stat., had the Circuit Court of the Southern District of New York jurisdiction to put him to trial upon an indictment under § 5347 Rev. Stat., charging him with cruel and unusual punishment of the same man, he being one of the crew of an American vessel of which the defendant was an officer, and such punishment consisting of the identical acts proved in the extradition proceedings?

United States Government in this affair. The only possible excuse for it is the assertion that the Spanish American States do not possess all the rights of sovereign states, and that there should be an exceptional rule adopted in their case, in regard to asylum on merchant ships, as there is in the case of legations.

For a careful study of the right of asylum, see an article by Professor J. B. Moore, in the "Political Science Quarterly" for 1892. See also, 1 "Wharton's Digest of International Law," § 104.

"The treaty with Great Britain, under which the defendant was surrendered by that government to ours upon a charge of murder, is that of August 9, 1842. * * * The tenth article of the treaty is as follows: 'It is agreed that the United States and her Britannic Majesty shall, upon mutual requisitions by them, or their ministers, officers, or authorities, respectively made, deliver up to justice all persons who, being charged with the crime of murder, or assault with intent to commit murder, or piracy, or arson, or robbery, or forgery, or the utterance of forged paper, committed within the jurisdiction of either, shall seek an asylum, or shall be found, within the territories of the other: provided that this shall only be done upon such evidence of criminality as, according to the laws of the place where the fugitive or person so charged shall be found, would justify his apprehension and commitment for trial, if the crime or offense had there been committed; and the respective judges and other magistrates of the two Governments shall have power, jurisdiction, and authority, upon complaint made under oath, to issue a warrant for the apprehension of the fugitive or person so charged, that he may be brought before such judges or other magistrates, respectively, to the end that the evidence of criminality may be heard and considered; and if, on such hearing, the evidence be deemed sufficient to sustain the charge, it shall be the duty of the examining judge or magistrate to certify the same to the proper executive authority, that a warrant may issue for the surrender of such fugitive.'

"Not only has the general subject of the extradition of persons, charged with crime in one country, who have fled to and sought refuge in another, been matter of much consideration of late years by the executive departments and statesmen of the governments of the civilized portion of the world, by various publicists and writers on international law, and by specialists on that subject, as well as by the courts and judicial tribunals of different countries, but the precise questions arising under this treaty, as presented by the certificate of the judges in this case, have recently been very much discussed in this country, and in Great Britain.

"It is only in modern times that the nations of the earth have imposed upon themselves the obligation of delivering up these fugitives from justice to the states where their crimes were committed, for trial and punishment. This has been done generally by treaties made by one independent government with another. Prior to these treaties, and apart from them, it may be stated as the general result of the writers upon international law, that there was no well-defined obligation on one country to deliver up such fugitives to another, and though such delivery was often made, it was upon the principle of comity, and within the discretion of the government whose action was invoked; and it has never been recognized as among those obligations of one government towards another which rest upon established principles of international law.

"Whether in the United States, in the absence of any treaty on the subject with a foreign nation from whose justice a fugitive may be found in one of the states, and in the absence of any act of Congress upon the subject, a state can, through its own judiciary or executive, surrender him for trial to such foreign nation, is a question which has been under consideration by the courts of this country without any very conclusive result. * * *

"There can be little doubt of the soundness of the opinion of Chief-Justice Taney, that the power exercised by the governor of Vermont is a part of the foreign intercourse of this country, which has undoubtedly been conferred upon the Federal government; and that it is clearly included in the treaty making power and the corresponding power of appointing and receiving ambassadors and other public ministers. There is no necessity for the states to enter upon the relations with foreign nations which are necessarily implied in the extradition of fugitives from justice found within the limits of the state, as there is none why they should, in their own name, make demand upon foreign nations for the surrender of such fugitives.

"At this time of day, and after the repeated examinations which have been made by this court into the powers of the Federal government to deal with all such international questions exclusively, it can hardly be admitted that, even in the absence of treaties or acts of Congress on the subject, the extradition of a fugitive from justice can become the subject of negotiation between a state of this Union and a foreign government.

"Fortunately, this question, with others which might arise in the absence of treaties or acts of Congress on the subject, is now of very little importance, since, with nearly all the nations of the world with whom our relations are such that fugitives from justice may be found within their dominions or within ours, we have treaties which govern the rights and conduct of the parties in such cases. These treaties are also supplemented by acts of Congress, and both are in their nature exclusive.

"The case we have under consideration arises under one of these treaties made between the United States and Great Britain, the country with which, on account of our intimate relations, the cases requiring extradition are likely to be most numerous. This treaty of 1842 is supplemented by the acts of Congress of August 12, 1848, 9 Stat., 302, and March 3, 1869, 15 Stat., 337, the provisions of which are embodied in §§ 5270, 5272 and 5275 of the Revised Statutes, under Title LXVI., Extradition.* * *

"The treaty of 1842 being, therefore, the supreme law of the land, which the courts are bound to take judicial notice of and to enforce in any appropriate proceeding the rights of persons growing out of that treaty, we proceed to inquire, in the first place, so far as pertinent to the question certified by the circuit judges, into the true construction of the treaty. We have already seen that, according to the doctrine of publicists and writers on international law, the country receiving the offender against its laws from another country had no right to proceed against him for any other offense than that for which he had been delivered up. This is a principle which commends itself as an appropriate adjunct to the discretionary exercise of the power of rendition because it can hardly be supposed that a government which was under no treaty obligation nor any absolute obligation of public duty to seize a person who had found an asylum within its bosom and turn him over to another country for trial, would be willing to do this, unless a case was made of some specific offense, of a character which justified the government in depriving the party of his asylum. It is unreasonable that the country of the asylum should be expected to deliver up such person to be dealt with by the demanding government without any limitation, implied or otherwise, upon its prosecution of the party. In exercising its discretion, it might be very willing to deliver up offenders against such laws as were essential to the protection of life, liberty and person, while it would not be willing to do this on account of minor misdemeanors or of a certain class of political offenses in which it would have no interest or sympathy. Accordingly, it has been the policy of all governments to grant an asylum to persons who have fled from their homes on account of political disturbances and who might be there amenable to laws framed with regard to such subjects, and to the personal allegiance of the party. In many of the treaties of extradition between the civilized nations of the world, there is an express exclusion of offenders against such laws, and in none of them is this class of offenses mentioned as being the foundation of extradition proceedings. Indeed, the enumeration of offenses in most of these treaties, and especially in the treaty now under consideration, is so specific, and marked by such a clear line in regard to the magnitude and importance of those offenses, that it is impossible to give any other interpretation to it than that of the exclusion of the right of extradition for any others.

"It is, therefore, very clear that this treaty did not intend to depart in this respect from the recognized public law which had prevailed in the absence of treaties, and that it was not intended that this treaty should be used for any other purpose than to secure the trial of the person extradited for one of the offenses enumerated in the treaty. This is not only apparent from the general principle that the specific enumeration of certain matters and things implies the exclusion of all others, but the entire face of the treaty, including the processes by which it is to be carried into effect, confirms this view of the subject. It is unreasonable to suppose that any demand for rendition framed upon a general representation to the government of the asylum (if we may use such an expression) that the party for whom the demand was made was guilty of some violation of the laws of the country which demanded him, without specifying any particular offense with which he was charged, and even without specifying an offense mentioned in the treaty, would receive any serious attention; and yet such is the effect of the construction that the party is properly liable to trial for any other offense than that for which he was demanded, and which is described in the treaty. There would, under that view of the subject, seem to be no need of a description of a specific offense in making the demand. But, so far from this being admissible the treaty not only provides that the party shall be charged with one of the crimes mentioned, to wit, murder, assault with intent to commit murder, piracy, arson, robbery, forgery or the utterance of forged paper, but that evidence shall be produced to the judge or magistrate of the country of which such demand is made, of the commission of such an offense, and that this evidence shall be such as according to the law of that country would justify the apprehension and commitment for trial of the person so charged. If the proceedings under which the party is arrested in a country where he is peaceably and quietly living, and to the protection of whose laws he is entitled, are to have no influence in limiting the prosecution in the country where the offense is charged to have been committed, there is very little use for this particularity in charging a specific offense, requiring that offense to be one mentioned in the treaty, as well as sufficient evidence of the party's guilt to put him upon trial for it. Nor can it be said that, in the exercise of such a delicate power under a treaty so well guarded in every particular, its provisions are obligatory alone on the State which makes the surrender of the fugitive, and that that fugitive passes into the hands of the country which charges him with the offense, free from all the positive requirements and just implications of the treaty under which the transfer of his person takes place. A moment before he is under the protection of a government which has afforded him an asylum from which he can only be taken under a very limited form of procedure, and a moment after he is found in the possession of another sovereignty by virtue of that proceeding, but divested of all the rights which he had the moment before, and of all the rights which the law governing that proceeding was intended to secure.

"If upon the face of this treaty it could be seen that its sole object was to secure the transfer of an individual from the jurisdiction of one sovereignty to that of another, the argument might be sound; but as this right of transfer, the right to demand it, the obligation to grant it, the proceedings under which it takes place, all show that it is for a limited and defined purpose that the transfer is made, it is impossible to conceive of the exercise of jurisdiction in such a case for any other purpose than that mentioned in the treaty, and ascertained by the proceedings under which the party is extradited, without an implication of fraud upon the rights of the party extradited, and of bad faith to the country which permitted his extradition. No such view of solemn public treaties between the great nations of the earth can be sustained by a tribunal called upon to give judicial construction to them.

"The opposite view has been attempted to be maintained in this country upon the ground that there is no express limitation in the treaty of the right of the country in which the offense was committed to try the person for the crime alone for which he was extradited, and that once being within the jurisdiction of that country, no matter by what contrivance or fraud or by what pretense of establishing a charge provided for by the extradition treaty he may have been brought within the jurisdiction, he is, when here, liable to be tried for any offense against the laws as though arrested here originally. This proposition of the absence of express restriction in the treaty of the right to try him for other offenses than that for which he was extradited, is met by the manifest scope and object of the treaty itself. The caption of the treaty, already quoted, declaring that its purpose is to settle the boundary line between the two governments; to provide for the final suppression of the African slave trade; adds, 'and for the giving up of criminals, fugitive from justice, *in certain cases*.' The treaty, then, requires, as we have already said, that there shall be given up, upon requisitions respectively made by the two governments, all persons charged with any of the seven crimes enumerated, and the provisions giving a party an examination before a proper tribunal, in which, before he shall be delivered up on this demand, it must be shown that the offense for which he is demanded is one of those enumerated, and that the proof is sufficient to satisfy the court or magistrate before whom this examination takes place that he is guilty and such as the law of State of the asylum requires to establish such guilt, leave no reason to doubt that the fair purpose of the treaty is, that the person shall be delivered up to be tried for that offense and for no other.

"If there should remain any doubt upon this construction of the treaty itself, the language of two acts of Congress, heretofore cited, incorporated in the Revised Statutes, must set this question at rest. Rev. Stat. §§ 3272, 3275. * * *

"The obvious meaning of these two statutes, which have reference to all treaties of extradition made by the United States, is that the party shall not be delivered up by this government to be tried for any other offense than that charged in the extradition proceedings; and that, when brought into this country upon similar proceedings, he shall not be arrested or tried for any other offense than that with which he was charged in those proceedings, until he shall have had a reasonable time to return unmolested to the country from which he was brought. This is undoubtedly a congressional construction of the purpose and meaning of extradition treaties such as the one we have under consideration, and whether it is or not, it is conclusive upon the judiciary of the right conferred upon persons bought from a foreign country into this under such proceedings.

"That right, as we understand it, is that he shall be tried only for the offense with which he is charged in the extradition proceedings, and for which he was delivered up, and that if not tried for that, or after trial and acquittal, he shall have a reasonable time to leave the country before he is arrested upon the charge of any other crime committed previous to his extradition. * * *

"Upon a review of these decisions of the Federal and State courts, to which may be added the opinions of the distinguished writers which we have cited in the earlier part of this opinion, we feel authorized to state that the weight of authority and of sound principle are in favor of the proposition, that a person who has been brought within the jurisdiction of the court by virtue of proceedings under an extradition treaty, can only be tried for one of the offenses described in that treaty, and for the offense with which he is charged in the proceedings for his extradition, until a reasonable time and opportunity have been given him, after his release or trial upon such charge, to return to the country from whose asylum he had been forcibly taken under those proceedings."

WAIT, C. J., dissented from the opinion of the court.[1]

[1] The decision in Rauscher's case put an end to a controversy between the United States and England, of some years' standing, as to the interpretation of the extradition clause of the treaty of 1842. England had contended that a person surrendered

TRIMBLE'S CASE, 1884.

(*Moore on Extradition*, I., 166.)

The question as regards the power and duty of a State to surrender its own citizens under treaties of extradition.

The question of the power of the government of the United States to surrender its citizens under the treaty with Mexico of 1861, was discussed in 1884, in the case of Alexander Trimble, an American citizen, whose extradition was demanded on charges of robbery and murder.

The first article of the treaty stipulates that the contracting parties shall, on requisition "deliver up to justice persons, who, etc." But in the sixth article, it is further declared that "neither of the contracting parties shall be bound to deliver up its own citizens under the stipulations of this treaty."

The government of the United States declined to order the surrender of the prisoner, on the ground that, as the treaty negatived any obligation to do so, the President was not invested with legal authority to act.

Mr. Frelinghuysen said, "It appears that, by the opinions of several Attorneys-General, by the decisions of our courts, and by the rulings of the Department of State, the President has not, independent of

under the treaty, could be tried for no offense except the specific one for which extradition was accorded. The government of the United States had insisted, on the other hand, that a person once extradited could be indicted and tried for offenses other than that charged in the demand for extradition. (See the cases of Lawrence and Winslow, Moore's Extradition, I., 196–219; Wharton's Digest, II., § 270; U. S. Foreign Relations, 1876.)

The Supreme Court, in Rauscher's case, upholds the English view of the question. Previous to this authoritative decision, judicial opinion had been divided. In *accord* with this decision: *Com.* v. *Hawes*, 1877, 13 Bush., 697; *Blanford* v. *The State*, 1881, 10 Texas App., 627; *Watt's Case*, 1882, 14 Fed. Rep., 139; *State* v. *Vanderpool*, 1881, 39 Ohio State, 237. *Contra*: *Caldwell's Case*, 1871, 8 Blatch, 131; *Lagarve's Case*, 1873, 14 Abb. Pr. (N. S.), 333; *In re Miller*, 1885, 23 Fed. Rep., 32; *Ex parte Hibbs*, 1886, 26 Fed. Rep., 422.

The decisions of the French court of Cassation are in accord with that of the United States Supreme Court: Dalloz, 1867, p. 281, No. 6, and Ib., 1874, p. 502 and notes.

In Rauscher's case, the Supreme Court expressed the opinion that, in the absence of treaty, there was under international law no right of extradition.

And further that, in the United States, extradition is a matter exclusively in the control of the Federal government. (See *Ex parte Holmes*, 1840, 12 Vt., 631; *Holmes* v. *Jennison*, 14 Peters, 540; *People* v. *Curtis*, 50 N. Y., 321.)

treaty provision, the power of extraditing an American citizen; and the only question to be considered is whether the treaty with Mexico confers that power.

"By the treaty with Mexico proclaimed June 20, 1862, this country places itself under obligations to Mexico to surrender to justice persons accused of enumerated crimes committed within the jurisdiction of Mexico who shall be found within the territory of the United States; and further provides that that obligation shall not extend to the surrender of American citizens. The treaty confers upon the President no affirmative power to surrender an American citizen. The treaty between the United States and Mexico creates an obligation on the part of the respective governments, and does no more, and where the obligation ceases the power falls. It is true that treaties are the laws of the land, but a statute and a treaty are subject to different modes of construction. If a statute by the first section should say, The President of the United States shall surrender to any friendly power any person who has committed a crime against the laws of that power, but shall not be bound so to surrender American citizens, it might be argued, perhaps correctly, that the President had a discretion whether he would or would not surrender an American citizen. But a treaty is a contract, and must be so construed. It confers upon the President only the power to perform that contract. I understand the treaty with Mexico as reading thus: The President shall be bound to surrender any person guilty of crime, unless such person is a citizen of the United States.

"Such being the construction of the treaty, and believing that the time to prevent a violation of the law of extradition was before the citizens left the jurisdiction of the United States, I telegraphed the Governor of Texas that an American citizen could not legally be held under the treaty for extradition.

"It would be a great evil that those guilty of high crime, whether American citizens or not, should go unpunished; but even that result could not justify an usurpation of power.

"On further reflection, in view of the fact that fourteen of our treaties with other nations contain provisions identical with that contained in our treaty with Mexico, and impressed also with the fact that the safety and peace of society on the frontier would be greatly injured if criminals, because citizens of this country, could here find an asylum and go unpunished, I concluded that the question was one of too much importance to be settled by the dictum of any individual, but should receive judicial determination, and to this end I telegraphed the officers to hold the accused until they received other direction. The accused had, however, after my first telegram, been discharged

"I now propose to inform the officers in Texas, who, subject to the supervision of the President, are authorized to determine whether a surrender of the accused should be made, that if another arrest is made and a case of guilt is made out, the President will not, on the ground of citizenship, interfere with an order of surrender if such be made, but requires that the accused be informed that if he or they wish a hearing before the Supreme Court of the United States on *habeas corpus* as to the power of the President in the matter of extradition, or as to the true construction of the treaty before the surrender be actually made, every facility for such hearing will be afforded. Should the court hold that the President has a discretionary power of extraditing citizens proven guilty of crime, the evil apprehended will not be realized; and should the court hold that the President has the power to extradite only when bound by treaty to do so, Congress can then, if it should be its pleasure, by statute confer the discretionary power."[1]

[1] In a similar case, in 1893, not yet reported, it is understood that the Federal District Court of Texas discharged the prisoner, on the grounds stated by Mr. Frelinghuysen, thus preventing a review of the question by the Supreme Court.

"The exemption of citizens from extradition has been maintained on various grounds. The only one which need seriously be noticed is that by the laws of most countries provision is made for the trial and punishment of their citizens for offenses committed abroad, and that a State should not deliver up one of its citizens to be tried before a foreign tribunal when he can be punished at home under its own laws. By England and the United States alone are offenses, even when committed by their citizens or subjects, treated as entirely local." (Moore's Extradition, I., 153.)

In negotiating extradition treaties these two states have therefore been willing to stipulate for the rendition of their own subjects or citizens. Indeed, the United States for a time refused to enter into extradition treaties on any other basis; but since 1852 this objection appears to have been waived, and a large number of our treaties of extradition, as that with Mexico, exempts each party from the obligation to surrender its own citizens.

But as this exemption from the obligation to surrender citizens was doubtless inserted in these treaties in deference to the opinion of other states, it is not probable that it was intended as an absolute prohibition upon the President of the United States; indeed, the wording of the clause would seem to imply a discretion on the part of the contracting parties.

In 1880, the Institute of International Law, after an exhaustive discussion of the subject of extradition, adopted a series of resolutions, the sixth of which was as follows:—

"Between countries whose criminal legislation rests on similar foundations, and which have confidence in each other's judicial institutions, the extradition of their own citizens would be a means of securing the good administration of criminal justice, because it ought to be desirable that the authorities of the *forum delicti commissi* should, if possible, be called upon to try the case."

See on this subject: Moore's Extradition, I., 152; Dana's Wheaton, pp. 189–191, notes.

CASE OF CAZO, 1887.

(*Moore on Extradition*, I., 324.)

What constitutes a political offense?

On February 3, 1887, the Mexican minister presented a request for the extradition of one "Francisco J. Cazo and his accomplices," charged with murder, assault with intent to commit murder, and robbery, committed in the town of Agualeguas, in the state of Nuevo Leone, Mexico, on the 11th, 12th, and 13th of July, 1886, who had taken refuge in Texas.

The evidence disclosed that three or four days previously to the 11th of July, it was reported that Cazo was coming to attack the town. Just before midnight on the 10th of July, a number of persons were observed to leave the place armed, and about two o'clock on the morning of the 11th an attack was made by a party of thirty or more persons, who could not be identified, but who kept shouting, "Hurrah for Don Francisco J. Cazo, and death to the Garra party!" The raiders kept possession of the town for nearly three days, during which time they had armed encounters with the inhabitants, seized horses and other property, and committed other acts of violence. When they departed, Cazo left a proclamation with a citizen of the town with directions to publish it. In reply to the application for extradition, Mr. Bayard, then Secretary of State, on February 7, 1887, wrote as follows:

"After a careful examination of the papers enclosed in your note, I am unable to avoid the conclusion that the acts of Cazo and his associates, who were about thirty or forty in number. were clearly of a political character, and consequently, under the express terms of article VI. of the treaty above mentioned, are not a proper basis for extradition. The character of the outbreak, the kind and quantity of the property taken, and the mode of attack all lead to that conclusion.

"Although the first assault of Cazo's party was made in the night, there was no effort to conceal the personal identity of the leader, and such property as was seized was taken manifestly for the purpose of military equipment, for which it was adapted. The evidence offered of the fact that Cazo led the attack is the testimony of several witnesses that the assailants cried, 'Hurrah for Don Francisco J. Cazo!" and at least one witness testifies to the additional and accompanying exclamation of, 'Death to the Garra party!' Another witness states that Cazo left a proclamation in the hands of a resident of Agualeguas, with a view to its publication. Indeed, all the circumstances point to the conclusion that the affair was an avowed partisan political conflict."

THE ST. ALBANS RAID, 1864.

(Moore on Extradition, I. 322.)

What constitutes a political offense?

On October 19, 1864, one Bennett H. Young and thirteen or fourteen associates, all of whom had come over from Canada for the purpose, raided the town of St. Albans, in the State of Vermont; pillaged the bank; set fire to several buildings; took and held a number of citizens as prisoners; and committed other acts of violence. While in possession of the bank they seized a man named Breck, who had entered on private business, and by threats of violence compelled him to give up a sum of money which he had in his possession. They were finally driven away by the citizens of the town, one of whom was killed. On October 25 and 29, and November 1, 1864, Mr. Seward made requisitions for their surrender on charges of murder, assault with intent to commit murder, and robbery. They were all arrested in Canada, and lodged in jail at Montreal. Passing over other proceedings, which will be noticed in their proper place, they were brought before Justice Coursol, of the city of Montreal, by whom they were, on December 13, 1864, discharged on the ground that, as there was no warrant from the Governor-general to authorize their arrest, as required by the Imperial extradition act then in force, there was no jurisdiction to hear the case, and no justification for the fugitives' further detention. Immediately upon their discharge, a warrant was issued by Mr. Justice Smith, of the superior court, for their re-arrest. On this warrant only five of the fugitives were taken, and these were brought back to Montreal and lodged in jail. Their examination was proceeded with before Judge Smith from time to time until March 25, when he discharged them. Various grounds were taken on behalf of the prisoners. The only one to be noticed in this place is the claim made that the acts with which they were charged were belligerent, and therefore not within the extradition treaty. It was shown that Young held a commission as a first lieutenant in the army of the Confederate States, under an appointment by President

Davis, dated June 16, 1864, and signed by Jas. A. Seddon as Secretary of War. It was contended that in the attack on St. Albans he was acting as an officer under his commission, and that the other prisoners were soldiers of the Confederate army, acting under his command. After an extended discussion of the facts and the law, Judge SMITH states his conclusions in the following language:—

"I am therefore constrained to hold that the attack on St. Albans was a hostile expedition, authorized both expressly and impliedly by the Confederate States; and carried out by a commissioned officer of their army in command of a party of their soldiers. And, therefore, that no act committed in the course of, or as incident to, that attack can be made the ground of extradition under the Ashburton treaty. And that if there had been any breach of neutrality in its inception, upon which point I state no opinion, it does not affect this application, which must rest entirely upon the acts of the prisoners within the territories of the state demanding their extradition, and upon their own *status* and authority as belligerents."[1]

In Re CASTIONI.

QUEEN'S BENCH, 1890.

(*L. R. Queen's Bench Div.*, 149.)

What constitutes a political offense?

On an application for a writ of *habeas corpus*, the motion was made on behalf of Angelo Castioni, for an order *nisi* calling upon the solicitor to the Treasury, Franklin Lushington, Esq., a metropolitan police magistrate, and the consul-general of Switzerland, as representative of the Swiss Republic, to show cause why a writ of *habeas corpus* should not issue to bring up the body of Castioni in order that he might be discharged from custody.

The prisoner Castioni had been arrested in England on the requisition of the Swiss Government, and brought before the magistrate at the police court at Bow Street, and by him committed to prison for the purpose of extradition, on a charge of willful murder, alleged to have been committed in Switzerland.

The facts, which were contained in depositions sent from Switzerland, in the depositions taken before the magistrate at Bow Street,

[1] In the case of Burley, 1864, who was charged with similar hostile acts against United States vessels on Lake Erie, the accused was arrested in Canada, and surrendered up to the United States. But on his trial, in Ohio, the court held that his acts were belligerent and not committed *animo furandi*. (Moore's Extradition, I., 319.)

and in affidavits used on the hearing of the motion were shortly as follows: —

The prisoner was charged with the murder of Luigi Rossi, by shooting him with a revolver on September 11, 1890, in the town of Bellinzona, in the canton of Ticino, in Switzerland. The deceased, Rossi, was a member of the State Council of the canton of Ticino, and was about twenty-six years of age. The prisoner, Castioni, was a citizen of the same canton; he had resided for seventeen years in England, and arrived at Bellinzona on September 10, 1890. For some time previous to this date much dissatisfaction had been felt and expressed by a large number of the inhabitants of Ticino at the mode in which the political party then in power were conducting the government of the canton. A request was presented to the Government for a revision of the constitution of the canton, under art. 15 of the constitution, which provides that "The constitution of the canton may be revised wholly or partially. * * * (b) at the request of 7,000 citizens presented with the legal formalities. In this case the council shall within one month submit to the people the question whether or not they wish to revise the constitution," and a law of May 9, 1877, prescribes the course to be adopted for the execution of letter (b) of art. 15.

The Government having declined to take a popular vote on the question of the revision of the constitution, on September 11, 1890, a number of the citizens of Bellinzona, among whom was Castioni, seized the arsenal of the town, from which they took rifles and ammunition, disarmed the gendarmes, arrested and bound or handcuffed several persons connected with the Government, and forced them to march in front of the armed crowd to the municipal palace. Admission to the palace was demanded in the name of the people, and was refused by Rossi and another member of the Government, who were in the palace. The crowd then broke open the outer gate of the palace, and rushed in, pushing before them the Government officials whom they had arrested and bound; Castioni, who was armed with a revolver was among the first to enter. A second door, which was locked, was broken open, and at this time, or immediately after, Rossi, who was in the passage, was shot through the body with a revolver, and died very soon afterwards. Some other shots were fired, but no one else was injured. Two witnesses, who were present when the shot was fired, and were called before the magistrate at Bow Street, identified Castioni as the person who fired the shot. One of the witnesses called for the prisoner was an advocate named Bruni, who had taken a leading part in the attack on the municipal palace. In cross-examination he said: "The death of

Rossi was a misfortune, and not necessary for the rising." There was no evidence that Castioni had any previous knowledge of Rossi. The crowd then occupied the palace, disarmed the gendarmes who were there, and imprisoned several members of the Government. A provisional Government was appointed, of which Bruni was a member, and assumed the Government of the canton, which it retained until dispossessed by the armed intervention of the Federal Government of the Republic.

The magistrate was of opinion that the identification of Castioni was sufficient, and held upon the evidence that the bar to extradition specified in § 3 of the Extradition Act, 1870: "A fugitive criminal shall not be surrendered if the offence in respect, of which his surrender is demanded is one of a political character, or if he prove to the satisfaction of the police magistrate, or the court before whom he is brought on *habeas-corpus*, or to the Secretary of State, that the requisition for his surrender has in fact been made with a view to try or punish him for an offence of a political character," did not exist, and committed Castioni to prison. By the extradition treaty with Switzerland, dated Nov. 26, 1880, article 11: "A fugitive criminal shall not be surrendered if the offence in respect of which his surrender is demanded is one of a political character, or if he prove that the requisition for his surrender has in fact been made with a view to try and punish him for an offence of a political character."

Sir Charles Russell, for the prisoner; the Attorney-General, for the Crown.

DENMAN, J.:—"Looking at the extreme importance of this case, I should have been disposed, if I had felt any serious doubt as to the course we ought to pursue, to have taken time, not so much to consider what our judgment should be, as to take care to put it in the best possible shape, or even to reduce it to writing. But there are many considerations which apply to cases of this sort. One is, that here is a man in custody who has been in custody for a considerable time, and no greater delay than is reasonably necessary ought to be interposed if our decision should be one to the effect that he ought not to be in custody any longer. I am unable to entertain a doubt that this is a case in which we ought to order that the prisoner be discharged.

"There has been no legal decision as yet upon the meaning of the words contained in the act of 1870, upon the true meaning of which this case mainly depends. We have had many definitions suggested, and great light has been thrown upon the possible and probable meaning of the words by the arguments that have been addressed to us, applying not only the language of judges, but language used in text-books, language used by great political authorities, and in one case by a most learned philosopher. I think it has been useful in such a case as this that we should hear a discussion as to the possible meaning of the words, as it has occurred that they ought to be construed to people such as those whose opinions have been cited, and especially I may apply that observation to the case of my very learned brother whose assistance we have on this occasion in deciding the present case. I do not think it is necessary or desirable that we should attempt to put into language, in the shape of an exhaustive definition, exactly the whole state of things, or every state of things which bring a particular case within the description of an offence of a political character. I wish, however, to express an opinion as to one matter upon which I entertain a very strong opinion. That is, that if the description given by Mr. John Stuart Mill, 'Any offence committed in the course of or furthering of civil war, insurrection, or political commotion,' were to be construed in the sense that it really means any act which takes place in the course of a political rising without reference to the object and intention of it, and other circumstances connected with it, I should say that it was a wrong definition and one which could not be legally applied to the words in the Act of Parliament. Sir Charles Russell suggested that 'in the course of' was to be read with the words following, 'or in furtherance of,' and that 'in furtherance of' is equivalent to 'in the coufse of.' I cannot quite think that this was the intention of the speaker, or is the natural meaning of the expression; but I entirely concur with the observation of the Solicitor-General that in the other sense of the words, if they are not to be construed as merely equivalent expressions, it would be a wrong definition. I think that in order to bring the case within the words of the Act and to exclude extradition for such an act as murder, which is one of the extradition offences, it must at least be shown that the act is done in furtherance of, done with the intention of assistance, as a sort of overt act in the course of acting in a political matter, a political rising, or a dispute between two parties in the state as to which is to have the government in its hands, before it can be brought within the meaning of the words used in the act.

"Sir Charles Russell has argued that in every case it is for the party seeking extradition to bear the onus of affirmatively bringing it within the meaning of those words. On the other hand, it has been contended that if there be an extraditable offence, the onus is upon the person seeking the benefit of those words to show a case in which extradition can be avoided. I do not myself think that it is possible to decide a case such as this, or the true meaning of those words, by applying any such test as on whom is the onus. I do not think it is intended that a scrap of a *prima facie* case on the one side should have the effect of throwing upon the other side the onus of proving or disproving his position. I look at the words of the act themselves and I think that they are against any such narrow technical mode of dealing with the case. The words of s. 3, subd. 1, are 'a fugitive criminal shall not be surrendered if the offence in respect of which his surrender is demanded is one of a political character.' The section itself begins: 'The following restrictions shall be observed with respect to the surrender of fugitive criminals.' There is nothing said as to upon whom is the *onus probandi*, or that it shall be made to appear by one side or the other in such a case. It is a restriction upon the surrender of a fugitive criminal, and however it appears, if it does appear, that the act was, in the judgment of the court, an offence which would otherwise be an offence according to the laws of this country, but an offence of a political character, then wholly irrespective of any doctrine of onus on the one side or the other, that is within the jurisdiction, and he cannot be surrendered. It was at first contended, in opposition to the application for a *habeas corpus*, that if the magistrate upon this question once made up his mind, the court had no jurisdiction to deal with it. It appears to me that this proposition cannot be maintained on the very face of the act itself, which requires by s. 11 that the magistrate shall inform the prisoner that he may apply for a *habeas corpus*, and if he is entitled to apply for a *habeas corpus*, I think it follows that this court must have power to go into the whole matter, and in some cases, certainly if there be fresh evidence, or perhaps upon the same evidence, might take a different view of the matter from that taken by the magistrate.

"It seems to me that it is a question of mixed law and fact—mainly indeed of fact—as to whether the facts are such as to bring the case within the restriction of s. 3, and to show that it was an offence of a political character. I do not think it is disputed, or that now it can be looked upon as in controversy, that there was at this time existing in Ticino a state of things which would certainly show that there was more than a mere small rising of a few people against the law of the State. I think it is clearly made out by the facts of this case, that there was something of a very serious character going on—amounting, I should go so far as to say, in that small community, to a state of war. There was an armed body of men who had seized arms from the arsenal of the State; they were rushing into the municipal council chamber in which the government of the State used to assemble; they demanded admission; admission was refused; some firing took place; the outer gate was broken down; and I think it also appears perfectly plain from the evidence in the case that Castioni was a person who had been taking part in that movement at a much earlier stage. He was an active party in the movement; he had taken part in the binding of one member of the government. Some time before he arrived with his pistol in his hand at the seat of government, he had gone with multitudes of men, armed with arms from the arsenal, in order to attack the seat of government, and I think it must be taken that it is quite clear that from the very first, he was an active party, one of the rebellious party who was acting and in the attack against the government. Now, that being so, it resolves itself into a small point, depending on the evidence which was taken before the magistrate, and anything that we can collect from the evidence that we have before us and from the whole circumstances of the case.

"Before dealing with the evidence, I will say one thing about the message which was objected to and which was read after a slight discussion, upon the understanding that we were not going to use that document as evidence of any particular fact, but that it would be only used as an important document showing that the government of the country had themselves looked upon this as a serious political rising, and a serious state of violence by a very large body of the people against the government. I mean so to use it, and I have never thought of using it in any other way. I think that was the understanding upon which we allowed it to be read, and I feel that I am not justified in using it for any other purpose. Then it is reduced to the question of whether, upon the depositions sent over, and upon the depositions before the magistrate and upon the fresh facts, if there be any, which are brought before us on the affidavits, we think that this was an act done, not only in the course of a political rising, but as part of a political rising. Here I must say at once that I assent entirely to the observation that we cannot decide that question merely by considering whether the act done at the moment at which it was done was a wise act in the sense of being an act which the man who did it would have been wise in doing with the view of promoting the cause in which he was engaged. I do not think it would be at all consistent with the real meaning of the words of the statute if we were to attempt so to limit it. I mean, I do not think it would be right to limit it in the way suggested by the cross-examination of Bruni, namely, by considering whether it was necessary at that time that the act should be done. The question really is whether, upon the facts, it is clear that the man was acting as one of a number of persons engaged in acts of violence of a political character with a political object, and as part of the political movement and rising in which he was taking part. Now, the only shadow of a suggestion of evidence to the contrary, I think, is the suggestion which appears on the face of some of the documents that he said something about his brother having been assassinated some years before. It was said in the message, which I have already said I do not rely upon as a statement of fact, that he did at the time he fired use the expression, 'My brother's death cries for vengeance!' That is in the document, and is a statement of fact which I do not rely upon, and I do not think that I am justified in relying upon it, though if I commented on that, I should certainly say it was quite as capable of the construction put upon it by Sir Charles Russell, that he was not intending to murder Rossi, of whom he knew nothing, and of whose connection with any injury towards his brother there is not the slightest particle of evidence, as that it means anything of the kind suggested. Then it amounts to a very little, and it comes to discussion as to the facts of the case, and as to what was taking place at the exact moment at which the shot was fired. I have carefully followed the discussion as to the facts of the case, and if it were necessary I could go through them all one by one, and point out, I think, that, looking at the way in which that evidence was given, and at the evidence itself, there is nothing in my judgment to displace the view which I take of the case, that at the moment at which Castioni fired the shot, the reasonable presumption is, not that it is a matter of absolute certainty (we cannot be absolutely certain about anything as to men's motives) but the reasonable assumption is that he, at the moment knowing nothing about Rossi, having no spite or ill-will against Rossi, as far as we know, fired that shot; that he fired it thinking it would advance, and that it was an act which was in furtherance of, and done intending it to be in furtherance of the very object which the rising had taken place in order to promote, and to get rid of the Government, who, he might, until he had absolutely got into the place, have supposed were resisting the entrance of the people to that place. That, I think, is the fair and reasonable presumption to draw from the facts of the case. I do not know that it is necessary to give any opinion as to the exact moment when the shot was fired; there is some conflict about it. There is evidence that there was great confusion; there is evidence of shots fired after the shot which Castioni fired; and all I can say is, that looking at it as a question of fact, I have come to the conclusion that at the time at which that shot was fired he acted in the furtherance of the unlawful rising to which at that time he was a party, and an active party—a person who had been doing active work from a very much earlier period, and in which he was still actively engaged. That being so, I think the writ ought to issue, and that we should be acting contrary to the spirit of this enactment, and to the fair meaning of it, if we were to allow him to be detained in custody longer."

HAWKINS, J., said, among other things, "Now what is the meaning of crime of a political character? I have thought over this matter very much indeed, and I have thought whether any definition can be given of the political character of the crime—I mean to say, in language which is satisfactory. I have found none at all, and I can imagine for myself none so satisfactory, and to my mind so complete, as that which I find in a work which I have now before me, and the language of which for the purpose of my present judgment I entirely adopt, and that is the expression of my brother Stephen in his History of the Criminal Law of England in vol. ii., pp. 70, 71. I will not do more than refer to the interpretations, other than those with which he agrees, which have been given upon this expression, 'political character'; but I adopt his definition absolutely. 'The third meaning which may be given to the words, and which I take to be the true meaning, is somewhat more complicated than either of those I have described. An act often falls under several different definitions. For instance, if a civil war were to take place, it would be high treason by levying war against the Queen. Every case in which a man was shot in action would be murder. Whenever a house was burnt for military purposes arson would be committed. To take cattle, etc., by requisition would be robbery. According to the common use of language, however, all such acts would be political offences, because they would be incidents in carrying on a civil war. I think, therefore, that the expression in the Extradition Act ought (unless some better interpretation of it can be suggested) to be interpreted to mean that fugitive criminals are not to be surrendered for extradition crimes, if those crimes were incidental to and formed a part of political disturbances. I do not wish to enter into details beforehand on a subject which might at any moment come under judicial consideration.' The question has come under judicial consideration, and having had the opportunity before this case arose of carefully reading and considering the views of my learned brother, having heard all that can be said upon the subject, I adopt his language as the definition that I think is the most perfect to be found or capable of being given as to what is the meaning of the phrase which is made use of in the Extradition Act. * * *

"I cannot help thinking that everybody knows there are many acts of a political character done without reason, done against all reason; but at the same time, one cannot look too hardly and weigh in golden scales the acts of men hot in their political excitement. We know that in heat and in heated blood men often do things which are against and contrary to reason; but none the less an act of this description may be done for the purpose of furthering and in furtherance of a political rising, even though it is an act which may be deplored and lamented, as even cruel and against all reason, by those who can calmly reflect upon it after the battle is over.

"For the reasons I have expressed, I am of opinion that this rule ought to be made absolute, and that the prisoner ought to be discharged." [1]

[1] *Political offenses*:—"Most codes extend their definitions of treason to acts not really against one's country. They do not distinguish between acts against the *Government* and acts against the *oppressions* of the *Government*. The latter are virtues, yet have furnished more victims to the executioner than the former * * * The unsuccessful strugglers against tyranny have been the chief martyrs of treason laws in all countries. * * * Treasons, then, taking the *simulated* with the *real*, are sufficiently punished by exile." (Jefferson to Carmichael and Short, 1792. 1 Am. St. Pap. For. Rel., 258.)

In recent years there has been much discussion as to the nature of the crime committed in the assassination of the head of a government and of other public officials; whether it is to be put upon the footing of ordinary murder, or whether it shall be classed among those political offences which are exempt from extradition proceedings. Is it possible to make a distinction, as Mr. Jefferson suggests, between acts directed against tyranny, and those of a mere common-law character? Some such distinction has probably influenced statesmen in their dealings with the question of extradition. But as offences of this class have become more common and have invaded the dominions of the most liberal governments, public opinion would seem to be undergoing a change in regard to them.

Soon after the assassination of President Garfield, the United States Government entered into two treaties of extradition—that with Belgium of 1882, and that with Luxembourg of 1883—in which it is stipulated that "an attempt against the life of the head of a foreign government or against that of any member of his family, when such attempt comprises the act either of murder or assassination or of poisoning, shall not be considered a political offence or an act connected with such an offence." An extradition treaty between the United States and Russia, 1893, contains a similar clause.

By an agreement between the governments of Russia and Prussia in 1888, for the basis of an extradition convention, attempts against the life of the Emperor of Russia or the members of his family are to be considered as extraditable offences. And further, "the fact that the crime or offence, in respect whereof extradition is demanded, has been committed for a political object, shall in no case be a reason for refusing extradition." (Lowe's Life of Bismarck, II., 19.)

On this subject, see Moore's Extradition., I., 303–326.

SECTION 15.—JURISDICTION OF OFFENSES COMMITTED ABROAD.

CUTTING'S CASE, 1886.

(*Report on the Cutting Case, by J. B. Moore*, 1887.)

May the courts of a State take jurisdiction in the case of offenses against its citizens, committed by foreigners in foreign countries?

A. K. Cutting, a citizen of the United States, was arrested in Paso del Norte, Mexico, on the 23d of June, 1886, for the publication in Texas of a libel against a Mexican citizen. Cutting had been for some time a resident of Paso del Norte, engaged in editing a newspaper called *El Centinela*, in a recent number of which he had reflected upon the character of one Medina, a Mexican, who proposed to start a rival newspaper in the same town. For this publication Cutting was, at the instance of Medina, arrested, brought before a local court, and required to sign a "reconciliation," which is in the nature of a compromise or settlement between the parties, in consideration of which the party who feels himself aggrieved abandons penal proceedings. Cutting then had the following notice inserted in the *El Paso Herald*, in Texas:

"To Emigdio Medina, of El Paso del Norte:

"El Paso, Texas, June 18th, 1886.

"In a late issue of *El Centinela*, published in Paso del Norte, Mexico, I made the assertion that said Emigdio Medina was a 'fraud' and that the Spanish newspaper he proposed to issue in Paso del Norte was a scheme to swindle advertisers, etc. This morning said Medina took the matter to a Mexican court, and I was forced to sign a reconciliation.

"Now I do hereby reiterate my original assertion that said Emigdio Medina is a fraud and add 'dead beat' to the same. Also that his taking advantage of the Mexican law and forcing me to a 'reconciliation' was contemptible and cowardly and in keeping with the odorous reputation of said Emigdio Medina.

"And should said Medina desire American satisfaction for this reiteration, I will be pleased to grant him all he may desire, at any time, in any manner.

"A. K. CUTTING."

Article 186 of the Mexican Penal Code, under which Cutting was arrested, is as follows:

Penal offenses committed in a foreign country by a Mexican against Mexicans or foreigners, or by a foreigner against Mexicans, may be punished in the Republic (Mexico) and according to its laws, subject to the following conditions:

I. That the accused be in the Republic, whither he has come voluntarily or has been brought by extradition proceedings.

II. That, if the offended party be a foreigner, he shall have made proper legal complaint.

III. That the accused shall not have been definitively tried in the country where the offense was committed, or, if tried, that he shall not have been acquitted, included in an amnesty, or pardoned.

IV. That the breach of law of which he is accused shall have the character of a penal offense, both in the country in which it was committed and in the Republic.

V. That by the laws of the Republic the offense shall be subject to a severer penalty than that of "arresto mayor" (detention for from one to eleven months).

Notwithstanding the demand of the United States (July 19th) for the "instant release" of Cutting, "now unlawfully imprisoned at Paso del Norte," the court at that place proceeded to try Cutting; and on the 6th of August sentenced him to serve a year at hard labor and pay a fine of $600. On appeal to the supreme court of Chihuahua, that court on the 21st of August, fully approved the decision of the lower court; but the prisoner was released on the ground that the plaintiff having withdrawn from the prosecution of the suit, the principal motive of its continuance had ceased to exist, it appearing, moreover, that the withdrawal had "for its principal object the quieting of the alarm consequent upon his complaint."

The government of the United States then demanded an indemnity, for the imprisonment of Cutting; and further, requested of Mexico the abolishment or modification of the offensive article of her code. Mr. Bayard, Secretary of State, wrote: "This government is still compelled to deny, what it denied on the 19th of July, 1886, and what the Mexican government has since executively and judicially maintained, that a citizen of the United States can be held under the rules of International Law to answer in Mexico for an offense committed in the United States, simply because the object of that offense happened to be a citizen of Mexico. The government of Mexico has endeavored to sustain this pretension on two grounds: First that such a claim is justified by the rules of International Law and the positive legislation of various countries; and, secondly, on the ground that such a claim being made in the legislation of Mexico, the question is one solely for the decision of the Mexican tribunals." Again, "there is no principle better settled than that the penal laws of a country have no extraterritorial force. Each may, it is true, provide for the punishment of its own citizens for acts committed by them outside of its territory; but this makes the penal law a personal statute, and while it may give rise to inconvenience and injustice in many cases, it is a matter in which no other government has the right to interfere. To say, however, that the penal laws of a country can bind foreigners and regulate their conduct, either in their own or any other foreign country, is to assert a jurisdiction over such countries, and to impair their independence. Such is the *concensus* of opinion of the leading authorities on International Law at the present day."[1]

[1] *Jurisdiction of extraterritorial offenses.*—The position of the government of the United States in the *Cutting* case, that the Mexican law giving to its courts the jurisdiction of extraterritorial offenses, is contrary to custom and international law, and that the principles involved in it are practically obsolete in practice, would seem not to be borne out by facts. Aside from the question whether the common-law doctrine of territorial jurisdiction is the more expedient practical rule, it may at least be said that it is by no means so universally prevalent as to warrant the assertion that it has become a rule of international law. Not only are there many codes which go quite as far in the direction of extraterritorial jurisdiction as that of Mexico, but there is probably not a state which adheres strictly to the territorial theory. In the first place, practically, all states punish their own citizens for offenses of one kind or another committed in foreign countries. Even England punishes not only for treasonable acts, but also for bigamy, murder, and manslaughter committed abroad by her subjects. The laws of the United States, too, provide for the punishment of certain offenses committed abroad by their citizens. (Revised Statutes, § 5335; and see acts of Aug. 18, 1856, and Feb. 25, 1863).

Secondly, In regard to foreigners, there is a large number of codes which take jurisdiction of offenses against the state committed by them in foreign states; and a lesser number which go further, and extend their jurisdiction to offenses against individuals. Of this number, are Austria, Hungary, Italy, Norway, Sweden, Russia, Greece, and Brazil, as well as Mexico.

Again, there are many cases in the state courts of the United States, where acts, done by persons without the state but which take effect within the state, are held to be done by persons constructively within the state, and jurisdiction is assumed. Thus, if a man in one state fires a gun over the boundary line and kills a man in another state, he is triable in the latter state. (*United States* v. *Davis*, 2 Sumner, 482; *State* v. *Wyckoff*, 2 Vroom, N. J., 68; *Com.* v. *Macloon*, 101 Mass., 1). So, the author of a libel, uttered by him in one country, and published by others in another country, is triable in the latter country. (*Com.* v. *Blanding*, 3 Pickering (Mass.), 304; *R.* v. *Johnson*, 7 East., 65).

The *Cutting* case is similar to that of *Com.* v. *Blanding*, being a libel uttered in Texas, but being circulated and having its effect in Mexico; is the offense different in principle from that of wounding a man in one state by firing across the boundary from another state?

SECTION 16.—EXTRATERRITORIAL ACTS BY ORDER OF THE STATE.

McLEOD'S CASE, 1837.

(*Halleck's International Law*, I., 429.)

An individual is not to be held personally responsible for acts done by him in a foreign State by order of his government.

"During the disturbances in Upper Canada, in the winter of 1837, a steamboat called the 'Caroline,' belonging to an American owner, had been actively engaged in conveying arms and stores from the American side of the river to the Canadian rebels, who were in possession of Navy Island, and had been boarded in the night time by a party of Canadian Royalists, while she was lying within the jurisdiction of the territory of New York, set on fire, and sent down the stream, when she was precipitated over the falls of Niagara and dashed to pieces. An American citizen, named Durfee, was killed in the affray, and several others wounded.

"In the month of January, 1841, a British subject domiciled in Canada, named Alexander McLeod, was suddenly arrested while engaged in some business, within the territory of the State of New York, and thrown into prison by the authorities, on the charge of having been concerned in the destruction of the 'Caroline' and the alleged murder of Durfee.

"McLeod was, in the month of May, removed by *habeas corpus* from Lockport to New York, in the custody of the sheriff of Niagara County. Previously to this, the following note, dated March 12, 1841, was sent by Mr. Fox to Mr. Webster, the new American Secretary of State:—

"'Her Majesty's Government have had under consideration the subject of the arrest and imprisonment of Alexander McLeod, on a pretended charge of arson and murder; and I am directed to make known to the Government of the United States, that the British Government entirely approved of the course pursued by him. I am

Among jurists there is a wide difference of opinion in regard to the merits of the two systems—the "territorial" and the "personal" theories of jurisdiction. (T. E. Holland: Jurisprudence, 2d Ed., p. 318; F. Wharton: Philosophy of Criminal Law, p. 309, *et seq.*; L. Bar: *Private International Law*, Translation by G. R. Gillespie, p. 620 *et seq.*; Wharton's Conflict of Law, § 1810; "Case of A. K. Cutting, by the Minister of Foreign Relations of the Republic of Mexico," 1888.)

instructed to demand formally, and in the name of the British Government, the immediate release of Alexander McLeod, for the reason that the transaction was of a public character, planned and executed by persons duly authorized by the Colonial Government to take such measures as might be necessary for protecting the property and lives of Her Majesty's subjects; and being, therefore, an act of public duty, they cannot be held responsible to the laws and tribunals of any foreign country.'

"Mr. Webster, in his correspondence with Mr. Fox, the British minister, said that 'The Government of the United States entertains no doubt that, after the avowal of the transaction as a public transaction, authorized and undertaken by the British authorities, individuals concerned in it ought not, by the principles of public law and the general usage of civilized States, to be holden personally responsible in the ordinary tribunals of law for their participation in it. And the President presumes that it can hardly be necessary to say that the American people, not distrustful of their ability to redress public wrongs by public means, cannot desire the punishment of individuals when the act complained of is declared to have been an act of government itself. * * *

"'The indictment against McLeod is pending in a State court, but his rights, whatever they may be, are no less safe, it is to be presumed, than if he were holden to answer in one of the courts of this government. He demands impunity from personal responsibility, by virtue of the law of nations, and that law, in civilized States, is to be respected in all courts.'

"The Supreme Court of the State of New York (25 Wend. R., 483), held that a subject of a foreign State was liable to be proceeded against individually, and tried on an indictment in the criminal courts for arson and murder, notwithstanding the acts for which the indictment was made had been subsequently avowed by his government, and it, consequently, refused to discharge him from custody. The opinion of the court was delivered by Mr. Justice Cowen, and is of great length. So far as the question of national law is concerned, the opinion rests upon the proposition, that till war is declared by the war-making power, the officers or citizens of a foreign government, who enter our territory, are as completely obnoxious to punishment by our law as if they had been born and always resided in this country; that while two nations are at peace with each other, the acts of hostility by individuals must be regarded as private and not public acts, and that the courts will hold the parties individually responsible, notwithstanding the avowal of such acts by their government."

[McLeod was therefore put upon his trial, but the failure of the jury to convict him, on the evidence, put a practical termination to the matter. But to prevent the recurrence of such controversies in the future, by which the action of one of the States might jeopardize the foreign relations of the federal government, the act of August 29, 1842 (U. S. Stat. at Large, V., 539), was passed by Congress for bringing such cases, by writ of *habeas corpus*, under the cognizance of the courts of the United States at the inception of the proceedings.—F. S.]

SECTION 17.—EXTRATERRITORIAL ACTS BY A STATE, IN SELF-DEFENSE.

THE "CAROLINE," 1837.

(*Wharton's Digest*, § 50 c.)

A violation of foreign territory may be justified on the ground of the necessity of self-defense.

In 1837 an insurrectionary movement was made in Upper Canada, having in view a reform in the Government of that province. A proclamation had been issued from Navy Island, in the Niagara River, signed by William Lyon Mackenzie, chairman *pro tem.* of the provisional government, calling upon the reformers to make that island their place of rendezvous, and to aid otherwise in revolutionizing the province. It stated that the command of the forces was given to General Van Rensselaer, a son of General Solomon Van Rensselaer, of Albany. The sympathy manifested by some citizens of the United States with the Canadian insurgents, induced the governors of New York and Vermont to issue proclamations, warning the citizens of these states to refrain from any unlawful acts within the territory of the United States. Notwithstanding these proclamations, the insurgents were joined by citizens of the United States; whence also they received arms and munitions of war. The steamboat *Caroline* owned by an American citizen, was said to be engaged in transporting recruits and supplies to the rendezvous on Navy Island; and it was further presumed that this boat would be the means of transferring the expedition to the Canadian shore. Under these circumstances, the British officer in command determined to destroy the *Caroline*. A force was accordingly despatched for that purpose on the night of the 29th of December, 1837. Not finding her at Navy Island, the party proceeded to her moorings at

12

Schlosser on the American shore, attacked the crew, one of whom was killed, took the boat into the stream and left it to be carried over Niagara Falls. A proclamation was promptly issued (January 5, 1838), by President Van Buren, enjoining on all citizens obedience to the laws and warning them that the violation of our neutrality would subject the offenders to punishment. General Scott was forthwith ordered to the Canadian frontier to assume the military command there; and requisitions were made upon the Governors of New York and Vermont for such militia force as General Scott might require for the defense of the frontier.

On the other hand, the act was made a subject of complaint by the American government, on the ground of a violation of territory; but it was justified by Great Britain on the ground of the necessity of self-preservation.

The question remained unsettled till 1842, when Mr. Webster, in correspondence with Lord Ashburton, contended, that for such an infringement of territorial rights, the British government must show "a necessity of self-defense, instant, overwhelming, and leaving no choice of means and no moment for deliberation;" and it should further appear that the Canadian authorities, in acting under this exigence, "did nothing unreasonable or excessive, since the act, justified by the necessity of self-defense, must be limited by that necessity and kept clearly within it." Lord Ashburton admitted the correctness of Mr. Webster's doctrine, and asserted that the destruction of the *Caroline* came fully within its limits: and, though the act was justifiable, an apology for the violation of territory should have been made at the time. This was accepted by the United States as satisfactory, and the subject was allowed to drop. (Parliamentary Papers, 1843, lxi. 46–51; Wharton's Digest of International Law, I., § 50 *c*; Benton's Thirty Years in the Senate, II., 289, 455.)

SEIZURE OF SAINT MARK'S.

(1 *Wharton's Digest*, 224.)

Necessity justifies an invasion of foreign territory so as to subdue an expected assailant.

In 1815, under orders of Mr. Monroe, measures were taken for the destruction of a fort held by outlaws of all kinds on the Appalachicola River, then within the Spanish territory, from which parties had gone forth to pillage within the United States. The governor of Pensacola had been called upon to suppress the evil and punish the marauders, but had refused; and on his refusal, the Spanish territory was entered, and the fort attacked and destroyed on the ground of necessity.

General Jackson put his seizure and occupation of the fort at Saint Mark's, which was within Spanish territory, expressly on the ground of necessity. In his letter to the governor of Saint Mark's, he declared that the Spanish garrison, from its feebleness, would be unable to resist the attacks of Indians who intended to make it a base for their operations against the United States.

"To prevent the recurrence of so gross a violation of neutrality, and to exclude our savage enemies from so strong a hold as Saint Mark's, I deem it expedient to garrison that fortress with American troops until the close of the present war. This measure is justifiable on the immutable principles of self-defense, and cannot but be satisfactory, under existing circumstances, to his Catholic Majesty the King of Spain. Under existing treaties between the two governments, the King of Spain is bound to preserve in peace with the citizens of the United States, not only his own subjects, but all Indian tribes residing within his territory. When called upon to fulfill that part of the treaty in relation to a savage tribe who have long depredated with impunity on the American frontier, incompetency is alleged, with an acknowledgment that the same tribe have acted in open hostility to the laws, and invaded the rights of his Catholic Majesty. As a mutual enemy, therefore, it is expected that every facility will be afforded by the agents of the King of Spain to chastise these lawless and inhuman savages. In this light is the possession of Saint Mark's by the American forces to be viewed."[1]

THE "VIRGINIUS," 1873.

(*U. S. Foreign Relations*, 1874; *Parl. Papers*, 1874, *vol.* 76.)

Seizure, on the high seas, of a vessel carrying a foreign flag, on the ground of self-defense.

The *Virginius* was registered in the United States and carried the American flag; but, as it eventually appeared, she was really the property of certain Cuban insurgents, and was employed in aid of the rebellion in Cuba. On the 9th of July, 1873, she arrived at Kingston, Jamaica, and on the 23d of October she cleared ostensibly for

[1] The seizure of Amelia Island, in 1817, by authority of the government of the United States, was put upon similar ground. (1 Wharton's Digest, § 50 *a*.)

Limon Bay in Costa Rica, but really for the coast of Cuba. Being chased by a Spanish war-ship, she put into Port-au-Prince, Hayti. Thence she proceeded again to the coast of Cuba, and was again chased by a Spanish war-vessel the *Tornado* and was captured ten or fifteen miles from the coast of Jamaica, on the 31st of October. She was taken to Santiago de Cuba, where a court was assembled for the trial of the persons found on board—155 in number: Of these four were tried on the 3d of November, and shot on the 4th, thirty-seven on the 7th, and sixteen on the 8th. Among those executed were nine Americans and sixteen British subjects.

The government of the United States supposing that its rights on the high seas had been violated, demanded reparation. And by an agreement of the 29th of November, Spain stipulated to restore the *Virginius* and the survivors of the passengers and crew, and to salute the flag of the United States on the 25th of December following, unless Spain should in the meantime prove that the vessel was not entitled to carry said flag. The matter was submitted to the Attorney-General of the United States, who, after careful examination, reported on the 12th of December, that the registry of the *Virginius* was fraudulent, and that she had therefore no right to carry the American flag. But he added, "I am also of opinion that she was as much exempt from interference on the high seas by any other power, on that ground, as though she had been lawfully registered. Spain, no doubt, has a right to capture a vessel, with an American register, and carrying the American flag, found in her own waters assisting, or endeavoring to assist, the insurrection in Cuba, but she has no right to capture such a vessel on the high seas upon an apprehension that, in violation of the neutrality or navigation laws of the United States, she was on her way to assist said rebellion. Spain may defend her territory and people from the hostile attacks of what is, or appears to be an American vessel; but she has no jurisdiction whatever over the question as to whether or not such vessel is on the high seas in violation of any law of the United States." Spain having proved her point, the salute to the flag was dispensed with. The vessel was delivered to the United States authorities on the 16th of December, 1873; but on her way north, sank, off Cape Fear, on the 26th of that month.

Both the United States and England demanded reparation for the persons of their respective nationalities who had been executed by the captors of the *Virginius*; and this Spain eventually agreed to make. Even assuming that the vessel was lawfully seized, it was contended that there could be no justification of the summary execution of foreigners by order of a drum-head court-martial.

The position of the Attorney-General, that Spain had no right to capture such a vessel on the high seas, etc., has called forth much adverse criticism. Both Woolsey and Dana justified the capture at the time. "The register of a foreign nation," said Dana, "is not, and by the law of nations is not recognized as being, a national voucher and guaranty of national character to all the world, and nations having cause to arrest a vessel, would go behind such a document to ascertain the jurisdictional fact which gives character to the document, and not the document to the fact." It was the duty of the Spanish captain, says Woolsey, to defend the coasts of Cuba against a vessel which was known to be under the control of the insurgents, for which he had been on the lookout, and against which the only effectual security was capture on the high seas. (Woolsey's International Law, 6th Ed., pp. 368, 369).

In a pamphlet on the "Case of the *Virginius*," Mr. George Ticner Curtis took similar ground. "We rest the seizure of this vessel," he says, "on the great right of self-defense, which, springing from the law of nature, is as thoroughly incorporated into the law of nations as any right can be."

SECTION 18.—INJURY TO FOREIGNERS BY MOB VIOLENCE.

NEW ORLEANS RIOT, 1851.

(*2 Wharton's Digest*, 600.)

A State is not responsible for injuries to aliens, through civil commotions or mob violence which it is unable to control.

On the receipt of intelligence from Havana, in 1851, of the summary execution in Cuba of a number of American citizens, who had accompanied Lopez on his filibustering expedition to that island, riots immediately took place in New Orleans and Key West, directed against the Spanish residents of those cities. The Spanish consulate in New Orleans was attacked; and much injury was done to persons and property. For these injuries, the Spanish government demanded reparation from the government of the United States. To these demands, Mr. Webster, Secretary of State, replied, November 13, 1851, as follows :—

"The assembling of mobs happens in all countries; popular violences occasionally break out everywhere, setting law at defiance, trampling on the rights of citizens and private men, and sometimes on those of public officers, and the agents of foreign governments, especially entitled to protection. In these cases public faith and national honor require, not only that such outrages should be disavowed, but also that the perpetrators of them should be punished wherever it is possible to bring them to justice; and, further, that full satisfaction should be made in cases in which a duty to that effect rests with the government, according to the general principles of law, public faith, and the obligation of treaties. Mr. Calderon thinks that the enormity of this act of popular violence is heightened by its insult to the flag of Spain. The government of the United States would earnestly deprecate any indignity offered in this country in time of peace to the flag of a nation so ancient, so respectable, so renowned as Spain.

"It appears, however, that in point of fact no flag was actually flying or publicly exhibited when the outrage took place; but this can make no difference in regard to the real nature of the offense or its enormity. The persons composing the mob knew that they were offering insult and injury to an officer of Her Catholic Majesty, residing in the United States under the sanction of laws and treaties; and therefore their conduct admits of no justification. Nevertheless, Mr. Calderon and his government are aware that recent intelligence had then been received from Havana, not a little calculated to excite popular feeling in a great city, and to lead to popular excesses. If this be no justification, as it certainly is none, it may still be taken into view, and regarded as showing that the outrage, however flagrant, was committed in the heat of blood, and not in pursuance of any predetermined plan or purpose of injury or insult. * * *

"While this government has manifested a willingness and determination to perform every duty which one friendly nation has a right to expect from another, in cases of this kind, it supposes that the rights of the Spanish consul, a public officer residing here under the protection of the United States government, are quite different from those of the Spanish subjects who have come into the country to mingle with our own citizens, and here to pursue their private business and objects. The former may claim special indemnity, the latter are entitled to such protection as is afforded to our own citizens. While, therefore, the losses of individuals, private Spanish subjects, are greatly to be regretted, yet it is understood that many American citizens suffered equal losses from the same cause. And these private individuals, subjects of Her Catholic Majesty, coming voluntarily to reside in the United States, have certainly no cause of complaint, if they are protected by the same law and the same administration of law, as native born citizens of this country.

"They have in fact some advantages over the citizens of the State in which they happen to be, inasmuch as they are enabled, until they become citizens themselves, to prosecute for any injuries done to their persons or property in the courts of the United States, or the State courts, at their election.

"The President is of opinion, as already stated, that, for obvious reasons, the case of the consul is different, and that the government of the United States should provide for Mr. Laborde a just indemnity; and a recommendation to that effect will be laid before Congress, at an early period of its approaching session. This is all which it is in his power to do. The case may be a new one, but the President being of opinion that Mr. Laborde ought to be indemnified, has not thought it necessary to search for precedents."

It would appear, by the resolution of Congress, March 3, 1853, that Congress did not limit the indemnity to the losses incurred by the consul. The resolution is as follows:—

"Resolved, etc., That the President of the United States be, and is hereby, requested to cause an investigation to be made of any losses that may have been sustained by the consul of Spain and other persons residing at New Orleans or at Key West in the year eighteen hundred and fifty-one, and who at that time were subjects of the Queen of Spain, by the violence of individuals arising out of intelligence then recently received at those places of the execution of certain persons at Havana, in Cuba, by the Spanish authorities of that island, and that such losses so ascertained to persons at that time subjects as aforesaid, on the certificate of the Secretary of State that the same are proven to the satisfaction of the President, together with the reasonable costs of the investigation, shall be paid to those entitled out of any money in the Treasury not otherwise appropriated." [1]

[1] *The New Orleans Mob*, 1891.—The questions growing out of this New Orleans affair, in 1891, present some peculiar features; and forcibly illustrate certain defects, as regards the conduct of foreign relations, in the federal system of the United States.

The Chief of Police of New Orleans had been assassinated in a most dastardly manner; and strong suspicions of complicity in the murder rested on the members of an Italian society called the "Mafia." A number of Italians were finally arrested and put upon their trial, but in the end were acquitted by the jury. Believing that the jury had been tampered with, and that there was, in this case, a signal failure of justice, a public indignation meeting was held, which was attended by the better class of citizens; inflammatory addresses were made, and measures apparently adopted to take the matter out of the hands of the court. Accordingly, a mob assembled the next morning, and, as it would appear, without any protest from state or city governments, broke open the jail where the accused were still incarcerated, and shot or hanged a number of the suspected Italians. Among this

CHAPTER III.

JURISDICTION ON THE HIGH SEAS.

SECTION 19.—MERCHANT VESSELS.

THE "ATALANTA," 1856.

(8 *Opin. Att-Gen.*, 73.)

Merchant ships on the high seas are subject to the jurisdiction of the country of their flag.

In 1856, a case arose in reference to seamen, supposed not to be citizens of the United States, who, having committed a mutiny at

number were several who were not naturalised, and were, therefore, still citizens of Italy.

The President, by the Secretary of State, expressed regret for the occurrence and declared his purpose to lay the matter before Congress at its next session, and to recommend that an indemnity be granted to the families of the murdered men.

The Italian government was not satisfied with this position of the United States, but demanded further that the leaders of the mob be criminally prosecuted and punished according to law.

With this demand the government of the United States could not comply, however willing it might be to do so. It is well known that the federal courts have no common-law jurisdiction in criminal matters; it was impossible, therefore, to institute a criminal suit against these persons in those courts; and as the states are wholly independent of the Federal Government in respect of such jurisdiction, it was equally impossible to compel the government of the State of Louisiana to institute such proceedings. The government of the United States was therefore quite helpless in this aspect of the case, and could only listen to the complaints of Italy, and try to explain to her statesmen the intricacies of the United States constitution.

It is undoubtedly within the competence of Congress to confer upon the federal courts jurisdiction in this class of cases; but as yet it has not been done.

In regard to the merits of this case, it would seem that the United States should accept the responsibility as in fact they have done, for the acts of the mob. In the first place these persons were in the custody of the state government and for the purposes of international law, in that of the national government,—and therefore entitled to special protection. In the second place, there was no serious attempt sea, on board of the American vessel *Atalanta*, were brought back in the vessel to Marseilles, where, on the application of the consul of the United States, they were received and imprisoned by the local authorities on shore.

Six of them were afterwards on his application taken from prison and placed on board the *Atalanta* for conveyance to the United States under charge of crime. Then, with notice to the consul, but in spite of his remonstrances, the local authorities went on board of the *Atalanta*, forcibly resumed possession of the prisoners, and replaced them in confinement on shore. Mr. Mason, in a note of the 27th of June, 1856, says:

"It is the first instance, in which a vessel wearing the flag of the United States, lying in a French port, or a French ship lying in a port of the United States has, since the date of the treaty, been visited by police officers without the authority of the consul." (MS. Department of State.) The correspondence between the two governments having been submitted to the Attorney-General of the United States, he concurred in opinion with the American Minister, "that the local authority of Marseilles exceeded its lawful power in substance, as well as in form, and that there could be no conflict on the part of France with other powers on account of the nationality of the prisoners, for they were always in the constructive, if not in the actual, custody of the United States."

CASE OF JOHN ANDERSON.

Evarts, Sec. of State, to Welch, July 11, 1879.

(1 *Wharton's Digest*, 123, 125.)

An offense committed on an American merchant vessel on the high seas is exclusively within the jurisdiction of the courts of the United States, whatever be the nationality of the accused.

"I enclose herewith a copy of a dispatch recently received from

on the part of the proper authorities to quell the riot; and it is generally understood that a government is liable internationally for injuries done to "alien residents by a mob which by due diligence it could have suppressed."

The Italian government eventually withdrew the demand for the punishment of the actors in the affair, and accepted a money indemnity instead.

For other cases under the subject of this section, see 1 Wharton's Digest, pp. 473, 482–486; Calvo: Droit International, 4th Ed., vol. III., pp. 142–156. And see the case of *Don Pacifico*, *infra*, section 26, in which the claim for damages was enforced against Greece, on the ground that it was impossible to obtain justice through the ordinary channels—the courts.

A. C. Litchfield, Esq., consul-general of the United States at Calcutta, in relation to the case of one John Anderson, an ordinary seaman on board the American bark *C. O. Whitemore*, who, it appears, stabbed and killed the first officer of the ship on the 31st of January last, while that vessel was on her way from New York to Calcutta, sixteen days from her port of departure, and on the high seas in latitude 25° 35′ N. and longitude 35° 50′ W.

"You will perceive that the consul-general invoked the aid of the local police authorities in securing the safe custody of the accused, who was a prisoner of the United States, until he could complete the necessary arrangements for sending him to this country for trial, against whose municipal laws only he was accused of having offended, and that while thus in the temporary custody of the local police, the colonial authorities took judicial cognizance of the matter, claiming, under the advice of the advocate-general of the colony, that, under a colonial statute, which confers upon the courts of the colony jurisdiction of crimes committed by a British subject on the high seas, even though such crimes be committed on the ship of a foreign nation, and that inasmuch as the accused, although appearing on the ship's articles under the name of John Anderson, subject of Sweden, had declared that his real name was Alfred Hussey, and that he was a native of Liverpool and therefore a British subject, the case came within the jurisdiction of those courts.

"The matter is now believed to have reached that point in the judicial proceedings where effective measures for asserting the jurisdictional rights of the United States would be unavailable in this particular case. And whilst I entertain no doubt that the accused will receive as fair a trial in the high court of Calcutta, where it is understood he is to be tried, as he would in the circuit court of the United States, in which tribunal he would be arraigned were he sent here for trial, I deem it proper, at the same time to instruct you to bring the question to the attention of Her Majesty's Government, in order to have it distinctly understood that this case cannot be admitted by this Government as a precedent for any similar cases that may arise in the future. No principle of public law is better understood nor more universally recognized than that merchant vessels on the high seas are under the jurisdiction of the nation to which they belong, and that as to common crimes committed on such vessels while on the high seas, the competent tribunals of the vessels' nation have *exclusive* jurisdiction of the questions of trial and punishment of any person thus accused of the commission of a crime against its municipal laws; the nationality of the accused can have no more to do with the question of jurisdiction than it would had he committed the same crime within the geographical territorial limits of the nation against whose municipal laws he offends. The merchant ship, while on the high seas, is, as the ship of war everywhere, a part of the territory of the nation to which she belongs.

"I pass over the apparent breach of comity in the proceeding of the colonial officials as being rather the result of inadvertence and possible misconception on the part of the Government law officer of the colony, than any design to question the sovereignty of the United States in this or cases of a similar nature."

"I have to acknowledge the receipt of your dispatch No. 17, of the 16th ultimo, inclosing a copy of the correspondence between your legation and the foreign office in relation to the case of John Anderson, who was tried in Calcutta for a crime alleged to have been committed on board a vessel of the United States on the high seas, which correspondence contains an expression of the regret of Her Majesty's Government that the action of the authorities at Calcutta in the case in question, should have been governed by a view of the law which, in the opinion of Her Majesty's Government, cannot be supported.

"In reply I have to instruct you to convey to the proper quarter an expression of this Department's appreciation of the candor and goodwill with which Her Majesty's Government have considered this matter, and I say, moreover, that it has afforded this Government great satisfaction to learn that the action of the authorities of Calcutta in the case of Anderson is to be attributed to a misconception, and not to any design to question the jurisdiction of the United States in that or any similar case." (Mr. Hay to Mr. Lowell, July 7, 1880).

REGINA v. LESLEY.

Court for Crown Cases Reserved, 1860.

(*Bell's Crown Cases*, 220.)

The master of a British ship may detain Chilian outlaws on board his ship, against their will, while in Chilian waters, by agreement with the Chilian government; but he cannot lawfully transport them on the high seas under such agreement.

The prosecutor and others were Chilians who were banished by their government from Chili to England. The government of Chili hired the defendant to take the banished men to England in his vessel, then lying in the territorial waters of Chili. This plan was carried out and now the defendant is prosecuted for false imprisonment.

Judgment, by ERLE, C. J.:—"In this case the question is whether a conviction for false imprisonment can be sustained upon the following facts. (Stating substantially as above.)

"Then, can the conviction be sustained for that which was done within the Chilian waters? We answer no.

"We assume that in Chili the act of the government toward its subjects was lawful; and although an English ship in some respects carries with her the laws of her country in the territorial waters of a foreign state, yet in other respects she is subject to the laws of that state as to acts done to the subjects thereof.

"We assume that the government could justify all that it did within its own territory, and we think it follows that the defendant can justify all that he did there as agent for the government and under its authority.

"In *Dobree* v. *Napier*, 2 Bing. N. C., 781, the defendant, on behalf of the Queen of Portugal, seized the plaintiff's vessel for violating a blockade of a Portuguese port in time of war. The plaintiff brought trespass; and judgment was for the defendant, because the Queen of Portugal, in her own territory, had a right to seize the vessel and to employ whom she would to make the seizure; and therefore the defendant, though an Englishman seizing an English vessel, could justify the act under the employment of the Queen.

"We think that the acts of the defendant in Chili became lawful on the same principle, and that there is therefore no ground for the conviction.

"The further question remains, Can the conviction be sustained for that which was done out of the Chilian territory? and we think it can.

"It is clear that an English ship on the high sea, out of any foreign territory, is subject to the laws of England; and persons, whether foreign or English, on board such ship, are as much amenable to English law as they would be on English soil.

"In *Regina* v. *Sattler*, Dears. & Bell's C. C., 525, this principle was acted on, so as to make the prisoner, a foreigner, responsible for murder on board an English ship at sea. The same principle has been laid down by foreign writers on international law among which it is enough to cite Ortolan, 'Sur la Diplomatie de la Mer,' liv. 2, cap. 13.

"The merchant shipping Act, 17 & 18 Vict. C. 104, § 267, makes the master and seamen of a British ship responsible for all offences against property or person committed on the sea out of her Majesty's dominions as if they had been committed within the jurisdiction of the admiralty of England.

"Such being the law, if the act of the defendant amounted to a false imprisonment, he was liable to be convicted. Now, as the contract of the defendant was to receive the prosecutor and the others as prisoners on board his ship and to take them, without their consent, over the sea to England, although he was justified in first receiving them in Chili, yet that justification ceased when he passed the line of Chilian jurisdiction and after that it was a wrong which was intentionally planned and executed in pursuance of the contract, amounting in law to a false imprisonment.

"It may be that transportation to England is lawful by the law of Chili, and that a Chilian ship might so lawfully transport Chilian subjects; but for an English ship, the laws of Chili, out of the state, are powerless, and the lawfulness of the acts must be tried by English law.

"For these reasons, to the extent above mentioned, the conviction is affirmed."

THE "BELGENLAND."

SUPREME COURT OF THE UNITED STATES, 1884.

(114 *United States Reports*, 355.)

In a case arising out of the collision of two foreign ships, which afterwards arrive in an American port, the admiralty courts of the United States may take jurisdiction.

This case grew out of a collision in mid-ocean between the Norwegian barque *Luna* and the Belgian steamer *Belgenland*, in consequence of which the *Luna* was run down and sunk. Part of the crew of the *Luna*, including the captain, were rescued by the steamer and brought to Philadelphia. The captain at once libelled the *Belgenland*. The District Court decided in favor of the libellant, giving a verdict for $50,000.

The Circuit Court confirmed the verdict, and the libellee now appeals to the U. S. Supreme Court. Only so much of the case is given as refers to jurisdiction.

Mr. Justice BRADLEY delivered the opinion of the court, from which the following extracts are taken:

"* * * We shall content ourselves with inquiring what rule is followed by Courts of Admiralty in dealing with maritime causes arising between foreigners and others on the high seas.

"This question is not a new one in these courts. Sir William Scott had occasion to pass upon it in 1799. An American ship was taken by the French on a voyage from Philadelphia to London, and afterwards rescued by her crew, carried to England, and libelled for salvage; and the court entertained jurisdiction. The crew, however, though engaged in the American ship, were British born subjects, and weight was given to this circumstance in the disposition of the case. The judge, however, made the following remarks: 'But, it is asked, if they were American seamen, would this court hold plea of their demands? It may be time enough to answer this question whenever the fact occurs. In the meantime, I will say without scruple that I can see no inconvenience that would arise if a British court of justice was to hold plea in such a case; or conversely, if American courts were to hold pleas of this nature respecting the merits of British seamen on such occasions. For salvage is a question of *jus gentium*, and materially different from the question of a mariner's contract, which is a creature of the particular institutions of the country, to be applied and construed and explained by its own particular rules. There might be good reason, therefore, for this court to decline to interfere in such cases and to remit them to their own domestic forum; but this is a general claim, upon the general ground of *quantum meruit*, to be governed by a sound discretion, acting on general principles; and I can see no reason why one country should be afraid to trust to the equity of the courts of another on such a question of such a nature, so to be determined.' *The Two Friends*, 1 Ch. Rob., 271, 278.

"The law has become settled very much in accord with these views. That was a case of salvage; but the same principles would seem to apply to the case of destroying or injuring a ship, as to that of saving it. Both, when acted on the high seas between persons of different nationalities, come within the domain of the general law of nations, or *communis juris*, and are *prima facie* proper subjects of inquiry in any court of admiralty which first obtains jurisdiction of the rescued or offending ship at the solicitation in justice of the meritorious, or injured, parties.

"The same question of jurisdiction arose in another salvage case which came before this court in 1804, *Mason* v. *The Blaireau*, 2 Cranch, 240.

"There a French ship was saved by a British ship, and brought into a port of the United States; and the question of jurisdiction was raised by Mr. Martin, of Maryland, who, however, did not press the point, and referred to the observations of Sir William Scott in *The Two Friends*. Chief Justice MARSHALL, speaking for the court, disposed of the question as follows:—'A doubt has been suggested,' said he, 'respecting the jurisdiction of the court, and upon reference to the authorities, the point does not appear to have been ever settled. These doubts seem rather founded on the idea that upon principles of general policy, this court ought not to take cognizance of a case entirely between foreigners, than from any positive incapacity to do so. On weighing the considerations drawn from public convenience, those in favor of the jurisdiction appear much to overbalance those against it, and it is the opinion of this court, that, whatever doubts may exist in a case where the jurisdiction may be objected to, there ought to be none where the parties assent to it.' * * *

"In the absence * * * of treaty stipulations, however, the case of foreign seamen is undoubtedly a special one, when they sue for wages under a contract which is generally strict in its character, and framed according to the laws of the country to which the ship belongs; framed also with a view to secure, in accordance with those laws, the rights and interests of the ship-owners as well as those of master and crew, as well when the ship is abroad as when she is at home. Nor is this special character of the case entirely absent when foreign seamen sue the master of their ship for ill-treatment. On general principles of comity, Admiralty Courts of other countries will not interfere between the parties in such cases unless there is special reason for doing so, and will require the foreign consul to be notified, and, though not absolutely bound by, will always pay due respect to, his wishes as to taking jurisdiction.

"But, although the courts will use a discretion about assuming jurisdiction of controversies between foreigners in cases arising beyond the territorial jurisdiction of the country to which the courts belong, yet where such controversies are *communis juris*, that is, where they arise under the common law of nations, special grounds should appear to induce the court to deny its aid to a foreign suitor when it has jurisdiction of the ship or party charged. The existence of jurisdiction in all such cases is beyond dispute; the only question will be, whether it is expedient to exercise it. * * *

"In another case, Justice STORY examined the subject very fully, and came to the conclusion that, wherever there is a maritime lien on the ship, an Admiralty Court can take jurisdiction on the principle of the civil law, that in proceedings *in rem* the proper forum is the *locus rei sitæ*. He added: 'With reference, therefore, to what may be deemed the public law of Europe, a proceeding *in rem* may well be maintained in our courts where the property of a foreigner is within our jurisdiction. Nor am I able to perceive how the exercise of such judicial authority clashes with any principles of public policy.'

"That, as we have seen, was a case of bottomry, and Justice STORY in answer to the objection that the contract might have been entered into in reference to the foreign law, after showing that such law might be proven here, said: 'In respect to maritime contracts, there is still less reason to decline the jurisdiction, for in almost all civilized countries these are in general substantially governed by the same rules.'

"Justice Story's decision in this case was referred to by Dr. Lushington with strong approbation in the case of the *Golubchick* 1 W. Rob., 143, decided in 1840, and was adopted as authority for his taking jurisdiction in that case. * * *

"A Danish ship was sunk by a Bremen ship, and on the latter being libelled, the respondents entered a protest against the jurisdiction of the court. But jurisdiction was retained by Dr. LUSHINGTON who, amongst other things, remarked: 'An alien friend is entitled to sue (in our courts) on the same footing as a British-born subject, and if the foreigner in this case had been resident here, and the cause of action had originated *infra corpus comitatus*, no objection could have been taken. Reference being made to the observations of Lord Stowell in cases of seamen's wages, the judge said: 'All questions of collision are questions *communis juris;* but in case of mariners' wages, whoever engages voluntarily to serve on board a foreign ship, necessarily undertakes to be bound by the law of the country to which such ship belongs, and the legality of his claim must be tried by such law. One of the most important distinctions, therefore, respecting cases where both parties are foreigners is, whether the case be *communis juris* or not. * * * If these parties must wait until the vessel that has done the injury returned to its own country, their remedy might be altogether lost, for she might never return, and, if she did, there is no part of the world to which they might not be sent for their redress.'

"In the subsequent case of the *Griefswald*, 1 Swabey, 430, decided by the same judge in 1859, which arose out of a collision between a British barque and a Persian ship in the Dardanelles, Dr. LUSHINGTON said: 'In cases of collision, it has been the practice of this country, and, so far as I know, of the European States and of the United States of America, to allow a party alleging grievance by a collision to proceed *in rem* against the ship wherever found, and this practice, it is manifest, is most conducive to justice, because in very many cases a remedy *in personam* would be impracticable.'

"The subject has frequently been before our own Admiralty Courts of original jurisdiction, and there has been but one opinion expressed, namely, that they have jurisdiction in such cases, and that they will exercise it unless special circumstances exist to show that justice would be better subserved by declining it. * * *

"Indeed, where the parties are not only foreigners, but belong to different nations, and the injury or salvage service takes place on the high seas, there seems to be no good reason why the party injured, or doing the service, should ever be denied justice in our courts; neither party has any peculiar claim to be judged by the municipal law of his own country, since the case is pre-eminently one *communis juris*, and can generally be more impartially and satisfactorily adjudicated by the court of a third nation having jurisdiction of the *res* or parties, than it could be by the courts of either of the nations to which the litigants belong. As Judge DEADY very justly said, in a case before him in the district of Oregon: 'The parties cannot be remitted to a home forum, for, being subjects of different governments, there is no such tribunal. The forum which is common to them both by the *jus gentium* is any court of admiralty within the reach of whose process they may both be found.' *Bernhard* v. *Greene*, 3 Sawyer, 230, 235.

"As to the law which should be applied in cases between parties, or ships, of different nationalties, arising on the high seas, not within the jurisdiction of any nation, there can be no doubt that it must be the general maritime law, as understood and administered in the courts of the country in which the litigation is prosecuted."

SECTION 20.—MUNICIPAL SEIZURES BEYOND THE THREE-MILE LIMIT.

CHURCH v. HUBBART.

SUPREME COURT OF THE UNITED STATES, 1804.

(2 *Cranch*, 187.)

Held, that a State may seize foreign merchant vessels beyond a marine league from the coast, in order to enforce its navigation and revenue laws.

While the American vessel *Aurora* was between four and five leagues from the Brazilian coast she was seized by the government of Brazil for attempting to carry on illicit trade with its citizens.

Upon the controversy as to whether the government of Brazil had a right to seize a foreign vessel so situated, MARSHALL, C. J., says:

"* * * As a general principle, the nation which prohibits commercial intercourse with its colonies must be supposed to adopt measures to make that prohibition effectual. They must, therefore, be supposed to seize vessels coming into their harbors or hovering on their coasts in a condition to trade. * * *

"To reason from the extent of protection a nation will afford to foreigners to the extent of the means it may use for its own security does not seem to be perfectly correct. It is opposed by principles which are universally acknowledged. The authority of a nation within its own territory is absolute and exclusive. The seizure of a vessel within the range of its cannon by a foreign force is an invasion of that territory and is a hostile act, which it is its duty to repel. But its power to secure itself from injury may certainly be exercised beyond the limits of its territory. Upon this principle the right of a belligerent to search a neutral vessel on the high seas for contraband of war, is universally admitted, because the belligerent has a right to prevent the injury done to himself by the assistance intended for his enemy; so, too, a nation has a right to prohibit any commerce with its colonies. Any attempt to violate the laws made to protect this right, is an injury to itself which it may prevent, and it has a right to use the means necessary for its prevention. These means do not appear to be limited within any certain marked boundaries, which remain the same at all times and in all situations. * * *

"In different seas and on different coasts, a wider or more contracted range, in which to exercise the vigilance of the government of the country, will be assented to. Thus in the channel * * * the seizure of vessels on suspicion of attempting an illicit trade must necessarily be restricted to very narrow limits, but on the coast of South America, seldom frequented by vessels but for the purpose of illicit trade, the vigilance of the government may be extended somewhat further. * * *

"The right of the Spaniards was supposed to be exercised unreasonably and vexatiously, but it never was contended that it could only be exercised within the range of the cannon from their batteries. Indeed, the right given to our own revenue cutters, to visit vessels four leagues from our coast, is a declaration that in the opinion of the American government, no such principle as that contended for, has a real existence." [1]

[1] Mr. Dana, in speaking of this decision (Dana's Wheaton, p. 259, note), says, as to the assertion that the seizure of a vessel four leagues from the coast does not render the seizure invalid, "this remark must now be treated as an unwarranted admission. * * * It may be said that the principle is settled, that municipal seizures cannot be made, for any purpose, beyond territorial waters. It is also settled, that the limit of these waters is, in the absence of treaty, the marine league or the cannon-shot. It cannot now be successfully maintained, either that municipal visits and search may be made beyond the territorial waters for special purposes, or that there are different bounds of that territory for different objects. * * * In

SECTION 21.—PIRACY.

OPINION OF SIR LEOLINE JENKINS.

CHARGE TO THE JURY, 1668.

(*Life of Sir Leoline Jenkins*, I., 86.)

Definition and character of Piracy.

"There are some sorts of felonies and offences, which cannot be committed anywhere else but upon the sea, within the jurisdiction of the Admiralty. These I shall insist upon a little more particularly, and the chiefest in this kind is piracy.

"You are therefore to inquire of all Pirates and sea-rovers; they are in the eye of the law *hostes humani generis*, enemies not of one nation or of one sort of people only, but of all mankind. They are outlawed, as I may say, by the laws of all nations, that is, out of the protection of all princes and of all laws whatsoever. Everybody is commissioned, and is to be armed against them, as against rebels and traitors, to subdue and to root them out.

"That which is called robbing upon the highway, the same being done upon the water is called piracy. Now robbery, as 'tis dis-

the earlier cases, the courts were not strict as to standards of distance, where no foreign powers intervened in the causes. In later times, it is safe to infer that judicial as well as political tribunals will insist on a line of marine territorial jurisdiction for the exercise of force on foreign vessels in time of peace for all purposes alike."

There still stands upon the Statute Book of the United States a law passed in 1799 authorizing their revenue officers to stop and visit foreign vessels four leagues from the coast. The British "Hovering Act," passed in 1784, and which doubtless suggested the American Act, contained a similar provision. But this, says Mr. Boyd (Boyd's Wheaton, p. 241), has long since been repealed. "The present customs' legislation makes a distinction as regards the extent of jurisdiction claimed for revenue purposes, between ships belonging to British subjects and ships belonging to foreigners." There is no longer any authority under English laws to visit a foreign vessel beyond the three-mile limit. (See Customs Consolidations Act, 1876, Sec. 134.)

See further on this subject, the case of *Rose* v. *Himely*, 1808, 4 Cranch, 241, in which the Supreme Court of the United States held that a seizure, under customs' regulations, of a foreign vessel beyond the territorial waters of a State was not valid. See also, the case of *Hudson* v. *Guestier*, 1810, 6 Cranch, 281.

tinguished from thieving or larceny, implies not only the actual taking away of my goods, while I am, as we say, in peace, but also the putting me in fear, by taking them away by force and arms out of my hands, or in my sight and presence; when this is done upon the sea, without a lawful commission of war or reprisals, it is down-right piracy.

"And such was the generosity of our ancient English, such the abhorrence of our laws against pirates and sea-rovers, that if any of the King's subjects robbed or murdered a foreigner upon our seas or within our ports, though the foreigner happened to be of a nation in hostility against the King, yet if he had the King's passport, or the Lord Admiral's, the offender was published, not as a felon only, but this crime was made high treason, in that great Prince Henry the Fifth's time; and not only himself, but all his accomplices were to suffer as traitors against the crown and dignity of the King."

UNITED STATES v. SMITH.

SUPREME COURT OF THE UNITED STATES, 1820.

(5 *Wheaton*, 153.)

The Constitution of the United States confers upon Congress the power to "define and punish piracies." In legislating upon the subject—acts of 1790 and 1819—Congress, instead of defining piracy, merely referred to the offense of piracy, "as defined by the law of nations."

***Held*, that this definition was sufficient to meet the requirements of the Constitution.**

This was an indictment for piracy against the prisoner Thomas Smith, before the circuit court of Virginia, under the act of Congress, of the 3d of March, 1819, c. 76, which provides (s. 5) "That if any person or persons whatsoever, shall, on the high seas, commit the crime of piracy, *as defined by the law of nations*, and such offender or offenders shall afterwards be brought into, or found in, the United States, every such offender or offenders shall, upon conviction thereof, before the circuit court of the United States for the district into which he or they may be brought, or in which he or they shall be found, be punished with death."

The jury found a special verdict as follows: "We, of the jury, find, that the prisoner, Thomas Smith, in the month of March, 1819, and others, were part of the crew of a private armed vessel, called the Creollo (commissioned by the government of Buenos Ayres, a colony then at war with Spain), and lying in the port of Margaritta;

that in the month of March, 1819, the said prisoner and others of the crew mutinied, confined their officers, left the vessel, and in the said port of Margaritta, seized by violence a vessel called the Irresistible, a private armed vessel, lying in that port, commissioned by the government of Artegas, who was also at war with Spain ; that the said prisoner and others, having so possessed themselves of the said vessel, the Irresistible, appointed their officers, proceeded to sea on a cruise, without any documents or commission whatever; and while on that cruise, in the month of April, 1819, on the high seas, committed the offence charged in the indictment, by the plunder and robbery of the Spanish vessel therein mentioned. If the plunder and robbery aforesaid be piracy under the act of the Congress of the United States, entitled, 'An act to protect the commerce of the United States, and punish the crime of piracy,' then we find the said prisoner guilty; if the plunder and robbery, above stated, be not piracy under the said act of Congress, then we find him, not guilty."

The circuit court divided on the question, whether this be piracy as defined by the law of nations, so as to be punishable under the act of Congress, of the 3d of March, 1819, and thereupon the question was certified to this court for its decision.

Mr. Justice STORY, delivered the opinion of the court:—"The act of Congress upon which this indictment is founded provides, that if any person or persons whatsoever, shall, upon the high seas, commit the crime of piracy, as defined by the law of nations, and such offender or offenders shall be brought into, or found in the United States, every such offender or offenders shall, upon conviction thereof, etc., be punished with death.

"The first point made at the bar is, whether this enactment be a constitutional exercise of the authority delegated to Congress upon the subject of piracies. The Constitution declares, that Congress shall have power 'to define and punish piracies and felonies, committed on the high seas, and offences against the law of nations.' The argument which has been urged in behalf of the prisoner is, that Congress is bound to define, in terms, the offence of piracy, and is not at liberty to leave it to be ascertained by judicial interpretation. If the argument be well founded, it seems admitted by the counsel that it equally applies to the 8th section of the act of Congress of 1790, ch. 9, which declares, that robbery and murder committed on the high seas shall be deemed piracy; and yet, notwithstanding a series of contested adjudications on this section, no doubt has hitherto been breathed of its conformity to the Constitution.

"In our judgment, the construction contended for proceeds upon too narrow a view of the language of the Constitution. The power given to Congress is not merely 'to define and punish piracies;' if it were, the words 'to define,' would seem almost superfluous, since the power to punish piracies would be held to include the power of ascertaining and fixing the definition of the crime. And it has been very justly observed, in a celebrated commentary, that the definition of piracies might have been left without inconvenience to the law of nations, though a legislative definition of them is to be found in most municipal codes. But the power is also 'given to define and punish felonies on the high seas, and offences against the law of nations.' The term 'felonies,' has been supposed in the same work, not to have a very exact and determinate meaning in relation to offences at the common law committed within the body of a country. However this may be, in relation to offences on the high seas, it is necessarily somewhat indeterminate, since the term is not used in the criminal jurisprudence of the admiralty in the technical sense of the common law. Offences, too, against the law of nations, cannot, with any accuracy, be said to be completely ascertained and defined in any public code recognized by the common consent of nations. In respect, therefore, as well to felonies on the high seas as to offences against the law of nations, there is a peculiar fitness in giving the power to define as well as to punish; and there is not the slightest reason to doubt that this consideration had very great weight in producing the phraseology in question.

"But, supposing Congress were bound in all the cases included in the clause under consideration to define the offence, still there is nothing which restricts it to a mere logical enumeration in detail of all the facts constituting the offence. Congress may as well define by using a term of a known and determinate meaning, as by an express enumeration of all the particulars included in that term. That is certain which is by necessary reference made certain. When the act of 1790 declares, that any person who shall commit the crime of robbery, or murder, on the high seas, shall be deemed a pirate, the crime is not less clearly ascertained than it would be by using the definitions of these terms as they are found in our treatises of the common law. In fact, by such a reference, the definitions are necessarily included, as much as if they stood in the text of the act. In respect to murder, where 'malice aforethought' is of the essence of the offence, even if the common-law definition were quoted in express terms, we should still be driven to deny that the definition was perfect, since the meaning of 'malice aforethought' would remain to be gathered from the common law. There would then be no end to our difficulties, or our definitions, for each would involve some terms which might still require some new explanation. Such a construction of the Constitution is, therefore, wholly inadvisable. To define piracies, in the sense of the Constitution, is merely to enumerate the crimes which shall constitute piracy; and this may be done, either by a reference to crimes having a technical name, and determinate extent, or by enumerating the acts in detail, upon which the punishment is inflicted.

"It is next to be considered, whether the crime of piracy is defined by the law of nations with reasonable certainty. What the law of nations on this subject is, may be ascertained by consulting the works of jurists, writing professedly on public law; or by the general usage and practice of nations; or by judicial decisions recognizing and enforcing that law. There is scarcely a writer on the law of nations, who does not allude to piracy as a crime of a settled and determinate nature; and whatever may be the diversity of definitions in other respects all writers concur, in holding that robbery, or forcible depredations upon the sea, *animo furandi*, is piracy. The same doctrine is held by all the great writers on maritime law, in terms that admit of no reasonable doubt.

"The common law, too, recognizes and punishes piracy as an offence, not against its own municipal code but as an offence against the law of nations (which is part of the common law), as an offence against the universal law of society, a pirate being deemed an enemy of the human race. Indeed, until the statute of 28th of Henry VIII., ch. 15, piracy was punished in England only in the admiralty as a civil law offence; and that statute, in changing the jurisdiction, has been universally admitted not to have changed the nature of the offence. Sir Charles Hedges, in his charge at the admiralty sessions, in the case of *Rex* v. *Dawson*, 5 State Trials, declared in emphatic terms that 'piracy is only a sea term for robbery, piracy being a robbery committed within the jurisdiction of the admiralty.' Sir Leoline Jenkins, too, on a like occasion, declared that 'a robbery, when committed upon the sea, is what we call piracy;' and he cited the civil-law writers, in proof.

"And it is manifest from the language of Sir William Blackstone, 4 Bl. Comm., 73, in his comments on piracy, that he considered the common law definition as distinguishable in no essential respect from that of the law of nations. So that, whether we advert to writers on the common law, or the maritime law, or the law of nations, we shall find that they universally treat of piracy as an offence against the law of nations, and that its true definition by that law is robbery upon the sea. And the general practice of all nations in punishing all persons, whether natives or foreigners, who have committed this offence against any persons whatsoever, with whom they are in amity, is a conclusive proof that the offence is supposed to depend, not upon the particular provisions of any municipal code, but upon the law of nations, both for its definition and punishment. We have, therefore, no hesitation in declaring that piracy, by the law of nations, is robbery upon the sea, and that it is sufficiently and constitutionally defined by the fifth section of the act of 1819.

"Another point has been made in this case, which is, that the special verdict does not contain sufficient facts upon which the court can pronounce that the prisoner is guilty of piracy. We are of a different opinion. The special verdict finds that the prisoner is guilty of the plunder and robbery charged in the indictment; and finds certain additional facts from which it is most manifest that he and his associates were, at the time of committing the offence, freebooters upon the sea, not under the acknowledged authority, or deriving protection from the flag or commission of any government. If, under such circumstances, the offence be not piracy, it is difficult to conceive any which would more completely fit the definition.

"It is to be certified to the Circuit Court, that upon the facts stated, the case is piracy, as defined by the law of nations, so as to be punishable under the act of Congress of the 3d of March, 1819."

Mr. Justice LIVINGSTONE dissented, on the ground that the act of Congress did not contain such a definition of piracy as the Constitution requires.

UNITED STATES v. THE "AMBROSE LIGHT."

U. S. DISTRICT COURT FOR SO. DIST. OF N. Y., 1885.

(25 *Federal Reporter*, 408.)

Held, by District Court, Judge Brown, that a vessel found on the high seas in the hands of insurgents who have not been recognized as belligerents by any independent nation, may be regarded as piratical.

The libel in this case was filed to procure the condemnation of the brig *Ambrose Light*, which was brought into this port as prize on June 3, 1885, by Lieut. Wright and a prize crew, detached from the United States gun-boat *Alliance*, under Commander Clarke, by whose orders the brigantine had been seized on the twenty-fourth of April. The seizure was made in the Caribbean sea, about twenty miles to the westward of Cartagena.

The commander was looking for the insurgent Preston, by whose order Colon had shortly before been fired, to the great loss and injury of our citizens.

Observing the brigantine displaying a strange flag, viz., a red cross on a white ground, he bore down upon her, and brought her to by a couple of shots across her bows. Before coming to, she exhibited the Colombian flag. On examination, some sixty armed soldiers were found concealed below her decks, and one cannon was aboard, with a considerable quantity of shot, shell, and ammunition. Preston was not found. Her papers purported to commission her as a Colombian man-of-war, and read as follows: (Translation.)

"I, Pedroa Lara, governor of the province of Barranquilla, in the state of Bolivia, in the United States of Colombia, with full powers conferred by the citizen president of the state, I give to whom it may concern this *patente* of the sailing vessel *Ambrose Light*, that she may navigate as a Colombian vessel-of-war in the waters touching the coast of this republic, in the Atlantic ocean.

"Therefore, the general commandants and captains of the vessels of war of the friendly nations of Colombia are requested to give this vessel all the consideration that by right belongs to the vessels of the class of the *Ambrose Light* of all civilized nations. In the faith of which we have given these presents, and signed with rubric with the secretary of my office, in the city of Barranquilla, on the eighteenth day of the month of April, 1885.

(Signed) "Pedroa Lara

The Secretary [Sig.], "R. A. Del Valle.

(Indorsed:) "Office of the Military,

"Barranquilla, April 18, 1885.

"Registered and noted in folio and book, respectively.

"The General in Chief, N. Juneno Collante.

"Adjutant and Secretary, A. Solanom."

Believing this commission to be irregular, and to show no lawful authority to cruise as a man-of-war on the high seas, Commander Clarke reported her under seizure, in accordance with the naval regulations, to Admiral Jowett, commanding the North Atlantic squadron, then cruising in the Central American waters, and the admiral directed the vessel to be taken to New York for adjudication as prize. The vessel was at first supposed to belong to citizens of the United States. The proofs showed that she had been sold to, and legally belonged to, Colente, one of the chief military leaders of the insurgents at Barranquilla. None of her officers or crew were citizens of the United States. She was engaged upon a hostile expedition against Cartagena, and designed to assist in the blockade and siege of that port by the rebels against the established government of the United States of Colombia. She had left Sabanilla on April 20th, bound for Baru, near Cartagena, where she expected the soldiers aboard to disembark. She was under the orders of the colonel of the troops, whose instructions were to shoot the captain if disobedient to his orders. Further instructions were to fight any Colombian vessel not showing the white flag with a red cross.

Sabanilla, and a few other adjacent sea-ports, and the province of Barranquilla, including the city of Barranquilla, had been for some months previous, and still were, under the control of the insurgents. The proofs did not show that any other depredations or hostilities were intended by the vessel than such as might be incident to the struggle between the insurgents and the government of Colombia, and to the so-called blockade and siege of Cartagena.

As respects any recognition of the insurgents by foreign powers, it did not appear in evidence that up to the time of the seizure of the vessel, on April 24, 1885, a state of war had been recognized as existing, or that the insurgents had ever been recognized as a *de facto* government, or as having belligerent rights, either by the Colombian government, or by our own government, or by any other nation. The claimants introduced in evidence a diplomatic note from our Secretary of State to the Colombian minister, dated April 24, 1885, which, it was contended, amounted to a recognition by implication of a state of war. The government claimed the forfeiture of the ship as piratical, under the law of nations, because she was not sailing under the authority of any acknowledged power. The claimants contended that, being actually belligerent, she was in no event piratical by the law of nations; but if so, that the subsequent recognition of belligerency by our government by implication entitles her to a release.

Judgment.—Brown, J., (extracts): —"6. That recognition by at least some established government of a 'state of war,' or of the belligerent rights of insurgents, is necessary to prevent their cruisers from being held legally piratical by the courts of other nations injuriously affected, is either directly affirmed, or necessarily implied from many adjudged cases; and I have found no adjudication in which a contrary view is even intimated.

"This great weight of authority, drawn from every source that authoritatively makes up the law of nations, seems to me fully to warrant the conclusion that the public vessels of war of all nations, for the preservation of the peace and order of the seas, and the security of their own commerce, have the *right* to seize as piratical all vessels carrying on, or threatening to carry on, unlawful private warfare to their injury; and that privateers, or vessels of war, sent out to blockade ports, under the commissions of insurgents, unrecognized by the government of any sovereign power, are of that character, and derive no protection from such void commissions.

"It thus appears that the rules laid down and implied in the decisions of our supreme court in the cases of *Rose* v. *Himely* and *U. S.* v. *Palmer*, nearly 70 years ago, have been since almost universally followed. The practical responsibility of determining whether insurgent vessels of war shall be treated as lawful belligerents, or as piratical, rests where the supreme court then in effect decided that it ought to rest, viz., with the political and executive departments of the government. These departments have it in their power, at any moment, through the granting or withholding of recognition of belligerency, and through the extent of such recognition as they may choose to accord, virtually to determine how such cruisers shall be treated by the courts.

"Even after judgment and sentence the prisoners may, like Smith and his associates, convicted before Mr. Justice Grier, be treated, and exchanged, as prisoners of war. And it is with those departments, exclusively, that the discretion ought to rest to determine when and how its technical rights against rebel cruisers shall be enforced. Its naval regulations will be framed accordingly; and any seizures made under such regulations may be enforced, or at any moment remitted, at the pleasure of those departments.

"Where insurgents conduct an armed strife for political ends, and avoid any infringement or menace of the rights of foreign nations on the high seas, the modern practice is, in the absence of treaty stipulations or other special ties, to take no notice of the contest. One of the earliest applications of this rule that I have met is in the answer of the states-general to Sir Josèph York's demand in 1779 for the surrender of Paul Jones' prizes as piratically captured, in which their Mightinesses say that 'they had for a century past strictly observed the maxim that they will in no respect presume to judge of the legality or illegality of the actions of those who, upon the open sea, have taken any vessels that do not belong to this country.' On this point Prof. Lawrence, in his recent Hand-book of Int. Law (London, 1884), says:

"'When a community, not being a state in the eye of international law, resorts to hostilities, it may, in respect of war, be endowed with the rights and subjected to the obligations of a state if other powers accord it what is called recognition of belligerency. Neutral powers should not do this * * * unless it affect by the struggle the interests of the recognizing state. If the struggle is maritime, recognition is almost a necessity. The controversy of 1861 illustrates the whole question.'

"The practice is stated by Hall as follows: 'When, however, piratical acts have a political object, and are directed solely against a particular state, it is not the practice for states other than that attacked to seize, and still less to punish, the persons committing them. It would be otherwise, so far as seizure is concerned, with respect to vessels manned by persons acting with a political object, if the crew, in the course of carrying out their object, committed acts of violence against ships of other states than that against which their political operation was aimed; and the mode in which the crew were dealt with would probably depend on the circumstances of the case.' Int. Law, § 81, p. 223.

"Whether a foreign nation shall exercise its rights only when its own interests are immediately threatened, or under special provocations only after injuries inflicted by the insurgents, as in this case, at Colon, is a question purely for the executive department. But when a seizure has been made by the navy department, under the regulations, and the case is prosecuted before the court by the government itself, claiming *summum jus*,—its extreme rights—the court is bound to apply to the case the strict technical rules of international law. The right here asserted may be rarely enforced; the very knowledge that the right exists tends, effectually, in most cases, to prevent any violation of it, or at least any actual interference by insurgents with the rights of other nations. But if the right itself were denied, the commerce of all nations would be at the mercy of every petty contest carried on by irresponsible insurgents and marauders under the name of war.

"In the absence of any recognition of these insurgents as belligerents, I therefore hold the *Ambrose Light* to have been lawfully seized, as bound upon an expedition technically piratical."[1]

[On the other ground, however, that the Secretary of State, by his note to the Colombian Minister, April 24, 1885, had recognized by implication a state of war, the vessel was released.]

[1] The judgment in the case of the *Ambrose Light* has called forth much adverse criticism; and on the whole the weight of opinion would seem to be against the position, that insurgent vessels not molesting the ships of other nations may be treated as pirates. See a criticism of this case by Mr. Francis Wharton, in 3 Wharton's Digest, 469.

In the case of *United States* v. *Baker*, 1861, 5 Blatch., 6, Judge NELSON charged the jury that "if it were necessary on the part of the government to bring the crime charged against the prisoners (officers of the privateer *Savannah*, within the definition of robbery and piracy as known to the common law of nations, there would be great difficulty in so doing, perhaps, upon the counts, certainly upon the

THE MAGELLAN PIRATES.

ECCL. AND ADM. COURT, 1853.

(1 *Spinks' Eccl. & Adm. Rep.*, 81.)

Insurgents may become, by depredations against third powers, pirates as well as insurgents.

LUSHINGTON, J. (extract):—

"I apprehend that in the administration of our criminal law, generally speaking, all persons are held to be pirates who are found guilty of piratical acts, and piratical acts are robbery and murder upon the high seas. I do not believe that, even where human life was at stake, our courts of common law ever thought it necessary to extend their inquiry further, if it was clearly proved against the accused that they had committed robbery and murder upon the high seas. In that case they were adjudged to be pirates, and suffered accordingly. * * * It was never, so far as I am able to find, deemed necessary to inquire whether the parties so convicted had intended to rob or to murder on the high seas indiscriminately. Though the municipal law of different countries may and does differ in many respects as to its definition of piracy, yet I apprehend that all nations agree in this, that acts such as those which I have mentioned, when committed on the high seas, are piratical acts, and contrary to the

evidence. For that shows, if anything, an intent to depredate upon the vessels and property of one nation only, the United States, which falls far short of the spirit and intent which are said to constitute the essential elements of the crime. But the robbery charged in this case is that which the act of Congress (1820) describes as a crime, and may be denominated a statute offence as contra-distinguished from that known to the law of nations. The act declares the person a pirate, punishable by death, who commits the crime of robbery upon the high seas, against any ship or vessel, etc." The jury did not agree in this case. But in Philadelphia four individuals were convicted for the same offence.—These arrests led to retaliatory action on the part of the Confederate States. And on the 31st of January, 1862, an order was issued by the Secretary of State, to the marshals, directing the transfer of all prisoners charged with piracy, including those who had been convicted at Philadelphia, to a military prison for the purpose, it was understood, of exchanging them as prisoners of war. (Lawrence's Wheaton, 1863, p. 253, note; 3 Wharton's Digest, p. 465., For other judicial decisions touching the status of the rebels in the civil war in the United States, see the Golden Rocket cases—viz., *Dole* v. *The N. E. M. M. Ins. Co.*, 1 Allen, 392; and same in U. S. Circuit Court for Massachusetts; in which it was held that the rebels in that war were not pirates *jure gentium*.

law of nations. * * * I think it does not follow that, because persons who are rebels and insurgents may commit against the ruling powers of their own country acts of violence, they may not be, as well as insurgents and rebels, pirates also; pirates for other acts committed towards other persons. It does not follow that rebels and insurgents may not commit piratical acts against the subjects of other States, especially if such acts were in no degree with the insurrection or rebellion. Even an independent State may, in my opinion, be guilty of piratical acts. What were the Barbary tribes of olden times ? what are many of the African tribes at this moment? It is, I believe, notorious that tribes now inhabiting the African coast of the Mediterranean will send out their boats and catch any ships becalmed upon their coasts ?

"Are they not pirates because, perhaps, their sole livelihood may not depend upon piratical acts? I am aware that it has been said that a State cannot be piratical, but I am not disposed to assent to such *dictum* as a universal proposition."

THE "MONTEZUMA," 1877.

(Calvo: Droit International, 4th Ed., I., 591.)

Ships belonging to insurgents, and confining their hostile acts to the parent government, are not to be treated as pirates by foreign powers.

"Le vapeur *Montezuma*, dans l'origine navire marchand espagnol, passé au service de l'insurrection cubaine, se trouvait dans un cas analogue à celui du *Porteña*.

"Au commencement de 1877, ce navire étant parvenu dans les eaux de Cuba ou dans le voisinage, des insurgés de cette île, qui se trouvaient à bord comme passagers, s'en emparèrent, lui donnèrent le nom du *Cespedes;* puis, ayant arboré le pavillon cubain, ils l'employèrent à attaquer les navires marchands de l'Espagne dans le Rio de la Plata.

"Le légation d'Espagne à Rio de Janeiro, demanda au gouvernement brésilien que, si le *Montezuma* arrivait dans quelque port de l'Empire, il fût traité comme pirate et soumis à toute la rigueur des lois. En réponse à cette demande, le baron de Cotejipe, ministre des affaires étrangères du Brésil, adressa, le 12 janvier, la dépêche suivante à M. de Estefani, chargé d'affaires d'Espagne :

"'Le gouvernement de Sa Majesté Catholique peut soumettre le *Montezuma* à toute la rigueur de ses lois comme pirate. Personne ne lui déniera ce droit; mais le gouvernement impérial, qui est étranger à la question de l'île de Cuba, ne se trouve pas obligé d'agir de la même façon; et en refusant de le faire il suit une règle généralement admise, qui est la première à laquelle il doive se conformer dans la question actuelle. Comme preuve de ce que je dis et sans appliquer le principe au cas de l'île précitée, qu'il me soit permis de signaler que tout gouvernement qui n'est pas intéressé dans une insurrection, a dans de certaines circonstances la faculté de reconnaître aux insurgés le caractère de belligérants.

"'Il n'est pas douteux que l'île de Cuba soit en état de rébellion et que les individus qui se sont emparés du *Montezuma*, soient des insurgés de cette île. Cette circonstance à laquelle M. de Estefani lui-même fait allusion dans sa première note suffit pour donner au fait de ces individus la signification politique qui leur méconnaît dans sa seconde. Bien plus M. de Estefani dit que les insurgés destinaient le vapeur à attaquer les navires marchands de l'Espagne dans le Rio de la Plata; d'où il resulte, le cas étant bien examiné, que ces insurgés paraissent être des agents politiques agissant dans des fins politiques.

"Les pirates, à proprement parler, sont ceux qui courent les mers pour leur propre compte, *sans autorisation compétente*, dans le but de s'emparer de force des navires qu'ils rencontrent, en commettant des déprédations contre toutes les nations indistinctement. Cette définition ne peut certainement s'appliquer à ceux qui ont pris le *Montezuma*. A cela s'opposent les arguments mêmes mis en avant par la législation de Sa Majesté Catholique. Les hostilités qu'elle dénonce et prévoit ne sont pas dirigées contre toutes les nations, mais uniquement contre l'Espagne; elles n'ont pas pour but de commettre des déprédations, mais d'aider la cause d'une colonie en insurrection.

"'C'est pour ces considérations, qui me paraissent concluantes, que le gouvernement impérial ne se croit pas autorisé à ordonner la saisie du vapeur; et en admettant qu'il s'y déterminât, les tribunaux, envisageant le cas sous un autre aspect, ne se jugeraient pas compétents, parce que ledit acte aurait été accompli sur un navire espagnol par des individus qui se trouvaient à bord ou dans des eaux qui n'étaient pas brésiliennes.

"'On ne saurait invoquer le traité d'extradition entre le Brésil et l'Espagne. Le chargé d'affaires ne demande pas qu'on livre les gens qui ont pris le *Montezuma*, mais qu'on les punisse au Brésil. Le traité n'éclaircit donc pas la question et ne fournit point d'arguments contre la décision du gouvernement espagnol.

"'M. de Estefani ne se juge pas compétent pour apprécier l'analogie qui peut exister entre le cas du *Montezuma* et celui d'autres navires. Je me permettrai de lui rappeler que l'analogie entre le *Montezuma* et le *Porteña* est compléte. Tous les deux, etrangers au Brésil et naviguant dans des eaux qui ne sont pas brésiliennes, ont été pris par des individus qui étaient à bord comme passagers et servaient d'agents aux insurgés. S'il y a une différence, c'est celle qui provient de la durée de la lutte dans la province argentine et dans la colonie espagnole.

"'Le gouvernement impérial respecte les principes acceptés par les nations civilisées; c'est pourquoi il ne croit pas de son devoir de consentér à la demande de la légation d'Espagne.'"

THE "HUASCAR," 1877.

(3 *Wharton's Digest*, p. 474.)

Rebels of one State may be treated as pirates by other States, if they extend their hostile acts to the ships or citizens of the latter States.

"The crew of the Peruvian monitor, the *Huascar*, anchored at Callao, revolted on May 6, 1877, and declared for the insurgent government of Pierola. The *Huascar* proceeded to sea without opposition from other Peruvian vessels in the harbor. On May 8 the titular government of Peru issued a decree calling the crew of the *Huascar* 'rebels,' and authorizing her capture (and stating further that the Peruvian government would not be responsible for the acts of the *Huascar*.) The *Huascar* then stopped several British vessels, taking out of one of them two officers who were going to Peru to enter government service. The British admiral on these coasts being advised of these proceedings, and also of the seizure of certain lighters of coal belonging to British subjects, sent the *Shah*, a British cruiser, to sea to seize the *Huascar*. An engagement took place, which was only partially successful, the *Huascar* ultimately eluding her assailant. The *Huascar* subsequently surrendered to Peru, and Peru claimed indemnity from Great Britain for the conduct of the British admiral. The law officers of the Crown, on the question being referred to them, held that as the *Huascar* was sailing under no national flag, and was an irresponsible depredating cruiser, approved the conduct of the admiral."

LE "LOUIS."

HIGH COURT OF ADMIRALTY, 1817.

(2 *Dodson*, 210.)

The slave trade is not piracy by the law of nations.

This was the case of a French vessel which sailed from Martinique on the 30th of January, 1816, destined on a voyage to the coast of Africa and back, and was captured ten or twelve leagues to the southward of Cape Mesurada, by the *Queen Charlotte* cutter, on the 11th of March in the same year, and carried to Sierra Leone.

She was proceeded against in the vice-admiralty court of that colony, and the information pleaded,—1st, that the seizors were duly and legally commissioned to make captures and seizures. 2d, That the seizure was within the jurisdiction of the court. 3d, That the vessel belonged to French subjects or others, and was fitted out, manned and navigated for the purpose of carrying on the African slave-trade, after that trade had been abolished by the internal laws of France, and by the treaty between Great Britain and France. 4th, That the vessel had bargained for twelve slaves at Mesurada, and was prevented by the capture alone from taking them on board. 5th, That the brig being engaged in the slave-trade, contrary to the laws of France, and the law of nations, was liable to condemnation, and could derive no protection from the French or any other flag. 6th, That the crew of the brig resisted the Queen Charlotte, and piratically killed eight of her crew, and wounded twelve others. 7th, That the vessel being engaged in this illegal traffic resisted the King's duly commissioned cruisers, and did not allow of search until overpowered by numbers. And 8th, That by reason of the circumstances stated, the vessel was out of the protection of any law, and liable to condemnation. The ship was condemned to His Majesty in the vice-admiralty court at Sierra Leone, and from this decision an appeal was made to this court.

Sir William Scott delivered the judgment, extracts from which are as follows:—"Upon the first question, whether the right of search exists in time of peace, I have to observe that two principles of public law are generally recognized as fundamental. One is the perfect equality and entire independence of all distinct states.

"Relative magnitude creates no distinction of right, relative imbecility, whether permanent or casual, gives no additional right to the more powerful neighbor; and any advantage seized upon that ground is mere usurpation. This is the great foundation of public law, which it mainly concerns the peace of mankind, both in their public and private capacities, to preserve inviolate. The second is, that all nations being equal, all have an equal right to the uninterrupted use of the unappropriated parts of the ocean for their navigation. In places where no local authority exists, where the subjects of all states meet upon a footing of entire equality and independence, no one state, or any of its subjects, has a right to assume or exercise authority over the subjects of another. I can find no authority that gives the right of interruption to the navigation of states in amity upon the high seas, excepting that which the rights of war give to both belligerents against neutrals. This right, incommodious as its exercise may occasionally be to those who are subjected to it, has been fully established in the legal practice of nations, having for its foundation the necessities of self-defence, in preventing the enemy from being supplied with the instruments of war, and from having his means of annoyance augmented by the advantages of maritime commerce. Against the property of his enemy each belligerent has the extreme rights of war. Against that of neutrals, the friends of both, each has the right of visitation and search, and of pursuing an inquiry whether they are employed in the service of his enemy, the right being subject, in almost all cases of an inquiry wrongfully pursued, to a compensation in costs and damages. * * *

"The right of visitation being in this present case exercised in time of peace, the question arises, how is it be legalized? And looking to what I have described as the known existing law of nations, evidenced by all authority and all practice, it must be upon the ground that the captured vessel is to be taken legally as a pirate, or else some new ground is to be assumed on which this right which has been distinctly admitted not to exist generally in time of peace can be supported. Wherever it has existed it has existed upon the ground of repelling injury, and as a measure of self-defence. No practice that exists in the world carries it farther.

"It is perfectly clear, that this vessel cannot be deemed a pirate from any want of a national character legally obtained. She is the property, not of sea-rovers, but of French acknowledged domiciled subjects. She has a French pass, French register, and all proper documents, and is an acknowledged portion of the mercantile marine of that country. If, therefore, the character of a pirate can be impressed upon her, it must be only on the ground of her occupation as a slave-trader; no other act of piracy being imputed. The question then comes to this:—can the occupation of this French vessel be legally deemed a piracy, inferring as it must do, if it be so, all the pains and penalties of piracy? I must remember, that in discussing the question, I must consider it, not according to any private moral apprehensions of my own (if I entertained them ever so sincerely) but as the law considers it; and, looking at the question in that direction, I think it requires no labour of proof to shew that such an occupation cannot be deemed a legal piracy. The very statute lately passed which makes it a transportable offence in any British subject to be concerned in this trade, affords a decisive proof that it was not liable to be considered as a piracy, and a capital offence, as it would be in foreigners as well as British subjects, if it was a piracy at all. In truth it wants some of the distinguishing features of that offence. It is not the act of freebooters, enemies of the human race, renouncing every country, and ravaging every country in its coasts and vessels indiscriminately, and thereby creating an universal terror and alarm; but of persons confining their transactions (reprehensible as they may be) to particular countries, without exciting the slightest apprehension in others. It is not the act of persons insulting and assaulting coasts and vessels against the will of the governments and the course of their laws, but of persons resorting thither to carry on a traffic (as it is there most unfortunately deemed, not only recognized but invited by the institutions of those barbarous communities. But it is unnecessary to pursue this topic further. It has not been contended in argument, that the common case of dealing in slaves could be deemed a piracy in law. In all the fervor of opinion which the agitation of all questions relating to this practice has excited in the minds of many intelligent persons in this country, no attempt has ever been thought of, at least with any visible effect, to submit any such question to the judgment of the law by such a prosecution of any form instituted in any court; and no lawyer, I presume, could be found hardy enough to maintain, that one indictment for piracy could be supported by the mere evidence of a trading in slaves. Be the malignity of the practice what it may, it is not that of piracy in legal consideration.* * *

"If I felt it necessary to press the consideration further, it would be by stating the gigantic mischief which such a claim is likely to produce. It is no secret, particularly in this place, that the right of search in time of war, though unquestionable, is not submitted to without complaints, loud and bitter, in spite of all the modifications that can be applied to it. If this right of war is imported into peace by convention it will be for the prudence of states to regulate by that convention the exercise of the right with all the softenings of which it is capable.

"Treaties, however, it must be remembered, are perishable things, and their obligations are dissipated by the first hostility. The covenants, however solemn, for the abolition of the trade, or for the exercise of modes of prevention, co-exist only with the relations of amity among the confederate states. At the same time it may be hoped, that so long as the treaties do exist, and their obligations are sincerely and reciprocally respected, the exercise of a right, which *pro tanto* converts a state of peace into a state of war, may be so conducted as not to excite just irritation. But if it be assumed by force, and left at large to operate reciprocally upon the ships of every state (for it must be a right of all against all), without any other limits as to time, place, or mode of inquiry than such as the prudence of particular states, or their individual subjects, may impose, I leave the tragedy contained in this case to illustrate the effects that are likely to arise in the very first stages of the process, without adding to the account what must be considered as a most awful part of it, the perpetual irritation and the universal hostility which are likely to ensue." (For other cases upon the subject of the slave trade, see *The Amédie*, 1 Acton's Adm. Rep., 240; *The Fortuna*, 1 Dodson, 81; *The Diana*, 1 Dodson, 95; *Madrazo* v. *Willes*, 3 Barnwell & Alderson, 353; *The Antelope*, 10 Wheaton, 66. See, also, Dana's Wheaton, pp. 203–218.)

CHAPTER IV.

NATIONALITY.

SECTION 22.—INDELIBLE ALLEGIANCE—EXPATRIATION.

OPINION OF COCKBURN.

(*Cockburn's Nationality*, 6-14.)

"Nationality by birth or origin depends, according to the law of some nations, on the place of birth; according to that of others on the nationality of the parents. In many countries both elements exist, one or other, however, predominating. Thus, by the law of England, the status of a subject depends generally on the place of birth: nevertheless, the descendants, of a natural-born subject, for two generations, though born out of the dominions of the Crown, are, to all intents and purposes, subjects. In like manner, by the law of France, though, generally speaking, it is necessary to be born of French parents to be a Frenchman, an exception is made in favour of the child of a foreigner, if born in France, subject only to the condition of the French nationality, being claimed within a prescribed period.

"By the common law of England, every person born within the dominions of the Crown, no matter whether of English or of foreign parents, and, in the latter case, whether the parents were settled, or merely temporarily sojourning in the country, was an English subject; save only the children of foreign ambassadors (who were excepted because their fathers carried their own nationality with them), or a child born to a foreigner during the hostile occupation of any part of the territories of England. No effect appears to have been given to descent as a source of nationality. * * *

"The law of the United States of America agrees with our own. The law of England as to the effect of the place of birth in the matter of nationality became the law of America as part of the law of the mother country, which the original settlers carried with them. * * *

"By the law of France, anterior to the revolution, a child born on French soil, though of foreign parents, was a Frenchman, as it was termed, *jure soli;* a child born of French parents out of French territory, was a Frenchman *jure sanguinis.* The framers of the Code Napoleon, adopting a sounder principle, excluded the place of birth as the source of nationality in itself; but compromising, as it were, with the old rule, they allowed the place of birth to have effect so far as to give to the offspring of an alien the right of claiming French nationality on attaining full age. The example set by the framers of the French Code has been followed by the nations by which that Code has been adopted, as also by others in remodelling their Constitutions or Codes. The result has been that, throughout the European States generally, descent, and not the place of birth, has been adopted as the primary criterion of nationality, though with a reservation in some, of a right to persons born within the territory to claim nationality within a fixed period. Thus, while in some of these countries nationality is derived from parentage alone, in others the right becomes complicated by reason that in addition to parentage, birth within the dominions of the particular country confers citizenship on the offspring of alien parents—in some absolutely—though subject to the right of the individual concerned to reject it at majority—in others on the right being claimed on certain specified conditions."

MACDONALD'S CASE, 1745.

(Cockburn's Nationality, 64, note.)

Held, that it was not in the power of a private person (subject of Great Britain) to shake off his allegiance and to transfer it to a foreign prince.

"In the case of Æneas Macdonald, who was tried for high treason, for having borne arms in the rebellion of 1745, it appeared that the prisoner had been born in England, brought up from his early infancy in France, had in his riper years been employed in that country, and that he held a commission from the French King.

"After a faint attempt to make out that the prisoner had been born in France, his counsel, despairing of establishing that fact, addressed the jury on the great hardship of such a prosecution against a person so circumstanced, and speaking of the doctrine of natural allegiance, represented it as a slavish principle, derogating from the principles of the Revolution. But the Court interposed, and said it never was doubted that a subject-born, taking a commission from a foreign Prince and committing high treason, may be punished as a subject for such treason, notwithstanding his foreign commission; that it was not in the power of any private person to shake off his allegiance and to transfer it to a foreign prince nor was it in the power of any foreign prince, by naturalizing or employing a subject of Great Britain, to dissolve the bond of allegiance between that subject and the Crown. And the Lord Chief Justice Lee, in charging the jury, told them that, the overt acts laid in the indictment having been proved against the prisoner, and admitted by him, the only fact to be tried by them, was whether he was a subject of Great Britain; as in that case he must be found guilty.

"The prisoner was accordingly found guilty, but received a pardon on condition of banishment."[1]

[1] In the case of *Isaac Williams*, 1799, Wharton's State Trials, 652, ELLSWORTH, C. J., said:—

"The common law of this country remains the same as it was before the Revolution. The present question is to be decided by two great principles; one is, that all the members of a civil community are bound to each other by compact. The other is, that one of the parties to this compact cannot dissolve it by his own act. The compact between our community and its members is, that the community will protect its members; and on the part of the members, that they will at all times be obedient to the laws of the community and faithful in its defence. This compact distinguishes our government from those which are founded in violence and fraud. It necessarily results, that the members cannot dissolve this compact, without the consent or default of the community. There has been here no consent—no default. Default is not pretended. Express consent is not claimed; but it has been argued, that the consent of the community is implied by its policy—its conditions, and its acts. * * * Consent has been argued from the acts of our government, permitting the naturalization of foreigners." But in the opinion of the Chief Justice no such inference could be drawn from this fact. When foreigners became naturalized in the United States, the question of their right to renounce their native allegiance was one between them and their native country, with which we were not concerned.

Proclamation of the Prince Regent, July 24, 1814, Cockburn's Nationality, 77:—

"A proclamation by the Prince Regent, of the 24th July, especially directed against America, after prohibiting all natural-born subjects of His Majesty from serving in the ships and armies of the United States, and charging all such persons at once to quit such service, proceeds as follows:

"And whereas it has been further represented to us that divers of our natural-born subjects as aforesaid have been induced to accept Letters of Naturalization or Certificates of Citizenship from the said United States of America, vainly supposing that by such Letters or Certificates they are discharged from that duty and allegiance which, as our natural-born subjects, they owe to us: Now we do hereby warn all such our natural-born subjects, that no such Letters of Naturalization or Certificates of Citizenship do, or can, in any manner discharge our natural-born subjects of the allegiance, or in any degree alter the duty which they owe to us, their natural Sovereign. * * *

"Moreover, that all such, our subjects, as aforesaid, who have voluntarily en-

MESSAGE OF PRESIDENT GRANT, 1873.

(2 *Wharton's Digest*, 312).

"I invite the earnest attention of Congress to the existing laws of the United States respecting expatriation and the election of nationality by individuals.

"Many citizens of the United States reside permanently abroad

tered, or shall enter, or voluntarily continue to serve on board of any such ships of war, or in the land forces of the said United States of America, at enmity with us, are, and will be guilty of high treason."

Opinion of Chancellor Kent:—From the "historical review of the principal discussions in the Federal Courts on this interesting subject in American jurisprudence, the better opinion would seem to be, that a citizen cannot renounce his allegiance to the United States without the permission of government, to be declared by law; and that, as there is no existing legislative regulation on the case, the rule of the English common law remains unaltered." (2 Kent's Commentaries, p 60.)

An Act concerning American citizens in foreign States, July 27, 1868.

"Whereas the right of expatriation is a natural and inherent right of all people, indispensable to the enjoyment of the rights of life, liberty, and the pursuit of happiness; and whereas in the recognition of this principle this Government has freely received emigrants from all nations, and invested them with the rights of citizenship; and whereas it is claimed that such American citizens, with their descendants, are subjects of foreign states, owing allegiance to the governments thereof; and whereas it is necessary to the maintenance of public peace that this claim of foreign allegiance should be promptly and finally disavowed: Therefore,

"*Be it enacted by the Senate and House of Representatives of the United States of America in Congress assembled*, That any declaration, instruction, opinion, order, or decision of any officers of this Government which denies, restricts, impairs, or questions the right of expatriation, is hereby declared inconsistent with the fundamental principles of this Government.

"SEC. 2. *And be it further enacted*, That, all naturalized citizens of the United States, while in foreign states, shall be entitled to and shall receive from this Government, the same protection of persons and property that is accorded to native-born citizens in like situations and circumstances.

"SEC. 3. *And be it further enacted*, That whenever it shall be made known to the President that any citizen of the United States has been unjustly deprived of his liberty by or under the authority of any foreign government, it shall be the duty of the President forthwith to demand of that government the reasons for such imprisonment, and if it appears to be wrongful and in violation of the rights of American citizenship, the President shall forthwith demand the release of such citizen, and if the release so demanded is unreasonably delayed or refused, it shall be the duty of the President to use such means, not amounting to acts of war, as he may think necessary and proper to obtain or effectuate such release, and all the facts and proceedings relative thereto shall as soon as practicable be communicated by the President to Congress."

with their families. Under the provisions of the act approved February 10, 1855, the children of such persons are to be deemed and taken to be citizens of the United States, but the rights of citizenship are not to descend to persons whose fathers never resided in the United States.

"It thus happens that persons who have never resided within the United States have been enabled to put forward a pretension to the protection of the United States against the claim to military service of the Government under whose protection they were born and have been reared. In some cases even naturalized citizens of the United States have returned to the land of their birth, with intent to remain there, and their children, the issue of a marriage contracted there after return, and who have never been in the United States, have laid claim to our protection, when the lapse of many years had imposed upon them the duty of military service to the only Government which had ever known them personally.

"Until the year 1868 it was left embarrassed by conflicting opinions of courts and of jurists to determine how far the doctrine of perpetual allegiance derived from our former colonial relations with Great Britain was applicable to American citizens. Congress then wisely swept these doubts away by enacting that 'any declaration, instruction, opinion, order, or decision of any officer of this Government which denies, restricts, impairs, or questions the right of expatriation, is inconsistent with the fundamental principles of this Government.' But Congress did not indicate in that statute, nor has it since done so, what acts are deemed to work expatriation. For my own guidance in determining such questions, I required (under the provisions of the Constitution) the opinion in writing of the principal officer in each of the Executive Departments upon certain questions relating to this subject. The result satisfies me that further legislation has become necessary. I therefore commend the

An Act concerning Aliens and British Subjects, May 12, 1870. Extract :—" 4. Any person who by reason of his having been born within the dominions of Her Majesty is a natural-born subject, but who also at the time of his birth became, under the law of any foreign state, a subject of such state, and is still such subject, may, if of full age and not under any disability, make a declaration of alienage in manner aforesaid, and from and after the making of such declaration shall cease to be a British subject. 5. From and after the passing of this act an alien shall not be entitled to be tried by a jury *de medietate linguæ*, but shall be triable in the same manner as if he were a natural-born subject. " 6. Any British subject who has at any time before, or may at any time after the passing of this act, when in any foreign state and not under any disability, voluntarily become naturalized in such state, shall, from and after the time of his so having become naturalized in such foreign state, be deemed to have ceased to be a British subject and be regarded as an alien;" etc.

subject to the careful consideration of Congress, and I transmit herewith copies of the several opinions of the principal officers of the Executive Department, together with other correspondence and pertinent information on the same subject.

"The United States, who led the way in the overthrow of the feudal doctrine of perpetual allegiance, are among the last to indicate how their own citizens may elect another nationality. The papers submitted herewith indicate what is necessary to place us on a par with other leading nations in liberality of legislation on this international question. We have already in our treaties assented to the principles which would need to be embodied in laws intended to accomplish such results. We have agreed that citizens of the United States may cease to be citizens, and may voluntarily render allegiance to other powers. We have agreed that residence in a foreign land, without intent to return, shall of itself work expatriation. We have agreed in some instances upon the length of time necessary for such continued residence to work a presumption of such intent."

ALIBERT'S CASE, 1852.

(*Report on Naturalization, United States, p.* 133.)

A citizen of France loses his French nationality by being naturalized in a foreign state.

Alibert was a native of Digne, Basses Alpes. He went to the United States in 1838, at the age of 18, and, after going through the usual formalities, was naturalized in 1846. In 1852 he returned to France and was arrested while on a visit to Digne as an "insoumis" of 1839, and pleaded his naturalization as exempting him from service. The United States consul at Marseilles applied to the general commanding the district, who informed him that Alibert's claim was founded in right, if his naturalization was really dated in 1846, as his naturalization would incapacitate him from serving in the French army, and the date of it would prove that more than three years had elapsed since the offense was committed (that being the period of limitation required by the penal code), and that he could not consequently be proceeded against for insubordination. Nevertheless Alibert was brought before a "conseil de guerre" at Marseilles, and condemned to a month's imprisonment.

The cause was then brought by appeal before a superior military court at Toulon, and the sentence quashed, thereby establishing Alibert's immunity from conscription.[1]

SECTION 23.—CITIZENSHIP—NATURALIZATION.

Ex Parte CHIN KING.

Ex Parte CHAN SAN HEE.

U. S. CIRCUIT COURT FOR OREGON, 1888.

(35 *Federal Reporter*, 354.)

Children born in the United States of Chinese parents are citizens of the United States.

Application for writ of *habeas corpus.*

DEADY, J.—"The writ of *habeas corpus* in these cases was allowed and issued on June 25, 1888, and they were heard together on the same day.

"The petition of Chin King states that she was born in San Francisco, Cal., on October 10, 1868; while that of Chan San Hee states that she was born in Portland, Or., on March 15, 1878; and they each state that they are restrained of their liberty by William Robert Laird, the master of the British bark 'Kitty,' because the collector of customs for this port refuses to allow them to land from said bark on the ground that the petitioners are Chinese, and have no return certificate, as required by the act of Congress on that subject; but

[1] In the case of Michael Zeiter, 1869, before the court of first instance of Wissembourg, the question was whether he was exempt from military service. And this depended upon whether he was a citizen of France, for, by the 2d article of the law of March 21, 1832, as the court say, "nul ne peut être admis dans les troupes françaises s'il n'est français."

Zeiter contended that he had been naturalized in the United States, and had thereby lost his French nationality. The court assented to this view of the law but demanded further proof of his naturalization in America. When he had procured satisfactory proofs, the court decreed as follows:

"Attendu que, par la production du certificat qui lui a été delivré le vingt-huit mai dernier, par le consul des Etats Unis à Paris, et qui a été enregistré à Wissembourg aujourd'hui, le demandeur a justifié qu'il est citoyen américain: le tribunal donne acte au demandeur de ce que, par la production du dit certificat, il a satisfait au jugement rendu en ce siége le vingt-cinq avril dernier.

"En conséquence dit et reconnait que le demandeur, Michel Zeiter, par sa naturalisation en pays étranger, a perdu la qualité de français."

they aver that they are native-born citizens of the United States and therefore not included within the terms of said act.

"The return of the master to each writ states that the 'Kitty' sailed from Hong Kong for Portland, on April 19, 1888, and that the petitioners were passengers thereon during said voyage, and are now in custody on board the same, for the reasons stated in the petitions.

"On application the United States district attorney was allowed to intervene on behalf of the United States, and allege that he had no knowledge or information sufficient to form a belief, as to whether the petitioners were born in the United States, as alleged, or not.

"On the hearing it appeared that Chung Yip Gen is a Chinese merchant, who has lived and done business in this city for the past 13 years and for 12 years prior thereto in San Francisco; that he was married in San Francisco about 23 years ago, and the petitioners are his daughters, the older one having been born in San Francisco, and the younger one in Portland, and that in 1881 the father sent them and their mother to China, from whence they were to return when they pleased.

"By the common law, a child born within the allegiance—the jurisdiction—of the United States, is born a subject or citizen thereof, without reference to the political *status* or condition of its parents. *McKay* v. *Campbell*, 2 Sawy., 118; *In re Look Tin Sing*, 10 Sawy., 353; 21 Fed. Rep., 905; *Lynch* v. *Clarke*, 1 Sandf. Ch., 583. In the latter case it was held that Julia Lynch, who was born in New York in 1849, of alien parents during a temporary sojourn by them in that city, and returned with them the same year to their native country, where she resided until her death, was an American citizen.

"The vice-chancellor, after an exhaustive examination of the law, declared that every citizen born within the dominion and allegiance of the United States was a citizen thereof, without reference to the situation of his parents.

"This, of course, does not include the children born in the United States of parents engaged in the diplomatic service of foreign governments, whose residence, in contemplation of public law, is a part of their own country.

"The rule of the common law on this subject has been incorporated into the fundamental law of the land.

"The fourteenth amendment declares; 'All persons born or naturalized in the United States, and subject to the jurisdiction thereof, are citizens of the United States, and of the state wherein they reside.'

"In *In re Look Tin Sing*, 10 Sawy., 353; 21 Fed. Rep., 905, it was held that a person born within the United States, of Chinese parents, not engaged in any diplomatic or official capacity under the emperor of China, is a citizen of the United States. The case is similar to that of the petitioners. The party in question was born in California in 1870, of Chinese parents. In 1879, he went to China, and returned to California in 1884, without the certificate provided for in the restriction act of 1882, or that of 1884, and was therefore denied the right to land.

"Mr. Justice FIELD, in delivering the opinion of the court, in which Sawyer, Sabin, and Hoffman concurred, says (p. 859): 'The inability of persons to become citizens under those laws (of naturalization) in no respect impairs the effect of their birth, or of the birth of their children, upon the *status* of either, as citizens of the United States.'

"The only point made by the district attorney against the petitioners on the question of their citizenship is that they left this country without, as he claims, any definite or fixed purpose to return.

"But I think the evidence does not warrant so strong a statement. For aught that appears they intended to return; and the fact that they have returned gives strength to the inference. The most that can be said is, there was no time fixed for their return. And that is the case with hundreds of minor American citizens, who go abroad yearly for nurture and education. But it seems that the citizenship of the petitioners would not be affected by the fact, if they had never come back, unless it also appears that they had in some formal and affirmative way renounced the same.

"However, in my judgment, a father cannot deprive his minor child of the *status* of American citizenship, impressed upon it by the circumstances of its birth under the Constitution and within the jurisdiction of the United States.

"This *status*, once acquired, can only be lost or changed by the act of the party when arrived at majority, and the consent of the government.

"By section 2 of article 4 of the Constitution it is provided: 'The citizens of each state shall be entitled to all privileges and immunities of citizens in the several states.'

"It has always been held that the privileges and immunities there referred to are fundamental; and that a citizen of one state may at least, under this provision, pass through or reside in any other state of the union for the ordinary pursuits or purposes of life. *Corfield* v. *Coryell*, 4 Wash. C. C., 380; *Paul* v. *Virginia*, 8 Wall., 180.

"The action of the collector in these cases has the effect, and is so intended, to deny these citizens of the United States the right of free locomotion within the same,—the right to come into, pass through, or reside in this state, and is therefore contrary to and in violation of the constitutional provision guaranteeing such right to every citizen. Sections 751, 752, and 753 of the Revised Statutes provide, in effect, that the courts of the United States and the judges thereof shall have power, by *habeas corpus,* to deliver a person held in custody or restrained of his liberty in violation of the Constitution or of a law or treaty of the United States.

"The petitioners, as we have seen, are restrained of their liberty in violation of the Constitution, and therefore this court has jurisdiction to discharge them on *habeas corpus.*

"The petitioners are discharged from custody."

HAUSDING'S CASE.

FRELINGHUYSEN, SEC. OF STATE, TO KASSON, 1885.

(2 *Wharton's Digest*, 399.)

Children born in the United States of alien parents, and never dwelling in the United States are not citizens thereof.

The "case of Ludwig Hausding, appears to have been decided according to the law and the facts. It is stated that having been born in the United States of a Saxon subject, he was removed to his father's native land, where he has ever since remained, although his father has subsequently become a citizen of the United States. You refused a passport on the ground that the applicant was born of Saxon subjects, temporarily in the United States, and was never 'dwelling in the United States,' either at the time of or since his parent's naturalization, and that he was not, therefore, naturalized by force of the statute, section 2172, Revised Statutes.

"It does not appear from your statement whether Wilhelm Hausding, the father, had declared his intention to become an American citizen before the birth of Ludwig. While this, if it were established, would lend an appearance of hardship to an adverse decision upon his claim to be deemed a citizen, yet, even in this case, as the statutes stand, your decision would conform to the letter of the law, section 2168, which admits to citizenship, on taking the oath prescribed by law, the widow and children of an alien who has declared his intention but dies before completing his naturalization.

"By providing for special exemption excludes the idea of any other exemption, as for instance in the case of the non-completion of the father's naturalization before the permanent removal of the minor son from the jurisdiction of the United States.

"Not being naturalized by force of the statute, Ludwig Hausding could only assert citizenship on the ground of birth in the United States; but this claim would, if presented, be untenable, for by section 1992, Revised Statutes, it is made a condition of citizenship by birth that the person be not subject to any foreign power.

"This last consideration serves only to answer the 'quære' which you annex to your statement of the Hausding case.

"You ask: 'Can one, born a foreign subject, but within the United States, make the option after his majority, and while still living abroad, to adopt the citizenship of his birthplace? It seems not, and that he must change his allegiance by emigration and legal process of naturalization.' Sections 1992 and 1993 of the Revised Statutes clearly show the extent of existing legislation; that the fact of birth, under circumstances implying alien subjection, establishes of itself no right of citizenship; and that the citizenship of a person so born is to be acquired in some legitimate manner through the operation of statute. No statute contemplates the acquisition of the declared character of an American citizen by a person not at the time within the jurisdiction of the tribunal of record which confers that character."

EMDEN'S CASE.

PORTER, ACTING SEC. OF STATE, TO WINCHESTER, 1885.

(2 *Wharton's Digest*, 410.)

Children born abroad of citizens of the United States and continuing to reside abroad, are not citizens thereof unless they elect to become such on coming of age.

Robert Emden was born in Switzerland, in 1862, and at the time of his application in 1885 for a passport, had never been in the United States. His father, a Swiss by origin, was naturalized in New York in 1854, but soon afterwards returned to Switzerland, where he continued afterwards to reside.

"Undoubtedly, by the law of nations, an infant child partakes of his father's nationality and domicile. But there are two difficulties in the way of applying this rule to the present case. In the first place a parent's nationality cannot, especially when produced by naturalization, be presumed to be adhered to after a residence in the country of origin for so long a period as in the present case.

"In the second place, the rule as to children only applies to minors, since when the child becomes of age he is required to elect between the country of his residence and the country of his alleged technical allegiance. Of this election two incidents are to be observed: when once made it is final; and it requires no formal act, but may be inferred from the conduct of the party from whom the election is required.

"Applying these tests to the present case it can hardly be said that Mr. Robert Emden's claim to be a citizen of the United States is, as a matter of international law, made out. The burden of proof is always on the applicant for the passport, and here there is no evidence to prove either his father's non-abandonment of his United States citizenship, or his own election of such citizenship, save the applications of father and son for passports."

A PRUSSIAN SUBJECT.

Opinion of the Att.-General, 1875.

(2 *Wharton's Digest*, 412.)

Under the treaty between the United States and the North German Confederation of 1868, a Prussian by birth, naturalized in the United States, is presumed to have renounced his American citizenship, if he returns to Prussia, and resides there two years.

"A Prussian subject by birth emigrated to the United States in 1848, became naturalized in 1854, and shortly afterwards returned to Germany with his family, in which was a son born in the United States, and became domiciled at Wiesbaden, where, together with his family, he has since continuously resided. The son having reached the age of twenty years, has been called upon by the German Government for military duty. The father invoked the intervention of the United States legation at Berlin, but declined in behalf of the son to give any assurance of intention on the part of the latter to return to the United States within a reasonable time and assume his duties as a citizen.

"Article IV. of the naturalization treaty between the United States and North Germany of 1868, reads as follows: 'If a German naturalized in America renews his residence in North Germany without intent to return to America, he shall be held to have renounced his naturalization in the United States. * * * The intent not to return may be held to exist when the person naturalized in the one country resides more than two years in the other country.'

"It was held (1) that under the above article, the father must be deemed to have abandoned his American citizenship and to have resumed the German nationality; (2) that the son, being a minor, acquired under the laws of Germany the nationality of his father, but did not thereby lose his American nationality; (3) that upon attaining his majority, the son may, at his own election, return and take the nationality of his birth or remain in Germany and retain his acquired nationality; (4) yet that during his minority and while domiciled with his father in Germany, he cannot rightfully claim exemption from military duty there."

SECTION 24.—PROTECTION TO CITIZENS ABROAD.

WAGNER'S CASE.

FRELINGHUYSEN, SEC. OF STATE, TO HUNT, 1883.

(2 *Wharton's Digest*, 892.)

What are the rights of a foreign minor who emigrates to the United States, and becomes naturalized there, and then returns to his native land? May he be forced to serve in the army of his original State?

"From the responses previously made to your inquiries in Mr. Wagner's behalf, it appears that the brunt of the charge against him was that he, a minor, quitted Russian jurisdiction in advance of attaining the age when he might have been called upon for military service. He was born at Lodz, 1852, and in 1874 became liable to military service. He came to the United States in 1869, five years before the liability could rest upon him. When the technical offense, styled evasion of military duty, which is the sole charge against him, began to exist as a tangible accusation, Reinhardt Wagner had already, by residence in the United States for more than three years preceding his majority, acquired under our statutes the preliminary rights of citizenship. No nation should assert an absolute claim over one of its subjects under circumstances like these, and it is thought improbable that Russia will persist in such a claim, even if made. There would be no limit to such a pretension, for the taking of a male infant out of Russia might be regarded with equal propriety as an 'evasion' of eventual military service.

"It is tantamount to asserting a right to punish any male Russian who, having quitted Russian territory and become a citizen of another state, may afterward return to Russia.

"This claim is different from that put forth by some governments for the completion of military duty fully accruing while the subject is within their jurisdiction, and actually left unfulfilled. It is, for example, claimed that a subject who leaves the country when called upon to serve in the army, and becomes a citizen or subject of another state, may, if he returns to the former jurisdiction while yet of age for military duty, be compelled to serve out his term. This rule appears harsh to us, and yet it goes no further, as a matter of fact, than a contention that an obligation of service accruing and unpaid while the subject is a resident of the country, continues, and is to be extinguished in kind by performance of the alleged defaulted service.

"But, harsh as it is, it is wholly different from the infliction of vindictive punishment, as, for instance, exile for the constructive evasion of an inchoate obligation. To exact the fulfillment of an existing obligation is one thing; to inflict corporal punishment for not recognizing a future contingent obligation is another."

KOSZTA'S CASE.

(*Cockburn's Nationality*, 118.)

Status of a foreigner who has "declared his intention" to become a citizen of the United States, and who has a domicil in the country, when he is temporarily out of their jurisdiction.

Koszta was a Hungarian, and one of the refugees of 1848–9. He went to Turkey, where he was arrested and imprisoned at Kutahieh, but released on condition of leaving the country. He went to the United States and made the usual declaration of an intention to become naturalized. In 1853 he returned to Turkey, and went to Smyrna on commercial business, and there obtained from the United States' Consul a traveling pass, stating that he was entitled to American protection. On the 21st of June, 1853, he was seized by some persons in the pay of the Austrian Consulate and taken out into the harbor in a boat; he was then thrown into the sea, and was picked up by a boat from the Austrian man-of-war "Hussar." The United States Consul went on board to rémonstrate, but the Captain of the "Hussar" persisted in retaining Koszta. Thereupon the United States' Chargé d'Affaires at Constantinople requested the Captain of the United States' ship of war "St. Louis" to demand Koszta's release, and, if necessary, to have recourse to force.

The "St. Louis" accordingly went to Smyrna, and the Captain in pursuance of his instructions, stated to the Commander of the "Hussar" that unless Koszta was at once delivered to him he should take him by force of arms.

As a conflict between the two ships of war would have been attended with great danger to the shipping in the port and to the town, the French Consul offered his mediation, and Koszta was then given over to his care to be kept until the decision of the respective governments was ascertained.

On the 29th of August, 1853, the Austrian Chargé d'Affaires at Washington presented a formal remonstrance to the United States Government, protesting against the claim of the United States to afford protection to Koszta, and calling on them to disavow the conduct of their agents and to grant reparation for the insult offered to the Austrian flag.

Mr. Marcy replied on the 26th of September, 1853, contending, first, for the general right of every citizen or subject, "having faithfully performed the past and present duties resulting from his relation to the Sovereign Power, to release himself at any time from the obligation of allegiance, freely quit the land of his birth and adoption, seek through all countries a home, or select anywhere that which offers him the fairest prospect of happiness for himself and his posterity;" secondly, that Koszta was not an Austrian subject, as by a "decree of the Emperor of Austria of the 24th of March, 1832, Austrian subjects leaving the dominions of the Emperor without permission of the magistrate and a release of Austrian citizenship, and with an intention never to return, become 'unlawful emigrants,' and lose all their civil and political rights at home." Thirdly, Mr. Marcy put forward the somewhat startling proposition that although Koszta had not yet been naturalized and become a citizen of the United States, yet having become domiciled in the latter country, he was entitled to be treated in all respects as a citizen of the United States. In support of this proposition Mr. Marcy writes as follows:—

"It is an error to assume that a nation can properly extend its protection only to native-born or naturalized citizens. This is not the doctrine of international law, nor is the practice of nations circumscribed within such narrow limits. This law does not, as has been before remarked, complicate questions of this nature by respect for municipal codes. In relation to this subject it has clear and distinct rules of its own. It gives the national character of the country, not only to native-born and naturalized citizens, but to all residents in it who are there with, or even without, an intention to become citizens, provided they have a domicile therein. Foreigners may, and often do, acquire a domicile in a country, even though they have entered it with the avowed intention not to become naturalized citizens, but to return to their native land at some remote and uncertain period, and whenever they acquire a domicile, international law at once impresses upon them the national character of the country of that domicile.

"It is a maxim of international law that domicile confers a national character; it does not allow any one who has a domicile to decline the national character thus conferred; it forces it upon him often very much against his will, and to his great detriment. International law looks only to the national character in determining what country has the right to protect. If a person goes from this country abroad, with the nationality of the United States, this law enjoins upon other nations to respect him, in regard to protection, as an American citizen. It concedes to every country the right to protect any and all who may be clothed with its nationality."

TOUSIG'S CASE, 1854.

(*Lawrence's Wheaton, Ed. of* 1863, 929.)

A foreigner who has "declared his intention" to become a citizen of the United States is not entitled to their protection if he returns to his native country.

Tousig, a native of Austria, had acquired a domicile in the United States, but had not become naturalized. He returned to Austria, with an American state passport, and was arrested on the charge of offenses committed before leaving Austria. He appealed to the United States Minister for protection, and the latter having brought the case before the state department, Mr. Marcy, on the 10th January, 1854, writes to Mr. Jackson, Chargé d' Affaires at Vienna, as follows:—

"I have carefully examined your despatches relating to the case of Simon Tousig, and regret to find that it is one which will not authorize a more effective interference than that which you have already made in his behalf. It is true he left this country with a passport issued from this department; but as he was neither a native-born nor naturalized citizen, he was not entitled to it. It is only to citizens that passports are issued.

"Assuming all that could possibly belong to Tousig's case,—that he had a domicile here and was actually clothed with the nationality of the United States,—there is a feature in it which distinguishes it from that of Koszta. Tousig voluntarily returned to Austria, and placed himself within the reach of her municipal laws. He went by his free act under their jurisdiction, and thereby subjected himself to them. If he had incurred penalties or assumed duties while under these laws, he might have expected they would be enforced against him, and should have known that the new political relation he had acquired, if indeed he had acquired any, could not operate as a release from these penalties. Having been once subject to the municipal laws of Austria, and while under her jurisdiction violated these laws, his withdrawal from that jurisdiction and acquiring a different national character would not exempt him from their operation whenever he again chose to place himself under them. Every nation, whenever its laws are violated by any one owing obedience to them, whether he be a citizen or a stranger, has a right to inflict the penalities incurred upon the transgressor, if found within its jurisdiction. The case is not altered by the character of the laws, unless they are in derogation of the well-established international code. No nation has a right to supervise the municipal code of another nation, or claim that its citizens or subjects shall be exempted from the operation of such code, if they have voluntarily placed themselves under it.

"The character of the municipal laws of one country does not furnish a just ground for other states to interfere with the execution of these laws, even upon their own citizens, when they have gone into that country and subjected themselves to its jurisdiction. If this country can rightfully claim no such exemption for its native-born or naturalized citizens, surely it cannot claim it for those who have at most but inchoate rights of citizens.

"The principle does not at all interfere with the right of any state to protect its citizens, or those entitled to its protection, when abroad, from wrongs and injuries,—from arbitrary acts of oppression or deprivation of property, as contradistinguished from penalties and punishments incurred by the infraction of the laws of the country within whose jurisdiction the sufferers have placed themselves. I do not discover any principle in virtue of which this government can claim, as a matter of right, the release of Tousig.

"He has voluntarily placed himself within the jurisdiction of the laws of Austria, and is suffering, as appears by the case as you present it, for the acts he had done in violation of those laws while he was an Austrian subject."

SECTION 25.—STATUS OF AMERICAN INDIANS.

ELK v. WILKINS.

SUPREME COURT OF THE UNITED STATES, 1884.

(112 *United States Reports*, 94.)

This was an action brought by an Indian in the Circuit Court of the United States for the District of Nebraska, against the registrar of one of the wards of the city of Omaha, for refusing to register him as a qualified voter therein.

Mr. Justice GRAY delivered the opinion of the court, extracts from which are as follows:

"* * * The question then, is, whether an Indian, born a member of one of the Indian tribes within the United States, is, merely by reason of his birth within the United States, and of his afterwards voluntarily separating himself from his tribe and taking up his residence among white citizens, a citizen of the United States, within the meaning of the first section of the Fourteenth Amendment to the Constitution.

"Under the Constitution of the United States, as originally established, 'Indians not taxed,' were excluded from the persons according to whose numbers representatives and direct taxes were apportioned among the several states; and Congress had and exercised the power to regulate commerce with the Indian tribes, and the members thereof, whether within or without the boundaries of one of the States of the Union. The Indian tribes, being within the territorial limits of the United States, were not, strictly speaking, foreign states; but they were alien nations, distinct political communities, with whom the United States might and habitually did deal, as they thought fit, either through treaties made by the President and Senate, or through acts of Congress in the ordinary forms of legislation. The members of those tribes owed immediate allegiance to their several tribes, and were not part of the people of the United States. They were in a dependent condition, a state of pupilage resembling that of a ward to his guardian. Indians and their property exempt from taxation by treaty or statute of the United States, could not be taxed by any State. General acts of Congress did not apply to Indians, unless so expressed as to clearly manifest an intention to include them. Constitution, art. 1, secs. 2, 8; art. 2, sec. 2; *Cherokee Nation* v. *Georgia*, 5 Pet. 1; *Worcester* v. *Georgia*, 6 Pet., 515; . . . *Crow Dog's Case*, 109 U. S. 556. * * *

"The alien and dependent condition of the members of the Indian tribes could not be put off at their own will, without the action or assent of the United States. They were never deemed citizens of the United States, except under explicit provisions of treaty or statute to that effect, either declaring a certain tribe, or such members of it as chose to remain behind on the removal of the tribe westward, to be citizens, or authorizing individuals of particular tribes to become citizens on application to a court of the United States for naturalization and satisfactory proof of fitness for civilized life. * * *

"Chief Justice TANEY, in the passage cited for the plaintiff from his opinion in *Scott* v. *Sandford*, 19 How., 393, 404, did not affirm or imply that either the Indian tribes, or individual members of those tribes, had the right, beyond other foreigners, to become citizens of their own will, without being naturalized by the United States. His words were: 'They' (the Indian tribes) 'may without doubt, like the subjects of any foreign government, be naturalized by the authority of Congress, and become citizens of a State, and of the United States; and if an individual should leave his nation or tribe, and take up his abode among the white population, he would be entitled to all the rights and privileges which would belong to an emigrant from any other foreign people.' But an emigrant from any foreign state cannot become a citizen of the United States without a formal renunciation of his old allegiance, and an acceptance by the United States of that renunciation through such form of naturalization as may be required by law.

"The distinction between citizenship by birth and citizenship by naturalization is clearly marked in the provisions of the Constitution, by which 'no person, except a natural born citizen or a citizen of the United States at the time of the adoption of this Constitution, shall be eligible to the office of President;' and 'the Congress shall have power to establish an uniform rule of naturalization.' Constitution, art. 2, sec. 1; art. 1, sec. 8.

"By the Thirteenth Amendment of the Constitution slavery was prohibited. The main object of the opening sentence of the Fourteenth Amendment was to settle the question, upon which there had been a difference of opinion throughout the country and in this court, as to the citizenship of free negroes, *Scott* v. *Sandford*, 19 How., 393; and to put it beyond doubt that all persons, white or black, and whether formerly slaves or not, born or naturalized in the United States, and owing no allegiance to any alien power, should be citizens of the United States and of the State in which they reside. *Slaughter House Cases*, 16 Wall., 36, 73; *Strauder* v. *West Virginia*, 600 U. S., 303, 306.

"This section contemplates two sources of citizenship, and two sources only; birth and naturalization. The persons declared to be citizens are 'all persons born or naturalized in the United States, and subject to the jurisdiction thereof,' the evident meaning of these last words is not merely subject in some respect or degree to the jurisdiction of the United States, but completely subject to their political jurisdiction and owing them direct and immediate allegiance. And the words relate to the time of birth in the one case, as they do to the time of naturalization in the other. Persons not thus subject to the jurisdiction of the United States at the time of birth cannot become so afterwards, except by being naturalized, either individually, as by proceedings under the naturalization acts, or collectively, as by force of a treaty by which foreign territory is acquired.

"Indians born within the territorial limits of the United States, members of, and owing allegiance to, one of the Indian tribes (an alien, though dependent, power), although in a geographical sense born in the United States, are no more 'born in the United States and subject to the jurisdiction thereof,' within the meaning of the first section of the Fourteenth Amendment, than the children of subjects of any foreign government born within the domain of that government, or the children born within the United States, of ambassadors or other public ministers of foreign nations. * * *

"Such Indians, then, not being citizens by birth, can only become citizens in the second way mentioned in the Fourteenth Amendment, by being 'naturalized in the United States,' by or under some treaty or statute. * * *

"The act of July 27, 1868, ch. 249, declaring the right of expatriation to be a natural and inherent right of all people, and reciting that 'in the recognition of this principle this government has freely received emigrants from all nations, and invested them with the rights of citizenship,' while it affirms the right of every man to expatriate himself from one country, contains nothing to enable him to become a citizen of another, without being naturalized under its authority. 15 Stat., 223; Rev. Stat., § 1999.

"The provision of the act of Congress of March 3, 1871, ch. 120, that 'hereafter no Indian nation or tribe within the territory of the United States shall be acknowledged or recognized as an independent nation, tribe or power with whom the United States may contract by treaty,' is coupled with a provision that the obligation of any treaty already lawfully made is not to be thereby invalidated or impaired, and its utmost possible effect is to require the Indian tribes to be dealt with for the future through the legislative and not through the treaty-making power. 16 Stat., 566; Rev. Stat., § 2079. * * *

"The plaintiff, not being a citizen of the United States under the Fourteenth Amendment of the Constitution, has been deprived of no right secured by the Fifteenth Amendment, and cannot maintain this action.

"Judgment affirmed."

UNITED STATES v. KAGAMA.

SUPREME COURT OF THE UNITED STATES, 1886.

(118 *United States Reports*, 375.)

Mr. Justice MILLER delivered the opinion of the court.

"The case is brought here by certificate of division of opinion between the Circuit Judge and the District Judge holding the Circuit Court of the United States for District of California.

"The questions certified arise on a demurrer to an indictment against two Indians for murder committed on the Indian reservation of Hoopa Valley, in the State of California, the person murdered being also an Indian of said reservation. Though there are six questions certified as the subject of difference, the point of them all is well set out in the third and sixth, which are as follows:

"Whether the provisions of said section 9 (of the act of Congress of March 3, 1885), making it a crime for one Indian to commit murder upon another Indian, upon an Indian reservation situated wholly within the limits of a State of the Union, and making such Indian so committing the crime of murder within and upon such Indian reservation 'subject to the same laws' and subject to be 'tried in the same courts, and in the same manner, and subject to the same penalties as are all other persons' committing the crime of murder 'within the exclusive jurisdiction of the United States,' is a constitutional and valid law of the United States?'

"'6. Whether the courts of the United States have jurisdiction or authority to try and punish an Indian belonging to an Indian tribe for committing the crime of murder upon another Indian belonging to the same Indian tribe, both sustaining the usual tribal relations, said crime having been committed upon an Indian reservation made and set apart for the use of the Indian tribe to which said Indians both belong?'

"The indictment sets out in two counts that Kagama, alias Pactah Billy, an Indian, murdered Iyouse, alias Ike, another Indian, at Humboldt county, in the State of California, within the limits of the Hoopa Valley Reservation, and it charges Mahawaha, alias Ben, also an Indian, with aiding and abetting in the murder.

"The law referred to in the certificate is the last section of the Indian appropriation act of that year, and is as follows:

"'9. That immediately upon and after the date of the passage of this act all Indians committing against the person or property of another Indian or other person any of the following crimes, namely, murder, manslaughter, rape, assault with intent to kill, arson, burglary and larceny, within any territory of the United States, and either within or without the Indian reservation, shall be subject therefor to the laws of said Territory relating to said crimes, and shall be tried therefor in the same courts and in the same manner, and shall be subject to the same penalties, as are all other persons charged with the commission of the said crimes, respectively; and the said courts are hereby given jurisdiction in all such cases; and all such Indians committing any of the above crimes against the person or property of another Indian or other person, within the boundaries of any State of the United States, and within the limits of any Indian reservation, shall be subject to the same laws, tried in the same courts and in the same manner, and subject to the same penalties, as are all other persons committing any of the above crimes within the exclusive jurisdiction of the United States., 23 Stat. Ch., 341, 362, § 9, 385.

"The above enactment is clearly separable into two distinct definitions of the conditions under which Indians may be punished for the same crimes as defined by the common law. The first of these is where the offence is committed within the limits of a territorial government, whether on or off an Indian reservation. In this class of cases the Indian charged with the crime shall be judged by the laws of the Territory on that subject, and tried by its courts. This proposition itself is new in legislation of Congress, which has heretofore only undertaken to punish an Indian who sustains the usual relation to his tribe, and who commits the offence in the Indian country, or on an Indian reservation, in exceptional cases; as where the offence was against the person or property of a white man, or was some violation of the trade and intercourse regulations imposed by Congress on the Indian tribes. It is new, because it now proposes to punish these offences when they are committed by one Indian on the person or property of another.

"The second is where the offence is committed by one Indian

against the person or property of another, within the limits of a State of the Union, but on an Indian reservation. In this case, of which the State and its tribunals would have jurisdiction if the offence was committed by a white man outside an Indian reservation, the courts of the United States are to exercise jurisdiction as if the offence had been committed at some place within the exclusive jurisdiction of the United States. The first clause subjects all Indians guilty of these crimes, committed within the limits of a Territory, to the laws of that Territory, and to its courts for trial. The second, which applies solely to offences by Indians which are committed within the limits of a State and the limits of a reservation, subjects the offenders to the laws of the United States passed for the government of places under the exclusive jurisdiction of those laws, and to trial by the courts of the United States. This is a still further advance, as asserting this jurisdiction over the Indians within the limits of the States of the Union.

"Although the offence charged in this indictment was committed within a State and not within a Territory, the considerations which are necessary to a solution of the problem in regard to the one must in a large degree affect the other.

"The Constitution of the United States is almost silent in regard to the relations of the government which was established by it to the numerous tribes of Indians within its borders.

"In declaring the basis on which representation in the lower branch of the Congress and direct taxation should be apportioned, it was fixed that it should be according to numbers, *excluding Indians not taxed*, which, of course, excluded nearly all of that race, but which meant that if there were such within a State as were taxed to support the government, they should be counted for representation, and in the computation for direct taxes levied by the United States. This expression, excluding Indians not taxed, is found in the XIVth amendment, where it deals with the same subject under the new conditions produced by the emancipation of the slaves. Neither of these shed much light on the power of Congress over the Indians in their existence as tribes, distinct from the ordinary citizens of a State or Territory.

"The mention of Indians in the constitution which has received most attention is that found in the clause which gives Congress 'power to regulate commerce with foreign nations and among the several States, and with the Indian tribes.'

"This clause is relied on in the argument in the present case, the proposition being that the statute under consideration is a regulation of commerce with the Indian tribes. But we think it would be a very strained construction of this clause, that a system of criminal laws for Indians living peaceably in their reservations, which left out the entire code of trade and intercourse laws justly enacted under that provision, and established punishments for the common-law crimes of murder, manslaughter, arson, burglary, larceny, and the like, without any reference to their relation to any kind of commerce, was authorized by the grant of power to regulate commerce with the Indian tribes. While we are not able to see, in either of these clauses of the Constitution and its amendments, any delegation of power to enact a code of criminal law for the punishment of the worst class of crimes known to civilized life when committed by Indians, there is a suggestion in the manner in which the Indian tribes are introduced into that clause, which may have a bearing on the subject before us. The commerce with foreign nations is distinctly stated as submitted to the control of Congress. Were the Indian tribes foreign nations? If so, they came within the first of the three classes of commerce mentioned, and did not need to be repeated as Indian tribes. Were they nations, in the minds of the framers of the Constitution? If so, the natural phrase would have been 'foreign nations and Indian nations,' or, in the terseness of language uniformly used by the framers of the instrument, it would naturally have been 'foreign and Indian nations.' And so in the case of *The Cherokee Nation* v. *The State of Georgia*, 5 Pet., 1, 20, brought in the Supreme Court of the United States, under the declaration that the judicial power extends to suits between a State and foreign states, and giving to the Supreme Court original jurisdiction where a State is a party, it was conceded that Georgia as a State came within the clause, but held that the Cherokees were not a State or nation within the meaning of the Constitution, so as to be able to maintain the suit.

"But these Indians are within the geographical limits of the United States. The soil and the people within these limits are under the political control of the Government of the United States, or of the States of the Union. There exist within the broad domain of sovereignty but these two. There may be cities, counties, and other organized bodies with limited legislative functions, but they are all derived from, or exist in, subordination to one or the other of these. The territorial governments owe all their powers to the statutes of the United States conferring on them the powers which they exercise, and which are liable to be withdrawn, modified, or repealed at any time by Congress. What authority the State governments may have to enact criminal laws for the Indians will be presently considered. But this power of Congress to organize territorial governments, and make laws for their inhabitants, arises not so much from the clause in the Constitution in regard to disposing of and making rules and regulations concerning the Territory and other property of the United States, as from the ownership of the country in which the Territories are, and the right of exclusive sovereignty which must exist in the National Government, and can be found nowhere else. *Murphy* v. *Ramsey*, 114 U. S., 15, 44.

"In the case of *American Ins. Co.* v. *Canter*, 1 Pet., 511, 542, in which the condition of the people of Florida, then under a territorial government, was under consideration, MARSHALL, Chief Justice, said: 'Perhaps the power of governing a Territory belonging to the United States, which has not, by becoming a State, acquired the means of self-government, may result necessarily from the fact that it is not within the jurisdiction of any particular State, and is within the power and jurisdiction of the United States. The right to govern may be the inevitable consequence of the right to acquire Territory. Whichever may be the source whence the power is derived, the possession of it is unquestioned.'

"In the case of the *United States* v. *Rogers*, 4 How., 567, 572, where a white man pleaded in abatement to an indictment for murder committed in the country of the Cherokee Indians, that he had been adopted by and become a member of the Cherokee tribe, Chief Justice TANEY said: 'The country in which the crime is charged to have been committed is a part of the territory of the United States, and not within the limits of any particular State. It is true it is occupied by the Cherokee Indians. But it has been assigned to them by the United States as a place of domicil for the tribe and they hold with the assent of the United States, and under their authority.' After referring to the policy of the European nations and the United States in asserting dominion over all the country discovered by them, and the justice of this course, he adds: 'But had it been otherwise, and were the right and the propriety of exercising this power now open to question, yet it is a question for the law-making and political departments of the government, and not for the judicial. It is our duty to expound and execute the law as we find it, and we think it too firmly and clearly established to admit of dispute, that the Indian tribes, residing within the territorial limits of the United States, are subject to their authority, and when the country occupied by one of them is not within the limits of one of the States, Congress may by law punish any offence committed there, no matter whether the offender be a white man or an Indian.'

"The Indian reservation in the case before us is land bought by the United States from Mexico by the treaty of Guadaloupe Hidalgo, and the whole of California, with the allegiance of its inhabitants, many of whom were Indians, was transferred by that treaty to the United States.

"The relation of the Indian tribes living within the borders of the United States, both before and since the Revolution, to the people of the United States has always been an anomalous one and of a complex character.

"Following the policy of the European governments in the discovery of America towards the Indians who were found here, the colonies before the Revolution and the States and the United States since, have recognized in the Indians a possessory right to the soil over which they roamed and hunted and established occasional villages. But they asserted an ultimate title in the land itself, by which the Indian tribes were forbidden to sell or transfer it to other nations or people without the consent of this paramount authority. When a tribe wished to dispose of its land, or any part of it, or the State or the United States wished to purchase it, a treaty with the tribe was the only mode in which this could be done. The United States recognized no right in private persons, or in other nations, to make such a purchase by treaty or otherwise. With the Indians themselves these relations are equally difficult to define. They were, and always have been, regarded as having a semi-independent position when they preserved their tribal relations; not as States, not as nations, not as possessed of the full attributes of sovereignty, but as a separate people with the power of regulating their internal and social relations, and thus far not brought under the laws of the Union or of the State within whose limits they resided.

"Perhaps the best statement of their position is found in the two opinions of this court by Chief Justice Marshall in the case of the *Cherokee Nation* v. *Georgia*, 5 Pet., 1, and in the case of *Worcester* v. *State of Georgia*, 6 Pet., 515, 536. These opinions are exhaustive; and in the separate opinion of Mr. Justice Baldwin, in the former, is a very valuable resumé of the treaties and statutes concerning the Indian tribes previous to and during the confederation.

"In the first of the above cases it was held that these tribes were neither States nor nations, had only some of the attributes of sovereignty, and could not be so far recognized in that capacity as to sustain a suit in the Supreme Court of the United States. In the second case it was said that they were not subject to the jurisdiction asserted over them by the State of Georgia, which, because they were within its limits where they had been for ages, had attempted to extend her laws and the jurisdiction of her courts over them.

"In the opinions in these cases they are spoken of as 'wards of the nation,' 'pupils,' as local dependent communities. In this spirit the United States has conducted its relations to them from its organization to this time. But, after an experience of a hundred years of the treaty-making system of government, Congress has determined upon a new departure—to govern them by acts of Congress. This is seen in the act of March 3, 1871, embodied in § 2079 of the Revised Statutes:

"'No Indian nation or tribe, within the territory of the United States shall be acknowledged or recognized as an independent nation, tribe, or power, with whom the United States may contract by treaty; but no obligation of any treaty lawfully made and ratified with any such Indian nation or tribe prior to March third, eighteen hundred and seventy-one, shall be hereby invalidated or impaired.'

"The case of *Crow Dog*, 109 U. S., 556, in which an agreement with the Sioux Indians, ratified by an act of Congress, was supposed to extend over them the laws of the United States and the jurisdiction of its courts, covering murder and other grave crimes, shows the purpose of Congress in this new departure. The decision in that case admits that if the intention of Congress had been to punish, by the United States courts, the murder of one Indian by another, the law would have been valid. But the court could not see, in the agreement with the Indians sanctioned by Congress, a purpose to repeal § 2146 of the Revised Statutes, which expressly excludes from that jurisdiction the case of a crime committed by one Indian against another in the Indian country. The passage of the act now under consideration was designed to remove that objection, and to go further by including such crimes on reservations lying within a State.

"Is this latter fact a fatal objection to the law? The statute itself contains no express limitation upon the powers of a State or the jurisdiction of its courts. If there be any limitation in either of these, it grows out of the implication arising from the fact that Congress has defined a crime committed within the State, and made it punishable in the courts of the United States. But Congress *has* done this, and *can* do it, with regard to all offences relating to matters to which the Federal authority extends. Does that authority extend to this case?

"It will be seen at once that the nature of the offence (murder) is one which in almost all cases of its commission is punishable by the laws of the States, and within the jurisdiction of their courts. The distinction is claimed to be that the offence under the statute is committed by an Indian, that it is committed on a reservation set apart within the State for residence of the tribe of Indians by the United States, and the fair inference is that the offending Indian shall belong to that or some other tribe. It does not interfere with the process of the State Courts within the reservation, nor with the operation of State laws upon white people found there. Its effect is confined to the acts of an Indian of some tribe, of a criminal character, committed within the limits of the reservation.

"It seems to us that this is within the competency of Congress. These Indian tribes *are* the wards of the nation. They are communities *dependent* on the United States. Dependent largely for their daily food. Dependent for their political rights. They owe no allegiance to the States, and receive from them no protection. Because of the local ill-feeling, the people of the States where they are found are often their deadliest enemies. From their very weakness and helplessness, so largely due to the course of dealing of the Federal Government with them and the treaties in which it has been promised, there arises the duty of protection, and with it the power. This has always been recognized by the Executive and by Congress, and by this Court whenever the question has arisen.

"In the case of *Worcester* v. *The State of Georgia*, above cited, it was held that, though the Indians had by treaty sold their land within that State, and agreed to remove away, which they had failed to do, the State could not, while they remained on those lands, extend its laws, criminal and civil, over the tribes; that the duty and power to compel their removal was in the United States, and the tribe was under their protection, and could not be subjected to the laws of the State and the process of its courts.

"The same thing was decided in the case of *Fellows* v. *Blacksmith and Others*, 19 How., 366. In this case, also, the Indians had sold their lands under supervision of the States of Massachusetts and of New York, and had agreed to remove within a given time. When the time came a suit to recover some of the land was brought in the Supreme Court of New York, which gave judgment for the plaintiff. But this court held, on writ of error, that the State could not enforce this removal, but the duty and the power to do so was in the United States. See also the case of the *Kansas Indians*, 5 Wall., 737; *New York Indians*, 5 Wall., 761.

"The power of the General Government over these remnants of a race once powerful, now weak and diminished in numbers, is necessary to their protection, as well as to the safety of those among whom they dwell. It must exist in that government, because it never has existed anywhere else, because the theater of its exercise is within the geographical limits of the United States, because it has never been denied, and because it alone can enforce its laws on all the tribes.

"We answer the questions propounded to us, that the 9th section of the act of March, 1885, is a valid law in both its branches, and that the Circuit Court of the United States for the District of California has jurisdiction of the offence charged in the indictment in this case."

PART II.

INTERNATIONAL RELATIONS AS MODIFIED BY WAR.

CHAPTER I.

MEASURES SHORT OF WAR.

---

§ 26.—Reprisals.

SILESIAN LOAN, 1752.

(*Martens: Causes Célèbres*, II., 97.)

The controversy in this case was as regards the right of a State to confiscate, for any reason, its public debt, held by foreign creditors.

In 1735 the Emperor Charles VI. borrowed of several London merchants the sum of 1,000,000 écus (3,000,000 francs), and as security for repayment, gave them a mortgage on the revenues of the Province of Silesia. After the death of the Emperor (1740) Frederick II. of Prussia seized Silesia, which Maria Theresa was constrained to formally cede to him by the treaties of Breslau and Berlin, 1742. Frederick agreed, however, to assume the debt of the province and to pay the English creditors.

In 1744 war broke out between England on the one side and France and Spain on the other. And during the next four years the English seized eighteen Prussian vessels and thirty-three other neutral vessels, freighted in whole or in part by Prussian subjects, and laden with merchandise on account of French subjects. These ships and their cargoes were seized for carrying contraband of war or goods belonging to the enemy.

The government of England having refused to listen to the demand of the Prussian government for an indemnity to the claimants,

Frederick II. appointed a commission in 1751 to examine these claims and compensate the claimants out of the Silesian loan, the payment of which had been withheld for this purpose. The next year the commission gave judgment, transferring the English mortgage on the Silesian revenues to the Prussian claimants as indemnity for the seizure of their property.

The contention of the Prussian government was that England had acted illegally in capturing the property of her enemies on neutral vessels,—that the rule, supported by the practice of most of the nations of Europe, was "free ships, free goods;" and further that the treaties of England with the neutral powers, confirmed by the declarations of the English ministry to diplomatic agents of Prussia, had exempted such goods from capture. According to the law of nature, say the Prussian commissioners, the vessel of a neutral is his property wherever it may be found (*i. e.* on the high seas), and a belligerent has no more right to enter it to seize the goods of his enemy, than he has to enter a neutral port and seize the vessels of his enemy therein anchored.

As to contraband of war, the general rule of international law limited it to munitions of war, the only exception being things of *ancipitis usus* destined to a beseiged or blockaded port. It was shown that England herself had made several treaties in which provisions and articles of naval construction were expressly excluded from the list of contraband.

Finally, it was asserted, that the English admiralty court had no right of jurisdiction over Prussian vessels or cargoes seized in places not within English territory; and that these unjust confiscations furnished a just cause for reprisals on the part of Prussia.

The matter was referred by the English government to a commission, composed of Sir R. Lee, judge of the Supreme Court, Dr. Paul, the King's Advocate-General in the civil courts, Sir Dudley Ryder, the Attorney-General, and Mr. William Murray, Solicitor-General (celebrated later as Lord Mansfield). The report of this commission is mentioned by Montesquieu as *réponse sans réplique.* The following propositions were laid down:—

(1) When two powers are at war, each has the right to seize as prize of war, the ships and merchandise of the other, but the property of neutrals should not be captured so long as they preserved their neutrality. It follows, therefore, (2) That the goods of an enemy on board a neutral vessel may be seized. (3) That neutral goods, not contraband, on board the vessel of an enemy, should be released. (4) That contraband goods, although belonging to a neutral, may be seized as prize of war. (5) Before appropriation of

captured goods, there must be condemnation by a court of admiralty, judging according to the law of nations and treaties. (6) The only competent court for that purpose is the court of the captor. (7) All proofs, in the first instance, should come from the vessel seized, such as the ship's papers and the depositions of the master and principal officers of the ship. (8) Every vessel must be furnished with the customary papers. (9) If a seizure is made without sufficient grounds, the captor is to be condemned in damages and expenses. (10) Finally, the law of nations permits reprisals in only two cases: First, in the case of a violent wrong directed and supported by the sovereign, or second, of an absolute denial of justice on the part of all the tribunals, and the sovereign himself, in a matter that admits of no doubt.

The report then takes up the cases of the captured vessels in detail, and shows that they were judged with the utmost impartiality. It would seem that all the Prussian vessels were restored, and all the cargoes in both classes of vessels save fifteen were likewise restored. The Prussian arguments are then answered seriatim, and shown to be without foundation in law or custom. Perhaps the weakest part of the report is the answer to the Prussian contention that contraband was limited to munitions of war. The question, says Wheaton, was at that time in litigation between England and the states of the north who had an interest in the free exportation of the products of their soil, as naval stores and provisions. The commissioners only said that Prussia could not claim the advantage of modifications of international law which had been the result of mutual concessions between England and certain neutral states.

As to the Silesian loan, the King of Prussia had pledged his royal word to pay the debt due to private individuals. This debt was negotiable, and a large part of it may have been transferred to subjects of other states. It would be difficult to find a case where a sovereign had ever seized by way of reprisal a debt which he owed to private individuals. When individuals lend money to a sovereign, they have to trust to his honor; for a sovereign may not, like other men, be sued, and forced to pay by the interposition of courts of law. England, France, and Spain, it was asserted, had adhered religiously to the principle of the inviolability of the public faith.

The dispute was finally settled by a clause of the treaty of Westminster, January 16, 1756, by which Frederick stipulated to pay the English creditors, and the English government agreed to pay 20,000 pounds sterling to satisfy the Prussian claimant. (Wheaton: Histoire du Droit des Gens, I., 260.)

The importance of this case rests, more upon the able exposition of the law of maritime capture by the English commissioners, than upon the question of reprisals. The report of this commission was generally accepted as a correct statement of the law of prize as then existing; and indeed, it so continued with little change till 1856. On the other hand, the Prussian contention was an attempt to establish the principle of "free ships," free goods, which was not realized till a hundred years later.

As to the question of reprisal, England virtually yielded the point in controversy in consenting to indemnify the Prussian claimants. Perhaps political reasons may have influenced the final action. The alliance between France and Austria at this time forced England and Prussia into a counter-alliance, and their minor differences were smoothed over rather hastily.

CASE OF DON PACIFICO, 1850.

(*Brit. and For. Stat. Pap., vol. 39, pp. 333–932.*)

Is a state responsible for the lawless actions of its citizens, to foreign states whose citizens suffer injury? England so held in this case, and proceeded to reprisals to enforce her position.

David Pacifico was a Jew, born at Gibraltar, but in 1847 resident at Athens. By virtue of his birth, he was entitled to the character of a British subject; he had represented himself in that character and had a British passport.

It was customary in Greece for the people to signalize the festival of Easter by burning an effigy of Judas Iscariot; but out of a regard for Mr. Charles de Rothschild, who was at Athens in April, 1847, the police were ordered to prevent this popular ceremony in that year. The mob, attributing this action of the Athenian authorities to the influence of the Jews, was highly incensed against that sect; and proceeded to attack and plunder the house of M. Pacifico, which happened to stand near the place where the effigy was wont to be burned. While his house was being plundered, the family of M. Pacifico received the grossest ill-treatment. M. Pacifico lodged a complaint with the procureur-general of the king, who, on the very day of the riot, held an inquest on the spot, and heard the testimony of the injured parties, but the Greek government took no further action in the matter. M. Pacifico, believing that, by reason of the odium in which his race was held in Greece, he would not be likely to obtain redress through his own efforts, applied to the British minister at Athens, Sir Edmund Lyons. This gentleman called the attention of the Greek government to the facts of the case; but his note was left unanswered for nine months, although he wrote several times subsequently, and when, in January, 1848, he finally received an answer, it was quite unsatisfactory. The government of Greece suggested that M. Pacifico should collect his damages, through the ordinary courts, from the persons who took part in the riot.

There were other British claims pending against Greece, some of which were of long standing, and as no satisfaction could be obtained from the Greek government, Mr. Wyse, successor to Sir Edmund Lyons, was instructed, in December, 1849, to deliver an ultimatum to that government; and in case it was rejected, Admiral Parker, commanding the English fleet in the Mediterranean, was ordered to lay an embargo upon Greek shipping. The demands of the ultimatum were rejected, and the embargo was immediately enforced, several Greek ships of war and many merchant vessels being seized and detained in the Piræus.

Shortly afterwards, in February, 1850, French mediation was accepted, pending which, active measures were suspended on the part of the English fleet. Mr. Wyse and Baron Gros, the French mediator, came to an agreement upon all points at issue save one; namely, a demand of indemnity by Pacifico for the loss of papers which, he alleged, were evidences of a valid claim by him against the Portuguese government for twenty-one thousand pounds. Mr. Wyse proposed that the Greek government should put into his hands a sum of money as security for the payment of this claim, if, after investigation, it should appear to be well-founded. Baron Gros objected to this, because he not only considered the claim to be worthless, but he contended, further, that this demand was too humiliating for Greece. Failing to agree upon this point, Baron Gros withdrew from the negotiations; thereupon, Mr. Wyse sent a new ultimatum to the Greek government, and this time it was accepted, and the indemnity demanded immediately paid.

The total amount of this indemnity was 6,408*l*, 10*s*, with the addition of a deposit of about 5,000*l* as security for the Portuguese claim. The indemnity awarded included the following items: For personal injury, 500*l*; for loss of household effects, jewelry, etc., 4,267*l*, 8*s*. As to his Portuguese claim, a commission, having investigated the case reported in 1851, that it could not be substantiated; but in view of the expense he had incurred, and a small amount due him, he was awarded 150*l*.

Don Pacifico has usually been represented as an adventurer who had little claim upon the sympathy of his fellow-men; and England has generally been severely criticised for supporting his claim. Yet if he was a British subject, he had a right to be protected as such. He was born in British territory, Gibraltar, and his father was born in London. His letters relating to this affair are dignified, and show much ability. His chief crime would seem to have been that of being a Jew. The argument that Pacifico ought to have resorted to the ordinary courts of Greece to obtain his indemnity is quite untenable. What chance of success would he have had in a suit against a mob of several hundred persons, to him unknown, and with public opinion against him? Indeed he brought the matter to the notice of the judiciary department of the government; and it was then the duty of the government to take further proceedings. The fact would seem to be that the whole trouble lay in the weak and vacillating policy of the Greek government, which could easily have avoided all trouble by simply doing justice to M. Pacifico and the other claimants. Whether the British government was justified in resorting to such extreme measures may be questioned; but that some action was called for there can be little doubt.[1]

[1] *Other cases of Reprisal. The bombardment of Greytown*, 1854.—"Greytown was a port on the Mosquito coast, in which some United States citizens resided. These citizens, and others interested with them in business, were subjected to gross indignities and injuries by the local authorities, who were British, but who professed to act under authority from the king or chief of the Mosquito Islands. The parties injured accordingly appealed to the commander of the United States sloop-of-war Cyane, then lying near that port, for protection. To punish the authorities for their action, he bombarded the town. For this act he was denounced by the British residents, who claimed that the British government had a protectorate over that region. His action was sustained by the government of the United States, the ground being the necessity of punishing in this way a great wrong to citizens of the United States, and preventing its continuance." (1 Wharton's Digest, p. 229, and II., p. 595.)

A favorite form of reprisal in coercing weaker states has been by what are called "pacific blockades;" thus, in 1827 "the coasts of Greece were blockaded by the English, French and Russian squadrons, while the three powers professed to be at peace with Turkey."

"The Togus was blockaded by France in 1831, New Granada by England in 1861, Mexico by France in 1838, and La Plata from 1838 to 1840 by France, and from 1845 to 1848 by France and England." (Hall's International Law, Ed. 1890, p. 369.)

In like manner, without a declaration of war, France blockaded the Island of Formosa, and in 1893, the coast of Siam. In 1886 Greece was blockaded by the fleets of nearly all the great European powers.

SECTION 27.—HOSTILE EMBARGO.

THE "BOEDUS LUST."

HIGH COURT OF ADMIRALTY, 1803.

(5 *C. Robinson*, 245.)

This was the case of a Dutch ship on a voyage from Demerara to Batavia, embargoed at the Cape of Good Hope by an English squadron before the actual declaration of war against Holland in 1803, and afterwards condemned as enemy's property.

Sir W. SCOTT, J.—Extract:—"This was the state of the first seizure. It was at first equivocal; and if the matter in dispute had terminated in reconciliation, the seizure would have been converted into a mere civil embargo. That would have been the retroactive effect of that course of circumstances. On the contrary, if the transactions end in hostility, the retroactive effect is directly the other way. It impresses the direct hostile character upon the original seizure. It is declared to be no embargo, it is no longer an equivocal act, subject to two interpretations; there is a declaration of the *animus*, by which it was done, that it was done *hostili animo* and is to be considered as an hostile measure *ab initio*. The property taken is liable to be used as the property of persons, trespassers *ab initio*, and guilty of injuries, which they have refused to redeem by any amicable alteration of their measures. This is the necessary course, if no particular compact intervenes for the restitution of such property taken before a formal declaration of hostilities. No such convention is set up on either side, and the state, by directing proceedings against this property for condemnation, has signified a contrary intention. Accordingly the general mass of Dutch property has been condemned on this retroactive effect; and this property stands upon the same footing.[1]

[1] The object of a hostile embargo may be by way of reprisal to obtain satisfaction for an alleged injury; or, it may be, in the expectation of the outbreak of war, to get possession of property which will presumably be hostile, for the purpose of confiscating it later—after the actual outbreak of war. Although the government might restore such property at the breaking out of war, it has not been the practice to do so; and hence, as Dana says, embargo "refers itself directly to the

Section 28.—Declaration of War.

THE "TEUTONIA."

Privy Council, 1870.

(4 *Privy Council Reports*, 171.)

War may exist *de facto* without a declaration, but in that case there must be actual commencement of hostilities.

***Held*, that a state of war did not exist between France and Prussia, in 1870, prior to the 19th of July, when a formal declaration on the part of France was communicated to the Prussian Government.**

The Lord Chief Justice Mellish:—"This is an appeal in a cause instituted under the 6th section of the Admiralty Court Act, 1861,

question of the right, on breaking out of war, to seize ships and cargoes found in port." (Dana's Wheaton, p. 372, note.)

In the case of *Lindo v. Rodney*, Douglas, 615, Lord Mansfield said, "Ships not knowing of hostilities come in by mistake; upon the declaration of war, or hostilities, all the ships of the enemy are detained in our ports, to be confiscated as the property of the enemy, if no reciprocal agreement is made."

The earlier writers upon international law do not mention embargo, at least in the sense of hostile embargo. Until towards the end of the last century, there was really no distinction made between property found on land, and that found afloat. In both cases it was liable to capture. At the time of Bynkershoek and of Vattel, private property of the enemy was confiscated, though some treaties had exempted it from seizure at the commencement of war. (Bynkershoek, I., chapter II.) Bynkershoek mentions many cases, too, where it was seized before the declaration of war. It was left to the English admiralty courts to formulate the practice into legal maxims by their decisions. As to the retroactive effect of a declaration of war as applied by the courts, it is apparently a necessary invention of Sir William Scott to legalize a practice already in vogue.

Dr. Lushington said in 1854 (Spinks, 14), "With regard to an enemy's property coming to any part of the kingdom, *or being found there*, being seizable, I confess I am astonished that doubt should exist on the subject. I apprehend the law has been this, that it is competent for any person to take possession of such property, unless it had any protection by license, or by some declaration emanating by the authority of the crown, and to assist the crown to proceed against it to adjudication."

At the breaking out of the Crimean War in 1854, merchant vessels of the enemy were allowed by the belligerents six weeks for loading their cargoes and departing. And further, vessels of the same character sailing from foreign ports prior to the promulgation of these orders, were allowed to enter the ports of the enemy and on behalf of Messrs. Duncan, Fox, & Co., the consignees of a bill of lading of the cargo laden on board the ship *Teutonia*, against that ship and her freight, and against the owner of the vessel.

"The *Teutonia* was a Prussian brig, subject to the laws of Prussia, and her master and crew were subjects of the King of Prussia.

"And by the charter-party referred to in the bill of lading it was agreed that, 'after receiving on board the said cargo, the said vessel shall proceed either to Cork, Cowes, or Falmouth, at the option of the master, where he shall receive orders from charterer's agents within three days after his arrival to proceed to any one safe port in Great Britain or on the Continent between Havre and Hamburgh, both included, and there, according to bills of lading and charter-party, deliver the cargo, "the act of God, the Queen's enemies, fire, and all and every other risk, dangers, and accidents of the seas, rivers, and navigation of whatever nature and kind soever excepted," freight to be paid in manner herein mentioned on a true and right delivery of the cargo in the port of discharge at and after the rate of 45*s*. British sterling per ton.'

"The vessel arrived at Falmouth on 10th of July; and the master, whilst there, heard rumours that war was probable between France and Prussia. On the 11th of July, the master received orders from the consignees to discharge the cargo at Dunkirk; and he at once set sail for Dunkirk, and arrived at a distance of about fourteen miles off that port, at 12 o'clock at night of the 16th, which was a Saturday; and the master says that, after lying to for about two hours, a regular pilot, in official uniform, came on board; that he asked the pilot about the war; that the pilot told him it had been declared two days ago; that he asked the pilot where he could bring-to in safety, so that he might ascertain whether war was actually declared or not; that the pilot offered to take him to Flushing, or the Downs, or wherever he liked. The master elected to go to the Downs; and he anchored there on Sunday morning, the 17th, at 10 o'clock. He says, that on that day he could obtain no advice or

discharge their cargoes and to depart. The initiation of this modification of the old rule in this war seems to have been taken by Turkey in her declaration of war against Russia, October 4, 1853. "The Sublime Porte, however, does not consider it just that, agreeably to ancient usage, an embargo should be laid on Russian merchant vessels. Accordingly they will be warned to proceed within a period to be fixed hereafter to the Black Sea or to the Mediterranean, as they choose." (Halleck, p. 364. Hertslet, II., 1176.)

The departure from the old rule in this case, coupled with the numerous treaties stipulating for time for the removal of vessels in case of war, go far towards creating that change of practice which ultimately changes the law of nations. (Dana's Wheaton, note No. 156.)

information; that on the Monday, the 18th, he was on shore at Deal, and the German consul told him that war had broken out. He telegraphed to the owner, who was his father, and received an answer, forbidding him to go to Dunkirk; and on Tuesday the 19th he took the ship into Dover, as the nearest port.

"On the same 19th of July, the French declaration of war was delivered to the Prussian Government at Berlin, which was known the same day by telegraph in England. On the 23d of July, an agent of the plaintiffs went to Dover, and required the master to proceed to Dunkirk, which he refused to do. Afterwards, on the 1st of August, the plaintiffs required the master to deliver them the cargo at Dover, which he refused to do unless he was paid his freight.

"Under these circumstances, the plaintiffs allege that the master has committed two breaches of contract or duty: first in refusing to proceed to, and deliver the cargo at, Dunkirk; and secondly, they complain that, when the performance of the contract became impossible, and the contract was, as they allege, dissolved by the war, the master was not justified in refusing to deliver the cargo to the plaintiffs at Dover without payment of freight.

"The first question to be considered is, whether the master was bound to have entered the port of Dunkirk on the 17th of July; and on that question, the learned Judge (Sir R. PHILLIMORE) in the court below has found that on the 16th of July, the *Teutonia* could not have entered the port of Dunkirk with her cargo without being exposed to the penalties of trading with the enemy of her country; but that, if this was an erroneous application of the law to the facts at that date, the circumstances justified the master in pausing and making further inquiries as to the existing relations between his own country and France, and that he did not exceed the limits of a reasonable time in making the inquiry.

"Their Lordships have great difficulty in agreeing with the learned Judge that the *Teutonia* could not have entered Dunkirk without being exposed to the penalties of trading with the enemy of its country on the 16th of July. There does not appear to their Lordships to be any satisfactory evidence that a state of war existed between France and Prussia prior to the 19th of July.

"Their Lordships do not think that either the declaration made by the French Minister to the French Chambers on the 16th of July, or the telegram sent by Count Bismarck to the Prussian Ambassador in London, in which he states that that declaration appears to be equal to a declaration of war, amounts to actual declaration of war. And though it is true, as stated by the learned Judge, that a war may exist *de facto* without a declaration of war, yet it appears to their Lordships that this can only be effected by an actual commencement of hostilities, which, in this case, is not alleged.

"It is, however, unnecessary further to consider this part of the case, because their Lordships agree with the learned Judge that the master of the *Teutonia*, when he was informed, on his arrival off Dunkirk, by the pilot, although incorrectly, that war had been actually declared two days before, was entitled to pause and to take a reasonable time to make further inquiries, and that he did not exceed the limits of a reasonable time in making inquiries.

"If the master had entered Dunkirk, and it had turned out that war had been previously declared, he would have entered it with notice that he was entering an enemy's port, and this would have obviously exposed his ship to condemnation, and might have exposed himself to severe penalties when he returned to his own country. It seems obvious that, if a master receives credible information that, if he continues in the direct course of his voyage, his ship will be exposed to some imminent peril, as, for instance, that there are pirates in his course, or icebergs, or other dangers of navigation, he must be justified in pausing and deviating from the direct course, and taking any step which a prudent man would take for the purpose of avoiding the danger. And their Lordships agree, if authority was wanting, that the case of *Pole* v. *Cetcovitch*, 9 C. B. (n. s.), 430, is an authority in point. It was argued, however, on the part of the appellants, that, to justify this course, both ship and cargo must be exposed to a common peril, whilst in the present case the cargo, being the property of a neutral owner, would have been in no danger from being carried into a French port, and it was argued that though a master might be justified in deviating from the direct course of the voyage for the purpose of avoiding a danger to which both ship and cargo were exposed, although it might afterwards turn out that the information upon which the master acted was incorrect, yet that if the reported danger was a danger to the ship alone, the master would commit a breach of contract by deviating from the direct course of the voyage unless the danger actually existed, and the master could allege that he was prevented by one of the perils excepted in the bill of lading from pursuing his voyage in the direct course. It appears to their Lordships, however, that there is no sound ground for this distinction; if the cargo had been a Prussian cargo it would have been exposed to the same danger as the ship from entering the port at Dunkirk, and it appears to their Lordships that when an English merchant ships goods on board a foreign ship, he cannot expect that the master will act in any respect differently towards his cargo than he would towards a cargo shipped by one of his own country, and that it cannot be contended that the master is deprived of the right of taking reasonable and prudent steps for the preservation of his ship, because from the accident of the cargo not belonging to his own nation, the cargo is not exposed to the same danger as the ship.

"On the whole, therefore, their Lordships are of opinion, on this part of the case, that the master was justified in going to the Downs for the purpose of ascertaining whether war had actually been declared; and they also entirely agree with the opinion of the learned Judge, that the master was guilty of no unreasonable delay in not returning to Dunkirk before war was actually declared on the 19th of July."

[The Lords next consider "Whether the master was bound to deliver the cargo at Dover without any payment in respect of freight?"

The decision is made in accordance with English law, and, in substance, is as follows: While the breaking out of the war did render it illegal for the *Teutonia* to enter a French port, yet the contract, under the particular terms of the charter-party, could be legally performed by the delivery of the cargo at some of the other ports mentioned in the charter-party—that the contract was not dissolved by the impossibility of delivering the cargo at Dunkirk, and that the ship-owner had not lost his chartered freight nor his lien for it at the time when the cargo was demanded at Dover.]

THE PRIZE CASES. (1)

SUPREME COURT OF THE UNITED STATES, 1862.

(2 *Black.*, 665.)

The character of a civil war—A civil war is never solemnly declared—The powers of the President of the United States in the case of civil war.

Held, that the President had the right, under the Constitution, to institute the blockade of the ports of the rebellious States in 1861; and that the proclamation of blockade was itself official and conclusive evidence to the court that a state of war existed.

Judgment,—Mr. Justice GRIER:—"There are certain propositions of law which must necessarily affect the ultimate decision of these cases, and many others, which it will be proper to discuss and decide before we notice the special facts peculiar to each.

"They are, 1st. Had the President a right to institute a blockade of ports in possession of persons in armed rebellion against the Government, on the principles of international law, as known and acknowledged among civilized states?

"2d. Was the property of persons domiciled or residing within those States a proper subject of capture on the sea as 'enemies' property?'

"I. Neutrals have a right to challenge the existence of a blockade *de facto*, and also the authority of the party exercising the right to institute it. They have a right to enter the ports of a friendly nation for the purposes of trade and commerce, but are bound to recognize the rights of a belligerent engaged in actual war, to use this mode of coercion, for the purpose of subduing the enemy.

"That a blockade *de facto* actually existed, and was formally declared and notified by the President on the 27th and 30th of April, 1861, is an admitted fact in these cases.

"That the President, as the Executive Chief of the Government and Commander-in-chief of the Army and Navy, was the proper person to make such notification, has not been, and cannot be disputed.

"The right of prize and capture has its origin in the '*jus belli*,' and is governed and adjudged under the law of nations. To legitimate the capture of a neutral vessel or property on the high seas, a war must exist *de facto*, and the neutral must have a knowledge or notice of the intention of one of the parties belligerent to use this mode of coercion against a port, city, or territory, in possession of the other.

"Let us inquire whether, at the time this blockade was instituted, a state of war existed which would justify a resort to these means of subduing the hostile force.

"War has been well defined to be, 'That state in which a nation prosecutes its right by force.'

"The parties belligerent in a public war are independent nations. But it is not necessary to constitute war, that both parties should be acknowledged as independent nations or sovereign states. A war may exist where one of the belligerents claims sovereign rights as against the other. Insurrection against a government may or may not culminate in an organized rebellion, but a civil war always begins by insurrection against the lawful authority of the Government. A civil war is never solemnly declared; it becomes such by its accidents—the number, power, and organization of the persons who originate and carry it on. When the party in rebellion occupy and hold in a hostile manner a certain portion of territory; have declared their independence; have cast off their allegiance; have organized armies; have commenced hostilities against their former sovereign, the world acknowledges them as belligerents, and the contest a *war: They* claim to be in arms to establish their liberty and independence, in order to become a sovereign state, while the sovereign party treats them as insurgents and rebels who owe allegiance, and who should be punished with death for their treason.

"The laws of war, as established among nations, have their foundation in reason, and all tend to mitigate the cruelties and misery produced by the scourge of war. Hence the parties to a civil war usually concede to each other belligerent rights. They exchange prisoners, and adopt the other courtesies and rules common to public or national wars.

"'A civil war,' says Vattel, 'breaks the bands of society and government, or at least suspends their force and effect; it produces in the nation two independent parties, who consider each other as enemies, and acknowledge no common judge. Those two parties, therefore, must necessarily be considered as constituting, at least for a time, two separate bodies, two distinct societies. Having no common superior to judge between them, they stand in precisely the same predicament as two nations who engage in a contest and have recourse to arms.

"'This being the case, it is very evident that the common laws of war—those maxims of humanity, moderation, and honor—ought to be observed by both parties in every civil war. Should the sovereign conceive he has a right to hang up his prisoners as rebels the opposite party will make reprisals, etc., etc.; the war will become cruel, horrible, and every day more destructive to the nation.'

"As a civil war is never publicly proclaimed, *eo nomine* against insurgents, its actual existence is a fact in our domestic history which the court is bound to notice and to know. The true test of its existence as found in the writing of the sages of the common law, may be thus summarily stated: 'When the regular course of justice is interrupted by revolt, rebellion, or insurrection, so that the Courts of Justice cannot be kept open, *civil war exists* and hostilities may be prosecuted on the same footing as if those opposing the Government were foreign enemies invading the land.'

"By the Constitution, Congress alone has the power to declare a national or foreign war. It cannot declare war against a State, or any number of States, by virtue of any clause in the Constitution.

"The Constitution confers on the President the whole executive power. He is bound to take care that the laws be faithfully executed. He is Commander-in-chief of the Army and Navy of the United

States, and of the militia of the several States when called into the actual service of the United States. He has no power to initiate or declare a war either against a foreign nation or a domestic State. But by the Acts of Congress of February 28th, 1795, and 3d of March, 1807, he is authorized to call out the militia and use the military and naval forces of the United States in case of invasion by foreign nations, and to suppress insurrection against the government of a State or of the United States.

"If a war be made by invasion of a foreign nation, the President is not only authorized but bound to resist force by force. He does not initiate the war, but is bound to accept the challenge without waiting for any special legislative authority. And whether the hostile party be a foreign invader, or States organized in rebellion, it is none the less a war, although the declaration of it be 'unilateral.' Lord Stowell (1 Dodson, 247) observes, 'It is not the less a war on *that account*, for war may exist without a declaration on either side. It is so laid down by the best writers on the law of nations. A declaration of war by one country only, is not a mere challenge to be accepted or refused at pleasure by the other.'

"The battles of Palo Alto and Resaca de la Palma had been fought before the passage of the Act of Congress of May 13th, 1846, which recognized '*a state of war as existing by the act of the Republic of Mexico.* This act not only provided for the future prosecution of the war, but was itself a vindication and ratification of the Act of the President in accepting the challenge without a previous formal declaration of war by Congress. This greatest of civil wars was not gradually developed by popular commotion, tumultuous assemblies, or local unorganized insurrections. However long may have been its previous conception, it nevertheless sprung forth suddenly from the parent brain, a Minerva in the full panoply of *war*. The President was bound to meet it in the shape it presented itself, without waiting for Congress to baptize it with a name; and no name given to it by him or them could change the fact.

"It is not the less a civil war, with belligerent parties in hostile array, because it may be called an 'insurrection' by one side, and the insurgents be considered as rebels or traitors. It is not necessary that the independence of the revolted province or state be acknowledged in order to constitute it a party belligerent in a war according to the law of nations. Foreign nations acknowledge it as war by a declaration of neutrality. The condition of neutrality cannot exist unless there be two belligerent parties. In the case of the *Santissima Trinidad* (7 Wheaton, 337), this Court say: 'The Government of the United States has recognized the existence of a civil war between

Spain and her colonies, and has avowed her determination to remain neutral between the parties. Each party is therefore deemed by us a belligerent nation, having, so far as concerns us, the sovereign right of war.' (See also 3 Beim., 252.)

"As soon as the news of the attack on Fort Sumter, and the organization of a government by the seceding States, assuming to act as belligerents, could become known in Europe, to wit, on the 13th of May, 1861, the Queen of England issued her proclamation of neutrality, 'recognizing hostilities as existing between the Government of the United States of America and *certain States* styling themselves the Confederate States of America.' This was immediately followed by similar declarations or silent acquiescence by other nations.

"After such an official recognition by the sovereign, a citizen of a foreign state is estopped to deny the existence of a war with all its consequences as regards neutrals. They cannot ask a Court to affect a technical ignorance of the existence of a war, which all the world acknowledges to be the greatest civil war known in the history of the human race, and thus cripple the arm of the Government and paralyze its power by subtle definitions and ingenious sophisms.

"The law of nations is also called the law of nature; it is founded on the common consent as well as the common sense of the world. It contains no such anomalous doctrine as that which this Court are now for the first time desired to pronounce, to wit: That insurgents who have risen in rebellion against their sovereign, expelled her Courts, established a revolutionary government, organized armies, and commenced hostilities, are not *enemies*, because they are *traitors*; and a war levied on the Government by traitors, in order to dismember and destroy it, is not a *war*, because it is an 'insurrection.'

"Whether the President in fulfilling his duties as Commander-in-chief, in suppressing an insurrection, has met with such armed hostile resistance, and a civil war of such alarming proportions as will compel him to accord to them the character of belligerents, is a question to be decided *by him*, and this Court must be governed by the decisions and acts of the political department of the Government to which this power was entrusted. 'He must determine what degree of force the crisis demands.' The proclamation of blockade is itself official and conclusive evidence to the Court that a state of war existed which demanded and authorized a recourse to such a measure, under the circumstances peculiar to the case.

"The correspondence of Lord Lyons with the Secretary of State admits the fact and concludes the question.

"If it were necessary to the technical existence of a war, that it should have legislative sanction, we find it in almost every act passed at the extraordinary session of the Legislature of 1861, which was wholly employed in enacting laws to enable the Government to prosecute the war with vigor and efficiency. And finally, in 1861, we find Congress '*ex majore cautela*' and in anticipation of such astute objections, passing an act 'approving, legalizing and making valid all the acts, proclamations and orders of the President, etc., as if they had been *issued and done under the previous express authority* and direction of the Congress of the United States.'

"Without admitting that such an act was necessary under the circumstances, it is plain that if the President had in any manner assumed powers which it was necessary should have the authority or sanction of Congress, that on the well-known principle of law, '*omnis ratihabitio retrotrahitur, et mandato equiparatur*,' this ratification has operated to perfectly cure the defect. In the case of *Brown* v. *United States* (8 Cr., 131, 132, 133), Mr. Justice STORY treats of this subject, and cites numerous authorities to which we may refer to prove this position, and concludes, 'I am perfectly satisfied that no subject can commence hostilities or capture property of an enemy, when the sovereign has prohibited it. But suppose he did, I would ask if the sovereign may not ratify his proceedings, and thus by a retroactive operation give validity to them?'

"Although Mr. Justice STORY dissented from the majority of the Court on the whole case, the doctrine stated by him on this point is correct and fully substantiated by authority.

"The objection made to this act of ratification, that it is *ex post facto*, and therefore unconstitutional and void, might possibly have some weight on the trial of an indictment in a criminal court. But precedents from that source cannot be received as authoritative in a tribunal administering public and international law.

"On this first question, therefore, we are of opinion that the President had a right, *jure belli*, to institute a blockade of ports in possession of the States in rebellion, which neutrals are bound to regard." (See the remainder of this decision under § 83.)

CHAPTER II.

EFFECTS OF WAR AS BETWEEN ENEMIES.

SECTION 29.—ENEMY'S PROPERTY WITHIN THE TERRITORY, AND DEBTS DUE TO THE ENEMY.

WARE v. HYLTON.

SUPREME COURT OF THE UNITED STATES, 1796.

(3 *Dallas*, 199.)

All the justices admitted—some however with great reluctance—that, in strict law, debts due to an enemy might be confiscated. But this point was not necessary to the decision; for the act of confiscation in question (of Virginia) was *held* to be annulled by the 4th article of the treaty of 1783 with England.

CHASE, J.—"The defendant in error, on the * * * day of July, 1774, passed their penal bond to Farrell and Jones for the payment of £2,976 11*s*. 6*d*., of good British money. In 1777, the war of the revolution having broken out, the legislature of Virginia passed a law to sequester British property; the 3d section of which was as follows:

"'That it should be lawful for any citizen of Virginia, owing money to a subject of Great Britain) to pay the same, or any part thereof, etc., * * * into the loan-office, taking thereout a certificate for the same, in the name of the creditor, with the endorsement, under the hand of the commissioner of said office, expressing the name of the payer.' The Governor and council were to see to the safekeeping of such sums, subject to the future directions of the legislature. In 1780 the defendants (in error) paid into the loan-office a part of their debt, in accordance with stipulations of the above law. After the return of peace, they were sued in the above bond in the circuit court of Virginia; and pleaded the said law of the legislature of

Virginia, and the payment thereunder, in bar of so much of the plaintiff's debt. The plaintiff, to avoid this bar, replied the fourth article of the Treaty of Peace between Great Britain and the United States, of 1783. For this replication there was a general demurrer and rejoinder. The circuit court allowed the demurrer, and the plaintiff brought the present writ of error.

"The counsel for the plaintiff denied that the Virginia legislature was competent to pass such a law; first, because it was contrary to the law of nations, relying on Vattel (lib. 3, c. 5, sec. 77); and, secondly, that the legislature was not competent inasmuch as all such power belonged exclusively to Congress. But it was held by the court that at the time of passing the law, Virginia was a free and independent state, inasmuch as Congress as well as the several individual states had declared their independence; and the articles of confederation had not yet been ratified. Supposing a general right to confiscate British property is admitted to be in Congress, then the same right belonged to the legislature of Virginia at the time of passing the act. 'The legislative power of every nation can only be restrained by its own constitution; and it is the duty of its courts of justice not to question the validity of any law made in pursuance of the constitution. In this case the law is obligatory on the courts of Virginia, and in my opinion on the courts of the United States.' If Virginia, as a sovereign state, violated the ancient or modern law of nations, in making the law of the 20th Oct., 1777, she was answerable in her political capacity to the British nation, whose subjects have been injured in consequence of that law.'

"It appears to me that every nation at war with another is justified, by the general and strict law of nations, to seize and confiscate all movable property of its enemy (of any kind or nature whatever) wherever found, whether within its territory or not." (Bynkershoek, Q. J. P. de rebus bellices, lib. 1, c. 7, pp. 175, 177; Vattel, B. 4, sec. 221; Sir Thomas Parker's Rep., 267.)[1]

[1] The case reported in Parker (11 William III.) is *Attorney-General* v. *Weeden and Shales*. This was the case of a naturalized Frenchman who died during the war, leaving in his will several legacies to Frenchmen living in Bordeaux. A commission was issued to investigate the matter; but peace was made meantime ten days before the inquisition was found and returned. And after long debate, it was resolved: "First, that chose in action which belonged to an alien enemy were forfeitable to the crown.

"Secondly, that this ought to be found by inquisition to make a title to the King; and that this was an inquisition of entitling, and not of instruction. (*Page's Case*, 5 Co., 52).

"Thirdly, that the peace being concluded before the inquisition was taken, discharged the cause of forfeiture.

"The right to confiscate the property of enemies during war is derived from a state of war; and is called the rights of war. This right originates from self-preservation, and is adopted as one of the means to weaken an enemy, and to strengthen ourselves. Justice, also, is another pillar on which it may rest; to wit, a right to reimburse the expense of an unjust war. (Vattel, lib. 3, c. 8, sec. 138; and c. 9, sec. 161.)

"Vattel is the only author relied on (or that can be found) to maintain the distinction between confiscating private debts, and other property of an enemy. Mr. Lee says, 'By the law of nations, rights and credits are not less in our power than other goods; why, therefore, should we regard the rights of war in regard to one, and not as to the others? And when nothing occurs which gives room for a proper distinction, the general law of nations ought to prevail.' He gives many examples of confiscating debts, and concludes (p. 119), 'All which prove, that not only actions, but all other things whatever, are forfeited in time of war.' (Lee on Capture, c. 8, p. 118.) * * *

"If a nation, during war, conducts herself contrary to the law of nations, and no notice is taken of such conduct in the treaty of peace, it is thereby so far considered lawful, as never afterwards to be revived, or to be a subject of complaint. * * *

"The validity of such a law (the act of the Virginia legislature) would not be questioned in the Court of Chancery of Great Britain; and the doctrine seemed strange to me in an American court of justice." (See Lord Chancellor Thurlow in *Wright* v. *Nutt*, 1782, H. Black. Rep., p. 135, 149; 3 Term. Rep., 726.)

[The sixth article of the present Constitution of the United States, "That all treaties made or which shall be made, under the authority of the United States, shall be the supreme law of the land; and the judges in every state shall be bound thereby, anything in the constitution, or laws, of any state to the contrary notwithstanding," was held to have a retroactive effect, and to be considered in the same light as if the Constitution had been established before the making of the treaty of 1783; and that Congress was competent to make the fourth article of the said treaty, which is to the following effect: "It is agreed that creditors, on either side, shall meet with no lawful impediment to the recovery of the full value, in sterling money, of all *bona fide* debts, heretofore contracted." And further, the said fourth article of the treaty annulled the act of confiscation of the legislature of Virginia, and the payment under it. And on that ground the

"Fourthly, that the inquisition taken afterwards did not relate to set up this forfeiture, for the cause was but temporary; and that cause being removed before the King's title was found, the finding after should not relate."

judgment of the circuit court was reversed; and judgment on the demurrer for plaintiff in error with costs in the circuit court, and the costs of the appeal.

The other justices expressed their individual opinions in the case.

PATTERSON, J., admitted, that in strict law, debts might be confiscated, but spoke strongly against the policy of doing so.

WILSON, J., thought the confiscation of debts disreputable.

CUSHING, J., admitted the right to confiscate debts, but thought the fourth article of the treaty annulled the statute of Virginia; and further that the state ought to be responsible to the debtor for the amount paid into the loan office.—F. S.]

BROWN v. THE UNITED STATES.

SUPREME COURT OF THE UNITED STATES, 1814.

(8 *Cranch*, 110.)

There is no difference in principle between the confiscation of debts due to the enemy and the confiscation of the property of the enemy found in the country at the outbreak of war. *Held*, that by the strict law of war both may be confiscated; but, under the Constitution of the United States, it can only be done by the authority of Congress.

The *Emulous*, owned by John Delano and others, citizens of the United States, was chartered to a company carrying on trade in Great Britain, one of whom was an American citizen, for the purpose of carrying a cargo from Savannah to Plymouth (England). After the cargo was put on board, the vessel was stopped in port by the embargo of the 4th of April, 1812. On the 25th of the same month, it was agreed between the master of the ship and the agent of the shippers, that she should proceed with her cargo to New Bedford, where her owners resided. While the ship was lying at New Bedford, war was declared (18th of June); and in October or November the cargo, consisting of pine timber, staves, and laths, was unloaded, the timber being put in a salt-water creek—not navigable, and on the 7th November was sold by the agent of the owners, an American citizen, to the claimant, Armitz Brown, who was also an American citizen. On the 19th April, 1813, a libel was filed by the attorney for the United States in the district court of Massachusetts against the said cargo, as well on behalf of the United States as for and in behalf of John Delano, and for all others concerned. The attorney had no instructions from his superior, the president of the United States, but acted at the instance of Delano, the owner of the *Emulous*.

The district court dismissed the libel. The circuit court (STORY, Justice), reversed this sentence, and condemned the pine timber as enemy's property forfeited to the United States. The claimant appealed to the supreme court.

Judgment, by MARSHALL, C. J:—

"The material question made at bar is this: can the pine timber, even admitting the property not to be changed by the sale in November, be condemned as prize of war? The cargo of the *Emulous* having been legally acquired and put on board the vessel, having been detained by an embargo not intended to act on foreign property, the vessel having sailed before the war, from Savannah, under a stipulation to reland the cargo in some port of the United States, the re-landing having been made with respect to the residue of the cargo, and the pine timber having been floated into shallow water, where it was secured and in the custody of the owner of the ship, an American citizen, the Court cannot perceive any solid distinction, so far as respects confiscation, between this property and other British property found on land at the commencement of hostilities. It will therefore be considered as a question relating to such property generally, and to be governed by the same rule.

"Respecting the power of government no doubt is entertained. That war gives to the sovereign full right to take the persons and confiscate the property of the enemy, wherever found, is conceded. The mitigations of this rigid rule, which the humane and wise policy of modern times has introduced into practice, will more or less affect the exercise of this right, but cannot impair the right itself. That remains undiminished, and when the sovereign authority shall choose to bring it into operation, the judicial department must give effect to its will. But until that will shall be expressed, no power of condemnation can exist in the court.

"The questions to be decided by the court are:

"1st. May enemy's property, found on land at the commencement of hostilities, be seized and condemned as a necessary consequence of the declaration of war?

"2d. Is there any legislative act which authorizes such seizure and condemnation?

"Since, in this country, from the structure of our government, proceedings to condemn the property of an enemy found within our territory at the declaration of war, can be sustained only upon the principle that they are instituted in execution of some existing law, we are led to ask:

"Is the declaration of war such a law? Does that declaration, by its own operation, so vest the property of the enemy in the government, as to support proceedings for its seizure and confiscation, or does it vest only a right, the assertion of which depends on the will of the sovereign power?

"The universal practice of forbearing to seize and confiscate debts and credits, the principle universally received, that the right to them revives on the restoration of peace, would seem to prove that war is not an absolute confiscation of this property, but simply confers the right of confiscation.

"Between debts contracted under the faith of laws, and property acquired in the course of trade, on the faith of the same laws, reason draws no distinction; and, although, in practice, vessels with their cargoes, found in port at the declaration of war, may have been seized, it is not believed that modern usage would sanction the seizure of the goods of an enemy on land, which were acquired in peace in the course of trade. Such a proceeding is rare, and would be deemed a harsh exercise of the right of war. But although the practice in this respect may not be uniform, that circumstance does not essentially affect the question. The inquiry is whether such property vests in the sovereign by the mere declaration of war, or remains subject to a right of confiscation, the exercise of which depends on the national will: and the rule which applies to one case so far as respects the operation of a declaration of war on the thing itself, must apply to all others over which war gives an equal right. The right of a sovereign to confiscate debts being precisely the same with the right to confiscate other property found in the country, the operation of a declaration of war on debts and on other property found in the country must be the same. What, then, is this operation?

"Even Bynkershoek, who maintains the broad principle, that in war everything done against an enemy is lawful; that he may be destroyed, though unarmed and defenceless; that fraud or even poison, may be employed against him; that a most unlimited right is acquired to his person and property; admits that war does not transfer to the sovereign a debt due to his enemy; and, therefore, if payment of such debt be not exacted, peace revives the former right of the creditor; 'because,' he says, 'the occupation which is had by war consists more in fact than in law.' He adds to his observations on this subject, 'let it not, however, be supposed that it is only true of actions, that they are not condemned *ipso jure*, for other things also belonging to the enemy, may be conceded and escape condemnation.'

"Vattel says, that 'the sovereign can neither detain the persons nor the property of those subjects of the enemy who are within his dominions at the time of the declaration.'

"It is true that this rule is, in terms, applied by Vattel to the property of those only who are personally within the territory at the commencement of hostilities; but it applies equally to things in action and to things in possession; and if war did, of itself, without any further exercise of the sovereign will, vest the property of the enemy in the sovereign, his presence would not exempt it from this operation of war. Nor can a reason be perceived for maintaining that the public faith is more entirely pledged for the security of property trusted in the territory of the nation in time of peace, if it be accompanied by its owner, than if it be confided to the care of others.

"Chitty, after stating the general right of seizure, says, 'but, in strict justice, that right can take effect only on those possessions of a belligerent which have come to the hands of his adversary after the declaration of hostilities.' (P. 67.)

"The modern rule, then, would seem to be, that tangible property belonging to an enemy and found in the country at the commencement of war, ought not to be immediately confiscated; and in almost every commercial treaty an article is inserted stipulating for the right to withdraw such property.

"This rule seems to be totally incompatible with the idea that war does of itself vest the property in the belligerent government. It may be considered as the opinion of all who have written on the *jus belli*, that war gives the right to confiscate, but does not itself confiscate the property of the enemy; and their rules go to the exercise of this right."

Having thus decided that war gives the right, in accordance with international law, to confiscate enemy's property in the situation of this cargo, but not of its own force, the court next proceeded to inquire whether the Constitution or laws of the United States had authorized such confiscation. The Constitution confers upon Congress the power "to declare war, grant letters of marque and reprisal, and make rules concerning captures on land and water." It is evident then that the power to confiscate is vested in Congress, and that it is not included in the power to declare war. The declaration of war, therefore, did not authorize confiscation; and Congress had enacted no other law to that effect.

"Neither is it admitted that the executive, in executing the laws of war, may seize and the courts condemn all property which, according to the modern law of nations, is subject to condemnation. The rule is in its nature flexible. It is subject to infinite modifications; it is not an immutable rule of law, but depends on political considerations which may continually vary. It is a question rather of policy than of law; and like all other questions of policy, it is proper for the consideration of a department which can modify it at will; not for the consideration of a department which can pursue only the law as it is written. It is proper for the consideration of the legislature, and not of the executive or judiciary.

"The court is therefore of opinion that there is error in the sentence of condemnation pronounced in the circuit court in this case, and doth direct that the same be reversed and annulled, and that the sentence of the district court be affirmed."

Mr. Justice STORY with a minority of the court, held that, the right of confiscation existing, it was within the power of the executive to enforce confiscation, in the same manner that the executive established blockades and authorized the capture of the enemy's property at sea, and contraband goods.

Ex Parte BOUSSMAKER.

CHANCERY, 1806.

(13 *Vesey Jun.*, 71.)

Held, that property of an enemy, in the form of a dividend arising from a contract made before the war, could not be confiscated.

This was a petition to be admitted to prove a debt under a commission of bankruptcy; which the commissioners refused to admit, upon the objection that the creditors applying to prove were alien enemies.

The Lord Chancellor, ERSKINE, said: "If this had been a debt arising from a contract with an alien enemy, it could not possibly stand; for the contract would be void. But, if the two nations were at peace at the date of the contract, from the time of war taking place the creditor could not sue; but the contract being originally good, upon the return of peace the right would revive. It would be contrary to justice, therefore, to confiscate this dividend. Though the right to recover is suspended, that is no reason why the fund should be divided among the other creditors. The point is of great moment, from the analogy to the case of an action; and it is true, a court of law would not take notice of the objection without a plea. It must appear upon the record. * * * The policy, avoiding contracts with an enemy is sound and wise; but when the contract was originally good, and the remedy is only suspended, the proposition, that therefore the fund should be lost, is very different.

"Let the claim be entered; and the dividend reserved."

WOLFF v. OXHOLM.

KING'S BENCH, 1817.

(6 *Maule and Selwyn*, 92.)

Held, that the confiscation of private debts due to an enemy was not in conformity with the usage of nations.

Oxholm, a Danish subject, was indebted, February 7, 1800, to the firm of Wolff & Dorville, English subjects, in the sum of £2,101 7*s*. 5*d*. sterling money, for which a suit was instituted in the Danish courts by Wolff & Dorville through their proctor, resident in Denmark. The defendant set up certain counter-claims in defense. To avoid this, the plaintiffs in 1806 assigned the debt to a Danish subject, who should sue and recover in his own name, thus avoiding some technicality in the Danish laws which affected the case.

The defendant, in Sept., 1806, instituted a cross-suit. In 1807, whilst these suits were pending, a war broke out between Great Britain and Denmark; and an ordinance was made by the government of Denmark, August 16, 1807, by which all ships, goods, money, and money's worth, of or belonging to English subjects, were declared to be sequestrated and detained; and by another law or ordinance of the Danish government, dated Sept. 9, 1807, all persons were commanded with in three days after the publication thereof (wherever it was not then already done) to transmit an account of the debts due to English subjects, of whatsoever nature or quality they might be, the whole of which were directed to be paid into the Danish treasury, and in case of concealment the person so offending was to be proceeded against by the officers of the exchequer. In virtue of this law and ordinance, commissioners were appointed to receive the debts declared to be sequestrated: and as a consequence of the ordinance, the suit of Mountford (the assignee of Wolff & Co.) against the defendant was not further prosecuted, and in 1807, the proctor gave information to the commissioners of the debt. The commissioners authorized such payments at the then current rate of exchange, six Danish dollars to the pound sterling.

In 1812 the defendant paid to the commissioners the amount of the debt with the accrued interest, and took their receipt for the same; upon the production of which, the court quashed the cause depending between Mountford and the defendant. It is said the rate of exchange at the time of payment, was forty-five to fifty dollars to the pound sterling. In 1814, the defendant arrived in this country and was arrested, and held to bail by the plaintiffs for the debt.

Judgment of ELLENBOROUGH, C. J.:—This judgment is a long and elaborate discussion, in which the opinions of Grotius, Puffendorf, Vattel, and some older authorities are analyzed; and the conclusion reached, that the practice of Europe in refraining from the confiscation of debts had become so general that confiscation must be considered as a violation of the public faith. It is admitted that Bynkershoek mentions several cases of confiscation in the 16th and 17th centuries which that writer considered as warranted by the law of nations. A similar case is cited as decided by a court at Paris in the middle of the 16th century. Moreover, Sir Matthew Hale is quoted as saying "that by the law of England debts and goods found in the realm belonging to alien enemies belong to the King, and may be seized by him." But, say the court, the books referred to do not furnish an instance of the seizure of debts, or a decided case in support of the legality of such a seizure. Magna Charta, Cap. 30, is referred to in support of the position of the court.

And finally, in the midst of all the extraordinary violence of our own times, say the court, "this ordinance of the court of Denmark stands single and alone, not supported by any precedent, nor adopted as an example in any other state." Not being therefore conformable to the usage of nations, the quashing of the suit of the plaintiffs thereunder could form no bar to the present suit.

"Postea to the plaintiffs." [1]

[1] This decision is directly at variance with the American cases above quoted. Sir ROBERT PHILLIMORE (International Law, III, 723) in reviewing this judgment, shows that the inferences from the language of Vattel, Grotius, and Puffendorf were not warranted; while the authority of Bynkershoek and the Dutch tribunals was hardly touched upon. That, moreover, to the high authority of Story and the American tribunals no allusion appears to have been made by counsel or judge. "Perhaps," he continues, "if the occasion should present itself, the decision of Lord Ellenborough might be reversed in England. It was the decision of a single court not much accustomed to deal with questions of international law."

The provocation for the act of the Danish government was very great. An English squadron had taken violent possession of the Danish fleet in time of peace between the two countries (1807); and at the breaking out of war in consequence of this act, the English government had confiscated all the Danish ships found in English ports as droits of admiralty.

SECTION 30.—PRIVATE CONTRACTS.

HANGER v. ABBOTT.

SUPREME COURT OF THE UNITED STATES, 1867.

(6 *Wallace*, 532.)

Held, that, in the case of contract debts, as between persons who become enemies, the remedy is suspended during the period of the war, and revives on the return of peace. In such case, the statute of limitations does not run during the war.

Error to the Circuit Court for the Eastern District of Arkansas.

J. & E. Abbott, of New Hampshire, sued Hanger, of Arkansas, in assumpsit. The latter pleaded the statute of limitations of Arkan-

In the case of the *Johanna Emilie*, Spinks' Prize Cases, 14 (1854), Dr. LUSHINGTON said, "If the property was on land, according to the ancient law, it was also seizable; and certainly during the American war there were not wanting instances in which such property was seized and condemned by law,—not by the authority of this court, but of another. That rigor was afterwards relaxed. I believe no such instance has occurred from the time of the American war to the present day—no instance in which property inland was subject to search or seizure, but no doubt it would be competent to the authority of the crown if it thought fit."

During the civil war in the United States (1861), the Congress of the Confederate States confiscated by act of Congress all property, movable or immovable, and all rights, credits, and interests held within the Confederacy by or for any alien enemy, except public stocks and securities. And all persons domiciled within the enemy's country were held to be subject to the provisions of the act. (Act of August 6th, 1861. McPherson, History of the Rebellion, 203.)

It would seem to be clear that, by the strict law, tangible property and debts are still subject to confiscation by a belligerent. But it is equally clear that the entire drift of modern opinion and practice is opposed to the exercise of that right. In the case of *Hanger* v. *Abbott*, 1867, the Supreme Court of the United States said "in strictness it (the right of confiscating such debts) may still be said to exist, but it may well be considered as a naked and impolitic right, condemned by the enlightened conscience of modern times."

On the other hand, property of the enemy found afloat in ports at the outbreak of war, as ships with their cargoes, has generally in the absence of a contrary agreement, been confiscated, following the rules still in practice in respect of private property of the enemy at sea. In *Brown* v. *The United States*, the Supreme Court was careful to exclude from the rule of the decision property found afloat in ports. But here, too, there are strong indications of a milder rule, if indeed it is not already pretty firmly established.

sas, which limits such action to three years. The former replied the rebellion, which broke out after the cause of action accrued, and closed for more than three years all lawful courts. On demurrer, and judgment against it, and error to this court, the question here was, simply, whether the time during which the courts in Arkansas were closed on account of the rebellion, was to be excluded from the computation of time fixed by the Arkansas statute of limitations within which suits on contracts were to be brought, there being no exception by the terms of the statute itself for any such case.

Extracts from the opinion of the court, delivered by Mr. Justice CLIFFORD:—

"Proclamation of blockade was made by the President on the nineteenth day of April, 1861, and, on the thirteenth day of July, in the same year, Congress passed a law authorizing the President to interdict all trade and intercourse between the inhabitants of the States in insurrection and the rest of the United States. 12 Stat. at Large.

"War, when duly declared or recognized as such by the war-making power, imports a prohibition to the subjects, or citizens, of all commercial intercourse and correspondence with citizens or persons domiciled in the enemy's country. Upon this principle of public law it is the established rule in all commercial nations, that trading with the enemy, except under a government license, subjects the property to confiscation, or to capture and condemnation.

"Partnership with a foreigner is dissolved by the same event which makes him an alien enemy, because there is in that case an utter incompatibility created by operation of law between the partners as to their respective rights, duties, and obligations, both public and private, which necessarily dissolves the relation, independent of the will or acts of the parties. Direct consequence of the rule as established in those cases is, that as soon as war is commenced all trading, negotiation, communication, and intercourse between the citizens of one of the belligerents with those of the other, without the permission of the government, is unlawful. No valid contract, therefore, can be made, nor can any promise arise by implication of law, from any transaction with an enemy. Exceptions to the rule are not admitted; and even after the war has terminated, the defendant, in an action founded upon a contract made in violation of that prohibition, may set up the illegality of the transaction as a defence. * * *

"Executory contracts also with an alien enemy, or even with a neutral, if they cannot be performed except in the way of commercial intercourse with the enemy, are dissolved by the declaration of war, which operates for that purpose with a force equivalent to an act of Congress. *Exposito* v. *Bowden*, 4 Ellis & Blackburne, 963.

"In former times the right to confiscate debts was admitted as an acknowledged doctrine of the law of nations, and in strictness it may still be said to exist, but it may well be considered as a naked and impolitic right, condemned by the enlightened conscience and judgment of modern times. Better opinion is that executed contracts, such as the debt in this case, although existing prior to the war, are not annulled or extinguished, but the remedy is only suspended, which is a necessary conclusion, on account of the inability of an alien enemy to sue or to sustain, in the language of the civilians, *a persona standi in judicio*. *Flint* v. *Waters*, 15 East., 260.

"Trading, which supposes the making of contracts, and which also involves the necessity of intercourse and correspondence, is necessarily contradictory to a state of war, but there is no exigency in war which requires that belligerents should confiscate or annul the debts due by the citizens of the other contending party. * * *

"Under the thirty-fourth section of the Judiciary Act, the statutes of limitations of the several States, where no special provision has been made by Congress, form the rule of decision in the courts of the United States, and the same effect is given to them as is given in the courts of the State. * * *

"When our ancestors immigrated here, they brought with them the statute of 21 Jac. 1, c. 16, entitled 'An act for limitation of actions, and for avoiding of suits in law,' known as the statute of limitations. * * *

"Persons within the age of twenty-one years, *femes covert*, *non compos mentis*, persons imprisoned or beyond the seas, were excepted out of the operation of the third section of the act, and were allowed the same period of time after such disability was removed. Just exceptions indeed are to be found in all such statutes, but when examined it will appear that they were framed to prevent injustice and never to encourage laches or to promote negligence. Cases where the courts of justice are closed in consequence of insurrection or rebellion are not within the express terms of any such exception, but the statute of limitations was passed in 1623, more than a century before it came to be understood that debts due to alien enemies were not subject to confiscation. Down to 1737, says Chancellor KENT, the opinion of jurists was in favor of the right to confiscate, and many maintained that such debts were annulled by the declaration of war. Regarding such debts as annulled by war, the law-makers of that day never thought of making provision for the collection of the same on the restoration of peace between the belligerents. Commerce and civilization have wrought great changes in the spirit of nations touching the conduct of war, and in respect to the principles of international law applicable to the subject.

"Constant usage and practice of belligerent nations from the earliest times subjected enemy's goods in neutral vessels to capture and condemnation as prize of war, but the maxim is now universally acknowledged that 'free ships make free goods' which is another victory of commerce over the feelings of avarice and revenge. Individual debts, as a general remark, are no longer the subject of confiscation, and the rule is universally admitted that if not confiscated during the war, the return of peace brings with it both 'the right and the remedy.' *Wolf* v. *Oxholm*, 6 Maule & Selwyn, 92. * * *

"Old decisions, made when the rule of law was that war annulled all debts between the subjects of the belligerents, are entitled to but little weight, even if it is safe to assume that they are correctly reported, of which, in respect to the leading case of *Prideaux* v. *Webber*, 1 Levinz, 31, there is much doubt. *Miller* v. *Prideaux*, 1 Keble, 157; *Lee* v. *Rogers*, 1 Levinz, 110; *Hall* v. *Wybourne*, 2 Salked., 420; *Aubrey* v. *Fortescue*, 10 Modern, 205, are of the same class, and to the same effect. All of those decisions were made between parties who were citizens of the same jurisdiction, and most of them were made nearly a hundred years before the international rule was acknowledged, that war only suspended debts due to an enemy, and that peace had the effect to restore the remedy. The rule of the present day is, that debts existing prior to the war, but which made no part of the reasons for undertaking it, remain entire, and the remedies are revived with the restoration of peace. * * *

"Text writers usually say, on the authority of the old cases referred to, that the non-existence of courts, or their being shut, is no answer to the bar of the statute of limitations, but Plowden says that things happening by an invincible necessity, though they be against common law, or an act of Parliament, shall not be prejudicial, that, therefore, to say that the courts were shut, is a good excuse on voucher of record. Exceptions not mentioned in the statutes have sometimes been admitted, and this court held that the time which elapsed while certain prior proceedings were suspended by appeal, should be deducted, as it appeared that the injured party in the meantime had no right to demand his money, or to sue for the recovery of the same; and in view of those circumstances, the court decided that his right of action had not accrued so as to bar it, although not commenced within six years. *Montgomery* v. *Hernandez*, 12 Wheaton, 129.

"But the exception set up in this case stands upon much more solid reasons, as the right to sue was suspended by the acts of the government, for which all the citizens are responsible. Unless the rule be so, then the citizens of a state may pay their debts by entering into an insurrection or rebellion against the government of the Union, if they are able to close the courts, and to successfully resist the laws, until the bar of the statute becomes complete, which cannot for a moment be admitted. Peace restores the right and the remedy, and as that cannot be if the limitation continues to run during the period the creditor is rendered incapable to sue, it necessarily follows that the operation of the statute is also suspended during the same period.

"Judgment affirmed with costs." [1]

GRISWOLD v. WADDINGTON.

COURT OF APPEALS OF NEW YORK, 1818.

(15 *Johnson's Reports*, 57.)

Held, that commercial partnerships existing between citizens of two States are dissolved by the breaking out of war between those States.

And, that the declaration of war itself furnishes the necessary legal notice of such dissolution.

Before the breaking out of the war between the United States and England, in 1812, Joshua Waddington, an American citizen residing in New York, and Henry Waddington, a British subject residing in London, were partners in a commercial business. During the war, N. L. and G. Griswold had transactions with J. Waddington, in the United States. After the close of the war, the Griswolds sued to recover a balance of account arising out of those transactions; and their contention was that H. Waddington, the London partner, was liable for the debt.

Judgment, by SPENCER, J.:—

"It appears to me, that the declaration of war did, of itself work a dissolution of all commercial partnerships existing at the time between British subjects and American citizens.

"By dealing with either party, no third person could acquire a legal right against the other, because one alien enemy cannot, in that capacity, make a private contract binding upon the other. This conclusion would seem to be an inevitable result from the new relations

[1] See also *Semmes* v. *Hartford Ins. Co.*, 13 Wallace, 160; and *Brown* v. *Hiatts*, 15 Chil., 177. That interest does not run during the war, see *Brown* v. *Hiatts*, 15 Wallace, 177.

created by the war. It is a necessary consequence of the other proposition, that it is unlawful to have communication or trade with an enemy. To suppose a commercial partnership (such as this was) to be continued, and recognized by law as subsisting, when the same law had severed the subjects of the two countries, and declared them enemies to each other, is to suppose the law chargeable with inconsistency and absurdity. For what use or purpose could the law uphold such a connection, when all further intercourse, communication, negotiation, or dealing between the partners, was prohibited, as unlawful? Why preserve the skeleton of the firm, when the sense and spirit of it has fled, and when the execution of any one article of it by either, would be a breach of his allegiance to his country? In short, it must be obvious to every one, that a state of war creates disabilities, imposes restraints, and exacts duties altogether inconsistent with the continuance of that relation. Why does war dissolve a charter-party, or a commercial contract for a particular voyage? Because, says Valin, (tom. 1 p. 626,) the war imposes an insurmountable obstacle to the accomplishment of the contract; and this obstacle arising from a cause beyond the control of the party, it is very natural, he observes, that the charter-party should be dissolved, as of course. Why should the contract of partnership continue by law when equally invincible obstacles are created by law to defeat it? If one alien enemy can go and bind his hostile partner, by contracts in time of war, when the other can have no agency, consultation, or control concerning them, the law would be as unjust as it would be extravagant. The good sense of the thing as applicable to this subject, is the rule prescribed by the Roman law, that a copartnership in any business ceased when there was an end put to the business itself. *Item si alicujus rei societas sit, et finis negotio impositus est, finitur societas.* (Inst. 3, 26, 6.)

"The doctrine, that war does not interfere with private contracts, is not to be carried to an extent inconsistent with the rights of war.

"Suppose that H. & J. W. had entered into a contract before the war, which was to continue until 1814, by which one of them was to ship, half yearly, to London, consigned to the other, a cargo of provisions, and the other, in return, to ship to New York a cargo of goods. The war which broke out in 1812, would surely have put an end to the further operation of this contract, lawful and innocent as it was when made. No person could raise a doubt on this point; and what sanctity or magic is there in a contract of copartnership, that it must not yield to the same power?

"If we examine, more particularly, the nature and objects of commercial partnerships, it would seem to be contrary to all the rules by which they are to be construed and governed, that they should continue to exist, after the parties are interdicted by the government, from any communication with each other, and are placed in a state of absolute hostility. It is of the essence of the contract that each party should contribute something valuable, as money, or goods, or skill and labor on joint account, and for the common benefit; and that the object of the partnership should be lawful, and honest business.

"But how can the partners have any unity of interest, or any joint object that is lawful, when their pursuits, in consequence of the war, and in consequence of the separate allegiance which each owes to his own government, must be mutually hostile?

"The commercial business of each country, and of all its people, is an object of attack, and of destruction to the other. One party may be engaged in privateering, or in supplying the fleets and armies of his country with provisions, or with munitions of war; and can the law recognize the other partner as having a joint interest in the profits of such business? It would be impossible for the one partner to be concerned *in any commercial business*, which was not auxiliary to the resources and efforts of his country in a maritime war. And shall the other partner be lawfully drawing a revenue from such employment of capital, and such personal services directed against his own country? We cannot contemplate such a confusion of obligation between the law of partnership and the law of war, or such a conflict between his interest as a partner, and his duty as a patriot, without a mixture of astonishment and dread. Shall it be said that the partnership must be deemed to be abridged during war, to business that is altogether innoxious and harmless?

"But I would ask, how can we cut down a partnership in that manner, without destroying it? The very object of the partnership, in this case, was, no doubt, commercial business between England and the United States, and which the hostile state of the two countries interdicted; or it may have been business in which the personal communication and advice of each partner was deemed essential, and without which the partnership would not have been formed. It is one of the principles of the law of partnership, that it is dissolved by the death of any one of its members, however numerous the association may be; and the reason is this; the personal qualities of each partner enter into the consideration of the contract, and the survivors ought not to be held bound without a new assent, when perhaps, the character of the deceased partner was the inducement to the connection.

"Shall we say that the partnership continues during war, in a quiescent state, and that the hostile partners do not share in each other's profits, made in carrying on the hostile commerce of each country?

"It would be then most unjust to make the party who did not share in profit to share in loss, and to be bound by the other's contracts; but if one partner does not share in profit, that alone destroys a partnership. It would be what the Roman lawyers called *Societas leonina*, in allusion to the fable of the lion, who, having entered into a partnership with the other animals of the forest in hunting, appropriated to himself all the prey.

"It is one of the fundamental principles of every commercial partnership, that each partner has the power to buy and sell and pay and receive, and to contract and bind the firm. But then, again, as a necessary check to this power, each partner can interfere and stop any contract about to be made by any one of the rest. This is an elementary rule, derived from the civil law. In *re pari potiorem causam esse prohibentis constat.* (Pothier, Trait. du Cont. sec. n. 90.)

"But if the partnership continues in war between hostile associates, this salutary power is withdrawn, and each partner is left defenceless. If the law continues the connection, after it has destroyed the check, the law is then cruel and unjust.

"In speaking of the dissolution of partnerships, the French and civil law writers say, that partnerships are dissolved by a change of the condition of one of the parties which disables him to perform his part of the duty, as by a loss of liberty, or banishment, or bankruptcy, or a judicial prohibition to execute his business, or by confiscation of his goods.

"The English law of partnership is derived from the same source; and as the cases arise, the same principles are applied. The principle here is, that when one of the parties becomes disabled to act, or when the business of the association becomes impracticable, the law, as well as common reason, adjudges the partnership to be dissolved. * * *

"Another objection was raised, from the want of notice of the dissolution of the partnership. The answer to this is extremely easy, and perfectly conclusive. Notice is requisite when a partnership is dissolved by the act of the parties, but it is not necessary when the dissolution takes place, by the act of the laws. The declaration of war, from the time it was duly made known to the nations, put an end to all future dealings between the subjects and citizens of the two countries, and, consequently, to the future operation of the copartnership in question.

"The declaration of war was, of itself, the most authentic and monitory notice. Any other notice, in a case like this, between two public enemies, who had each his domicil in his own country, would have been useless. All mankind were bound to take notice, of the war, and of its consequence. The notice, if given, could only be given by each partner in his own country; and there it would be useless, as his countrymen could not hold any lawful intercourse with the enemy. It could not be given as a joint act, for the partners cannot lawfully commune together.

"But, it was said, that the peace had a healing influence, and restored the parties to all their rights, and arrested all confiscations, and forfeitures, which had not previously and duly attached. I do not know that I differ from the counsel in any just application of this doctrine.

"As far as the war suspended the right of action existing in the adverse party prior to the war, that right revived; but if the contract in this case was unlawful, peace could not revive it, for it never had any legal existence. So, too, the copartnership being once dissolved by the war, it was extinguished forever, except as to matters existing prior to the war."

NEW YORK LIFE INS. CO. v. STATHEM.

SAME v. SEYMS.

MANHATTAN LIFE INS. CO. v. BUCK, Executor.

Supreme Court of the United States, 1876.

(93 *United States Reports*, 24.)

Executory contracts between persons who become enemies, where time is material and of the essence of the contract, are annulled by the war.

Life insurance policies are of this character; but the assured is entitled to recover the equitable value of the policy, at the time of the outbreak of the war.

The first of these cases is here on appeal from, and the second and third on writs of error to, the Circuit Court of the United States for the Southern District of Mississippi.

The first case is a bill in equity, filed to recover the amount of a policy of life assurance, granted by the defendant (now appellant) in 1851, on the life of Dr. A. D. Stathem, of Mississippi, from the proceeds of certain funds belonging to the defendant attached in the hands of its agent at Jackson, in that State. It appears from the statements of the bill that the annual premiums accruing on the policy were all regularly paid, until the breaking out of the late civil war, but that, in consequence of that event, the premium due on the 8th of December, 1861, was not paid; the parties assured being residents of Mississippi, and the defendant a corporation of New York. Dr. Stathem died in July, 1862.

The other cases are similar.

Each policy contained various conditions, upon the breach of which it was to be null and void; and amongst others the following: "That in case the said (assured) shall not pay the said premium on or before the several days hereinbefore mentioned for the payment thereof, then and in every such case the said company shall not be liable to the payment of the sum insured, or in any part thereof, and this policy shall cease and determine."

The Manhattan policy contained the additional provision, that, in every case where the policy should cease or become null and void, all previous payments made thereon should be forfeited to the company.

The non-payment of the premiums in arrear was set up in bar of the actions; and the plaintiffs respectively relied on the existence of the war as an excuse, offering to deduct the premiums in arrear from the amounts of the policies.

The decree and judgments below were against the defendants.

Mr. Justice BRADLEY, after stating the case, delivered the opinion of the court.

"We agree with the court below, that the contract is not an assurance for a single year, with a privilege of renewal from year to year by paying the annual premium, but that it is an entire contract of assurance for life, subject to discontinuance and forfeiture for non-payment of any of the stipulated premiums. Such is the form of the contract, and such is its character. * * *

"Each instalment is, in fact, part consideration of the entire insurance for life. It is the same thing, where the annual premiums are spread over the whole life. * * *

"The case, therefore, is one in which time is material and of the essence of the contract. Non-payment at the day involves absolute forfeiture, if such be the terms of the contract, as is the case here. Courts cannot with safety vary the stipulation of the parties by introducing equities for the relief of the insured against their own negligence.

"But the court below bases its decision on the assumption that, when performance of the condition becomes illegal in consequence of the prevalence of public war, it is excused, and forfeiture does not ensue. It supposes the contract to have been suspended during the war, and to have revived with all its force when the war ended.

"Such a suspension and revival do take place in the case of ordinary debts. But have they ever been known to take place in the case of executory contracts in which time is material? If a Texas merchant had contracted to furnish some Northern explorer a thousand cans of preserved meat by a certain day, so as to be ready for his departure for the North Pole, and was prevented from furnishing it by the civil war, would the contract still be good at the close of the war five years afterwards, and after the return of the expedition?

"If the proprietor of a Tennessee quarry had agreed, in 1860, to furnish, during the two following years, ten thousand cubic feet of marble, for the construction of a building in Cincinnati, could he have claimed to perform the contract in 1865, on the ground that the war prevented an earlier performance?

"The truth is, that the doctrine of the revival of contracts suspended during the war is one based on considerations of equity and justice, and cannot be invoked to revive a contract which it would be unjust or inequitable to revive.

"In the case of life insurance, besides the materiality of time in the performance of the contract, another strong reason exists why the policy should not be revived. The parties do not stand on equal ground in reference to such a revival.

"It would operate most unjustly against the company. The business of insurance is founded on the law of averages; that of life insurance eminently so. The average rate of mortality is the basis on which it rests. By spreading their risks over a large number of cases, the companies calculate on this average with reasonable certainty and safety. Anything that interferes with it deranges the security of the business. If every policy lapsed by reason of the war should be revived, and all the back premiums should be paid, the companies would have the benefit of this average amount of risk.

"But the good risks are never heard from; only the bad are sought to be revived, where the person insured is either dead or dying. Those in health can get new policies cheaper than to pay arrearages on the old. To enforce a revival of the bad cases, whilst the company necessarily lose the cases, which are desirable, would be manifestly unjust. An injured person, as before stated, does not stand isolated and alone. His case is connected with and correlated to the cases of all others insured by the same company.

"The nature of the business, as a whole, must be looked at to understand the general equities of the parties.

"We are of opinion, therefore, that an action cannot be maintained for the amount assured on a policy of life-insurance forfeited, like those in question, by non-payment of the premium, even though the payment was prevented by the existence of the war.

"The question then arises, Must the insured lose all the money which has been paid for premiums on their respective policies? If they must, they will sustain an equal injustice to that which the companies would sustain by reviving the policies. At the very first blush, it seems manifest that justice requires that they should have some compensation or return for the money already paid, otherwise the companies would be the gainers from their loss; and that from a cause for which neither party is to blame. The case may be illustrated thus: Suppose an inhabitant of Georgia had bargained for a house, situated in a Northern city, to be paid for by instalments, and no title to be made until all the instalments were paid, with a condition that on the failure to pay any of the instalments when due, the contract should be at an end, and the previous payments forfeited; and suppose that this condition was declared by the parties to be absolute and the time of payment material. Now, if some of the instalments were paid before the war, and others accruing during the war were not paid, the contract, as an executory one, was at an end. If the necessities of the vendor obliged him to avail himself of the condition, and to resell the property to another party, would it be just for him to retain the money he had received? Perhaps it might be just if the failure to pay had been voluntary, or could, by possibility, have been avoided.

"But it was caused by an event beyond the control of either party, —an event which made it unlawful to pay. In such case, whilst it would be unjust, after the war, to enforce the contract as an executory one against the vendor contrary to his will, it would be equally unjust in him, treating it as ended, to insist upon the forfeiture of the money already paid on it. An equitable right to some compensation or return for previous payments would clearly result from the circumstances of the case. The money paid by the purchaser, subject to the value of any possession which he may have enjoyed, should, *ex æquo et bono*, be returned to him. This would clearly be demanded by justice and right.

"And so, in the present case, whilst the insurance company has a right to insist on the materiality of time in the condition of payment of premiums, and to hold the contract ended by reason of non-payment, they cannot with any fairness insist upon the condition, as it regards the forfeiture of the premiums already paid; that would be clearly unjust and inequitable. The insured has an equitable right to have this amount restored to him, subject to a deduction for the value of the assurance enjoyed by him whilst the policy was in existence; in other words, he is fairly entitled to have the equitable value of his policy. * * *

"We are of opinion, therefore, first, that as the companies elected to insist upon the condition in these cases, the policies in question must be regarded as extinguished by the non-payment of the premiums, though caused by the existence of the war, and that an action will not lie for the amount insured thereon.

"Secondly, that such failure being caused by a public war, without the fault of the assured, they are entitled *ex æquo et bono* to recover the equitable value of the policies with interest from the close of the war. * * *

"In estimating the equitable value of a policy, no deduction should be made from the precise amount which the calculations give, as is sometimes done where policies are voluntarily surrendered, for the purpose of discouraging such surrenders; and the value should be taken as of the day when the first default occurred in the payment of the premium by which the policy became forfeited. In each case the rates of mortality and interest used in the tables of the company will form the basis of the calculation.

"The decree in the equity suit and the judgments in the actions at law are reversed, and the causes respectively remanded to be proceeded with according to law and the directions of this opinion.

CLIFFORD, J., (with whom concurred HUNT, J.,) dissenting:—

"Where the parties to an executory money-contract live in different countries, and the governments of those countries become involved in public war with each other, the contract between such parties is suspended during the existence of the war, and revives when peace ensues; and that rule, in my judgment, is as applicable to the contract of life-insurance as to any other executory contract.

"Consequently, I am obliged to dissent from the opinion and judgment of the court in these cases." [1]

[1] *Effect of war upon treaties.*—"General compacts between nations," says Wheaton (Lawrence's ed., p. 460), "may be divided into what are called *transitory conventions*, and *treaties* properly so termed. The first are perpetual in their nature, so that, being once carried into effect, they subsist independent of any change in the sovereignty and form of government of the contracting parties; and although their operation may, in some cases, be suspended during war, they revive on the return of peace without any express stipulation. Such are treaties of cession, boundary, or exchange of territory, or those which create a permanent servitude in favor of one nation within the territory of another."

SECTION 81.—TRADE WITH THE ENEMY.

THE "HOOP."

HIGH COURT OF ADMIRALTY, 1799.

(1 *C. Robinson*, 196.)

British merchants are not at liberty to trade with the enemy without the King's license; all property taken in such trade is confiscable as prize to the captor.

Judgment.—SIR W. SCOTT.—"This is the case of a ship laden with flax, madder, geneva, and cheese, and bound from Rotterdam ostensibly to Bergen; but she was in truth coming to a British port, and took a destination to Bergen to deceive the French cruisers; and, as the claim discloses (of which I see no reason to doubt the truth), the goods were to be imported on account of British merchants, being most of them articles of considerable use in the manufactures and commerce of this country, and being brought under an assurance from the commissioners of customs in Scotland that they might be lawfully imported without any license, by virtue of the statute 35 Geo. 3, c. 15, § 180. [1]

"It is said that these circumstances compose a case entitled to great indulgence; and I do not deny it. But if there is a rule of law on the subject binding the court, I must follow where that rule leads me; though it leads to consequences which I may privately regret, when I look to the particular intentions of the parties.

"In my opinion there exists such a general rule in the maritime jurisprudence of this country, by which all trading with the public enemy, unless with the permission of the sovereign, is interdicted. It is not a principle peculiar to the maritime law of this country; it is laid down by Bynkershoek as an universal principle of law.—'Ex naturâ belli commercia inter hostes cessare non est dubitandum. Quamvis nulla specialis sit commerciorum prohibitio, ipso tamen

[1] The 35 G. 3, c. 15 (March 16, 1795), enacts, "that it shall be lawful to import such goods belonging to subjects of the United Provinces, or to any who were subjects before the 19th of January, 1795, or to any subject of his majesty, to be landed and secured in warehouses for the benefit of the proprietor, and for the security of the revenue." Subsequent acts contain further regulations for property coming from Holland, in the ambiguous situation of the two countries at that time.

jure belli commercia esse vetita, ipsæ indictiones bellorum satis decarant, etc.' He proceeds to observe, that the interests of trade, and the necessity of obtaining certain commodities have sometimes so far overpowered this rule, that different species of traffic have been permitted, '*prout e re sua, subditorumque suorum esse censent principes*' (Bynk. Q. J. P. B. 1, c. 3.) But it is in all cases the act and permission of the sovereign. Wherever that is permitted, it is a suspension of the state of war *quo ad hoc*. It is, as he expresses it, '*pro parte sic bellum, pro parte pax inter subditos utriusque principes.*' It appears from these passages to have been the law of Holland; Valin, l. iii., tit. 6, art. 3, states it to have been the law of France, whether the trade was attempted to be carried on in national or in neutral vessels; it will appear in a case which I shall have occasion to mention, *The Fortuna*, to have been the law of Spain; and it may, I think, without rashness be affirmed to have been a general principle of law in most of the countries of Europe.

"By the law and constitution of this country, the sovereign alone has the power of declaring war and peace. He alone therefore who has the power of entirely removing the state of war, has the power of removing it in part, by permitting, where he sees proper, that commercial intercourse which is a partial suspension of the war. There may be occasions on which such an intercourse may be highly expedient. But it is not for individuals to determine on the expediency of such occasions on their own notions of commerce, and of commerce merely, and possibly on grounds of private advantage not very reconcilable with the general interest of the state. It is for the state alone, on more enlarged views of policy, and of all circumstances which may be connected with such an intercourse, to determine when it shall be permitted, and under what regulations. In my opinion, no principle ought to be held more sacred than that this intercourse cannot subsist on any other footing than that of the direct permission of the state. Who can be insensible to the consequences that might follow, if every person in a time of war had a right to carry on a commercial intercourse with the enemy, and under color of that, had the means of carrying on any other species of intercourse he might think fit? The inconvenience to the public might be extreme; and where is the inconvenience on the other side, that the merchant should be compelled, in such a situation of the two countries, to carry on his trade between them (if necessary) under the eye and control of the government, charged with the care of the public safety?

"Another principle of law, of a less public nature, but equally general in its reception and direct in its application, forbids this sort of communication as fundamentally inconsistent with the relation at that time existing between the two countries; and that is, the total inability to sustain any contract by an appeal to the tribunals of the one country, on the part of the subjects of the other. In the law of almost every country, the character of alien enemy carries with it a disability to sue, or to sustain in the language of the civilians *a persona standi in judicio.* The peculiar law of our own country applies this principle with great rigor. The same principle is received in our courts of the law of nations; they are so far British courts, that no man can sue therein who is a subject of the enemy, unless under particular circumstances that *pro hâc vice* discharge him from the character of an enemy; such as his coming under a flag of truce, a cartel, a pass, or some other act of public authority that puts him in the King's peace *pro hâc vice.* But otherwise he is totally *ex lex;* even in the case of ransoms which are contracts, but contracts arising *ex jure belli,* and tolerated as such, the enemy was not permitted to sue in his own proper person for the payment of the ransom bill; but the payment was enforced by an action brought by the imprisoned hostage in the courts of his own country, for the recovery of his freedom. A state in which contracts cannot be enforced, cannot be a state of legal commerce. If the parties who are to contract have no right to compel the performance of the contract, nor even to appear in a court of justice for that purpose, can there be a stronger proof that the law imposes a legal inability to contract? To such transactions it gives no sanction; they have no legal existence; and the whole of such commerce is attempted without its protection and against its authority. Bynkershoek expresses himself with great force upon this argument in his first book, chapter 7, where he lays down that the legality of commerce and the mutual use of courts of justice are inseparable; he says, that cases of commerce are undistinguishable from cases of any other species in this respect. 'Si hosti semel permittas actiones exercere, difficile est distinguere ex quâ causâ oriunter, nec potui animadvertere illam distinctionem usu fuisse servatam.'

"Upon these and similar grounds it has been the established rule of law of this court, confirmed by the judgment of the Supreme Court, that a trading with the enemy, except under a royal license, subjects the property to confiscation;—and the most eminent persons of the law sitting in the Supreme Court have uniformly sustained such judgments. * * *[1]

[1] In support of this rule Sir W. Scott reviews a large number of cases decided on appeal by the Lords of Appeal. These cases are the following: The Ringende Jacob, 1750; The Lady Jane, 1749; Deergaden, 1747; The Elizabeth, 1749; The

"I omit many other cases of the last and the present war merely on this ground that the rule is so firmly established, that no one case exists which has been permitted to contravene it,—for I take upon me to aver, that all cases of this kind which have come before that tribunal have received an uniform determination. The cases which I have produced, prove that the rule has been rigidly enforced:—where acts of parliament have on different occasions been made to relax the navigation-law and other revenue acts; where the government has authorized, under the sanction of an act of parliament, a homeward trade from the enemy's possession, but has not especially protected an outward trade to the same, though intimately connected with that homeward trade, and almost necessary to its existence; that it has been enforced where strong claim not merely of convenience, but almost of necessity, excused it, on behalf of the individual; that it has been enforced where carriages have been laden before the war, but where the parties have not used all possible diligence to countermand the voyage after the first notice of hostilities; and that it has been enforced not only against the subjects of the crown, but likewise against those of its allies in the war, upon the supposition that the rule was founded on a strong and universal principle, which allied states in war had a right to notice and apply, mutually, to each other's subjects. Indeed it is the less necessary to produce these cases, because it is expressly laid down by Lord Mansfield, as I understand him, that such is the maritime law of England." (*Gist* v. *Mason*, 1 T. R., 85.)

[In conclusion, Sir W. Scott held that the acts of Parliament in question were not intended to legalize the trade without special licenses; and that the law advisers of the commissioners were wrong in their conclusions to that effect. The property was therefore condemned according to the strict rule of law.]

Juffrow Louisa Margaretha, 1781; The St. Louis, 1781; The Victoria, 1781; The Comte de Wohrougoff, 1781; The Guldita, 1785: The Eenigheid, 1795; The Fortuna, 1795; The Freeden, 1795; The William, 1795.

These were all cases in which the property in question was condemned, though some of them, like the case of the *Hoop*, were cases of great hardship upon British merchants.

POTTS v. BELL.

KING'S BENCH, 1800.

(8 *Term Reports*, 548.)

Trading with the enemy without the King's license is illegal.

This was the case of a neutral ship captured by a French cruiser on a voyage from Rotterdam to Hull, for having on board enemy property (English). These goods were bought in Rotterdam by the agent of an English house, after the breaking out of hostilities between France and England, and insured in an English company. An action was brought on the insurance policy.

The defendant insisted that the plaintiff was not entitled to recover; because the policy was void, inasmuch as it was not lawful to trade with the enemy. The Common Pleas found for the plaintiffs. But on appeal, this judgment was reversed:

Judgment,—Lord KENYON, Ch., J.:—"The court had very fully considered the case immediately after the very learned argument which had been made by the King's advocate, Sir J. Nicholl, in the last term. That the reasons which he had urged and the authorities he had cited were so many, so uniform, and so conclusive to show that a British subject's trading with an enemy was illegal, that the question might be considered as finally at rest. That those authorities, it was true, were mostly drawn from the decisions of the admiralty courts; and that though all diligence had been used, there was only one direct authority on the subject to be found in the common-law books, and that one was to the same effect. But that the circumstances of there being that single case only was strong to show that the point had not been since disputed, and that it might now be taken for granted that it was a principle of the common law that trading with an enemy without the King's license was illegal in British subjects. That it was therefore needless in this case to delay giving judgment for the sake of pronouncing the opinion of the court in more formal terms; more especially as they could do little more than recapitulate the judgment with the long train of authorities, already to be found in the clearest terms in the principal report of the case of the *Hoop* published by Dr. Robinson. That the consequence was that the judgment of the court of Common Pleas must be reversed."

THE "RAPID."

SUPREME COURT OF THE UNITED STATES, 1814.

(8 *Cranch*, 155.)

After a declaration of war, an American citizen cannot legally send a vessel to the enemy's country to bring away his property.

This was an appeal from the sentence of the circuit court, for the district of Massachusetts.

The material facts in the case were these.

Jabez Harrison, a native American citizen, the claimant and appellant in this case, had purchased a quantity of English goods in England, before the declaration of war by the United States against that country, and deposited them on a small island, belonging to the English, called Indian Island, and situated near the line between Nova Scotia and the United States. Upon the breaking out of the war, Harrison's agents in Boston hired the *Rapid*, a vessel licensed and enrolled for the cod fishery, to proceed to the place of deposit and bring away the goods. The *Rapid* accordingly sailed from Boston, on the 3d of July, 1812, with Harrison, the claimant, on board, proceeded to Eastport, where Harrison was left, and from thence, agreeably to Harrison's orders, to Indian Island, where the cargo in question was taken on board. On the eighth of July, while on his return, she was captured by the Jefferson Privateer, on the high seas, and brought into Salem. The goods, being libeled as prize, and claimed by Harrison as his property, were condemned in the circuit court of Massachusetts to the captors, on the ground that by "trading with the enemy," they had acquired the character of enemies' property.

A claim was also interposed by the United States, on the ground of a violation, by the *Rapid*, of the non-intercourse act. This claim was also rejected. From the decree of the circuit court the United States and Harrison appealed; at the trial before the Supreme Court the government of the United States did not interpose its claim.

The Court dwelt at considerable length upon the general principles of the rule which prohibited trading between enemies; and as there was no question of the observance of this rule in international law, this part of the opinion is omitted. The claimant contended, however, that there was not a trading with the enemy in this case;

that on the breaking out of war, every citizen had a right to withdraw property lying in the enemy's country and purchased before the war. Only so much of the opinion as bears upon this point is given.

Judgment,—JOHNSON, J.:—

"* * * After taking this general view of the principal doctrine on this subject, we will consider the points made in behalf of the claimant in this case, and, 1. Whether this was a trading, in the eye of the prize law, such as will subject the property to capture?

"The force of the argument on this point depends upon the terms made use of. If by *trading*, in prize law, was meant that signification of the term which consists in negotiation or contract, this case would certainly not come under the penalties of the rule. But the object, policy, and spirit of the rule is to cut off all communication or actual locomotive intercourse between individuals of the belligerent states. Negotiation or contract has, therefore, no necessary connection with the offence. Intercourse inconsistent with actual hostility, is the offence against which the operation of the rule is directed; and by substituting this definition for that of trading with an enemy, an answer is given to this argument.

"2. Whether, on the breaking out of a war, the citizen has a right to remove to his own country with his property, is a question which we conceive does not arise in this case. This claimaint certainly had not a right to leave the United States, for the purpose of bringing home his property from an enemy's country; much less could he claim it as a right to bring into this country, goods, the importation of which was expressly prohibited. As to the claim for the vessel, it is founded on no pretext whatever; for the undertaking, besides being in violation of two laws of the United States, was altogether voluntary and inexcusable. With regard to the importations from Great Britain about this time, it is well known that the forfeiture was released on grounds of policy and a supposed obligation induced by the assurances which had been held out by the American chargé d'affaires in England. But this claimant could allege no such excuse.

"3. On the third point, we are of opinion that the foregoing observations furnish a sufficient answer.

"If the right to capture property thus offending, grows out of a state of war, it is enough to support the condemnation in this case, that the act of Congress should produce a state of war, and that the commission of the privateer should authorize the capture of any property that shall assume the belligerent character.

"Such a character we are of opinion this vessel and cargo took

19

upon herself; or at least, she is deprived of the right to prove herself otherwise.

"We are aware that there may exist considerable hardship in this case; the owners, both of vessel and cargo, may have been unconscious that they were violating the duties which a state of war imposed upon them. It does not appear that they meant a daring violation either of the laws or belligerent rights of their country. But it is the unenvied province of this court to be directed by the head, and not by the heart. In deciding upon principles that must define the rights and duties of the citizen and direct the future decisions of justice, no latitude is left for the exercise of feeling."

THE "ST. LAWRENCE."

SUPREME COURT OF THE UNITED STATES, 1814—1815.

(8 *Cranch*, 434, *and* 9 *Cranch*, 120.)

Without deciding whether an American citizen may, after the outbreak of war, withdraw with his property from the enemy's country, *held*, that he cannot do so *eleven months* after the declaration of war.

This was an appeal from the sentence of the United States Circuit Court for the district of New Hampshire.

The ship *St. Lawrence* was captured on the 20th of June, 1813, and, with her cargo, libeled as prize, in the District Court of New Hampshire. On the 5th of May, 1813, a license was granted by the privy council of Great Britain to Thomas White of London, and others, permitting them to export, direct to the United States, an enumerated cargo in the St. Lawrence, provided she cleared out before the last day of that month. On the 30th of May, 1813, she sailed from Liverpool for the United States with the cargo specified in the license. Mr. Alexander M'Gregor and his family were passengers on board.

It appeared from the examination of Mr. M'Gregor, that he was born in Scotland, was naturalized in the United States in 1795, had lived, the last seven years, in Liverpool, and was returning in the St. Lawrence, with his family to the United States.

There were several claimants, but only so much of the case is given as refers to the claims of M'Gregor and Penniman.

WEBSTER, for M'Gregor and Penniman, said:

"We contend that a distinction is to be taken between an American citizen, domiciled in England at the breaking out of the war, withdrawing his funds, and an American citizen who goes to England after the declaration of war, for the same purpose. That the former, whether a native or naturalized citizen, has a right (and perhaps it is his duty) to return to the United States with his effects. If he has no such right, why should the law of nations have provided a reasonable time for removing in case of war?

"This rule of the law of nations has been founded upon the necessity of the case, and upon the hardship which would attend the want of such a rule. A citizen of one country may lawfully go to any other country, in time of peace, and take up his residence there; and it would be very hard if he must suffer by the sudden and unexpected breaking out of a war—an event over which he had no control. A neutral would be permitted to withdraw his funds in such a case; and if we should allow the privilege to neutrals, why should we deny it to our own citizens? 1 Rob., 1, *The Vigilantià* 1; *Bos. and Pul.*, 355, *Bell* v. *Gitson*.

"The case of Escott, cited in *The Hoop*, 1 Rob., 165, 196, may perhaps be thought to make against our claim.

"But the cases are not alike. In that case, Escott *sent* for his property: here M'Gregor came with his.

"A character gained by residence, is lost by non-residence. When M'Gregor ceased to reside in England, his character, if hostile before, no longer continued hostile. That it was not his intention to continue his residence in England, is clearly evidenced by his actual return to the United States with his family.

"With regard to his half of the ship, we contend that if he had a right to return, he had a right to use the means necessary for that purpose—he had a right to purchase a ship for the conveyance of himself and his family. So if it was lawful for him to withdraw his funds, he might lawfully invest those funds in merchandise, if he could not otherwise withdraw them. 4 Rob., 161, 195, *The Madonna delle Gracie*; 3 Rob., 11, 12, *The Indian Chief*; 5 Rob., 248, *The President*; 5 Rob., 84, 90, *The Ocean*; 5 Rob., 60, *The Diana*."

Judgment:—

"It is not the intention, to express any opinion as to the right of an American citizen, on the breaking out of hostilities, to withdraw his property purchased before the war, from an enemy country. Admitting such right to exist, it is necessary that it should be exercised with due diligence, and within a reasonable time after the knowledge of hostilities. To admit a citizen to withdraw property from an enemy country, a long time after the war, under the pretence of its having been purchased before the war, would lead to the most injurious consequences, and hold out strong temptations to every species of fraudulent and illegal traffic with the enemy. To such an unlimited extent we are all satisfied that the right cannot exist. The present shipment was not made until more than eleven months had elapsed after war was declared; and we are all of opinion that it was then too late for the party to make the shipment, so as to exempt him from the penalty attached to an illegal traffic with the enemy. The consequence, is that the property of Mr. Penniman must be condemned.

"And their decision is fatal, also, to the claim of Mr. M'Gregor. Independent, indeed, of the principle, there are many circumstances in the case unfavorable to the latter gentleman. In the first place, it is not pretended that the goods included in his claim were purchased before the war. In the next place, he was the projector of the present voyage, and became, as to one moiety, the charterer or purchaser of the ship. Nearly all the cargo consisted of goods belonging (as it must now be deemed) exclusively to British merchants. He was, therefore, engaged in an illegal traffic of the most noxious nature; a traffic not only prohibited by the law of war, but by the municipal regulations of his adopted country. His whole property, therefore, embarked in such an enterprise, must alike be inflicted with the taint of forfeiture."

THE BRIG "JOSEPH."

U. S. CIRCUIT COURT FOR MASSACHUSETTS, 1813.

(1 *Gallison*, 545.)

When a citizen of the United States is residing in the enemy's country at the outbreak of war, he is not permitted to bring his property back in such a way as to involve a trade with the enemy.

The following is an extract from the opinion of Mr. Justice STORY:—"It has been farther argued, that a declaration of war is, in effect, a command to the citizens of the belligerent country abroad at the time, to return home, and that the law allows a reasonable time and way to effect it.

"I am not aware of any principle of public law, which obliges every absent citizen to return to his country, on the breaking out of the war, nor has any authority been produced, which countenances the position. It may be admitted, that the sovereign power of the country has a right to require the services of all its citizens, in time of war, and for this purpose may recall them home under penalties for disobedience. But until the sovereign power has promulgated such command, the citizens of the country have a perfect right to pursue their ordinary business and trade in and with all other countries, except that of the enemy. Upon any other supposition, all foreign commerce would, during war, be suspended; for if it were the duty of absent citizens to return, it would, upon the same principle, be the duty of those at home to remain there. As to citizens in the hostile country, the declaration of war imports a suspension of all farther commerce with such country, and obliges them to return, unless they would be involved in all the consequences of the hostile character. If they wish to return, they must do it in a manner, which does not violate the laws; and their property cannot be removed with safety from the enemy country, unless under the sanction of their own government.

"But even if the position were generally true, that is contended for, the law would never deem that a reasonable mode of conveying property home, which involved it in a noxious trade with the public enemy. That can never be held to be a reasonable mode of returning a ship to the United States, which involves her in a traffic forbidden by the laws."

THE "WILLIAM BAGALAY."

SUPREME COURT OF THE UNITED STATES, 1866.

(5 *Wallace*, 408.)

As to the duty of an American citizen to return home when the United States becomes involved in war with the country of his residence.

Extract from the judgment,—CLIFFORD, J.:—

"The duty of a citizen when war breaks out, if it be a foreign war, and he is abroad, is to return without delay; and if it be a civil war, and he is a resident in the rebellious section, he should leave it as soon as practicable and adhere to the regular established government. Domicil in the law of prize becomes an important consideration, because every person is to be considered in such proceedings as belonging to that country where he has his domicil, whatever may be his native or adopted country.

"Personal property, except such as is the product of the hostile soil, follows as a general rule the rights of the proprietor; but if suffered to remain in the hostile country after war breaks out, it becomes impressed with the national character of the belligerent where it is situated. Promptitude is therefore justly required of citizens resident in the enemy country, or having personal property there, in changing their domicil, severing those business relations, or disposing of their effects, as matter of duty to their own government, and as tending to weaken the enemy. Presumption of the law of nations is against one who lingers in the enemy's country, and if he continues there for much length of time, without satisfactory explanations, he is liable to be considered as remorant, or guilty of culpable delay, and an enemy." [1]

[1] In the case of the *Gray Jacket*, 5 Wallace, 370, Mr. Justice SWAYNE, in giving the opinion of the court, said: "The only qualification of these rules (property coming from the enemy country to be condemned) is that when, upon breaking out of hostilities, or as soon after as possible, the owner escapes with such property as he can take with him, or in good faith thus early removes his property, with the view of putting it beyond the dominion of the hostile power, the property in such cases is exempt from the liability which would otherwise attend it."

In the case of *Fifty-two Bales Cotton*, Blatchford's Prize Cases, 664 (1863), the cotton was captured on a flat-boat fastened to a wharf in Texas, and belonged to a citizen of New York, who went to Texas before the war to collect debts due to him. The proceeds had been invested in this cotton, with a view to leave the hostile country after the breaking out of the war.

Mr. Justice NELSON, in the circuit court for Southern New York held that "the only pretext for condemnation is that the property in question was enemy's property, which I think is not sustained. It appears to me that the claimant used all diligence to collect his effects, with a view to leave the hostile country, after the breaking out of the war, and is brought fairly within the principle of international law that protects him."

In the case of the *Sarah Starr and Cargo*, Blatchford, 650, the same judge held, that after the breaking out of war citizens of the loyal States resident in the States in rebellion should be accorded a reasonable time to convert their property into funds which could be conveniently carried, and to withdraw from their business connections in the enemy's country. To the same effect the case of the *John Gilpin*, Blatchford, 661, in which NELSON, J., overruled the decision of the district court.

Mr. Justice NELSON would seem to be more lenient in this class of cases than the majority of his colleagues on the supreme bench. In the Prize Cases, he dissented from the opinion of the majority, and asserted that there could be no illegal trading with the enemy prior to the proclamation of the President, on the 16th of August, 1861.

See further on the removal of property on the outbreak of war, the case of the *Ocean*, 5 C. Robinson, 90 (1804); and the *President*, 5 C. Robinson, 277 (1804).

KERSHAW v. KELSEY.

SUPREME COURT OF MASSACHUSETTS, 1868.

(100 *Massachusetts Reports*, 561.)

A citizen of Massachusetts, residing in Mississippi during the civil war, leased a plantation and planted it with crops; but was driven away by soldiers of the Confederate States, and returned to Massachusetts. The lessor then took charge of the plantation, harvested the crops, and delivered to the lessee's son, in Mississippi, cotton of the value of $10,000. The cotton was shipped to the lessee at Boston by his son. After the close of the war, the lessor sued to recover rent, etc.

Held, that, as between lessor and lessee, there was no trading between enemies, and that the lessor could recover on the contract of lease.

Judgment,—GRAY, J.:—

"The defendant, a citizen of Massachusetts, in February, 1864, in Mississippi, took from the plaintiff, then and ever since a citizen and resident of Mississippi, a lease for one year of a cotton plantation in that state, and therein agreed to pay a rent of ten thousand dollars, half in cash, and half 'out of the first part of the cotton crop, which is to be fitted for market in reasonable time.' The lessor also agreed to deliver, and the lessee to receive and pay the value of the corn then on the plantation. It does not appear whether the defendant went into Mississippi before or after the beginning of the war of the rebellion; and there is no evidence of any intent on the part of either party to violate or evade the laws or oppose or injure the government of the United States. The defendant paid the first instalment of rent, took possession of the plantation and corn, used the corn on the plantation, provided it with supplies to the amount of about five thousand dollars, and planted and sowed it, but early in March was driven away by rebel soldiers and never returned to the plantation, except once in April following, after which he came back to Massachusetts. The plaintiff continued to reside on the plantation, raised a crop of cotton there, and delivered it in Mississippi to the defendant's son, by whom it was forwarded in the autumn of the same year to the defendant; and he sold it and retained the profits amounting to nearly ten thousand dollars.

"The plaintiff sues for the unpaid instalment of rent and the value of the corn. The claims made in the other counts of the declaration have been negatived by the special findings of the jury.

"The defendant, in his answer, denied all the plaintiff's allegations;

and at the trial contended that the lease, having been made during the civil war, was illegal and void, as well by the principles of international law, as by the terms of the act of Congress of 1861, c. 3, § 5, and the proclamation issued by the President under that act, (declaring all intercourse with states in rebellion unlawful).[1] * * *

"The result is, that the law of nations, as judicially declared, prohibits all intercourse between citizens of the two belligerents which is inconsistent with the state of war between their countries; and that this includes any act of voluntary submission to the enemy, or receiving his protection; as well as any act or contract which tends to increase his resources; and every kind of trading or commercial dealing or intercourse, whether by transmission of money or goods, or by orders for the delivery of either, between the two countries, directly or indirectly, or through the intervention of third persons or partnerships, or by contracts in any form looking to or involving such transmission, or by insurances upon trade with or by the enemy. Beyond the principle of these cases the prohibition has not been carried by judicial decision. The more sweeping statements in the text books are taken from the *dicta* which we have already examined, and in none of them is any other example given than those just mentioned. At this age of the world, when all the tendencies of the law of nations are to exempt individuals and private contracts from injury or restraint in consequence of war between their governments, we are not disposed to declare such contracts unlawful as have not been heretofore adjudged to be inconsistent with a state of war.

"The trading or transmission of property or money which is prohibited by international law is from or to one of the countries at war. An alien enemy residing in this country may contract and sue like a citizen. 2. Kent, Com., 63. When a creditor, although a subject of the enemy, remains in the country of the debtor, or has a known agent there authorized to receive the amount of the debt, throughout

[1] GRAY, J., then reviews the authorities on the subject at great length. The following are the principal cases reviewed:—

The *Hoop*; The *Indian Chief*; *Bell* v. *Chapman*, 10 Johnson, 185; *Ricord* v. *Bettenham*, 1 W. Blackstone, 563; *Hutchinson* v. *Brock*, 11 Mass., 122; *Sparenburgh* v. *Bannatyne*, 1 B. & P., 170; *Potts* v. *Bell*; *Antoine* v. *Morshead*; *Willison* v. *Patterson*, 1 Moore, 133; *Exposito* v. *Bowden*, 7 El. & Bl. 763; *Kennet* v. *Chambers*, 14 Howard, 38; *Bentzen* v. *Boyle*, 9 Cranch, 191; *Prize Cases*, 2 Black., 635; The *Rapid*; The *Julia*; The *Emulous*; *Brown* v. *United States*; The *Joseph*; *Jecker* v. *Montgomery*; 18 Howard, 110; *Hanger* v. *Abbott*, 6 Wallace, 532; The *Ouachita Cotton*, 6 Wallace, 521; *United States* v. *Lane*, 18 Wallace, 195; *McKee* v. *United States*, 8 Wallace, 166; *Griswold* v. *Waddington*, 16 Johnson, 38; *Alexander's Cotton*, 2 Wallace, 404; *Ex parte Boussmaker*, 13 Ves., 71; *Coolidge* v. *Inglee*, 13 Mass., 26; *Paton* v. *Nichols*, 3 Wheaton, 204; *Musson* v. *Fales*, 16 Mass., 332; *Capen* v. *Barrows*, 1 Grey, 380.

the war, payment then to such creditor or his agent can in no respect be construed into a violation of the duties imposed by a state of war upon the debtor; it is not made to an enemy, in contemplation of international or municipal law; and it is no objection that the agent may possibly remit the money to his principal in the enemy's country; if he should do so, the offence would be imputable to him, and not to the person paying him the money. (*Com.* v. *Penn.*, Peters, C. C., 496; *Denniston* v. *Imbrie*, 3 Wash. C. C., 396; *Ward* v. *Smith*, 7 Wall., 447; *Buchanan* v. *Cury*, 19 Johns., 137.)

"The same reasons cover an agreement made in the enemy's territory to pay money there, out of funds accruing there, and not agreed to be transmitted from within our own territory; for, as was said by the Supreme Court of New York—the last case cited, 'This rule is founded in public policy, which, forbids, during war, that money or other resources shall be transferred so as to aid or strengthen our enemies. The crime consists in exporting the money or property, or placing it in the power of the enemy.

"The lease now in question was made within the rebel territory where both parties were at the time, and would seem to have contemplated the continued residence of the lessee upon the demised premises throughout the term. No agreement appears to have been made as part of a contract contemporaneously with the lease, that the cotton crop should be transported, or the rent sent back, across the line between the belligerents, and no contract or communication appears to have been made across that line, relating to the lease, the delivery of possession of the premises or of the corn, or the payment of the rent of the one or the value of the other. The subsequent forwarding of the cotton by the defendant's son from Mississippi to Massachusetts may have been unlawful; but that cannot affect the validity of the agreements contained in the lease. Neither of these agreements involved or contemplated the transmission of money or property, or other communication, between the enemy's territory and our own. We are therefore unanimously of opinion that they did not contravene the law of nations or the public acts of the government, even if the plantation was within the enemy's lines; and that the plaintiff, upon the case reported, is entitled to recover the unpaid rent, and the value of the corn."

UNITED STATES v. GROSSMAYER.

SUPREME COURT OF THE UNITED STATES, 1869.

(9 *Wallace*, 72.)

A merchant residing in New York, could not legally transmit orders by a third person to his agent in Georgia, during the civil war. *Held*, that all acts of the agent, in carrying out such orders, in dealing with the property or debts of his principal, were null and void.

This case was an appeal from the Court of Claims.

Elias Einstein, a resident of Macon, Georgia, was indebted, when the late rebellion broke out, to Grossmayer, a resident of New York, for goods sold and money lent, and while the war was in progress a correspondence on the subject was maintained through the medium of a third person, who passed back and forth several times between Macon and New York. The communication between the parties resulted in Grossmayer requesting Einstein to remit the amount due him in money or sterling exchange, or, if that were not possible, to invest the sum in cotton and hold it for him until the close of the war.

In pursuance of this direction—and, as it is supposed, because money or sterling exchange could not be transmitted—Einstein purchased cotton for Grossmayer, and informed him of it; Grossmayer expressing *himself satisfied with the arrangement.* The cotton was afterwards shipped at Grossmayer's request to one Abraham Einstein, at Savannah, who stored it there in his own name, in order to prevent its seizure by the rebel authorities. It remained in store in this manner until the capture of Savannah, in December, 1864, by the armies of the United States, when it was reported to our military forces as Grossmayer's cotton, and taken by them and sent to New York and sold.

Grossmayer now preferred a claim in the Court of Claims for the residue of the proceeds, asserting that he was within the protection of the Captured and Abandoned Property Act.

That court considering that the purchase by Elias Einstein for Grossmayer was not a violation of the war intercourse acts set forth in the preceding case, decided that he was so, and gave judgment in his favor. The United States appealed.

Judgment,—DAVIS. J.:—

"Grossmayer insists that he is within the protection of the Captured and Abandoned Property Act, but it is hard to see on what ground he can base this claim for protection. It was natural that Grossmayer should desire to be paid, and creditable to Einstein to wish to discharge his obligation to him, but the same thing can be said of very many persons who were similarly situated during the war, and if all persons in this condition had been allowed to do what was done in this case it is easy to see that it would have produced great embarrassment and obstructed very materially the operations of the army. It has been found necessary, as soon as war is commenced, that business intercourse should cease between the citizens of the respective parties engaged in it, and this necessity is so great that all writers on public law agree that it is unlawful, without any express declaration of the sovereign on the subject.

"But Congress did not wish to leave any one in ignorance of the effect of war in this regard, for as early as the 13th of July, 1861, it passed a Non-intercourse Act, which prohibited all commercial intercourse between the States in insurrection and the rest of the United States. It is true the President could allow a restricted trade, if he thought proper; but, in so far as he did allow it, it had to be conducted according to regulations prescribed by the Secretary of the Treasury.

"There is no pretence, however, that this particular transaction was authorized by any one connected with the Treasury Department, and it was, therefore, not only inconsistent with the duties growing out of a state of war, but in open violation of a statute on the subject.

"A prohibition of all intercourse with an enemy during the war affects debtors and creditors on either side, equally with those who do not bear that relation to each other. We are not disposed to deny the doctrine that a resident in the territory of one of the belligerents may have, in time of war, an agent residing in the territory of the other, to whom his debtor could pay his debt in money, or deliver to him property in discharge of it, but in such a case the agency must have been created before the war began, for there is no power to appoint an agent for any purpose after hostilities have actually commenced, and to this effect are all the authorities. The reason why this cannot be done is obvious, for while the war lasts nothing which depends on commercial intercourse is permitted.

"In this case, if Einstein is to be considered as the agent of Grossmayer to buy the cotton, the act appointing him was illegal, because it was done by means of a direct communication through a messenger who was in some manner not stated in the record able to pass, during the war, between Macon and New York. It was not necessary to make the act unlawful that Grossmayer should have communicated personally with Einstein. The business intercourse through a middleman, which resulted in establishing the agency, is equally within the condemnation of the law.

"Besides, if, as is conceded, Grossmayer was prohibited from trading directly with the enemy, how can the purchase in question be treated as lawful when it was made for him by an agent appointed after his own disability to deal at all with the insurgents was created?

"It is argued that the purchase by Einstein was ratified by Grossmayer, and that being so, the case is relieved of difficulty; but this is a mistaken view of the principle of ratification, for a transaction originally unlawful cannot be made any better by being ratified.

"In any aspect of this case, whether the relation of debtor and creditor continued, or was changed to that of principal and agent, the claimant cannot recover.

"As he was prohibited during the war from having any dealings with Einstein, it follows that nothing which both or either of them did in this case could have the effect to vest in him the title to the cotton in question.

"Not being the owner of the property he has no claim against the United States.

"The judgment of the Court of Claims is reversed, and the cause is remanded to that court with directions to enter an order

"Dismissing the petition."

THE "SEA LION."

SUPREME COURT OF THE UNITED STATES, 1866.

(5 *Wallace*, 630.)

The act of Congress of July 13, 1861, authorizing the President to license certain commercial intercourse with the States in rebellion did not contemplate the exercise of that authority by subordinate officers of the executive department without the express order of the President.

An act of Congress passed during the late rebellion (July 13th, 1861), prohibited all commercial intercourse between the inhabitants of any State which the President might declare in a state of insurrection, and the citizens of the rest of the United States; and enacted that all merchandise coming from such territory into other ports of the United States with the vessel conveying it should be forfeited.

The act provided, however, that "the *President*" might "in *his* discretion *license and permit commercial intercourse*" with any such part of a State the inhabitants of which had been so declared in a state of insurrection, "in such articles, and for such time, and by such persons, as he, in *his* discretion, may think most conducive to the public interest." And that, "such intercourse, so far as by *him* licensed, shall be conducted and carried on only in pursuance of rules and regulations prescribed by the secretary of the treasury."

The President having soon after declared several Southern States, and among them Alabama, in a state of insurrection, and the Secretary of the Treasury having issued a series of commercial regulations on the subject of intercourse with them, Brott, Davis & Shons, a commercial firm of New Orleans, obtained from Mr. G. S. Denison, special agent of the Treasury Department, and acting Collector of Customs at New Orleans, a paper, dated February 16th, 1863, as follows:

"The United States military and other authorities at New Orleans permit cotton to be received here from beyond the United States military lines, and such cotton is exempt from seizure or confiscation. An *order is in my hands from Major-General Banks approving and directing this policy*. The only condition imposed is that cotton or other produce must not be bought with specie. All cotton or other produce brought hither from the Confederate lines by Brott, Davis & Shons will not be interfered with in any manner, and they can ship it direct to any foreign or domestic port."

This paper was indorsed by Rear-Admiral Farragut, in command of the blockading force on that coast, "approved." The Rear-Admiral had given also the following instructions to his commanders of the Mobile blockade:

"Should any vessel come out of Mobile and deliver itself up as the property of a Union man desiring to go to New Orleans, take possession and send it into New Orleans for an investigation of the facts, and if it be shown to be as represented, the vessel will be considered a legal trader, under the general order permitting all cotton and other produce to come to New Orleans."

With this paper of the collector of New Orleans in their hands, Brott, Davis & Shons had, through their agents in Mobile, seventy-two bales of cotton shipped at that port on the vessel *Sea Lion* to be carried to New Orleans.

The vessel was captured by the blockading fleet off Mobile, and taken to Key West, and there libeled as prize. The district court condemned the property, and an appeal was taken to the Supreme Court.

Mr. Justice SWAYNE, in delivering the opinion of the court, said as to the question of license:—

"The effect of this paper depends upon the authority under which it was issued. The fifth section of the act of July 13th, 1861, authorized the President to proclaim any State or part of a State in a condition of insurrection, and it declared, that thereupon all commercial intercourse between that territory and the citizens of the rest of the United States, should cease and be unlawful, so long as the condition of hostility should continue, and that all goods and merchandise coming from such territory, into other parts of the United States, and all proceeding to such territory by land or water, and the vessel or vehicle conveying them, or conveying persons to or from such territory, should be forfeited to the United States: *Provided, however*, 'That the President may, in his discretion, license and permit commercial intercourse with any such part of said State or section, the inhabitants of which are so declared in a state of insurrection in such articles, and for such time, and by such persons, as he, in his discretion, may think most conducive to the public interest; and such intercourse, so far as by him licensed, shall be conducted and carried on only in pursuance of rules and regulations prescribed by the Secretary of the Treasury.'

"There is no other statutory provision bearing upon the subject material to be considered.

"On the 16th day of August, 1861, the President issued his proclamation declaring the inhabitants of the rebel States, including Alabama, to be in a state of insurrection.

"On the 28th of the same month the Secretary of the Treasury, pursuant to the provisions of the act referred to, issued a series of regulations upon the subject of commercial intercourse with those States.

"These regulations continued in force until the 31st of March, 1863, when a new series were issued by the same authority. The former were in force when the alleged license bears date; the latter when the vessel and cargo left Mobile and when they were captured. It is unnecessary to analyze them. It is sufficient to remark that they contain nothing which affords the slightest pretext for issuing such a paper. It is in conflict with rules and requirements contained in both of them. It finds no warrant in the statute. The statute prescribes that the President shall license the trade. The only function of the Secretary was to establish the rules by which it should be regulated, when thus permitted. The order of General

Banks is not produced. If it were as comprehensive as the special agent assumed it to be, it covered shipments to New Orleans from Wilmington, Charleston, and all points in the rebel States. It embraced merchandise, coming alike from places within, and places beyond his military lines. With respect to the latter it was clearly void. The President only could grant such a license. Mobile was then in possession of the enemy. The vessel and cargo bore the stamp of the enemy's property. The paper relied upon was a nullity, and gave them no protection. They were as much liable to capture and condemnation as any other vessel or cargo, leaving a blockaded port and coming within reach of a blockading vessel.

"The decree below was rightly rendered, and it is

"Affirmed."

Mr. Justice GRIER:—

"I do not concur in this judgment. The vessel went out of Mobile by permission of the commander of the blockade there. To condemn such property would be a violation of good faith. No English court has ever condemned under such circumstances."

FURTADO v. RODGERS.

COMMON PLEAS, 1802.

(3 *Bos. & Pull.* 191.)

An insurance effected in Great Britain on a French ship previous to the commencement of hostilities between Great Britain and France does not cover a loss by British capture.

This was the case of the ship *Petronelli*, which sailed from Bayonne in France, Oct., 1792, for Martinique insured in an English company, the policy dating 19th Oct., 1792. The next year, while still at Martinique the war between France and England broke out; and the island of Martinique with all the shipping in the harbors was captured by the English. After the peace of Amiens in 1802, the owner of the ship brought suit in Common Pleas in England, to recover the insurance on the ship.

Judgment,—Lord ALVANLEY, C. J.:—

"As it is of infinite importance to the parties that this case should be decided as speedily as possible, and as we entertain no doubts upon the subject, we think it right to deliver the judgment of the court without any further delay; at the same time considering the magnitude of the question we shall allow the parties to convert this case into a special verdict, in order that the opinion of the highest court in this kingdom may be taken, if it should be thought necessary. There are two questions for our consideration: 1st, whether it be lawful for a British subject to insure an enemy from the effect of capture made by his own government? 2dly, whether, if that be legal, the insurance in this case having been made previous to the commencement of hostilities will make any difference? As to the first point, it has been understood for some years to have been the opinion of all Westminster-Hall, and I believe of the nation at large, that such insurances are not strictly legal or capable of being enforced in a court of justice.

"The cases upon the subject are all brought into a small compass in the two valuable books of Mr. Park and my Brother Marshall. Mr. Park seems to consider the cases of *Brandon* v. *Nesbitt* and *Bristow* v. *Towers* as having decided the point; but after looking very accurately into all the cases, I am ready to admit that there is no direct determination. The above two cases proceeded on the short ground of alienage, which was sufficient to support the decision of the Court without entering into the other question; and I do not think the latter words of Lord Kenyon in *Brandon* v. *Nesbitt*, applied as they are to the case of *Ricord* v. *Bettenham*, support the inference which has been drawn by my Brother Marshall, the Law of Insurance, pp. 37, 600, viz., that his Lordship thought that a policy effected previous to the war might be sued upon in the event of peace, even though the loss sustained by the assured arose from British capture. It is well known that for a considerable time, not only some politicians entertained an opinion that insurances on enemy's property was beneficial, but that a great Judge went so far as to try causes in which this point directly appeared, and permitted foreigners in their own names, and for their own benefit during the war, to recover on policies of insurance on foreign goods against British capture. The opinion of that learned Judge, as to the policy of such insurances, is well known, and it was supposed he would not have sanctioned them unless his opinion in point of law had been equally favorable. But we have now the best evidence that his sentiments in that respect were different from what they were supposed to be. Though he did try causes upon such insurances, he always entertained doubts upon the law, and endeavored to keep out of sight a question which might oblige him to decide against what he thought for the benefit of the country. This takes off materially from the effect of those cases which have been cited, to induce a supposition that the law of England had tolerated such insurances. How far it is consistent with good faith, after so long an acquiescence, to set up a defence which the foreigner may say he had no reason to expect, is a question for the decision of defendant and not that of the Court. We can only say, that although many persons have recovered in such actions it is equally true that doubts have been entertained by many persons as to their right to recover, and that most of those who were informed upon the subject were firmly persuaded that the objection might have been made with success. This affords a sufficient vindication to the courts of this country in now deciding this point against a foreigner.

"In 1748 an act, 21 Geo. 2, c. 4, passed prohibiting the insurance of French ships and goods during the war; this was at least a legislative declaration of the impolicy of such insurances at that time. From the expiration of that act to the passing of the 33 Geo. 3, c. 27, s. 4, no legislative interference upon the subject ever took place, and previous to the last mentioned act the policy in question was effected. By the terms of the policy, the underwriters certainly undertake to indemnify the plaintiff against all captures and detentions of princes, without any exception in respect of the acts of the government of their own nation. The question then is, whether the law does not make that exception, and whether it be competent to an English underwriter to indemnify persons who may be engaged in war with his own sovereign against the consequences of that war? We are all of opinion, that on the principles of the English law, it is not competent to any subject to enter into a contract to do anything which may be detrimental to the interests of his own country; and that such a contract is as much prohibited as if it had been expressly forbidden by an act of parliament. It is admitted that if a man contract to do a thing which is afterwards prohibited by act of parliament, he is not bound by his contract. This was expressly laid down in *Brewster* v. *Kitchell*, 1 Salk., 198. And on the same principle, where hostilities commence between the country of the underwriter and the assured, the former is forbidden to fulfil his contract. With respect to the expediency of these insurances, it seems only necessary to cite a single line from Bynkershoek (Quaes. Juris. Pub. lib. 1, c. 21) and part of a passage from Valin, p. 32. The former says, '*Hostium pericula in se suscipere quid est aliud quam eorum commercia maritima promovere*,' and the latter, speaking of the conduct of the English during the war of 1756, who permitted these insurances, says, 'The consequence was, that one part of that nation restored to us by the effect of insurance, what the other took from us by the rights of war.' Lord Hardwicke indeed, in *Henckle* v. *The Royal Exchange Assurance Company*, 1 Ves., 320, uses these words: 'No determination has been that insurance on enemies' ships during the war is unlawful; it might be going too far to say all trading with enemies is unlawful, for that general doctrine would go a great way, even where only English goods are exported, and none of the enemies' imported, which may be very beneficial. I do not go on a foundation of that kind, and there have been several insurances of this sort during the war which a determination upon that point might hurt.' This however is but a doubtful opinion as to the legality of such insurances, and not very favorable to them. In *Plancke* v. *Fletcher*, Lord MANSFIELD is certainly reported to have said, 'It is indifferent whether the goods were English or French, the risk insured extends to all captures,' which seems at first to go a great way towards giving effect to insurances against British capture. But we must suppose this to have been said because the defendant did not press the objection; and if the party acquiesced, the expression gives no more weight to the case than belongs to any of the other cases which have been cited, such as *Bermon* v. *Woodbridge*, *Eden* v. *Parkinson*, and *Tyson* v. *Gurney*, in which the question was not raised at all. On the other hand, the cases of *Brandon* v. *Nesbitt* and *Bristow* v. *Towers* certainly proceed on the ground of alienage. There is no express declaration therefore of the Court of King's Bench, either for or against the legality of such insurances, and the question comes now to be decided for the first time. We are all of opinion that to insure enemies' property was at the common law illegal, for the reasons given by the two foreign jurists (Bynkershoek and Valin) to whom I have referred. If this be so, a contract of this kind entered into previous to the commencement of hostilities must be equally unavailing in a court of law, since it is equally injurious to the interests of the country; for if such a contract could be supported, a foreigner might insure previous to the war against all the evils incident to war. But it is said that the action is suspended, and that the indemnity comes so late that it does not strengthen the resources of the enemy during the war. The enemy however is very little injured by captures for which he is sure at some period or other to be repaid by the underwriter. Since the case of *Bell* v. *Potts*, it has been universally understood that all commercial intercourse with the enemy is to be considered as illegal at common law [though previous to that case a very learned judge (Mr. Justice BULLER, in *Bell* v. *Gitson*, 1 Bos. & Pull., 345) appears to have entertained doubts on that subject], and that consequently all insurances founded on such intercourse are also illegal. Why are they illegal? Because they are in contravention of his Majesty's object in making war, which is by the capture of the enemies' property, and by the prohibition of any beneficial intercourse between them and his own subjects to cripple their commerce. The same reasoning which influenced the Court of King's Bench in their decision in Bell against Potts, seems decisive in the present case. For it being determined that during war all commercial intercourse with the enemy is illegal at common law, it follows that whatever contract tends to protect the enemy's property from the calamities of war, though effected antecedent to the war, is nevertheless illegal. 'It has been supposed that the doctrine which has prevailed respecting ransom bills tends to favor these insurances; but no action was ever maintained upon a ransom bill in a court of common law until the case of *Ricord* v. *Bettenham*, 3 Bur., 1734; 1 Bl., 563, and I have the authority of Sir Wm. Scott for saying, that in the Admiralty Court the suit was always instituted by the hostage. The case of *Ricord* v. *Bettenham*, however, certainly tended to show that such an action might be maintained in the courts of common law at the suit of an alien enemy. In consequence of this, a similar action was brought in *Cornu* v. *Blackburn* (Doug., 641), and after argument, the Court of King's Bench held that it might be sustained. But in *Anthon* v. *Fisher* (Doug., 649, 650, in notes), the contrary was expressly determined upon a writ of error in the Exchequer Chamber. I forbear to enter into the arguments suggested at the bar in favor of the defendant, that the law will not enforce a contract founded on a transaction detrimental to the public policy of the state. The ground upon which we decide this case is, that when a British subject insures against captures, the law infers that the contract contains an exception of captures made by the government of his own country; and that if he had expressly insured against British capture, such a contract would be abrogated by the law of England. With respect to the argument insisted upon by way of answer to the public inconvenience likely to arise from permitting such contracts to be enforced, viz., that all contracts made with an enemy enure to the benefit of the King during the war, and that he may enforce payment of any debt due to an alien enemy from any of his subjects, we think it is not entitled to much weight. Such a course of proceeding never has been adopted; nor is it very probable that it ever will be adopted, as well from the difficulties attending it, as the disinclination to put in force such a prerogative. The plaintiff, I am sorry to say, is not entitled to a return of premium, because the contract was legal at the time the risk commenced, and was a good insurance against all other losses but that arising from capture by the forces of Great Britain.

"Judgment for the defendant."

ANTOINE v. MORSHEAD.

COMMON PLEAS, 1815.

(6 *Taunton*, 237.)

A British prisoner in France drew five bills of exchange on his son in England —the defendant—made payable to certain of his fellow-prisoners, also British subjects. The payees endorsed the bills to the plaintiff, a French banker at Verdun, and they were accepted by the defendant.

In a suit, after the close of the war, *held*, that the plaintiff could recover on the bills.

This was an action upon five bills of exchange, all drawn by the father of the defendant, a British subject, on the 12th of September, 1806, while he was detained a prisoner at Verdun in France during the late war with that country, payable, some to Tyndall, some to Estwicke, both British subjects in like manner detained prisoners there, at one year after date, indorsed to the plaintiff, who was a French subject and a banker at Verdun, and accepted by the defendant. The cause was tried at Guildhall at the sittings after Easter term, 1815, before C. J., when it was contended on the part of the defendant, that it would be treason to pay the bills, by the statute 34 G. 3, c. 9, §§ 1, 4. GIBBS, C. J., refused to hear the objection: he did not know to what extent it might be carried, but if it could be supported to its full extent, many of our miserable fellow-subjects detained in France must have starved. It was also objected, that this being a contract with an alien enemy, was not merely suspended during the war, but absolutely void; the Chief Justice thought otherwise, and the jury found a verdict for the plaintiff.

Vaughan, Serjt., on a former day in this term moved for a rule *nisi* on both these objections, when, it being suggested on the part of the plaintiff, that the statute 34 G. 3, c. 9, had expired at the peace of 1800 and never been re-enacted, the court gave time to ascertain that fact, and that being found to be the case, Vaughan now moved upon the second objection only, namely, that the indorsement of the bill to an alien enemy was void. For this he cited *Anthon* v. *Fisher*, where it is held that no action can be maintained by an alien in the courts of this country on a ransom bill, because it is a right claimed to be acquired by him in actual war. Lord Ashburton's argument in *Ricord* v. *Bettenham*, 3 Burr., 1734, which decision is overruled by *Anthon* v. *Fisher*, is to be called in aid. If a bond be given to an alien enemy, it is good *quoad* the obligor, that is, it enures only for the benefit of the Crown. And if so of a bond, the law must be the like on a bill of exchange. So is it of contracts of insurance made with an alien enemy. *Flindt* v. *Waters*, 15 East., 266, Lord ELLENBOROUGH, C. J., says the defense of alien enemy may go to the contract itself, on which the plaintiff sues, and operate as a perpetual bar; though in that case the contracting party having become an enemy after the contract, it was held to be only a temporary suspension of the right to sue, but he showed a disposition to confirm the cases of *Brandon* v. *Nesbitt*, 6 T. R., 23, and *Bristow* v. *Towers*, 6 T. R., 35. No case has decided that a contract made with an alien enemy in time of war may be ever afterwards enforced. Chief Baron Gilbert lays it down, that upon the plea of alien enemy the right of the plaintiff is forfeited to the crown, as a species of reprisal upon the state committing hostility.

GIBBS, C. J.:—"It will not be useless to consider what legal propositions can be deduced from the cases cited on behalf of the defendant, and to try how far they are applicable to the present case. This is no bill of exchange drawn in favour of an alien enemy, but by one subject in favour of another subject, upon a subject resident here, the two first being both detained prisoners in France; the drawer might legally draw such a bill for his subsistence. After the bill is so drawn, the payee indorses it to the plaintiff, then an alien enemy. How was he to avail himself of the bill, except by negotiating it, and to whom could he negotiate it, except to the inhabitants of that country in which he resided? I can recollect but two principles from the cases cited by the counsel for the defendant, and they are principles on which there never was the slightest doubt. First, that a contract made with an alien enemy in time of war and that of such a nature that it endangers the security, or is against the policy of this country, is void. Such are policies of insurance to protect an enemy's trade. Another principle is, that however valid a contract originally may be, if the party become an alien enemy he cannot sue. The Crown, during the war, may lay hands on the debt, and recover it, but if it do not, then, on the return of peace the rights of the contracting alien are restored, and he may himself sue. No other principle is to be deduced. The first may be laid out of the case, for this was not in its creation a contract made with an alien enemy. The second question is, whether the bill came to the hands of the plaintiff by a good title? Under the circumstances of this case, not meaning to lay down any general rule beyond this case, I am of opinion that the indorsement to the plaintiff conveyed to him a legal title in this bill, on which the king might have sued in the time of the war, and he not having so done, the plaintiff might sue after peace was proclaimed."

HEATH, J., was absent.

CHAMBRE, J.—"I am perfectly of the same opinion, and it would be of very mischievous consequence if it were otherwise."

DALLAS, J.—"This is not a contract between a subject of this country and an alien enemy, nor is it a contract of that sort to which the principle can be applied. That principle is, that there shall be no communication with the enemy in time of war, but this is a contract between two subjects in an enemy's country, which is perfectly legal.

"Ruled refused."

SECTION 32.—RANSOM BILLS.

CORNU v. BLACKBURNE.

KING'S BENCH, 1781.

(2 *Douglas*, 640.)

A French captor had ransomed a British vessel, taken a hostage, and was then in turn captured by British cruisers; but he concealed the ransom bill, and afterward sued upon it. *Held*, that he could recover in the action.

This was the case of an English vessel and cargo captured by a French privateer and ransomed and a hostage taken as security; but the privateer was in turn captured by two English frigates and taken into an English port. The ransom bill was concealed, however, by the first captor, and not given up; and the present suit is on the ransom bill. This document is as follows:

"No. 66. Registered the present ransom bill at the Admiralty office, Boulogne, the 25th October, 1779, and delivered in double to Captain Robert Cornu, commanding, the cutter, the *Princesse de Robecq* privateer, of this port, by me underwritten Chief Register. Signed, Merlin, Boulogne.'—We the underwitten Robert Cornu of Boulogne, commander of the ship the *Princesse de Robecq*, privateer of Boulogne, and Thomas Finchett of Liverpool, master of the ship the *Dolly* of Liverpoole, have agreed as followeth, viz.—That I, Robert Cornu, commander of the said privateer, acknowledge to have ransomed the said ship the *Dolly* of Liverpoole, belonging to John Blackburne, burgher of Liverpoole, burthen 105 tons, on the 6th of June, in the year 1780, at the heighth of Edinburgh, going from Lynn to Liverpoole in England, under English colours, and passport of said England, loaded with wheat, for the account of John Blackburne, burgher of Liverpoole; which vessel I have agreed to ransom for the sum of 1300*l.* sterling, to be paid to Mr. Hauffoullier, fitter of the said privateer at Dunkirk; in consideration of which I have set the said vessel at liberty to go to the port of Liverpoole, where she is to be arrived in the time and space of three months, after the expiration of which this present agreement shall not clear her from being taken by any other privateers. For security of which ransom, I have received for hostage on board of the said ship, John Butler, cousin to the captain of the said vessel, desiring all friends and allies to let safely and freely proceed the said vessel to the port of Liverpoole, without any let or molestation, during the said time or course of her voyage; and I, Thomas Finchett, owner of the said ship and merchandizes, have voluntarily submitted to the payment of the said ransom, viz. 1300*l.* sterling; for surety whereof I have delivered up the said John Butler of Liverpoole for hostage, promising not to go against the conditions of this present contract, whereof each of us have a copy by us, which we have signed, with the said hostage. Signed on board the said ship, the 6th of June in the year 1780. And it is further expressly covenanted and agreed, that I the said Thomas Finchett do bind and oblige myself, and engage my vessel and cargo, to pay or cause to be paid to the owners of the said privateer, the full amount of the said ransom, should the said hostage come to die, or to desert, or that the said privateer should perish, or be taken with the hostage on board, *without* which condition the captain of the said privateer would not have consented to the above ransom, which, in all cases whatsoever, shall be well and truly paid.—(Signed) Robert Cornu. Thomas Finchett. John Butler."

Lord MANSFIELD:—"It is sound policy, as well as good morality, to keep faith with an enemy in time of war. This is a contract which arises out of a state of hostility, and is to be governed by the law of nations, and the eternal rules of justice. The additional clause is particularly adapted to this case. There is no pretext to impeach it, on the ground of fraud or extortion. The bill was registered before the French ship sailed, with this clause in it. Nor does any inference arise, from its insertion, that the general law was understood to be otherwise; for it is, also, stipulated, that the death of the hostage shall not vacate the contract, which stipulation the parties must be presumed to have known to be unnecessary, because the decision in *Ricord* v. *Bettenham* was notorious over all Europe. Learned lawyers were written to on that occasion, both in France and Holland, and Mr. Justice BLACKSTONE shewed me several letters he had received from abroad, on the subject. It is said, that, by the law of nations, the recapture puts an end to the ransom bill; and the argument is, that the court of Admiralty decrees salvage for retaking the ransom bill.

"But what are the cases brought to prove this position? None of them were litigated but the last, and, there, no ransom bill was forthcoming. Upon what was salvage given in that case? They seem to have mistaken the nature of salvage. They seem to consider it as a debt which may be exacted. But no man can be compelled to pay salvage, unless he chooses to have the property back. They have confounded distinct subjects. What is the eighth part of a ransom bill? Can the eighth part of an hostage be claimed as salvage? Could the recaptor make use of the ransom bill?

"Could he bring an action on it in the foreign captain's name? When the owner gets possession of the ransom bill, it may be a different consideration. But the present case is clear on two grounds. 1. The special clause is decisive; and, 2. Independent of that clause, there never has been any capture of the ransom bill.

"The authority from Grotius is very strong on this last ground."

WILLES, and ASHHURST, Justices, "of the same opinion."

BULLER, Justice, "of the same opinion.—The last ground goes all the length; for the bill was never taken.

"The Postea to be delivered to the plaintiff." [1]

THE "CHARMING NANCY."

OPINION OF G. HAY, 1761.

(*Marsden's Admiralty Cases*, 398.)

Who may sue on a ransom bill?

The ship *Charming Nancy* (whereof James Fanneson now is or lately was master) being taken as prize by the French, was with her cargo ransomed by the master for the sum of £ ; and Francis Burt and one of the crew, whose name is unknown, consented to go as hostages for the payment of the said ransom; in consequence whereof the said ship and cargo were released. The ship afterwards arrived at her destined port, and has there unlivered part of her cargo, but the said ransom has not been paid, and the said hostages still remain prisoners. A suit is intended to be commenced in the Court of Admiralty by the relations of Burt to compel the payment of the said ransom, and thereby procure the release of the hostage, and it is uncertain whether the ship, and that part of the cargo which remains unlivered may be sufficient to answer the said ransom.

[1] The case of *Ricord* v. *Bettenham*, 3 Burrow, 1734 (1762), referred to by Lord Mansfield, was that of a British ship captured and ransomed by a French captor, a hostage—Joseph Bell—being taken. The hostage died in prison; and the present action was subsequently brought on the ransom bill by the captor.

It was objected that, the plaintiff being an alien enemy at the time of the contract, the ransom bill was void, the hostage alone being entitled to bring an action. But the court overruled these objections and gave judgment for the plaintiff.

Query.—"Have not Burt's relations a right to bring an action against the master, for the performance of whose contract the hostages became bound, as well [as] against the ship and goods, so that they may, if necessary, proceed against both? And can a warrant on such action be refused? And, as the name of the other hostage is not at present known, may not such action be entered in the name of Burt and company as hostages?"

Answer.—"I do not know any instance of a warrant issuing against the master in such a case. The ship and goods are in the first place answerable for the redemption of a hostage.

"These may be arrested, and the suit may be brought by Burt's relations on behalf of both the hostages, naming the one and describing the other of name at present unknown."

G. HAY, January 24, 1761.

"In the first instance I think you cannot proceed against the master. If the ship and goods will not produce the sum stipulated for the ransom, and you can show that the master fraudulently ransomed, I think he may then be prosecuted on behalf of the hostages."

THE "PATRIXENT."

OPINION OF WM. WYNNE, 1781.

(*Marsden's Admiralty Cases*, 398.)

A British ship was ransomed by an American captor, and a hostage taken. The bill was sent to Holland to be forwarded to England for collection. The opinion was that a suit on the ransom bill could be maintained against the master and owners of the ransomed vessel, but, it must first be shown that the hostage was detained or dead.

The ship *Patrixent*, Hannibal Lush, master, was taken by an American privateer, and was ransomed for £5,500 sterling, and an hostage delivered, who was carried to America. For the above sum the captain of the ransomed ship drew a bill upon Messrs. John Glassford & Co., merchants in Glasgow, a copy of which is underwritten, who are owners of the vessel.

The ransom-bill was sent to Amsterdam, and from thence remitted to merchants in London, to recover the value of it. When it was first presented to the gentlemen upon whom it was drawn, they offered £1,000, part of it, as the value of the ship; but it not being thought prudent to receive a part of the money, their offer was then refused: since which the said gentlemen, together with the owners of the cargo, have refused to pay the bill or any part of it.

Your opinion is desired whether the holder of this ransom bill can maintain a suit in the Admiralty Court against the owners of the ship and cargo for the recovery of the sum for which such bill was given? And whether such suit must be brought against every individual owner of the ship and cargo.

COPY OF THE BILL.

"£5,500. On board the schooner *Hanna.*

July 26, 1779.

"At ninety days' sight my second bill of exchange, first and third of the same tenor not paid, pay to Richard Jackson or order the sum of five thousand five hundred pound sterling, for the ransom of the ship *Patrixent* and her cargo.

HANNIBAL LUSH.

"To Messrs. JOHN GLASSFORD & Co.,
"Merchants, Glasgow."

Answer.—"I think that the owner of this ransom-bill may maintain a suit in the Court of Admiralty for the recovery of the sum for which the bill was given; but I apprehend they must make it appear that the hostage is not at liberty, if he is living, before they can obtain payment of the money. The proper way of commencing such a suit would be by arresting the ransomed ship with the cargo on board. But if that cannot be done, I think it will be sufficient to bring the suit against Lush, the master, who drew the bill, and Messrs. Glassford & Co., the owners of the vessel, upon whom it is drawn."

WM. WYNNE, Doctors' Commons, July 25th, 1781.[1]

[1] *Ransom Contracts.*—In a subsequent case, *Anthon* v. *Fisher*, 2 Douglas, 649, note, it was settled in English law that an alien enemy cannot sue on a ransom bill for want of a *persona standi in judicio.*

And so in the case of the *Hoop*, 1 C. Rob., 201, Sir W. Scott said, "even in the case of ransoms which were contracts, but contracts arising *ex jure belli*, and tolerated as such, the enemy was not permitted to sue in his own proper person for the payment of the ransom bill; but the payment was enforced by an action by the imprisoned hostage in the courts of his own country, for the recovery of his freedom."

"But the effect of such a contract," says Wheaton, Ed. of 1863, p. 695, "like that of every other which may be lawfully entered into between belligerents, is to suspend the character of an enemy, so far as respects the parties to the ransom bill; and, consequently, the technical objection of the want of a *persona standi in judi-*

SECTION 33.—COMMERCIAL DOMICIL.

THE "INDIAN CHIEF."

HIGH COURT OF ADMIRALTY, 1801.

(3 *C. Robinson*, 12.)

This was the case of a ship and cargo seized in the harbor of Cowes, on a voyage from Batavia to Hamburg, in which two questions arose, respecting the national character of the owners of the ship and cargo respectively, both American citizens residing in British territory, and charged with trading with the enemy.

Held, That a neutral merchant residing in a belligerent country is to be regarded as a belligerent trader; but that the moment he puts himself in motion *bona fide* to return to his native country *sine animo revertendi*, he loses his belligerent character, and resumes that of a neutral.

Judgment,—Sir W. SCOTT:—

"This is the case of a ship seized in the port of Cowes, where she came to receive orders respecting the delivery of a cargo taken in at Batavia, with a professed original intention of proceeding to Hamburg; but on coming into this country for particular orders, the ship and cargo were seized in port. It does not appear clear to the court, that it might not be a cargo intended to be delivered in this country, as many such cargoes have been, un-

cio cannot, on principle, prevent a suit being brought by the captor, directly on the ransom bill." And this appears to be the practice in the maritime courts of the European continent. (Valin, Ord. de la Marine, liv. 3, tit. 9, art. 19; Pistoye et Duverdy, I., 280 *et seq.*)

"If the ransomed vessel," says Wheaton, Ed. of 1863, p. 694, "is lost by the perils of the sea, before her arrival, the obligation to pay the sum stipulated for her ransom is not thereby extinguished. * * * Even where it is expressly agreed that the loss of the vessel by these perils shall discharge the captured from the payment of the ransom, this clause is restrained to the case of a total loss on the high seas, and is not extended to shipwreck or stranding, which might afford the master a temptation fraudulently to cast away his vessel, in order to save the most valuable part of the cargo, and avoid the payment of the ransom. * * * So, if the captor, after having ransomed a vessel belonging to the enemy, is himself taken by the enemy, together with the ransom bill, of which he is the bearer, this ransom bill becomes a part of the capture made by the enemy; and the persons of the hostile nation who were debtors of the ransom are thereby discharged from their obligation."

On the subject of ransom generally, see Judge STORY's opinion in *Maisonnare* v. *Keating*, 2 Gallison, 337.

der the Dutch property act: I mention this to meet an observation that has been thrown out, 'that it is doubtful whether the ship might not be confiscable on the ground of being a neutral ship coming from a colony of the enemy, not to her own ports or the ports of this country.' I cannot assume it as a demonstrated fact in the case, that the cargo was to be delivered at Hamburg.—The vessel sailed in 1795, and as an American ship with an American pass, and all American documents; but nevertheless if the owner really resided here, such papers could not protect his vessel; if the owner was resident in England, and the voyage such as an English merchant could not engage in, an American residing here, and carrying on trade, could not protect his ship merely by putting American documents on board; his interest must stand or fall according to the determination which the court shall make on the national character of such a person.

"There are two propositions which are not to be controverted; that Mr. Johnson is an American generally by birth, which is the circumstance that first impresses itself on the mind of the Court; and also by the part which he took on the breaking out of the American war. He came hither when both countries were open to him; but on the breaking out of hostilities, he made his election which country he would adhere to, and in consequence thereof went to France. As to the doubt that has been suggested, whether he would be deemed an American, not having been personally there at the time of the declaration of the independence of that country; I think that is sufficiently cleared up, by the circumstances of his being adopted as such by the act of the American government, declaring him and his family to be American subjects, and by the official character which that government has intrusted to him; I am of opinion, therefore, that he has not lost the benefit of his native American character. He came however to this country in 1783, and engaged in trade, and has resided in this country till 1797; during that time he was undoubtedly to be considered as an English trader; for no position is more established than this, that if a person goes into another country, and engages in trade, and resides there, he is, by the law of nations, to be considered as a merchant of that country; I should therefore have no doubt in pronouncing that Mr. Johnson was to be considered as a merchant of this country, at the time of sailing of this vessel on her outward voyage. That leads me to take a view of the circumstances of this case; the ship went out in 1795 with Mr. Hewlet on board, and Mr. Johnson says, 'he sent out Mr. Hewlet as supercargo, and put the vessel under his control to take freight for America, but that his designs were frustrated by various circumstances;' and the ship actually went to Madeira, Madras, Tranquahar, and Batavia, and from thence to Cowes where she was arrested.

"Now there can be no doubt that if Mr. Johnson had continued where he was at the time of sailing, if he had remained resident in England, it must be considered as a British transaction; and therefore a criminal transaction, on the common principle that it is illegal in any person owing an allegiance, though temporary, to trade with the public enemy. But it is pleaded that he had quitted this country before the capture, and that he had done this in consequence of an intention he had formed of removing much earlier, but that he had been prevented by obstacles that obstructed his wish; to this effect the letter of March 1797, is exhibited, which must have been preceded by private correspondence and application to some of his creditors. It does, I think, breathe strong expressions of intention, and of an ardent desire to get over the restraint that alone detained him; and it affords conclusive reason to believe that if he had been a free man, and at liberty to go where he pleased, he would have removed long before; and that he was detained here as a hostage, as he describes himself, to his creditors, on motives of honor creditable to his character. On the 9th of September 1797 he did actually retire; of the sincerity of his quitting this country there can hardly be a doubt entertained; it is almost impossible to represent stronger or more natural grounds for such a measure; and I do not think the Court runs any risk of encountering a fraudulent pretension, put forward to meet the circumstances of the moment, without anything of an original and *bona fide* intention at the bottom of it.

The ship was sent out under the management of the supercargo, and it is said that Mr. Hewlet exceeded his commission. The affidavit does not go so far; it does not appear from that, that the agent had not the power to enter into such an engagement; but this, I think, appears clearly, that it was the understanding both of Mr. Johnson, and of his agent, Mr. Hewlet, who had been his clerk, and to whom he refers for a confirmation of his avowed design of removing, that before the completion of such a voyage Mr. Johnson would be in America; therefore if the illegality of the voyage must be supposed to have presented itself to their minds, as a British transaction, owing to Mr. Johnson's residence in England, there was reason enough for them to conclude that Mr. Johnson would be removed; and, on that view of the matter, although it is certain that an agent would bind his employer in such a case, there is ground sufficient to presume that the agent acted fairly and *bona fide*, and under the expectation that Mr. Johnson would be returned to America.

"The ship arrives a few weeks after his departure; and taking it to be clear, that the national character of Mr. Johnson as a British merchant was founded in residence only, that it was acquired by residence, and rested on that circumstance alone; it must be held that from the moment he turns his back on the country where he has resided, on his way to his own country, he was in the act of resuming his original character, and is to be considered as an American: The character that is gained by residence ceases by residence: It is an adventitious character which no longer adheres to him, from the moment that he puts himself in motion, *bona fide*, to quit the country, *sine animo revertendi*. The courts that have to apply this principle, have applied it both ways, unfavorably in some cases, and favorably in others. This man had actually quitted the country. Stronger was the case of Mr. Curtissos (The *Snelle Zeylder*, Lds. Ap. 25, 1783); he was a British born-subject, that had been resident in Surinam and St. Eustatius, and had left those settlements with an intention of returning to this country; but he had got no farther than Holland, the mother country of those settlements, when the war broke out. It was determined by the Lords of Appeal, that he was *in itinere*, that he had put himself in motion, and was in pursuit of his native British character: and as such, he was held to be entitled to the restitution of his property. So here, this gentleman was in actual pursuit of his American character; and, I think, there can be no doubt that his native character was strongly and substantially revived, not occasionally, nor colorably, for the mere purpose of the present claim; and therefore I shall restore the ship."

[The cargo of this vessel belonged to Mr. Millar, resident in Calcutta as American consul. He was held to be a British merchant engaged in trade with the enemy, and his goods were therefore condemned as droits of admiralty, being seized in a British port. His consular character made no difference whatever in protecting his trade.]

THE "VENUS."

SUPREME COURT OF THE UNITED STATES, 1814.

(8 *Cranch*, 253.)

If a citizen of the United States establishes his domicil in a foreign country between which and the United States hostilities afterwards break out, any property shipped by such citizen before knowledge of the war, and captured by an American cruiser after the declaration of war, must be condemned as lawful prize.

Judgment,—WASHINGTON, J.:—

" * * * The great question involved in this, and many other of the prize cases which have been argued, is, whether the property of these claimants who were settled in Great Britain, and engaged in the commerce of that country, shipped before they had a knowledge of the war, but which was captured, after the declaration of war, by an American cruiser, ought to be condemned as lawful prize. It is contended by the captors, that as these claimants had gained a domicil in Great Britain, and continued to enjoy it up to the time war was declared, and when these captures were made, they must be considered as British subjects, in reference to this property, and, consequently, that it may legally be seized as prize of war, in like manner as if it had belonged to real British subjects. But, if not so, it is then insisted that these claimants, having, after their naturalization in the United States, returned to Great Britain, the country of their birth, and there resettled themselves, they became redintegrated British subjects, and ought to be considered by this court in the same light as if they never had emigrated. On the other side it is argued, that American citizens settled in the country of the enemy, as these persons were, at the time war was declared, were entitled to a reasonable time to elect, after they knew of the war, to remain there, or to return to the United States; and that until such election was, *bona fide*, made, the courts of this country are bound to consider them as American citizens, and their property shipped before they had an opportunity to make this election, as being protected against American capture.

"There being no dispute as to the facts upon which the domicil of these claimants is asserted, the questions of law alone remain to be considered. They are two.—First, by what means and to what extent, a national character may be impressed upon a person different from that which permanent allegiance gives him? and, secondly, what are the legal consequences to which this acquired character may expose him, in the event of a war taking place between the country of his residence and that of his birth, or in which he had been naturalized?

"1. The writers upon the law of nations distinguish between a temporary residence in a foreign country, for a special purpose, and a residence accompanied with an intention to make it a permanent place of abode. The latter is styled by Vattel, *domicil*, which he defines to be, 'a habitation fixed in any place with an intention of always staying there.' * * *

"The question whether the person to be affected by the right of domicil had sufficiently made known his intention of fixing himself permanently in the foreign country, must depend upon all the circumstances of the case. If he had made no express declaration on the subject, and his secret intention is to be discovered, his acts must be attended to, as affording the most satisfactory evidence of his intention. On this ground it is, that the courts of England have decided, that a person who removes to a foreign country, settles himself there, and engages in the trade of the country, furnishes by these acts such evidence of an intention permanently to reside there, as to stamp him with the national character of the state where he resides. In questions on this subject, the chief point to be considered, is the *animus manendi;* and courts are to devise such reasonable rules of evidence as may establish the fact of intention. If it sufficiently appear that the intention of removing was to make a permanent settlement, or for an indefinite time, the right of domicil is acquired by a residence even of a few days. This is one of the rules of the British courts, and it appears to be perfectly reasonable. Another is, that a neutral or subject, found residing in a foreign country is presumed to be there *animo manendi;* and if a state of war should bring his national character into question, it lies upon him to explain the circumstance of his residence—(the *Bernon*, 1 C. Rob., 86, 102). * * *

"2. The next question is, what are the consequences to which this acquired domicil may legally expose the person entitled to it, in the event of a war taking place between the government under which he resides and that to which he owes a permanent allegiance? A neutral in his situation, if he should engage in open hostilities with the other belligerent would be considered and treated as an enemy. A citizen of the other belligerent could not be so considered, because he could not by any act of hostility, render himself, strictly speaking, an enemy, contrary to his permanent allegiance. But although he cannot be considered an enemy, in the strict sense of the word, yet he is deemed such, with reference to the seizure of so much of his property concerned in the trade of the enemy, as is connected with his residence. It is found adhering to the enemy. He is himself adhering to the enemy, although not criminally so, unless he engages in acts of hostility against his native country, or, probably, refuses, when required by his country, to return. The same rule, as to property engaged in the commerce of the enemy, applies to neutrals; and for the same reason. The converse of this rule inevitably applies to the subject of a belligerent state domiciled in a neutral country; he is deemed a neutral by both belligerents, with reference to the trade which he carries on with the adverse belligerent, and with all the rest of the world.

"But this national character which a man acquires by residence may be thrown off at pleasure, by a return to his native country, or even by turning his back on the country in which he has resided, on his way to another. To use the language of Sir W. Scott, it is an adventitious character gained by residence, and which ceases by non-residence. It no longer adheres to the party from the moment he puts himself in motion, *bona fide*, to quit the country *sine animo revertendi* (3 C. Rob., 17,12, *The Indian Chief*). The reasonableness of this rule can hardly be disputed. Having once acquired a national character by residence in a foreign country, he ought to be bound by all the consequences of it, until he has thrown it off, either by an actual return to his native country, or to that where he was naturalized, or by commencing his removal *bona fide*, and without an intention of returning. If anything short of actual removal be admitted to work a change in the national character acquired by residence, it seems perfectly reasonable that the evidence of a *bona fide* intention to remove should be such as to leave no doubt of its sincerity. Mere declaration of such an intention ought never to be relied upon, where contradicted, or at least rendered doubtful, by a continuance of that residence which impressed the character. They may have been made to deceive; or, if sincerely made, they may never be executed. Even the party himself ought not to be bound by them, because he may afterwards find reason to change his determination, and ought to be permitted to do so. But when he accompanies those declarations with acts which speak a language not to be mistaken, and can hardly fail to be consummated by actual removal, the strongest evidence is afforded which the nature of such a case can furnish. And is it not proper that the courts of a belligerent nation should deny to any person the right to use a character so equivocal, as to put it in his power to claim whichever may best suit his purpose, when it is called in question?

If his property be taken trading with the enemy, shall he be allowed to shield it from confiscation, by alleging that he had intended to remove from the country of the enemy to his own, then neutral, and, therefore, that, as a neutral, the trade was lawful? If war exists between the country of his residence and his native country, and his property be seized by the former, or by the latter, shall he be heard to say in the former case, that he was a domiciled subject of the country of the captor, and in the latter, that he was a native subject of the country of that captor also, because he had declared an intention to resume his native character; and thus to parry the belligerent rights of both? It is to guard against such inconsistencies, and against the frauds which such pretensions, if tolerated, would sanction, that the rule above mentioned has been adopted. Upon what sound principle can a distinction be framed between the case of a neutral, and the subject of one belligerent domiciled in the country of the other at the breaking out of the war? The property of each, found engaged in the commerce of their adopted country, belonging to them, before the war, in their character of subjects of that country, so long as they continued to retain their domicil; and a state of war takes place between that country and any other, by which the two nations and all their subjects become enemies to each other, it follows that all the property, which was once the property of a friend, belongs now, in reference to that property, to an enemy. This doctrine of the common-law and prize courts of England is founded, like that mentioned under the first head, upon national law; and it is believed to be strongly supported by reason and justice. It is laid down by Grotius, p. 563, 'that all the subjects of the enemy who are such from a permanent cause, that is to say, settled in the country, are liable to the law of reprisals, whether they be natives or foreigners; but not so if they are only trading or sojourning for a little time.' And why, it may be confidently asked, should not the property of such subjects be exposed to the law of reprisals and of war, so long as the owner retains his acquired domicil, or, in the words of Grotius, continues a permanent residence in the country of the enemy? They were before, and continue after the war, bound, by such residence, to the society of which they are members, subject to the laws of the state, and owing a qualified allegiance thereto; they are obliged to defend it (with an exception in favor of such a subject, in relation to his native country), in return for the protection it affords them, and the privileges which the laws bestow upon them as subjects. The property of such persons, equally with that of the native subjects in their totality, is to be considered as the goods of the nation, in regard to other states. It belongs, in some sort, to the state, from the right which she has over the goods of its citizens, which make a part of the sum total of its riches, and augment its power. Vatt., 147, and also B., 1, c. 14., § 182. In reprisals, continues the same author, we seize on the property of the subject, just as we would that of the sovereign; everything that belongs to the nation is subject to reprisals, wherever it can be seized, with the exception of a deposit entrusted to the public faith. B., 2, c. 18, § 344. Now if a permanent residence constitutes the person a subject of the country where he is settled, so long as he continues to reside there, and subjects his property to the law of reprisals, as a part of the property of the nation, it would seem difficult to maintain that the same consequences would not follow in the case of an open and public war, whether between the adopted and native countries of persons so domiciled, or between the former and any other nation. If, then, nothing but an actual removal, or *bona fide* beginning to remove, can change a national character acquired by domicil, and if, at the time of the inception of the voyage, as well as at the time of capture, the property belonged to such domiciled person in his character of a subject, what is there that does, or ought to exempt it from capture by the privateers of his native country, if, at the time of capture, he continues to reside in the country of the adverse belligerent? It is contended that a native or naturalized subject of one country, who is surprised, in the country where he was domiciled, by a declaration of war, ought to have time to make his election to continue there, or to remove to the country to which he owes a permanent allegiance, and that, until such election is made, his property ought to be protected from capture by the cruisers of the latter. This doctrine is believed to be as unfounded in reason and justice, as it clearly is in law. In the first place, it is founded upon a presumption that the person will certainly remove, before it can possibly be known whether he may elect to do so or not. It is said that this presumption ought to be made, because, on receiving information of the war, it will be his duty to return home. This position is denied. It is his duty to commit no acts of hostility against his native country, and to return to her assistance when required to do so; nor will any just nation, regarding the mild principles of the law of nations, require him to take arms against his native country, or refuse her permission to him to withdraw whenever he wishes to do so, unless under peculiar circumstances, which, by such removal at a critical period, might endanger the public safety. The conventional law of nations is in conformity with these principles. It is not uncommon to stipulate in treaties that the subjects of each shall be allowed to remove with their property, or to remain unmolested. Such a stipulation does not coerce those subjects either to remove or to remain. They are left free to choose for themselves; and when they have made their election, they claim the right of enjoying it under the treaty. But until the election is made, their former character continues unchanged.

"Until this election is made, if his property found upon the high seas, engaged in the commerce of his adopted country, should be permitted by the cruisers of the other belligerent to pass free, under the notion that he may elect to remove, upon notice of the war, and should arrive safe, what is to be done in case the owner of it should afterwards elect to remain where he is? or if captured and brought immediately to adjudication, it must, upon this doctrine, be acquitted until the election to remain is made known. In short, the point contended for would apply the doctrine of relation to cases where the party claiming the benefit of it may gain all, and can lose nothing. If he, after the capture, should find it his interest to remain where he is domiciled, his property embarked before his election was made, is safe; and if he finds it best to return, it is safe of course. It is safe whether he goes or stays. This doctrine, producing such contradictory consequences, is not only unsupported by any authority, but it would violate principles long and well established in the prize courts of England, and which ought not, without strong reasons which may render them inapplicable to this country, to be disregarded by this court. The rule there is, that the character of the property, during war, cannot be changed *in transitu*, by any act of the party, subsequent to the capture. The rule indeed goes farther: as to the correctness of which in its greatest extension, no opinion need now be given; but it may safely be affirmed that this charge cannot and ought not to be affected by an election of the owner and shipper of it made subsequent to the capture, and, more especially, after a knowlege of the capture is obtained by the owner. Observe the consequences which would result from it. The capture is made and known. The owner is allowed to deliberate whether it is his interest to remain a subject of his adopted, or of his native country. If the capture be made by the former, then he elects to be a subject of that country; if by the latter, then a subject of that. Can such a privileged situation be tolerated by either belligerent? Can any system of law be correct, which places an individual who adheres to one belligerent, and, to the period of his election to remove, contributes to increase her wealth, in so anomalous a situation as to be clothed with the privilege of a neutral, as to both belligerents? This notion about a temporary state of neutrality impressed upon a subject of one of the belligerents, and the consequent exemption of his property from capture by either, until he has had notice of the war and made his election, is altogether a novel theory, and seems, from the course of the argument, to owe its origin to a supposed hardship to which the contrary doctrine exposes him. But if the reasoning employed on this subject be correct, no such hardship can exist. For if, before the election is made, his property on the ocean is liable to capture by the cruisers of his native and deserted country, it is not only free from capture by those of his adopted country, but is under its protection. The privilege is supposed to be equal to the disadvantage, and is therefore just. The double privilege claimed seems too unreasonable to be granted. * * *

"Condemnation was pronounced in all the cases." [1]

[1] Chief-Justice MARSHALL and LIVINGSTON, J., dissented from a part of the judgment.

Mr. Duer ("Insurance," I., 505) has given an admirable summary of the dissenting opinion of Chief-Justice MARSHALL in the *Venus*, the principles of which he seems inclined to think are more in accordance with reason than the one laid down by the majority of the bench.

Mr. Duer says: "From this opinion of the majority of the court Chief-Justice MARSHALL, and Mr. Justice LIVINGSTON, dissented, and the former supported his dissent in an elaborate argument, which, as it bears, in an eminent degree, the impress of his vigorous and comprehensive mind, claims, and will amply reward, the diligent perusal of the student. The basis of his argument was the position, that, a mere commercial domicil, wholly acquired in time of peace, necessarily ceases at the commencement of hostilities between the country of the merchant's residence, and that of his allegiance; and this position he expands and illustrates by a great variety of arguments, from various sources. It is only a very condensed view of his reasoning that I shall attempt to exhibit. Where a merchant removes to a foreign country, for commercial purposes, in time of peace, it is reasonable to believe, that he intends to remain only so long as he can carry on his trade, lawfully and advantageously, without a violation of duty to the country of his affections and his allegiance; but the intervention of a war between the country of his residence and his own country, renders the prosecution of a trade, such as he alone contemplated, no longer practicable. Such a war, we are bound to believe, removes the causes, and supersedes the motives that alone induced his foreign residence; and an intention of continued residence, under so material a change of circumstances, ought no longer to be imputed to him. On the contrary, when we consider that the right of the merchant to remain and prosecute the trade in which he was engaged, is now forfeited—that he has become the enemy of the country in which he resides—that his continuance in it will, probably, expose him to many and serious inconveniences—that his interests and his duty and most probably, his inclinations, call him home—it seems, not only a fair, but almost a necessary inference, that the change in his situation has produced a change of his intentions; it, therefore, justifies the presumption, that he means not to continue, but as soon as practicable, to terminate his residence. It is alike impolitic and unjust, to build any argument upon his first residence, of his intention to throw off permanently his original character and allegiance.

THE "HARMONY."

HIGH COURT OF ADMIRALTY, 1800.

(2 *C. Robinson*, 322.)

In considering the evidence which shall constitute domicil, time is the most important ingredient.

This was one of several American vessels in which a claim had been reserved for part of the cargo, on farther proof to be made of the national character of G. W. Murray, who appeared in the original

"The very commerce, in which he was engaged, may have had a direct relation to the interest of his own country, may have tended to augment its resources and wealth. No nation that takes an interest in the prosperity of its own commerce, can wish to restrain its own citizens from residing abroad for commercial purposes; nor will it hastily construe such a residence into a change of national character, to the certain injury of the individual, and probably to its own. Nor is this all. It is the doctrine of the most approved writers on the law of nations, that a citizen of one country, who is residing, but not naturalized, in another, is not incorporated into the foreign society; but is still considered as a member of that to which he originally belonged. If a war breaks out between the two nations he is to be permitted, and it is, in truth, his duty to restore himself, by a speedy removal, to his proper allegiance. It is his duty to free himself from a position, that, by its voluntary continuance, would render him an enemy of his own country; and we are bound to presume that he will avail himself of the earliest means and opportunity to discharge a duty, that the dictates of patriotism, and the law of his allegiance, alike impose. Whilst this presumption continues in force, it is unjust to consider him as an enemy. It is a harsh proceeding of his native country to confiscate the property of one, who, for aught that appears, may deserve to be ranked among its most attached and devoted citizens. But this presumption, that, while it exists, should shield his property from condemnation, continues to exist, not only till he is proved to have a knowledge of the war, but until a reasonable and sufficient time has been allowed him to disengage himself and effect a removal. It exists until there is evidence, that after a knowledge of the war, he had continued to reside, without compulsion, or justifiable cause, in the hostile country. When it is proved to be his real intention to change permanently his national character; where it is his choice to remain in the hostile country, there is no injustice or harshness in treating him as an enemy; but if, while prosecuting his business in a foreign country, he retained his attachment, and contemplated a return, to his own, it is pressing admiralty principles too far; it is drawing conclusions that the premises do not warrant, to infer absolutely his intention to continue in a country which has become hostile, merely from his residence and trading in that country while it was friendly, and to punish him by a confiscation of his goods, as if he had been fully convicted of this intention.

"The Chief-Justice concluded by remarking, that in applying the principles he case, as a partner of a house of trade in America, but personally resident in France; restitution had been decreed in the several claims to the house of trade in America, with a reservation of the share of this partner.

G. W. Murray, a partner in a house of trade in New York, had gone to France, in 1794, as supercargo of a vessel, in behalf of his firm, to there dispose of the cargo; but with the exception of a brief visit to America in 1795–96, he continued to reside in France, and to receive and dispose of cargoes sent out from New York.

At the time of the first trial, Mr. G. W. Murray had not been in France a year; but from the evidence of letters, etc., Sir W. SCOTT thought the intention was to form a permanent residence and correspondence in France. This belief was strengthened by the fact that Mr. Murray had returned to France in 1796 and remained there till 1800. Hence his return to America in 1795–96 was probably but temporary, and he was considered to have had a residence in France for six years.

Judgment,—Sir W. SCOTT, (Extract):—

"This is a question which arises on several parcels of property claimed on behalf of G. W. Murray; and it is in all of them a ques-

had laid down to the claimants, the court ought to be regulated by the conduct they had pursued, after a *knowledge of the war*. If they had continued their residence and trade, after a knowledge of the war, it was clear, that their claim to a restitution could not be sustained; but if they had taken immediate measures for returning to the United States, and had since actually returned, or had assigned sufficient reasons for not returning, their property was, in his judgment, capable of restitution, and that by this discrimination some of the claimants, although not all, were entitled to the restoration of their goods.

"In the course of this opinion, which I have reluctantly abridged, the Chief-Justice subjected most of the leading decisions of the English admiralty on the question of domicil, to a strict and searching analysis, and he arrived at the conclusion that they gave no support to the assertion that Sir W. SCOTT had ever advanced or intimated, or would probably maintain, a doctrine repugnant to that he sought to establish. Indeed, the exact case, under circumstances analogous to those in which it was presented to the Supreme Court of the United States, seems never to have arisen in the courts of England.

"It is necessary, in conclusion, to remark that the claimants in the case which was the subject of this controversy, although naturalized citizens of the United States, were native-born subjects of Great Britain, and consequently their residence in England was not properly the acquisition of a new domicil, but, by its necessary effect, a restoration to their original allegiance. Whether the reasoning and views of the Chief-Justice were applicable in their full extent, if at all, to such a case, may be seriously doubted; and these doubts may be felt even by those, who assent without difficulty to the soundness and truth of his doctrine, when limited in its application to native subjects or citizens, residing merely, and not naturalized, in a foreign country."

tion of residence or domicil, which I have often had occasion to observe, is in itself a question of considerable difficulty, depending on a great variety of circumstances, hardly capable of being defined by any general precise rules. The active spirit of commerce now abroad in the world, still farther increases this difficulty by increasing the variety of local situations, in which the same individual is to be found at no great distance of time; and by that sort of extended circulation, if I may so call it, by which the same transaction communicates with different countries, as in the present cases, in which the same trading adventures have their origin (perhaps) in America, travel to France, from France to England, from England back to America again, without enabling us to assign accurately the exact legal effect of the local character of every particular portion of this divided transaction.

"In deciding such cases, the necessary freedom of commerce imposes likewise the duty of a particular attention and delicacy; and strict principle of law must not be pressed too eagerly against it; and I have before had occasion to remark, that the particular situation of America, in respect to distance, seems still more particularly to entitle the merchants of that country to some favourable distinctions. They live at a great distance from Europe; they have not the same open and ready and constant correspondence with individuals of the several nations of Europe, that these persons have with each other; they are on that very account more likely to have their mercantile confidence in Europe abused, and therefore to have more frequent calls for a personal attendance to their own concerns; and it is to be expected that when the necessity of their affairs calls them across the Atlantic, they should make rather a longer stay in the country where they are called, than foreign merchants who step from a neighbouring country in Europe, to which every day offers a convenient opportunity of return.

"In considering this particular case, it may not be improper to remark, that circumstances occur in the evidence that address themselves forcibly to private commiseration, remarking, however, at the same time, that public duty can allow only a very limited effect to such considerations, and still less to another, that has been pressed upon me, that the money, if restored, is to go in payment of debts due to British creditors, from the bankrupt estate of this unfortunate person.

"My business is to inquire whether he is entitled to recover it, without regard to the probable application of it, if it finds its way again into his possession.

"Of the few principles that can be laid down generally, I may venture to hold, that time is the grand ingredient in constituting domicil. I think that hardly enough is attributed to its effects; in most cases it is unavoidably conclusive; it is not unfrequently said, that if a person comes only for a special purpose, *that* shall not fix a domicil. This is not to be taken in an unqualified latitude, and without some respect had to the time which such a purpose may or shall occupy; for if the purpose be of a nature that *may*, *probably*, or *does actually* detain the person for a great length of time, I cannot but think that a general residence might grow upon the special purpose.

"A special purpose may lead a man to a country, where it shall detain him the whole of his life. A man comes here to follow a law-suit, it may happen, and indeed is often used as a ground of vulgar and unfounded reproach (unfounded as matter of just reproach though the fact may be true,) on the laws of this country, that it may last as long as himself. Some suits are famous in our juridical history for having even outlived generations of suitors. I cannot but think that against such a long residence, the plea of an original special purpose could not be averred; it must be inferred in such a case, that other purposes forced themselves upon him and mixed themselves with his original design, and impressed upon him the character of the country where he resided.

"Suppose a man comes into a belligerent country at or before the beginning of a war; it is certainly reasonable not to bind him too soon to an acquired character, and to allow him a fair time to disengage himself; but if he continues to reside during a good part of the war, contributing, by payment of taxes, and other means, to the strength of that country, I am of opinion, that he could not plead his special purpose with any effect against the rights of hostility. If he could, there would be no sufficient guard against the fraud and abuses of masked, pretended, original, and sole purposes of a long-continued residence. There is a time which will estop such a plea; no rule can fix the time *a priori*, but such a time there *must* be.

"In proof of the efficacy of mere time, it is not impertinent to remark, that the same quantity of business, which would not fix a domicil in a certain space of time, would nevertheless have that effect, if distributed over a large space of time. Suppose an American comes to Europe, with six contemporary cargoes, of which he had the present care and management, meaning to return to America immediately; they would form a different case from that, of the same American, coming to any particular country of Europe, with one cargo, and fixing himself there, to receive five remaining cargoes, one in each year successively. I repeat, that time is the great agent in this matter; it is to be taken in a compound ratio, of the time and the occupation, with a great preponderance on the article of time: be the occupation what it may, it cannot happen, but with few exceptions, that mere length of time shall not constitute a domicil."

BENTZEN v. BOYLE.

SUPREME COURT OF THE UNITED STATES, 1815.

(9 *Cranch*, 191.)

The produce of enemy soil while unsold is hostile, whatever be the domicil of the owner of the soil.

Judgment,—MARSHALL, C. J.:—

"The Island of Santa Cruz, belonging to the kingdom of Denmark, was subdued during the late war, by the arms of his Britannic Majesty. Adrien Benjamin Bentzen, an officer of the Danish government, and a proprietor of land therein, withdrew from the island on its surrender, and has since resided in Denmark. The property of the inhabitants being secured to them, he still retained his estate in the island under the management of an agent, who shipped thirty hogsheads of sugar, the product of that estate, on board a British ship, to a commercial house in London, on account and risk of the said A. B. Bentzen. On her passage she was captured by the American privateer, the *Comet*, and brought into Baltimore, where the vessel and cargo were libelled as enemy property. A claim for these sugars was put in by Bentzen; but they were condemned with the rest of the cargo; and the sentence was affirmed by the circuit court. The claimant then appealed to this court.

Some doubt has been suggested whether Santa Cruz, while in the possession of Great Britain, could properly be considered as a British island. But, for this doubt there can be no foundation. Although acquisitions made during war are not considered as permanent until confirmed by a treaty, yet to every commercial and belligerent purpose, they are considered as a part of the domain of the conqueror, so long as he retains the possession and government of them. The island of Santa Cruz, after its capitulation, remained a British island until it was restored to Denmark.

"Must the product of a plantation in that island, shipped by the proprietor himself, who is a Dane residing in Denmark, be considered as British, and therefore enemy property?

"In arguing this question, the counsel for the claimant has made two points. 1. That this case does not come within the rule applicable to shipments from an enemy country, even as laid down in the British courts of admiralty. 2. That the rule has not been rightly laid down in those courts and consequently will not be adopted in this. 1. Does the rule laid down in the British courts of admiralty embrace this case?

"It appears to the court that the case of the *Phœnix* [1] is precisely in point. In that case a vessel was captured on a voyage from Surinam to Holland, and a part of the cargo was claimed by persons residing in Germany, then a neutral country, as the produce of their estates in Surinam.

"The counsel for the captors considered the law of the case as entirely settled. The counsel for the claimant did not controvert this position. They admitted it; but endeavoured to extricate their case from the general principle by giving it the protection of the treaty of Amiens. In pronouncing his opinion, Sir WILLIAM SCOTT lays down the rule thus: 'Certainly nothing can be more decided and fixed, as the principles of this court and the Supreme Court upon very solemn arguments, than that the possession of the soil does impress upon the owner the character of the country, whatever the local residence of the owner may be. This has been so repeatedly decided, both in this and the Superior Court, that it is no longer open to discussion. No question can be made on the point of law, at this day.'

"Afterwards, in the case of the *Vrow Anna Catharina*, 5 C. Rob., 167, Sir WILLIAM SCOTT lays down the rule, and states its reason. 'It cannot be doubted,' he says, 'that there are transactions so radically and fundamentally national as to impress the national character, independent of peace or war, and the local residence of the parties. The produce of a person's own plantation in the colony of the enemy, though shipped in time of peace, is liable to be considered as the property of the enemy, by reason that the proprietor has incorporated himself with the permanent interests of the nation as a holder of the soil, and is to be taken as a part of that country, in that particular transaction, independent of his own personal residence and occupation.'

"This rule laid down with so much precision, does not, it is contended, embrace Mr. Bentzen's claim, because he has not 'incorporated himself with the permanent interests of the nation.' He acquired the property while Santa Cruz was a Danish colony, and he withdrew from the island when it became British.

[1] 5 C. Rob., 20.

"This distinction does not appear to the court to be a sound one. The identification of the national character of the owner with that of the soil, in the particular transaction, is not placed on the disposition with which he acquires the soil, or on his general character. The acquisition of land in Santa Cruz binds him, so far as respects that land, to the fate of Santa Cruz, whatever its destiny may be. While that island belonged to Denmark, the produce of the soil, while unsold, was, according to this rule, Danish property, whatever might be the general character of the particular proprietor. When the island became British, the soil and its produce, while that produce remained unsold, were British.

"The general commercial or political character of Mr. Bentzen could not, according to this rule, affect this particular transaction. Although incorporated, so far as respects his general character, with the permanent interests of Denmark, he was incorporated so far as respects his plantation in Santa Cruz, with the permanent interests of Santa Cruz, which was at that time British; and though as a Dane, he was at war with Great Britain, and an enemy, yet, as a proprietor of land in Santa Cruz, he was no enemy; he could ship his produce to Great Britain in perfect safety.

"The case is certainly within the rule as laid down in the British courts. The next inquiry is: how far that rule will be adopted in this country?

"The law of nations is the great source whence we derive those rules, respecting neutral and belligerent rights, which are recognized by all civilized and commercial states throughout Europe and America. This law is in part unwritten, and in part conventional. To ascertain that which is unwritten, we resort to the great principles of reason and justice; but, as these principles will be differently understood by different nations under different circumstances, we consider them as being in some degree, fixed and rendered stable by a series of judicial decisions. The decisions of the courts of every country, so far as they are founded on a law common to every country, will be received, not as authority, but with respect. The decisions of the courts of every country show how the law of nations, in the given case, is understood in that country, and will be considered in adopting the rule which is to prevail in this.

"Without taking a comparative view of the justice or fairness of the rules established in the British courts, and of those established in the courts of other nations, there are circumstances not to be excluded from consideration, which give to those rules a claim to our attention, that we cannot entirely disregard. The United States having, at one time, formed a component part of the British Empire, *their* prize law was our prize law. When we separated, it continued to be our prize law, so far as it was adapted to our circumstances and was not varied by the power which was capable of changing it.

"It will not be advanced, in consequence of this former relation between the two countries, that any obvious misconstruction of public law made by the British courts, will be considered as forming a rule for the American courts, or that any recent rule of the British courts is entitled to more respect than the recent rules of other countries. But a case professing to be decided on ancient principles will not be entirely disregarded, unless it be very unreasonable, or be founded on a construction rejected by other nations.

"The rule laid down in the *Phœnix* is said to be a recent rule, because a case solemnly decided before the Lords Commissioners in 1783, is quoted in the margin as its authority. But that case is not suggested to have been determined contrary to former practice or former opinions. Nor do we perceive any reason for supposing it to be contrary to the rule of other nations in a similar case.

"The opinion that the ownership of the soil does, in some degree, connect the owner with the property, so far as respects that soil, is an opinion which certainly prevails very extensively. It is not an unreasonable opinion. Personal property may follow the person anywhere; and its character, if found on the ocean, may depend on the domicil of the owner. But land is fixed. Wherever the owner may reside, that land is hostile or friendly according to the condition of the country in which it is placed. It is no extravagant perversion of principle, nor is it a violent offense to the course of human opinion to say that the proprietor, so far as respects his interest in this land, partakes of this character; and that the produce, while the owner remains unchanged, is subject to the same disabilities. In condemning the sugars of Mr. Bentzen as enemy property, this court is of opinion that there was no error, and the sentence is affirmed with costs."

THE "PRIZE CASES."

SUPREME COURT OF THE UNITED STATES, 1862.

(2 *Black.*, 671.)

The property of all persons resident within the territory of the states in rebellion, during the civil war in the United States, and engaged in commerce upon the sea, is enemy property and subject to condemnation as prize.

II. "We come now to the consideration of the second question. What is included in the term 'enemies' property?'

"Is the property of all persons residing within the territory of the states now in rebellion, captured on the high seas, to be treated as 'enemy's property' whether the owner be in arms against the government or not?

"The right of one belligerent not only to coerce the other by direct force, but also to cripple his resources by the seizure or destruction of his property, is a necessary result of a state of war. Money and wealth, the products of agriculture and commerce, are said to be the sinews of war, and as necessary in its conduct as numbers and physical force. Hence it is, that the laws of war recognize the right of a belligerent to cut these sinews of the power of the enemy, by capturing his property on the high seas.

"The appellants contend that the term 'enemy' is properly applicable to those only who are subjects or citizens of a foreign state at war with our own. They quote from the pages of the common law, which say, 'that persons who wage war against the king may be of two kinds, subjects or citizens. The former are not proper enemies, but rebels and traitors; the latter are those that come properly under the name of enemies.'

"They insist, moreover, that the President himself, in his proclamation, admits that great numbers of the persons residing within the territories in the possession of the insurgent government, are loyal in their feelings, and forced by compulsion and the violence of the rebellious and revolutionary party and its '*de facto* government' to submit to their laws and assist in their scheme of revolution; that the acts of the usurping government cannot legally sever the bond of their allegiance; they have, therefore, a co-relative right to claim the protection of the government for their persons and property, and to be treated as loyal citizens, till legally convicted of having renounced their allegiance and made war against the government by treasonably resisting its laws.

"They contend, also, that insurrection is the act of individuals, and not of a government or sovereignty; that the individuals engaged are the subjects of law. That confiscation of their property can be effected only under a municipal law. That by the law of the land such confiscation cannot take place without the conviction of the owner of some offence, and finally that the secession ordinances are nullities and ineffectual to release any citizen from his allegiance to the national government, and consequently that the constitution and laws of the United States are still operative over persons in all the states for punishment as well as protection.

"This argument rests on the assumption of two propositions, each of which is without foundation on the established law of nations.

"It assumes that where a civil war exists, the party belligerent claiming to be sovereign, cannot for some unknown reason, exercise the rights of belligerents, although the revolutionary party may. Being sovereign, he can exercise only sovereign rights over the other party.

"The insurgents may be killed on the battle-field or by the executioner; his property on land may be confiscated under the municipal law; but the commerce on the ocean, which supplies the rebels with means to support the war, cannot be made the subject of capture under the laws of war, because it is 'unconstitutional'!!! Now, it is a proposition never doubted, that the belligerent party who claims to be sovereign, may exercise both belligerent and sovereign rights; (see 4 Cr., 272). Treating the other party as a belligerent and using only the milder modes of coercion which the law of nations has introduced to mitigate the rigors of war, cannot be a subject of complaint by the party to whom it is accorded as a grace or granted as a necessity. We have shown that a civil war such as that now waged between the Northern and Southern states, is properly conducted according to the humane regulations of public law as regards capture on the ocean.

"Under the very peculiar constitution of this government, although the citizens owe supreme allegiance to the Federal government, they owe also a qualified allegiance to the state in which they are domiciled.

"Their persons and property are subject to its laws.

"Hence, in organizing this rebellion, they have *acted as states* claiming to be sovereign over all persons and property within their respective limits, and asserting a right to absolve their citizens from their allegiance to the Federal government. Several of these states have combined to form a new confederacy, claiming to be acknowledged by the world as a sovereign state. Their right to do so is now being decided by wager of battle.

"The ports and territory of each of these states are held in hostility to the general government. It is no loose, unorganized insurrection, having no defined boundary or possession. It has a boundary marked by lines of bayonets, and which can be crossed only by force,—south of this line is enemies' territory, because it is claimed and held in possession by an organized, hostile and belligerent power.

"All persons residing within this territory whose property may be used to increase the revenues of the hostile power are, in this contest, liable to be treated as enemies, though not foreigners. They have cast off their allegiance and made war on their government, and are none the less enemies because they are traitors.

"But in defining the meaning of the term 'enemies' property,' we shall be led into error if we refer to Fleta and Lord Coke for their definition of the word 'enemy'. It is a technical phrase peculiar to prize courts, and depends upon principles of public policy as distinguished from the common law.

"Whether property be liable to capture as 'enemies' property' does not in any manner depend on the personal allegiance of the owner. 'It is the illegal traffic that stamps it as "enemies' property." It is of no consequence whether it belongs to an ally or a citizen. 8 Cr., 384. The owner, *pro hac vice*, is an enemy.' 3 Wash. C. C. R., 183.

"The produce of the soil of the hostile territory, as well as other property engaged in the commerce of the hostile power, as the source of its wealth and strength, are always regarded as legitimate prize, without regard to the domicil of the owner, and much more so if he reside and trade within their territory."[1]

[1] For the first part of this case see § 28, *supra*.

Domicil.—"A commercial domicil," says Mr. DICEY, "is such a residence in a country for the purpose of trading there as makes a person's trade or business contribute to or form part of the resources of such country, and renders it, therefore, reasonable that his hostile, friendly, or neutral character should be determined by reference to the character of such country. When a person's civil domicil is in question, the matter to be determined is whether he has or has not so settled in a given country as to have made it his home. When a person's commercial domicil is in question, the matter to be determined is whether he is or is not residing in a given country with the intention of continuing to trade there." (Dicey on Domicil, 345.)

In the case of the *Antonia Johanna*, 1 Wheaton, 159, the Supreme Court of the United States held, that the share of a partner in a neutral house is, *jure belli*, sub-

"LE HARDY" *contre* "LA VOLTIGEANTE."

CONSEIL DES PRISES, AN IX.

(*Pistoye et Duverdy*, I., 321.)

A neutral merchant domiciled in a belligerent country does not acquire a belligerent character; and his property at sea is neutral property.

Le navire neutre *le Hardy*, chargé pour le compte de Coste Lanfreda, citoyen ragusais, consul de Raguse à Messine, avait été arrêté par *la Voltigeante*. La France était alors en guerre avec le roi des Deux-Siciles; il s'agissait de savoir si Coste Lanfreda, citoyen et consul d'une nation neutre, devait être considéré comme ennemi ou comme neutre.

Le CONSEIL,—Oui le rapport du citoyen Lacoste, membre du Conseil;

Au moyen de ce qu'il résulte principalement des pièces qu'il n'a point existé de contravention sérieuse sur la régularité des pièces relatives au navire, qui a été emmené aussitôt après le jugement du tribunal de commerce;—Qu'à l'égard de la cargaison, Coste Lanfreda, qui en est propriétaire, exerçant à Messine les fonctions de consul de Raguse, a prouvé, devant le tribunal d'appel, qu'il était originaire de Raguse, ce qui ne permet pas de s'arrêter à l'assertion vague du capitaine, portant qu'il le croyait sujet de Naples;—Qu'il n'y a point eu de double destination constatée, et que, lors même qu'elle l'eût été, les deux ports indiqués étant également l'un neutre, l'autre allié, il ne pouvait y avoir lieu à aucune suspicion raisonnable;—Que la loi du 29 nivôse an VI, ne concernant que les marchandises du cru anglais,

ject to confiscation where his own domicil is in a hostile country. (3 Wharton's Digest, 343.)

In the case of the *Friendschaft*, 4 Wheaton, 105, the court held, that the property of a house of trade established in the enemy's country is condemnable as prize, whatever may be the personal domicil of the partners. (3 Wharton's Digest, 343.)

Other cases on *Commercial Domicil* are: *Bell* v. *Reid*, 1 Maul. & Selw., 726 (1813); *Wilson* v. *Maryat*, 8 T. R., 45 (1798); The *San Jose Indiano*, 2 Gall., 268 (1814); The *Junge Klassina*, 5 C. Rob., 302–304 (1804); The *Herman*, 4 C. Rob., 228 (1802); *Sparenburg* v. *Bannatyne*, 1 Bos. & Pul., 163 (1797); The *Abo*, 1 Spinks, 349 (1854); The *Gerasimo*, 11 Moo. P. C. C., 88 (1857); The *Baltica*, 11 Moo. P. C. C., 141 (1857); *Mrs. Alexander's Cotton*, 2 Wall., 404 (1864); The *Flying Scud*, 6 Wall., 263 (1867).

ne pouvait s'appliquer à celles du cru des Deux-Siciles, qui n'ont pas été occupées à titre de conquête par les troupes de la Grande-Bretagne;—Qu'alors, pour décider la qualité de la cargaison du navire *le Hardy*, il suffit d'examiner si elle peut être considérée comme ennemie, sur le rapport que Coste Lanfreda, originaire de Raguse et consul, résidait en cette qualité et faisait le commerce à Messine, pays alors en guerre avec la République française;—Que cette question de droit public se résoudra facilement pour la négative, en faisant attention que la résidence en pays étranger n'empêche pas un individu d'appartenir au pays qui l'a vu naître;—Que, pour ne plus tenir à sa patrie, il faut qu'il ait volontairement choisi une patrie nouvelle, et qu'elle l'ait régulièrement adopté;—Que sans cette renonciation de sa part à son ancienne patrie, sans cette adoption nécessaire, il est toujours ce qu'il était originairement, ami des amis, ennemi des ennemis de sa patrie native; que, lorsque cette patrie est neutre, il reste neutre lui-même, et doit jouir, pour sa personne comme pour ses biens, de tous les avantages de la neutralité, parce que les biens n'ont pas par eux-mêmes de caractère neutre ou hostile, mais prenant toujours celui dont se trouve revêtu leur propriétaire;—Que d'ailleurs la guerre n'étant point une relation d'homme à homme, ni des sociétés aux individus, mais bien des Etats entre eux, on ne peut forcer à y prendre part celui qui n'a pas manifesté la volonté expresse de s'incorporer à la puissance belligérante chez laquelle il habite;—Que les inconvénients, les abus que peut entraîner le système contraire, quelque graves qu'ils soient, sont plus que balancés par l'avantage que retire le monde commerçant de la protection et de la faveur accordées par les belligérants au commerce neutre, quelque part qu'il s'exerce;—Que les ennemis d'origine, quoique établis dans un pays neutre et y faisant le commerce sous la protection et le pavillon neutre, ne perdant point le caractère ennemi, il serait tout à la fois déloyal et contradictoire d'assimiler, suivant l'occurence et les chances variables de la guerre, les neutres d'origine à des ennemis, uniquement parce qu'ils résideraient et commerceraient en pays ennemis;—Que les publicistes, dans des temps déjà reculés, où la force tenait encore plus ou moins lieu du droit, ont bien pu énoncer des faits contraires et professer des principes opposés; mais que les progrès successifs de la civilisation, le besoin, universellement senti, de l'accroissement et de la liberté des relations commerciales entre les peuples, en amenant des idées plus saines, ont fait prévaloir des idées plus libérales que le gouvernement s'empresse de proclamer aujourd'hui, comme le type de sa politique et le gage de son amour de l'humanité;—Qu'en reportant ces considérations sur l'espèce actuelle, on voit un propriétaire neutre d'origine, qui, par sa résidence en pays devenu momentanément ennemi, et par ses spéculations commerciales, n'a pu perdre les avantages de sa neutralité, avec d'autant plus de raison, qu'y exerçant les fonctions de consul de sa patrie originaire, il n'a pas cessé de lui appartenir de fait et de droit, et, dans aucun cas, ni pour sa personne ni pour son commerce, qui en est inséparable, n'a pu être considéré comme ennemi;

DECIDE que la prise faite par le corsaire français *la Voltigeante*, du navire ragusais *le Hordy*, est nulle et illégale, en fait pleine entière mainlevée aux propriétaires tant du navire que de la cargaison.

SECTION 34.—OWNERSHIP OF GOODS IN TRANSIT.

THE PACKET "DE BILBOA."

HIGH COURT OF ADMIRALTY, 1799.

(2 *C. Robinson*, 133.)

In time of war, or in contemplation of war, goods *in transitu* on the ocean are held to belong to the consignee.

This was a case of a claim of an English house for goods shipped on the order of a Spanish merchant, before hostilities with Spain, and captured December, 1796, on a voyage from London to Corunna. *Held*, that the contract was valid and the goods were restored.

Judgment,—Sir W. SCOTT:—

"This is a claim of a peculiar nature for goods sent by British subjects to Spain, shipped before hostilities, during the time of that situation of the two countries, of which it was unknown, even to our government, what would be the issue between them. There appears to be no ground to say that this contract was influenced by speculations on the prospect of a war, or that anything has been specially done to avoid the risks of war. It is shown in the affidavit of the claimant 'that this is the constant habit and practice of this trade;' whether it is the practice of the Spanish trade generally, or only the particular mode of these individuals in carrying on commerce together is not material, as the latter would be quite sufficient to raise the subject of this claim. The question is, in whom is the legal title? Because, if I should find that the interest was in the Spanish consignee, I must then condemn, and leave the British party to apply to the Crown for that grace and favor which it is always ready to shew; the property being condemnable to the Crown as taken before hostilities.

"The statement of the claim sets forth that these goods have not been paid for by the Spaniard;—that would go but little way,—that alone would not do; there must be many cases in which British merchants suffer from capture, by our own cruisers, of goods shipped for foreign account before the breaking out of hostilities. It goes on to state, 'that, according to the custom of the trade, a credit of six, nine, or twelve months is usually given, and that it is not the custom to draw on the consignee till the arrival of the goods; that the sea risk in peace as well as war is on the consignor; that he insures, and has no remedy against the consignee for any accident that happens during the voyage.' Under these circumstances, in whom does the property reside? The ordinary state of commerce is, that goods ordered and delivered to the master are considered as delivered to the consignee, whose agent the master is in this respect; but that general contract of the law may be varied by special agreement or by a particular prevailing practice, that presupposes an agreement amongst such a description of merchants. In time of profound peace, when there is no prospect of approaching war, there would unquestionably be nothing illegal in contracting, that the whole risk should fall on the consignor, till the goods came into possession of the consignee. In time of peace they may divide their risk as they please, and nobody has a right to say they shall not; it would not be at all illegal, that goods not shipped in time of war, or in contemplation of war, should be at the risk of the shipper. In time of war this cannot be permitted, for it would at once put an end to all captures at sea; the risk would in all cases be laid on the consignor, where it suited the purpose of protection; on every contemplation of a war, this contrivance would be practiced in all consignments from neutral ports to the enemy's country, to the manifest defrauding of all rights of capture; it is therefore considered to be an invalid contract in time of war; or, to express it more accurately, it is a contract which, if made in war, has this effect; that the captor has a right to seize it and convert the property to his own use; for he having all the rights that belong to his enemy, is authorized to have his taking possession considered as equivalent to an actual delivery to his enemy; and the shipper who put it on board during a time of war, must be presumed to know the rule, and to secure himself in his agreement with the consignee against the contingence of any loss to himself that can arise from capture. In other words, he is a mere insurer against sea risk, and he has nothing to do with the case of capture, the loss of which falls entirely on the consignee. If the consignee refuses payment and throws it upon the shipper, the shipper must be supposed to have guarded his own interests against that hazard, or he has acted improvidently and without caution.

"The present contract is not of this sort; it stands as a lawful agreement, being made whilst there was neither war nor prospect of war. The goods are sent at the risk of the shipper: if they had been lost, on whom would the loss have fallen but on him? What surer test of property can there be than this? It is the true criterion of property that, if you are the person on whom the loss will fall, you are to be considered as the proprietor. The bill of lading very much favors this account. The master binds himself to the shipper, 'to deliver for you and in your name,' by which it is to be understood that the delivery had not been made to the master for the consignee, but that he was to make the delivery in the name of the shipper to the consignee, till which time the inference is that they were to remain the property of the shipper: as to the payment of freight, that is not material, as in the end the purchaser must necessarily pay the carriage. The other consideration—who bears the loss? much outweighs that,—neither does the case put shew the contrary. The case put is—supposing Spain and England both neutral and that these goods had been taken by the French and sold to great profit, to whose advantage would it have been? The answer is, if the goods were to continue the property of the shipper till delivery, it must have enured to *his* benefit, and not that of the consignee. To make the loss fall upon the shipper in the case of the present shipment would be harsh in the extreme. He ships his goods in the ordinary course of traffic, by an agreement mutually understood between the parties, and in no wise injurious to the rights of any third party; an event subsequently happens which he could in no degree provide against. If he is to be the sufferer he is a sufferer without notice and without the means of securing himself; he was not called upon to know that the injustice of the other party would produce a war before the delivery of his goods. The consignee may refuse payment, referring to the terms of the contract which was made when it was perfectly lawful; and under what circumstances and on what principles the shipper could ever enforce payment against the consignee is not easy to discover. The goods have never been delivered in Spain; they were to have been at the risk of the shipper until delivery, and this under a perfectly fair contract. I must consider the property to reside still in the English merchant. It is a case altogether different from other cases which have happened on this subject *flagrante bello*. I am of opinion that, on all just considerations of ownership, the legal property is in the British merchant; that the loss must have fallen on the shipper, and the delivery was not to have been made till the last stage of the business, till they had actually arrived in Spain and had been put into the hands of the consignee; and therefore I shall decree restitution of the goods to the shipper."

On prayer that the captor's expenses might be paid, it was answered that they had already had the benefit of the condemnation of the ship.

Court.—"I think there has been a great service performed to the shipper. If the goods had not been captured they would have gone into the possession of the enemy. The captor did right in bringing the question before the court, and he ought by no means to be a loser. I shall not give salvage, but shall direct the expenses of the captor to be paid out of the proceeds."

THE "SAN JOSE INDIANO."

U. S. CIRCUIT COURT FOR MASSACHUSETTS, 1814.

(2 *Gallison*, 268.)

Title to goods *in transitu*—stoppage *in transitu*.

Extract from the opinion of STORY, J.:—

"The next is the claim of Mr. J. Lizaur, of ——, in Brazil.

"The shipment was made by Messrs. Dyson Brothers & Co., and by the bill of lading the goods are consigned to Messrs. Dyson Brothers and Finney, Rio de Janeiro.

"The accompanying invoices express the shipment to be made by order and for account of Mr. J. Lizaur, and contain charges of freight, commission and insurance, and an acknowledgment of giving credit for three and six months. In a letter of the 4th of May, 1814, addressed by the shippers to the consignees, they say, 'for Mr. Lizaur we open an account in our books here, and debit him 1764*l.* 11*s.* 7*d.* for 16 cases of cambrics, etc., at three months' credit; we cannot yet ascertain proceeds of his hides, etc., but find his order will far *exceed amount of these shipments, therefore consign the whole to you, so as you may come to a proper understanding.* We have charged our usual commission of two and a half per cent. in the invoices, but should you have made any stipulation to the contrary, he can again bring same to our debit. Invoices, bills of lading and patterns of what goods are requisite we forward as usual in a small box to your address.'

"The single question presented in this claim is, in whom the property vested during its transit; if in Mr. Lizaur, then it is to be restored; if in the shippers, then it is to be condemned. It is contended on behalf of the claimant, that the goods, having been purchased by order of Mr. Lizaur, the property vested in him immediately by the purchase, and the contract being executed by the sale, no delivery was necessary to perfect the legal title; that nothing was reserved to the shippers, but a mere right of stoppage *in transitu*, and that if they had been burnt before the shipment, or lost during the voyage, the loss must have fallen on Mr. Lizaur.

"As to the doctrine of stoppage *in transitu*, I do not conceive it can apply to this case. That right exists in the single case of insolvency, and presupposes, not only that the property in the goods has passed to the consignee, but that the possession is in a third person in their transit to the consignee. It cannot, therefore, touch a case, where the actual or constructive possession still remains in the shipper or his exclusive agents.

"I agree also to the position, that in general the rules of the prize court, as to the vesting of property, are the same as those of the common law, by which the thing sold, after the completion of the contract, is properly at the risk of the purchaser. But the question still recurs, when is the contract executed? It is certainly competent for an agent abroad, who purchases in pursuance of orders, to vest the property, immediately on the purchase, in his principal. This is the case, when he purchases on the credit of his principal, or makes an absolute appropriation and designation of the property for his principal. But where a merchant abroad, in pursuance of orders, sells either his own goods, or purchases goods on his own credit (and thereby in reality becomes the owner), no property in the goods vests in his correspondent, until he has done some notorious act to divest himself of his title, or has parted with the possession by an actual and unconditional delivery for the use of such correspondent. Until that time he has in legal contemplation the exclusive property, as well as possession; and it is not a wrongful act for him to convert them to any use, which he pleases. He is at liberty to contract upon any new engagements, or substitute any new conditions in relation to the shipment. And this, I understand, not only as the general law, but as the prize law pronounced by that high tribunal, whose decisions I am bound to obey.

"In the *Venus*, 1814, on the claim of Magee and Jones, in delivering the opinion of the court, Mr. Justice WASHINGTON observed: 'to effect a change of property, as between seller and buyer, it is essential, that there should be a contract of sale agreed to by both parties, and if the thing agreed to be purchased is to be sent by the vendor to the vendee it is necessary to the perfection of the contract, that it should be delivered to the purchaser or to his agent, which the master (of a ship) to many purposes is considered to be.'

"And adverting to the facts of that claim he further says: 'The delivery of the goods to the master of the vessel was not for the use of Magee and Jones, any more than it was for the shipper solely, and consequently it amounted to nothing, so as to divest the property out of the shipper, until Magee should elect to take them on joint account, or to act as the agent of Jones.'"

THE "SALLY."

LORDS, 1795.

(3 *C. Robinson*, 300, *note.*)

Merchandise shipped to become the property of the enemy on arrival, if taken *in transitu*, is to be condemned as enemy's property. Supposing it was to become the property of the enemy on delivery, capture is considered as delivery.

The *Sally* was a case of a cargo of corn shipped March, 1793, by Steward and Plunket, of Baltimore, ostensibly for the account and risk of Conyngham, Nesbit & Co., of Philadelphia, and consigned to them *or their assigns:* By an endorsement of the bill of lading, it was further agreed that the ship should proceed to Havre de Grace, and there wait such time as might be necessary, the orders of the consignee of the said cargo (the mayor of Havre) either to deliver the same at the port of Havre, or proceed therewith to any one port without the Mediterranean, on freight at the rate of 5*s.* per barrel on delivery at Havre, and 5*s.* 6*d.* at a second port, the freight to be settled by the shippers in America according to agreement.

Amongst the papers was a concealed letter from Jean Ternant, the minister of the French Republic to the United States, in which he informs the minister of foreign affairs in France. "The house of Conyngham & Co., already known to the ministers, by their former operations for France, is charged by me to procure without delay, a consignment of 22,000 bushels of wheat, 8,000 barrels of fine flour, 900 barrels of salted beef from New England. The conditions stipulated are the same as those of the contract of 2d November, 1792, with the American citizens, Swan & Co., for a like supply to be made to the Antilles, namely, that the grain, flour, and beef are to be paid at the current price of the markets at the time of their being shipped; that the freights shall be at the lowest course in the ports; that an insurance should be on the whole; and that a commission of five per cent. shall be allowed for all the merchants' expenses and fees. It has been, moreover, agreed, considering the actual reports of war, that the whole shall be sent as American property to Havre and to Nantes, with power to our government of sending the ships to other ports conditional on the usual freight. As you have not signified to me to whom these cargoes ought to be delivered in our ports, I shall provide each captain with a letter to the mayor of the place."

There was also a letter from Jean Ternant to the mayor of the municipality of Havre. "Our government having ordered me to send supplies of provisions to your port, I inform you that the bearer of this, commanding the American ship, the *Sally*, is laden with a cargo of wheat, of which he will deliver you the bill of lading."

To the 12th and 20th interrogatories the master deposed, "that he believes the flour was the property of the French government, and, on being *unladen, would have immediately become the property* of the French government."

In the argument it was insisted, *on the part of the claimants*, that the cargo was to be considered as the property of the American merchants; that it had been ordered by them, to be supplied and delivered at a certain place; and that under the general principle of law, property was not considered to be divested between the vendor and vendee till actual delivery.

It was contended, that the contract remained *executory* till the completion by delivery in Europe; that the payment was contingent on the completion of the contract in this form, and that no money had passed, nor any compensation or agreement had intervened to produce an absolute conversion of the property; and it was prayed that the court would admit farther proof to ascertain that circumstance.

On the part of the captors it was replied, that the general rule of law subsisting between vendor and vendee in a commercial transaction, referring only to the contracting parties, and not affecting the rights of third persons, could not apply to contracts made in time of war, or in contemplation of war, where the rights of a belligerent nation intervened; that the effect of such a contract as the present would be to protect the trade of the contracting belligerent from his enemy; and that if it could be allowed, it would put an end to all capture. It was said to be a known principle of the prize court, that neutral property must be proved to be neutral at all periods from the time of shipment, without intermission, to the arrival and subsequent *sale* in the port of the enemy; that the twelfth and twentieth interrogatories were framed with this view to inquire, "whether on its arrival, etc., it shall and will belong to the same owner and no other, etc.," and a reference was made to the case of the Charles Havenerswerth in 1741, in which the form of attestation was directed to be prepared by the whole bar, and was established in the present form to ascertain the property at the several periods of *shipment*, and *arrival in the enemy's ports*,—in cases where affidavits were to be received to supply the defects of the original evidence, in the place of plea and proof.

The Court:—"It has always been the rule of the prize courts, that property going to be delivered in the enemy's country, and under a contract to become the property of the enemy immediately on arrival, if taken *in transitu*, is to be considered as enemies' property. Where the contract is made in time of peace or without any contemplation of a war, no such rule exists:—But in a case like the present, where the form of the contract was framed directly for the purpose of obviating the danger apprehended from approaching hostilities, it is a rule which unavoidably must take place. The bill of lading expresses account and risk of the American merchants; but papers alone make no proof, unless supported by the depositions of the master. Instead of supporting the contents of his papers, the master deposes, 'that on arrival the goods would become the property of the French government,' and all the concealed papers strongly support him in this testimony: The *evidentia rei* is too strong to admit farther proof. Supposing that it was to become the property of the enemy on delivery, *capture* is considered as *delivery:* The captors, by the rights of war, stand in the place of the enemy, and are entitled to a condemnation of goods passing under such a contract, as of enemy's property. On every principle on which Prize Courts can proceed, this cargo must be considered as enemy's property.

"Condemned."

THE "ANNA CATHARINA."

High Court of Admiralty, 1802.

(4 *C. Robinson*, 107.)

Goods going to become the property of the enemy immediately on arrival, condemned.

This was a case of a cargo of dry goods, etc., taken October, 1801, on a voyage from Hamburgh to La Guayra, and described in the ostensible papers and depositions, "as going to take the chance of the market." By the discovery of a letter, it afterwards appeared, that these goods were going under a special agreement and contract with the Spanish government of the Caracas.

Judgment,—Sir W. SCOTT :—

* * * Taking the shippers to be neutral merchants "how does the character of the goods stand in this transaction? Was it not, in the first place, a cargo going to become the property of the Spanish government immediately on arrival? Was not the Spanish government entitled to possession? It was only on the violation of the contract, on the part of the Spanish government, that these goods were to take the chance of the market. The shippers considered themselves as bound to deliver them to the use of the Spanish government, under the agreement; as entitled to the benefit, and subject to the obligations of that contract. Were there any intermediate acts to be done after the arrival of the vessel? Or were the acts such, as would have the effect of substantially distinguishing this case from the *Sally*, and other cases? Is there any act of ownership which the claimant was at liberty to exercise, so as to prevent the delivery? If not the goods must be considered as having substantially become, *in itinere*, the property of the enemy. * * *

"It is said * * * that these goods do not exactly correspond with the enumeration in the agreement, that *they are not contract goods;* and consequently, that without any violation of public faith, the acceptance of them was merely optional and contingent. But, I cannot think, that it is now open to the parties to make this averment; when it is evident, on the face of their own letters, that they had relied on the clear and absolute obligation of the Spanish government to take them *as such.* * * *

"These distinctions are, in my judgment, totally insufficient to take the case out of the authority of the precedents alluded to. Where the goods are sent under a contract by the party, it surely cannot be permitted to the claimant himself to aver, that the goods so sent are not contract goods. * * * Under these circumstances, I am strongly disposed to hold, that this cargo was going in time of war to the port of a belligerent, there to become the property of the belligerent, immediately on arrival, and that the legal consequence of condemnation would on that ground alone attach upon it." [1]

[1] Only so much of this case is given as refers to the shipment of goods under contract to a belligerent port.

LES "TROIS FRERES."

COMITÉ DE SALUT PUBLIC, AN III.

(*Pistoye et Duverdy*, I., 357.)

Semble, that, by the French rule, the neutral shipper may assume the risk of goods in transit to an enemy country.

Le navire danois *les Trois-Frères*, chargé à Gênes de 535 futailles d'huile, à destination d'Ostende et Amsterdam (qui, en juin 1793, étaient des pays ennemis de la France), fut capturé le 3 juin 1793 par le corsaire *le Passe-Partout*, de Bordeaux, et le 6 de juillet suivant la prise fut amenée à Bayonne. Le 24 brumaire an II, un jugement du tribunal de commerce de cette ville, sur l'opposition de négociants génois, le sieur Strafforello et Cie, qui avaient revendiqué une partie de la cargaison (150 futailles), fit mainlevée de la capture et condamna les capteurs à payer le prix de la marchandise, valuer d'Ostende et d'Amsterdam, par application du droit de présomption créé par la loi du 9 mai 1793, bien que les capteurs n'eussent pas demandé à user de cette faculté, qui était devenue très-onéreuse par suite du *maximum* récemment décrété pour toutes les denrées. Ce jugement rendu, les pièces relatives à la capture des *Trois-Frères* furent envoyées au Conseil exécutif après la loi du 18 brumaire an II, et le Comité de salut public, qui se substitua à ce conseil exécutif, rendit sur cette affaire la décision suivante :

"Sur le rapport fait au Comité de salut public par le commissaire de la marine et des colonies, que, le 3 juin 1793, le corsaire *le Passe-Partout*, de Bordeaux, prit et conduisit à Bayonne le navire danois *les Trois-Frères*, que le tribunal de commerce à Bayonne ayant statué sur la validité de la prise du navire et l'ayant déclaré neutre, le capitaine a reçu son fret et l'indemnité réglée par le même tribunal ;

"Que, ne s'agissant plus de la cargaison, l'examen des pièces qui la concernent et l'état de la procédure apprennent qu'une partie a été chargée par des Génois, amis de la République française, et pour leur compte et risque ; que c'est la propriété de citoyens génois ; que conséquemment la saisie qui en a été faite est illégale et nulle, et que la restitution en doit être faite à leurs propriétaires ;

"Que la propriété de celles chargées par des Génois pour le compte de qui il appartiendrait ne se trouvant point désignée, ces marchandises sont de droit présumées ennemies, dès le moment qu'il ne se trouve aucune preuve contraire propre à détruire cette présomption ; que, comme telles, elles sont bien saisies et deviennent sujettes à confiscation ;

"LE COMITÉ DE SALUT PUBLIC,—statuant en conséquence de son arrêté du 4 floréal dernier, arrête :

"'1° Est confirmé le jugement du tribunal de commerce de Bayonne, du 30 août 1793, rendu en faveur du capitaine danois du navire *les Trois-Frères*, et par lequel ce navire a été déclaré propriété neutre, et relâché avec payement de son fret et une indemnité ;

"'2° Sont déclarées propriétés génoises et neutres les marchandises chargées à bord du navire *les Trois-Frères* pour compte et risque des citoyens Strafforello et autres ;

"'3° Les marchandises appartenant aux citoyens Strafforello et autres Génois leur seront restituées, dans les quantités marquées et qualités désignées dans les connaissements ; et, en cas de vente de ces marchandises, les armateurs du corsaire *le Passe-Partout* en rembourseront la valeur, suivant le cours dans le lieu de leur destination au moment de la prise, avec intérêt de la valeur des objets restitués, les dits intérêts tenant lieu de toute indemnité d'indue rétention ;

"'4° Sont déclarées propriétés ennemies et comme telles acquises par confiscation aux armateurs et à l'équipage du corsaire *le Passe-Partout*, toutes autres parties de la cargaison du navire *les Trois-Frères* et qui ont été chargées pour le compte de qui il appartiendra ;

"'5° Les marchandises de cette cargaison, si elles existent encore en nature, qui pourraient être jugées utiles au service de la République, seront achetées pour son compte, et la valeur en sera payée dès la remise au magasin à ceux à qui elles appartiennent, aux termes du présent arrêté.'" (Cette cause était usuelle au temps du Comité de salut public. Voyez Merlin, *Questions de droit* V. *Prises maritimes*, § II.) [1]

[1] Observations.—"Aujourd'hui, que le principe que le pavillon couvre la cargaison est admis sans conteste, cette décision peut paraître au premier abord n'avoir qu'un intérêt historique ; elle a cependant aussi un intérêt juridique. En effet, la déclaration de l'Empereur, du 29 mars 1854, annonce que les marchandises neutres chargées sur navires ennemis ne seront pas confisquées. L'arrêté du Comité de salut public juge que des marchandises chargées par des neutres avec d'autres marchandises reconnues neutres et destinées à un port ennemi, doivent être réputées ennemies, si le destinataire n'est pas connu. Cette décision pourrait s'appliquer aujourd'hui à des marchandises chargées sur un navire ennemi. En effet, il s'agissait dans l'espèce de savoir quelle était la nationalité des marchandises, et cette question était tout à fait indépendante de la nationalité du navire vecteur."

Section 35.—Transfer in Transitu.

THE "VROW MARGARETHA."

High Court of Admiralty, 1799.

(1 *C. Robinson*, 336.)

This was the case of a cargo of brandies shipped by Spanish merchants in Spain in May, 1794, before Spanish hostilities, and transferred to Mr. Berkeymyer at Hamburgh, during their voyage to Holland. *Held*, to be a *bona fide* transaction, and the rule against transfer *in transitu* was not applied.

Judgment,—Sir W. Scott:—

"This is a claim of Mr. Ph. Berkeymyer, of Hamburgh, for some parcels of wine which were seized on board three Dutch vessels detained by order of government in 1795. The ships have been since condemned; the cargoes were described in the ship's papers, as far as the property was expressed, as belonging to Spanish merchants. It is material, in this case, to consider the relative situation of the countries from which, and to which these cargoes were going. Spain and Holland were then in alliance with this country and at war with France; it might, therefore, be an inducement with a Spanish merchant to conceal the property of his goods, although it *does not* appear to have existed in any great degree, as the goods were coming under an English convoy, and as they were shipped 'as Spanish wines,' and destined, avowedly, to Holland; there was, therefore, nothing in this part of the case to mislead our cruisers. Mr. Berkeymyer is allowed to be an inhabitant of Hamburgh, although he had made a journey, a short time previous to the shipment of these cargoes, to Spain (where he had resided some years before), to settle his affairs, and bring off the property which he had left behind him. He had quitted Spain, however, previous to the breaking out of Spanish hostilities, and had resumed his original character of a merchant of Hamburgh. The account which he gives of his transactions in Spain, as far as they regard this case, is, that he entered into a contract with two Spanish houses for some wines, which were at the time actually shipped, and *in itinere* towards Holland. The first objection that has been taken is, that such a transfer is invalid, and cannot be set up in a Prize Court, where the property is always considered to remain in the same character in which it was shipped till the delivery. If that could be maintained there would be an end of the question, because it has been admitted that these wines were shipped as Spanish property, and that Spanish property is now become liable to condemnation. But I apprehend it is a position which cannot be maintained in that extent. In the ordinary course of things in time of peace—for it is not denied that such a contract may be made, and effectually made (according to the usage of merchants,) such a transfer *in transitu* might certainly be made. It has even been contended that a mere delivering of the bill of lading is a transfer of the property. But it might be more correctly expressed, perhaps, if said that it transfers only the right of delivery; but that a transfer of the bill of lading, with a contract of sale accompanying it, may transfer the property in the ordinary course of things, so as effectually to bind the parties, and all others, cannot well be doubted. When war intervenes, another rule is set up by Courts of Admiralty, which interferes with the ordinary practice. In a state of war, existing or imminent, it is held that the property shall be deemed to continue as it was at the time of shipment till the actual delivery; this arises out of the state of war, which gives a belligerent a right to stop the goods of his enemy. If such a rule did not exist all goods shipped in the enemy's country would be protected by transfers which it would be impossible to detect. It is on that principle held, I believe, as a general rule, that property cannot be converted *in transitu*; and in that sense I recognize it as the rule of this Court. But this arises, as I have said, out of a state of war, which creates new rights in other parties, and cannot be applied to transactions originating, like this, in a time of peace. The transfer, therefore, must be considered as not invalid in point of law, at the time of the contract; and being made before the war it must be judged according to the ordinary rules of commerce.

"It has been farther objected to the validity of this contract, that a part of the wines did actually reach Hamburgh, where they were sold, and the money was detained by the consignees in payment of the advances which they had made. It is said that this annuls the contract—to the extent of that part it may do so, and the deficiency must be made up to the purchaser by other means; but it appears that it has been actually supplied by bills of exchange, and an assignment of other wines sent to Petersburgh. It is not for me to set aside the whole contract on that partial ground, or to construe the defect in the execution of the contract so rigorously as to extend it to those wines which never went to Holland, and which never became *de facto* subject to be detained by the consignees. They are free for the contract to act upon; and if the parties are desirous of adhering to their contract in its whole extent, it does not become other persons to obstruct them.

"It comes then to a question of fact, whether it was a *bona fide* transfer or not? I think the time is a strong circumstance to prove the fairness of the transaction. Had it happened three months later there might have been reason to alarm the prudence of Spanish merchants, and induce them to resort to the expedient of covering their property. But at the time of the contract there seems to have been no reason for apprehension, and therefore there is nothing to raise any suspicion on that point.

"The instruments of sale have been produced, and no observation has been made upon them. The correspondence has been exhibited, and there is certainly some confusion in the dates. Explanations have been given, which are probable enough; still they are but conjectural. If the counsel for the captors require it I will order the original documents in proof of these explanations to be produced; although I must say, at the same time, that the impression upon my mind is, that it is a fair transaction.

"The originals decreed to be produced.

"January 15th, 1800. The captors being satisfied with the farther proof produced, Mr. Berkeymyer's claims were restored without opposition."

THE "JAN FREDERICK."

HIGH COURT OF ADMIRALTY, 1804.

(5 *C. Robinson*, 128.)

A contract in contemplation of war, for the transfer of colonial produce *in transitu*, held illegal.

Judgment,—Sir W. SCOTT:—

"This question arises on parts of several cargoes put on board Dutch ships in January and February, 1803, and brought in under the general embargo on Dutch property, previous to hostilities, in the month of May. The property is documented for the account and risk of certain estates in Surinam; and certainly, if it was not allowable under any considerations to aver against the evidence of the ship's documents, it must be subject to condemnation as Dutch property. But the Court has opened a door to such claims, in opposition to the averment of the ship's papers; and it has done this, on a consideration of the fair course of mercantile speculation in time of peace. It has even allowed a change of property *in transitu*, by the transfer of the bills of lading, where it had been done without any view of accommodation to relieve the seller from the pressure or prospect of war. In the present instance, there is no proof of any transfer of the bills of lading, except as to one or two parcels of goods belonging to the widow Noble, which do, indeed, bear an endorsement, but whether they were so endorsed before or after the war, it does not appear. This alone would be sufficient to defeat the claim; since, till the bill of lading was so endorsed, the contract would, I apprehend, be a thing remaining in covenant only: it might subject the party to an action *damni dati*, but it would not amount to a transfer, being only an engagement that the goods should be transferred when they arrived. That a transfer may take place *in transitu*, has, I have already observed, been decided in two or three cases, where there had been no actual war, nor any prospect of war, mixing itself with the transaction of the parties. But in time of war this is prohibited as a vicious contract, being a fraud on belligerent rights, not only in the particular transaction, but in the great facility which it would necessarily introduce, of evading those rights beyond the possibility of detection. It is a road that, in time of war, must be shut up; for although honest men might be induced to travel it with very innocent intentions, the far greater proportion of those who passed would use it only for sinister purposes, and with views of fraud on the rights of the belligerent.

"This, however, is not a contract made in time of war; and therefore an important question is raised, whether the *contemplation of war* would have the same effect in vitiating these contracts as actual war? It cannot be said that all engagements in the proximity of war, into which the speculation of war might enter, as for instance, with regard to the price, would therefore be invalid. The contemplation of war is undoubtedly to be taken in a more restricted sense. But if the contemplation of war leads immediately to the transfer, and becomes the foundation of a contract, that would not otherwise be entered into on the part of the seller; and this is known to be so done, in the understanding of the purchaser, though on his part there may be other concurrent motives, as in the case of the *Rendsborg* (4 C. Rob., 121), such a contract cannot be held good, on the same principle that applies to invalidate a transfer *in transitu* in time of actual war. The motive may indeed be difficult to be proved —but that will be the difficulty of particular cases. Supposing the fact to be established, that it is a sale under an admitted necessity, arising from a certain expectation of war; that it is a sale of goods not in the possession of the seller, and in a state where they could not, during war, be legally transferred, on account of the fraud on belligerent rights. I cannot but think that the same fraud is committed against the belligerent, not, indeed as an actual belligerent, but as one who was, in the clear expectation of both the contracting parties, likely to become a belligerent before the arrival of the property, which is made the subject of their agreement. The nature of both contracts is identically the same, being equally to protect the property from capture of war—not indeed in either case from capture at the present moment when the contract is made, but from the danger of capture, when it was likely to occur. The object is the same in both instances, to afford a guarantee against the same crisis. In other words, both are done for the purpose of eluding a belligerent right, either present or expected. Both contracts are framed with the same *animo fraudandi*, and are, in my opinion, justly subject to the same rule. * * *

"I am of opinion, therefore, that if the papers and letters which have been produced, do sufficiently establish the purpose attributed to the contract, if it is proved to have been built immediately and fundamentally on the contemplation of war, on the part of the seller, and that it would not otherwise have fallen into the hands of the purchaser, it is an illegal contract, and must be held on every ground, on which similar contracts in time of war have been held to be invalid. * * *

"But taking it to be a *bona fide* contract, yet being formed *in transitu*, for the purpose of withdrawing the property from capture, it does intimately partake of the nature of those contracts, which have, in the repeated decisions of this, and of the Supreme Court, been pronounced null and invalid; and I pronounce this property subject to condemnation."

THE SHIP "ANN GREEN."

U. S. CIRCUIT COURT FOR MASSACHUSETTS, 1812.

(1 *Gallison*, 274.)

Property not permitted to change character in transit; nor shall property consigned, to become the property of the enemy on arrival, be protected by the neutrality of the shipper.

Extract from the opinion of STORY, J.:—

"It has been further argued, that this capture, being made while the property was *in transitu*, and war intervening, it is to be considered as enemy's property, because it would have become such upon arrival at the port of destination: and at all events it would have been liable to seizure and confiscation. As to the fact that the property was taken *in transitu*, I do not perceive how of itself it can affect the rights of the parties either way; nor do I perceive how this property was to have become enemy's property on its arrival. The case proved is, that it was American property consigned for sale only, and not a consignment where the property was, at the time of shipment or of arrival, to belong to the consignee. The cases are, as I think, settled upon just principles, that decide that in time of war, property shall not be permitted to change character in its transit; nor shall property consigned, to become the property of the enemy on arrival, be protected by the neutrality of the shipper. Such contracts, however valid in time of peace, are considered, if made in war or in contemplation of war, as infringements of belligerent rights, and calculated to introduce the grossest frauds. In fact, if they could prevail, not a single bale of enemy's goods would ever be found upon the ocean." (*Vrow Margaretha*, 1 C. Rob., 336; *Carl Walter*, 4 C. Rob., 207; *Jan Frederick*, 5 C. Rob., 128; The *Constantia*, 6 C. Rob., 321; The *Anna Catharina*, 4 C. Rob., 107; Packet *De Bilboa*, 2 C. Rob., 133.)[1]

[1] In the case of the ship *Francis and Cargo*, 1 Gallison, 445, approved by the Supreme Court, 8 Cranch, 354 (1818), a shipment made by an enemy shipper to his correspondent in America, to belong to the latter at his election, in twenty-four hours after the arrival thereof, was held liable to condemnation as hostile property.

In war property cannot change its character *in transitu*; and in this case, an election during the transit would not merge the hostile character of the property.

On the subject of the sale *in transitu* by a belligerent to a neutral, see an article by T. S. M. Browne, in the Law Magazine and Review, 1870, vol. 29, p. 283.

SECTION 36.—FREIGHT.

THE "VROW HENRICA."

HIGH COURT OF ADMIRALTY, 1803.

(4 *C. Robinson*, 348.)

Where a neutral vessel carrying enemy's goods is captured, the neutral master is, as a general rule, entitled to his freight, which is a lien on the cargo. On account of the peculiar circumstances of this case, the freight was postponed to the captor's *law expenses*.

This was a case of a Danish vessel taken on a voyage from Valencia to London. The ship had been restored with freight to be a charge on the cargo, which was condemned, but the proceeds not being sufficient to pay the freight and the expenses of the captor, it was prayed on the part of the neutral ship, that the priority of payment might be given to freight, on the authority of the *Bremen Flugge*, 4 C. Rob., 90.

Judgment,—Sir W. SCOTT:—

"I have considered the cases which I directed to be looked up, and I see no reason to alter the opinion which I before expressed, that freight is, in all ordinary cases, a lien which is to take place of all others. The captor takes *cum onere:* It is the allowed privilege of neutral trade to carry the property of the enemy, subject to its capture, and to the temporary detention of his vessel; and if the party does not prevaricate, or conduct himself in any respect with ill-faith, he is entitled to his freight. This is the rule which I am disposed to apply in all cases of neutral ships carrying on their ordinary commerce. It is the *general* rule, which may nevertheless be liable to be altered by circumstances. There is one class of cases to which I think it *ought not* to be applied—I mean the case of ships carrying on a trade between ports of allied enemies—a trade which may be said to arise in a great measure out of the circumstances of war, though not altogether: I say not altogether, because such a trade exists in a limited degree in times of peace.

"In such a course of trade, although the Court has not altogether refused freight to the neutral ship, yet it may not think it unreasonable that the captor should, in preference, be entitled to his expenses, inasmuch as the nature of such a trade cannot but very much influence the judgment which he must unavoidably form of his duty to bring in the cargo for adjudication. In the present case, the voyage is not between the ports of allied enemies, but between the ports of two belligerents, from Valencia to London; that constitutes, I think, a sort of middle case, with respect to the obligation by which the captor might conceive himself bound to bring the cargo to adjudication. There might be a presumption, undoubtedly, that the property belonged to the enemy exporter; but there is a foundation also for presuming that it might belong to the consignee, and that it would not have been sent on a destination to this country, but under the protection of a license.

"It is, therefore, a case of a mixed nature, to which I shall apply a sort of a middle judgment. I will allow the captor his law expenses, and direct the other expenses to be postponed to the payment of freight."

THE "FORTUNA."

High Court of Admiralty, 1802.

(4 *C. Robinson*, 278.)

Freight is due to the captor, in virtue of the ship, which had been condemned, when the cargo (neutral) is carried by them to the place of its destination.

This was a case on petition of the captors, praying to be allowed freight for a cargo, which had been restored as neutral property. The demand for freight was founded on a suggestion, that the ship, which had been condemned, had actually performed the contract of the original affreightment, by carrying the cargo to the place of its destination.

Judgment,—Sir W. Scott:—

"This is the case of a ship which had carried a cargo of corn to Lisbon, the original port of destination. In such a case I apprehend the rule to be, that the captor *is* entitled to freight, and on the same principle, on which he would be held *not to be* entitled, where he does *not* proceed, and perform the original voyage. The specific contract is performed in the one case, and not performed in the other. It is the rule of practice laid down in the case of the *Vreyheid*, Lords, 1784, a case perfectly within my recollection as a case very deliberately considered at the Cockpit. It is conformable to the text law, and the opinion of eminent jurists. 'Quod additur de vecturæ pretiis solvendis (says Bynkershoek), ejus juris rationem non adsequor. Satis intelligo, qui navem hostilem occupant, etiam occupasse omne jus quod navi, sive navarcho debebatur, ob merces translatas in portum destinatum. Proponitur autem, navem in ipso itinere fuisse captam. Eccur igitur capienti solvam mercedes? Si qui cepit navem, eam cum mercibus in locum destinatum perducere paratus sit, ejus juris rationem intelligerem, ceteroquin non intelligo.'

"In the case of the *Vreyheid*, all the considerations that could be applied to this question were fully canvassed, and it was then recognized as the true rule, that the captor *who has performed* the contract of the vessel is, as a matter of right, and *de cursu*, entitled to freight; although, if he has done anything to the injury of the property, or has been guilty of any misconduct, he may remain answerable for the effect of such misconduct, or injury, in the way of a set-off against him.

"The case then is reduced to a question, whether the captor, in this instance, *has* done anything to forfeit the right, which, under the general rule, he had acquired. * * *

"Under the circumstances of this case, I am of opinion, that the captor has not forfeited the interest which he had acquired.

"Freight decreed to the captor."

SECTION 37.—RECAPTURE—RESCUE.

THE "SANTA CRUZ."

HIGH COURT OF ADMIRALTY, 1798.

(1 *C. Robinson*, 49.)

General rules of recapture and salvage.
The law of England, on recapture of property of allies, is the law of reciprocity.

This was the case of a Portuguese vessel taken by the French, August 1, 1796, and retaken by English cruisers, on the 28th, after being a month in the possession of the enemy.

Judgment,—Sir W. SCOTT:—

"* * * In the arguments of the counsel, I have heard much of the rules which the law of nations prescribes on recapture, respecting the time when property vests in the captor; and it certainly is a question of much curiosity to inquire what is the true rule on this subject; when I say the *true rule*, I mean only the rule to which civilized nations, attending to just principles, ought to adhere; for the moment you admit, as admitted it must be, that the practice of nations is various, you admit there is no rule operating with the proper force and authority of a general rule.

"It may be fit there should be some rule, and it might be either the rule of immediate possession or the rule of pernoctation and twenty-four hours' possession; or it might be the rule of bringing *infra præsidia;* or it might be a rule requiring an actual sentence of condemnation; either of these rules might be sufficient for general practical convenience, although in theory perhaps one might appear more just than another; but the fact is, there is no such rule of practice; nations concur in principle, indeed, so far as require firm and secure possession; but their rules of evidence respecting the possession are so discordant and lead to such opposite conclusions that the mere unity of principle forms no uniform rule to regulate the general practice. But were the public opinion of European States more distinctly agreed on any principle as fit to form the rule of the law of nations on this subject, it by no means follows that any one nation would lie under an obligation to observe it.

"That obligation could arise only from a reciprocity of practice in other nations; for from the very circumstance of the prevalence of a different rule among other nations, it would become not only lawful, but necessary to that one nation to pursue a different conduct: for instance, were there a rule prevailing among other nations that the immediate possession and the very act of capture should divest the property from the first owner, it would be absurd in Great Britain to act towards them on a more extended principle; and to lay it down as a general rule, that a bringing *infra præsidia*, though probably the true rule should in all cases of recapture be deemed necessary to divest the original proprietor of his rights; for the effect of adhering to such a rule would be gross injustice to British subjects. * * *

"If I am asked, under the known diversity of practice on this subject, what is the proper rule for a State to apply to the recaptured property of its allies, I should answer that the liberal and rational proceeding would be, to apply in the first instance the rule of that country to which the recaptured property belongs. * * *

"If there should exist a country in which no rule prevails, the recapturing country must then of necessity apply its own rule and rest on the presumption that that rule will be adopted and administered in the future practice of its allies. * * *

"I understand [the law of England] to be clearly this: That the maritime law of England, having adopted a most liberal rule of restitution on salvage, with respect to the recaptured property of its own subjects, gives the benefit of that rule to its allies, till it appears that they act towards British property on a less liberal principle. In such a case it adopts their rule and treats them according to their own measure of justice. * * *"

[As Portugal had adopted the twenty-four-hour rule, that principle was applied to those ships recaptured during the time that rule prevailed in Portugal, and the rate of salvage decreed was the Portuguese rate, one-eighth to ships of war and one-fifth to privateers. The English rule allowed one-sixth to privateers.]

THE "CARLOTTA."

HIGH COURT OF ADMIRALTY, 1803.

(5 *C. Robinson*, 54.)

Salvage on neutral property, retaken out of the hands of the enemy, not given—unless it can be shown by references to the ordinances or to the practice of the prize courts of the enemy, that the first seizure was made under such circumstances as would have exposed the goods to condemnation in the hands of the enemy.

This was a question of salvage, on the recapture of a Spanish ship and cargo from a French cruiser.

Judgment,—Sir W. SCOTT:—

"The question now to be decided is, whether salvage is due on the neutral property in this ship which has been recaptured out of the possession of the enemy. It certainly has not been the practice of this court to decree salvage under such circumstances generally; but, in consequence of the violent conduct of France during the last war, it was thought not unreasonable on the part of neutral merchants themselves, that salvage should be allowed. * * *

"I am, therefore, not disposed to hold generally that neutral property recaptured from French cruisers shall be subject to salvage. The rule, so far as it can be considered a general rule, is rather to be laid down the other way. At the same time, if any edict can be appealed to or any fact established, by which it can be shewn that the property would have been exposed to condemnation in the courts of France, I shall hold that to be sufficient ground to induce me to pronounce for salvage in that particular case. With regard to the precedent of the *Jonge Lambert* (5 C. Rob., 54, note), I think I am warranted to consider the authority of that case as in a great measure done away by the subsequent decision of the Lords in the late war, in which they have repeatedly pronounced for salvage on the recapture of neutral property. In departing from the old rule they have in some degree disclaimed the principle; and, I think, with great propriety, as far as it could be considered as an universal principle, governing the practice of our prize courts in all possible cases, without any possible exception. In the present instance there does not appear to me to be any grounds on which it can be supposed that this property would have been condemned, merely because it came out of the hands of a British privateer, or because the original voyage had been the colony of Spain to London. No edict has been produced from the French code to shew that this property would have been subject to any such penalty on either of those accounts, in the prize courts of France. The expenses of the recaptors must be fully paid; but I shall not pronounce salvage to be due."[1]

THE "EMILY ST. PIERRE."

(*Lawrence's Wheaton*, 667, 1021.)

It is not the duty of a neutral government to restore a private vessel of one of its citizens which has been rescued by her crew from a belligerent captor before condemnation.

This was a British vessel, captured by the United States blockading squadron, in the act of breaking the blockade of Charleston, S. C., and ordered to Philadelphia for adjudication in charge of a prize crew. The original crew, by fraud and force, regained possession, and took the vessel to Liverpool and restored her to the possession of her owners. Mr. Adams applied to Earl Russell for a restoration of the vessel, on the ground that the rescue was a violation of the law of nations, which furnished sufficient cause for condemnation, and a breach of the duty of a neutral, who is bound to submit to the adjudication of the prize court of the captor. Earl Russell refused the demand on two grounds,—*first*, that, as the rescue

[1] For an account of the laws of different countries on the subject of recapture and salvage, see Dana's Wheaton, pp. 466–472.

was not a violation of any municipal law of England, and as the vessel was not in the custody of the British Government, that government had no legal right to take her from the hands of her owners, or to prosecute or proceed against the vessel or the owners for any violation of law; and, *second*, that, in addition to the technical objection, the offense was solely one against the laws of war made for the benefit of captors, which the captors could assert and vindicate only in their own tribunals. Admitting that rescue was ground for condemnation, he contended that the decree could only be made by the belligerent prize court. No other court, either of the belligerent or of a neutral country, had jurisdiction to condemn or restore property taken in war. If the private neutral rescues his vessel by force he takes all risks of the captor's rights of force recognized by nations, but nothing more. The courts and government of the neutral country cannot decide that the title to the vessel has passed to the captor before condemnation by the prize courts of the captor's country. All they can do is to restore to the captor the temporary possessory right, which he has between capture and condemnation. Such possessory right he held to be one of force, which the captor's government could guard and assert by condemnation or other penalty on the property, if in its possession, through its prize court; but, even by the courts of the captor, the neutral rescuer could not be personally punished, as for a crime. He contended that it was not incumbent on neutral governments to make laws to enforce such belligerent possessory rights against their own citizens, any more than it is in case of crimes committed by their own citizens abroad, whom they do not even deliver up to the offended government for trial, except by treaty stipulation; or in case of violations of the revenue or embargo laws of other countries, which they never even indirectly take active cognizance of; or in case of successful breach of blockade.

In the course of the correspondence Mr. Adams cited a parallel case, in which the position of the two governments was reversed, as early as 1799, that of the brig *Experience*. She was an American vessel, captured (with two other vessels) by a British cruiser, rescued by her crew, and brought to Philadelphia. By direction of Lord Grenville, of Oct. 21, 1799, Mr. Liston demanded her restoration by the American government, by letter of May 2, 1800.

The Secretary of State, Mr. Pickering, by letter to Mr. Liston, of May 3, 1800, declined to interfere, and upon the ground that it was an inchoate and belligerent right of captors, which the neutral government cannot be expected to enforce against its own subjects; but referred the British Minister to the Admiralty Courts of the United

States, giving no opinion on the question beyond declining executive intervention.

The papers on the interesting question of the brig *Experience* were searched for and exchanged between the two governments by both Earl Russell and Mr. Adams; and Earl Russell stated that there was no evidence in the Foreign Office that the opinion of the law-officer of the crown had been taken in that case, or that any further proceedings were had after the reply of Mr. Pickering. Mr. Adams, on his part, did not press further the case of the *Emily St. Pierre*, nor attempt proceedings in the Admiralty Courts of Great Britain.

It may, therefore, be considered as settled by these two cases, that a neutral government is not required, by executive action, to restore a private vessel of one of its citizens which has been rescued by her crew from her captors before condemnation, on demand of the government of the captors. The possessory, belligerent right of the captors, is not to be enforced by neutral powers by any positive action in the way of penalty or seizure for restitution. Whether the right can be vindicated by a possessory suit by the captors in the Admiralty Courts of the neutral, has not been judicially determined; but the course of the political departments of both governments, and the reasoning on which they proceeded, seem to settle the judicial, as well as the political question. (Dana's Wheaton, 475.)[1]

[1] In the case of the *Lone*, 3 Op. Atty.-Gen., 377, this vessel had entered the port of Matamoras while it was blockaded by a French squadron (1838), and sailed thence for New Orleans. On the voyage she was captured by a French cruiser; but some days later she was rescued by her captain, who brought her into New Orleans. A demand was made on the President by the French Government for her return to the captors. Attorney-General Grundy advised that the President had no power to grant the demand, the case involving questions to be settled by the courts, and not by the executive, and that the claimants must go into the courts. He also advised that if a vessel, after escaping from her captors, terminated her voyage in safety, her liability to condemnation for the escape entirely ceases. (3 Wharton's Digest, 179.)

SECTION 38.—HOSTILE OCCUPATION—CONQUEST.

UNITED STATES v. RICE.

SUPREME COURT OF THE UNITED STATES, 1819.

(4 *Wheaton*, 246.)

Held, That, while Castine, in Maine, was in the military possession of the British forces, it was not a port of the United States, within the meaning of the revenue laws, so that, after the evacuation of the place, the United States could collect duties on goods imported into it during the occupation.

STORY, J., delivered the opinion of the court:—

"The single question arising on the pleadings in this case is, whether goods imported into Castine, during its occupation by the enemy, are liable to the duties imposed by the revenue laws upon goods imported into the United States. It appears, by the pleadings, that on the first day of September, 1814, Castine was captured by the enemy, and remained in his exclusive possession, under the command and control of his military and naval forces, until after the ratification of the treaty of peace, in February, 1815. During this period, the British government exercised all civil and military authority over the place; and established a custom-house, and admitted goods to be imported, according to regulations prescribed by itself, and, among others, admitted the goods upon which duties are now demanded. These goods remained at Castine until after it was evacuated by the enemy, and upon the reëstablishment of the American government, the collector of the customs, claiming a right to American duties on the goods, took the bond in question from the defendant, for the security of them.

"Under these circumstances, we are of opinion, that the claim for duties cannot be sustained. By the conquest and military occupation of Castine, the enemy acquired that firm possession which enabled him to exercise the fullest rights of sovereignty over that place. The sovereignty of the United States over the territory was, of course, suspended, and the laws of the United States could no longer be rightfully enforced there, or be obligatory upon the inhabitants who remained and submitted to the conquerors. By the surrender the inhabitants passed under a temporary allegiance to the

British government, and were bound by such laws, and such only, as it chose to recognize and impose. From the nature of the case, no other laws could be obligatory upon them; for where there is no protection, or allegiance, or sovereignty, there can be no claim to obedience. Castine was, therefore, during this period, so far as respected our revenue laws, to be deemed a foreign port; and goods imported into it by the inhabitants, were subject to such duties only as the British government chose to require. Such goods were, in no correct sense, imported into the United States. The subsequent evacuation by the enemy, and resumption of authority by the United States, did not, and could not, change the character of the previous transactions.

"The doctrines respecting the *jus postliminii* are wholly inapplicable to the case. The goods were liable to American duties, when imported, or not at all. That they were not so liable at the time of importation, is clear from what has been already stated; and when, upon the return of peace, the jurisdiction of the United States was reassumed, they were in the same predicament as they would have been if Castine had been a foreign territory ceded by treaty to the United States, and the goods had been previously imported there. In the latter case, there would be no pretence to say that American duties could be demanded; and, upon principles of public or municipal law, the cases are not distinguishable.

"The authorities cited at the bar, would, if there were any doubt, be decisive of the question. But we think it too clear to require any aid from authority." [1]

FLEMING v. PAGE.

SUPREME COURT OF THE UNITED STATES, 1850.

(9 *Howard*, 603.)

Held, that goods imported into the United States from Tampico, Mexico, while in the military occupation of the United States forces, are to be considered as importations from a foreign country.

This action is brought by the plaintiffs, merchants, residing in the city of Philadelphia, against the defendant, the late collector of the port of Philadelphia, to recover the sum of one thousand five hun-

[1] In the *United States* v. *Hayward*, 2 Gallison, 485 (1815), Mr. Justice STORY held that Castine was to be considered a "foreign port," with reference to the non-importation acts.

dred and twenty-nine dollars, duties paid on the 14th of June, 1847, under protest, on goods belonging to the plaintiffs, brought from Tampico while that place was in the military occupation of the forces of the United States.

On the 15th of November, 1846, Commodore Conner took military possession of Tampico, a seaport of the State of Tamaulipas, and from that time until the treaty of peace it was garrisoned by American forces, and remained in their military occupation.

Justice was administered there by courts appointed under the military authority, and a custom-house was established there, and a collector appointed, under the military and naval authority.

Upon a certificate of division in opinion in the Circuit Court the case came up to this court.

Judgment,—TANEY, C. J. :—

"The question certified by the Circuit Court turns upon the construction of the act of Congress of July 30, 1846.

"The duties levied upon the cargo of the schooner *Catharine* were duties imposed by this law upon goods imported from a foreign country. And if at the time of this shipment Tampico was not a foreign port, within the meaning of the act of Congress, then the duties were illegally charged, and, having been paid under protest, the plaintiffs would be entitled to recover in this action the amount exacted by the collector.

"The port of Tampico, at which the goods were shipped, and the Mexican State of Tamaulipas, in which it is situated, were undoubtedly at the time of the shipment subject to the sovereignty and dominion of the United States. The Mexican authorities had been driven out, or had submitted to our army and navy; and the country was in the exclusive and firm possession of the United States, and governed by its military authorities acting under the orders of the President. But it does not follow that it was a part of the United States, or that it ceased to be a foreign country, in the sense in which these words are used in the acts of Congress.

"The country in question had been conquered in war. But the genius and character of our institutions are peaceful, and the power to declare war was not conferred upon Congress for the purposes of aggression or aggrandizement, but to enable the general government to vindicate by arms, if it should become necessary, its own rights and the rights of its citizens.

"A war, therefore, declared by Congress, can never be presumed to be waged for the purpose of conquest or the acquisition of territory; nor does the law declaring the war imply an authority to the President to enlarge the limits of the United States by subjugating the enemy's country. The United States, it is true, may extend its boundaries by conquest or treaty, and may demand the cession of territory as the condition of peace, in order to indemnify its citizens for the injuries they have suffered, or to reimburse the government for the expenses of the war. But this can be done only by the treaty-making power or the legislative authority, and is not a part of the power conferred upon the President by the declaration of war. His duty and his power are purely military. As commander-in-chief, he is authorized to direct the movements of the naval and military forces placed by law at his command, and to employ them in the manner he may deem most effectual to harass and conquer and subdue the enemy. He may invade the hostile country, and subject it to the sovereignty and authority of the United States. But his conquests do not enlarge the boundaries of this Union, nor extend the operation of our institutions and laws beyond the limits before assigned to them by the legislative power.

"It is true, that, when Tampico had been captured, and the State of Tamaulipas subjugated, other nations were bound to regard the country, while our possession continued, as the territory of the United States, and to respect it as such. For, by the laws and usages of nations, conquest is a valid title, while the victor maintains the exclusive possession of the conquered country. The citizens of no other nation, therefore, had a right to enter it without the permission of the American authorities, nor to hold intercourse with its inhabitants, nor to trade with them. As regarded all other nations, it was a part of the United States, and belonged to them as exclusively as the territory included in our established boundaries.

"But yet it was not a part of this Union. For every nation which acquires territory by treaty or conquest holds it according to its own institutions and laws. And the relation in which the port of Tampico stood to the United States, while it was occupied by their arms, did not depend upon the laws of nations, but upon our own Constitution and acts of Congress. The power of the President, under which Tampico and the State of Tamaulipas were conquered and held in subjection, was simply that of a military commander prosecuting a war, waged against a public enemy, by the authority of his government. And the country from which these goods were imported was invaded and subdued, and occupied as the territory of a foreign hostile nation, as a portion of Mexico, and was held in possession in order to distress and harass the enemy. While it was occupied by our troops they were in an enemy's country, and not in their own; the inhabitants were still foreigners and enemies, and owed to the United States nothing more than the submission and obedience, sometimes called temporary allegiance, which is due from a conquered enemy, when he surrenders to a force which he is unable to resist. But the boundaries of the United States, as they existed when war was declared against Mexico, were not extended by the conquest; nor could they be regulated by the varying incidents of war, and be enlarged or diminished as the armies on either side advanced or retreated. They remained unchanged. And every place which was out of the limits of the United States, as previously established by the political authorities of the government, was still foreign; nor did our laws extend over it. Tampico was, therefore, a foreign port when this shipment was made.

"Again, there was no act of Congress establishing a custom-house at Tampico, nor authorizing the appointment of a collector; and, consequently, there was no officer of the United States authorized by law to grant the clearance and authenticate the coasting manifest of the cargo, in the manner directed by law, where the voyage is from one port of the United States to another. The person who acted in the character of collector in this instance, acted as such under the authority of the military commander, and in obedience to his orders; and the duties he exacted, and the regulations he adopted, were not those prescribed by law, but by the President in his character of commander-in-chief. The custom-house was established in an enemy's country, as one of the weapons of war. It was established, not for the purpose of giving to the people of Tamaulipas the benefits of commerce with the United States, or with other countries, but as a measure of hostility, and as a part of the military operations in Mexico; it was a mode of exacting contributions from the enemy to support our army, and intended also to cripple the resources of Mexico, and make it feel the evils and burdens of the war. The duties required to be paid were regulated with this view, and were nothing more than contributions levied upon the enemy, which the usages of war justify when an army is operating in the enemy's country. The permit and coasting manifest granted by an officer thus appointed, and thus controlled by military authority, could not be recognized in any port of the United States, as the documents required by the act of Congress when the vessel is engaged in the coasting trade, nor could they exempt the cargo from the payment of duties.

"This construction of the revenue laws has been uniformly given by the administrative department of the government in every case that has come before it. And it has, indeed, been given in cases where there appears to have been stronger ground for regarding the place of shipment as a domestic port. For, after Florida had been ceded to the United States, and the forces of the United States had taken possession of Pensacola, it was decided by the Treasury Department, that goods imported from Pensacola before an act of Congress was passed erecting it into a collection district, and authorizing the appointment of a collector, were liable to duty. That is, that although Florida had, by cession, actually become a part of the United States, and was in our possession, yet, under our revenue laws, its ports must be regarded as foreign until they were established as domestic, by act of Congress; and it appears that this decision was sanctioned at the time by the Attorney-General of the United States, the law officer of the government. And, although not so directly applicable to the case before us, yet the decisions of the Treasury Department in relation to Amelia Island, and certain ports in Louisiana, after that province had been ceded to the United States, were both made upon the same grounds. And, in the latter case, after a custom-house had been established by law at New Orleans, the collector at that place was instructed to regard as foreign ports Baton Rouge and other settlements still in the possession of Spain, whether on the Mississippi, Iberville, or the sea-coast. The Department in no instance that we are aware of, since the establishment of the government, has ever recognized a place in a newly-acquired country as a domestic port, from which the coasting trade might be carried on, unless it had been previously made so by act of Congress.

"The principle thus adopted and acted upon by the executive department of the government has been sanctioned by the decisions in this court and the circuit courts whenever the question came before them. We do not propose to comment upon the different cases cited in the argument. It is sufficient to say, that there is no discrepancy between them. And all of them, so far as they apply, maintain, that under our revenue laws every port is regarded as a foreign one, unless the custom-house from which the vessel clears is within a collection district established by act of Congress, and the officers granting the clearance exercise their functions under the authority and control of the laws of the United States.

"In the view we have taken of this question, it is unnecessary to notice particularly the passages from eminent writers on the laws of nations which were brought forward in the argument. They speak altogether of the rights which a sovereign acquires and the powers he may exercise in a conquered country, and they do not bear upon the question we are considering. For in this country the sovereignty of the United States resides in the people of the several States, and they act through their representatives according to the delegation and distribution of powers contained in the constitution. And the constituted authorities to whom the power of making war and concluding peace is confided, and of determining whether a conquered country shall be permanently retained or not, neither claimed nor exercised any rights or powers in relation to the territory in question but the rights of war. After it was subdued it was uniformly treated as an enemy's country and restored to the possession of the Mexican authorities when peace was concluded. And certainly its subjugation did not compel the United States, while they held it, to regard it as a part of their dominions, nor to give to it any form of civil government, nor to extend to it our laws.

"Neither is it necessary to examine the English decisions which have been referred to by counsel. It is true that most of the States have adopted the principles of English jurisprudence, so far as it concerns private and individual rights, and when such rights are in question we habitually refer to the English decisions, not only with respect, but in many cases as authoritative. But in the distribution of political power between the great departments of government, there is such a wide difference between the power conferred on the President of the United States and the authority and sovereignty which belong to the English crown, that it would be altogether unsafe to reason from any supposed resemblance between them, either as regards conquest in war or any other subject where the rights and powers of the executive arm of the government are brought into question. Our own constitution and form of government must be our only guide. And we are entirely satisfied that, under the constitution and laws of the United States, Tampico was a foreign port, within the meaning of the act of 1846, when these goods were shipped, and that the cargoes were liable to the duty charged upon them, and we shall certify accordingly to the circuit court."

Mr. Justice McLEAN dissented.

Order.—"This cause came on to be heard on the transcript of the record from the circuit court of the United States for the eastern district of Pennsylvania, and on the point or question on which the judges of the said circuit court were opposed in opinion and which was certified to this court for its opinion, agreeably to the act of Congress in such case made and provided, and was argued by counsel.—On consideration whereof, it is the opinion of this court, that Tampico was a foreign port within the meaning of the act of Congress of July 30, 1846, entitled 'An act reducing the duties on imports, and for other purposes,' and that the goods, wares, and merchandise as set forth and described in the record were liable to the duties charged upon them under said act of Congress. Whereupon it is now here ordered and adjudged by this court that it be so certified to the said circuit court."

CROSS v. HARRISON.

SUPREME COURT OF THE UNITED STATES, 1853.

(16 *Howard*, 164.)

Character of the military and civil government set up in California under the military occupation of the United States army.

In the war with Mexico the port of San Francisco was conquered by the arms of the United States, in the year 1846, and shortly afterwards the United States had military possession of all of Upper California. Early in 1847 the President of the United States, as constitutional commander-in-chief of the army and navy, authorized the military and naval commanders of the United States forces in California to exercise the belligerent rights of a conqueror and to form a civil and military government for the conquered territory, with power to impose duties on imports and tonnage for the support of such government and of the army which had the conquest in possession.

This was done, and tonnage and import duties were levied under a war tariff, which had been established by the civil government for that purpose until official notice was received by the civil and military governor of California, that a treaty of peace had been made with Mexico, by which Upper California had been ceded to the United States.

Upon receiving this intelligence the governor directed that import and tonnage duties should thereafter be levied in conformity with such as were to be paid in the other ports of the United States, by the acts of Congress; and for such purpose he appointed the defendant in this suit collector of the port of San Francisco.

The plaintiffs now seek to recover from him certain tonnage duties and imposts upon foreign merchandise paid by them to the defendant as collector between the 3d of February, 1848 (the date of the treaty of peace), and the 13th of November, 1849 (when the collector appointed by the President, according to law, entered upon the duties of his office), upon the ground that they had been illegally exacted. The formation of the civil government in California, when it was done, was the lawful exercise of a belligerent right over a conquered territory. It was the existing government when the territory was ceded to the United States, as a conquest, and did not cease as a matter of course, or as a consequence of the restoration of peace; and it was rightfully continued after peace was made with Mexico, until Congress legislated otherwise, under its constitutional power, to dispose of and make all needful rules and regulations respecting the territory or other property belonging to the United States.

The tonnage duties and duties upon foreign goods imported into San Francisco were legally demanded and lawfully collected by the civil governor, whilst the war continued, and afterwards, from the ratification of the treaty of peace until the revenue system of the United States was put into practical operation in California under the acts of Congress passed for that purpose.

THE AMERICAN INSURANCE COMPANY v. CANTER.

SUPREME COURT OF THE UNITED STATES, 1828.

(1 *Peters*, 511.)

Status of the people of Florida after the cession of that territory to the United States.

The following is an extract from the judgment:—

MARSHALL, C. J.:—"The course which the argument has taken will require, that, in deciding this question, the Court should take into view the relation in which Florida stands to to the United States.

"The Constitution confers absolutely on the government of the Union the powers of making war and of making treaties; consequently, that government possesses the power of acquiring territory either by conquest or by treaty.

"The usage of the world is, if a nation be not entirely subdued, to consider the holding of conquered territory as a mere military occupation, until its fate shall be determined at the treaty of peace. If it be ceded by the treaty, the acquisition is confirmed and the ceded territory becomes a part of the nation to which it is annexed; either on the terms stipulated in the treaty of cession, or on such as its new master shall impose. On such transfer of territory, it has never been held, that the relations of the inhabitants with each other undergo any change. Their relations with their former sovereign are dissolved, and new relations are created between them and the government which has acquired their territory. The same act which transfers their country, transfers the allegiance of those who remain in it; and the law, which may be denominated political, is necessarily changed, although that which regulates the intercourse and general conduct of individuals, remains in force until altered by the newly-created power of the State.

"On the 2d of February, 1819, Spain ceded Florida to the United States. The 6th article of the treaty of cession contains the following provision: 'The inhabitants of the territories which his Catholic majesty cedes to the United States by this treaty, shall be incorporated in the Union of the United States as soon as may be consistent with the principles of the federal Constitution; and admitted to the enjoyment of the privileges, rights, and immunities of the citizens of the United States.'

"This treaty is the law of the land and admits the inhabitants of Florida to the enjoyment of the privileges, rights, and immunities of the citizens of the United States. It is unnecessary to inquire whether this is not their condition, independent of stipulation. They do not, however, participate in political power; they do not share in the government, till Florida shall become a state. In the meantime Florida continues to be a territory of the United States; governed by virtue of that clause in the Constitution which empowers Congress 'to make all needful rules and regulations respecting the territory or other property belonging to the United States.'"

JECKER v. MONTGOMERY.

SUPREME COURT OF THE UNITED STATES, 1851.

(13 *Howard*, 498.)

Neither the President of the United States, nor any inferior executive officer, can establish a court of prize, in territory occupied by American troops, competent to take jurisdiction of a case of capture *jure belli*.

After California had been occupied by the United States forces, during the war with Mexico, a Prize Court was set up at Monterey, at the request of Commodore Biddle, and sanctioned by the President.

An American vessel—the *Admittance*—was captured for trading with the enemy, April 7, 1847, and condemned by this court at Monterey; and the vessel and cargo were sold under the sentence.

The question finally came before the Supreme Court.

Chief Justice TANEY, in pronouncing the judgment, said in respect of the power of establishing courts:—

"* * * In relation to the proceedings in the court at Monterey, which is the subject of the first demurrer, the decision of the circuit court is correct.

"All captures *jure belli* are for the benefit of the sovereign under whose authority they are made; and the validity of the seizure and the question of prize or no prize can be determined in his own courts only, upon which he has conferred jurisdiction to try the question. And under the Constitution of the United States the judicial power of the general government is vested in one supreme court, and in such inferior courts as Congress shall, from time to time, ordain and establish. Every court of the United States, therefore, must derive its jurisdiction and its authority from the Constitution or the laws of the United States. And neither the President nor any military officer can establish a court in a conquered country, and authorize it to decide upon the rights of the United States, or of individuals in prize cases, nor to administer the law of nations.

"The courts established or sanctioned in Mexico during the war by the commanders of the American forces were nothing more than the agents of the military power, to assist in preserving order in the conquered territory, and to protect the inhabitants in their persons and property while it was occupied by the American arms; they were subject to the military power, and their decisions under its control, whenever the commanding officer thought proper to interfere. They were not courts of the United States, and had no right to adjudicate upon a question of prize or no prize. And the sentence of condemnation in the court at Monterey is a nullity, and can have no effect upon the rights of any party.

"The second demurrer denies the authority of the district court to adjudicate, because the property had not been brought within its jurisdiction. But that proposition cannot be maintained; and a prize court, when a proper case is made for its interposition, will proceed to adjudicate and condemn the captured property or award restitution, although it is not actually in the control of the court. It may always proceed *in rem* whenever the prize or proceeds of the prize can be traced to the hands of any person whatever." [1]

[1] See also *Leitensdorfer* v. *Webb*, 20 Howard, 176:

In the case of the *Grapeshot*, 9 Wallace, 129 (1869), the Supreme Court decided that, during the civil war, when the national forces occupied parts of the revolted territory it was within the authority of the President, as commander-in-chief, to establish provisional courts to try causes arising under the laws of the State or of the United States. And see *Mechanics and Traders' Bank* v. *Union Bank*, 22 Wallace, 276; *U. S.* v. *Diekelman*, 92 U. S., 520; *Dow* v. *Johnson*, 100 U. S., 158.

UNITED STATES v. MORENO.

SUPREME COURT OF THE UNITED STATES, 1863.

(1 *Wallace*, 400.)

Conquest or cession of territory works no change in private titles to land.

The following is an extract from the opinion of the court delivered by Mr. Justice SWAYNE:—

"California belonged to Spain by the rights of discovery and conquest. The government of that country established regulations for transfers of the public domain to individuals. When the sovereignty of Spain was displaced by the revolutionary action of Mexico, the new government established regulations upon the same subject. These two sovereignties are the spring heads of all the land titles in California, existing at the time of the cession of that country to the United States by the treaty of Guadalupe Hidalgo. That cession did not impair the rights of private property. They were consecrated by the law of nations, and protected by the treaty.

"The treaty stipulation was but a formal recognition of the pre-existing sanction in the law of nations. The act of March 3d, 1851, was passed to assure to the inhabitants of the ceded territory the benefit of the rights of property thus secured to them. It recognizes alike legal and equitable rights, and should be administered in a large and liberal spirit. A right of any validity before the cession was equally valid afterwards, and while it is the duty of the court in the cases which may come before it to guard carefully against claims originating in fraud, it is equally their duty to see that no rightful claim is rejected. No nation can have any higher interest than the right administration of justice."

CASE OF GUERIN.

COURT OF APPEAL OF NANCY, 1872.

(*Dalloz*, 1872, II., p. 185.)

The occupation of a department of France by the troops of the enemy does not suspend therein the civil and criminal laws of France; which continue obligatory upon all Frenchmen, so long at least as they have not been expressly and specifically abrogated by the exigencies of the war.

During the military occupation of various departments of France, by the German army, in 1870–71, the German authorities therein caused the trees in the forests of the state to be cut down and sold, deriving therefrom a certain revenue. In this case, a French citizen engaged in a traffic in these trees, purchasing them from the Germans. After the war he was prosecuted for a breach of the forestry laws of France.

LA COUR.—"Attendu qu'il n'appartient pas à la cour de se prononcer sur le caractère légitime ou illégal des actes émanés de l'autorité allemande; que la seule question soumise à son appréciation par le système de défense du prévenu qui se dégage nettement des conclusions par lui prises en première instance, est celle de savoir si, dans le cas même où l'ennemi envahisseur n'aurait fait qu'user d'un droit en vendant les coupes de la Bousule et de la Maquinière, dans la forêt domaniale de Champenoux, il pouvait être permis à des sujets français de s'en rendre adjudicataires et d'exploiter ces coupes, avant et après la conclusion de la paix, en violation de la loi française, en se passant de toute délivrance et autorisation de l'administration forestière, sans encourir les pénalités édictées par le code forestier;—Attendu qu'il est de principe que l'occupation du territoire par l'ennemi n'entraine pas la suspension du droit politique ou privé du pays occupé; que les lois civiles et pénales conservent au contraire tout leur empire, à moins qu'elles n'aient été l'objet d'abrogations expresses et spéciales commandées par les exigences de la guerre; que telle est l'opinion des auteurs les plus accrédités qui ont écrit sur le droit international;—Attendu qu'en constituant en Lorraine un gouvernement militaire, avec adjonction d'un commissaire civil, le souverain envahisseur, loin d'abroger les lois françaises, a, au contraire, admis qu'elles resteraient en vigueur; que le commissaire civil de Lorraine, lorsqu'il a pris possession de ses fonctions, a confirmé leur maintien en disant dans sa proclamation du 4 sept. 1870: 'Toutes vos lois, en tant que l'état de guerre n'en réclame pas la suspension, seront respectées. La justice conservera son libre cours';—Attendu qu'il suit de là que les citoyens français n'ont jamais été déliés, par le fait de l'invasion, de leur devoir d'obéissance envers les lois de leur pays; que le code forestier français, toutes ses prescriptions et ses défenses n'ont donc pas cessé de s'imposer aux sujets français, et que, dès lors, ceux-ci n'ont pu légitimement enlever quoi que ce soit dans les forêts domaniales sans la permission des agents français, qui sont toujours restés la seule autorité forestière légitime du pays;—Attendu que si des français, mus par un sentiment de cupidité assez fort pour éteindre en eux tout patriotisme, se sont rendus comme Guérin adjudicataires à vil prix de coupes vendues par l'autorité allemande, ils ont agi à leurs risques et périls, à charge par eux d'obtenir, s'ils le pouvaient, de l'administration forestière, la permission d'exploiter ces coupes, sinon en encourant les rigueurs de la loi pénale qui pourrait leur être appliquée lorsque l'autorité française aurait recouvré, par la conclusion de la paix, toute sa liberté d'action et la plénitude de sa puissance répressive."[1]

MOHR AND HAAS v. HATZFELD.

Court of Appeals of Nancy, 1872.

(*Dalloz*, 1872, II., *p.* 229.)

The military occupation of a territory confers upon the invader the right to the usufruct and revenues only of the public domain; the French courts will not recognize as valid the sale of old trees (during the war of 1870–71) on the public domain, which were reserved at the time of the annual cutting. They are as inalienable as the soil of the forest itself.

La Cour:—"En ce qui touche l'appel principal (des sieurs Mohr et Haas):—Attendu que, le 24 oct. 1870, le gouvernement allemand, représenté par le comte de Villers, son commissaire civil en Lorraine, a vendu aux sieurs Samelsohn et Sackür, banquiers à Berlin à raison de 3 thalers l'un, plus de 15,000 chênes d'au moins 5 mètres de hauteur et de 50 centimètres de diamètre, mesurés à 1 mètre 25 centimètres au-dessus du sol, à prendre dans les forêts domaniales des départements de la Meuse et de la Meurthe;—Que, dès le 8 nov. suivant, les acquéreurs rétrocédaient purement et simplement le bénéfice de leur marché aux sieurs Mohr et Haas, négociants à Manheim, lesquels, après avoir fait abattre environ 9,000 arbres, ont, à leur tour, transmis tous leurs droits au sieur Hatzfeld, de Nancy, par acte sous signatures privées du 15 mars 1871;—Qu'aux termes de cet acte, le sieur Hatzfeld devait payer, par arbre abattu ou sur pied dont il prendrait possession, non plus 3 thalers, mais 40 fr., plus 140,000 fr. pour frais d'exploitation et dépenses de toutes sortes;—Qu'il versa 150,000 fr. comptant, et que, pour le surplus, il souscrivit

[1] The same rule, says Dalloz, was enforced in respect to the customs laws; and even in that part of the occupied territory where the Germans collected and appropriated the duties.

"Les introductions de marchandises faites en fraude auxdites lois de douane pendant l'occupation, encore même qu'elles auraient été tolérés par les autorités étrangères commandant dans ces départements, sont poursuivies à bon droit après le retablissement du service de la douane française." (Dalloz, 1872, II., 185, notes 3 and 4.)

les traites jusqu'à concurrence de 300,000 fr.;—Attendu que, mis en demeure d'exécuter les conventions par lui souscrites le 15 mars 1871, et confirmées le 16 avril de la même année, le sieur Hatzfeld se refuse à cette exécution, en excipant de nullités que la cour a, après le tribunal, le droit et le devoir d'apprécier;—Que sa compétence résulte d'abord de la clause par laquelle les parties se sont engagées à saisir, le cas échéant, les tribunaux de la ville de Nancy, où elles feraient élection de domicile au greffe du tribunal de commerce, de toutes les contestasions qui pourraient s'élever entre elles à l'occasion de leur traité;—Qu'elle a été de plus formellement reconnue par l'ambassadeur d'Allemagne, qui, prié d'intervenir pour la conservation des droits des sieurs Mohr et Haas, a répondu à ces derniers, le 8 sept. 1871, au nom de son gouvernement, que 'l'affaire devait être jugée suivant le droit civil français.'

"Attendu que la première et la plus délicate des questions a examiner et à résoudre est celle de savoir si le gouvernement allemand pouvait faire ce qu'il a fait le 24 octobre 1870, et qu'à cet égard le droit international, bien plus que le droit civil, pose des règles inspirées par la conscience publique, et dont il appartient à la magistrature, en les appliquant sans faiblesse, d'assurer la diffusion et le succès;—Qu'il ne s'agit point de méconnaître le droit du vainqueur, mais de le maintenir dans les limites que lui assignent les précédents, l'usage, la raison et la justice;—Que ce droit, en ce qui touche les immeubles, ne consiste que dans la prise de possession temporaire des domaines de l'Etat ennemi, et dans la perception de leurs fruits et de leurs revenus;—Qu'en cela tous les auteurs sont d'accord, et que deux des plus récents et des moins suspects, les célèbres professeurs de l'école allemande, Bluntschli (art. 646), et Heffter. * * * Qu'il faut donc proclamer que les fruits et les revenus des propriétés domaniales appartiennent seuls au vainqueur, et que, lorsque celui-ci dispose d'autre chose, il dispose de ce qui ne lui appartient pas;

"Attendu que, réduite à ces termes, la question ne présente plus la moindre difficulté, puisqu'il ne reste plus qu'à rechercher si les chênes anciens vendus le 24 oct. 1870 aux sieurs Samelsohn et Sackür, puis revendus le 15 mars 1871 au sieur Hatzfeld, constituent des fruits ou des revenus, ce que personne n'oserait prétendre;—Que ces vieux chênes, l'honneur et la richesse de la forêt, marqués en réserve lors des coupes annuelles, font partie intégrante du sol lui-même, au repeuplement duquel ils concourent, et ne sont pas moins inaliénables que lui;—Que leur vente isolée, après les coupes ordinaires et en dehors de ces coupes, présente tous les caractères d'un fait anormal, exceptionnel, et ne peut s'opérer, aux termes de l'art. 16 c. for., qu'en vertu d'un décret spécial;—Qu'en vendant les arbres objet du litige, sans l'accomplissement de formalités protectrice, en contravention à un aménagement régulier, le comte de Villers, et après lui les sieurs Mohr et Haas, ont donc vendu ce qu'ils n'avaient pas le droit de vendre, ce que le propriétaire aurait dû retrouver après l'invasion et l'occupation, en un mot la chose d'autrui, et en tous cas une chose qui n'était pas dans le commerce. * * *

"Que le Gouvernement allemand lui-même a montré, par son attitude et son language, qu'il considérait comme inefficace le contrat intervenu entre les sieurs Mohr et Haas et le sieur Hatzfeld, en n'insistant pas pour son insertion dans le traité de paix, en refusant ensuite de prévenir par son intervention le procès actuel, en laissant enfin sans un mot de réponse la déclaration suivant des plénipotentiaires français, consignée au protocole de signature de la convention additionnelle au traité de paix du 10 mai 1871: 'Des aliénations de coupes de bois dans les forêts de l'Etat ont été consenties durant la guerre, sur le territoire français, par les autorités civiles et militaires allemandes. A raison des circonstances au milieu desquelles ont été souscrits les contrats passés à ce sujet, le Gouvernement français ne saurait, en ce qui le concerne, reconnaître à ces contrats ni valeur légale ni force obligatoire, et entend repousser toute responsabilité pécuniaire ou autre que les tiers intéressés pourraient de ce chef vouloir faire peser sur lui;'—Que cette déclaration solennelle du Gouvernement français, non contredite par les plénipotentiaires allemands, a, au point de vue du droit international, une importance dont les juges du droit civil sont autorisés à s'emparer, pour rendre plus manifeste encore le bien jugé de la sentence frappée d'appel;

"En ce qui touche l'appel incident du sieur Hatzfeld:—Attendu qu'il ne suffisait pas de condamner les sieurs Mohr et Haas à restituer les 150,000 fr. par eux indûment reçus; qu'il fallait aussi les condamner à payer une somme équivalente au profit que le sieur Hatzfeld aurait tiré de ce capital, s'il ne s'en était pas dessaisi;—Que sans cela les appelants s'enrichiraient au préjudice d'autri, ce que ne permettent ni l'équité ni la justice;

"Par ces motifs, rejette comme mal fondé l'appel principal;—Reçoit au contraire l'appel incident, et, y faisant droit, réforme le jugement de première instance en ce qu'il a refusé à Hatzfeld toute espèce de dommages-intérêts;—Condamne les appelants à payer à l'intimé, à titre de dommages-intérêts, la somme de 11,600 fr., avec intérêts à partir de ce jour, tant du capital que de la somme allouée à titre de dommages-intérêts;—Condamne les sieurs Mohr et Haas à l'amende et aux frais, etc."

VILLASSEQUE'S CASE.

COUR DE CASSATION, 1818.

(*Ortolan: Diplomatie de la Mer*, 2d *Ed.*, I., 324.)

A crime committed by a French citizen in Spanish territory, occupied and administered by the French army, *held*, to be committed in a foreign country.

Villasseque, a Frenchman, was charged with the crime of assassination, committed in the territory of Catalonia, Spain, during the military occupation by France in the summer of 1811. It was contended by the prosecution that, inasmuch as Catalonia was occupied by French troops, and the government administered by French authorities, it must be considered as French territory. On appeal from "la Cour d'assises des Pyrénées Orientales," "La Cour de Cassation" pronounced the following judgment:

"Attendu. . . ., qu'en règle générale, le droit de poursuivre un crime n'appartient qu'au magistrat du territoire sur lequel le crime a été commis ou s'est prolongé;

"Que les seules exceptions admises à ce principe par le Code d'instruction criminelle sont renfermées dans les articles 5, 6 et 7, ci-dessus cités;

"Que la demande de Villasseque, tendante à ce que le crime porté dans le premier chef d'accusation ne fût point soumis à des débats, parce qu'il aurait été commis en pays étranger et sur la personne d'un étranger, et qu'il ne rentrait dans aucune des exceptions desdits articles 5, 6 et 7, a été rejetée par la Cour d'assises, d'après le seul motif qu'à l'époque de ce crime la Catalogne était occupée par les troupes françaises et administrée par des autorités françaises, ce qui suffisait pour qu'elle fût alors réputée partie intégrante du territoire français;

"Mais que cette occupation et cette administration par des troupes et des autorités françaises n'avaient pas communiqué aux habitants de la Catalogne le titre de Français, ni à leur territoire la qualité de territoire français; que cette communication n'aurait pu résulter que d'un acte de réunion émané de l'autorité publique, lequel n'a jamais existé; Casse, etc."

THE ELECTOR OF HESSE CASSEL.

(*Phillimore's International Law*, III., 841.)

Hesse Cassel was conquered by the first Napoleon in 1806, and remained for about a year under his immediate control; when it was annexed to the new kingdom of Westphalia, and formed a part of that kingdom till after the battle of Leipzig, in 1813.

The question was whether debts owing to the Elector were validly discharged by a payment to Napoleon and receiving from him a quittance in full.

The legal title of the Emperor was set forth as follows:—

"Que par suite de la conquête de l'Electorat de Hesse, l'Empereur a confisqué au profit de son *domaine extraordinaire* les créances appartenantes, soit au ci-divant Electeur de Hesse, soit aux états et provinces, dont il avait été pris possession, et a déclaré, qu'il entendait, qu'aucun débiteur ne pût se libérer valablement qu'au trésor dudit domaine."

One of the debtors of the Elector was Count von Hahn, a subject of Mecklenburg, and having large estates in that duchy. The mortgage of these estates held by the Elector of Hesse, was duly registered in the proper office in Mecklenburg.

The Duke of Mecklenburg, at the instance of Napoleon, issued an order (circular Rescript), which, after reciting that Napoleon, being possessed of the sovereignty of Hesse Cassel, was possessed, as an accessory to the principal, of the debts due to that sovereign, directed the Court of Registration to record as extinguished those mortgages in favor of Hesse Cassel, for which a particular discharge or receipt had been given by Napoleon, or by his appointee for that purpose.

The Rescript was dated the 15th of June, 1810. It appears that it was obeyed, but that a particular minute of the circumstance of the extinguishment of the mortgage was also recorded, so as in some measure to leave open the question of the lawfulness of the discharge.

The affairs of the Count became embarrassed, and after his death creditors claimed his property; among them was the restored Prince of Hesse Cassel. The *actor communis* (or *official assignee*) of the creditors brought the question into court.

The Mecklenburg court of justice at Güstrow first entertained the question. The Prince denied both the validity of the discharge and the legality of the Mecklenburg order of 1810, and asserted that Napoleon possessed himself of the money in the character of a robber, and not of a conqueror.

This matter was then remitted to the Prussian University of Breslau. The decision of this tribunal (May 29, 1824) was in substance that the Prince might recover that part of the debt which had not been actually paid in money to Napoleon, but no more. It had happened that in many cases Napoleon had remitted, no doubt in order to induce payment, a considerable portion of the original debt, giving, however, a discharge from the whole.

Both parties, being dissatisfied with this judgment, appealed to the Holstein University of Kiel, which, however, confirmed, with some difference as to the costs, the sentence (March 24, 1831). But from this sentence the court itself sanctioned an appeal "*ad impartiales exteras*," that is, to another German University.

This learned body (name not given) delivered at great length the reasons of their judgment.

They rightly said that the real question was, whether Napoleon had, or had not, become the true creditor of the Hesse Cassel funds. They drew a broad distinction between the validity of acts done by a mere transient conqueror and acts done by him after the kingdom had been wholly subdued, and the subjects had either expressly, or by necessary implication, accepted him as their ruler.

In the former case the conqueror's right was confined to the effects of his private acts, to the *occupatio bellica*, and required actual seizure and possession for its valid exercise.

In the latter case the rights and title of the conqueror had been ratified by the public act of the state. As Napoleon's right and title was of the latter kind, the fact that these funds were the private property of the Prince, and not the public property of the state, became of no importance. They rejected the consideration of the justice or injustice of the war which Napoleon had waged against the Prince, wisely holding that the presumption of law, upon which they were bound to act, was in favor of its justice. Nor did it matter that the Prince, instead of giving battle to Napoleon, had departed, and resigned his country to the military occupation of the enemy. They pointed out that the Prince had, from the time of his departure or abdication, been an active enemy of the new government established under Napoleon and Jerome, and that, by the laws of all countries, the property of a person, *qui sub publico egit* against the state, was confiscable.

They rejected the doctrine that, because the Prince had retained possession of the instruments containing the written acknowledgments of the debtors, he therefore had constructive possession of the debts, the circumstances being considered under which the money had been borrowed—adopting the principle of the Roman Law, "*Dissolutæ quantitatis retentum instrumentum inefficax penes creditorem remanere* * * * *non est ambigui juris.*"

They considered how the question was affected by the return of the Prince, and by his reclamation of his former property, and they held that the principle of the decision of the Amphictyons in the case of the Thebans and Thessalians was sound law, and that it had been so treated by almost all jurists, ancient and modern.

They considered the general question whether, after peace, there did or did not take place a *restitutio in integrum* with respect to those who had been dispossessed by war. They held that, even according to the letter of the Roman Law, the restored owner must take the property as he found it, and was entitled to no compensation for the damage which it might have suffered in the interval; that what was actually gone he could not claim to have replaced; and especially that what the public exchequer (*fiscus*) had alienated was not to be restored.

That as to such alienations the principle of all law, whether private, public, or international, was expressed in the words of the Roman Law, "*Non debet quod ritè et secundum leges ab initio actum est, ex alio eventu resuscitari.*"

It was impossible, these judges observed, to consider the return of the Prince as a continuation of his former government.

He had not been constantly in arms against Napoleon, and at last successful, by force of arms, in recovering his domains. He had been treated by the peaces of Tilsit and Schönbrunn as politically extinct, and the King of Westphalia had been recognized by the continental powers as Regent of Hesse Cassel.

They remarked that the Prince's own tribunals of Hesse Cassel had pronounced (June 27, 1818,) that those subjects of the King of Westphalia who had paid to him or his exchequer their debts, and received due discharges, could not be legally called upon to pay a second time; and they thought the principle of that decision, as well as the authorities which they had referred to, led them to the judicial conclusion that all the debts, whether the whole sum had been paid or not, for which discharges in full had been given by Napoleon, were validly and effectually paid; and they, therefore, so far, reversed the former sentences, leaving, it should seem, both parties to pay their costs.

OCCUPATION OF NAPLES BY CHARLES VIII., 1495.

(*Phillimore's International Law*, III., 888.)

May citizens legally discharge the debts which they owe to the sovereign by paying the amounts to the temporary conqueror or military occupier of the territory of the state?

In the year 1495, Charles the Eighth of France overran Italy, and replaced for a moment the House of Anjou upon the throne of Naples. During his brief tenure of that kingdom the French king bestowed upon his adherents all that he could lay hands upon. Amongst other devices for enriching the Angevin party, that of calling in debts due to the state from the opposite faction was adopted. Many of these debtors paid honestly the full amount of their debt. Some tried to drive a bargain to their advantage, paying only a portion of their debt, and obtaining a receipt for the whole. Some contrived to pay nothing, and obtain a written discharge from everything. Four months afterwards, when the French king, with the Angevins, was driven out, and Ferdinand, with the Arragonese, was restored, the question as to the validity of these payments and receipts was sharply contested. Among other jurists invoked to adjudicate or arbitrate upon it, was one *summæ auctoritatis*, named *Matthæus de Afflictis*. His conclusions on this important subject are as follows:—

"*Prima conclusio:* Quod illi debitores dictorum regum de Arragoniâ, qui fuerunt in morâ solvendi dictis regibus pecuniam debitam in genere, et jussu regis Caroli et suorum officialium solverunt ipsis donatariis, quod *non sunt liberati*, et tenentur solvere dictis regibus, veris creditoribus.

"*Secunda conclusio* sit ista, quod illi debitores qui non fuerunt in morâ solvendi dictis creditoribus, sed jussi ab officialibus regis Franciæ, quod solvant illis Gallis, virtute largitatis regis, et ipsi fecerunt, quidquid eis fuit possible, ut non solverent, et realiter eis solverunt propter jussum pœnale, quod isti *sunt liberati*.

"*Tertia conclusio* sit ista, quod si debitor fuit in morâ, sed erat infra tempus purgandi moram, et infra illud tempus sit exactus ab illis Gallis jussu magistratûs tunc solvendo Gallis perindè habetur ac si non esset in morâ, et sic *erit liberatus*.

"*Quarta conclusio* sit ista, quod debitor, qui solvit Gallis illam pecuniam debitam regibus de Arragoniâ virtute jussûs magistratûs, cui non potuit resistere, et pecuniam illam debitam post diem solutionis faciendæ erat solitum quod ipsi debitores penes se retinebant pro expensis occurrentibus in administratione officii nomine regio, si ipsam pecuniam Gallis solverunt, *sunt liberati*, etiam quod fuerint in morâ.

"*Quinta conclusio* sit ista, quod illi debitores, qui solutionem probant per confessionem Gallorum publicam vel privatam, ita, quod non probant veram numerationem pecuniæ eis factum, *non sunt liberati*, sed debent solvere veris creditoribus, quantumcunque ostenderint dictum jussum.

"*Sexta conclusio*, quod illi debitores, qui se concordaverunt, quod si non ostendunt veram solutionem in totum vel in partem, *non sunt liberati*.

"Exitus rei approbavit istas conclusiones."

SECTION 39.—TERMINATION OF WAR.

THE "MENTOR."

HIGH COURT OF ADMIRALTY.

(1 *C. Robinson*, 179.)

Hostile acts committed after the conclusion of peace are illegal; and the injured party may sustain an action for damages against the wrongdoer. But if an officer commits such act in ignorance of the ending of the war, his own government should protect him.

The following is an extract from the judgment of Sir W. SCOTT:—

"The circumstances of the case, as far as it is necessary to state them, are these: The ship being American property, was on a voyage from Havannah to Philadelphia, in 1783; off the Delaware she was pursued by His Majesty's ships, the *Centurion* and the *Vulture*, then cruising off that river, under the command of the admiral on that station, Admiral Digby. All parties were in complete ignorance of the cessation of hostilities; not only the persons on board the King's ships, but the Americans, as well those on the shore, as those on board the vessel. In the pursuit, shots were fired on both sides, and, it is alleged on the part of the British, that the ship was set on fire by her own crew, who took to the shore.

"Now, I incline to assent to Dr. Lawrence's position, that if an act of mischief was done by the King's officers, though through ignorance, in a place where no act of hostility ought to have been exercised, it does not necessarily follow that mere ignorance of *that fact* would protect the officers from civil responsibility. If by articles, a place or district was put under the King's peace, and an act of hostility was afterwards committed therein, the injured party might have a right to resort to a court of prize; to show that he had been injured by this breach of the peace, and was entitled to compensation; and if the officer acted *through ignorance*, his own government must protect him: for it is the duty of government, if they put a certain district within the King's peace, to take care that due notice shall be given to those persons by whose conduct that peace is to be maintained; and if no such notice has been given, nor due diligence used to give it, and a breach of the peace is committed through the ignorance of those persons, they are to be borne harmless, at the expense of that government whose duty it was to have given that notice."[1]

THE "NYMPH."

Conseil des Prises, 1801.

(*Merlin; Repertoire de Jurisprudence, t.* 25, *p.* 181.)

It was stipulated by the Peace of Amiens, between England and France, that two months should be allowed for the news of the close of the war to reach their respective cruisers in the West Indies. A British vessel was captured before the two months had expired, but after news of the peace had reached the captors, coming, however, through British sources. The ship was restored.

The *Nymph*, a British vessel, was captured by the privateer *Petite-Renommée* at the island of Guadeloupe before the two months granted by the treaty of Amiens for these seas had expired. But the *Petite-Renommée* had received the commission and sailed from Guadeloupe five days after the signing of the treaty of peace had been communicated by the English governor of the island of Dominica to the authorities of Guadeloupe, and acknowledged by the latter. The conseil therefore held this to be a case of bad faith on the part of the captor; and although information of peace was communicated

[1] This case had been in the courts ten or more years previously, but no records of the proceedings were produced. On this account, and from the further fact that the present action was brought against the admiral of the station, instead of against the actual wrongdoer, the court refused to give relief.

by the enemy, it was sufficient to stop any aggressive acts of war until the truth of the news could be ascertained officially. Consequently the *Nymph* was restored with damages.

Conclusions du Commaissaire du Gouvernement. M. Collet-Descotils:—

"Une chaloupe, la *Petite-Renommée*, armée en course, partit du port de la Liberté, île de la Guadeloupe, le 2 frimaire an X, et, le 9 du même mois, aborda le brick Anglais, *la Nymbhe*, à l'ancre dans la rade de l'île de Saint-Christophe, coupa son câble et l'enleva.

"Plusieurs jours auparavant, les préliminaires de la paix avaient été publiés dans les îles Anglaises de ces parages; le capitaine de la frégate Anglaise, *le Tamer*, avait envoyé un parliamentaire à la Guadeloupe pour en donner la nouvelle, qui etait confirmée en même temps par le gouverneur de la Dominique. Tout en accusant réception de ces deux communications au gouvernement Anglais, à la date du 24 brumaire, le mulâtre Pélage qui avait usurpé le gouvernement militaire de la Guadeloupe, se hâta d'expédier des pouvoirs à des corsaires, qui mirent immédiatement à la mer, dans le dessein de profiter de la sécurité des Anglais. Une de ces commissions, délivrée à la *Petite-Renommée*, portait la date du 29 brumaire, et était, par conséquent, postèrieure de cinq jours à la réponse de Pélage. Dans sa protestation contre la capture, le capitaine Anglais declara que la *Petite-Renommée* avait surpris son navire pendant la nuit; qu'apres avoir coupé son câble, les corsaires étaient montés a bord où tout l'equipage dormait, et avaient usé de leurs armes, quoiqu 'aucun des Anglais ne fût armé; qu'ils avaient pillé l'équipage, ainsi que les marchandises de la cargaison.

"Par décision du 24 frimaire an X, le commissaire de la marine au port de la Liberté, assisté du contrôleur de la marine et du sous—commissaire chargé de l'inscription maritime, prononça la confiscation du navire et du chargement, qui furent vendus, et dont le produit fût versé à la caisse des invalides de la marine jusqu' à ce qu'il fut statué définitivement.

"Sur l'appel porté devant les Conseil des prises, le procureur général conclut á l'annulation de la prise. Les armateurs avaient allégue qu'on ne devait reconnaître comme nouvelles de la paix que les nouvelles officielles, c'est à dire émanent du gouvernement; que, sans cela, on serait exposé à devenir victime de la ruse des ennemis et de la confiance qu'on aurait eue dans une fausse nouvelle.

"C'est se tromper étrangement, dit M. Collet-Descotils, commissaire du Gouvernement, que de confondre la perfidie avec la ruse; et ce serait une perfidie dont il n'est point d'exemple dans l'histoire des nations de l'Europe, qu'une fausse nouvelle de paix, donnée officiellement par des commandmants militaires d'une nation avec laquelle le premiere serait en guerre.

"Du reste, je suis loin de prétendre que l'on soit obligé de donner une confiance aveugle aux nouvelles de paix ainsi transmises, et que l'on doive négliger les mesures de sûreté dans les lieux où elles parviennent; mais il y a une grande différence entre se tenir sur une sage défensive, jusqu' à ce qu'on ait reçu des instructions de son propre gouvernement, et se permettre des actes d'oppression, lors surtout que les circonstances rendent plus que probable la nouvelle de la paix, et que la conduite de l'ennemi est telle qu'elle n'offre point de motifs de craindre aucune surprise de sa part. Recevoir de notre ennemi la nouvelle de la paix, et, par consequent, recevoir en même temps l'assurance qu'il n'attaquera plus nos vaisseaux, exige au moins de notre part une suspension d'hostilités offensives : profiter de la sécurité que lui inspire la communication qu'il nous a donnée, pour faire enlever, soit à la mer, soit dans ses ports, ses navires, et sabrer les hommes qui les montent, est un acte de perfidie et de déloyauté qui ne convient qu' à des pirates et qui flétrirait l'honneur du nom Français, s'il demeurait impuni.

"Les armateurs du corsaire ont encore prétendu que toute prise faite avant l'expiration des délais était valable, puisque l'art. 11 des préliminaires fait connaître que ces délais ont été convenus par les puissances contractantes, pour prévenir les plaintes ou les réclamations. Rien de plus erroné que cette opinion. Les prises faites dans les délais portés par l'art. 11 des préliminaires ne peuvent donc être jugées valables, qu'autant que les bâtiments capteurs n'auraient pas eu une connaissance positive de la paix. Cette vérité, conforme aux principes professés par les publicistes que j'ai cités dans mes conclusions sur l'affaire du *Porcher*, est d'une évidence à laquelle on ne peut refuser de se rendre.

"LE CONSEIL déclare nulle, illégale, et contraire au droit des gens, la prise faite par le corsaire Français de la Guadeloupe, *la Petite-Renommée*, du navire Anglais *la Nymphe*."[1]

[1] The similar case of the *Swineherd* (*le Porcher*), Pistoge et Duverdy, i., 140, was that of an English vessel captured in the Indian seas by a French privateer, after the signing of the treaty of Amiens, but before the expiration of the five months allowed for the news of the peace to reach those seas.

In this case the English ship had been fitted out as a privateer. She sailed from Calcutta after the news of the peace had reached that place, and informed the captor of that fact. It was contended further by the claimant that the captor had received notice of the peace from a Portuguese vessel. On the other hand it was held by the Conseil des Prises that no sufficient notice of peace had reached the captor. "Il demeure donc pour constant que la capture est légitimée, d'un côté, par le fait de son antériorité aux époques fixé pour la restitution, tant par les prelim-

THE "THETIS."

CONSEIL DES PRISES, 1801.

(*Pistoye et Duverdy*, I., 148.)

A vessel captured between the dates of the signing of the preliminary treaty of Luneville, and the final ratification of the treaty, restored, on the ground of illegal capture in time of peace.

"La capture de *la Thétis* avait été faite le 8 mars, 1801, vingt-neuf jours après la signature du traité de Lunéville, qui est du 9 février précédent (20 pluviôse an IX); mais huit jours avant que ce traité fût ratifié, ce qui a eu lieu le 16 mars, 1801. Quant à la publication, elle est du 19 mars, 1801.

"Le commissaire du gouvernement a conclu de ces faits qu' à l'époque de la capture nous étions en paix avec la puissance sous le pavillon de laquelle voyageait *la Thétis*, navire autrichien.

"Dire que le traité de Lunéville n'etait pas encore ratifié, et que, par consequent, il ne pouvait pas encore avoir son execution, c'est soutenir une proposition vraiment dérisoire. Sans doute, un traité ne devient définitif entre deux puissances qu'après la ratification; mais le seul bon sens nous dit que, pour parvenir à cette ratification, chaque puissance respective est intéressée à executer sur-le-champ les clauses de ce traité, sans qu' un acte de cette nature, bien plus

inaires que par le traité de paix; de l'autre par le défaut de connaissance suffisantes de la cessation de toute hostilité; qu'au surplus, ce serait étrangement se méprendre sur l'objet de la course et les principes qui la dirigent, que de penser que de simples avis de l'existence de la paix, donnés vaguement en mer à un corsaire, par des navigateurs étrangers, ou sou la foi d'une gazette, dussent, en paralysant ses lettres de marque, être pour lui le signal de l'abandon de la croisière, au risque même de tomber entre les mains de l'ennemi; qu'un semblable effet n'appartient qu'à l'ordre qui lui serait intimé, au nom du gouvernement dont il tient l'autorisation formelle de capturer; que si cependant la communication de la paix lui était faite par la voie de l'ennemi, en vertu d'instructions spéciales et officielles dont il serait porteur, la juste déférence pour les actes émanés de l'autorité d'un souverain déterminerait sans doute le corsaire a respecter cette sauvegarde, pourvu qu'elle fût rèciproque; mais que ce serait être pas trop libéral à son préjudice, et lui enlever arbitrairement le bénéfice des réglements et des traités, que de restituer une prise qu'il a faite dans les termes précis de son droit, et lorsque les avis qu'il aurait reçus ne porteraient point avec eux le cachet de l'authenticité, et encore le gage de sa sécurité particulière." The vessel was therefore condemned as lawful prize.

sérieux qu'une simple trêve, ne produirait pas néanmoins le même effet, puisque l'effet de la trêve est de suspendre toutes les hostilités reciproques. Or, si la trêve, qui n'est qu'un repos momentané, suspend les hostilités, comment pourrait—on s'en permettre après la signature d'un traité qui n'a d'autre but que de réclamer une paix durable?

"A mon avis, une pareille proposition répugne autant à la politique qu'au bon sens. Mais, dira-t-on, ce traité ne peut tout au plus être exécutoire pour les sujets des puissances contractantes que du moment où il leur est légalement connu. D'abord, je fais observer ici que le traité dont est cas ayant une existence de vingt-neuf jours a l'epoque de la prise, il est difficile de penser que le corsaire n'en fût pas instruit. En second lieu, en supposant qu'il n'en fût pas réellement instruit qu'en résulterait-il? Rien, sinon que sa bonne foi le mettrait à l'abri des domages-intérêts à l'égard du capturé; mais non pas que la capture fût valide, puisqu' une capture ne peut être valide que quand elle est faite sur un ennemi. Or, nous ne pouvons pas qualifier d'ennemi celui avec lequel nous avons signé un traité de paix: s'il en était autrement, on adjugerait à un corsaire une prise que le gouvernement serait obligé de restituer.

"Mais, a-t-on dit encore, la cargaison doit au moins encore être réputée ennemie: 1° parce, qu'elle comportait des objets de contrebande; 2° parce qu'elle était destinée pour des ennemis.

"A cela, je crois devoir faire observer: 1° que pour qu'une cargaison soit réputée de contrebande, il faut que les objets prohibés surpassent les trois quarts de cette cargaison, et ici 50 caisses de fusils se sont trouvées confondues entre 120 caisses de vitriol et une quantité considérable de bougies, de livres et de tables de pierre; 2° les armes ne sont des objets de contrebande que lorsqu'elles sont destinées pour un port ennemi; et, à l' instant de la capture de *la Thétis* qui se rendait en Sicile, un armistice était signé entre la Republique et le roi de Naples. Il est vrai que cet armistice date du 29 pluviôse an IX, c'est-à-dire treize jours après la sortie de *la Thétis* de Venise; en sorte que, lorsque ce navire était en armement, nous étions encore en guerre ouverte avec la puissance pour les Etats de laquelle elle était destinée.

"Mais, outre que ce serait vraiment une question que celle de savoir si on doit juger une prise ou d'aprés l'état de choses existant à l'epoque de son armement, ou d'aprés celui existant au moment de sa capture; d'un autre côté, dès lorsque les caisses de fusils trouvées à bord de *la Thétis* ne montaient pas aux trois quarts de sa cargaison, elles ne pouvaient pas en faire confisquer la totalité de la cargaison, et seraient tout au plus, elles seules, sujettes à confiscation.

"Je conclus à la restitution du navire et de sa cargaison.

"Du 7 ventôse an IX.—Decision du Conseil des prises, qui invalide la prise de *la Thétis.*"

THE "PROTECTOR."

SUPREME COURT OF THE UNITED STATES, 1871.

(12 *Wallace*, 700.)

The beginning and termination of the civil war in the United States in reference to statutes of limitation, is to be determined by some public act of the political department.

The war did not begin or close at the same time in all the States.

The question in this case was whether the suit was barred by the statute of limitations in Alabama. As the statute did not run during the period of the war, it was necessary to determine precisely the dates of beginning and end of the war.

Judgment,—CHASE, C. J.:—

"The question, in the present case is, when did the rebellion begin and end? In other words, what space of time must be considered as excepted from the operation of the statute of limitations by the war of the rebellion?

"Acts of hostility by the insurgents occurred at periods so various, and of such different degrees of importance, and in parts of the country so remote from each other, both at the commencement and the close of the late civil war, that it would be difficult, if not impossible, to say on what precise day it began or terminated. It is necessary, therefore, to refer to some public act of the political departments of the government to fix the dates; and, for obvious reasons, those of the executive department, which may be, and, in fact, was, at the commencement of hostilities, obliged to act during the recess of Congress, must be taken.

"The proclamation of intended blockade by the President may, therefore, be assumed as marking the first of these dates, and the proclamation that the war had closed, as marking the second. But the war did not begin or close at the same time in all the States. There were two proclamations of intended blockade: the first of the 19th of April, 1861 (12 Stat. at Large, 1258), embracing the States of South Carolina, Georgia, Alabama, Florida, Mississippi, Louisiana and Texas; the second, of the 27th of April, 1861 (12 Stat. at L., 1259), embracing the States of Virginia, and North Carolina; and there were two proclamations declaring that the war had closed; one issued on the 2d of April, 1866, (14 Stat. at Large, 811), embracing the States of Virginia, North Carolina, South Carolina, Georgia, Florida, Mississippi, Tennessee, Alabama, Louisiana, and Arkansas, and the other issued on the 20th of August, 1866 (13 Stat. at Large, 814), embracing the State of Texas.

"In the absence of more certain criteria, of equally general application, we must take the dates of these proclamations as ascertaining the commencement and the close of the war in the states mentioned in them. Applying this rule to the case before us, we find that the war began in Alabama on the 19th of April, 1861, and ended on the 2d of April, 1866. More than five years, therefore, had elapsed from the close of the war till the 17th of May, 1871, when this appeal was brought. The motion to dismiss, therefore, must be

"Granted."[1]

[1] See *Brown* v. *Hiatts*, 15 Wallace, 177.

In the case of *Philips* v. *Hatch*, 1 Dillon, 571 (1871), the United States Circuit Court for Iowa held that a contract entered into in the spring of 1866 between a resident of the State of Iowa and a resident of the State of Texas, was void as a contract between enemies.

CHAPTER III.

RELATIONS BETWEEN BELLIGERENTS AND NEUTRALS.

SECTION 40.—BELLIGERENT CAPTURE IN NEUTRAL WATERS.

THE "ANNA."

HIGH COURT OF ADMIRALTY, 1805.

(5 *C. Robinson*, 373.)

The capture of the ship of an enemy in neutral waters is illegal; and the ship will be restored by the prize court of the captor.

Territorial waters extend three miles from the shore, or from islands near shore.

This was the case of a ship under American colors, with a cargo of logwood, and about 13,000 dollars on board, bound from the Spanish main to New Orleans, and captured by the *Minerva* privateer near the mouth of the river Mississippi. A claim was given under the direction of the American Minister for the ship and cargo, as taken within the territory of the United States, at the distance of a mile and a half from the western shore of the principal entrance of the Mississippi, and within view of a port protected by a gun, and where is stationed an officer of the United States.

The following is an extract from the judgment of Sir W. SCOTT:—

"When the ship was brought into this country a claim was given of a grave nature, alleging a violation of the territory of the United States of America. This great leading fact has very properly been made a matter of much discussion, and charts have been laid before the court to show the place of capture, though with different representations from the adverse parties. The capture was made, it seems, at the mouth of the river Mississippi, and, as it is contended in the claim, within the boundaries of the United States. We all know that the rule of law on this subject is 'terræ dominium finitur, ubi finitur armorum vis,' and since the introduction of fire-arms that distance has usually been recognized to be about three miles from the shore. But it so happens in this case, that a question arises as to what is to be deemed the shore, since there are a number of little mud islands composed of earth and trees drifted down by the river, which form a kind of portico to the main-land. It is contended that these are not to be considered as any part of the territory of America, that they are a sort of 'no man's land,' not of consistency enough to support the purposes of life, uninhabited, and resorted to, only, for shooting and taking birds' nests. It is argued that the line of territory is to be taken only from the Balise, which is a fort raised on made land by the former Spanish possessors. I am of a different opinion; I think that the protection of territory is to be reckoned from these islands; and that they are the natural appendages of the coast on which they border, and from which, indeed, they are formed. Their elements are derived immediately from the territory, and on the principle of alluvium and increment, on which so much is to be found in the books of law. *Quod vis fluminis de tuo prædio detraxerit*, and *vicino prædio attulerit, palam tuum remanet*, even if it had been carried over to an adjoining territory. Consider what the consequence would be if lands of this description were not considered as appendant to the main-land, and as comprised within the bounds of territory.

"If they do not belong to the United States of America, any other power might occupy them; they might be embanked and fortified. What a thorn would this be in the side of America! It is physically possible at least that they might be so occupied by European nations, and then the command of the river would be no longer in America, but in such settlements. The possibility of such a consequence is enough to expose the fallacy of any arguments that are addressed to show that these islands are not to be considered as part of the territory of America. Whether they are composed of earth or solid rock, will not vary the right of dominion, for the right of dominion does not depend upon the texture of the soil.

"I am of opinion that the right of territory is to be reckoned from those islands. That being established, it is not denied that the actual capture took place within the distance of three miles from the islands, and at the very threshold of the river. But it is said that the act of capture is to be carried back to the commencement of the pursuit, and that if a contest begins before, it is lawful for a belligerent cruiser to follow, and to seize his prize within the territory of a neutral state. And the authority of Bynkershoek is cited on this point. True it is, that that great man does intimate an opinion of his own to that effect; but with many qualifications, and as an opinion, which he did not find to have been adopted by any other writers. I confess I should have been inclined to have gone along with him, to this extent, that if a cruiser, which had before acted in a manner entirely unexceptionable, and free from all violation of territory, had summoned a vessel to submit to examination and search, and that vessel had fled to such places as these, entirely uninhabited, and the cruiser had without injury or annoyance to any person whatever, quietly taken possession of his prey, it would be stretching the point too hardly against the captor, to say that on this account only it should be held an illegal capture. If nothing objectionable had appeared in the conduct of the captors before, the mere following to such a place as this is, would, I think, not invalidate a seizure otherwise just and lawful.

"But that brings me to a part of the case, on which I am of opinion that the privateer has laid herself open to great reprehension. Captors must understand that they are not to station themselves in the mouth of a neutral river, for the purpose of exercising the rights of war from that river, much less in the river itself. It appears from the privateer's own log-book that this vessel has done both; and as to any attempt to shelter this conduct under the example of King's ships, which I do not believe, and which, if true, would be no justification to others, captors must, I say, be admonished, that the practice is altogether indefensible, and that if King's ships should be guilty of such misconduct, they would be as much subject to censure as other cruisers.

"It is unnecessary to go over all the entries in the log. The captors appear by their own description *to have been standing off and on*, obtaining information at the Balise, overhauling vessels in their course down the river, and making the river as much subservient to the purposes of war, as if it had been a river of their own country. This is an inconvenience which the states of America are called upon to resist, and which this court is bound on every principle to discourage and correct.

"With respect to one vessel, it appears that the *Bilboa*, under Spanish colors, and an undoubted Spanish ship, had been captured and carried into the river; and it was stated in an affidavit which was exhibited to account for the absence of the usual witnesses in that case, *that the prisoners had escaped.* The cause was brought on upon the evidence of the releasing witnesses under this representation. It now appears by an entry in this log, '*that the prisoners were set on shore;*' an act highly unjustifiable, in its own nature, independent of the deception with which it has been accompanied. The prisoners are the King's prisoners, and captors are particularly enjoined by the instructions not to release any prisoners belonging to the ships of the enemy, and they violate their duty whenever they do. When I advert to the imposition that has been put upon the court in that transaction, how can I trust myself to any representation coming from the same persons. Indeed, I think, I can perceive strong traits of bad faith running throughout the whole conduct of the captors in the present case. In answer to the complaint that has been made against the captors for bringing this prize to England, it was said, that it was done at the desire of the master of the captured vessel; though in the affidavit of the master, which is not contradicted, it is sworn, 'that the captors offered to set him on shore, but that he refused to be separated from his cargo.'

"The conduct of the captors has on all points been highly reprehensible. Looking to all the circumstances of previous misconduct, I feel myself bound to pronounce, that there has been a violation of territory, and that as to the question of property, there was not sufficient ground of seizure; and that these acts of misconduct have been further aggravated, by bringing the vessel to England, without any necessity that can justify such a measure. In such a case it would be falling short of the justice due to the violated rights of America, and to the individuals who have sustained injury by such misconduct, if I did not follow up the restitution which has passed on the former day, with a decree of costs and damages."

THE "GENERAL ARMSTRONG."

LOUIS NAPOLEON, ARBITRATOR, 1851.

(2 *Wharton's Digest*, 604.)

Where a capture has been made in neutral waters, claims for damages by the injured belligerent against the neutral state not allowed, if the captured ship resisted, instead of asking protection of the neutral.

"The destruction of the American armed brig *General Armstrong* by a British man-of-war, in the harbor of Fayal, in 1814, gave rise to a long-continuing correspondence, which resulted, in 1851, in an agreement to refer the claims growing out of it to the 'arbitrament of a sovereign, potentate, or chief of some nation in amity with both the high contracting parties.' The President of the French Republic (afterwards Napoleon III.) was selected as the arbiter. This decision was adverse to the United States."

The following is a translation of the material parts of the decision:

"Considering that it is clear, in fact, that the United States were at war with Her Britannic Majesty, and Her Most Faithful Majesty preserving her neutrality, the American brig the *General Armstrong*, commanded by Captain Reid, legally provided with letters of marque, and armed for privateering purposes, having sailed from the port of New York, did, on the 26th of September, 1814, cast anchor in the port of Fayal, one of the Azores Islands, constituting part of Her Most Faithful Majesty's dominions.

"That it is equally clear that, on the evening of the same day, an English squadron, commanded by Commodore Lloyd, entered the same port;

"That it is no less certain that, during the following night, regardless of the rights of sovereignty and neutrality of Her Most Faithful Majesty, a bloody encounter took place between the Americans and the English; and that on the following day, the 27th of September, one of the vessels belonging to the English squadron came to range herself near the American privateer for the purpose of cannonading her; that this demonstration, accompanied by the act, determined Captain Reid, followed by his crew, to abandon his vessel and to destroy her;

"Considering that if it be clear that, on the night of the 26th of September, some English long-boats, commanded by Lieutenant Robert Fausset, of the British navy, approached the American brig, the *General Armstrong*, it is not certain that the men who manned the boats aforesaid were provided with arms and ammunition;

"That it is evident, in fact, from the documents which have been exhibited, that the aforesaid long-boats, having approached the American brig, the crew of the latter, after having hailed them and summoned them to be off, immediately fired upon them, and that some men were killed on board the English boats, and others wounded —some of whom mortally—without any attempt having been made on the part of the crew of the boats to repel at once force by force;

"Considering that the report of the governor of Fayal proves that the American captain did not apply to the Portuguese government for protection until blood had already been shed, and, when the fire had ceased, the brig *General Armstrong* came to anchor under the castle at a distance of a stone's-throw; that the said governor states that it was only then that he was informed of what was passing in the port; that he did, on several occasions, interpose with Commodore Lloyd with a view of obtaining a cessation of hostilities, and to complain of the violation of a neutral territory;

"That he effectively prevented some American sailors, who

were on land, from embarking on board the American brig for the purpose of prolonging a conflict which was contrary to the law of nations;

"That the weakness of the garrison of the island and the constant dismantling of the forts, by the removal of the guns which guarded them, rendered all armed intervention on his part impossible;

"Considering, in this state of things, that Captain Reid, not having applied from the beginning for the intervention of the neutral sovereign, and having had recourse to arms in order to repel an unjust aggression, of which he pretended to be the object, has thus failed to respect the neutrality of the territory of the foreign sovereign, and released that sovereign of the obligation in which he was, to afford him protection by any other means than that of a pacific intervention;

"From which it follows that the government of Her Most Faithful Majesty cannot be held responsible for the results of the collision which took place in contempt of her rights of sovereignty, in violation of the neutrality of her territory, and without the local officers or lieutenants having been required in proper time, and enabled to grant aid and protection to those having a right to the same;

"Therefore, we have decided, and we declare, that the claim presented by the government of the United States against Her Most Faithful Majesty has no foundation, and that no indemnity is due by Portugal in consequence of the loss of the American brig, the *General Armstrong*, armed for privateering purposes."

THE "PERLE."

CONSEIL DES PRISES, AN VIII.

(*Pistoye et Duverdy*, I., 100.)

A belligerent capture in neutral waters, held to be illegal, whether under the guns of a fort or on the undefended coast; and the captured ship will be restored by the courts (French) of the captor's country.

Le navire *la Perle*, sous pavillon américain, parti de New York pour Saint-Sébastien, sous la consignation de Jean Holmière, fut pris par le corsaire *l'Effronté*, le 30 nivôse an VII. Le corsaire *la Légère*, voulant concourir à cette prise, jeta quelques hommes à bord de ce navire, qui fut conduit le même jour au port de Socoa.

Le capturé prétendait que la prise, avait été faite sous le canon du fort Saint-Sébastien, et il se plaignait de cette violation du droit des gens.

Le capteur soutenait, au contraire, que le droit des gens n'avait pas été violé, et que la prise n'avait été faite qu'à trois lieues de Saint-Sébastien.

En fait, le capturé avait raison, la capture avait eu lieu dans les eaux espagnoles. M. Portalis, commissaire du gouvernement, déposa les conclusions suivantes:

"La capture du navire *la Perle* n'ayant été faite qu'à une demi-lieue d'un port d'Espagne, que faut-il penser de la validité ou de l'invalidité de cette capture?

"Il serait inutile de discuter les divers systèmes qui ont été publiés relativement aux droits de chaque souverain sur les mers qui environnent son empire. Ces systèmes n'offrent que des questions d'école, abandonnées depuis longtemps à la dispute et à la discussion des publicistes.

"Mais, par le droit conventionnel des puissances maritimes et par la coutume générale, il est reconnu qu'un corsaire ne peut se permettre aucun acte d'hostilité, ni même aucune visite, contre un navire ennemi ou pretendu tel, si ce navire n'est à une distance convenable du territoire de toute puissance neutre. Cette distance a été fixée à deux lieues.

"Plusieurs auteurs avaient déterminé la distance que tout armateur en course doit respecter, par la portée du canon; mais on a très-judicieusement observé qu'il est plus raisonnable de décider que toute prise faite à moins de deux lieues de distance des côtes du pays neutre est contre le droit des gens quoiqu'il n'y ait sur la côte ni forteresse ni canons; car le territoire neutre doit être respecté, indépendamment de la force, et à cause de lui-même.

"Il faut rendre justice à nos temps modernes: on a cherché à diminuer les maux de la guerre. Ce sont moins les jalousies de juridiction que les principes d'une philosophie plus humaine qui ont fixé le droit conventionnel des puissances maritimes sur les égards respectifs qu'elles se doivent: de là, elles ont cherché à transformer les prérogatives de leur souverainete en droit d'asile pour les navigateurs; et, sous ce point de vue, les rivalités même de pouvoir, avouées par l'humanité, ont mérité d'être consacrées comme utiles au bien du commerce et au bonheur universel des nations.

"Des doutes s'élèvant encore sur la fixation du territoire de chaque souverain, quand il ne s'agit que de l'intérêt particulier de ses Etats. Ainsi, le voeu des publicistes les plus estimables est de restreindre le plus que l'on peut les prétentions de territoire, lorsque ces prétentions ne sont motivées que par des idées ambitieuses ou fiscales : mais comme, dans la question présente, la règle des deux lieues suppose moins dans les souverains le désir d'étendre leur domination que celui de protéger le malheur et de lui offrir un asile cette règle a été applaudie et adoptée comme un vrai bien public.

"Dans la cause présente, M. l'Ambassadeur d'Espagne a réclamé. Le ministre des relations extérieures, écrivant au ministre de la justice, l'a invité à rappeler les règles internationales à tous les tribunaux qui étaient alors chargés de la matière des prises. La capture soumise à la décision du Conseil ne peut donc être autorisée, si elle a été faite à moins de deux lieues de distance d'un port ou d'une côte espagnole. Or, il est démontré, en point de fait, que la capture du navire *la Perle* a été faite à demi-lieue du port de Saint-Sébastien ou de celui du Passage. Donc, elle offre une violation manifeste du droit des gens et de la foi publique; et ce n'est pas vis-à-vis d'un allié fidèle que l'on pent tolérer une pareille violation, aussi condamnable aux yeux de l'humanité qu'à ceux de la politique.

"Je conclus à ce que l'arrestation et la prise du navire *la Perle* soient déclarées invalides.

"Le Conseil décide que la prise du navire *la Perle* et de son chargement, faite par les corsaires francais *la Légère* et *l'Effronté*, est nulle et de nul effet."

THE "ANNE."

SUPREME COURT OF THE UNITED STATES, 1818.

(3 *Wheaton*, 435.)

If the captured ship first commences hostilities in neutral waters, she thereby forfeits neutral protection.

A capture made in neutral waters is, as between enemies, deemed to all intents and purposes a legal capture. The neutral sovereign can alone call its validity in question.

This was the case of a British ship captured while lying at anchor near the Spanish part of the island of St. Domingo, by the American privateer *Ultor*.

Extract from the judgment of STORY, J. :—

"The claim of the Spanish government for the violation of its neutral territory being thus disposed of, it is next to be considered whether the British claimant can assert any title founded upon that circumstance.

"By the return of peace, the claimant became rehabilitated with the capacity to sustain a suit in the courts of this country; and the argument is, that a capture made in a neutral territory is void; and, therefore, the title by capture being invalid, the British owner has a right to restitution. The difficulty of this argument rests in the incorrectness of the premises. A capture made within neutral waters is, as between enemies, deemed, to all intents and purposes, rightful; it is only by the neutral sovereign that its legal validity can be called in question; and as to him and him only, is it to be considered void. The enemy has no rights whatsoever, and if the neutral sovereign omits or declines to interpose a claim, the property is condemnable, *jure belli*, to the captors. This is the clear result of the authorities; and the doctrine rests on well established principles of public law.

"There is one other point in the case which, if all other difficulties were removed, would be decisive against the claimant. It is a fact, that the captured ship first commenced hostilities against the privateer. This is admitted on all sides; and it is no excuse to assert that it was done under a mistake of the national character of the privateer, even if this were entirely made out in the evidence. While the ship was lying in neutral waters, she was bound to abstain from all hostilities, except in self-defence. The privateer had an equal title with herself to the neutral protection, and was in no default in approaching the coast without showing her national character. It was a violation of that neutrality which the captured ship was bound to observe, to commence hostilities for any purpose in these waters; for no vessel coming thither was bound to submit to search, or to account to her for her conduct or character. When, therefore, she commenced hostilities, she forfeited the neutral protection, and the capture was no injury for which any redress could be rightfully sought from the neutral sovereign.

"The conclusion from all these views of the case is, that the ship and cargo ought to be condemned as good prize of war." [1]

[1] In the case of the *Lilla*, 2 Sprague, 177, it is said that, "it is undoubtedly true that no private person can rest a claim for the restoration of prize in the courts of the captor on the ground that the capture was made in neutral waters, and that the neutral nation whose rights have been infringed alone can interpose." See also, The *Sir William Peel*, 5 Wall., 517; The *Adela*, Wall., 266.

In the case of the British ship *Grange*, captured in Delaware Bay by a French privateer (1793), it was held by Attorney-General Randolph (1 Op. Att-Gen., 15,) that if the captured ship was brought within the jurisdiction of the United States, it was their duty as neutrals to restore her to the owners. To the same effect, see *La Estrella*, 4 Wheaton, 298.

SECTION 41.—EQUIPMENT OF VESSELS OF WAR IN NEUTRAL TERRITORY.

UNITED STATES NEUTRALITY ACTS OF 1794 AND 1818.

(*U. S. Statutes at Large*, I., 381, *and Revised Stat.*, § 5289.)

Act of June 5, 1794:

SECTION 3.—"If any person shall within any of the ports, harbors, bays, rivers, or other waters of the United States, fit out and arm, or attempt to fit out and arm, or procure to be fitted out and armed, or shall knowingly be concerned in the furnishing, fitting out or arming of any ship or vessel with intent that such ship or vessel shall be employed in the service of any foreign prince or state [or of any colony, district or people], to cruise or commit hostilities upon the subjects, citizens or property of another foreign prince or state [or of any colony, district or people], with whom the United States are at peace, or shall issue or deliver a commission within the territory or jurisdiction of the United States for any ship or vessel to the intent that she may be employed as aforesaid, every such person so offending shall, upon conviction, be adjudged guilty of a high misdemeanor, and shall be fined and imprisoned at the discretion of the court in which the conviction shall be had, so as the fine to be imposed shall in no case be more than five thousand [ten thousand by the act of 1818] dollars, and the term of imprisonment shall not exceed three years, and every such ship or vessel with her tackle, apparel and furniture together with all materials, arms, ammunition and stores which may have been procured for the building and equipment thereof shall be forfeited, one-half to the use of any person who shall give information of the offence, and the other half to the use of the United States.

SECTION 7.—By this section the President is authorized to employ the land and naval forces or militia to execute the law.

On account of the complaints of Spain and Portugal (1815-17), of infractions of neutrality on the part of citizens of the United States in the war which those states were then waging with their revolted South American colonies, President Madison sent a special message on the subject to Congress, and the result was the more stringent act of April 20, 1818. From a suggestion of the Spanish Minister, that the South American provinces in revolt, and not recognized as independent, might not be included in the word "State," the words "colony, district, or people," were added, as given in brackets above. The new clauses of the act of 1818 of chief importance are those authorizing the detention of vessels on suspicion, and requiring the owners to give bonds on clearance.

Act of 1818 (Revised Statutes, § 5289):

SECTION 10.—"The owners or consignees of every armed vessel sailing out of the ports of the United States, belonging wholly or in part to citizens thereof, shall, before clearing out the same, give bond to the United States, with sufficient sureties, in double the amount of the value of vessel and cargo on board, including armament, conditioned that the vessel shall not be employed by such owners to cruise or commit hostilities against the subjects, citizens, or property of any foreign prince or state, or of any colony, district, or people, with whom the United States are at peace."

SECTION 11.—"The several collectors of customs shall detain any vessel manifestly built for warlike purposes, and about to depart the United States, the cargo of which principally consists of arms and munitions of war, when the number of men shipped on board, or other circumstances, render it probable that such vessel is intended to be employed by the owners to cruise or commit hostilities upon the subjects, citizens, or property of any foreign prince, etc., with whom the United States are at peace, until the decision of the President is had thereon, or until the owner gives such bond and security as is required of the owners of armed vessels by the preceding section."

BRITISH FOREIGN ENLISTMENT ACTS, OF 1819 AND 1870.

(59 *Geo.* III., c. 69, *and* 33 *and* 34 *Vict.*, 90.)

Act of July 3, 1819.—SECTION 7.

"If any person, within any part of the United Kingdom, or in any part of His Majesty's dominions beyond the seas, shall, without the leave and license of His Majesty for that purpose first had and obtained as aforesaid, equip, furnish, fit out, or arm, or attempt or endeavor to equip, furnish, fit out, or arm, or procure to be equipped, furnished, fitted out, or armed, or shall knowingly aid, assist, or be concerned in the equipping, furnishing, fitting out, or arming of any ship or vessel, with intent, or in order that such ship or vessel shall be employed in the service of any foreign prince, state, or potentate, or of any foreign colony, province, or part of any province, or people; or if any person or persons exercising or assuming to exercise any powers of government in or over any foreign state, colony, province, or part of any province or people, as a transport or store-ship, or with intent to cruise or commit hostilities against any prince, state, or potentate, or against the persons exercising or assuming to exercise the powers of government in any colony, province, or part of any province or country, or against the inhabitants of any foreign colony, province, or part of any province or country, with whom His Majesty shall not then be at war; or shall, within the United Kingdom, or any of His Majesty's dominions, or in any settlement, colony, territory, island, or place belonging or subject to His Majesty, issue or deliver any commission for a ship or vessel, to the intent that such ship or vessel shall be employed as aforesaid, every such person so offending shall be deemed guilty of a misdemeanor, and shall, upon conviction thereof, upon any information or indictment, be punished by fine and imprisonment, or either of them, at the discretion of the court in which such offender shall be convicted; and every such ship or vessel, with the tackle, apparel, and furniture, together with all the materials, arms, ammunition, and stores, which may belong to or be on board of any such ship or vessel, shall be forfeited, and it shall be lawful for any officer of His Majesty's customs or excise, or any officer of His Majesty's navy, who is by law empowered to make seizures, for any forfeiture incurred under any of the laws of customs, or excise, or the laws of trade and navigation, to seize such ships and vessels aforesaid, and in such places and in such manner in which the officers of His Majesty's customs or excise, and the officers of His Majesty's navy are empowered respectively to make seizures under the laws of customs and excise, or under the laws of trade and navigation; and that every such ship and vessel, with the tackle, apparel, and furniture, together with all the materials, arms, ammunition, and stores which may belong to or be on board of such ship, or vessel, may be prosecuted and condemned in the like manner, and in such courts as ships or vessels may be prosecuted and condemned for any breach of the laws made for the protection of the revenues of customs and excise, or of the laws of trade and navigation.

Section 8 imposes penalties for the augmentation of force in British ports.

The defect in this act was in the procedure under it rather than in the intention of the act itself. The evidence required in order to arrest or detain a vessel must be sufficient to satisfy a jury of the probable breach of the provisions of the act; and such evidence may be difficult to obtain. The local officers were wary of taking action for which they might be held liable in damages. The act of 1870 removed this defect of procedure, as well as any ambiguity there might be in the act itself. The question of the breach of the act is not to be determined by the mere "intent" of the builder.

Act of 1870:

SECTION 8.—"If any person within Her Majesty's dominions, etc., (1) Builds or agrees to build, or causes to be built, any ship with intent or knowledge or having reasonable cause to believe that the same shall or will be employed in the military or naval service of any foreign State at war with any friendly State; or

"(2) Issues or delivers any commission for any ship with intent or knowledge, etc.; or

"(3) Equips any ships with intent or knowledge, etc.; or

"(4) Despatches, or causes or allows to be despatched, any ship with intent or knowledge, etc.

"Such persons shall be deemed to have committed an offence against this Act, etc."

Section 23 empowers the Secretary of State on "reasonable and probable cause for believing" that a ship is being built contrary to this Act, to issue a warrant to seize and search such ship and to detain the same until it has been either condemned or released by process of law, or in manner hereinafter mentioned.

Section 24 provides that "where it is represented to any local authority" that there is reasonable and probable cause for believing that a ship has been or is being built, commissioned or equipped contrary to this Act, it shall be the duty of such local authority to detain such ship, and forthwith to communicate the fact of such detention to the Secretary of State or chief executive authority, who may then issue a warrant for detention, or release the vessel.

THE "CASSIUS" OR "LES JUMEAUX."

1794—1796.

(3 *Dallas*, 121; *Wharton's State Trials*, 93.)

The questions in respect to this vessel are discussed in the cases of *United States* v. *Guinet*, Wharton's State Trials, 93; *United States* v. *Peters*, 3 Dallas, 121; and *Ketland* v. *The Cassius*, 2 Dallas, 365.

This was the first case under the neutrality act of 1794. Originally a British cutter, this vessel came into the hands of French owners, who brought her to Philadelphia as a merchant vessel, though carrying several guns. She was here repaired, and was being fitted out with additional guns and munitions when an attempt was made to arrest her; but making her escape, she proceeded to San Domingo—then a French island—where she was sold to the French government, February 4th, 1795, her armament completed, and regularly commissioned as a ship of war, *le Cassius*. August 4, 1794, she came to Philadelphia. A civil suit in admiralty for damages was immediately brought against her by the owners of the *William Lindsay*, a vessel that the *Cassius* had captured in May of that year. On a writ of prohibition from the Supreme Court the vessel was released (*U. S.* v. *Peters*); but a new libel was immediately filed in the Circuit Court by one of the former plaintiffs, on the ground of illegal equipment of the vessel the year before. At the October term, 1796, the question arose, whether the Circuit Court could take original cognizance of informations for forfeiture under the Act of 1794; and the court dismissed the proceedings, on the ground that such proceedings must be instituted in the District Court. No further action was taken in the courts; and it will thus be seen that the question of international law was left undecided. The French minister, M. Adet, had dismantled the ship and had formally abandoned her to the government of the United States. The practical result was that a foreign ship of war was libeled and detained by the courts of the United States, and the Federal Executive seemed unable to prevent it.

In the *United States* v. *Guinet*, the accused was tried and condemned to fine and imprisonment for aiding in fitting out the *Cassius* in contravention of the Act of 1794.

LA "AMISTAD DE RUES."

SUPREME COURT OF THE UNITED STATES, 1820.

(5 *Wheaton*, 385.)

A civil court of a neutral country cannot adjudicate upon the validity of a capture *jure belli*, as between the captor and the prize. Its only function is to vindicate the offended sovereignty of its own country, when the capture was made in violation of its neutrality.

"A Venezuelan privateer captured a Spanish vessel on the high seas, and sent her towards New Orleans. On her way, she was taken possession of by a United States ship, and carried into that port. She was there libelled by the Spanish owner in the Court of Admiralty for restitution, on the ground that the privateer which captured her had increased its force within the United States before the capture, in violation of the neutrality laws. The court decreed restitution, and made a further decree condemning the commander of the privateer to pay damages to the owner of the vessel for loss occasioned by the capture. An appeal from both decrees was taken to the Supreme Court. That court, on examination of the proofs, decided that the privateer had not violated our neutrality laws by the work done upon her, and dismissed the libel. This was, it will be seen, only a decision on a question of evidence; and by that decision the whole suit failed. But STORY, J., in delivering the opinion of the court, thought proper to go beyond what was necessary for terminating the suit, and said, that, if the privateer had violated our neutrality laws, so as to have warranted the decree of restitution of the prize, that would not have justified the decree for damages. In explanation of this distinction, the learned judge shows that a civil court of a neutral country cannot adjudicate upon the validity of a capture *jure belli*, as between the captor and the prize. Its only function is to vindicate the offended sovereignty of its own country. If a prize is taken in war, in violation of the territory or other rights of a neutral, the neutral may undo the act, and put the parties in *statu quo ante*, by releasing the prize and restoring it to the owner. And the owner of the prize may demand that. The neutral does this solely to vindicate its own sovereignty, and not with any regard to the validity or invalidity of the capture as between the parties. Into that, it need not and cannot inquire. The fact that a capture is made in violation of the rights of a neutral sovereign, is no legal objection to the capture, as between the parties. Consequently, the neutral court cannot award damages to the owner of the captured vessel, as for a capture made without probable cause, or as otherwise illegal. The neutral nation should fairly execute its own laws, and give no asylum to the property unjustly captured. It is bound, therefore, to restore the property, if found within its own ports. Beyond this, it is not bound to interpose between the belligerents." (Quoted from Dana's Wheaton, p. 552, note.) [1]

[1] In the case of *The Nereyda*, 8 Wheaton, 108 (1828), a Spanish ship of war was captured by the privateer *Irresistible*, which was fitted out, owned, and commanded by American citizens, cruising under a commission from Artigas, as chief of the Oriental Republic of Rio de la Plata. The prize was taken to Margarita, an island of Venezuela, and there condemned as prize, Venezuela being an ally of the Oriental Republic. She was there commissioned as a Venezuelan privateer, and came to Baltimore. Here she was libelled on behalf of the King

THE "SANTISSIMA TRINIDAD."

SUPREME COURT OF THE UNITED STATES, 1822.

(7 *Wheaton*, 283.)

Held, that neutral citizens may send armed vessels to belligerent ports for sale, provided it be done as a *bona fide* commercial transaction, a ship in this situation being considered as merely an article of contraband of war.

The augmentation of the force of a belligerent cruiser, in neutral territory, is illegal; and will entail the restoration of a prize made by such vessel, if brought within the jurisdiction of the offended neutral.

This was a libel filed by the consul of Spain, in the district court of Virginia, in April, 1817, against eighty-nine bales of cochineal, two bales of jalap, and one box of vanilla, originally constituting part of the cargoes of the Spanish ships *Santissima Trinidad* and *St. Ander*, and alleged to be unlawfully and piratically taken out of those vessels on the high seas by a squadron consisting of two armed vessels called the *Independencia del Sud* and the *Altravida*, and manned and commanded by persons assuming themselves to be citizens of the United Provinces of the Rio de la Plata. The libel was filed, in behalf of the original Spanish owners, by Don Pablo Chacon, consul of his Catholic Majesty for the port of Norfolk; and as amended, it insisted upon restitution, principally for three reasons:

(1) That the commanders of the capturing vessels, the *Independencia* and the *Altravida*, were native citizens of the United States, and were prohibited by our treaty with Spain of 1795, from taking commissions to cruise against that power. (2) That the said capturing vessels were owned in the United States, and were originally

of Spain on the ground that the *Irresistible* had been illegally fitted out in an American port. A claim was set up by one Franceschi, who alleged that he had bought her at the prize sale. The Supreme Court (STORY, J., giving the opinion) held that this purchase was not proved, and that she was still in the hands and ownership of the owners of the *Irresistible*; that their title was not improved by the condemnation, if valid otherwise; and restored her to the King of Spain. (Dana's Wheaton, 555, note.)

Other early cases in the United States courts on this question are: *The Betsey*, Bee, 67; *The Brothers*, Bee, 76; *The Nancy*, Bee, 73; *The Sloop Betsey*, 3 Dallas, 6; *The Magdalena*, 1796 (*Talbot* v. *Jansen*, 3 Dallas, 133); *The Alfred*, 1796, 3 Dallas, 307; *The Phœbe Ann*, 1796, 3 Dallas, 319; *The Invincible*, 1816, 1 Wheaton, 238; *Bello Corrunes*, 1821, 6 Wheaton, 152; *Gran Para*, 1822, 7 Wheaton, 471; *Arrogante Barcelones*, 1822, 7 Wheaton, 496; *The Fanny*, 1824, 9 Wheaton, 658.

equipped, fitted out, armed and manned in the United States, contrary to law. (3) That their force and armament had been illegally augmented within the United States.

The district court, upon the hearing of the cause, decreed restitution to the original Spanish owners. That sentence was affirmed in the circuit court, and from the decree of the latter the cause was brought by appeal to this court.

Judgment,—STORY, J.:—

"Upon the argument at the bar several questions have arisen, which have been deliberately considered by the court; and its judgment will now be pronounced. The first in the order, in which we think it most convenient to consider the cause, is, whether the *Independencia* is in point of fact a public ship, belonging to the government of Buenos Ayres. The history of this vessel, so far as is necessary for the disposal of this point, is briefly this: She was originally built and equipped at Baltimore as a privateer during the late war with Great Britain, and was then rigged as a schooner, and called the *Mammoth*, and cruised against the enemy. After the peace she was rigged as a brig, and sold by her original owners. In January, 1816, she was loaded with a cargo of munitions of war, by her new owners, who are inhabitants of Baltimore, and being armed with twelve guns, constituting a part of her original armament, she was despatched from that port, under the command of the claimant, on a voyage, ostensibly to the Northwest Coast, but in reality to Buenos Ayres. By the written instructions given to the supercargo on this voyage, he was authorized to sell the vessel to the government of Buenos Ayres, if he could obtain a suitable price. She duly arrived at Buenos Ayres, having exercised no act of hostility, but sailed under the protection of the American flag, during the voyage. At Buenos Ayres the vessel was sold to Captain Chaytor and two other persons; and soon afterwards she assumed the flag and character of a public ship, and was understood by the crew to have been sold to the government of Buenos Ayres; and Captain Chaytor made known these facts to the crew, and asserted that he had become a citizen of Buenos Ayres; and had received a commission to command the vessel as a national ship; and invited the crew to enlist in the service; and the greater part of them accordingly enlisted. From this period, which was in May, 1816, the public functionaries of our own and other foreign governments at that port, considered the vessel as a public ship of war, and such was her avowed character and reputation. No bill of sale of the vessel to the government of Buenos Ayres is produced, and a question has been made principally from this defect in the evidence, whether her character as a public ship is established. It is not understood that any doubt is expressed as to the genuineness of Captain Chaytor's commission, nor as to the competency of the other proofs in the cause introduced, to corroborate it. We are of opinion that they do. In general the commission of a public ship, signed by the proper authorities of the nation to which she belongs, is complete proof of her national character. A bill of sale is not necessary to be produced. Nor will the courts of a foreign country inquire into the means by which the title to the property has been acquired. It would be to exert the right of examining into the validity of the acts of the foreign sovereign, and to sit in judgment upon them in cases where he has not conceded the jurisdiction, and where it would be inconsistent with his own supremacy. The commission, therefore, of a public ship, when duly authenticated, so far at least as foreign courts are concerned, imports absolute verity, and the title is not examinable. The property must be taken to be duly acquired, and cannot be controverted. This has been the settled practice between nations; and it is a rule founded in public convenience and policy, and cannot be broken in upon, without endangering the peace and repose, as well of neutral as of belligerent sovereigns. The commission in the present case is not expressed in the most unequivocal terms; but its fair purport and interpretation must be deemed to apply to a public ship of the government. If we add to this the corroborative testimony of our own and the British consul at Buenos Ayres, as well as that of private citizens, to the notoriety of her claim of a public character; and her admission into our own ports as a public ship, with the immunities and privileges belonging to such a ship, with the express approbation of our own government, it does not seem too much to assert, whatever may be the private suspicion of a lurking American interest, that she must be judicially held to be a public ship of the country whose commission she bears. * * *

"The next question growing out of this record, is whether the property in controversy was captured in violation of our neutrality, so that restitution ought, by the law of nations, to be decreed to the libellants. Two grounds are relied upon to justify restitution: *First*, that the *Independencia* and *Altravida* were originally equipped, armed, and manned as vessels of war in our ports. *Secondly*, that there was an illegal augmentation of the force of the *Independencia* within our ports. Are these grounds, or either of them, sustained by the evidence? * * *

"The question as to the original illegal armament and outfit of the *Independencia* may be dismissed in a few words. It is apparent, that though equipped as a vessel of war, she was sent to Buenos Ayres on a commercial adventure, contraband, indeed, but in no shape violating our laws on our national neutrality. If captured by a Spanish ship of war during the voyage she would have been justly condemned as good prize, and for being engaged in a traffic prohibited by the law of nations. But there is nothing in our laws, or in the law of nations, that forbids our citizens from sending armed vessels, as well as munitions of war, to foreign ports for sale. It is a commercial adventure which no nation is bound to prohibit; and which only exposes the persons engaged in it to the penalty of confiscation. Supposing, therefore, the voyage to have been for commercial purposes, and the sale at Buenos Ayres to have been a *bona fide* sale (and there is nothing in the evidence before us to contradict it), there is no pretence to say, that the original outfit on the voyage was illegal, or that a capture made after the sale was, for that cause alone, invalid.

"The most material consideration is as to the augmentation of her force in the United States, at a subsequent period. * * *

"The Court is, therefore, driven to the conclusion, that there was an illegal augmentation of the force of the *Independencia* in our ports by a substantial increase of her crew; and this renders it wholly unnecessary to enter into an investigation of the question, whether there was not also an illegal increase of her armament. * * * This view of the question renders it unnecessary to consider another which has been discussed at the bar respecting what is denominated the right of expatriation. * * *

"And here we are met by an argument on behalf of the claimant, that the augmentation of the force of the *Independencia* within our ports, is not an infraction of the law of nations, or a violation of our neutrality; and that so far as it stands prohibited by our municipal laws the penalties are personal, and do not reach the case of restitution of captures made in the cruise, during which such augmentation has taken place. It has never been held by this court that an augmentation of force or illegal outfit affected any captures made after the original cruise was terminated. By analogy to other cases of violations of public law the offence may well be deemed to be deposited at the termination of the voyage, and not to affect future transactions. But as to captures made during the same cruise, the doctrine of this court has long established that such illegal augmentation is a violation of the law of nations, as well as of our own municipal laws, and as a violation of our neutrality, by analogy to other cases, it infects the captures subsequently made with the character of torts, and justifies and requires a restitution to the parties who have been injured by such misconduct. It does not lie in the mouth of wrongdoers to set up a title derived from a violation of our neutrality.

"The cases in which this doctrine has been recognized and applied, have been cited at the bar, and are so numerous and so uniform, that it would be a waste of time to discuss them, or to examine the reasoning by which they are supported. More especially as no inclination exists on the part of the court to question the soundness of these decisions. If, indeed, the question were entirely new, it would deserve very grave consideration, whether a claim founded on a violation of our neutral jurisdiction could be asserted by private persons, or in any other manner than a direct intervention of the government itself. In the case of a capture made within a neutral territorial jurisdiction, it is well settled, that as between the captors and the captured, the question can never be litigated. It can arise only upon a claim of the neutral sovereign asserted in his own courts or the courts of the power having cognizance of the capture itself for the purposes of prize. And by analogy to this course of proceeding, the interposition of our own government might seem fit to have been required before cognizance of the wrong could be taken by our courts. But the practice from the beginning in this class of causes, a period of nearly 30 years, has been uniformly the other way; and it is now too late to disturb it. If any inconvenience should grow out of it, from reasons of state policy or executive discretion, it is competent for Congress to apply at its pleasure the proper remedy. * * *

"Upon the whole, it is the opinion of the court that the decree of the circuit court be affirmed, with costs."

UNITED STATES v. QUINCY.

SUPREME COURT OF THE UNITED STATES, 1832.

(6 *Peters*, 445.)

Held, that, if a vessel be fitted out in the United States with the intent that she shall engage in hostilities against a friendly nation, it is an infringement of the neutrality act of 1818, and subjects the owner to the penalties attached to that act.

But if the intention was to send the vessel to the West Indies in search of funds with which to complete her armament, with no present intention of preying upon the commerce of a friendly state, he was not guilty.

So, if there was no fixed intention, but a mere wish to fit her out, etc., it would not be illegal.

Mr. Justice THOMPSON delivered the opinion of the court:—

"This case comes up from the Circuit Court of the United States for the Maryland district, on a division of opinion of the judges, upon certain instructions prayed for to the jury.

"The indictment upon which the defendant was put upon his trial, contains a number of counts, to which the testimony did not apply, and which are not now drawn in question. The twelfth and thirteenth are the only counts to which the evidence applied; and the offence charged in each of these is substantially the same; to wit, that the said John D. Quincy, on the 31st day of December, 1828, at the district of Maryland, etc., with force and arms, was knowingly concerned in the fitting out of a certain vessel called the *Bolivar*, otherwise called *Las Damas Argentinas*, with intent that such vessel should be employed in the service of a foreign people, that is to say, in the service of the United Provinces of Rio de la Plata, to commit hostilities against the subjects of a foreign prince; that is to say, against the subjects of his imperial majesty, the constitutional emperor and perpetual defender of Brazil, with whom the United States then were, and still are at peace, against the form of the act of Congress in such case made and provided.

"The act of Congress under which the indictment was found, 6th Vol., Laws U. S., 321, sect. 3, declares, 'that if any person shall, within the limits of the United States, fit out and arm, or attempt to fit out and arm, or procure to be fitted out and armed, or shall knowingly be concerned in the furnishing, fitting out, or arming of any ship or vessel, with intent that such ship or vessel shall be employed in the service of any foreign prince or state, or of any colony, district or people, to cruise or commit hostilities against the subjects, citizens or property of any foreign prince or state, or of any colony, district or people with whom the United States are at peace, etc., every person so offending, shall be deemed guilty of a high misdemeanor, and shall be fined not more than ten thousand dollars, and imprisoned not more than three years, etc.'

"The testimony being closed, several prayers, both on the part of the United States and of the defendant, were presented to the court for their opinion and direction to the jury; and upon which the opinions of the judges were opposed, and which will now be noticed in the order in which they were made.

"On the part of the defendant the court was requested to charge the jury, that if they believe that when the *Bolivar* left Baltimore, and when she arrived at St. Thomas, and during the voyage from Baltimore to St. Thomas, she was not armed, or at all prepared for war, or in a condition to commit hostilities, the verdict must be for the defendant.

"The prayer on the part of the United States upon this part of the case, was, in substance, that if the jury find from the evidence that the defendant was, within the district of Maryland, knowingly concerned in the fitting out the privateer *Bolivar*, with intent that she should be employed in the manner alleged in the indictment, then the defendant was guilty of the offence charged against him, although the jury should find that the equipments of the said privateer were not complete within the United States, and that the cruise did not actually commence until men were recruited, and further equipments were made at the island of St. Thomas in the West Indies.

"The instruction which ought to be given to the jury under these prayers involves the construction of the act of Congress, touching the extent to which the preparation of the vessel for cruising or committing hostilities must be carried before she leaves the limits of the United States, in order to bring the case within the act.

"On the part of the defendant it is contended, that the vessel must be fitted out *and* armed, if not complete, so far at least as to be prepared for war, or in a condition to commit hostilities.

"We do not think this is the true construction of the act. It has been argued that, although the offence created by the act is a misdemeanor, and there cannot, legally speaking, be principal and accessory, yet the act evidently contemplates two distinct classes of offenders. The principal actors, who are directly engaged in preparing the vessel, and another class, who, though not the chief actors, are in some way concerned in the preparation.

"The act, in this respect, may not be drawn with very great perspicuity. But should the view taken of it by the defendant's counsel be deemed correct (which, however, we do not admit), it is not perceived how it can affect the present case. For the indictment, according to this construction, places the defendant in the secondary class of offenders. He is only charged with being knowingly concerned in the fitting out the vessel, with intent that she should be employed, etc.

"To bring him within the words of the act, it is not necessary to charge him with being concerned in fitting out *and* arming. The words of the act are, fitting out *or* arming. Either will constitute the offence. But it is said such fitting out must be of a vessel armed and in a condition to commit hostilities, otherwise the minor actor may be guilty when the greater would not. For, as to the latter, there must be a fitting out *and* arming in order to bring him within the law. If this construction of the act be well founded, the indictment ought to charge, that the defendant was concerned in fitting out the *Bolivar, being a vessel fitted out and armed, etc.* But this, we apprehend, is not required. It would be going beyond the plain meaning of the words used in defining the offence. It is sufficient if the indictment charges the offence in the words of the act; and it cannot be necessary to prove what is not charged. It is true, that, with respect to those who have been denominated at the bar the chief actors, the law would seem to make it necessary that they should be charged with fitting out *and* arming. These words may require that both should concur; and the vessel be put in a condition to commit hostilities, in order to bring her within the law. But an *attempt* to fit out *and* arm is made an offence. This is certainly doing something short of a complete fitting out and arming. To attempt to do an act does not, either in law or in common parlance, imply a completion of the act, or any definite progress towards it. Any effort or endeavor to effect it will satisfy the terms of the law.

"This varied phraseology in the law was probably employed with a view to embrace all persons of every description who might be engaged, directly or indirectly in preparing vessels with intent that they should be employed in committing hostilities against any powers with whom the United States were at peace. Different degrees of criminality will necessarily attach to persons thus engaged. Hence the great latitude given to the courts in affixing the punishment, viz., a fine not more than ten thousand dollars and imprisonment not more than three years.

"We are, accordingly, of opinion, that it is not necessary that the jury should believe or find that the *Bolivar*, when she left Baltimore, and when she arrived at St. Thomas, and during the voyage from Baltimore to St. Thomas, was armed, or in a condition to commit hostilities, in order to find the defendant guilty of the offence charged in the indictment.

"The first instruction, therefore, prayed on the part of the defendant, must be denied, and that on the part of the United States given.

"The second and third instructions asked on the part of the defendant, were:

"That if the jury believe that, when the *Bolivar* was fitted and equipped at Baltimore, the owner and equipper intended to go to the West Indies in search of funds, with which to arm and equip the said vessel and had *no present intention* of using or employing the said vessel as a privateer, but intended, when he equipped her, to go to the West Indies, to endeavor to raise funds to prepare her for a cruise; then the defendant is not guilty.

"Or if the jury believe that, when the *Bolivar* was equipped at Baltimore, and when she left the United States, the equipper *had no fixed intention to employ* her as a privateer, but had a wish so to employ her, the fulfilment of which wish depended on his ability to obtain funds in the West Indies, for the purpose of arming and preparing her for war; then the defendant is not guilty.

"We think these instructions ought to be given. The offence consists principally in the intention with which the preparations were made. These preparations, according to the very terms of the act, must be made within the limits of the United States; and it is equally necessary that the intention with respect to the employment of the vessel should be formed before she leaves the United States. And this must be a fixed intention; not conditional or contingent, depending on some future arrangements. This intention is a question belonging exclusively to the jury to decide. It is the material point on which the legality or criminality of the act must turn; and decides whether the adventure is of a commercial or warlike character.

"The law does not prohibit armed vessels belonging to citizens of the United States from sailing out of our ports; it only requires the owners to give security (as was done in the present case) that such vessels shall not be employed by them to commit hostilities against foreign powers at peace with the United States. The collectors are not authorized to detain vessels, although manifestly built for warlike purposes, and about to depart from the United States, unless circumstances shall render it probable that such vessels are intended to be employed by the owners to commit hostilities against some foreign power, at peace with the United States.

"All the latitude, therefore, necessary for commercial purposes, is given to our citizens; and they are restrained only from such acts as are calculated to involve the country in war.

"The second and third instructions, asked on the part of the United States, ought also to be given. For, if the jury shall find (as the instructions assume) that, the defendant was knowingly concerned in fitting out the *Bolivar* within the United States, with the intent that she should be employed as set forth in the indictment, that intention being defeated by what might afterwards take place in the West Indies, would not purge the offence, which was previously consummated. It is not necessary that the design or intention should be carried into execution in order to constitute the offence.

"The last instruction or opinion asked on the part of the defendant, was:

"That, according to the evidence in the cause, the United Provinces of Rio de la Plata is, and was, at the time of the offence alleged in the indictment, a government acknowledged by the United States, and thus was a *state*, and not a *people*, within the meaning of the act of Congress, under which the defendant is indicted; the word *people* in that act being intended to describe communities under an existing government, not recognized by the United States; and that the indictment cannot be supposed on this evidence.

"The indictment charges that the defendant was concerned in fitting out the *Bolivar*, with intent that she should be employed in the service of a foreign *people;* that is to say, in the service of the United Provinces of Rio de la Plata. It was in evidence, that the United Provinces of Rio de la Plata had been regularly acknowledged as an independent nation by the executive department of the government of the United States, before the year 1827. And, therefore, it is argued that the word *people* is not properly applicable to that nation or power.

"The objection is one purely technical, and we think not well-founded. The word *people*, as here used, is merely descriptive of the power in whose service the vessel was intended to be employed; and it is one of the denominations applied by the act of Congress to a foreign power. The words are, 'in the service of any foreign prince or state; or of any colony, district or *people*.' The application of the word *people* is rendered sufficiently certain by what follows under the videlicet, 'that is to say, the United Provinces of Rio de la Plata.' This particularizes that which by the word *people* is left too general. The descriptions are no way repugnant or inconsistent with each other, and may well stand together. That which comes under the videlicet, only serves to explain what is doubtful and obscure in the word *people*.

"This instruction must therefore be denied, and the one asked on the part of the United States, viz., that the indictment is sufficient in law, must be given.

"These answers must accordingly be certified to the circuit court."

THE "METEOR."

U. S. CIRCUIT COURT FOR SO. NEW YORK, 1866.

(3 *Wharton's Digest*, 561.)

A vessel may be fitted out in the United States for war, whether with armament, or without, and sent to a belligerent port in search of a market.

The case of the *Meteor*, which has been the subject of much discussion in this relation is reported in brief in 1 American Law, Rev., 401. According to this report, the *Meteor* was built in the United States in 1865, during the war then pending between Chile and Spain, and sold to the Chilean government, without armament, and then, it was alleged, commissioned, when in the United States, as a Chilean privateer. She was libeled in New York and seized January 23, 1866; and on the hearing before Judge BETTS it was maintained by the claimant to "be no offense (under the act of 1818) to issue a commission within the United States for a vessel fitted and equipped to cruise or commit hostilities, and intended to cruise and commit hostilities, so long as such vessel was not armed at the time, and was not intended to be armed within the United States, although it could be shown that a clear intent existed, on the part of the person issuing or delivering the commission, that the vessel should receive her armament the moment she should be beyond the jurisdiction of the United States." It was said, however, by Judge BETTS, that "the court cannot give any such construction to the statute. Such a construction was repudiated by the supreme court. * * * The *Meteor*, although not completely fitted out for military operations, was a vessel-of-war, and not a vessel of commerce. She has in no manner been altered from a vessel-of-war so as to fit her to be only a merchantman and so as to unfit her to be a vessel-of-war. It needed only that she should reach a point beyond the jurisdiction of the United States, and there have her armament and ammunition put on board of her, to become an armed cruiser of the Chilean government against the government of Spain. * * * To say that the neutrality laws of the United States have never prohibited the sale of a vessel-of-war as an article of commerce, is merely to say that they have not prohibited the fitting out and arming, or the attempting to fit out and arm, or the furnishing or fitting out or arming, of a vessel, within the limits of the United States, provided the unlawful and prohibited intent did not exist." The court relied as authority on Dana's Wheaton, 562, 563, note 215, where it is said that "an American merchant may build and fully arm a vessel and supply her with stores, and offer her for sale in our own market. If he does any acts, as an agent or servant of a belligerent, or in pursuance of an arrangement or understanding with a belligerent, that she shall be employed in hostilities when sold, he is guilty. He may, without violating our law, send out such a vessel, so equipped, under the flag and papers of his own country, with no more force of crew than is suitable for navigation, with no right to resist search or seizure, and to take the chances of capture as contraband merchandise, of blockade, and of a market in a belligerent port. In such case the extent and character of the equipment is as immaterial as in the other class of cases. The intent is all. The act is open to great suspicions and abuse, and the line may often be scarcely traceable; yet the principle is clear enough. Is the intent one to prepare an article of contraband merchandise, to be sent to the market of a belligerent, subject to the chances of capture and of the market? Or, on the other hand, is it to fit out a vessel which shall leave our port to cruise, immediately or ultimately, against the commerce of a friendly nation? The latter we are bound to prevent. The former the belligerent must prevent. Judge BETTS then proceeded to say: "The evidence in the present case leaves no rational doubt that what was done here in respect to the *Meteor* was done with the intent that she should be employed in hostile operations in favor of Chile against Spain; and that what was done by her owners towards dispatching her from the United States was done in pursuance of an arrangement with the authorized agents of Chile for her sale to that government, and for her employment in hostilities against Spain, and that the case is not one of a *bona fide* commercial dealing in contraband of war. With these views, there must be a decree condemning and forfeiting the property under seizure, in accordance with the prayer of the libel."

Judge BETTS' decree was reversed in the circuit court, where the following opinion was delivered by Mr. Justice NELSON:—

"This is an appeal in admiralty from a decree of condemnation in a libel of information for the violation of the neutrality laws of the United States. We have examined the pleadings and proofs in the case, and have been unable to concur in the judgment of the court below, but from the pressure of other business have not found time to write out at large the grounds and reasons for the opinion arrived at. We must, therefore, for the present, be content in the statement of our conclusions in the matter.

"1. Although negotiations were commenced and carried on between the owners of the *Meteor* and agents of the Government of Chile, for the sale of her to the latter, with the knowledge that she would be employed against the Government of Spain, with which Chile was at war, yet these negotiations failed and came to an end from the inability of the agents to raise the amount of the purchase-money demanded; and if the sale of the vessel, in its then condition and equipment, to the Chilean Government would have been a violation of our neutrality laws, of which it is unnecessary to express any opinion, the termination of the negotiation put an end to this ground of complaint.

"2. The furnishing of the vessel with coal and provisions for a voyage to Panama, or some other port of South America, and the purpose of the owners to send her thither, in our judgment, was not in pursuance of an agreement or understanding with the agents of the Chilean Government, but for the purpose and design of finding a market for her, and that the owners were free to sell her on her arrival there to the Government of Chile or of Spain, or of any other Government or person with whom they might be able to negotiate a sale.

"3. The witnesses chiefly relied on to implicate the owners in the negotiations with the agents of the Chilean Government, with a view and intent of fitting out and equipping the vessel to be employed in the war with Spain, are persons who had volunteered to negotiate on behalf of the agents with the owners in expectation of large commissions in the event of a sale, or persons in the expectation of employment in some situation in the command of the vessel, and very clearly manifest their disappointment and chagrin at the failure of the negotiations, and whose testimony is to be examined with considerable distrust and suspicion. We are not satisfied that a case is made out, upon the proofs, of a violation of the neutrality laws of the United States, and must, therefore, reverse the decree below, and enter a decree dismissing the libel."

An appeal was taken by the Government from the decision of the circuit court to the Supreme Court of the United States, but was not prosecuted to a hearing, being dismissed by consent November 9, 1868.[1]

[1] In a criticism on Judge BETTS' ruling, in the "North American Review" for October, 1866 (vol. 103, p. 188), we have the following :—

"It has been by many supposed that the decision in this *Meteor* case will be of great weight and importance as a precedent in the question of the *Alabama* and other Confederate vessels, now pending between this country and Great Britain, and the suspicion has been intimated by some that the law was a little warped by

THE TERCEIRA AFFAIR, 1827.

(*Phillimore, 3d Ed.*, III., 287.)

An expedition having left English ports to attack the government of Portugal, a British squadron was despatched in pursuit; finding the vessels of the expedition in Portuguese waters, the English captain kept a close watch upon them, and finally ordered them out of the neigborhood.

"In 1827, Don Pedro, having retained to himself the empire of the Brazils, formally renounced the throne of Portugal in favor of his daughter, Donna Maria, having delegated to his brother, Don Miguel,

the learned judge with the charitable intent of aiding Mr. Seward in the controversy. To justify either of these ideas, it is of course primarily necessary that the cases should be at least substantially parallel. That they are far from being so may be briefly shown. The *Meteor* was built as a purely commercial enterprise to be sent to a foreign land, there to take her chance of finding a market, subject to the risk of capture on the way, to be followed by confiscation as contraband of war, and to the further risk, should she reach her destination in safety, of finding no market in case the war should be drawing to a close, or terms could not be agreed on; liable, also, to be sold to any other bidder who would pay a better price. She differed nowise from any other contraband merchandise, except in the wholly insignificant fact that instead of being of such a nature as to require to be carried she was able to move herself. She was simply a mercantile speculation in contraband merchandise, which is of all men and nations confessedly and avowedly legitimate. The *Alabama* presents no one of these characteristics. * * * The question then being as Mr. Dana says, of *intent*, the vital difference is readily distinguishable. The English builders had assured their trade before they entered upon the undertaking; the American merchants only had in view a quite probable purchaser. The former were not free to dispose of their ship to any person who might offer her price, for she was bespoken; the latter would have been very glad to have received and closed with a fair offer from any source. In short, the action of the former betrays clearly the *intent*, the element of illegality, but how the action of the latter can have been regarded in the same light we must confess ourselves unable to see. Where, then, is the similarity? Or why should it have been conceived necessary to sacrifice the *Meteor*, to overrule old and good law, to create a new necessity requiring to be met by new statutes of untried efficiency, simply for the purpose of creating a precedent which is after all no precedent?"

Dana says of the Practice of the United States (note to Wheaton, p. 562): "As to the preparing of vessels within our jurisdiction for subsequent hostile operations, the test we have applied has not been the extent and character of the preparations, but the intent with which the particular acts are done. If any person does any act, or attempts to do any act, towards such preparation, with the intent that the vessel shall be employed in hostile operations, he is guilty, without refer-the office of Regency of the kingdom, with the intention that he should marry his niece.

"Donna Maria II. was recognized by Great Britain and the other great powers of Europe as the legitimate sovereign of Portugal.

ence to the completion of the preparations, or to the extent to which they have gone, and although his attempt may have resulted in no definite progress towards the completion of the preparations. The procuring of materials to be used, knowingly and with the intent, etc., is an offence. * * *

"On the point of the intent, more nicety and discrimination are necessary. If the person charged has himself the control of the vessel, to put her into foreign belligerent service, the question of the intent to employ her is simple. If he has not, he is still chargeable with doing acts, or being knowingly concerned in the doing of acts, of or towards the preparation, with the intent that the vessel shall be so employed though others may control her during the preparations. But the intent must be that she shall be so employed; and the intent must be a fixed and present intent, and not a wish or desire merely that she may be. If there is a contingency, it must, to exculpate the party, be one which forms a condition precedent to the intent, and not merely a condition precedent to the employment, or a condition subsequent which may defeat the intent. Thus, if the owner of a vessel, not completely ready for hostile operations, with instructions to her commander to complete her preparation and obtain letters of marque in the port of destination, and, in case of failure in obtaining the commission and equipment, to take a cargo and return, he would doubtless be guilty; for he has entered on the execution of his purpose, and those are only the ordinary contingencies to all employments, by which they may be defeated. But the purpose to which he shall put his vessel after her arrival may depend on circumstances so entirely contingent and fortuitous, as to relieve from the charge of a fixed intent at the time he sends her out.

"It will be seen at once, by these abstract definitions, that our rules do not interfere with *bona fide* commercial dealings in contraband of war. An American merchant may build and fully arm a vessel, and supply her with stores, and offer her for sale in our own market. If he does any acts, as an agent or servant of a belligerent, or in pursuance of an arrangement or understanding with a belligerent, that she shall be employed in hostilities when sold, he is guilty. He may, without violating our law, send out such a vessel, so equipped, under the flag and papers of his own country, with no more force of crew than is suitable for navigation, with no right to resist search or seizure, and to take the chances of capture as contraband merchandise, of blockade, and of a market in a belligerent port. In such case, the extent and character of the equipments is as immaterial as in the other class of cases. The intent is all. The act is open to great suspicions and abuse, and the line may often be scarcely traceable; yet the principle is clear enough. Is the intent one to prepare an article of contraband merchandise, to be sent to the market of a belligerent, subject to the chances of capture and of the market? Or, on the other hand, is it to fit out a vessel which shall leave our port to cruise, immediately or ultimately, against the commerce of a friendly nation? The latter we are bound to prevent. The former the belligerent must prevent. In the former case, the ship is merchandise, under *bona fide* neutral flag and papers, with a port of destination, subject to search and capture as contraband merchandise by the other belligerent, or to the risks of blockade, and with no

"Don Miguel, however, after a very short period, violated all his engagements, placed himself at the head of the Absolutists, procured himself to be proclaimed king in 1828, proscribed the Constitutionalists, and plunged the country into the horrors of a civil war.

"The sovereigns of Europe, except the King of Spain, still kept aloof from any communication with the usurper—from any act which might be considered a recognition of his title. The Portuguese refugees, and the Ministers of Don Pedro, insisted that they ought to do more, and drive him from his throne by positive interference. These applications were addressed particularly to the British Ministry.

"The British Government refused, however, to interfere in this domestic quarrel; and, holding that it was not entitled to make any distinction between the claimants of the Portuguese crown, in so far as their respective pretensions were supported only by domestic force, considered itself bound to observe, in regard to all military operations, a strict neutrality. A great number of Portuguese refugees, most of them military men, had arrived in England, taking up their residence principally in Portsmouth, Falmouth, and the neighborhood. As it was believed that they were meditating to fit out some expedition from these ports against Don Miguel, the British government, holding that to permit this would be a breach of neutrality, informed the Brazilian minister that it would not allow such designs to be carried on in British harbors, and that, for security's sake, the refugees must remove farther from the coast. The Envoy then stated that those troops were about to be conveyed to Brazil; and accordingly four vessels, having on board 652 officers and men, under the command of General Count Saldanha, who had been the constitutional Minister of War, sailed from Plymouth. The British government suspected that the true design was to land these troops at Terceira, although the ostensible destination was Brazil. Notice was given to them before they sailed, that any such attempt would be resisted, and a small force of armed vessels, under the command of Captain Walpole, of the *Ranger*, was despatched beforehand to Terceira, to enforce the prohibition. His instructions were to cruise

right to resist search and seizure, and liable to be treated as a pirate by any nation, if she does any act of hostility to the property of a belligerent, as much as if she did it to that of a neutral. Such a trade in contraband, a belligerent may cut off by cruising the seas and by blockading his enemy's ports. But, to protect himself against vessels sailing out of a neutral port to commit hostilities, it would be necessary for him to hover off the ports of the neutral; and, to do that effectually, he must maintain a kind of blockade of the neutral coast; which, as neutrals will not permit, they ought not to give occasion for."

off the island, to inform the Portuguese if they appeared that he had authority to prevent their landing; 'and, should they persist, notwithstanding such warning, in hovering about, or in making any efforts to effect a landing, you are then to use force to drive them away from that neighborhood, and keep sight of them until you shall be convinced, by the course they may steer, and the distance they may have proceeded, that they have no intention of returning to the Western Islands, or to proceed to Madeira.'

"The expedition of Count Saldanha appeared off Terceira on the 16th of January, and was discovered by Captain Walpole standing right in for Port Praya. He fired two shots to bring them to, but they continued their course. The vessel, on board of which was Saldanha, although now within point-blank range of the *Ranger's* guns, seemed determined to push in at all hazards. To prevent him from effecting his object Captain Walpole was under the necessity of firing a shot at the vessel, which killed one man and wounded another. The vessels then lay to, and to a note from Captain Walpole, inquiring what was their object in coming thither, Saldanha answered, 'My object in appearing here is to fulfil the orders of Her Majesty the Queen of Portugal, and which prescribe me to conduct, unarmed, without any hostile appearance, to the isle of Terceira, the men that are on board the four vessels in sight, which island has never ceased to obey and acknowledge, as its legitimate sovereign, Her Faithful Majesty Donna Maria II. As a faithful subject and soldier, I think it unnecessary to assure you that I am determined to fulfil my duty at all peril.' Captain Walpole replied, that he too had instructions to obey, and an imperious duty to perform; that both of them prevented him from allowing the Count, or any part of his force, to land, either at Terceira, or on any of the Western Islands or the Azores, or even to continue in that neighborhood; that, therefore, unless the Count immediately quitted the vicinity of the islands he should be obliged, and was determined, to use force to compel him to do so. Saldanha then declared that he considered himself and his men as being, in these circumstances, Captain Walpole's prisoners.

"Count Saldanha, and his squadron, instead of returning to England proceeded to Brest.

"The act of the British Government produced a great excitement in England, and very animated debates in Parliament, in which the principles of International Law were laid down with great precision, and discussed with no ordinary ability.

"The Government defended the instructions given to Captain Walpole upon the ground that the refugees had fitted out a warlike armament in a British port; that the armament having been equipped under the disguise of a destination to Brazil, had not been prevented from sailing, as it otherwise would have been, out of the port of Plymouth; and that they were, therefore, bound, by the duties of neutrality, to prevent by force an armament so equipped from disembarking, even in the harbor of the Queen of Portugal's dominions. The Government were supported by a majority in both Houses of Parliament; but in the protest of the House of Lords, or in the resolutions of the House of Commons, the true principles of International Law are to be found.

"The protest of the House of Lords is as follows:—

"'Because the forcible detention or interruption of the subjects of a belligerent state, upon the high seas, or within the legitimate jurisdiction of either of the belligerents, by a neutral, constitutes a direct breach of Neutrality, and is an obvious violation of the Law of Nations. And such an act of aggression, illegal and unjust at all times against a people with whom the interfering power is not actually at war, assumed in this instance a yet more odious and ungenerous aspect, inasmuch as it was exercised against the unarmed subjects of a defenseless and friendly sovereign, whose elevation and right to the Crown of Portugal had been earnestly recommended and openly recognized by His Majesty, and whose actual residence in Great Britain, bespeaking confidence in the friendship and protection of the king, entitled both her and her subjects to especial favor and countenance, even if considerations of policy precluded His Majesty's government from enforcing her just pretensions by arms.'"

Resolutions moved in the House of Commons suggested, "That the use of force in intercepting these unarmed vessels, and preventing them from anchoring and landing their passengers in the harbor of Porto Praira, was a violation of the sovereignty of the state to which the island of Terceira belonged; and that the further interference to compel those merchant ships or transports to quit the neighborhood of the Azores was an assumption of jurisdiction upon the high seas, neither justified by the necessity of the case, nor sanctioned by the general Law of Nations." (Quoted from Cobbett's "Cases," p. 264.)

THE "ALABAMA," 1862.

(Papers Relating to the Treaty of Washington.)

The *Alabama*, known in the shipyard as the "290," was built at Liverpool by Messrs. Laird & Co., and launched on the 15th of May, 1862. Mr. Dudley, United States consul at Liverpool, having obtained evidence that the "290" was constructed as a vessel of war and was being built for the Confederate government, transmitted this information to Mr. Adams, the United States minister in London. On the 23d of June, 1862, Mr. Adams wrote to Earl Russell, foreign secretary, enclosing the letter of Mr. Dudley, and said: "This vessel has been built and launched from the dockyard of persons, one of whom is now sitting as a member of the House of Commons, and is fitting out for the especial and manifest object of carrying on hostilities by sea. It is about to be commanded by one of the insurgent agents, the same who sailed in the *Oreto*. The parties engaged in the enterprise are persons well known at Liverpool to be agents and officers of the insurgents in the United States, the nature and extent of whose labors are well explained in the copy of an intercepted letter of one of them, which I received from my government some days ago, and which I had the honor to place in your lordship's hands on Thursday last."

On the 1st of July, 1862, the commissioners of customs, to whom had been referred Mr. Adams' letter to Earl Russell, and its inclosure reported to the Lords Commissioners of the Treasury, that the vessel was undoubtedly intended for a ship of war, but as yet there were neither guns nor gun-carriages on board, "and, having referred the matter to our solicitor, he has reported his opinion that at present there is not sufficient ground to warrant the detention of the vessel or any interference on the part of this department, in which report we beg to express our concurrence." The commissioners further suggested that the American consul should submit any evidence he might procure to the collector of customs at Liverpool, "who would thereupon take such measures as the provisions of the Foreign Enlistment Act would require." This suggestion was acted upon by Mr. Dudley, and a mass of evidence, including six affidavits showing the true state of affairs, were laid before Mr. Edwards, the collector at Liverpool. This evidence was again referred to the commissioners of customs, who again advised, July 22d, that there was not sufficient evidence to detain the vessel. The same evidence having been submitted to Mr. R. P. Collier, barrister, he gave the following opinion on July 23d: "I have perused the above affidavits and am of opinion that the collector of customs would be justified in detaining the vessel. Indeed, I should think it his duty to detain, and that if, after the application which has been made to him, supported by the evidence which has been laid before me, he allows the vessel to leave Liverpool, he will incur a heavy responsibility, of which the board of customs, under whose direction he appears to be acting, must take their share.

"It appears difficult to make out a stronger case of infringement of the Foreign Enlistment Act, which, if not enforced on this occasion, is little better than a dead letter.

"It well deserves consideration whether, if the vessel be allowed to escape, the Federal government would not have serious grounds of remonstrance."

Finally, on July 24th, Mr. Adams sent to Earl Russell copies of two additional affidavits, and of Mr. Collier's opinion, and on the same day the commissioners of customs referred the matter to the law officers of the Crown, as did Earl Russell on the 26th.

On Tuesday, the 29th, the law officers, before whom all the evidence had been laid, reported to the Secretary of State for Foreign Affairs their opinion that the vessel should be detained.

But on the morning of the 29th of July the "290" went to sea, without a clearance, ostensibly on a trial trip, carrying with her a party of ladies and gentlemen, who were, however, sent back by a tug from the mouth of the river. She proceeded to Moelfra Bay, on the coast of Anglesea, where she remained at anchor until the morning of July 31st, and took on board about 40 men, who had been sent after her from Liverpool in a tug. And although it was known to the customs officers at Liverpool on July 30th that the tug was to take men to the "290," no steps were taken to follow or seize her.

On July 31st the "290" sailed for Terceira, in the Azores, where she was met by two vessels,the *Agrippina*, from London, and the *Bahama*, from Liverpool, which brought out her armament and additional supplies and seamen. Here the transshipment of the armament was effected, and the "290," now the *Alabama*, under the command of Captain Semmes, and a crew nearly all British seamen, proceeded on her cruise to destroy the commerce of the United States.

From this time until her destruction by the *Kearsarge*, on the 19th of June, 1864, the *Alabama* was received in British ports as a foreign belligerent ship of war, being allowed the privilege of refitting and of procuring coal and provisions.

The *Alabama* captured 70 United States vessels, of which 9 were bonded, 2 released, 2 detained, and 57 burned.

THE "FLORIDA," 1862.

(Papers Relating to the Treaty of Washington.)

The *Florida*, originally known as the *Oreto*, was an iron screw gunboat of about seven hundred tons burden, built in 1861–1862, by Fawcet, Preston & Co., of Liverpool, on the order of the government of the Confederate States. To avoid suspicion, it was given out that she was to be built for the Italian government, but the Italian consul at Liverpool disclaimed all knowledge of her, and Mr. Charles Francis Adams, the United States minister in London, informed Earl Russell on the 18th of February, 1862, that she was intended for the Confederate Government. As the result of inquiries set on foot by the British government, the commissioners of customs reported on February 22d, that the *Oreto* was a vessel pierced for guns, but had neither guns nor gun-carriages on board, and that she was intended for the use of Thomas Brothers, of Palermo. Mr. Adams again on the 26th of March, called the attention of Earl Russell to the probable destination of this vessel; but on March 22d she had sailed with a general cargo and a crew of 52 men for Palermo and Jamaica. Next appearing at Nassau, in New Providence, she aroused the suspicions of the American consul and of British naval officers, who strongly recommended her arrest. Other vessels had arrived from England with equipment and guns. The arrest was finally made, but the Vice-Admiralty Court released her for alleged lack of evidence. Sailing from Nassau on July 7th, ostensibly for St. Johns, N. B., she was followed by vessels bearing her armament, to Green Cay, another of the Bahama islands, and was there equipped as a vessel of war.

After leaving British waters the *Oreto*, now the *Florida*, proceeded to Cuba, and soon after entered the port of Mobile, eluding the blockading fleet by the ruse of carrying the British flag. Issuing from that port January 16, 1863, she again appeared at Nassau and was permitted to take in a supply of coal. After that she was received at various ports of the British West Indies, and in some cases remained several days, refitting and procuring coal and provisions.

She had by October, 1864, destroyed 36 vessels belonging to the merchant marine of the United States.

The end of her career was now reached. While lying in the neutral port of Bahia, Brazil, the U. S. war steamer *Wachusetts* cut her out and towed her to sea, and on reaching the waters of the United States, she accidentally sank in Hampton Roads. For this violation of neutral rights the United States made every possible reparation to the government of Brazil.

The *Florida* captured 36 United States vessels, of which 4 were bonded and 32 destroyed.

THE "SHENANDOAH," 1864.

(*Papers Relating to the Treaty of Washington.*)

The *Shenandoah* was originally a British merchant vessel known as the *Sea King*. On October 8, 1864, she cleared from London to Bombay with a large supply of coal and a crew of forty-seven men. The *Laurel* having sailed the same day from Liverpool with guns, equipment and men, the two vessels met off the island of Madeira, and as in the case of the *Alabama* and *Florida*, the *Sea King* was transformed into a Confederate cruiser, under the name of the *Shenandoah*, and proceeded to prey upon the commerce of the United States. She crossed the Atlantic, rounded Cape Horn, and arrived at Melbourne on the 25th of January, 1865. Notwithstanding the remonstrance of the United States consul at Melbourne, she was allowed to make extensive repairs, to take in supplies and coal and to enlist more than forty seamen. Proceeding on her cruise, she destroyed many United States whaling vessels in the Northern Pacific, and a considerable number after the war had ended. Finally, having made her way back to Liverpool, she was surrendered to the English government, by whom she was transferred to the United States consul. The *Shenandoah* captured 36 United States vessels, 31 of which were destroyed, 3 bonded, and 2 ransomed.

THE "GEORGIA," 1863.

(*Papers Relating to the Treaty of Washington.*)

The *Georgia*, previously known as the *Japan*, and the *Virginia*, was built at Dumbarton, on the Clyde, and was equipped by a Liverpool firm. Her crew were shipped by the same Liverpool firm for Shanghai, and sent round to Greenock by steamer. She was entered on the 31st of March, 1863, as for Point de Galle and Hong

Kong, with a crew of forty-eight men. She cleared on the 1st of April, and left her anchorage on the 2d, ostensibly to try her engines, but did not return. She had no armament on leaving Greenock, but a few days after her departure a small steamer named the *Allar*, freighted with guns and ammunition, and having on board a partner of the Liverpool firm who had equipped her, left Newhaven and met the *Georgia* off the coast of France, near Ushant. The cargo of the *Allar* was transferred to the *Georgia* on the 8th or 9th of April, and the *Allar* put into Plymouth on the 11th, bringing the Liverpool merchant who had directed the proceedings throughout, and bringing also fifteen seamen who had refused to proceed in the *Georgia*, on learning her real character. The rest of the crew, British subjects, remained.

The *Georgia* was received in various British ports as a Confederate man-of-war; but not being very successful in capturing ships she returned to Liverpool on May 2, 1864, and at Birkenhead was dismantled, her stores sold, and the vessel disposed of to an English merchant. The United States did not, however, recognize the validity of this transfer, and she was subsequently captured off Lisbon by an American cruiser, and condemned as prize. The *Georgia* captured 9 vessels, 2 of which were bonded.

Two members of the Liverpool firm, who had engaged in enlisting men for the *Georgia*, were indicted under the Foreign Enlistment Act, and, on conviction, sentenced to fines of £50.

CASES OF THE "SUMPTER" AND OTHER VESSELS,

1861–1865.

(*Papers Relating to the Treaty of Washington.*)

The *Sumpter*, previously the merchant steamer *Havana*, was fitted out at New Orleans as a vessel of war, and sailed the 30th of June, 1861, under the command of Captain Semmes. On the 30th of July she entered the harbor of Trinidad, and was the first of the Confederate cruisers to receive the recognition of England as a legitimate ship of war of a recognized belligerent. She remained six days, and was allowed to supply herself with coal and other necessary articles. The *Sumpter* having entered the port of Gibraltar, she was there practically blockaded by the United States steamer *Tuscarora*, and in consequence, was dismantled and sold to an agent of Frazer, Trenholm & Co., of Liverpool, at which port she arrived on the 17th of

February, 1863. She was subsequently wrecked in attempting to run the blockade of Charleston with a cargo of contraband. The *Sumpter* captured 18 vessels, 8 of which were released, 1 recaptured, 2 bonded, the rest destroyed.

The *Nashville* ran out of Charleston through the blockade in November, 1861. Her Confederate commission was recognized in the ports of Bermuda and Southampton, where she was permitted to repair ship and take in coal and provisions. She afterwards returned to Charleston, and was not heard of again as a cruiser. The *Nashville* destroyed 2 vessels.

The *Tallahassee* appeared off the coast of New York in July, 1864. She was probably built in an English port; little, however, is known of her construction and outfit, the chief complaint in her case being that she was received in British ports. She destroyed 29 United States vessels.

The *Tacony*, the *Tuscaloosa*, the *Clarence*, and the *Lapwing*, were tenders to the *Alabama* and the *Florida*. These were vessels captured by the *Alabama* and *Florida*, and converted into gunboats, at sea, and which acted as tenders to those two vessels. These tenders destroyed or bonded 24 United States vessels.

GENEVA AWARD, 1872.

(3 *Wharton's Digest*, 630.)

Article VI. of the Treaty of Washington of 1871, providing, among other things, for an arbitration to determine British liability for the depredations on the commerce of the United States by the *Alabama* and other Confederate cruisers which left British waters, is as follows:

"In deciding the matters submitted to the arbitrators they shall be governed by the following three rules, which are agreed upon by the high contracting parties, as rules to be taken as applicable to the case, and by such principles of international law, not inconsistent therewith, as the arbitrators shall determine to have been applicable to the case:—

"RULES.

"A neutral Government is bound—

"First. To use due diligence to prevent the fitting out, arming, or equipping, within its jurisdiction, of any vessel which it has reasonable ground to believe is intended to cruise or to carry on war against a power with which it is at peace; and also to use like diligence to prevent the departure from its jurisdiction of any vessel intended to cruise or carry on war as above, such vessel having been specially adapted, in whole or in part, within such jurisdiction, to warlike use.

"Secondly. Not to permit or suffer either belligerent to make use of its ports or waters as the base of naval operations against the other, or for the purpose of the renewal or augmentation of military supplies or arms, or the recruitment of men.

"Thirdly. To exercise due diligence in its own ports and waters, and as to all persons within its jurisdiction, to prevent any violation of the foregoing obligations and duties.

"Her Britannic Majesty has commanded her high commissioners and plenipotentiaries to declare that Her Majesty's Government cannot assent to the foregoing rules as a statement of the principles of international law which were in force at the time when the claims mentioned in Article I. arose, but that Her Majesty's Government, in order to evince its desire of strengthening the friendly relations between the two countries, and of making satisfactory provision for the future, agrees that in deciding the questions between the two countries, arising out of those claims, the arbitrators should assume that Her Majesty's Government had undertaken to act upon the principles set forth in these rules.

"And the high contracting parties agree to observe these rules as between themselves in future, and to bring them to the knowledge of other maritime powers, and to invite them to accede to them."

DECISION AND AWARD.

"The tribunal having since fully taken into their consideration the treaty and also the cases, counter-cases, documents, evidence, and arguments, and likewise all other communications made to them by the two parties during the progress of their sittings, and having impartially and carefully examined the same,

"Has arrived at the decision embodied in the present award:

"Whereas, having regard to the sixth and seventh articles of the said treaty, the arbitrators are bound under the terms of the said sixth article, 'in deciding the matters submitted to them, to be governed by the three rules therein specified and by such principles of international law, not inconsistent therewith as the arbitrators shall determine to have been applicable to the case;'

"And whereas the 'due diligence,' referred to in the first and third of the said rules, ought to be exercised by neutral governments in exact proportion to the risks to which either of the belligerents may be exposed, from a failure to fulfill the obligations of neutrality on their part;

"And whereas the circumstances out of which the facts constituting the subject-matter of the present controversy arose were of a nature to call for the exercise on the part of Her Britannic Majesty's Government of all possible solicitude for the observance of the rights and duties involved in the proclamation of neutrality issued by Her Majesty on the 13th day of May, 1861.

"And whereas the effects of a violation of neutrality, committed by means of the construction, equipment, and armament of a vessel is not done away with by any commission which the government of the belligerent power, benefited by the violation of neutrality, may afterwards have granted to that vessel; and the ultimate step, by which the offense is completed, cannot be admissible as a ground for the absolution of the offender, nor can the consummation of his fraud become the means of establishing his innocence.

"And whereas the privilege of extra-territoriality, accorded to vessels of war, has been admitted into the law of nations, not as an absolute right, but solely as a proceeding founded on the principle of courtesy and mutual deference between different nations, and, therefore, can never be appealed to for the protection of acts done in violation of neutrality;

"And whereas the absence of a previous notice cannot be regarded as a failure in any consideration required by the law of nations, in those cases in which a vessel carries with it its own condemnation;

And whereas, in order to impart to any supplies of coal a character inconsistent with the second rule, prohibiting the use of neutral ports or waters, as a base of naval operations for a belligerent, it is necessary that the said supplies should be connected with special circumstances, of time, of persons, or of place, which may combine to give them such character;

"And whereas, with respect to the vessel called the *Alabama*, it clearly results from all the facts relative to the construction of the ship, at first designated by the number '290,' in the port of Liverpool, and its equipment and armament in the vicinity of Terceira, through the agency of the vessels called the *Agrippina* and the *Bahama*, dispatched from Great Britain to that end, that the British Government failed to use due diligence in the performance of its neutral obligations, and especially that it omitted, notwithstanding the warnings and official representations made by the diplomatic agents of the United States during the construction of the said number '290,' to take in due time any effective measures of prevention, and that those orders which it did give at last, for the detention of the vessel, were issued so late that their execution was not practicable;

"And whereas, after the escape of that vessel, the measures taken for its pursuit and arrest were so imperfect as to lead to no result, and therefore cannot be considered sufficient to release Great Britain from the responsibility already incurred;

"And whereas, in despite of the violations of the neutrality of Great Britain, committed by the '290,' this same vessel, later known as the Confederate cruiser *Alabama*, was on several occasions freely admitted into the ports of the colonies of Great Britain, instead of being proceeded against as it ought to have been in any and every port within British jurisdiction in which it might have been found;

"And whereas the Government of Her Britannic Majesty cannot justify itself for a failure in due diligence on the plea of insufficiency of the legal means of action which it possessed:

"Four of the arbitrators for the reasons above assigned, and the fifth, for reasons separately assigned by him, are of opinion that Great Britain has in this case failed, by omission, to fulfill the duties prescribed in the first and the third of the rules, established by the sixth article of the treaty of Washington.

"And whereas, with respect to the vessel called the *Florida*, it results from all the facts relative to the construction of the *Oreto* in the port of Liverpool, and to its issue therefrom, which facts failed to induce the authorities in Great Britain to resort to measures adequate to prevent the violation of the neutrality of that nation, notwithstanding the warnings and repeated representations of the agents of the United States; that Her Majesty's government has failed to use due diligence to fulfill the duties of neutrality;

"And whereas it likewise results from all the facts relative to the stay of the *Oreto* at Nassau, to her issue from that port, to her enlistment of men, to her supplies, and to her armament, with the co-operation of the British vessel *Prince Alfred*, at Green Cay, that there was negligence on the part of the British colonial authorities;

"And whereas, notwithstanding the violation of the neutrality of Great Britain, committed by the *Oreto*, this same vessel, later known as the Confederate cruiser *Florida*, was, nevertheless, on several occasions freely admitted into the ports of British colonies;

"And whereas the judicial acquittal of the *Oreto* at Nassau cannot relieve Great Britain from the responsibility incurred by her under the principles of international law; nor can the fact of the entry of the *Florida* into the Confederate port of Mobile, and of its stay there during four months, extinguish the responsibility previously to that time incurred by Great Britain;

"For these reasons the tribunal, by a majority of four voices to one, is of opinion, that Great Britain has in this case failed, by omission, to fulfill the duties prescribed in the first, in the second, and in the third, of the rules established by Article VI., of the Treaty of Washington.

"And whereas, with respect to the vessel called the *Shenandoah*, it results from all the facts relative to the departure from London of the merchant vessel, the *Sea King*, and to the transformation of that ship into a Confederate cruiser under the name of the *Shenandoah*, near the island of Madeira, that the Government of Her Britannic Majesty is not chargeable with any failure, down to that date, in the use of due diligence to fulfill the duties of neutrality;

"But whereas it results from all the facts connected with the stay of the *Shenandoah* at Melbourne, and especially with the augmentation which the British Government itself admits to have been clandestinely effected of her force, by the enlistment of men within that port, that there was negligence on the part of the authorities at that place;

"For these reasons the tribunal is unanimously of opinion, that Great Britain has not failed, by any act or omission, 'to fulfill any of the duties prescribed by the three rules of Article VI. in the Treaty of Washington, or by the principles of international law not inconsistent therewith,' in respect to the vessel called the *Shenandoah*, during the period of time anterior to her entry into the port of Melbourne;

"And, by a majority of three to two voices, the tribunal decides that Great Britain has failed, by omission, to fulfill the duties prescribed by the second and third of the rules aforesaid, in the case of this same vessel, from and after her entry into Hobson's Bay, and is, therefore, responsible for all acts committed by that vessel after her departure from Melbourne, on the 18th day of February, 1865.

"And so far as relates to the vessels called the *Tuscaloosa* (tender to the *Alabama*), the *Clarence*, the *Tacony*, and the *Archer*, (tenders to the *Florida*), the tribunal is unanimously of opinion, that such tenders or auxiliary vessels, being properly regarded as accessories, must necessarily follow the lot of their principals, and be submitted to the same decision which applies to them respectively.

"And so far as relates to the vessel called *Retribution*, the tribunal, by a majority of three to two voices, is of opinion, that Great Britain has not failed, by any act or omission, to fulfill any of the duties prescribed by the three rules of Article VI., in the Treaty of Washington, or by the principles of international law not inconsistent therewith.

"And so far as relates to the vessels called the *Georgia*, the *Sumpter*, the *Nashville*, the *Tallahassee*, and the *Chickamauga*, respectively, the tribunal is unanimously of opinion, that Great Britain has not failed, by any act or omission, to fulfill any of the duties prescribed by the three rules of Article VI., in the Treaty of Washington, or by the principles of international law not inconsistent therewith.

"And so far as relates to the vessels called the *Sallie*, the *Jefferson Davis*, the *Music*, the *Boston*, and the *V. H. Joy* respectively, the tribunal is unanimously of opinion that they ought to be excluded from consideration for want of evidence.

"And whereas, so far as relates to the particulars of the indemnity claimed by the United States, the costs of pursuit of the Confederate cruisers are not, in the judgment of the tribunal, properly distinguishable from the general expenses of the war carried on by the United States:

"The tribunal is, therefore, of opinion, by a majority of three to two voices, that there is no ground for awarding to the United States any sum by way of indemnity under this head.

"And, whereas, prospective earnings cannot properly be made the subject of compensation, inasmuch as they depend in their nature upon future and uncertain contingencies:

"The tribunal is unanimously of opinion that there is no ground for awarding to the United States any sum by way of indemnity under this head.

"And, whereas, in order to arrive at an equitable compensation for the damages which have been sustained, it is necessary to set aside all double claims for the same losses, and all claims for 'gross freights,' so far as they exceed 'net freights';

"And, whereas, it is just and reasonable to allow interest at a reasonable rate;

"And, whereas, in accordance with the spirit and letter of the Treaty of Washington, it is preferable to adopt the form of adjudication of a sum in gross, rather than to refer the subject of compensation for further discussion and deliberation to a board of assessors, as provided by Article X., of the said treaty:

"The tribunal, making use of the authority conferred upon it by Article VII., of the said treaty, by a majority of four voices to one, awards to the United States a sum of $15,500,000 in gold, as the indemnity to be paid by Great Britain to the United States, for the satisfaction of all the claims referred to the consideration of the tribunal, conformably to the provisions contained in Article VII., of the aforesaid treaty.

"And, in accordance with the terms of Article XI. of the said treaty, the tribunal declares that 'all the claims referred to in the treaty as submitted to the tribunal are hereby fully, perfectly, and finally settled.'

"Furthermore, it declares that 'each and every one of the said claims, whether the same may or may not have been presented to the notice of, or made, preferred, or laid before the tribunal, shall henceforth be considered and treated as finally settled, barred, and inadmissible.'

"In testimony whereof this present decision and award has been made in duplicate, and signed by the arbitrators who have given their assent thereto, the whole being in exact conformity with the provisions of Article VII., of the said Treaty of Washington.

"Made and concluded at the Hotel de Ville of Geneva, in Switzerland, the 14th day of the month of September, in the year of our Lord one thousand eight hundred and seventy-two.[1]

"CHARLES FRANCIS ADAMS,
"FREDERICK SCLOPIS,
"STAMPFLI,
"VICOMTE D'ITAJUBA."

[1] *The Three Rules of the Treaty of Washington.*—These rules have been the subject of widespread interest and discussion. The question was immediately raised, whether they formed, at the time of the American civil war, or indeed since that time, a true expression of the accepted principles of International Law. The English government, at the time of the arbitration, announced that it did not accept them "as a statement of principles of International Law which were in force at the time when the claims arose;" and the view generally held in England was that they were *ex post facto* rules.

On the other hand, continental jurists are inclined to regard these rules as a fair statement of modern International Law upon the subject to which they apply. (See an article by Calvo in the Revue de Droit International, vol. VI., pp. 453–532.)

In considering this question, it should be remembered that, by the introduction of steam as the motive power of ships, and of iron and steel as the material of their construction, the conditions of maritime warfare have been very radically changed. What might have been a reasonable rule as applied in the time of sailing ships, might now, in the age of swift ironclads, be intolerably oppressive. In the cases of the *Santissima Trinidad*, *U. S.* v. *Quincy*, and the *Meteor*, the courts were dealing with small sailing vessels, which had been converted into privateers, the possession of which by one or the other belligerent made very little difference in the general result of the struggle: whereas, the possession of an ironclad ship might very well turn the scale one way or the other, as indeed it did in the war between Chili and Peru, in 1880–1881. This great power of inflicting injury upon one of the belligerents, it is fair to say,

SECTION 42.—AID TO INSURGENTS.

(*a*) *Loans of Money.*

DE WUTZ v. HENDRICKS.

COMMON PLEAS, 1824.

(9 *Moore*, 586.)

The question of the legality of a contract to negotiate a loan in aid of insurgents.

This was an action of trover for certain papers, and which were described in the declaration to be a power of attorney, and sundry engravings.

At the trial, before Lord Chief Justice BEST, at Guildhall, at the Sittings after the last Term, it appeared that the plaintiff had proposed to raise money by way of loan, to espouse the cause of the Greeks against the government of the Porte. That he stated publicly that he was authorized to do so, and, in consequence, applied to the defendant, a stockbroker, to negotiate the loan, who required certain securities to be left with him for that purpose; that the plaintiff accordingly lodged with him a power of attorney, which, he stated, was signed and executed abroad by the Exarch of Ravenna, authorizing him, the plaintiff, to raise money for the Greek cause; he also requested the defendant to procure certain scrip receipts to be engraved, which he accordingly did, and which were afterwards stamped at the stamp office, as such receipts. The defendant suspecting the accuracy of the plaintiff's statement or authority, the intended loan failed, and no money was raised by him. The plaintiff then claimed the power of attorney and engraved scrip receipts from the defendant, which he refused to deliver up, until the engraver's bill

ought not to be permitted to neutral citizens; and the neutral nation is alone in a position to restrain them.

In view of these facts, it is believed that the doctrine set up by the United States Neutrality Act and by the Federal Courts, that the "intent" of the owner or shipbuilder is the criterion by which his guilt or innocence is to be judged, is wholly inadequate; it would not for a moment stand the test of the rule of "due diligence," as applied by the Geneva tribunal.

The English Foreign Enlistment Act of 1870 is perhaps the best and fairest expression of the modern rule anywhere to be found in public laws.

and other expenses had been paid. On their amount being tendered, the defendant claimed a commission for scrip on part of the loan, which the plaintiff also offered to pay, provided the defendant would transfer the scrip to him, on which he claimed such commission; but none was in fact ever raised, as the projected loan fell to the ground in the first instance. The plaintiff having again formally demanded the above documents from the defendant, who refused to deliver them up, he commenced the present action.

For the defendant, it was submitted, that the whole of the transaction was a fraud on the part of the plaintiff, as he had no authority to negotiate the loan in question. And his Lordship being of opinion, that a resident in this country could not enter into an engagement to raise money by way of loan, to assist subjects of a foreign state, so as to enable them to prosecute a war against a government in alliance with our own, without the license of the Crown; the Jury accordingly found a verdict for the defendant.

Lord Chief Justice Best.—"I am of opinion, that the whole of the transaction on which the plaintiff rested his claim to recover the articles in question from the defendant, was bottomed in fraud; the Jury so found at the trial; and I am perfectly satisfied with their verdict.

"I then thought that it was contrary to the law of nations, for persons residing in this country, to enter into engagements to raise money, by way of loan, for the purpose of supporting subjects of a foreign state in arms against a government in alliance with our own; and that no right of action could arise out of such a transaction; and I consequently suggested a nonsuit; but as it was not insisted on by the defendants' counsel, I allowed the cause to proceed. A case in circumstances precisely similar to the present, except that a different loan was proposed to be raised, was lately decided in the Court of Chancery in which the Lord Chancellor entertained the same opinion as myself, and in which he is stated to have said, that English Courts of Justice will not take notice of, or afford any assistance to persons who set about raising loans for subjects of the King of Spain, to enable them to prosecute a war against that sovereign; or, at all events that such loans could not be raised without the license of the Crown. I left the question to the Jury on the merits, and they found that the power of attorney was an abrogated fabrication. It appeared on the face of it to have been executed in Greece, it was drawn up in the modern Greek language, and was pretended to have been sent from that country. The plaintiff, however, adduced no evidence to show that it was a genuine instrument; but, on the contrary, it was proved to have been executed in London, but by whom did not appear. The other articles sought to be recovered, and described in the declaration as engravings, were scrip receipts, which could be of no value, as the whole of the transaction to which they were intended to be applied fell to the ground, as it was founded and bottomed in fraud. It was proved for the defendant, that he was employed by the plaintiff to negotiate the loan in question; that many articles had been written on the subject, and that placards had been stuck up in the city, stating, that the plaintiff was not authorized by the Greek government to raise any money, and that it was altogether a fraud.

"I told the Jury, that, with respect to the power of attorney, the plaintiff could not be entitled to recover, unless he shewed that it was a genuine instrument, as it was so described in the declaration; and that to render it valid, he should have proved that it was executed in Greece; but there was no evidence whatever to shew that fact;—on the contrary, it was proved to have been concocted and executed in Mincing Lane. I also told the Jury, that if the plaintiff was attempting a fraud on the public by raising money under a false pretence, and that he caused the papers in question to be delivered to the defendant in furtherance of such attempt, he could not be entitled to recover them back in this action. The Jury, under these circumstances, were fully warranted in considering the transaction as fraudulent; and I am not only satisfied with their verdict, but am decidedly of opinion that there is no ground whatever to disturb it.

"The rest of the Court concurring, Rule refused."

THOMPSON v. POWLES.

CHANCERY, 1828.

(2 *Simon*, 194.)

Loans to unrecognized communities.

The contract in this case was for the purchase of Guatemala bonds, which were in the hands of the London agents of that government. The plaintiff was led into the venture by the fraud and misrepresentations of the agents and their partners in guilt, and now files a bill in Chancery for the recovery of his money, the Guatemalan government having repudiated its agents and all their engagements because of these frauds.

The following is an extract from the judgment of the Vice-Chancellor:—

"But there is this further consideration; that this is represented to have been a contract, by the plaintiff, to purchase the obligations of persons who were stated to be the Government of the Federal Republic of Central America.

"I confess that, after all I have heard fall from the mouth of Lord ELDON, on the subject of persons representing themselves to be Governments of Foreign Countries, which this Country had not acknowledged to be Governments, and which the courts cannot acknowledge them to be, till the Government of the country has recognized them to be so, it does appear to me that this is a contract entered into by the plaintiff for the purpose of purchasing that which, by the law of the land, he could not purchase. I think that the contract, being to purchase securities from these persons, who, as the plaintiff says, were the Government of Guatemala, cannot be considered as being a contract which this court ought to sanction. The whole case being founded on that, I do not think that I could give relief to the party, who builds his case for relief entirely on a transaction originating in such a manner; and it appears to me that, on that ground, I must allow this demurrer."

KENNETT v. CHAMBERS.

SUPREME COURT OF THE UNITED STATES, 1852.

(14 *Howard*, 88.)

Held, that a contract to raise money to aid the Texans in their war with Mexico, Texan independence not then being recognized by the United States, was invalid.

The following is an extract from the opinion of the court, delivered by Mr. Chief Justice TANEY:—

"To this bill the respondent (Chambers) demurred, and the principal question which arises on the demurrer is, whether the contract was a legal and a valid one, and such as can be enforced by either party in a court of the United States. It appears on the face of it, and by the averments of the appellants in their bill, that it was made in Cincinnati, with a general in the Texan army, who was then engaged in raising, arming, and equipping volunteers for Texas, to carry on hostilities with Mexico; and that one of the inducements of the appellants, in entering into this contract and advancing the money, was to assist him in accomplishing these objects.

"The District Court decided that the contract was illegal and void, and sustained the demurrer and dismissed the bill; and we think that the decision was right.

"The validity of this contract depends upon the relation in which this country then stood to Mexico and Texas; and the duties which these relations imposed upon the government and citizens of the United States.

"Texas had declared itself independent a few months previous to this agreement. But it had not been acknowledged by the United States; and the constituted authorities charged with our foreign relations, regarded the treaties we had made with Mexico as still in full force, and obligatory upon both nations.

"By the treaty of limits, Texas had been admitted by our government to be a part of the Mexican territory; and by the first article of the treaty of amity, commerce, and navigation, it was declared, 'that there should be a firm, inviolable, and universal peace, and a true and sincere friendship between the United States of America and the United Mexican States, in all the extent of their possessions and territories, and between their people and citizens respectively, without distinction of persons or place.'

"These treaties, while they remained in force, were, by the Constitution of the United States, the supreme law, and binding not only upon the government, but upon every citizen. No contract could lawfully be made in violation of their provisions.

"Undoubtedly, when Texas had achieved her independence, no previous treaty could bind this country to regard it as a part of the Mexican territory. But it belonged to the government, and not to individual citizens, to decide when that event had taken place. And that decision, according to the laws of nations, depended upon the question whether she had or had not a civil government in successful operation, capable of performing the duties and fulfilling the obligations of an independent power. It depended upon the state of the fact, and not upon the right which was in contest between the parties.

"And the President, in his message to the Senate, of December 22, 1836, in relation to the conflict between Mexico and Texas, which was still pending, says: 'All questions relative to the government of foreign nations, whether of the old or the new world, have been treated by the United States as questions of fact only, and our predecessors have cautiously abstained from deciding upon them until the clearest evidence was in their possession, to enable them not only to decide correctly, but to shield their decision from every unworthy imputation.' Senate Journal of 1836, 37, p. 54.

" * * * We, therefore, hold this contract to be illegal and void, and affirm the decree of the District Court."

Mr. Justice DANIEL and Mr. Justice GRIER dissented.

(b) *Ships, Munitions, and other Supplies.*

UNITED STATES v. TRUMBULL.

U. S. DISTRICT COURT FOR CALIFORNIA, 1891.

(48 *Federal Reporter*, 99.)

Held, that it is not in contravention of the neutrality laws of the United States, to deliver to a vessel belonging to Chilean insurgents, in our waters, arms and ammunitions.

Indictment of Trumbull and Burt for violation of neutrality laws.

The opinion was delivered by Ross, J.:—

"The indictment in this case contains 11 counts, the first 4 of which, in effect, charge that on the 9th day of May, 1891, at a certain designated place in this judicial district, near the island of San Clemente, the defendants unlawfully attempted to fit out and arm, fitted out and armed, procured to be fitted out and armed, and were knowingly concerned in furnishing, fitting out, and arming, a certain steamship called the *Itata*, which was then and there in the possession and under the control of certain citizens of the republic of Chile, known as the 'Congressional Party,' and who were then and there, in said republic, organized and banded together in great numbers in armed rebellion and attempted revolution, and carrying on war against the republic of Chile, and the government thereof, with which the United States, then and at the time of the finding of the indictment were at peace, with intent that said ship should be employed in the service of the aforesaid Congressional Party, to cruise or commit hostilities against the then established and recognized government of Chile, with which this government then was at peace, contrary to the provisions of section 5283 of the Revised Statutes of the United States, which section is as follows:—

"'Every person who, within the limits of the United States, fits out and arms, or attempts to fit out and arm, or procures to be fitted out and armed, or knowingly is concerned in the furnishing, fitting out, or arming of, any vessel, with intent that such vessel shall be employed in the service of any foreign prince or state, or of any colony, district or people, to cruise or commit hostilities against the subjects, citizens, or property of any foreign prince or state, or of any colony, district, or people, with whom the United States are at peace, or who issues and delivers a commission within the territory or jurisdiction of the United States, for any vessel, to the intent that she shall be so employed, shall be deemed guilty of a high misdemeanor, and shall be fined not more than ten thousand dollars, and imprisoned not more than three years. And every such vessel, her tackle, apparel, and furniture, together with all materials, arms, ammunition, and stores, which may have been procured for the building or equipment thereof, shall be forfeited, one-half to the use of the informer, and the other half to the use of the United States.'

"The next three counts of the indictment, in effect, charge that the defendants, at the same time and place, increased, unlawfully procured to be increased, and were knowingly concerned in increasing, the force of a certain ship of war and armed steamship called *Itata*, which arrived at the port of San Diego in this judicial district on the 2d day of May, 1891, and was at the time of her said arrival, and to and including the 9th day of May, 1891 (during which time she remained within the jurisdiction of the United States, and of this court), a ship of war in the service of a certain foreign people called the 'Congressional Party,' then citizens of and residing in the republic of Chile, and who were then and there banded together in large numbers, in open-armed rebellion, and attempted forcible revolution, and making war against, and being at war with a certain foreign state, namely, the republic of Chile, and the lawful government thereof, with which the United States then, and at the finding of the indictment, were at peace, by adding to the force of said armed vessel an equipment solely applicable to war, viz., by adding to her equipment 10,000 rifles, 10,000 bayonets, and 500,000 cartridges therefor, contrary to the provisions of Section 5285 of the Revised Statutes of the United States, which is as follows:—

"'Every person who, within the territory or jurisdiction of the United States, increases or augments, or procures to be increased or augmented, or knowingly is concerned in increasing or augmenting, the force of any ship of war, cruiser, or other armed vessel, which, at the time of her arrival within the United States, was a ship of war, or cruiser, or armed vessel, in the service of any foreign prince or state, or of any colony, district, or people, or belonging to the subjects or citizens of any such prince or state, colony, district or people, the same being at war with any foreign prince or state, or of any colony, district, or people, with whom the United States are at peace, by adding to the number of the guns of such vessel, or by changing those on board of her for guns of a larger caliber, or by adding thereto any equipment solely applicable to war, shall be deemed guilty of a high misdemeanor, and shall be fined not more than one thousand dollars, and imprisoned not more than one year.'

"The last four counts of the indictment, in effect, charge that the defendants, at the same time and place, began, set on foot, provided the means for, and prepared the means for, a certain military expedition to be carried on from thence against the territory and dominions of a foreign state, namely, the republic of Chile,—the United States, then and there, and at the time of the finding of the indictment, being at peace with said republic,—contrary to the provisions of section 5286 of the Revised Statutes of the United States, which is as follows:

"'Every person who, within the territory of the United States, begins or sets on foot, or provides or prepares the means for, any military expedition or enterprise, to be carried on from thence against the territory or dominions of any foreign prince or state, or of any colony, district, or people, with whom the United States are at peace, shall be deemed guilty of a high misdemeanor, and shall be fined not exceeding three thousand dollars, and imprisoned not more than three years.'

"The evidence introduced by the United States in support of the indictment being concluded, the court is asked by the defendants to direct the jury to return a verdict of not guilty, on the ground that the evidence introduced on the part of the prosecution is insufficient to sustain any count of the indictment. For the purposes of the motion, every fact that the evidence tends to establish must, of course, be considered as proven.

"Briefly stated, these facts are as follows: In January of this year the steamship *Itata* was an ordinary merchant vessel. Early in that month she was captured in the harbor of Valparaiso, Chile, by the people designated in this indictment as the 'Congressional Party,' and who were then engaged in an effort to overthrow the then established and recognized government of Chile, of which Balmaceda was the head. The *Itata* was by the Congressional Party put in command of one of its officers, and was used in their undertaking as a transport to convey troops, provisions, and munitions of war, and also as an hospital ship, and one in which to confine prisoners. Four small cannon were also put upon her decks and she carried a jack and pennant. Some time prior to the following April the defendant Trumbull came to the United States as an agent of the Congressional Party, and about the month of April went to the city of New York, and there bought from one of the large mercantile firms of that city, dealing in such matters, 5,000 rifles and 2,000,000 cartridges therefor, with the intention and for the purpose of sending them to the Congressional Party in Chile for use in their efforts to overthrow the Balmacedan government. The sale and purchase of the arms and ammunition were made in the usual course of trade. Trumbull caused them to be shipped by rail to San Francisco, and engaged the defendant Burt to accompany them, which he did. Arrangements had been made by Trumbull with his principals in Chile, by which they were to send a vessel to the United States to get the arms and ammunition, and convey them to Chile for the use of the Congressional Party there. The *Itata* was dispatched by that party for that purpose, and was accompanied as far as Cape San Lucas by the *Esmeralda*, a war ship then in the service of the Congressional Party. At one of the Chilean ports the *Itata* took on board some soldiers, with their arms, by one witness stated to be about 150, and by another to be about 12, in number.

"At San Lucas the captain of the *Esmeralda* took command of the *Itata*, and the captain of the latter was left there in command of the *Esmeralda*. The *Itata* then proceeded to San Diego, really in command of the *Esmeralda's* captain, but ostensibly in command of another, who represented to the customs officers at that port that she was an ordinary merchantman, and was bound to some port on the northern coast. Before coming into the port of San Diego, or into the waters of the United States, the *Itata* hauled down her jack and pennant, the cannon theretofore carried on her decks were removed and stowed in her hold, as were also the arms of the soldiers she carried; and their uniforms, as well as those of the officers, were removed, and all appeared in civilian's dress. At that port she laid in stores of coal and provisions, all of which were bought in the open market, and some of which were marked 'Esmeralda.'

"Meanwhile Trumbull had chartered a schooner, called the *Robert and Minnie*, in San Francisco to take the arms and ammunition from there to a point in this judicial district, then expected to be near the island of Catalina, where she could meet the *Itata*, and deliver them on board of her to be conveyed to Chile for the purposes already stated. The schooner *Robert and Minnie* accordingly took on board the arms and ammunition at the port of San Francisco, and, in charge of the defendant Burt, proceeded to the neighborhood of Catalina Island, where she expected to meet the *Itata*. In the meantime the suspicion of some of the officers of the United States that the neutrality laws were being violated was aroused, and the marshal of this district was directed by the attorney-general to detain the *Itata*, if such was found to be the case; and, acting upon those and certain instructions from the district attorney of the judicial district, he went on board the ship at San Diego, and put a keeper in charge of her, and then went in search of the *Robert and Minnie*, which he did not find in the waters of the United States. Communication was, however, had between the *Itata* and the schooner and a point near San Clemente Island was fixed upon as the place of meeting for the purpose of transferring the arms and ammunition from the schooner to the ship. Accordingly, the *Itata*, on the 6th of May, 1891, without obtaining clearance papers, and against the protest of the person left on board and in charge of her by the marshal, weighed anchor, and steamed out of the harbor of San Diego, with him on board, to meet the *Robert and Minnie*, and receive the arms and ammunition. The marshal's keeper was, however, put ashore at Point Ballast, before leaving the harbor. While steaming out of it, one or more of the *Itata's* cannon were brought on deck, and some of the soldiers on board of her appeared in uniform. On the 9th of May, the *Itata* and *Robert and Minnie* came together about a mile and a half southerly of San Clemente Island, and there the arms and ammunition in question were taken from the schooner, and put on board the ship in original packages, and the latter at once left with them for Chile.

"No evidence was introduced tending to show that the Congressional Party ever received any recognition of any character from the government of the United States until September 4th, when it was recognized as the established and only government of Chile.

"But since the argument and submission of the motion, the counsel for the United States have called the attention of the court to the following facts furnished by the respective departments, to-wit: On March 4th, the secretary of the navy cabled Admiral McCann 'to proceed to Valparaiso, and observe strict neutrality, and take no part in troubles between parties further than to protect American interests.' On March 26th, the secretary of the navy cabled Admiral Brown, who had superseded Admiral McCann, 'to abstain from proceedings in nature of assistance to either, that is, the Balmaceda or Congressional Party; that the ships of the latter were not to be treated as piratical, so long as they waged war only against the Balmaceda government.' On April 25th, Secretary of State Blaine cabled the American minister, 'You can act as mediator with Brazilian minister and French *chargé d'affaires*.' On May 5th, Minister Eagan cabled this government, 'Government of Chile and revolutionists have accepted mediation of the United States, Brazil, and France most cordially; those of England and Germany declined.' On May 7th, Acting Secretary of State Wharton acknowledged the dispatch of Minister Eagan, and 'expressed hope that through combined efforts of the governments in question, the strife which has been going on in Chile may be speedily and happily terminated.' On May 14th Acting Secretary of State Wharton cabled Minister Eagan that 'French minister reports threats to shoot the insurgent envoys by Balmaceda,' and directed that they should have ordinary treatment under flag of truce.

"The foregoing are the facts of the case as now presented, and the question the court is called upon to decide is whether they are sufficient to justify a verdict against the defendants upon any count of the indictment. The counsel for the United States concede that they are insufficient to justify a verdict against the defendants under either of the counts that are based on section 5285 of the Revised Statutes. It seems to me the same thing is equally true in respect to those counts that are based on section 5286. The very terms of that statute imply that the military expeditions or enterprises thereby prohibited are such as originate within the limits of the United States, and are to be carried on from this country. 'Every person who, within the limits or jurisdiction of the United States, begins or sets on foot, or provides or prepares the means for, any military expedition or enterprises, to be carried on from thence,'—that is to say, from the United States,—is the language of the statute.

"If the evidence shows that in this case there ever was any military expedition begun or set on foot, or provided or prepared for, within the sense of this statute, it was begun, set on foot, provided and prepared for in Chile, and was to be carried on from Chile, and not from the United States. But I think it perfectly clear that the sending of a ship from Chile to the United States, to take on board arms and ammunition purchased in this country, and carry them back to Chile, is not the beginning, setting on foot, providing or preparing the means for any military expedition or enterprise, within the meaning of section 5286 of the Revised Statutes.

"The cases of *The Mary A. Hogan*, 18 Fed. Rep., 529; *U. S.* v. *Two Hundred and Fourteen Boxes of Arms, etc.*, 20 Fed. Rep., 50; and *U. S.* v. *Rand*, 17 Fed. Rep., 142, cited by counsel for the United States in support of their position in respect to this point, do not at all support it. In each of those cases there was a military expedition, and it was organized within, started from, and was to be carried on from the United States. The facts of those cases are wholly different from the facts of the present case.

"There remains for consideration the four counts of the indictment that are based on section 5283 of the Revised Statutes. The first of these, as has been seen, charges that the defendants, on the 9th of May last, at a certain designated place within this judicial district, unlawfully fitted out and armed a certain steamship called the *Itata*, which was then and there in the possession and under the control of certain citizens of the republic of Chile, known as the 'Congressional Party,' and who were then and there, in said republic, organized and banded together in great numbers in armed rebellion and attempted revolution, and carrying on war against the republic of Chile and the government thereof, with which the United States then, and at the time of the finding of the indictment, were at peace, with intent that said ship should be employed in the service of the aforesaid Congressional Party, to cruise or commit hostilities against the then established and recognized government of Chile, with which this government then was at peace. The second count charges that the defendants, at the same time and place, attempted to do the same thing; the third count charges that, at the same time and place, they unlawfully procured the same thing to be done; and the fourth, that, at the same time and place, defendants were 'unlawfully and knowingly concerned in the furnishing, fitting out, and arming of the *Itata*, with intent, etc.

"It is contended on behalf of the defendants that section 5283 has no application to this case, for the reason that the people designated in the indictment as the 'Congressional Party' do not constitute a people, within the meaning of that section. It is beyond question that the *status* of the people composing the Congressional Party at the time of the commission of the alleged offense, is to be regarded by the court as it was then regarded by the political or executive department of the United States. This doctrine is firmly established. *Gelston* v. *Hoyt*, 3 Wheat., 246, 324; *U. S.* v. *Palmer*, Id., 610, 635; *Kennett* v. *Chambers*, 14 How., 38; Whart. Int. Law Dig., pp. 551, 552, and cases there cited.

"If the dispatches from the secretary of the navy, the secretary of state, and acting secretary of state, already referred to, are to be considered as indicating the light in which the people composing the Congressional Party of Chile were regarded by the executive department of this government prior to their recognition, on the 4th of September, the position of the United States towards them seems to have been similar to that taken by the United States towards the insurgents against Hayti in 1869. That position was thus stated by Mr. Fish, then secretary of state, in a letter dated September 14, 1869:—

"'(1) That we do not dispute the right of the government of Hayti to treat the officers and crew of the *Quaker City* and *Florida* (vessels in the service of the insurgents against Hayti) as pirates for all intents and purposes. How they are to be regarded by their own legitimate government is a question of municipal law, into which we have no occasion, if we had the right, to enter.

"'(2) That this government is not aware of any reason which would require or justify it in looking upon the vessel named in a different light from any other vessel employed in the service of the insurgents.

"'(3) That, regarding them simply as armed cruisers of the insurgents, not yet acknowledged by this government to have obtained belligerent rights, it is competent to the United States to deny and resist the exercises by those vessels, or any other agents of the rebellion, of the privileges which attend maritime war, in respect to our citizens or their property entitled to their protection. We may or may not, at option, as justice or policy may require, treat them as pirates in the absolute and unqualified sense, or we may, as the circumstances of any actual case shall suggest, waive the extreme right, and recognize, where facts warrant it, an actual intent, on the part of the individual offenders, not to depredate in a criminal sense and for private gain, but to capture and destroy *jure belli*. It is sufficient for the present purpose, that the United States will not admit any commission or authority proceeding from rebels as a justification or excuse for injury to persons or property entitled to the protection of this government. They will not tolerate the search or stopping, by cruisers in the rebel service, of vessels of the United States, nor any other act which is only privileged by recognized belligerency.

"'(4) While asserting the right to capture and destroy the vessels in question, and others of similar character, if any aggression upon persons or property entitled to the protection of this government shall recommend such action, we cannot admit the existence of any obligation to do so in the interest of Hayti or of the general security of commerce.' 3 Whart. Int. Law Dig., pp. 465, 466.

"Does section 5283 of the Revised Statutes apply to any people whom it is optional with the United States to treat as pirates? That section is found in the chapter headed 'Neutrality,' and it was carried into the Revised Statutes, and was originally enacted in furtherance of the obligations of the nation as a neutral. The very idea of neutrality imports that the neutral will treat each contending party alike; that it will accord no right or privilege to one that it withholds from the other, and will withhold none from one that it accords to the other. In the case of *U. S.* v. *Quincy*, 6 Pet., 445, the Supreme Court of the United States said that the word 'people' in the 3d section of the act of April 20, 1818 (and from that carried into the Revised Statutes as section 5283), 'is one of the denominations applied by the act of Congress to a foreign power.' This can hardly mean an association of people in no way recognized by the United States, or by the government against which they are rebelling, whose rebellion has not attained the dignity of war, and who may, at the option of the United States, be treated by them as pirates. Prior to the passage of the act of April 20, 1818, the Supreme Court of the United States, in the case of *Gelston* v. *Hoyt*, 3 Wheat., 246, speaking through Mr. Justice STORY, held that section 3 of the act of 1794, prohibiting the fitting out any ship, etc., for the service of any foreign prince or state, to cruise against the subjects, etc., of any foreign prince or state, with which the United States were at peace, did not apply to any new government, unless it had been recognized by the United States or by the government of the country to which such new country belonged; and that a plea which set up a forfeiture under that act, in fitting out a ship to cruise against such new state, must aver such recognition, or it is bad.

"Congress, in passing the subsequent act of April 20, 1818, by which the provision referred to of the act of 1794 was, in substance, reenacted, must be presumed to have known the construction that had been theretofore put by the Supreme Court upon the words 'prince or state' in the act of 1794, and with that knowledge, in passing the act of 1818, inserted in the same clause the words 'colony, district, or people.'

"This was done, according to Dana's Wheat. Int. Law, § 439, note 215, and Wharton's Int. Law Dig., p. 561, upon the suggestion of the Spanish minister that the South American provinces, then in revolt, and not recognized as independent, might not be included in the word 'state.' But in every one of those instances the United States had acknowledged the existence of a state of war, and, as a consequence, the belligerent rights of the provinces. *The Ambrose Light*, 25 Fed. Rep., 414, and references there made.

"It will be observed that the Supreme Court, in the case of *Gelston* v. *Hoyt* did not say that the independence of the new government must have been recognized by the United States to make the statute of which it was speaking applicable. There are different kinds or degrees of recognition, but can it be properly said that, in passing an act in furtherance of the obligations of the nation as a neutral, Congress was legislating with reference to a people not in any way recognized by the government of the United States, and whom it might, at its option, treat as pirates? 'To fall within the statute,' said Judge BROWN, in the case of *The Carondelet*, 37 Fed. Rep., 800, 'the vessel must be intended to be employed in the service of one foreign prince, state, colony, district, or people, to cruise or commit hostilities against the subjects, citizens, or property of another, with whom the United States are at peace. The United States can hardly be said to be at peace, in the sense of the statute, with a faction which they are unwilling to recognize as a government; nor could the cruising or committing of hostilities against such a mere faction well be said to be committing hostilities against the 'subjects, citizens, or property of a district or people, within the meaning of the statute. So on the other hand, a vessel, in entering the service of the opposite faction of Hippolyte, could hardly be said to enter the service of a foreign 'prince or state, or of a colony, district or people,' unless our government had recognized Hippolyte's faction as at least constituting a belligerent, which it does not appear to have done.' Attorney-General Hoar, however, in a letter to Mr. Fish, secretary of state, of date December 16, 1869 (13 Op. Atty. Gen. U. S., 177), said:—

"'Undoubtedly the ordinary application of the statute [in question] is to cases where the United States intends to maintain its neutrality in wars between two other nations, or where both parties to a contest have been recognized as belligerents; that is, as having a sufficiently organized political existence to enable them to carry on war. But the statute is not confined in its terms, nor, as it seems to me, in its scope and proper effect, to such cases. Under it, any persons who are insurgents, or engaged in what would be regarded under our law as levying war against the sovereign power of the nation, though few in number and occupying however small a territory, might procure the fitting out and arming of vessels with intent to commit hostilities against a nation with which we were at peace, and with intent that they should be employed in the service of a colony, district, or people, not waging a recognized war.'

"The attention of Attorney-General Hoar does not appear to have been attracted to the decisions of the Supreme Court and other cases above cited, nor are any authorities cited in support of the views expressed by him. In my opinion, it is, to say the least, extremely doubtful whether section 5283 of the Revised Statutes applies to the present case. But, assuming that it does, the evidence does not sustain the charges based upon it. It does not show, or tend to show, that the defendants, or either of them, attempted to do, or procured to be done, or were concerned in doing, anything that they did not in fact do.

"What the evidence shows that they did do has already been stated. If none of those acts constituted the arming, fitting out, or furnishing the *Itata* with the intent that she should be employed to cruise or commit hostilities against the then established government of Chile, it necessarily follows that the prosecution has failed to prove the case alleged against the defendants, and the motion made on their behalf should be granted. One of the counsel for the United

States conceded, on the argument, that the evidence is insufficient to show that the defendants fitted out and armed the *Itata*, but he contended strenuously that it is sufficient to show that they were knowingly concerned in 'furnishing' her. Of course, if he is right in the concession, it results that the first count is not established by proof; and, since the evidence does not tend to show that the defendants, or either of them, attempted to do, or procured to be done, anything they did not in fact do, the second and third counts would also fall. If, as is thus conceded, and as seems to me to be clear, the putting on board the *Itata* of the arms and ammunition, under the circumstances and for the purposes stated, did not constitute the fitting out and arming of that vessel, it is difficult to understand how the same acts, committed under the same circumstances and for the same purposes, constituted the 'furnishing' of her. There is nothing in the evidence tending to show that any of the arms or ammunition were intended for use by the *Itata*. On the contrary, the whole case shows that the defendants caused them to be put on board of her with the intention that she should transport them to Chile, for the use of the insurrecting party there.

"This does not constitute the fitting out, arming, or furnishing of the *Itata*, with intent that she should be employed to cruise or commit hostilities in the service of the insurrectionary party against the then government of Chile. In principle, the case is, I think, much like that of *The Florida*, decided by Judge Blatchford in 1871, and reported in 4 Ben., 452. This was a suit against the *Florida* for an alleged forfeiture incurred under the third section of the act of April 20, 1818, now, in substance, section 5283 of the Revised Statutes.

"The court said:—

"'Admitting that persons acting as agents of the insurrectionary party in Cuba were the real owners of the vessel and her cargo of arms and munitions of war, and that the transaction of the borrowing, by Darr from Castillo, of the money wherewith the vessel and her cargo were purchased, was a sham, and that the vessel was to proceed with her cargo to Vera Cruz, and there vessel and cargo were to be transferred by Darr, their nominal owner, to persons acting for the insurrectionary party in Cuba, and that thence the vessel was to take the cargo to some point off the coast of Cuba, and land it on the shore by the use of rafts made out of the lumber on board, towed by the steam-launch on board, through shallow water, to the shore, and that Darr and such real owners of the vessel and cargo had an intent to do all this in fitting out the vessel, and putting her cargo on board, still a violation of the third section of the act 1818 is not thereby made out. A vessel fitted out with intent to do this, is not fitted out with intent to cruise or commit hostilities, within the sense of that section. If so, then every vessel fitted out to run a blockade, with a cargo of munitions of war, is necessarily fitted out, within the sense of that section, to commit hostilities against the country whose forces have instituted the blockade. * * * There is no satisfactory evidence that the vessel was furnished or fitted out or armed, or attempted to be furnished or fitted out or armed, with intent that she should be employed to cruise or commit hostilities, in the sense of the third section of the act, in the service of the insurrectionary party in Cuba, against the government of Spain. There is no evidence that she was intended to do anything more than transport her cargo to the coast of Cuba, and cause it to be landed there on rafts, by the aid of the launch on board. To do this was no violation of the third section of the act, which is the one on which the libel is founded.'

"In a letter from Attorney-General Speed to Mr. Seward, then secretary of state, he said:—

"'I know of no law or regulation which forbids any person or government, whether the political designation be real or assumed, from purchasing arms from the citizens of the United States, and shipping them at the risk of the purchaser.' 11 Op. Atty.-Gen. U. S., 452.

"The fact that secrecy and deception were resorted to in the present case, as was also done in the case of the *Florida*, cannot bring it within the purview of the statute, if not otherwise within it; nor can the circumstance that the *Itata*, in leaving the port of San Diego in the manner disclosed by the evidence, violated other provisions of law. The case alleged must, of course, be proved; otherwise the defendants are entitled to a verdict of not guilty.

"Entertaining the views above expressed, it becomes unnecessary to decide what effect, if any, should otherwise be given in this case to the recognition by the United States, on the 4th of September, of the government established by the Congressional Party, or to determine other questions raised, all of which have been elaborately and very ably argued by counsel.

"The evidence introduced on behalf of the prosecution being, in my opinion, insufficient to warrant a conviction under either count of the indictments, the motion made on behalf of the defendants is granted, and the jury are instructed to find a verdict of not guilty."[1]

[1] This decision has since been affirmed by the Circuit Court for California.

THE "SALVADOR."

PRIVY COUNCIL, 1870.

(3 *Privy Council Rep.*, 218.)

Held, that a British vessel fitted out in aid of insurgents in the island of Cuba, was liable to forfeiture under the 7th section of the Foreign Enlistment Act of 1819.

The Proclamation of the 24th of March, 1869, stated that an insurrection against the Government of Spain was reported to have taken place, and to be then existing in the Island of Cuba, and upon the fact of that report being well-founded, and a state of insurrection actually existing in Cuba, the Proclamation against Her Majesty's subjects in the Bahamas enlisting or engaging in a Foreign service in aid of such insurrection was legally and properly issued.

All the witnesses show, and the learned Judge of the Vice-Admiralty Court below himself admits, that there was a very serious insurrection or revolt in the Island of Cuba against the Spanish Government. But the learned Judge, though apparently satisfied that there was a state of insurrection in Cuba, hesitates to apply the penal section of the "Foreign Enlistment Act, because he cannot find that such insurrection is in favor of any persons assuming the powers of Government, or pretended Government, in the Island of Cuba; though the nature and object of the expedition for which the *Salvador* was equipped and fitted-out is from the evidence proved to have been in aid of this insurrection, and she, being a British vessel, was engaged in and for a military expedition, for the purpose of attacking the dominions of a friendly Power, yet the Judge of the Vice-Admiralty Court refused to declare the vessel liable to forfeiture within the meaning of the 7th section of the Act.

Their Lordships' judgment was delivered by Lord CAIRNS:—

"This is an appeal from the decision of the Vice-Admiralty Court of the Bahamas, upon an information filed on behalf of the Crown before that Court under the Foreign Enlistment Act, with regard to the ship *Salvador*, and seeking her confiscation.

"The section in the Foreign Enlistment Act which has to be considered is the seventh. It has frequently been remarked, that the interpretation of that section is attended with some difficulty, mainly owing to the great quantity of words which are used in the clause; but endeavoring for the moment to set aside the verbiage of the section, it is obvious that, in order to constitute an offence under it, five propositions must be established. In the first place, the ship, which in other respects is found to be acting within the meaning of the section, must be acting without the leave and license of the Sovereign of this Country. That is the first element of the charge under the section. The second is this, the ship must be equipped, furnished, fitted-out or armed, or there must be a procuring, or an attempt or endeavor to equip, furnish, fit-out, or arm the ship. The third is, that the equipping, furnishing, fitting-out, or arming of the ship must be done with the intent or in order that the ship or vessel shall be employed in the service of some 'foreign Prince, State, or Potentate, or some foreign colony, province, or part of any province or people, or of any person or persons exercising, or assuming to exercise, any powers of government in or over any foreign State, colony, province, or part of any province or people.'

"Then the fourth element in the section is this, there must be an intent to employ the ship in one of two capacities either 'as a transport or storeship, against any Prince, State, or Potentate,' or 'with intent to cruise or commit hostilities against any Prince, State, or Potentate.' I pause for the purpose of observing that the words are not very happily chosen which represent her as being employed 'as a transport or storeship against any Prince, State, or Potentate;' but it is clear, open as the words may be to criticism, that the intent is, that the ship should be employed in one of the two capacities I have mentioned, and not only so, but employed 'against,' that is in the way of aggression against, some foreign Prince, Potentate, or State. This should be done, as I have already said, against some Prince, State, or Potentate, 'or against the subjects or citizens of any Prince, State, or Potentate, or against the persons exercising or assuming to exercise the powers of government in any colony, province, or part of any province or country, or against the inhabitants of any foreign colony, province, or part of any province or country.' And the fifth element is, that this foreign State or Potentate, and so on, should be one with whom the Sovereign of this country should not then be at war.

"Those are the five elements which go to make up the whole charge under the 7th section.

"Now, with regard to the first which I have mentioned, the absence of leave and licence on the part of Her Majesty, no question arises.

"With regard to the second, namely, that there must be an equipping, furnishing, fitting-up, or arming, or a procuring, or an attempt to do so, no question can arise in this case when we read the evidence of Mr. Dumaresq, the Receiver-General and Treasurer of the Island, who states the condition in which he found the ship, and the preparations made on board of her, which seem to their Lordships to amount to a fitting-out or arming, or an attempt to do so, within the meaning of this section. The learned Judge of the Vice-Admiralty Court seems to have entertained no doubt himself upon this part of the case.

"I pass over the third element which I mentioned, for the moment, in order to say that upon the fourth and fifth heads to which I have referred there can also be no doubt entertained, as it seems to their Lordships; and here, again, no doubt was entertained by the learned Judge of the Court below. It is quite clear, that the ship was intended to be used as a transport or storeship against a Prince, State, or Potentate with whom Her Majesty was not at war. She was to be used obviously as a transport or storeship for the purpose of conveying to Cuba men and materials; and in that way to do the duty of a transport ship, and so to inflict injury upon the Spanish government, who, at that time were, and are now, the lawful authority having the dominion over Cuba. Here, again, no doubt was entertained by the learned Judge in the Court below, and no doubt could be entertained by any one who looks at the evidence of Mr. Dumaresq, to whom I have already adverted, and also the evidence of Mr. Butler, the collector of revenue, both of whom state what the report was which was made to themselves by Carlin, the master of this vessel, as to her conduct when she went to the coast of Cuba—how she landed all the men she had on board, plainly for the purpose of taking part in the insurrection which was going on in Cuba—how they abandoned the ship when they saw a Spanish ship of war in sight—how they were prepared to set fire to their ship if the Spanish ship approached them—and how afterwards, when they found that they were unnoticed, they took possession of the *Salvador* again, and brought her back to Nassau.

"That leaves uncovered only the third element of charge in this section, and it is upon that alone that the learned Judge of the Vice-Admiralty Court entertained any doubt.

"The third element is, that the ship must be employed in this way in the service of some 'foreign Prince, State, or Potentate, or of any foreign colony, province, or part of any province or people, or of any person or persons exercising or assuming to exercise any powers of Government in or over any foreign State, colony, province, or part of any province or people.' It is to be observed that this part of the section is in the alternative. The ship may be employed in the service of a foreign Prince, State, or Potentate, or foreign State, colony, province, or part of any province or people; that is to say, if you find any consolidated body in the foreign State, whether it be the Potentate, who has the absolute dominion, or the Government, or a part of the province or of the people, or the whole of the province or the people acting for themselves, that is sufficient.

"But by way of alternative, it is suggested that there may be a case where, although you cannot say that the province, or the people, or a part of the province or people are employing the ship, there yet may be some person or persons who may be exercising, or assuming to exercise, powers of Government in the foreign colony or State, drawing the whole of the material for the hostile proceedings from abroad; and, therefore, by way of alternative, it is stated to be sufficient, if you find the ship prepared or acting in the service of 'any person or persons exercising, or assuming to exercise, any powers of Government in or over any foreign State, colony, province, or part of any province or people;' but that alternative need not be resorted to, if you find the ship is fitted-out and armed for the purpose of being 'employed in the service of any foreign State or people, or part of any province or people.'

"Upon that the observation of the learned Judge was this:—'We have no evidence of the object of the insurrection, who are the leaders, what portion of Cuba they have possession of, in what manner this insurrection is controlled or supported, or in what manner they govern themselves. How, therefore, can I say that they are assuming the powers of Government in or over any part of the Island of Cuba?'

"Now, it appears to their Lordships, that the error into which the learned Judge below fell, was in confining his attention to what I have termed the second alternative of this part of the section, and in disregarding the first part of the alternative. It may be (it is not necessary to decide whether it is so or not) that you could not state who were the person or persons, or that there were any person or persons exercising, or assuming to exercise, powers of Government in Cuba, in opposition to the Spanish authorities.

"That may be so: their Lordships express no opinion upon that subject, but they will assume that there might be a difficulty in bringing the case within that second alternative of the section; but their Lordships are clearly of opinion, that there is no difficulty in bringing the case under the first alternative of the section, because their Lordships find these propositions established beyond all doubt, —there was an insurrection in the Island of Cuba; there were insurgents who had formed themselves into a body of people acting together, undertaking and conducting hostilities; these insurgents, beyond all doubt, formed part of the province or people of Cuba; and beyond all doubt the ship in question was to be employed, and was employed, in connection with and in the service of this body of insurgents.

"Those propositions being established, as their Lordships think they clearly are established, both by the evidence of Dumaresq and Butler, to which I have already referred, and further, by the evidence of the three witnesses, Loinaz, Wells, and Mama, their Lordships think that the requisitions of the seventh section in this respect are entirely fulfilled, and that the case is made out under this head, as it is upon all other heads of the section.

"Their Lordships, therefore, will humbly recommend to Her Majesty that the decision of the Vice-Admiralty Court should be reversed, and that judgment should be pronounced for the Crown, according to the prayer of the information.

"It has been intimated to their Lordships, that on the 7th of February last, there was a decree by their Lordships for the appraisement and sale of the vessel. She has been sold, and the net proceeds, £163, 4*s*. 8*d*., paid into Her Majesty's Commissariat Chest in the Bahamas. The Colonial Government, it appears, have incurred expenses to the amount of £145, 5*s*. 10*d*. in keeping the vessel while she was under arrest, and they claim to be reimbursed those expenses out of the proceeds of the sale. That, of course, will be proper, and if it is necessary to make that part of this Order, it will be done."

Section 43.—The Sale of Munitions of War by a Neutral State.

THE SALE OF ARMS, ETC., TO FRANCE, 1870.

Report of Senate Committee, 1870.

(3 *Wharton's Digest*, 512.)

During the Franco-Prussian war, the government of the United States proceeded to sell a quantity of arms and munitions which it had accumulated during the civil war, but with no intention that these articles should go into the hands of either belligerent. The committee reported that the sale was lawful and proper, and would have been so, if the sale had been made directly to one of the belligerents.

Early in 1872 complaints were made to the Senate of the United States that certain "sales of ordinance stores" had been "made by the Government of the United States during the fiscal year ending the 30th of June, 1871, to parties who were agents of the French Government, such stores to be used by France in the war then pending with Germany. A committee was appointed to investigate the subject, and on June 30, 1871, this committee, through Mr. Carpenter, chairman, submitted a report, in which it was observed that the Government being in possession, at the close of the civil war, of a large quantity of "muskets and other military stores," for which it had no occasion, a statute was passed in 1868 (15 Stat. L., 250), authorizing the sale of such arms and stores as were "unsuitable" for use. Under this provision certain large sales were made "without" (as the report stated) "the least preference to purchasers as to opportunities or conditions of purchase, except that persons were excluded from the opportunity to purchase who were suspected of being agents of France, then at war with Germany."

On the question whether the sales were "made under such circumstances as to violate the obligations of the United States as a neutral power pending the war between France and Germany," the committee reported as follows:

"This subject involves two questions—one in regard to the law applicable to the transactions or the question what the Government *might* do under the circumstances, and the other a question of fact, *What was done?* As to the first question, it is the duty of a power desiring to respect the obligations of neutrality, to maintain strict impartiality in regard to the belligerent powers. This, however, is more a question of intention than of fact. If a nation be under treaty obligations with another, the treaty having been entered into when no war was existing or anticipated, to furnish such other nation ships or other supplies in the event of a future war, the obligations of such a treaty may be discharged during the existence of such war without impairing the position of the contracting nation as a neutral. So if a nation has a fund on hand which it is accustomed to loan, or is engaged in the manufacture and sale of arms and other military supplies, it may loan such money or prosecute such sale during the existence of war between other nations, provided it does so in the fair pursuit of its own interest, and without any intention of influencing the strife."

After quoting Vattel to sustain this position, the committee went on to say:

"Congress having, by the act of 1868, directed the Secretary of War to dispose of these arms and stores, and the Government being engaged in such sales prior to the war between France and Germany, had a right to continue the same during the war, and might, in the city of Washington, have sold and delivered any amount of such stores to Frederick William or Louis Napoleon in person, without violating the obligations of neutrality, providing such sales were made in good faith, not for the purpose of influencing the strife, but in execution of the lawful purpose of the Government to sell its surplus arms and stores."

It was then stated that *after* certain sales to Remington & Sons had been agreed on, but before delivery, the Secretary of War received a telegram, which led him "to suspect that Remington & Sons might be purchasing as agents of the French Government," and he then gave orders that no further sales should be made to them. The sale already made, however, was not repudiated, and the articles were delivered subsequent to the reception of the telegram.

The committee, after an examination of the facts, reported as follows:

"Your committee, without hesitation, report that the sales of arms and military stores during the fiscal year ending June 30, 1871, were not made under such circumstances as to violate the obligations of our Government as a neutral power; and this, to recapitulate, for three reasons: (1) The Remingtons were not, in fact, agents of France during the time when sales were made to them; (2) if they were such agents, such fact was neither known nor suspected by our Government at the time the sales were made; and (3) if they had been such agents, and if that fact had been known to our Government, or if, instead of sending agents, Louis Napoleon or Frederick William had personally appeared at the War Department to purchase arms it would have been lawful for us to sell to either of them, in pursuance of a national policy adopted by us prior to the commencement of hostilities." [1]

[1] See the Senate Report, 42d Cong., 2d sess., Rep. 183. And see House Report, 46, 42d Cong., 2d sess.

Perels, Int. Seerecht, 251, says that the Government of the United States sold in October, 1870, at public auction, 500,000 muskets, 163 carbines, 35,000 revolvers, 40,000 sabers, 20,000 horse-trappings, and 50 batteries with ammunition; and that the export from New York to France from September to the middle of December of that year included 378,000 muskets, 45,000,000 *patronen*, 55 cannon, and 2,000 pistols. (3 Wharton's Digest, p. 513.)

It is to be hoped that the report of the Senate committee does not express the settled law of the United States upon this subject. It confounds the rights and duties of a neutral state with those of the private citizens of a neutral state, which is a very different matter. Such a transaction, however innocent the intention, can hardly fail to raise the suspicion of bad faith on the part of the neutral government. For it is undoubtedly true that a war between foreign states provides just the opportunity for the sale of such articles to the best advantage.

SECTION 44.—CONTRABAND OF WAR.

PROCLAMATION OF CHARLES I., 1625.

(*Collectanea Maritima*, 54.)

"Forasmuch as the many injuries and indignities obtruded upon the King's most excellent Majesty, and his most deare and onlie Sister and her children, and his royal Father, of ever blessed memory, deceased, by the King of Spaine, under colour of treaties and alliances, the many violences offered by him to divers of his Majestie's subjects, in taking, slaying and ransoming divers of them, in a hostile manner, whilest they intended onely their merchandize at sea. The King of Spayne's restlesse ambition to aspire to an universall monarchye, discover'd to the whole world, to the disquieting of that peace which other Princes and States, his neighbours, would gladly rest in and enjoy, have, out of an unavoidable necessity, drawn his most excellent Majestie to take up armes against the said King, for defence of himselfe, his dominions, and subjects, and of other Princes and States, his confederates and allies, there being none other safe meanes for the obteyning of an assured peace to himself and his subjects, and to his confederates and allyes, which his highness shall be ever most ready to imbrace, when with safety and honour it may be had. His Majestie, in his princely wisedome and providence, foreseeing that whilst the said King of Spaine contynneth in these termes and courses of hostilitye, itt is neither agreeable with the rules of policie, or law of nations, to permitt the said King, or his subjects, to be furnished and supplyed with corne, victual, armes, or provision for his shipping, navye, or armes, if the same can be prevented; for although theis violent hostilities of the said King of Spayne, to the trouble of a great part of the Christian domynions, are mightily maynteyned by the aboundance of his treasure from the Indyes, wherein he trusteth, and with the opinion whereof he is puffed up. Yett itt is manifest, that to maynteyne his armes, and renew his shipping, his monies in their propper nature would not suffice, if he were not contynually supplied with corne, and other victualls, and furnished with munition, and materialls for armes and shipping, from foreigne countries, whereof neither his Indies, nor Spayne, nor any other parte of his owne dominions, are able to serve, but the same are knowne to be brought into Spayne, Portugall, Burgundie, and other his countryes from forraigne parts, not in his owne subjection, and that especially from the Hans Towns, and Marchants of the Northeast countries, whoe for the desire of gayne are contented to furnish the said King, though to their owne extreame hazard and prejudice of their neighbours, with all things requisite to mayntayne his unjust warrs.

"For this cause his Majestye,

"Being amongst other Princes and States herein principally interested, for the defence of hymselfe, his countries and subjects, against the said King of Spayne's great preparations of his navyes and armies by sea and by land; and his Majesty being persuaded, that if such his provisions for hostilitie to be brought unto him by sea from forrayne parts might be stayed, or interrupted, until the said King might be disposed to live in peace, his Majestie might the sooner forbeare to continue his charge in maintaineing his forces both by sea and land, which he is now constrained yearlie to renewe, only for the just defence of himselfe and his dominions, and of his confederates and allies.

"Doth by these presents, by the advice of his Privy Councell, notifye to all manner of persons of all conditions, that shall send or carrie into Spayne, Portugall, Burgundy, or any other the said King of Spaine's countries, or dominions, any manner of graine, or other victualls, or any manner of provisions to serve to build, furnish, or arme any shipps of warr, or any kind of munition for the warr, or materialls for the same, being not of the nature of meere merchandize; that as it is lawful for his Majesty, being a Monarch and Prince Sovereigne, and as other Kings, in like cases, have alwayes used to doe, he will not only authorize his owne admiralls, and captaines of his owne shipps of warr, serving on the seas, but will also allow and approve all other his subjects, to arme their shipps at their will, and with them to impeach and arrest all shipps that shall sayle, either out of the East parts, or out of the Lowe Countries, or from any other parts, with intention to passe to Spaine, Portugall, Burgundy, or any other the King of Spain's countries or dominions, or to any the King of Spain's shipps, being on the seas, haveing on board any such graine, victuals, or provisions of warre, or furniture for shipping, or materialls for the same; and the same to bring in to the next good port, there to be ordered as goods duely forfeited for the benefitt of his Majesty, where his Majestie's shipps shall arrest the same, and to the benefitt of such others as being not in his Majestie's wages, shall, by their travell and adventure, have stay'd and arrested such shipps and goods prohibited, provided that all others, besides the captaines of his Majesties owne shipps, that shall be disposed to arme their shipps for this purpose, shall notifie their intent to the Lord High Admiral of England, making declaration of their condition, of their manner of shipping of the furniture thereof, of the number of men requisite to serve therein, with their quantity of victualls and munition, and of all other things requisite to be certified to the Lord Admirall, which being by him allowed thereuppon, the owners of the said shipps, and captaines and conductors thereof, to be bound to his Majesty's use, in good sommes of money for themselves, and, as cause shall require, to the Lord Admirall, with sufficient sureties, that they do their best endeavour without fraud, for gaine, or composition, to arrest such shipps having, as aforesaid, grane, victuall, armes, munition, or furniture for shipping, or any materiall for the same, intended to be carryed to any of the King of Spayne's dominions, or countries as aforesaid; and likewise to be bound, as is aforesaid, that with the said shipps noe harme shall be wittingly done to any person on the seas being in friendship with his Majestie, and that shall not be privy to the carriage of any such grane, victuall, provision, furniture, or materialls, into any the said King of Spaine's dominions, or towards any of his countries, or to any the King of Spaine's shippes, being on the seas. And in case any shall be found to have committed any such offence, whereby their bonds shall be forfeited, the partes dampnified, shall be fully recompenced for all their losses and damages, with the sommes of money forfeited, and otherwise as there shall be cause, and the offendors alsoe severely punished according to their offences, by due course of lawe.

"Given at our Honor of Hampton Court, the one and thirtieth day of December.

Per ipsum Regem.[1]

[1] In a supplementary proclamation of the next year, to make more definite the list of prohibited goods, it is decreed as follows:

"Concerninge therefore those kindes wherewith his Majestie maie not suffer his said enemyes to be furnished, his Majestie doth by these presents publish and notifie that he houldeth theis things following, to be of that quality and condition, videlicet, ordinance, armes of all sortes, powder, shott, match, brimstone, copper, iron, cordage of all kindes, hempe, saile, canvas, danuce pouldavis, cables, anchors, mastes, rafters, boat ores, balks, capraves, deale board, clap board, pipe staves, and vessels and vessel staffe, pitch, tarr, rosen, okam, corne graine, and victualls of all sortes, all provisions of shipping, and all munition of warr, or of provisions for the same, according to former declarations and acts of state, made in this behalfe in the tyme of Queen Elizabeth, of famous memorie.

"And therefore if any person whatsoever, after three moneths from the pub-

THE "PETERHOFF."

SUPREME COURT OF THE UNITED STATES, 1866.

(5 *Wallace*, 28, 58.)

Classification of contraband; non-contraband goods belonging to the owner of contraband on board the same ship are subject to confiscation.

The following is an extract from the opinion of the court, delivered by Mr. Chief-Justice CHASE :—

"The classification of goods as contraband or not contraband has much perplexed text-writers and jurists. A strictly accurate and satisfactory classification is perhaps impracticable; but that which is best supported by American and English decisions may be said to divide all merchandise into three classes. Of these classes, the first consists of articles manufactured and primarily and ordinarily used for military purposes in time of war; the second, of articles which may be and are used for purposes of war or peace, according to circumstances; and the third, of articles exclusively used for peaceful purposes.

"Merchandise of the first class, destined to a belligerent country or places occupied by the army or navy of a belligerent, is always contraband; merchandise of the second class is contraband only when actually destined to the military or naval use of a belligerent; while merchandise of the third class is not contraband at all, though liable to seizure and condemnation for violation of blockade or siege.

lication of theis presentes, shall, by anie of his Majesties owne shippes, or of the shippes of anie his subjects authorized to that effect, be taken sayling towards the places aforesaid, *or returning thence in the same voyage*, having vented or disposed of the said prohibited goods, his Majestie will hould both the shipps and goods soe taken for lawful prize, and cause them to be ordered as duely forfeited, whereby as his Majestie doth putt in practice noe innovation, since the same course hath been held, and the same penalties have been heretofore inflicted by other States and Princes, upon the like occasions, and avowed and maintayned by public wrytings and apologies, so nowe his Majestie is in a manner inforced thereunto, by proclamations set forth by the King of Spaine and the Archduchesse, in which the same and greater severity is professed against those that shall carry or have carried without limitation the like commodities into theis his Majesties domynions.

"Given att our Court att Newmarket, the fowerth day of March.

"*Per ipsum regem.*"

"A considerable portion of the cargo of the *Peterhoff* was of the third class, and need not be further referred to.

"A large portion, perhaps, was of the second class, but is not proved, as we think, to have been actually destined to belligerent use, and cannot therefore be treated as contraband. Another portion was, in our judgment, of the first class, or, if of the second, destined directly to the rebel military service. This portion of the cargo consisted of the cases of artillery harness, and of articles described in the invoices as 'men's army bluchers,' 'artillery boots,' and 'government regulation gray blankets.' These goods come fairly under the description of goods primarily and ordinarily used for military purposes in time of war. They make part of the necessary equipment of an army.

"It is true that even these goods, if really intended for sale in the market of Matamoras, would be free of liability; for contraband may be transported by neutrals to a neutral port, if intended to make part of its general stock in trade. But there is nothing in the case which tends to convince us that such was their real destination, while all the circumstances indicate that these articles, at least, were destined for the use of the rebel forces then occupying Brownsville, and other places in the vicinity.

"And contraband merchandise is subject to a different rule in respect to ulterior destination than that which applies to merchandise not contraband. The latter is liable to capture only when a violation of blockade is intended; the former when destined to the hostile country, or to the actual military or naval use of the enemy, whether blockaded or not.

"The trade of neutrals with belligerents in articles not contraband is absolutely free, unless interrupted by blockade; the conveyance by neutrals to belligerents of contraband and articles is always unlawful, and such articles may always be seized during transit by sea. Hence, while articles, not contraband, might be sent to Matamoras and beyond to the rebel region, where the communications were not interrupted by blockade, articles of a contraband character, destined in fact to a state in rebellion, or for the use of the rebel military forces, were liable to capture, though primarily destined to Matamoras.

"We are obliged to conclude that the portion of the cargo which we have characterized as contraband must be condemned.

"And it is an established rule that the part of the cargo belonging to the same owner as the contraband portion must share its fate. This rule is well stated by Chancellor KENT, thus: 'Contraband articles are infectious, as it is called, and contaminate the whole cargo belonging to the same owners, and the invoice of any particular article is not usually admitted, to exempt it from general confiscation.'

"So much of the cargo of the *Peterhoff*, therefore, as actually belonged to the owner of the artillery harness, and the other contraband goods, must be also condemned."

THE "JONGE MARGARETHA."

HIGH COURT OF ADMIRALTY, 1799.

(1 *C. Robinson*, 189.)

Provisions going to a port of naval equipment of the enemy may be treated as contraband of war. And if the ship belongs to the owner of the contraband, it is also condemned.

This was a case of a Papenberg ship, taken on a voyage from Amsterdam to Brest with a cargo of cheese, April, 1797.

Judgment,—Sir W. SCOTT:—

"There is little reason to doubt the property in this case, and therefore passing over the observations which have been made on that part of the subject, I shall confine myself to the single question: Is this a legal transaction in a neutral, being the transaction of a Papenberg ship carrying Dutch cheese from Amsterdam to Brest, or Morlaix (it is said), but certainly to Brest; or, as it may be otherwise described, the transaction of a neutral carrying a cargo of provisions, not the product and manufacture of his own country, but of the enemy's ally in the war—of provisions which are a capital ship's store—and to the great port of naval equipment of the enemy.

"If I adverted to the state of Brest at this time, it might be no unfair addition to the terms of the description, if I noticed, what was notorious to all Europe at this time, that there was in that port a considerable French fleet in a state of preparation for sallying forth on a hostile expedition; its motions at that time were watched with great anxiety by a British fleet which lay off the harbor for the purpose of defeating its designs. Is the carriage of such a supply to such a place, and on such an occasion, a traffic so purely neutral as to subject the neutral trader to no inconvenience?

"If it could be laid down as a general position, in the manner in which it has been argued, that cheese being a provision is universally contraband, the question would be readily answered: but the court lays down no such position. The catalogue of contraband has varied very much, and sometimes in such a manner as to make it very difficult to assign the reason of the variations; owing to particular circumstances, the history of which has not accompanied the history of the decisions. In 1673, when many unwarrantable rules were laid down by public authority respecting contraband, it was expressly asserted by Sir R. Wiseman, the King's advocate, upon a formal reference made to him, that by the practice of the English Admiralty, corn, wine, and oil were liable to be deemed contraband. 'I do agree,' says he, reprobating the regulations that had been published, and observing that rules are not to be so hardly laid down as to press upon neutrals, 'that corn, wine, and oil will be deemed contraband.'

"These articles of provisions then were at that time confiscable, according to the judgment of a person of great knowledge and experience in the practice of this court. In much later times many other sorts of provisions have been condemned as contraband. In 1747, in the *Jonge Andreas*, butter, going to Rochelle, was condemned. How it happened that cheese at the same time was more favourably considered, according to the case cited by Dr. Swabey, I don't exactly know. The distinction appears nice. In all probability the cheeses were not of the species which is intended for ship's use. Salted cod and salmon were condemned in the *Jonge Frederick*, going to Rochelle, in the same year. In 1748, in the *Joannes*, rice and salted herrings were condemned as contraband. These instances show that articles of human food have been so considered, at least where it was probable that they were intended for naval or military use.

"I am aware of the favourable positions laid down upon this matter by Wolfius and Vattel, and other writers of the continent, although Vattel expressly admits that provisions may, under certain circumstances, be treated as contraband. And I take the modern established rule to be this, that generally they are not contraband, but may become so under circumstances arising out of the particular situation of the war, or the condition of the parties engaged in it. The court must therefore look to the circumstances under which this supply was sent.

"Among the circumstances which tend to preserve provisions from being liable to be treated as contraband, one is, that they are of the growth of the country which exports them. In the present case they are the product of another country, and that a hostile country; and the claimant has not only gone out of his way for the supply of the enemy, but he has assisted the enemy's ally in the war by taking off his surplus commodities.

"Another circumstance to which some indulgence, by the practice of nations, is shown, is, when the articles are in their native and unmanufactured state. Thus, iron is treated with indulgence, though anchors and other instruments fabricated out of it are directly contraband. Hemp is more favourably considered than cordage, and wheat is not considered as so noxious a commodity as any of the final preparations of it for human use. In the present case, the article falls under this unfavourable consideration, being a manufacture prepared for immediate use.

"But the most important distinction is, whether the articles were intended for the ordinary use of life, or even for mercantile ship's use; or whether they were going with a highly probable destination to military use? Of the matter of fact on which the distinction is to be applied, the nature and quality of the port to which the articles were going is not an irrational test; if the port is a general commercial port it shall be understood that the articles were going for civil use, although occasionally a frigate or other ships of war may be constructed in that port. *Contra*, if the great predominant character of a port be that of a port of naval military equipment, it shall be intended that the articles were going for military use, although merchant ships resort to the same place, and although it is possible that the articles might have been applied to civil consumption; for it being impossible to ascertain the final use of an article *ancipitis usus*, it is not an injurious rule which deduces both ways the final use from the immediate destination; and the presumption of a hostile use, founded on its destination to a military port, is very much inflamed if at the time when the articles were going, a considerable armament was notoriously preparing, to which a supply of those articles would be eminently useful.

"In the case of the *Eendraght*, cited for the claimant, the destination was to Bourdeaux; and though smaller vessels of war may be occasionally built and fitted out there, it is by no means a port of naval military equipment in its principal occupation, in the same manner as Brest is universally known to be.

"The court, however, was unwilling in the present case to conclude the claimant on the one point of destination, it being alleged that the cheeses were not fit for naval use, but were merely luxuries for the use of domestic tables. It therefore permitted both parties to exhibit affidavits as to their nature and quality. The claimant has exhibited none; but here are authentic certificates from persons of integrity and knowledge that they are exactly such cheeses as are used in British ships when foreign cheeses are used at all, and that they are exclusively used in French ships of war.

"Attending to all these circumstances, I think myself warranted to pronounce these cheeses to be contraband, and condemn them as As such, however, the party has acted without dissimulation in the case, and may have been misled by an inattention to circumstances, to which in strictness he ought to have adverted, as well as by something like an irregular indulgence on which he has relied; I shall content myself with pronouncing the cargo to be contraband without enforcing the usual penalty of the confiscation of the ship belonging to the same proprietor."[1]

THE "COMMERCEN."

SUPREME COURT OF THE UNITED STATES.

(1 *Wheaton*, 382.)

By the modern law of nations, provisions are not in general deemed contraband, but they may become so on account of the particular situation of the war, or on account of their destination to the military use of the enemy.

This was the case of a Swedish vessel captured on the 16th of April, 1814, by the private armed schooner *Lawrence*, on a voyage from Limerick, in Ireland, to Bilboa, in Spain. The cargo consisted of barley and oats, the property of British subjects, the exportation of which is generally prohibited by the British government; and, as well by the official papers of the custom-house as by the private letters of the shippers, it appears to have been shipped under the special permission of the government for the sole use of his Britannic Majesty's forces then in Spain.

The following is an extract from the opinion of the court, delivered by STORY, J.:—

"The single point now in controversy in this cause is, whether the ship is entitled to the freight for the voyage. The general rule that the neutral carrier of enemy's property is entitled to his freight, is now too firmly established to admit of discussion. But to this rule there are many exceptions. If the neutral be guilty of fraudulent or unneutral conduct, or has interposed himself to assist the enemy in carrying on the war, he is justly deemed to have forfeited his title to freight. Hence, the carrying of contraband goods to the enemy; the engaging in the coasting or colonial trade of the enemy; the

[1] See to the same effect: The *Frau Margaretha*, 6 C. Rob., 92; the *Zelden Rust*, 6 C. Rob., 93; the *Ranger*, 6 C. Rob., 125 (ship's biscuit condemned); the *Edward*, 4 C. Rob., 68.

spoliation of papers, and the fraudulent suppression of enemy interests have been held to affect the neutral with the forfeiture of freight, and in cases of a more flagrant character, such as carrying despatches or hostile military passengers, an engagement in the transport service of the enemy, and a breach of blockade, the penalty of confiscation of the vessel has also been inflicted. By the modern law of nations provisions are not, in general, deemed contraband, but they may become so, although the property of a neutral, on account of the particular situation of the war, or on account of their destination. If destined for the ordinary use of life in the enemy's country they are not, in general, contraband; but it is otherwise if destined for military use. Hence, if destined for the army or navy of the enemy, or for his ports of naval or military equipment, they are deemed contraband." [1]

[1] *Provisions.*—In the case of *Maissonnaire* v. *Keating*, 2 Gallison, the question was as to the validity of a Russian document, in which the legality of the capture had to be passed upon. It was the case of a cargo of provisions; and the court held that provisions going to a port of naval equipment of the enemy, and *a fortiori*, if destined for the supply of his army, became contraband, and subjected the vessel (probably belonging to owner of cargo) and cargo to confiscation by the other belligerent.

Res ancipitis usus.—As to the question: what articles shall be regarded as contraband of war? there has been, and still is, a wide difference of opinion. The English prize courts, as shown by the cases given, have treated provisions as contraband in certain circumstances; and the American courts followed this practice. The French decrees and decisions, on the other hand, have taken the opposite view, that provisions are in no case to be treated as contraband. And yet, in 1885, the French government announced that it proposed to treat rice bound for open Chinese ports as contraband of war.

As to other articles *ancipitis usus*, those most in controversy have been naval stores, including in that term everything used in the construction of ships of war. The cases in which these articles have been confiscated by the English prize courts are very numerous. A few of the leading cases are as follows:—

The *Staat Embden*, 1 C. Rob., 26 (masts); the *Endraught*, 1 C. Rob., 22 (timber); the *Jonge Tobias*, 1 C. Rob., 329 (tar); the *Sarah Christina*, 1 C. Rob., 237, 241 (tar and pitch); the *Ringende Jacob*, 1 C. Rob., 89 (hemp, iron bars); the *Neptunus*, 3 C. Rob., 108 (sail cloth).

The greater number of these articles were treated by Sir William SCOTT as goods absolutely contraband, if going to an enemy's port, without considering the nature of the port. The government of the United States, in 1797, held the same view: "Ship timber and naval stores," said the Secretary of State, "are by the law of nations contraband of war." It will be seen by the French cases *la Minerve* and others, that the French practice is the reverse of that of England and the United States.

The recent changes in naval warfare, brought about by the introduction of steam power and steel ships, have introduced a large number of new articles into the list of contraband or "occasional contraband" goods. This may be

"IL VOLANTE."

LE CONSEIL DES PRISES, 1807.

(*Pistoye et Duverdy*, I., 409.)

France does not regard timber for the construction of ships as contraband of war.

Le corsaire *l'Etoile de Bonaparte* avait capturé le navire autrichien *il Volante;* cette capture a donné lieu à la décision suivante du Conseil des prises.

"Le CONSEIL:—Attendu qu'il est constant, par les pièces de bord, que le navire et le chargement sont propriétés neutres; que le port de Messine, pour lequel l'expédition était destinée, malgré l'autorité que peuvent y exercer les Anglais, n'est point soumis au blocus qui, aux termes du décret du 21 novembre 1806, a lieu pour les ports et les Iles Britanniques; et que les sucres, suivant le manifeste et le connaissement, proviennent de Lisbonne, et ont été raffinés par la

seen in Mr. G. Lushington's "Manual of Naval Prize Law" (edition of 1866), in which goods absolutely contraband are enumerated as follows:—

"Arms of all kinds and machinery for manufacturing arms. Ammunition and materials for ammunition, including lead, sulphate of potash, muriate of potash, chlorate of potash, and nitrate of soda. Gunpowder and its materials, saltpetre and brimstone; also gun-cotton.

"Military equipments and clothing. Military stores.

"Naval stores, such as masts, spars, rudders, and ship timber, hemp and cordage, sail-cloth, pitch and tar; copper fit for sheathing vessels; marine engines, and the component parts thereof, including screw-propellers, paddle-wheels, cylinders, cranks, shafts, boilers, tubes for boilers, boiler-plates, fire-bars; marine cement and the materials in the manufacture thereof, as blue-lias and Portland cement. Iron in any of the following forms: Anchors, rivet-iron, angle-iron, round bars from ¾ to ⅝ of an inch diameter, rivets, strips of iron, sheet plate-iron exceeding ¼ of an inch, and low-moor and bowling plates."

Goods conditionally contraband comprise:

"Provisions and liquors fit for the consumption of army or navy; money; telegraph materials, such as wire, porous cups, platina, sulphuric acid, and zinc. Materials for the construction of a railway, as iron bars, sleepers, etc.

"Coals, hay, horses, rosin, tallow, timber."

Pre-emption.—See as to the doctrine of pre-emption set up by the English prize courts, the cases of the *Haabet*, 2 C. Rob., 182; the *Sarah Christina*, 1 C. Rob., 287.

Compagnie de Trieste et Fiume;—Attendu que le moyen déduit de la qualité des bois composant la majeure partie de la cargaison, et sur lequel les capteurs ont le plus insisté, ne peut être accueilli si l'on considère que, loin qu'il soit démontré que ces bois appartiennent exclusivement à la construction des bâtiments de guerre, comme l'ont pensé les experts qui ont opéré hors de la présence des parties intéressées, le contraire semble résulter, tant de la teneur du procès-verbal de visite qu'ils ont irrégulièrement dressé, que de la dimension des planches et de leur nombre comparé avec la capacité du navire;—Qu'au reste, et en abordant la question de contrebande élevée par le corsaire, il est facile de se convaincre que la solution lui en est contraire. En effet, les bois de construction ne sont déclarés contrebande de guerre par aucun traité particulier; c'est faute d'avoir lu le traité de 1742, conclu entre la France et le Danemark, qu'on a dit qu'il comprenait sous cette dénomination les bois de construction. Si, par l'arrêté du Directoire du 12 ventôse an V, ils ont été rangés parmi les objets prohibés, ce n'a été que relativement aux Américains qui avaient souffert, par leur traité de 1794 avec les Anglais, que ces objets fussent regardés comme de contrebande; et la disposition de cet arrêté, de droit annulée par la convention du 8 vendémiaire an IX, passée entre la France et les Etats-Unis d'Amérique, qui, en spécifiant tous les articles de contrebande, n'y a point compris les bois de construction. Lors même que l'on aurait pu soutenir avec quelque fondement que la prohibition contenue dans l'arrêté du 12 ventôse an V eût été applicable à tous les neutres, elle se trouverait implicitement rapportée par l'arrêté du 29 frimaire an VIII, qui, à l'égard de la navigation des neutres, a rétabli les dispositions du règlement du 26 juillet 1778, dont l'art. 15 ordonne l'exécution de l'ordonnance de la marine de 1681, laquelle, dans l'énumération des objets de contrebande de guerre, ne place point les bois de construction: d'où il faut conclure que la destination pour un port ennemi des planches chargées sur le navire *il Volante*, quel qu'en dût être l'emploi, ne les a point rendues confiscables, et que tout au plus elle serait susceptible, avec les autres circonstances de la prise, d'exempter les capteurs des dommages et intérêts;—Décide que la prise, faite par le corsaire français *l'Etoile de Bonaparte*, du navire autrichien *il Volante*, est invalide; en fait pleine et entière mainlevée au profit des propriétaires."[1]

[1] And see, *La Minerve*, Pistoye et Duverdy, I., 410.

THE "NEUTRALITET."

HIGH COURT OF ADMIRALTY, 1801.

(3 *C. Robinson*, 295.)

Penalty for carrying contraband. It does not as a rule involve the confiscation of the ship.

This was a case of a Danish ship taken with a cargo on a voyage from Archangel to Dordrecht. The ship had been a Dutch vessel, and was asserted to have been purchased by Mr. Schultz, of Altona. She then went from Holland to Altona, and was from thence sent on to Archangel, to carry a cargo to Dordrecht, under a charter party made by the asserted owner.

Judgment,—Sir W. SCOTT:—

"The modern rule of the law of nations is, certainly, that the ship shall not be subject to condemnation for carrying contraband articles.

"The ancient practice was otherwise, and it cannot be denied, that it was perfectly defensible on every principle of justice. If to supply the enemy with such articles is a noxious act with respect to the owner of the cargo, the vehicle which is instrumental in effecting that illegal purpose cannot be innocent. The policy of modern times has however introduced a relaxation on this point; and the general rule now is, that the vessel does not become confiscable for that act. But this rule is liable to exceptions: Where a ship belongs to the owner of the cargo, or where the ship is going on such service, under a false destination or false papers; these circumstances of aggravation have been held to constitute excepted cases out of the modern rule, and to continue them under the ancient one. The circumstances of the present case compose a case of exception also; for it is a case of singular misconduct on the part of the asserted ship owners. They are subjects of Denmark, and as such are under the peculiar obligations of a treaty not to carry goods of this nature for the use of the enemies of Great Britain.

"A reference has been made to ancient cases of Dantzick ships, which were restored, though taken carrying masts to Cadiz. The particulars of those cases are not very exactly stated; but they were clearly the cases of proprietors exporting the produce of their own territory, or of neighboring ports, without the breach of any obligation but such as the general law of nations imposed.

"In this instance the ship was freighted at Altona, to go to Archangel, for the purpose of carrying a cargo of tar to Holland, which is a commerce expressly prohibited by the Danish treaty. Tar is an article which a Danish ship cannot lawfully carry to an enemy's port, even when it is the produce and manufacture of Denmark. This ship goes to a foreign port, to effect that which she is prohibited from doing, even for the produce of her own country; in this respect, throwing off the character of a Danish ship by violating the treaties of her country; and all this is done with the full privity of the asserted owner, who is the person entering into the charter party. In such a case as the present, the known ground on which the relaxation was introduced, the supposition that freights of noxious or doubtful articles might be taken, without the personal knowledge of the owner, entirely fails; and the active guilt of the parties is aggravated by the circumstances, of its being a criminal traffic in foreign commodities, and in breach of explicit and special obligations. The confiscation of a ship so engaged will leave the general rule still untouched, that the carriage of contraband works a forfeiture of freight and expenses, but not of the ship.

"Ship condemned."

SETON v. LOW.

Supreme Court of New York, 1799.

(1 *Johnson*, 1.)

A trade by a neutral in articles of contraband is a lawful trade. And a contract of insurance on such goods is valid.

This was an action on a policy of insurance, which included "all kinds of lawful goods and merchandises" on board the *Hannah*, etc.

The ship having been captured and a part of the goods condemned as contraband, the defendants refused to pay the insurance, on the ground that the plaintiffs had not informed them of the nature of the cargo.

The following is an extract from the judgment:

Kent, J.—"Two questions were raised on the argument in this case.

"1. Whether the contraband goods were lawful, within the meaning of the policy.

"2. If lawful, whether the assured were bound to disclose to the defendant the fact, that part of the cargo was contraband of war.

"On the first point, I am of opinion, that the contraband goods were lawful goods, and that whatever is not prohibited to be exported, by the positive law of the country, is lawful. It may be said, that the law of nations is part of the municipal law of the land, and that by that law (and which, so far as it concerns the present question, is expressly incorporated into our treaty of commerce with Great Britain) contraband trade is prohibited to neutrals, and, consequently, unlawful. This reasoning is not destitute of force, but the fact is, that the law of nations does not declare the trade to be unlawful. It only authorizes the seizure of the contraband articles by the belligerent powers; and this it does from necessity. A neutral nation has nothing to do with the war, and is under no moral obligation to abandon or abridge its trade; and yet, at the same time, from the law of necessity, as Vattel observes, the powers at war have a right to seize and confiscate the contraband goods, and this they may do from the principle of self-defence. The right of the hostile power to seize, this same very moral and correct writer continues to observe, does not destroy the right of the neutral to transport. They are rights which may, at times, reciprocally clash and injure each other. But this collision is the effect of inevitable necessity, and the neutral has no just cause to complain. A trade by a neutral in articles contraband of war is, therefore, a lawful trade, though a trade, from necessity, subject to inconvenience and loss."

EX-PARTE CHAVASSE, IN RE GRAZEBROOK.

COURT OF APPEAL IN BANKRUPTCY, 1865.

(34 *L. J. n. s., Bankruptcy*, 17.)

Trade in contraband articles by a neutral is lawful.

Chavasse and Grazebrook went into partnership in the furnishing of contraband articles to the Confederacy. Both parties became bankrupt, and the assignees of Chavasse presented a petition to have the proceeds of these transactions apportioned, Chavasse never having received anything from them. This petition was dismissed with costs on the ground of the illegality of the contract. An appeal was allowed, the Lord Chancellor considering that there was a valid partnership. He cites the *Santissima Trinidad* (7 Wheat., 340), and quotes the following passage to be a very correct representation of the present state of the law of England also:—"There is nothing in our laws, or in the law of nations, that forbids our citizens from sending armed vessels as well as munitions of war to foreign ports for sale. It is a commercial adventure which no nation is bound to prohibit, and which only exposes the persons engaged in it to the penalty of confiscation."

He also said: "But this commerce, which was perfectly lawful for the neutral with either belligerent country before the war, is not made by the war unlawful or capable of being prohibited by both or either of the belligerents; and all that international law does is to subject the neutral merchant who transports the contraband of war to the risk of having his ship and cargo captured and condemned by the belligerent power for whose enemy the contraband is destined." [1]

SECTION 45.—DESPATCHES AND PERSONS AS CONTRABAND.

THE "ATALANTA."

HIGH COURT OF ADMIRALTY, 1808.

(6 *C. Robinson*, 440.)

Carrying dispatches from the Governor of the Isle of France to the Minister of Marine, at Paris, is cause of confiscation of the ship.

This was a case of a Bremen ship and cargo, captured on a voyage from Batavia to Bremen, on the 14th of July, 1797, having come last from the Isle of France; where a packet containing dispatches from the Government of the Isle of France to the Minister of Marine, at Paris, was taken on board by the master and one of the supercargoes, and was afterwards found concealed in the possession of the second supercargo, under circumstances detailed in the judgment.

Extract from judgment,—Sir W. SCOTT:—

"The question then is, what are the legal consequences attaching on such a criminal act?—for that it is criminal and most noxious is scarcely denied. What might be the consequences of a *simple* transmission of dispatches, I am not called upon by the necessities of the present case to decide, because I have already pronounced this to be a *fraudulent* case. That the simple carrying of dispatches, between

[1] The only penalty by the modern law of nations for carrying contraband is the loss of freight and expenses. The *Ringende Jacob*, 1 C. Rob., 90; the *Sarah Christina*, Ib., 242, and others.

the colonies and the mother country of the enemy, is a service highly injurious to the other Belligerent, is most obvious. In the present state of the world, in the hostilities of *European* powers, it is an object of great importance to preserve the connection between the mother country and her colonies; and to interrupt that connection, on the part of the other Belligerent, is one of the most energetic operations of war. The importance of keeping up that connection, for the concentration of troops, and for various military purposes, is manifest; and I may add, for the supply of civil assistance, also, and support, because the infliction of civil distress, for the purpose of compelling a surrender, forms no inconsiderable part of the operations of war. It is not to be argued, therefore, that the importance of these dispatches might relate only to the civil wants of the colony, and that it is necessary to shew a military tendency; because the object of compelling a surrender being a measure of war, whatever is conducive to that event must also be considered in the contemplation of law, as an object of hostility, although not produced by operations strictly military. How is this intercourse with the mother country kept up, in time of peace? by ships of war or by packets in the service of the state. If a war intervenes and the other Belligerent prevails to interrupt that communication, any person stepping in to lend himself to effect the same purpose, under the privilege of an ostensible neutral character, does, in fact, place himself in the service of the enemy-state, and is justly to be considered in that character. Nor let it be supposed, that it is an act of light and casual importance. The consequence of such a service is indefinite, infinitely beyond the effect of any contraband that can be conveyed. The carrying of two or three cargoes of stores is necessarily an assistance of a limited nature; but in the transmission of dispatches may be conveyed the entire plan of a campaign, that may defeat all the projects of the other Belligerent in that quarter of the world. It is true, as it has been said, that *one ball* might take off a *Charles* the XIIth, and might produce the most disastrous effects in a campaign; but that is a consequence so remote and accidental, that in the contemplation of human events it is a sort of evanescent quantity of which no account is taken; and the practice has been *accordingly*, that it is in considerable quantities only that the offence of contraband is contemplated. The case of dispatches is very different; it is impossible to limit a letter to so small a size, as not to be capable of producing the most important consequences in the operations of the enemy. It is a service, therefore, which, in whatever degree it exists, can only be considered in one character, as an act of the most noxious and hostile nature.

"This country, which—however much its practice may be misrepresented by foreign writers, and sometimes by our own, has always administered the law of nations with lenity, adopts a more indulgent rule, inflicting on the ship only a forfeiture of freight in ordinary cases of contraband. But the offence of carrying dispatches is, it has been observed, greater. To talk of the confiscation of the noxious article, *the dispatches*, which constitutes the penalty in contraband, would be ridiculous. There would be *no* freight dependent on it, and therefore the same precise penalty cannot, in the nature of things, be applied. It becomes absolutely necessary, as well as just, to resort to some other measure of confiscation, which can be no other than that of the vehicle.

"Then comes the other question, whether the penalty is not also to be extended further, to the cargo, being the property of the same proprietors—not merely *ob continentiam delicti*, but likewise because the representatives of the owners of the cargo, are directly involved in the knowledge and conduct of this guilty transaction? On the circumstances of the present case I have to observe, that the offence is as much the act of those who are the constituted agents of the cargo, as of the master, who is the agent of the ship. The general rule of law is, that, where a party has been guilty of an interposition in the war, and is taken *in delicto*, he is not entitled to the aid of the court, to obtain the restitution of any part of his property involved in the same transaction. It is said, that the term, 'interposition in the war' is a very general term and not to be loosely applied. I am of opinion, that this is an aggravated case of active interposition in the service of the enemy, concerted and continued in fraud, and marked with every species of malignant conduct. In such a case I feel myself bound, not only by the general rule, *ob continentiam delicti*, but by the direct participation of guilt in the agents of the cargo. Their own immediate conduct not only excludes all favourable distinction, but makes them pre-eminently the object of just punishment. The conclusion therefore is, that I must pronounce the ship and cargo subject to condemnation.

"The court observed afterwards:—I will mention, though it is a circumstance of no great consequence, that I have seen the dispatches in this case, and that they are of a noxious nature, stating the strength of the different regiments, &c., and other particulars entirely military."

THE "RAPID."

HIGH COURT OF ADMIRALTY, 1810.

(*Edwards*, 228.)

As a rule, carrying dispatches to the enemy involves the confiscation of the ship; but where the master denied all knowledge of the presence of the dispatch, he was subjected to loss of expenses and time only.

This was the case of an American ship which was captured on her voyage from New York to Tonningen, on suspicion of an intention to push into the *Texel*. But the question of destination being abandoned by the captors, they now contended that the case came within the principle laid down by the court in the case of the *Atalanta*, as it had been discovered, that among the papers given up by the master at the time of capture, there was a dispatch addressed to the Dutch colonial minister at the Hague, under cover to a commercial house at Tonningen.

Judgment,—Sir WILLIAM SCOTT:—

"The question of destination being disposed of, I have now only to consider what will be the legal effect of carrying these dispatches; and as it appears that the practice of conveying papers of this description, for the enemy, prevails to a considerable extent, I must take occasion to remind the proprietors of neutral vessels, that wherever it is indulged without sufficient caution, they will inevitably subject themselves to very grievous inconveniences. I should certainly be extremely unwilling to incur the imputation of imposing any restrictions upon the correspondence which neutral nations are entitled to maintain with the enemy, or, as it was suggested in argument, to lay down a rule which would in effect deter masters of vessels from receiving on board any private letters, as they cannot know what they may contain. But it must be understood, that where a party, from want of proper caution, suffers dispatches to be conveyed on board his vessel, the plea of ignorance will not avail him. His caution must be proportioned to the circumstances under which such papers are received. If he is taking his departure from a hostile port in a hostile country, and still more, if the letters which are brought to him are addressed to persons resident in an hostile country, he is called upon to exercise the utmost jealousy with regard to what papers he takes on board. On the other hand, it is to be observed, that where the commencement of the voyage is in a neutral country, and it is to terminate at a neutral port, or, as in this instance, at a port to which, though not neutral, an open trade is allowed, in such a case there is less to excite his vigilance, and, therefore, it may be proper to make some allowance for any imposition which may be practiced upon him. But when a neutral master receives papers on board in a hostile port, he receives them at his own hazard and cannot be heard to aver his ignorance of a fact which, by due enquiry, he might have made himself acquainted with. The party in the present case has the benefit of the favourable distinction: these papers, with some others, were put on board in an envelope, addressed to a person at Tonningen, who was instructed to forward them to Holland, but of this the master swears he knew nothing. They turn out to be of a public nature, conveying intelligence of importance to the government of the enemy at the Hague, and they begin, I observe, with an assertion which I hope is not true. The writer says: 'The letter and accompanying inclosures which I this day dispatch to His Excellency, the minister of the colonies, *via* Tonningen, will, I expect, be communicated to you. I trust my conduct will be approved of by His Excellency, and that he will please explain himself, both with regard thereto, as also respecting the contents of my letter to the Marshal Daandels. The surest mode of correspondence, is by way of England or Paris, through the channel of the Dutch minister, as the American minister *will not refuse to inclose for him a letter to me in his dispatches*.' This, I hope, is rashly and injuriously said; the court cannot bring itself to believe, that the accredited minister of a country in amity with this would so far lend himself to the purposes of the enemy as to be the private instrument of conveying the dispatches of the enemy's government to their agent. The papers in question come from a person who seems to be invested with something of a public character, though of a peculiar kind, and they are upon public business, but I do not know whether they come strictly within the definition of dispatches. The writer of them had been sent to America from Batavia by the governor, to beat up for volunteers among the American merchants, in the hope of inducing them to embark themselves in the trade of that settlement. How far he had been acknowledged by the American government does not appear; from the contents of the papers themselves he seems to have been stationed in America, not by the government of Holland, but by the Dutch governor of Batavia, rather as a commercial agent to drive a bargain with individuals, and to induce them to join in these speculations for the relief of the Batavian trade, than for any

31

purposes of a more diplomatic nature. His commission was such that it might exist without his being acknowledged as a public accredited minister by the American government, and therefore the claimant is, perhaps, entitled to the benefit of the distinction which has been taken, that these papers, though mischievous in their own nature, proceed from a person who is not clothed with any public official character. They came to the hands of this American master among a variety of other letters from private persons; they were concealed in an envelope, addressed to a private person, and were taken on board in a neutral country; these are circumstances which would rather induce the court to consider this case as excepted from the general rule which does not permit a neutral master, carrying dispatches for the enemy, to shelter himself under the plea of ignorance. In the present instance the American master denies all knowledge of the contents of these papers, and the benefit of that denial will extend to the cargo; it is not, therefore, a case in which the property is to be confiscated, although in this, as in every other instance in which the enemy's dispatches are found on board a vessel, he has justly subjected himself to all the inconveniences of seizure and detention and to all the expenses of those judicial inquiries which they have occasioned."

THE "MADISON."

High Court of Admiralty, 1810.

(*Edwards*, 224.)

Carrying dispatches from an enemy's government to its officials in a neutral country is lawful; and no penalty attaches to the ship therefor.

The following are extracts from the judgment, Sir Wm. Scott:—

"Now I am of opinion, that a communication from the Danish government to its own consul in America, does not necessarily imply anything that is of a nature hostile or injurious to the interests of this country. It is not to be so presumed; such communications must be supposed to have reference to the business of the consul-general's office, which is to maintain the commercial relations of Denmark with America. If such communications were interdicted the functions of the official persons would cease altogether. * * *

"A Danish consul-general in America is not stationed there merely for the purpose of Danish trade, but of Danish-American trade; his functions relate to the joint commerce in which the two countries are engaged, and the case, therefore, falls within the principle which has been laid down in the case of the *Caroline* in regard to dispatches from the enemy to his ambassador resident in a neutral country."

THE "OROZEMBO."

HIGH COURT OF ADMIRALTY, 1807.

(6 *C. Robinson*, 430.)

A neutral vessel chartered by the enemy to convey military persons is subject to confiscation as engaged in an unlawful commerce.

This was a case of an American vessel that had been ostensibly chartered by a merchant at Lisbon "to proceed in ballast to Macao, and there to take a cargo to America," but which had been afterwards, by his directions, fitted up for the reception of three military officers of distinction and two persons in civil departments in the government of Batavia, who had come from Holland to take their passage to Batavia, under the appointment of the Government of Holland.

There were also on board a lady, and some persons in the capacity of servants, making in the whole seventeen passengers.

Judgment,—Sir W. SCOTT:—

"This is the case of an admitted American vessel; but the title to restitution is impugned, on the ground of its having been employed, at the time of the capture, in the service of the enemy, in transporting military persons first to Macao and ultimately to Batavia. That a vessel hired by the enemy for the conveyance of military persons is to be considered as a transport subject to condemnation, has been in a recent case held by this court, and on other occasions.

"What is the number of military persons that shall constitute such a case, it may be difficult to define. In the former case there were many, in the present there are much fewer in number; but I accede to what has been observed in argument, that number alone is an insignificant circumstance in the considerations, on which the principle of law on this subject is built, since fewer persons of high quality and character may be of more importance, than a much greater number of persons of lower condition. To send out one veteran general of France to take the command of the forces at Batavia, might be a much more noxious act than the conveyance of a whole regiment. The consequences of such assistance are greater; and therefore it is what the belligerent has a stronger right to prevent and punish. In this instance the military persons are three, and there are, besides, two other persons, who were going to be employed in civil capacities in the government of Batavia. Whether the principle would apply to them alone, I do not feel it necessary to determine. I am not aware of any case in which that question has been agitated; but it appears to me, on principle, to be but reasonable that, whenever it is of sufficient importance to the enemy that such persons should be sent out on the public service, at the public expencé, it should afford equal ground of forfeiture against the vessel that may be let out for a purpose so intimately connected with the hostile operations.

"It has been argued, that the master was ignorant of the character of the service on which he was engaged, and that, in order to support the penalty, it would be necessary that there should be some proof of delinquency in him, or his owner. But, I conceive, that is *not* necessary; it will be sufficient if there is an injury arising to the belligerent from the employment in which the vessel is found. In the case of the Swedish vessel there was no *mens rea* in the owner, or in any other person acting under his authority. The master was an involuntary agent, acting under compulsion, put upon him by the officers of the French government, and, so far as intention alone is considered, *perfectly innocent.* In the same manner, in cases of *bona fide* ignorance, there may be no actual delinquency, but if the service is injurious, that will be sufficient to give the belligerent a right to prevent the thing from being done, or at least repeated, by enforcing the penalty of confiscation. If imposition has been practiced, it operates as force; and if redress in the way of indemnification is to be sought against any person, it must be against those, who have, by means either of compulsion or deceit, exposed the property to danger. If, therefore, it was the most innocent case on the part of the master, if there was nothing whatever to affect him with privity, the whole amount of this argument would be, that he must seek *his* redress against the freighter; otherwise such opportunities of conveyance would be constantly used, and it would be almost impossible, in the greater number of cases, to prove the knowledge, and privity of the immediate offender.

"It has been argued throughout, as if the ignorance of the master *alone* would be sufficient to exempt the property of the owner from confiscation. But may there not be other persons, besides the master, whose knowledge and privity would carry with it the same consequences?

"Suppose the owner himself had knowledge of the engagement, would not that produce the *mens rea*, if such a thing is necessary? or if those who had been employed to act for the owner, had thought fit to engage the ship in a service of this nature, keeping the master in profound ignorance, would it not be just as effectual, if the *mens rea* is necessary, that it should reside in those persons, as in the owner?

"The observations which I shall have occasion to make on the remaining parts of this case will, perhaps, appear to justify such a supposition, either that the owner himself, or those who acted for him in Lisbon or in Holland, were connusant of the nature of the whole transaction. But I will first state *distinctly*, that the principle on which I determine this case is, that the carrying military persons to the colony of an enemy, who are there to take on them the exercise of their military functions, will lead to condemnation, and that the court is not to scan with minute arithmetic the number of persons that are so carried. If it has appeared to be of sufficient importance to the government of the enemy to send them, it must be enough to put the adverse government on the exercise of their right of prevention; and the ignorance of the master can afford no ground of exculpation in favour of the owner, who must seek his remedy in cases of deception, as well as of force, against those who have imposed upon him." [1]

[1] See the cases of the *Friendship*, 6 C. Rob., 420; and the *Caroline*, 4 C. Rob., 256.

In all these cases the offense is rather the engagement of the vessel as an enemy transport than the mere carrying of hostile persons as passengers.

In a note to the case of the *Friendship*, Dr. Robinson says: "The act of carrying the soldiers of the enemy has been in former wars assimilated to contraband, by public proclamation and instructions, and has been declared to render the ship liable to condemnation. The declaration of war, 25th March, 1744, concludes with the following clause:

"'And we do hereby command our own subjects, and advertise all other persons of whatever nation soever, not to transport or carry any *soldiers*, arms, powder, ammunition, or other contraband goods, to any of their territories, lands, plantations, or countries of the said French king, declaring, that whatsoever ship or vessel shall be met withal transporting or carrying any *soldiers*, arms, powder, ammunition, or other contraband goods, etc. * * *, the same being taken, shall be condemned as good and lawful prize.'

"The same declaration is also inserted in the second article of the instruction to cruisers, of the same date; also in the second article of the instructions in the war with Spain, 20th Dec., 1768."

THE "TRENT," 1861.

(*Lawrence's Wheaton*, 939; *Dana's Wheaton*, 644.)

The *Trent* was carrying, as passengers, Messrs. Mason and Slidell, agents of the Confederate Government, between the neutral ports of Havana and St. Thomas; when these passengers were forcibly removed by Captain Wilkes of the United States steamer *San Jacinto*. Mr. Seward admitted that these persons could not be lawfully taken from the *Trent* at sea, but contended that she might have been brought in as prize.

At an early stage of the civil war in the United States, in October, 1861, the Confederate Government appointed Mr. Mason to England and Mr. Slidell to France, each with a secretary, to act as commissioners or ambassadors to those countries. The government had not been recognized by any nation, and could not maintain diplomatic relations; but it had been recognized as a lawful belligerent. The object of the mission of Mason and Slidell was to aid the insurgent government by all means in their power; to urge its recognition by the European States; to effect treaties of commerce or alliance; to procure, if desired by their government, the intervention of European powers.

It may be said to have been essential that these agents should make the passage under neutral flags. They succeeded in running the blockade in fast steamers to Havana. At Havana they took passage, on their way to Europe, in a British steamer, the *Trent*, bound from Havana to St. Thomas, from which latter place a regular line of steamers, connecting with the *Trent*, ran to England. The *Trent* carried the regular mails from the South American continent and Cuba to England, to transfer them at St. Thomas to the next steamer on the route. She had a large number of passengers, most of whom were also bound to England. Messrs. Mason and Slidell, and their secretaries, had dispatches and instructions from their own government, which were under their personal charge.

On the high seas, nine miles from the coast of Cuba, she was stopped and searched by the United States steamer *San Jacinto*, Captain Wilkes.

Messrs. Mason and Slidell were found on board; but the dispatches they secreted, and confided to some of the passengers to be taken to Europe. There was no evidence or charge that the commander of the *Trent* aided in the concealment or forwarding of these dispatches.

He did, however, deny the right of search, refused all facilities for it, and obstructed it by everything but actual force; and made it known to Captain Wilkes that he yielded only to superior power, and that, if made a prize, he and his crew would lend no aid in carrying the *Trent* into port. Captain Wilkes took Messrs. Mason and Slidell and their suite from the *Trent*, permitted her to proceed on her passage, and carried his prisoners to the United States.

Earl Russell, in his demand upon the United States Government (letter to Lord Lyons, Nov. 30, 1861), stated the proceeding as simply a case of a forcible taking of four passengers from an innocent British vessel at sea by an American ship of war, making no reference to their official character, or even to their nationality. Mr. Seward's reply (letter to Lord Lyons of Dec. 29, 1861) goes at length into the subject. He considers, first, whether these persons were, as he terms it, contraband of war. He cites Vattel as saying, "War allows us to cut off from our enemy all his resources, and to hinder him from sending ministers to solicit assistance," and Sir William Scott, as saying, "You may stop the ambassador of your enemy on his passage," and applies the test, in the words of Sir William Scott, "If it is of sufficient importance to the enemy that such persons should be sent out on the public service at the public expense, it should afford equal ground of forfeiture of the vessel that may be let out for a purpose so intimately connected with the hostile operations:" and he comes to the conclusion, that these persons were, from the nature of their office and destination, contraband.

Assuming, then, which was not denied, that Captain Wilkes had a right to visit and search the *Trent*, as an act of maritime belligerency, and showing that he exercised the right of search in a proper manner, he examines the last question, whether the taking of these persons out of the ship, by Captain Wilkes, was justifiable, under the accepted law of nations.

He at once disclaims, what Lord Russell assumed to be the ground of the act, a right to take rebels or other criminals or enemies, as such, from a neutral vessel, as an exercise of ocean police. He states that the whole course of Captain Wilkes was in the exercise of a belligerent right of search and capture. In this connection, he alludes to the claim long made and enforced by Great Britain, and resisted by us, of a right to take her own seamen from American vessels. As such seamen are not enemies, nor enemy's property, nor contraband, the exercise of that power was simply an exercise of ocean police, for municipal purposes, over vessels of a foreign country.

He treats this reclamation of Lord Russell as a renunciation of such a claim in the future by Great Britain; and agrees, that, if such had been the character of Captain Wilkes's act, it would have been indefensible. Having resolved the question of contraband in favor of the captors, he proceeds to discuss the rights and duties of a cruiser which finds contraband persons on board of a neutral vessel. He contends that it is clearly the right and duty of the cruiser to make the vessel a prize, and send her in for adjudication. He adverts to the fact that, in such cases, the prize proceedings can only be against the vessel. A prize court is not competent to decide abstractly upon the character of persons on board, and decree them to be either prize or prisoners of war. Its only function is to pronounce on property, whether it be prize or no prize; and it passes upon the *status* and character of persons, only as means of determining the *status* and predicament of the *res*. He remarks upon the unsatisfactory nature of such a circuitous proceeding as a mode of determining the character and fate of persons, owing to the liability of a defeat of the purpose by the accidents and incidents of all trials. The vessel may be restored or condemned on grounds independent of the character of the persons in question. The prize court has no power directly to control the persons found on board, after their evidence is given, or to restore them to the claimants; so that, after all, the question must be left to diplomacy.

Still, he considers that this process, though unsatisfactory, is all that the laws of war have provided, unless the cruiser can take the contraband persons from the vessel *jure belli*, leaving her to proceed on her course.

As to such a right, he says that the United States have always denied its existence, and that to claim it in this instance, would be to reverse the whole course of our history. After pointing to the evils that might follow the exercise of the right, he says, "I think all unprejudiced minds will agree, that, imperfect as the present judicial remedy may be supposed to be, it would be, as a general practice, better to follow it than to adopt the summary one of leaving the decision with the captor, and relying upon diplomatic debate to review his decision." Had the act of Captain Wilkes, therefore, been for the purpose of taking contraband persons out of a neutral vessel, it would have been disclaimed. But, having been for the purpose of making a prize of the vessel, with the contraband persons on board, Mr. Seward next proceeds to consider the effect of the release of the vessel.

He observes upon the fact that it was not a case in which, at the request or with the consent of the neutral, what had been seized was surrendered to the captors, upon a release of the vessel. The master of the *Trent* made no request or assent; and the release was the act of Captain Wilkes solely. Mr. Seward then refers to the exceptions to the rule that the captor must send in his prize for adjudication, and finds them all to be cases of substantial necessity, excusing the performance of what is else a duty. He then examines the statements of Captain Wilkes as to the motives which induced him to release the vessel, and finds that he was governed mainly by a desire to relieve the large number of passengers, and an unwillingness to subject the mails to the delays consequent upon the sending-in of the vessel; although it also appeared that the want of force to bring in both vessels, conveniently and safely, operated somewhat upon his mind. Mr. Seward concludes that, while the comity of Captain Wilkes, and his willingness to relinquish for himself and his crew their large possible interest as captors, are to be applauded, he did in fact, without being aware of it, take a step which made the detention and bringing in of Mason and Slidell unjustifiable, under those rules of war for which the United States have argued, negotiated, and fought.

Mr. Seward concludes by declaring that the persons in question, held as prisoners of war, would be liberated.

By an arrangement between Mr. Seward and Lord Lyons, they were placed on board an English war vessel, which took them to St. Thomas, the port of destination of the *Trent;* thus placing things, as far as possible, in *statu quo ante.*

Earl Russell, in his letter to Lord Lyons, of Jan. 23, 1862, reviews the letter of Mr. Seward on the point of the contraband character of Messrs. Mason and Slidell, and comes to a different result. As the affair was now settled, this letter was for the purpose of precluding an inference, in case of silence, that he agreed to Mr. Seward's position. He places his argument on two grounds,—*first*, that the office and character of the persons detained were not such as to make them contraband; and *second*, that, if contraband in the abstract, they were not, on board the *Trent*, contraband in such a sense as to involve her in any penalties, since her passage was between neutral ports.

On the first point, Earl Russell contends that Messrs. Mason and Slidell have the protection which is accorded to diplomatic agents, by the decisions of Sir William Scott. He argues that this protection cannot be confined to persons who have been already received as diplomatic agents, or persons sent from regularly recognized sovereignties. The nations of Europe having recognized the Confederate Government as belligerent, and their subjects having many important rights of person or property under the control of that *de facto* government, and the recognition of belligerency carrying with it rights as well as duties, neutral nations have an interest in such imperfect diplomatic relations as they may maintain with commissioners or other diplomatic agents from such *de facto* governments. "It appears to Her Majesty's Government to be a necessary and certain deduction from these principles, that the conveyance of public agents of this character on their way to Great Britain and France, and of their credentials and dispatches (if any), was not, and could not be, a violation of the duties of neutrality."

SECTION 46.—BLOCKADE.

THE "NEPTUNUS."

HIGH COURT OF ADMIRALTY, 1799.

(2 *C. Robinson*, 110.)

Blockade by notice, and blockade *de facto*. When is notice required?

This was a case of a vessel sailing on a voyage from Dantzick to Havre, 26th October, 1798, and taken in attempting to enter that port on 26th November.

Judgment,—Sir WM. SCOTT:—

"This is a case of a ship and cargo seized in the act of entering the port of Havre in pursuance of the original intention under which the voyage began. The notification of the blockade of that port was made on the 23d January, 1798, and this transaction happened in November in that year; the effect of a notification to any foreign government would clearly be to include all the individuals of that nation; it would be the most nugatory thing in the world, if individuals were allowed to plead their ignorance of it; it is the duty of foreign governments to communicate the information to their subjects, whose interests they are bound to protect. I shall hold therefore that a neutral master can never be heard to aver against a notification of blockade, that he is ignorant of it. If he is really ignorant of it, it may be a subject of representation to his own government, and may raise a claim of compensation from them, but it can be no plea in the court of a belligerent. In the case of a blockade *de facto* only, it may be otherwise, but this is the case of a blockade by notification; another distinction between a notified blockade and a blockade existing *de facto* only, is that in the former, the act of sailing to a blockaded place is sufficient to constitute the offence. It is to be presumed that the notification will be formally revoked, and that due notice will be given of it; till that is done, the port is to be considered as closed up, and from the moment of quitting port to sail on such a destination, the offence of violating the blockade is complete, and the property engaged in it subject to confiscation: it may be different in a blockade existing *de facto* only; there no presumption arises as to the continuance, and the ignorance of the party may be admitted as an excuse, for sailing on a doubtful and provisional destination. But this is a case of a vessel from Dantzick after the notification, and the master cannot be heard to aver his ignorance of it. He sails:—till the moment of meeting Admiral Duncan's fleet, I should have no hesitation in saying, that, if he had been taken, he would have been taken *in delicto*, and have subjected his vessel to confiscation; but he meets Admiral Duncan's fleet, and is examined, and liberated by the captain of an English frigate belonging to that fleet, who told him that he might proceed on his destination, and who, on being asked, Whether Havre was under a blockade? said, 'it was not blockaded,' and wished him a good voyage. The question is, In what light he is to be considered after receiving this information? That it was *bona fide* given cannot be doubted, as they would otherwise have seized the vessel; the fleet must have been ignorant of the fact; and I have to lament that they were so: When a blockade is laid on, it ought by some kind of communication to be made known not only to foreign governments, but to the King's subjects, and particularly to the King's cruisers; not only to those stationed at the blockaded ports, but to others, and especially considerable fleets, that are stationed *in itinere*, to such a port from the different trading countries that may be supposed to have an intercourse with it.

"Perhaps it would have been safer in the English captain to have answered, that he could not say anything of the situation at Havre; but the fact is (and it has not been contradicted), that the British officer told the master 'that Havre was not blockaded.' Under these circumstances, I think that after this information he is not taken *in delicto*. I do not mean to say that the fleet could give the man any authority to go to a blockaded port; it is not set up as an authority, but as intelligence affording a reasonable ground of belief; as it could not be supposed, that such a fleet as that was, would be ignorant of the fact.

"From that time I consider that a state of innocence commences; the man was not only in ignorance, but had received positive information that Havre was not blockaded. Under these circumstances,

I think it would be a little too hard to press the former offence against him; it would be to press a pretty strong principle rather too strongly; I think I cannot look retrospectively to the state in which he stood before the meeting with the British fleet, and therefore I shall direct this vessel *and cargo* to be restored."

THE "BETSY."

HIGH COURT OF ADMIRALTY, 1798.

(1 *C. Robinson*, 92 *a.*)

A declaration of blockade by a commander, without an actual investment, will not constitute a blockade.

What constitutes a breach of blockade?

Extract from judgment,—Sir W. SCOTT:—

"On the question of blockade three things must be proved: 1st, the existence of an actual blockade; 2dly, the knowledge of the party; and, 3dly, some act of violation, either by going in, or by coming out with a cargo laden after the commencement of blockade. The time of shipment would on this last point be very material, for although it might be hard to refuse a neutral liberty to retire with a cargo already laden, and by that act already become neutral property; yet, after the commencement of a blockade, a neutral cannot, I conceive, be allowed to interpose in any way to assist the exportation of the property of the enemy. After the commencement of the blockade, a neutral is no longer at liberty to make any purchase in that port.

"It is necessary, however, that the evidence of a blockade should be clear and decisive: but in this case there is only an affidavit of one of the captors, and the account which is there given is, 'that on the arrival of the British forces in the West Indies, a proclamation, inviting the inhabitants of Martinique, St. Lucie, and Guadaloupe to put themselves under the protection of the English; that on a refusal, hostile operations were commenced against them all;' but it cannot be meant that they began immediately against all at once; for it is notorious that they were directed against them separately and in succession. It is further stated, 'that in January, 1794 (but without any more precise date), Guadaloupe was summoned, and was then put into a state of complete investment and blockade.'

"The word complete is a word of great energy; and we might expect from it to find, that a number of vessels were stationed round the entrance of the port to cut off all communication: but, from the protest, I perceive that the captors entertained but a very loose notion of the true nature of a blockade; for it is there stated, 'that on the 1st of January, after a general proclamation to the French islands, they were put into a state of *complete* blockade.' It is a term, therefore, which was applied to all those islands at the same time, under the first proclamation.

"The Lords of Appeal have determined that such a proclamation was not in itself sufficient to constitute a legal blockade: it is clear, indeed, that it could not in reason be sufficient to produce the effect, which the captors erroneously ascribed to it: but from the misapplication of these phrases in one instance, I learn, that we must not give too much weight to the use of them on this occasion; and, from the generality of these expressions, I think, we must infer, that there was not that actual blockade which the law is now distinctly understood to require.

"But it is attempted to raise other inferences on this point, from the manner in which the master speaks of the difficulty and danger of entering; and from the declaration of the municipality of Guadaloupe, which states 'the island to have been in a state of siege.' It is evident the American master speaks only of the difficulty of avoiding the English cruisers generally in those seas; and as to the other phrase, it is a term of the new jargon of France, which is sometimes applied to domestic disturbances; and certainly is not so intelligible as to justify me in concluding, that the island was in a state of investment, from a foreign enemy, which we require to constitute blockade: I cannot, therefore, lay it down, that a blockade did exist, till the operations of the forces were actually directed against Guadaloupe in April.

"It would be necessary for me, however, to go much farther, and to say that I am satisfied also that the parties had knowledge of it: but this is expressly denied by the master. He went in without obstruction. Mr. Incledon's statement of his belief of the notoriety of the blockade is not such evidence as will alone be sufficient to convince me of it. With respect to the shipment of the cargo, it does not appear exactly under what circumstances or what time it was taken in: I shall therefore dismiss this part of the case. * * *"

THE "NANCY."

PRIVY COUNCIL, 1809.

(1 *Acton*, 57.)

If the blockading fleet is temporarily absent from the port blockaded, in order to accomplish other objects, no penalty attaches to a ship which enters and leaves the port during such absence.

This was a case of several appeals from Vice-Admiralty Courts in America and the West Indies, condemning the ships and cargoes for a breach of the blockade of the island of Martinique, in the year 1804.

A ship, belonging to American citizens, sailed from New York for St. Pierre, in Martinique, unless the same should be blockaded. If the island should be blockaded, the master was to go to St. Thomas, whence he was to return to New York with a cargo purchased with the proceeds of the outward cargo.

Arriving off Martinique the 29th of March, and finding no ship there, and not being given to understand that there existed any blockade at that time, he, in consequence of the vessel's having sprung a leak, repaired to the port of Trinity, in that island, to refit; from whence he sailed to St. Pierre, arriving the 3d of April.

While in the island he heard of no blockade, and no vessel of war had appeared off the island during his stay.

Having completed his cargo on the 15th, he sailed for New York, and was captured and carried into Halifax, in Nova Scotia, where the vessel and cargo were condemned as prize.

This statement was supported by the evidence of a passenger on board the vessel, by some of the crew, and by the tenor of a correspondence between persons in France, New York, and Martinique; which proved that the blockade was at that time removed, or left so far relaxed that no armed vessels had been seen off these ports during the period the vessel remained in the island.

For the captors it was contended that, although the blockading fleet had been dispatched to Surinam, a force had been left off the island to continue the blockade and apprise vessels of its existence. This appeared, even by the correspondence exhibited by the claimants, one of the letters admitting that a British fifty-gun ship continued off the island, and was now and then seen by the inhabitants.

Judgment:—

The court held that, to constitute a blockade, the intention to shut up the port should not only be generally made known to the vessels navigating the seas in the vicinity, but that it was the duty of the blockaders to maintain such a force as would be of itself sufficient to enforce the blockade. This could only be effected by keeping a number of vessels on the different stations, so communicating with each other as to be able to intercept all vessels attempting to enter the ports of the island. In the present instance no such measures had been resorted to, and this neglect necessarily led neutral vessels to believe these ports might be entered without any risk. The periodical appearance of a vessel of war in the offing could not be supposed a continuation of a blockade, which the correspondence mentioned had described to have been previously maintained by a number of vessels; and with such unparalleled rigor, that no vessel whatever had been able to enter the island during its continuance. Their Lordships were therefore pleased to order that the ship should be restored, the proof of property being sufficient, but directed further proof as to the cargo claimed for the American citizens mentioned.

THE "OCEAN."

HIGH COURT OF ADMIRALTY, 1801.

(3 *C. Robinson*, 297.)

Merchandise going by land or inland navigation from a blockaded port, and shipped from a port not blockaded, is not subject to confiscation for breach of blockade.

This was a question arising on the blockade of Amsterdam, respecting a cargo shipped for America at Rotterdam. It appeared that the persons ordering the shipment had ordered it of their agents at Amsterdam, as a shipment to be made *there*, subsequent to the date of the blockade of that place, but previous to *the blockade of the ports of* Holland. It was argued that in the intention of the claimants it was to be an exportation *actually from* Amsterdam, and that in effect the trade was the same, as the goods were ordered and *purchased* at Amsterdam, and were to be considered as part of the commerce of that place.

Judgment,—Sir W. SCOTT:—

"I am inclined to consider this matter favourably, as an exportation from Rotterdam only, the place in which the cargo becomes first connected with the ship. In what course it had travelled before that time, whether from Amsterdam at all, and if from Amsterdam, whether by land carriage or by one of their inland navigations, Rotterdam being the port of actual shipment, I do not think it material to inquire. On this view of the case it would be a little too rigorous to say, that an order for a shipment to be made at Amsterdam should be construed to attach on the owner, although not carried into effect. It has been said from the letter of the correspondent at Amsterdam, that the agents there had informed their correspondents in America that the blockade was not intended to prevent exportation: The representation of the enemy shipper could not have availed to exonerate the neutral merchants, if otherwise liable. Were this to be allowed, it would be in the power of the enemy to put an end to the blockade as soon as he pleased. If the general law is, that *egress* as well as ingress is prohibited by blockade, the neutral merchant is bound to know it; and if he entertains any doubt, he must satisfy himself by applying to the country imposing the blockade, and not to the party who has an interest in breaking it.

"It happens in this case, that the intended exportation did not take place. The only criminal act, if any, must have been the conveyance from Amsterdam to Rotterdam. It would be a little too much to say, that by that previous act the goods shipped at Rotterdam are affected. The legal consequences of a blockade must depend on the means of blockade; and on the actual or possible application of the blockading force. On the land side Amsterdam neither was nor could be affected by a blockading naval force. It could be applied only externally. The internal communications of the country were out of its reach, and in no way subject to its operation. If the exportation of goods from Rotterdam was at this time permitted, it could in no degree be vitiated by a previous inland transmission of them from the city of Amsterdam. Restored." [1]

[1] *Blockade.*—In the case of the *Circassian*, 2 Wallace, 135, it was held that a blockade may be made effectual by batteries on shore, as well as by ships afloat, supported by a naval force sufficient to warn off innocent, and capture offending vessels attempting to enter.

That a blockade regularly notified to neutral governments must, in the absence of clear proof of a discontinuance of it, be presumed to continue until notification is given by the blockading government of such discontinuance.

That a vessel sailing from a neutral port with intent to violate a blockade is liable to capture and condemnation as prize from the time of sailing. See also the decision of Sir WILLIAM SCOTT in the case of the *Columbia*, 1 C. Rob., 154.

In the *Prize Cases*, 2 Black., 635 (*supra*, § 28), it was held, that it is a settled rule that a vessel in a blockaded port is presumed to have notice of a blockade as

THE "HELEN."

HIGH COURT OF ADMIRALTY, 1865.

(*L. R.* 1 *Ad. and Ell.*, 1.)

A breach of blockade is not an offence against the laws of the country of the neutral owner or master. The only penalty for engaging in such trade is the liability to capture and condemnation by the belligerent.

In this case, the master sued for wages upon an agreement entered into between himself and the defendants, the owners of the *Helen*.

The defendants, in the fourth article of their answer, alleged that "the agreement was made and entered into for the purpose of running the blockade of the Southern ports of the United States of America, or one of them, and was and is contrary to law, and cannot be recognized or enforced by this Honourable Court."

Judgment, by Dr. LUSHINGTON:—

"This is a motion by the plaintiff to reject the fourth article of the defendant's answer. The parties in this cause are John Andrews Wardell, formerly the master of the *Helen*, plaintiff, and the Albion Trading Company, the owners of the ship, defendants. The master sues for wages (with certain premiums added), alleged to have been earned between July, 1864, and March, 1865. The answer states that according to the agreement as set forth by the defendants, the plaintiff has been paid all that was due to him. This part of the

soon as it commences. See also the *Vrow Judith*, 1 C. Rob., 150. In this case a *de facto* blockade may be broken without notice, by egress. But persons entering a place under *de facto* blockade are entitled to warning.

The French rule in respect of a violation of blockade differs essentially from that of the United States and England. Notwithstanding that a blockade has been publicly proclaimed, a ship sailing for a blockaded port is entitled to a warning, entered upon her papers, and is only liable to seizure and condemnation when she subsequently attempts to enter or leave a blockaded port. See the cases of *La Louisa*, Pistoye et Duverdy, I., 382; and the *Eliza Cornish*, ib., 387.

As to the blockades established by the "orders in council," during the wars with Napoleon I., see Edwards' Admiralty Reports, 381–416, and the appendix to that volume. See also in the same volume, pp. 249–251, and 311–326.

For other cases on the subject of blockade, see the *Baigorry*, 2 Wall., 474; the *Cheshire*, 3 Wall., 231, 235; the *Admiral*, 3 Wall., 604; the *Peterhoff*, 5 Wall., 28; the *Dashing Wave*, 5 Wall., 170; the *Teresita*, 5 Wall., 180; the *Pearle*, 5 Wall., 574; the *Wren*, 6 Wall., 582; the *Franciska*, Spinks, 111, and 10 Moore, P. C. C., 37; the *Henrick and Maria*, 1 C. Rob., 146.

32

answer is not objected to. The fourth and last article is the one objected to. It alleges that the agreement was entered into for the purpose of breaking the blockade of the Southern States of America; that such an agreement is contrary to law, and cannot be enforced by this Court. In the course of the argument, the judgment in *Ex parte Chavasse re Grazebrook*, 34 L. J. (Bkr.), 17, was cited as governing the case; a judgment recently delivered by Lord Westbury whilst he was Lord Chancellor. The law there laid down is briefly stated, that a contract of partnership in blockade-running is not contrary to the municipal law of this country; and by the decree the partnership was declared valid, and the accounts ordered accordingly. It was admitted that this decision is directly applicable to the present case, a suit to recover wages according to a contract with respect to an intended adventure to break the blockade.

"That a decision of the Lord Chancellor is to be treated by this court with the greatest respect there can be no doubt, but is it absolutely binding?

"There are three tribunals whose decisions are absolutely binding upon the Court of Admiralty: 1. The House of Lords. 2. The Privy Council. 3. The Courts of Common Law when deciding upon the construction of a statute. If a decision of any of these tribunals is cited, all that the Court of Admiralty can do is to inquire if the decision is applicable to the case. If so, then it is the duty of the Court to obey, whatever may be its own judgment.

"No other decisions are, I believe, absolutely binding on the Court. On the present occasion, no decision has been cited from the House of Lords or Privy Council. Whatever, therefore, may be the effect of the decisions of other tribunals, I am not relieved from the duty of reconsidering the whole question.

"An intimation has been given that this case will be carried to the Judicial Committee; if so, I apprehend that tribunal might be inclined to consider me remiss in my duty if I had omitted to form an independent judgment on the case, and to state it with my reasons. It is, I conceive, admitted on all hands, that the Court must enforce the agreement with the master, unless it is satisfied that such agreement is illegal by the municipal law of Great Britain. In order to prove this proposition, the defendants say that the agreement to break the blockade by a neutral ship is, on the part of all persons concerned, illegal according to the law of nations, and that the law of nations is a part of the municipal law of the land—*ergo*, this contract was illegal by municipal law.

"Now a good deal may depend on the sense in which the word 'illegal' is used. I am strongly inclined to think that the defendants attach to it a more extensive meaning than it can properly bear, or was intended to bear by those who used it. The true meaning, I think, is that all such contracts are illegal so far, that if carried out, they would lead to acts which might, under certain circumstances, expose the parties concerned to such penal consequences as are sanctioned by international law, for breach of blockade, or for the carrying of contraband. If so, the illegality is one of a limited character. For instance suppose a vessel after breaking the blockade completes her voyage home, and is afterwards seized on another voyage, the original taint of illegality—whatever it may have been—is purged, and the ship cannot be condemned; yet if the voyage was, *ab initio*, wholly and absolutely illegal, both by the law of nations and the municipal law, why should its successful termination purge the offence? Let me consider the relative situation of the parties. A neutral country has a right to trade with all other countries in time of peace. One of these countries becomes a belligerent, and is blockaded. Why should the right of the neutral be affected by the acts of the other belligerent? The answer of the blockading power is: 'Mine is a just and necessary war,' a matter which, in ordinary cases, the neutral cannot question, 'I must seize contraband, I must enforce blockade, to carry on the war.' In this state of things there has been a long and admitted usage on the part of all civilized states—a concession by both parties, the belligerent and the neutral—a universal usage which constitutes the law of nations. It is only with reference to this usage that the belligerent can interfere with the neutral. Suppose no question of blockade or contraband, no belligerent could claim a right of seizure on the high seas of a neutral vessel going to the port of another belligerent, however essential to his interest it might be so to do.

"What is the usage as to blockade? There are several conditions to be observed in order to justify the seizure of a ship for breach of blockade. The blockade must be effectual and (save accidental interruption by weather) constantly enforced. The neutral vessel must be taken *in delicto*. The blockade must be enforced against all nations alike, including the belligerent one. When all the necessary conditions are satisfied, then, by the usage of nations, the belligerent is allowed to capture and condemn neutral vessels without remonstrance from the neutral state. It never has been a part of admitted common usage that such voyages should be deemed illegal by the neutral state, still less that the neutral state should be bound to prevent them; the belligerent has not a shadow of right to require more than universal usage has given him, and has no pretence to say to the neutral: 'You shall help me to enforce my belligerent right by curtailing your own freedom of commerce, and making that illegal by your own law which was not so before.' This doctrine is not inconsistent with the maxim that the law of nations is part of the law of the land. The fact is, the law of nations has never declared that a neutral state is bound to impede or diminish its own trade by municipal restriction. Our own Foreign Enlistment Act is itself a proof that to constitute transactions between British subjects, when neutral and belligerents, a municipal offence by the law of Great Britain, a statute was necessary. If the acts mentioned in that statute were in themselves a violation of municipal law, why any statute at all? I am now speaking of fitting out ships of war, not of levying soldiers, which is altogether a different matter. Then how stands the case upon authority? I may here say, that in principle, there is no essential difference whether the question of breach of municipal law is raised with regard to contraband or breach of blockade.

"Mr. Duer, 'Marine Insurance,' vol. I., lect. VII., is the only text-writer who maintains an opinion contrary to what I have stated to be the law. He maintains it with much ability and acuteness, but he stands alone. He himself admits that an insurance of a contraband voyage is no offence against municipal law of a neutral country, according to the practice of all the principal states of continental Europe. In the American courts the question has been more than once agitated, but with the same result. In the case of *The Santissima Trinidad*, 7 Wheat., 340, Mr. Justice STORY says:—'It is apparent that, though equipped as a vessel of war, she (*The Independencia*) was sent to Buenos Ayres on a commercial adventure, contraband, indeed, but in no shape violating our laws or our national neutrality. If captured by a Spanish ship of war during the voyage, she would have been justly condemned as good prize, and for being engaged in a traffic prohibited by the law of nations. But there is nothing in our law or in the law of nations that forbids our citizens fron sending armed vessels as well as munitions of war to foreign ports for sale. It is a commercial adventure which no nation is bound to prohibit, and which only exposes the persons engaged in it to the penalty of confiscation.' * * *

"'There is no pretence for saying that the original outfit on the voyage was illegal.' Again, in *Richardson* v. *The Marine Insurance Company*, 6 Mass., 112, PARSONS, C. J., observes:—'The last class we shall mention is the transportation by a neutral of goods contraband of war to the country of either of the belligerent powers. And here, it is said, that these voyages are prohibited by the law of nations, which forms a part of the municipal law of every state, and, consequently, that an insurance on such voyages made in a neutral state is prohibited by the laws of that state, and therefore, as in the case of an insurance on interdicted commerce, is void. That there are certain laws which form a part of the municipal laws of all civilized states, regulating their mutual intercourse and duties, and thence called the law of nations, must be admitted: as, for instance, the law of nations affecting the rights and the security of ambassadors. But we do not consider the law of nations, ascertaining what voyages or merchandise are contraband of war, as having the same extent and effect. It is agreed by every civilized state that, if the subject of a neutral power shall attempt to furnish either of the belligerent sovereigns with goods contraband of war, the other may rightfully seize and condemn them as prize. But we do not know of any rule established by the law of nations that the neutral shipper of goods contraband of war, is an offender against his own sovereign, and liable to be punished by the municipal laws of his own country. When a neutral sovereign is notified of a declaration of war, he may, and usually does, notify his subjects of it, with orders to decline all contraband trade with the nations at war, declaring that, if they are taken in it, he cannot protect them, but not announcing the trade as a violation of his own laws. Should their sovereign offer to protect them, his conduct would be incompatible with his neutrality. And as, on the one hand, he cannot complain of the confiscation of his subjects' goods, so, on the other, the power at war *does not impute to him* these practices of his subjects. A neutral merchant is not obliged to regard the state of war between other nations, but if he ships goods prohibited *jure belli*, they may be rightfully seized and condemned. It is one of the cases where two conflicting rights exist, which either party may exercise without charging the other with doing wrong. As the transportation is not prohibited by the laws of the neutral sovereign, his subjects may lawfully be concerned in it; and, as the right of war lawfully authorizes a belligerent power to seize and condemn the goods, he may lawfully do it.' Lastly, in *Seton, Maitland & Co.* v. *Low*, 1 Johnson, 5, Mr. Justice KENT says:—'I am of opinion that the contraband goods were lawful goods, and that whatever is not prohibited to be exported by the positive law of the country is lawful. It may be said that the law of nations is part of the municipal law of the land, and that by that law contraband trade is prohibited to neutrals, and, consequently, unlawful. This reasoning is not destitute of force; but the fact is that the law of nations does not declare the trade to be unlawful. It only authorizes the seizure of the contraband articles by the belligerent powers.' * * *

"In the English Courts the only case in which the point has been actually decided is the recent case before the Lord Chancellor, which I have already adverted to. With regard to the cases in Mr. Duer's book, *Naylor* v. *Taylor*, *Medeiross* v. *Hill*, it is enough to say that, in the view which the court eventually took of the facts, the question of law did not arise. It is in these two cases impossible to say with certainty what was the opinion of the judges at *nisi prius*.

"I cannot entertain any doubt as to the judgment I ought to pronounce in this case. It appears that principle, authority, and usage unite in calling on me to reject the new doctrine that, to carry on trade with a blockaded port, is or ought to be a municipal offence by the law of nations. I must direct the 4th article of the answer to be struck out. I cannot pass by the fact that the attempt to introduce this novel doctrine comes from an avowed *particeps criminis*, who seeks to benefit himself by it. As he has failed on every ground, he must pay the cost of his experiment."

SECTION 47.—RULE OF THE WAR OF 1756.

THE "IMMANUEL."

HIGH COURT OF ADMIRALTY, 1799.

(2 *C. Robinson*, 186.)

Neutrals will not be permitted to engage in a trade, during a war, from which they were excluded in time of peace. This applies especially to the colonial trade.

This was the case of an asserted Hamburg ship, taken 14th August, 1799, on a voyage from Hamburg to St. Domingo, having in her voyage touched at Bourdeaux, where she sold part of the goods brought from Hamburg, and took a quantity of iron stores and other articles for St. Domingo. A question was first raised as to the property of the ship and cargo; 2dly, supposing it to be neutral property, whether a trade from the mother country of France to St. Domingo, a French Colony, was not an illegal trade, and such as would render the property of neutrals engaged in it liable to be considered as the property of enemies, and subject to confiscation?

The following are extracts from the judgment.

SIR WM. SCOTT.—"Upon the breaking out of a war, it is the right of neutrals to carry on their *accustomed trade*, with an exception of the particular cases of a trade to blockaded places, or in contraband articles (in both which cases their property is liable to be condemned), and of their ships being liable to visitation and search; in which case however they are entitled to freight and expenses. I do not mean to say that in the accidents of a war the property of neutrals may not be variously entangled and endangered; in the nature of human connections it is hardly possible that inconveniences of this kind should be altogether avoided. Some neutrals will be unjustly engaged in covering the goods of the enemy, and others will be unjustly suspected of doing it; these inconveniences are more than fully balanced by the enlargement of their commerce; the trade of the belligerents is usually interrupted in a great degree, and falls in the same degree into the lap of neutrals. But without reference to accidents of the one kind or other, the general rule is, that the neutral has a right to carry on, in time of war, his accustomed trade to the utmost extent of which that accustomed trade is capable.

"Very different is the case of a trade which the neutral has never possessed, which he holds by no title of use and habit in times of peace, and which, in fact, can obtain in war by no other title, than by the success of the one belligerent against the other, and at the expense of that very belligerent under whose success he sets up his title; and such I take to be the colonial trade, generally speaking.

"What is the colonial trade *generally speaking?* It is a trade generally shut up to the exclusive use of the mother country, to which the colony belongs, and this to a double use;—that, of supplying a market for the consumption of native commodities, and the other of furnishing to the mother country the peculiar commodities of the colonial regions; to these two purposes of the mother country, the general policy respecting colonies belonging to the states of Europe, has restricted them. With respect to other countries, generally speaking, the colony has no existence; it is possible that indirectly and remotely such colonies may affect the commerce of other countries. * * *

"Upon the interruption of a war, what are the rights of belligerents and neutrals respectively regarding such places? It is an indubitable right of the belligerent to possess himself of such places, as of any other possession of his enemy. This is his common right, but he has the certain means of carrying such a right into effect, if he has a decided superiority at sea: Such colonies are dependent for their existence, as colonies, on foreign supplies; if they cannot be supplied and defended they must fall to the belligerent of course—and if the belligerent chooses to apply his means to such an object, what right has a third party, perfectly neutral, to step in and prevent the execution? No existing interest of his is affected by it; he can have no right to apply to his own use the beneficial consequences of the mere act of the belligerent; and say, 'True it is, you have, by force of arms forced such places out of the exclusive possession of the enemy, but I will share the benefit of the conquest, and by sharing its benefits prevent its progress. You have in effect, and by lawful means, turned the enemy out of the possession which he had exclusively maintained against the whole world, and with whom we had never presumed to interfere; but we will interpose to prevent his absolute surrender, by the means of that very opening, which the prevalence of your arms alone has affected; supplies shall be sent and their products shall be exported; you have lawfully destroyed his monopoly, but you shall not be permitted to possess it yourself; we insist to share the fruits of your victories, and your blood and treasure have been expended, not for your own interest, but for the common benefit of others.'

"Upon these grounds, it cannot be contended to be a *right* of neutrals, to intrude into a commerce which had been uniformly shut against them, and which is now forced open merely by the pressure of war; for when the enemy, under an entire inability to supply his colonies and to export their products, affects to open them to neutrals, it is not his will but his necessity that changes his system; that change is the direct and unavoidable consequence of the compulsion of war, it is a measure not of French councils, but of British force.

"Upon these and other grounds, which I shall not at present enumerate, an instruction issued at an early period for the purpose of preventing the communication of neutrals with the colonies of the enemy, intended, I presume, to be carried into effect on the same footing, on which the prohibition had been legally enforced in the war of 1756; a period when, Mr. Justice Blackstone observes, the decisions on the law of nations proceeding from the Court of Appeals, were known and revered by every state in Europe.

"Condemned."

THE "EMANUEL."

HIGH COURT OF ADMIRALTY, 1799.

(1 *C. Robinson*, 296.)

Neutrals not allowed to carry on a trade during war, forbidden to them in time of peace. This rule applies to the coasting trade.

This was a case respecting the allowance of freight and expenses to a neutral ship, taken carrying on the coasting trade of the enemy.

The following are extracts from the judgment by Sir WM. SCOTT :—

"Now the ground upon which it is contended that the freight is not due to the proprietors of this vessel, is, that she is a Danish ship employed in the transmission of Spanish goods, from one Spanish port to another, and so carrying on the coasting-trade of that country. In our own country it has long been the system, that the coasting-trade should only be carried on by our own navigation. I observe, that in all the rage of novel experiment that has dictated the commercial regulations of France in its new condition, this policy is held sacred; it stands enacted, by a decree 21st Sept., 1793, that no goods, the growth or manufacture of France, shall be carried from one French port to another in foreign ships under pain of confiscation.—The same policy has directed the commercial system of other European countries; in the ordinary state of affairs, no indulgence is generally permitted to the ships of most other countries to carry on the coasting trade. I think therefore the *onus probandi* does at least lie on that side; and always makes it necessary to be shown by the claimants, that such a trade was not a mere indulgence, and a temporary relaxation of the coasting system of the state in question; but that it was a common and ordinary trade, open to the ships of any country whatever. * * *

"As to the coasting trade (supposing it to be a trade not usually opened to foreign vessels), can there be described a more effective accommodation that can be given to an enemy during a war than to undertake it for him during his own disability?"

SECTION 48.—CONTINUOUS VOYAGES.

THE "WILLIAM."

LORDS OF APPEAL IN PRIZE CASES, 1806.

(5 *C. Robinson*, 385.)

By the "Rule of the War of 1756," neutrals were not permitted to engage in the direct trade between the enemy and his colonies. And the mere touching at a neutral port to avoid this rule, will not make the voyage lawful.

This was a question on the continuity of a voyage in the colonial trade of the enemy, brought by appeal from the Vice-Admiralty

Court at Halifax, where the ship and cargo, taken on a destination to Bilboa in Spain, and claimed on behalf of Messrs. W. and N. Hooper of Marblehead in the state of Massachusetts, had been condemned 17th July, 1800.

Among the papers was a certificate from the collector of the customs, "that this vessel had entered and landed a cargo of cocoa belonging to Messrs. W. and N. Hooper, and that the duties had been secured agreeable to law, and that the said cargo had been reshipped on board this vessel bound for Bilboa.

Judgment,—Sir WILLIAM GRANT :—

"The question in this case is, whether that part of the cargo which has been the subject of further proof, and which, it is admitted, was, at the time of the capture, going to Spain, is to be considered as coming directly from Laguira within the meaning of his Majesty's instructions. According to our understanding of the law, it is only from those instructions that neutrals derive any right of carrying on with the colonies of our enemies, in time of war, a trade from which they were excluded in time of peace. The instructions had not permitted the direct trade between the hostile colony and its mother country, but had, on the contrary ordered all vessels engaged in it to be brought in for lawful adjudication; and what the present claimants accordingly maintain, is not that they could carry the produce of Laguira directly to Spain; but that they were not so carrying the cargo in question, inasmuch as the voyage in which it was taken was a voyage from North America, and not directly from a colony of Spain.

"What then, with reference to this subject, is to be considered as a direct voyage from one place to another? Nobody has ever supposed that a mere deviation from the straightest and shortest course, in which the voyage could be performed, would change its denomination, and make it cease to be a direct one within the intendment of the instructions.

"Nothing can depend on the degree or the deviation—whether it be of more or fewer leagues, whether towards the coast of Africa, or towards that of America. Neither will it be contended that the point from which the commencement of a voyage is to be reckoned changes as often as the ship stops in the course of it; nor will it the more change, because a party may choose arbitrarily by the ship's papers, or otherwise, to give the name of a distinct voyage to each stage of a ship's progress. The act of shifting the cargo from the ship to the shore, and from the shore back again into the ship, does not necessarily amount to the termination of one voyage and the commencement of another. It may be wholly unconnected with any purpose of importation into the place where it is done: Supposing the landing to be merely for the purpose of airing or drying the goods, or of repairing the ship, would any man think of describing the voyage as beginning at the place where it happened to become necessary to go through such a process?

"Again, let it be supposed that the party has a motive for desiring to make the voyage appear to begin at some other place than that of the original lading, and that he therefore lands the cargo purely and solely for the purpose of enabling himself to affirm, that it was at such other place that the goods were taken on board, would this contrivance at all alter the truth of the fact? Would not the real voyage still be from the place of the original shipment, notwithstanding the attempt to give it the appearance of having begun from a different place? The truth may not always be discernible, but when it is discovered, it is according to the truth and not according to the fiction, that we are to give to the transaction its character and denomination. If the voyage from the place of lading be not really ended, it matters not by what acts the party may have evinced his desire of making it appear to have been ended. That those acts have been attended with trouble and expence cannot alter their quality or their effect. The trouble and expence may weigh as circumstances of evidence, to shew the purpose for which the acts were done; but if the evasive purpose be admitted or proved, we can never be found to accept as a substitute for the observance of the law, the means, however operose, which have been employed to cover a breach of it. Between the actual importation by which a voyage is really ended, and the colourable importation which is to give it the appearance of being ended, there must necessarily be a great resemblance. The acts to be done must be almost entirely the same; but there is this difference between them.—The landing of the cargo, the entry at the custom-house, and the payment of such duties as the law of the place requires, *are necessary ingredients* in a genuine importation; the true purpose of the owner cannot be effected without them. But in a fictitious importation they are *mere voluntary ceremonies*, which have no natural connection whatever with the purpose of sending on the cargo to another market, and which, therefore, would never be resorted to by a person entertaining that purpose, except with a view of giving to the voyage which he has resolved to continue, the appearance of being broken by an importation, which he has resolved not really to make.

"Now, what is the case immediately before us? The cargo in question was taken on board at Laguira. It was at the time of the capture proceeding to Spain; but the ship had touched at an American port. The cargo was landed and entered at the custom-house, and a bond was given for the duties to the amount of 1,239 dollars. The cargo was re-shipped, and a debenture for 1,211 dollars by way of drawback was obtained. All this passed in the course of a few days. The vessel arrived at Marblehead on the 29th of May; on that day the bond for securing the duties was given. On the 30th and 31st the goods were landed, weighed, and packed. The permit to ship them is dated the 1st of June, and on the 3d of June the vessel is cleared out as laden, and ready to proceed to sea. We are frequently obliged to collect the purpose from the circumstances of the transaction. The landing thus almost instantaneously followed by the re-shipment, has little appearance of having been made with a view to actual importation; but it is not upon inference that the conclusion in this case is left to rest. The claimants, instead of showing that they really did import their cargo, have, in their attestation, stated the reasons which determined them not to import it. They say, indeed, that when they ordered it to be purchased, 'it was with the single view of bringing it to the United States, and that they had no intention or expectation of exporting it in the *said schooner* to Spain.' Supposing that from this somewhat ambiguous statement we are to collect that their original intention was to have imported this cargo into America, with a view only to the American market, yet their intention had been changed before the arrival of the vessel. For they state that *in the beginning of May* they had received accounts of the prices of cocoa in Spain, which satisfied them that it would sell much better there than in America, and that they had therefore determined to send it to the Spanish market. Nothing is alleged to have happened between the landing of the cargo and its re-shipment, that could have the least influence on their determination. It was not in that short interval that American prices fell, or that information of the higher prices in Spain had been received. Knowing beforehand the comparative state of the two markets, they neither tried nor meant to try that of America, but proceeded with all possible expedition to go through the forms which have been before enumerated. If the continuity of the voyage remains unbroken, it is immaterial whether it be by the prosecution of an original purpose to continue it, as in the case of the *Essex*, or, as in this case, by the relinquishment of an original purpose to have brought it to a termination in America. It can never be contended, that an intention to import once entertained is equivalent to importation. And it would be a contradiction in terms to say that by acts done after the original intention has been abandoned, such original intention has been carried into execution. Why should a cargo, which there was to be no attempt to sell in America, have been entered at an American custom-house, and voluntarily subjected to the payment of any, even the most trifling duty? Not because importation was, or in such a case could be intended, but because it was thought expedient that something should be done, which in a British Prize Court might pass for importation. Indeed, the claimants seem to have conceived that the inquiry to be made here was, *not*, whether the importation was real or pretended, but whether the pretence had assumed a particular form, and was accompanied with certain circumstances which by some positive rule were, in all cases, to stand for importation, or to be conclusive evidence of it. * * *

"But supposing that we had uniformly held that payment of the import duties furnished conclusive evidence of importation, would there have been any inconsistency or contradiction in holding that the mere act of giving a bond for an amount of duties, of which only a very insignificant part was ever to be paid, could not have the same effect as the actual payment of such amount? The further proof in the *Essex* first brought distinctly before us the real state of the fact in this particular. It has been already mentioned that we had called for an account of the drawbacks, if any, that had been received. This produced the information that although the duties secured amounted to 5,278 dollars, yet a debenture was immediately afterwards given for no less than 5,080 dollars; so that on that valuable cargo no more than 198 dollars would be ultimately payable, which sum is said to be more than compensated for the advantage arising from the negotiability of the debenture. * * *

"The consequence is, that the voyage was illegal, and that the sentence of condemnation must be affirmed."

THE "STEPHEN HART."

U. S. District Court for So. New York, 1863.

(*Blatchford's Prize Cases*, 387.)

The mere touching at a neutral port, or even a trans-shipment in such port, will not be considered as breaking the voyage, if the intention was, on sailing, to carry contraband goods to Confederate ports, or to break the blockade instituted against them.

The schooner *Stephen Hart* was captured, as lawful prize of war, by the United States vessel of war *Supply*, on the 29th of January,

1862, off the southern coast of Florida, about 25 miles from Key West, and about 82 miles from Point de Yeacos, in Cuba, bound ostensibly from London to Cardenas, in Cuba, with a cargo of munitions of war and army supplies.

Extract from the decision of BETTS, J.:—

"Many of the principle questions involved in the present case, and in the cases of the *Springbok* and the *Peterhoff*, are alike; and, as the conclusion at which the court has arrived in all of those cases is to condemn the vessels and their cargoes, I shall announce, in this case, the leading principles of public law which lead to a condemnation in all the cases.

"On behalf of the libellants, it is urged in this case, 1st. That the *Stephen Hart* and her cargo were enemy's property when the voyage in question was undertaken, and when the capture was made; 2d. That the schooner was laden with articles contraband of war, destined for the aid and use of the enemy, and on transportation by sea to the enemy's country at the time of capture; 3d. That, with a full knowledge, on the part of the owner of the vessel and of the owners of her cargo, that the ports of the enemy were under blockade, the vessel and her cargo were despatched from a neutral port with an intention, on the part of the owners of each, that in violation of the blockade, both the vessel and her cargo should enter a port of the enemy.

"On the part of the claimants, it is maintained, 1st. That the transportation of all articles, including arms and munitions of war, between neutral ports in a neutral vessel, is lawful in time of war; 2d. That if a neutral vessel, with a cargo belonging to neutrals, be in fact on a voyage from one neutral port to another, she cannot be seized and condemned as lawful prize, although she be laden with contraband of war, unless it be determined that she was actually destined to a port of the enemy upon the voyage on which she was seized, or unless she is taken in the act of violating a blockade.

"It is insisted, on the part of the claimants, that the *Stephen Hart* was, at the time of her capture, a neutral vessel, carrying a neutral cargo from London to Cardenas—both of them being neutral ports—in the regular course of trade and commerce. On the other side it is contended that the cargo was composed exclusively of articles contraband of war, destined, when they left London, to be delivered to the enemy, either directly, by being carried into a port of the enemy in the *Stephen Hart* or by being trans-shipped at Cardenas to another vessel; that Cardenas was to be used merely as a port of call for the *Stephen Hart*, or as a port of trans-shipment for her cargo; that the vessel and her cargo are equally involved in the forbidden transaction; and that the papers of the vessel were simulated and fraudulent in respect to her destination and that of her cargo. A condemnation is not asked if the cargo was in fact neutral property, to be delivered at Cardenas for discharge and general consumption or sale there, but is only claimed if the cargo was really intended to be delivered to the enemy at some other place than Cardenas, after using that port as a port of call or of trans-shipment, so as to thus render the representations contained in the papers of the vessel false and fraudulent as to the real destination of the vessel and her cargo.

"It would scarcely seem possible that there could be any serious debate as to the true principles of public law applicable to the solution of the questions thus presented; and, indeed, the law is so well settled as to make it only necessary to see whether the facts in this case bring the vessel and her cargo within the rules which have been laid down by the most eminent authorities in England and in this country.

"The principles upon which the government of the United States, and the public vessels acting under its commission, have proceeded, during the present war, in arresting vessels and cargoes as lawful prize upon the high seas, are very succinctly embodied in the instructions issued by the Navy Department on the 18th of August, 1862, to the naval commanders of the United States, and which instructions are therein declared to be a recapitulation of those theretofore from time to time given. The substance of those instructions, so far so they are applicable to the present case, is, that a vessel is not to be seized 'without a search carefully made, so far as to render it reasonable to believe that she is engaged in carrying contraband of war for or to the insurgents, and to their ports directly or indirectly by trans-shipment, or otherwise violating the blockade.'

"The main feature of these instructions, so far as they bear upon the questions involved in this case, is but an application of the doctrine in regard to captures laid down by the government of the United States at a very early day. In an ordinance of the Congress of the Confederation, which went into effect on the 1st of February, 1782, 5 Wheaton, Appendix, p. 120, it was declared to be lawful to capture and to obtain condemnation of all 'contraband goods, wares, and merchandises, to whatever nations belonging, although found in a neutral bottom, *if destined for the use of an enemy*.'

"The soundness of these principles, and the fact that the law of nations, as applicable to cases of prize, has been observed and applied by the government of the United States and its courts during the present war, was fully recognized by Earl Russell, her Britannic

Majesty's principal secretary of state for foreign affairs, in his remarks made in the House of Lords on the 18th of May last. Earl Russell there stated that the judgments of the United States prize courts, which had been reported to her Majesty's government during the present war, did not evince any disregard of the established principles of international law; that the law officers of the Crown, after an attentive consideration of the decisions which had been laid before them, were of opinion that there was no rational ground of complaint as to the judgments of the American prize courts; and that the law of nations in regard to the search and seizure of neutral vessels had been fully and completely acknowledged by the government of the United States. On the same occasion Earl Russell remarked: 'It has been a most profitable business to send swift vessels to break or run the blockade of the southern ports, and carry their cargoes into those ports. There is no municipal law in this or any country to punish such an act as an offence. I understand that every cargo which runs the blockade and enters Charleston is worth a million of dollars, and that the profit on these transactions is immense. It is well known that the trade has attracted a great deal of attention in this country from those who have a keen eye to such gains, and that vessels have been sent to Nassau in order to break the blockade at Charleston, Wilmington, and other places, and carry contraband of war into some of the ports of the Southern States.' He added: 'I certainly am not prepared to declare, nor is there any ground for declaring, that the courts of the United States do not faithfully administer the law; that they will not allow evidence making against the captors; or that they are likely to give decisions founded, not upon the law, but upon their own passions and national partialities.' He also said, that in a case of simulated destination—that is, a vessel pretending that she is going to Nassau, when she is in reality bound to a port of the enemy—the right of seizure exists.

"The then solicitor-general of England (Sir Roundell Palmer) stated, in the House of Commons, on the 29th of June last, referring to the cases of the *Dolphin* and the *Pearl*, decided by the district court for the southern district of Florida (those vessels having been captured while ostensibly on voyages from Liverpool to Nassau, and it having been held by the court that the intention of the owners of the vessels was that they should only touch at Nassau, and then go and break the blockade at Charleston), that 'if the owners imagined that the mere fact of the vessel touching at Nassau when on such an expedition exonerated her, they were very much mistaken;' that the principles of the judgment in the case of the Dolphin 'were to be found in every volume of Lord Stowell's decisions;' that it was well known to everybody that there was a large contraband trade between England and America by way of Nassau; that it was absurd to pretend to shut their eyes to it; and that the trade with Nassau and Matamoras had become what it was in consequence of the war.

"The Foreign Office of Great Britain, in a letter to the owner of the *Peterhoff*, on the 3d of April last, announced as its conclusion, after having communicated with the law officers of the Crown, that the government of the United States has no right to seize a British vessel *bona fide* bound from a British port to another neutral port, unless such vessel attempts to touch at, or has an intermediate or contingent destination to, some blockaded port or place, or is a carrier of contraband of war destined for the enemy of the United States; that her Majesty's government, however, cannot, without violating the rules of international law, claim for British vessels navigating between Great Britain and such neutral ports any general exemption from the belligerent right of visitation by the cruisers of the United States, or proceed upon any general assumption that such vessels may not so act as to render their capture lawful and justifiable; that nothing is more common than for those who contemplate a breach of blockade or the carriage of contraband, to disguise their purpose by a simulated destination and by deceptive papers; and that it has already happened, in many cases, that British vessels have been seized while engaged in voyages apparently lawful, and have been afterwards proved in the prize courts to have been really guilty of endeavoring to break the blockade, or of carrying contraband to the enemy of the United States.

"The cases of the *Stephen Hart*, the *Springbok*, the *Peterhoff*, and the *Gertrude* illustrate a course of trade which has sprung up during the present war, and of which this court will take judicial cognizance, as it appears from its own records and those of other courts of the United States as well as from public reputation. Those neutral ports have suddenly been raised from ports of comparatively insignificant trade to marts of the first magnitude. Nassau and Cardenas are in the vicinity of the blockaded ports of the enemy, while Matamoras is in Mexico, upon the right bank of the Rio Grande, directly opposite the town of Brownsville, in Texas. The course of trade, in respect to Nassau and Cardenas, has been generally to clear neutral vessels, almost always under the British flag, from English ports for those places, and, using them merely as ports either of call or of trans-shipment, to either resume new voyages from them in the same vessels, or to trans-ship their cargoes to fleet steamers, with which to run the blockade, the cargoes being composed, in almost all cases, more or less, of articles contraband of war. The character and course of this trade, and its sudden rise, are very properly commented upon in a despatch from the Secretary of State of the United States to Lord Lyons, of the 12th of May, 1863.

"The broad issue upon the merits in this case is, whether the adventure of the *Stephen Hart* was the honest voyage of a neutral vessel from one neutral port to another neutral, carrying neutral goods between those two ports only, or was a simulated voyage, the cargo being contraband of war, and being really destined for the use of the enemy, and to be introduced into the enemy's country by a breach of blockade by the *Stephen Hart*, or by trans-shipment from her to another vessel at Cardenas. It is conceded in the argument of the leading counsel for the claimants that if the property was owned by the enemy, and was fraudulently on its way to the enemy as neutral property, it was enemy's property, and was liable to capture, no matter whence it came or whither it was bound; and that, if the vessel were really intending and endeavoring to run the blockade, the property was liable to capture, no matter to whom it belonged or what was its character; but that if it was neutral property, in *lawful commerce*, it was safe from seizure.

"The question whether or not the property laden on board of the *Stephen Hart* was being transported in the business of lawful commerce, is not to be decided by merely deciding the question as to whether the vessel was documented for, and sailing upon, a voyage from London to Cardenas. The commerce is in the destination and intended use of the property laden on board of the vessel, and not in the incidental, ancillary, and temporary voyage of the vessel, which may be but one of many carriers through which the property is to reach its true and original destination. If this were not the rule of the prize law, a very wide door would be opened for fraud and evasion. A cargo of contraband goods, really intended for the enemy, might be carried to Cardenas in a neutral vessel sailing from England with papers which, upon their face, import merely a voyage of the vessel to Cardenas, while in fact, her cargo, when it left England, was destined by its owners to be delivered to the enemy by being trans-shipped at Cardenas into a swifter vessel. And such, indeed, has been the course of proceeding in many cases during the present war. * * *

"The law seeks out the truth, and never, in any of its branches, tolerates any such fiction as that under which it is sought to shield the vessel and her cargo in the present case. If the guilty intention, that the contraband goods should reach a port of the enemy, existed when such goods left their English port, that guilty intention cannot be obliterated by the innocent intention of stopping at a neutral port on the way. If there be, in stopping at such port, no intention of trans-shipping the cargo, and if it is to proceed to the enemy's country in the same vessel in which it came from England, of course there can be no purpose of lawful neutral commerce at the neutral port by the sale or use of the cargo in the market there; and the sole purpose of stopping at the neutral port must merely be to have upon the papers of the vessel an ostensible neutral terminus for the voyage.

"If, on the other hand, the object of stopping at the neutral port be to trans-ship the cargo to another vessel to be transported to a port of the enemy, while the vessel in which it was brought from England does not proceed to the port of the enemy, there is equally an absence of all lawful neutral commerce at the neutral port; and the only commerce carried on in the case is that of the transportation of the contraband cargo from the English port to the port of the enemy, as was intended when it left the English port. This court holds that, in all such cases, the transportation or voyage of the contraband goods is to be considered as a unit, from the port of lading to the port of delivery in the enemy's country; that if any part of such voyage or transportation be unlawful, it is unlawful throughout; and that the vessel and her cargo are subject to capture; as well before arriving at the first neutral port at which she touches after her departure from England, as on the voyage or transportation by sea from such neutral port to the port of the enemy. * * *

"There must, therefore, be a decree condemning both vessel and cargo."[1]

SECTION 49.—VISIT AND SEARCH.

THE "MARIA."

A vessel sailing under convoy of an armed ship for the purpose of avoiding visitation and search is liable to condemnation.

This was the leading case of a fleet of Swedish merchantmen, carrying pitch, tar, hemp, deals, and iron, to several ports of France,

[1] Cases involving the same principles, are the *Springbok*, 5 Wallace, 1; The *Peterhoff*, 5 Wallace, 28, and others. The judgment of BETTS, J., in the *Stephen Hart* was subsequently briefly affirmed by the Supreme Court, and it (BETTS' judgment) is on the whole the clearest and most forcible statement of the principles and the circumstances involved in these cases, to be found in the reports.

Portugal, and the Mediterranean; and taken, Jan., 1798, sailing under convoy of a ship of war, and proceeded against for resistance of visitation and search by British cruisers.

Judgment,—Sir W. Scott.—(Only so much of the judgment is here given as applies to general principles). "* * * This being the actual state of facts, it is proper for me to examine, 2dly, what is their legal state, or, in other words, to what considerations they are justly subject, according to the law of nations; for which purpose I state a few principles of that system of law which I take to be incontrovertible.

"1st, That the right of visiting and searching merchant ships upon the high seas, whatever be the ships, whatever be the cargoes, whatever be the destinations, is an incontestible right of the lawfully commissioned cruisers of a belligerent nation. I say, be the ships, the cargoes, and the destinations what they may, because, till they are visited and searched, it does not appear what the ships, or the cargoes, or the destinations are; and it is for the purpose of ascertaining these points that the necessity of this right of visitation and search exists. This right is so clear in principle, that no man can deny it who admits the legality of maritime capture; because if you are not at liberty to ascertain by sufficient inquiry whether there is property that can legally be captured, it is impossible to capture. Even those who contend for the inadmissible rule, that *free ships make free goods*, must admit the exercise of this right at least for the purpose of ascertaining whether the ships are free ships or not. The right is equally clear in practice; for practice is uniform and universal upon the subject. The many European treaties which refer to this right, refer to it as pre-existing, and merely regulate the exercise of it. All writers upon the law of nations unanimously acknowledge it, without the exception even of Hubner himself, the great champion of neutral privileges. In short, no man in the least degree conversant in subjects of this kind has ever, that I know of, breathed a doubt upon it. The right must unquestionably be exercised with as little of personal harshness and of vexation in the mode as possible; but soften it as much as you can, it is still a right of force, though of lawful force—something in the nature of civil process, where force is employed, but a lawful force, which cannot lawfully be resisted. For it is a wild conceit that wherever force is used, it may be forcibly resisted; a lawful force cannot lawfully be resisted. The only case where it can be so in matters of this nature, is in the state of war and conflict between two countries, where one party has a perfect right to attack by force, and the other has an equally perfect right to repel by force. But in the relative situation of two countries at peace with each other, no such conflicting rights can possibly coexist.

"2dly, That the authority of the Sovereign of the neutral country being interposed in any manner of mere force cannot *legally* vary the rights of a lawfully-commissioned belligerent cruiser; I say *legally*, because what may be given, or be fit to be given, in the administration of this species of law, to considerations of comity or of national policy, are views of the matter which, sitting in this Court, I have no right to entertain. All that I assert is, that *legally* it cannot be maintained, that if a Swedish commissioned cruiser, during the wars of his own country, has a right by the law of nations to visit and examine neutral ships, the King of England, being neutral to Sweden, is authorized by that law to obstruct the exercise of that right with respect to the merchant-ships of his country. I add this, that I cannot but think that if he obstructed it by force, it would very much resemble (with all due reverence be it spoken) an opposition of illegal violence to legal right. Two sovereigns may unquestionably agree, if they think fit, (as in some late instances they have agreed,) by special covenant, that the presence of one of their armed ships along with their merchant-ships shall be mutually understood to imply that nothing is to be found in that convoy of merchant-ships inconsistent with amity or neutrality; and if they consent to accept this pledge no third party has a right to quarrel with it any more than with any other pledge which they may agree mutually to accept. But surely no sovereign can legally compel the acceptance of such a security by mere force. The only security known to the law of nations upon this subject, independent of all special covenant, is the right of personal visitation and search, to be exercised by those who have the interest in making it. I am not ignorant, that amongst the loose doctrines which modern fancy, under the various denominations of philosophy and philanthropy, and I know not what, have thrown upon the world, it has been within these few years advanced, or rather insinuated, that it might possibly be well if such a security were accepted. Upon such unauthorized speculations it is not necessary for me to descant: the law and practice of nations (I include particularly the practice of Sweden when it happens to be belligerent) give them no sort of countenance; and until that law and practice are new-modelled in such a *way* as may surrender the known and ancient rights of some nations to the present convenience of other nations, (which nations may perhaps REMEMBER to *forget* them, when they happen to be themselves belligerent,) no reverence is due to them; they are the elements of that system which, if it is consistent, has for its real purpose an entire abolition of capture in war—that is, in other words, to change the nature of hostility, as it has ever existed amongst mankind, and to introduce a state of things not yet seen in the world, that of a military war and a commercial peace. If it were fit that such a state should be introduced, it is at least necessary that it should be introduced in an avowed and intelligible manner, and not in a way which, professing gravely to adhere to that system which has for centuries prevailed among civilized states, and urging at the same time a pretension utterly inconsistent with all its known principles, delivers over the whole matter at once to eternal controversy and conflict, at the expence of the constant hazard of the harmony of states, and of the lives and safeties of innocent individuals.

"3dly, That the penalty for the violent contravention of this right is the confiscation of the property so withheld from visitation and search. For the proof of this I need only refer to Vattel, one of the most correct and certainly not the least indulgent of modern professors of public law."[1] See Book III., c. vii., sect. 114.

SECTION 50.—PRIZE COURTS.

DECISIONS OF PRIZE COURTS.

(*Lawrence's Wheaton*, 960.)

The decision of a prize court is conclusive in respect of the title to the property.

"The constitution of prize courts is an anomaly in jurisprudence. Deriving their authority from one nation, they pass irrevocably on the title to the property belonging to the citizens or subjects of another. Tribunals exclusively of the belligerents, they pronounce on the rights of neutrals, who have no other appeal from the admiralty courts in the last resort than to the justice of the sovereign of the captor, through the diplomatic interposition of their own government.

"In England the common law courts, whatever protection they may have given to the rights of property as well as of person, have from an early day recognized the conclusiveness of foreign prize decisions on the question of title. A case in the King's Bench, which

[1] See also the case of the *Marianna Flora*, 11 Wheaton, 1.

For decisions on Visit and Search in time of peace, see *Le Louis*, *supra*, § 20 (c); The *Antelope*, 10 Wheaton, 119.

occurred in 1683 (34 Car. II.), while declaring the absence in such cases of jurisdiction in the court, points out the only remedy for the party aggrieved. Trover having been brought by the original owner, an English denizen, for a Dutch built ship taken in the war between the Dutch and French, as a Dutch prize, and condemned in the French admiralty court, the chief question was, whether the sentence should be examined by the common law courts. 'It was resolved that it shall not, because, though it be in another king's dominions, we ought to give credit to it, or else they will not give credit to the sentences of our court of admiralty. And the defendants are at no prejudice. The way is, if they find themselves aggrieved, to petition the king, who will examine the case, and, if he finds cause of complaint, will send to his ambassador residing with the prince or state where the sentence was given, and upon failure of redress, will grant letters of marque and reprisal.'"[1]

PRIZE COURTS ON BOARD SHIPS.

(*Captain Semmes: "Cruise of the Alabama,"* I., 346.)

Does International Law sanction the establishment of prize courts by commanders of belligerent cruisers, on board their ships?

Captain Semmes, of the Confederate steamer *Sumpter*, and later commander of the *Alabama*, would seem to have turned his cabin into a prize court on the occasion of every capture made by him. It has generally been held that the commander of a belligerent cruiser has no right to decide controverted questions arising in cases of prize. He seizes a vessel on the belief or suspicion that she is enemy's property, or that she is engaged in a forbidden commerce, it is left to the prize court of the captor's country to determine whether these suspicions are warranted or not.

During his cruises in the *Sumpter* and the *Alabama*, Captain Semmes had occasion to adjudicate in more than seventy cases of prize; in fifty-nine of these cases, ship and cargo were condemned as enemy's property, and burned; in nine cases the ships were released on ransom bonds, the cargoes being plainly neutral. But in a large number of the cases of those condemned and burned, there were claims for the cargoes as neutral property. Captain Semmes seems to have condemned the cargo, unless there was positive proof

[1] For the constitution and functions of prize courts, see Lawrence's Wheaton, 960; Baker's Halleck, II., 411; Phillimore, III., 648–679.

of its neutrality. This practice was carried on by him and others for four years, and was acquiesced in by neutral nations; who permitted their ships to be searched and their property adjudicated upon by these commanders. They received them into their ports, and supplied them with provisions and coal. Who shall say, therefore, that hereafter a prize court may not be established on the deck of every belligerent man-of-war, the commander constituting such court?

The following is a specimen of Captain Semmes' procedure, taken from his own memorandum.

Case of the *Lafayette* ("Cruise of the Alabama," I., 346):—

"Ship and cargo condemned. The cargo of this ship was condemned by me as enemy's property, notwithstanding there were depositions of the shippers that it had been purchased by them on neutral account. These *ex parte* statements are precisely such as every unscrupulous merchant would prepare, to deceive his enemy and save his property from capture."

After an extended discussion of the case, showing that there was fraud, and that the neutrality of the cargo was not established, Captain Semmes continues:—

"3d Phillimore, 599, to the effect, that 'further proof' is always necessary where the master cannot swear to the ownership of the property (as in this case). And as I cannot send my prizes in for adjudication, I must of necessity condemn in all cases where 'further proof' is necessary, since the granting of 'further proof' proceeds on the presumption that the neutrality of the cargo is not sufficiently established; and where the neutrality of the property does not fully appear from the ship's papers and the master's deposition, I had the right to act upon the presumption of enemy's property."

Again, in the case of the *Express* (*Ib.*, 167), in which ship and cargo were condemned. "It must be admitted that this is a case in which, perhaps, a prize court would grant 'further proof;' but as I cannot do this, and as a distinct neutral character is not impressed upon the property by former evidence, I must act under the presumption of law. See 3d Phill., 589."

The following is an extract from the "Cape Argus," giving an interview with Captain Semmes:—

"You English people won't be neighborly enough to let me bring my prizes into your ports and get them condemned, so that I am obliged to sit here a *court of myself*, try every case, and condemn the ships I take."

APPENDIX.

A.

THE BEHRING SEA ARBITRATION, 1893.[1]

May a State exercise jurisdiction on tho high seas for the purpose of protecting fur-seals, which, for several months in each year, remain on land in its territory.

The controversy in this case grew out of the seizure by United States revenue cutters, in Behring Sea, of sixteen Canadian vessels, between August 1st, 1886, and March 27th, 1890, for taking seals in that sea. These seizures were all made beyond the three-mile limit, at distances varying from fifteen to one hundred and fifteen miles from land. It was supposed that the United States acted upon the assumption that Behring Sea was *mare clausum*. That was the view taken of it by Judge Dawson, of the District Court of Alaska; who, in charging the jury in the case of one of these vessels (the *Thornton*), said: "All the waters within the boundary set forth to the western end of the Aleutian Archipelago and chain of islands are to be considered as comprised within the waters of Alaska. * * *

"If the jury believe the defendant killed any otter, mink, marten, sable, or fur-seal, or other fur-bearing animals on the shores of Alaska, or in the Behring Sea, east of the 193 8 of west longitude, they shall find him guilty. * * *"

So, Chief Justice Fuller, in delivering the opinion of the court in the Sayward case, assumed that the seizure was made by right of *mare clausum.*

But the government of the United States did not press that claim. Mr. E. J. Phelps, in a despatch to Mr. Blaine, September 12th, 1888, said:—

"Here is a valuable fishery, and a large and, if properly managed,

[1] On account of the recent date of this decision, it has been impossible to put it in its proper place in the body of the book ("Jurisdiction on the High Seas").

The arguments of the English counsel have not come to hand and therefore are not represented in this report.

permanent industry, the property of the nation on whose shores it is carried on. It is proposed by the colony of a foreign nation, in defiance of the joint remonstrance of all the countries interested, to destroy this business by the indiscriminate slaughter and extermination of the animals in question in the open neighboring sea, during the period of gestation, when the common dictates of humanity ought to protect them, were there no interests at all involved. And it is suggested that we are prevented from protecting ourselves against such depredations because the sea, at a certain distance from the coast, is free.

"The same line of argument would take under its protection piracy and the slave trade, when prosecuted in the open sea, or would justify one nation in destroying the commerce of another by placing dangerous obstructions and derelicts in the open sea near its coasts. There are many things that cannot be allowed to be done on the open sea with impunity, and against which every sea is *mare clausum*. And the right of self-defense as to person and property prevails there as fully as elsewhere. If the fish upon Canadian coasts could be destroyed by scattering poison in the open sea adjacent, with some small profit to those engaged in it, would Canada, upon the just principles of international law, be held defenseless in such a case? Yet that process would be no more destructive, inhuman, and wanton than this.

"If precedents are wanting for a defense so necessary and so proper, it is because precedents for such a course of conduct are likewise unknown. The best international law has arisen from precedents that have been established when the just occasion for them arose, undeterred by the discussion of abstract and inadequate rules."

The views thus expressed by Mr. Phelps were declared by Mr. Blaine, to be the views adopted by the Government of the United States.

Mr. Blaine's statement of the issues, January 22d, 1890, to Sir Julian Pauncefote:—

"In the opinion of the President, the Canadian vessels arrested and detained in the Behring Sea were engaged in a pursuit that was *contra bonos mores*, a pursuit which of necessity involves a serious and permanent injury to the rights of the government and people of the United States. To establish this ground it is not necessary to argue the question of the extent and nature of the sovereignty of this government over the waters of the Behring Sea; it is not necessary to explain, certainly to define, the powers and privileges ceded by His Imperial Majesty the Emperor of Russia in the treaty by which the Alaska Territory was transferred to the United States.

The weighty considerations growing out of the acquisition of that Territory, with all the rights on land and sea inseparably connected therewith, may be safely left out of view, while the grounds are set forth upon which this government rests its justification for the action complained of by Her Majesty's Government."

The grounds set forth are these:—

(1) The value of the sealeries and the absence of any interference with them down to 1886.

(2) That the taking of seals in the open water rapidly leads to their extermination, because of the indiscriminate slaughter of the animal, especially of the female; with which slaughter Mr. Blaine contrasts the careful methods pursued by the United States Government in killing seals upon the Islands.

(3) That the right of defense by the United States against such extermination is not confined to the three-mile limit, and Mr. Blaine remarks as follows: "does Her Majesty's Government seriously maintain that the law of nations is powerless to prevent such violation of the common rights of man? Are the supporters of justice of all nations to be declared incompetent to prevent wrongs so obvious and so destructive.

"In the judgment of this Government, the law of the sea is not lawlessness. Nor can the law of the sea, and the liberty which it confers, and which it protects, be perverted to justify acts which are immoral in themselves, which inevitably tend to results against the interests and against the welfare of mankind."

By the treaty of February 29, 1892, the two governments agreed to refer the questions in dispute to a tribunal of arbitration, to be composed of seven arbitrators, two to be named by each of the contracting powers, one by the President of the French Republic, one by the King of Italy, and one by the King of Sweden and Norway.

Article II. of the treaty contains the five points of dispute to be passed upon by the tribunal, as follows: Art. VI. "In deciding the matters submitted to the Arbitrators, it is agreed that the following five points shall be submitted to them, in order that their award shall embrace a distinct decision upon each of said five points, to wit:—

"1. What exclusive jurisdiction in the sea now known as the Behring's Sea, and what exclusive rights in the seal fisheries therein, did Russia assert and exercise prior and up to the time of the cession of Alaska to the United States?

"2. How far were these claims of jurisdiction as to the seal fisheries recognized and conceded by Great Britain?

"3. Was the body of water now known as the Behring Sea included in the phrase 'Pacific Ocean,' as used in the treaty of 1825 between Great Britain and Russia; and what rights, if any, in the Behring Sea were held and exclusively exercised by Russia after said Treaty?

"4. Did not all the rights of Russia as to jurisdiction, and as to the seal fisheries in Behring Sea east of the water boundary, in the Treaty between the United States and Russia of the 30th March, 1867, pass unimpaired to the United States under that Treaty?

"5. Has the United States any right, and if so, what right of protection or property in the fur-seals frequenting the islands of the United States in Behring Sea when such seals are found outside the ordinary three-mile limit?"

In the event of a decision against the United States on these points, the seventh article provides for the establishment of concurrent regulations for the waters beyond the jurisdiction of either party.

Under the provisions of this treaty, the tribunal met in Paris in the spring of 1893. The Arbitrators were as follows:—

Baron de Courcel, France (President); Marquis Emilio Visconti-Venosta, Italy; M. Gregero W. W. Gram, Sweden and Norway; Lord Hannen, and Sir John S. D. Thompson, England; and Justice John M. Harlan, and Senator John T. Morgan, United States.

The counsel on the part of the United States were Messrs. Edward J. Phelps, James C. Carter, Frederick R. Coudert, and Henry Blodgett; on the part of England, Sir Charles Russell, Sir Richard Webster, and others.

When the evidence was before the Tribunal, it appeared that the United States had a very weak case in respect of the first two points to be considered: and this was evident indeed from the moment of the discovery of the false translations of certain Russian documents, imposed upon the government of the United States by a person employed by it. On the third point, the decision was unanimous in favor of the English contention. That being the state of the case as to the first three points, the fourth was of no weight either way.

Thus the real issue before the tribunal was upon the fifth point, that the United States had a right of property in the seals, and a further right to protect this property on the high seas, and to these points the chief weight of the American argument was directed.

On the question of property in the seals, Mr. Carter said: "The United States hold that the ownership of the islands upon which seals breed; that the habit of the seals in regularly resorting thereto and rearing their young thereon; that their going out in search of food and regularly returning thereto, and all the facts and incidents of their relation to the islands, give to the United States a property interest therein; that this property interest was claimed and exercised by Russia during the whole period of its sovereignty over the land and waters of Alaska; that England recognized that property interest so far as recognition is implied by abstaining from all interference with it during the whole period of Russia's ownership of Alaska, and during the first nineteen years of the sovereignty of the United States.

Mr. Carter argues at great length to prove, from the Civil Law and the Common Law, the right of property in animals *feræ naturæ.* He quotes Justinian, Savigny, Puffendorf, Bracton, Bowyer, Vattel, Hautefeuille, Kent, and others; and the cases of *The Swans*, 7 Coke, 15b; *Keeble* v. *Hickeringill*, 11 East, 574; *Amory* v. *Flyn*, 10 John., 102; *Goff* v. *Kitts*, 15 Wend., 550; *Blades* v. *Higgs*, 12 C. B. N. S., 512; *Davis* v. *Powell*, Willes, 1737.

On the question of the right to protect the seals on the high seas, Mr. Phelps said, the case of the Government of the United States was:

"1st. That in view of the facts and circumstances established by the evidence, it has such a property in the Alaskan seal herd, as the natural product of its soil, made chiefly available by its protection and expenditure, highly valuable to its people, and a considerable source of public revenue, as entitles it to preserve the herd from destruction in the manner complained of, by an employment of such reasonable force as may be necessary.

"2d. That irrespective of the distinct right of property, in the seal herd, the United States Government has for itself and for its people, an interest, an industry, and a commerce derived from the legitimate and proper use of the produce of the seal herd on its territory, which it is entitled, upon all principles applicable to the case, to protect against wanton destruction by individuals, for the sake of the small and casual profits in that way to be gained; and that no part of the high sea is or ought to be open to individuals, for the purpose of accomplishing the destruction of national interests of such a character and importance.

"Third That the United States, possessing as they alone possess, the power of preserving and cherishing this valuable interest, are in a most just sense the trustee thereof for the benefit of mankind, and should be permitted to discharge their trust without hindrance."

In support of this view, Mr. Phelps quotes, Grotius, Kent, Twiss, etc., and the following cases: The *Marianna Flora*, 11 Wheaton, 41; *Church* v. *Hubbart*, 2 Cranch, 287, *Queen* v. *Keyn*, L. R., 2 Ex. Div., 63; *Rose* v. *Himely*, 4 Cranch, 287; The *Success*, 1 Dod., 133; The *Fox*, Ed., 314; The *Snipe*, Ed., 382.

DECISION.

After a preamble stating the case submitted for decision, the full text of the award runs as follows: (New York *Herald*, August 16, 1893.):—

"We decide and determine as to the five points mentioned in article 6, as to which our reward is to embrace a distinct decision upon each of them:—

"As to the first of said five points, we, Baron de Courcel, John M. Harlan, Lord Hannen, Sir John S. D. Thompson, Marquis Emilio Visconti-Venosta and Gregero W. W. Gram, being a majority of said arbitrators, do decide as follows:—

"By the ukase of 1821 Russia claimed jurisdiction in the sea now known as Behring Sea to the extent of one hundred Italian miles from the coasts and islands belonging to her, but in the course of the negotiations which led to the conclusion of the treaty of 1824 with the United States and the treaty of 1825 with Great Britain, Russia admitted that her jurisdiction in said sea should be restricted so as to reach a cannon shot from shore. It appears, that from that time up to the time of the cession of Alaska to the United States, Russia never asserted in fact or exercised any exclusive jurisdiction in Behring Sea or any exclusive rights to the seal fisheries therein beyond the ordinary limit of territorial waters.

"As to the second of the five points, we, Baron de Courcel, John M. Harlan, Lord Hannen, Sir John S. D. Thompson, Marquis Emilio Visconti-Venosta and Gregero W. W. Gram, being a majority of said arbitrators, decide and determine that Great Britain did not recognize or concede any claim upon the part of Russia to exclusive jurisdiction as to the seal fisheries in Behring Sea outside the ordinary territorial waters.

"As to the third point, as to so much thereof as requires us to decide whether the body of water now known as Behring Sea was included in the phrase 'Pacific Ocean' as used in the treaty of 1825 between Great Britain and Russia, we unanimously decide and determine that the body of water now known as Behring Sea was included in the phrase 'Pacific Ocean' as used in said treaty.

"On the fourth point we decide and determine that all the rights of Russia to jurisdiction and to the seal fisheries passed to the United States, limited by the cession."

On the fifth point the decision of the tribunal, Justice Harlan and Senator Morgan dissenting, was as follows:—

"On the fifth point, we, Baron de Courcel, Lord Hannen, Sir John S. D. Thompson, Marquis Emilio Visconti-Venosta and Gregero W.

W. Gram, being the majority of said arbitrators, decide and determine that the United States have no right to the protection of or property in the seals frequenting the islands of the United States in Behring Sea when the same are found outside the ordinary three-mile limit.

"And whereas the aforesaid determination of the foregoing questions as to the exclusive jurisdiction of the United States leaves the subject in such a position that the concurrence of Great Britain is necessary to the establishment of regulations for the proper protection and preservation of fur seals habitually resorting to Behring Sea, we, Baron de Courcel, Lord Hannen, Marquis Emilio Visconti-Venosta and Gregero W. W. Gram, being a majority of the arbitrators, assent to the whole of the nine articles of the following regulations as necessary outside of the jurisdiction limits of the respective governments, and that they should extend over the waters hereinafter mentioned:—

"Art. 1.—The United States and Great Britain shall forbid their citizens and subjects respectively to kill, capture or pursue at any time or in any manner whatever the animals commonly called fur seals within a zone of sixty miles around the Pribyloff Islands, inclusive of the territorial water, the miles being geographical miles, sixty to a degree of latitude.

"Art. 2.—The two governments shall forbid their citizens or subjects to kill, capture or pursue in any manner whatever during a season extending in each year from May 1 to July 31 inclusive fur seals on the high part of the sea in that part of the Pacific Ocean inclusive of Behring Sea, situated north of the thirty-fifth degree of north latitude, or eastward of the 180th degree of longitude from Greenwich until it strikes the water boundary described in article 1 of the treaty of 1867 between the United States and Russia, following that line up to Behring Straits.

"Art. 3.—During the period of time in the waters in which fur-sealing is allowed only sailing vessels shall be permitted to carry on or take part in fur-sealing operations. They will, however, be at liberty to avail themselves of the use of such canoes or undecked boats, propelled by paddles, oars or sails, as are in common use as fishing boats.

"Art. 4.—Each sailing vessel authorized to carry on fur-sealing must be provided with a special license issued for the purpose by its government. Each vessel so employed shall be required to carry a distinguishing flag prescribed by its government.

"Art. 5.—The masters of vessels engaged in fur-sealing shall enter accurately in an official log-book the date and place of each operation, the number and the sex of the seals captured daily. These entries shall be communicated by each of the two governments to each other at the end of each season.

"Art. 6.—The use of nets, firearms or explosives is forbidden in fur-sealing. This restriction shall not apply to shotguns when such are used in fishing outside of Behring Sea during the season when such may lawfully be carried on.

"Art. 7.—The two governments shall take measures to control the fitness of the men authorized to engage in sealing. These men shall have been proved fit to handle with sufficient skill the weapons by means of which seal fishing is carried on.

"Art. 8.—The preceding regulations shall not apply to Indians dwelling on the coast of the territories of the United States or Great Britain carrying on fur-sealing in canoes or undecked boats not transported by or used in connection with other vessels and propelled wholly by paddles, oars or sails, and manned by not more than five persons, in the way hitherto practised by the Indians, provided that such Indians are not employed by other persons, and provided that when so hunting in canoes or undecked boats the Indians shall not hunt fur seals outside the territorial waters under contract to deliver skins to anybody. This exemption is not to be construed to affect the municipal law of either country, nor shall it extend to the waters of Behring Sea or the waters around the Aleutian Islands. Nothing herein contained is intended to interfere with the employment of Indians as hunters or otherwise in connection with sealing vessels as heretofore.

"Art. 9.—The concurrent regulations hereby determined with a view to the protection and preservation of the fur seals shall remain in force until they have been wholly or in part abolished or modified by a common agreement between the United States and Great Britain. Said concurrent regulations shall be submitted every five years to a new examination in order to enable both governments to consider whether in the light of past experience there is occasion to make any modification thereof."

The arbitrators make a special finding on the facts agreed upon by the agents of both governments with reference to the seizure of British vessels in Behring Sea in 1887 and 1889. In addition the arbitrators make certain suggestions to the two governments, the most important being that they should come to an understanding to prohibit the killing of seals on land or sea for a period of from one to three years, and should enact regulations to carry out the findings of the arbitrators.[1]

[1] This decision forms a fitting end of the struggle of three hundred years for the freedom of the seas; it is to be hoped that it will not again be questioned.

B.

THE DECLARATION OF PARIS, 1856.

DECLARATION RESPECTING MARITIME LAW, SIGNED BY THE PLENIPOTENTIARIES OF GREAT BRITAIN, AUSTRIA, FRANCE, PRUSSIA, RUSSIA, SARDINIA, AND TURKEY, ASSEMBLED IN CONGRESS AT PARIS, APRIL 16, 1856.

THE Plenipotentiaries who signed the Treaty of Paris of the 30th of March, 1856, assembled in conference,—Considering:

That Maritime Law, in time of war, has long been the subject of deplorable disputes;

That the uncertainty of the law, and of the duties in such a matter, gives rise to differences of opinion between neutrals and belligerents which may occasion serious difficulties, and even conflicts;

That it is consequently advantageous to establish a uniform doctrine on so important a point;

That the Plenipotentiaries assembled in Congress at Paris cannot better respond to the intentions by which their governments are animated than by seeking to introduce into international relations fixed principles in this respect:

The above-mentioned Plenipotentiaries, being duly authorized, resolved to concert among themselves as to the means of attaining this object; and, having come to an agreement, have adopted the following solemn declaration:

1. Privateering is, and remains abolished.

2. The neutral flag covers enemy's goods, with the exception of contraband of war.

3. Neutral goods, with the exception of contraband of war, are not liable to capture under the enemy's flag.

4. Blockades, in order to be binding, must be effective, that is to say, maintained by a force sufficient really to prevent access to the coast of the enemy.

The Governments of the undersigned Plenipotentiaries engage to bring the present Declaration to the knowledge of the states which have not taken part in the Congress of Paris, and to invite them to accede to it.

Convinced that the maxims which they now proclaim cannot but be received with gratitude by the whole world, the undersigned Plenipotentiaries doubt not that the efforts of their governments to obtain the general adoption thereof will be crowned with full success.

The present Declaration is not and shall not be binding, except between those Powers who have acceded, or shall accede to it.

Done at Paris, April 16, 1856.

C.

THE DECLARATION OF ST. PETERSBURG, 1868.

Considering that the progress of civilization should have the effect of alleviating, as much as possible, the calamities of war;

That the only legitimate object which states should endeavor to accomplish during war is to weaken the military force of the enemy;

That for this purpose, it is sufficient to disable the greatest possible number of men;

That this object would be exceeded by the employment of arms which uselessly aggravate the sufferings of disabled men, or render their death inevitable;

That the employment of such arms would, therefore, be contrary to the laws of humanity;

The contracting parties engage, mutually, to renounce, in case of war among themselves, the employment, by their military or naval forces, of any projectile of less weight than four hundred grammes, which is explosive, or is charged with fulminating or inflammable substances.

They agree to invite all the states which have not taken part in the deliberations of the International Military Commission, assembled at St. Petersburg, by sending delegates thereto, to accede to the present engagement.

This engagement is obligatory only upon the contracting or acceding parties thereto, in case of war between two or more of themselves; it is not applicable with regard to non-contracting powers, or powers that shall not have acceded to it.

It will also cease to be obligatory from the moment when, in a war between contracting or acceding parties, a non-contracting party, or a non-acceding party, shall join one of the belligerents.

The contracting or acceding parties reserve to themselves the right to come to an understanding, hereafter, whenever a precise proposition shall be drawn up, in view of future improvements which may be effected in the armament of troops, in order to maintain the principles which they have established, and to reconcile the necessities of war with the laws of humanity.

D.

THE GENEVA CONVENTION FOR THE AMELIORATION OF THE CONDITION OF THE SICK AND WOUNDED OF ARMIES IN THE FIELD.

Art. I.—Ambulances and military hospitals shall be acknowledged to be neuter, and, as such, shall be protected and respected by belligerents so long as any sick or wounded may be therein. Such neutrality shall cease if the ambulances or hospitals should be held by a military force.

Art. II.—Persons employed in hospitals and ambulances, comprising the staff for superintendence, medical service, administration, transport of wounded, as well as chaplains, shall participate in the benefit of neutrality, while so employed, and so long as there remain any wounded to bring in or to succor.

Art. III.—The persons designated in the preceding article may, even after occupation by the enemy, continue to fulfill their duties in the hospital or ambulance which they serve, or may withdraw in order to rejoin the corps to which they belong.

Under such circumstances, when these persons shall cease from their functions, they shall be delivered by the occupying army to the outposts of the enemy.

Art. IV.—As the equipment of military hospitals remains subject to the laws of war, persons attached to such hospitals cannot, in withdrawing, carry away any articles but such as are their private property.

Under the same circumstances an ambulance shall, on the contrary, retain its equipment.

Art. V.—Inhabitants of the country who may bring help to the wounded shall be respected, and shall remain free. The generals of the belligerent powers shall make it their care to inform the inhabitants of the appeal addressed to their humanity, and the neutrality which will be the consequence of it.

Any wounded man entertained and taken care of in a house shall be considered a protection thereto. Any inhabitant who shall have entertained wounded men in his house shall be exempted from the quartering of troops, as well as from a part of the contributions of war which may be imposed.

Art. VI.—Wounded or sick soldiers shall be entertained and taken care of, to whatever nation they may belong.

Commanders-in-chief shall have the power to deliver immediately, to the outposts of the enemy, soldiers who have been wounded in an engagement, when circumstances permit this to be done, and with the consent of both parties.

Those who are recognized, after their wounds are healed, as incapable of serving, shall be sent back to their own country.

The others may also be sent back, on condition of not bearing arms during the continuance of the war.

Evacuations, together with the persons under whose direction they shall take place, shall be protected by an absolute neutrality.

Art. VII.—A distinctive and uniform flag shall be adopted for hospitals, ambulances, and evacuations. It must on every occasion be accompanied by the national flag. An arm badge (brassard) shall also be allowed for individuals neutralized, but the delivery thereof shall be left to military authority.

The flag and arm badge shall bear a red cross on a white ground.

Art. VIII.—The details of execution of the present convention shall be regulated by the commanders-in-chief of belligerent armies, according to the instructions of their respective governments, and in conformity with the general principles laid down in this convention.

Art. IX.—The high contracting powers have agreed to communicate the present convention to those governments which have not found it convenient to send plenipotentiaries to the International Convention at Geneva, with an invitation to accede thereto; the protocol is for that purpose left open.

Art. X.—The present convention shall be ratified, and the ratifications exchanged at Berne, in four months, or sooner if possible.[1]

E.

INSTRUCTIONS

FOR THE

GOVERNMENT OF ARMIES OF THE UNITED STATES IN THE FIELD.

GENERAL ORDERS, No. 100.

WAR DEPARTMENT,
ADJUTANT-GENERAL'S OFFICE,
Washington, April 24, 1863.

The following "Instructions for the Government of Armies of the United States in the Field," prepared by FRANCIS LIEBER, LL. D., and revised by a Board of Officers, of which Major-General E. A. HITCHCOCK is president, having been approved by the President of

[1] The text of the Geneva Convention and of the two preceding Declarations, is taken from the Appendix of Davis' International Law.

the United States, he commands that they be published for the information of all concerned.

BY ORDER OF THE SECRETARY OF WAR:

E. D. TOWNSEND,
Assistant Adjutant-General.

SECTION I.

MARTIAL LAW—MILITARY JURISDICTION—MILITARY NECESSITY—RETALIATION.

1. A place, district, or country occupied by an enemy stands, in consequence of the occupation, under the Martial Law of the invading or occupying army, whether any proclamation declaring Martial Law, or any public warning to the inhabitants, has been issued or not. Martial Law is the immediate and direct effect and consequence of occupation or conquest.

The presence of a hostile army proclaims its Martial Law.

2. Martial Law does not cease during the hostile occupation, except by special proclamation, ordered by the commander-in-chief; or by special mention in the treaty of peace concluding the war, when the occupation of a place or territory continues beyond the conclusion of peace as one of the conditions of the same.

3. Martial Law in a hostile country consists in the suspension, by the occupying military authority, of the criminal and civil law, and of the domestic administration and government in the occupied place or territory, and in the substitution of military rule and force for the same, as well as in the dictation of general laws, as far as military necessity requires this suspension, substitution, or dictation.

The commander of the forces may proclaim that the administration of all civil and penal law shall continue, either wholly or in part, as in times of peace, unless otherwise ordered by the military authority.

4. Martial Law is simply military authority exercised in accordance with the laws and usages of war. Military oppression is not Martial Law; it is the abuse of the power which that law confers. As Martial Law is executed by military force, it is incumbent upon those who administer it to be strictly guided by the principles of justice, honor, and humanity—virtues adorning a soldier even more than other men, for the very reason that he possesses the power of his arms against the unarmed.

5. Martial Law should be less stringent in places and countries fully occupied and fairly conquered. Much greater severity may be exercised in places or regions where actual hostilities exist, or are expected and must be prepared for. Its most complete sway is allowed—even in the commander's own country—when face to face with the enemy, because of the absolute necessities of the case, and of the paramount duty to defend the country against invasion.

To save the country is paramount to all other considerations.

6. All civil and penal law shall continue to take its usual course in the enemy's places and territories under Martial Law, unless interrupted or stopped by order of the occupying military power; but all the functions of the hostile government—legislative, executive, or administrative—whether of a general, provincial, or local character, cease under Martial Law, or continue only with the sanction, or if deemed necessary, the participation of the occupier or invader.

7. Martial Law extends to property, and to persons, whether they are subjects of the enemy or aliens to that government.

8. Consuls, among American and European nations, are not diplomatic agents. Nevertheless, their offices and persons will be subjected to Martial Law in cases of urgent necessity only: their property and business are not exempted. Any delinquency they commit against the established military rule may be punished as in the case of any other inhabitant, and such punishment furnishes no reasonable ground for international complaint.

9. The functions of Ambassadors, Ministers, or other diplomatic agents, accredited by neutral powers to the hostile government, cease, so far as regards the displaced government; but the conquering or occupying power usually recognizes them as temporarily accredited to itself.

10. Martial Law affects chiefly the police and collection of public revenue and taxes, whether imposed by the expelled government or by the invader, and refers mainly to the support and efficiency of the army, its safety, and the safety of its operations.

11. The law of war does not only disclaim all cruelty and bad faith concerning engagements concluded with the enemy during the war, but also the breaking of stipulations solemnly contracted by the belligerents in time of peace, and avowedly intended to remain in force in case of war between the contracting powers.

It disclaims all extortions and other transactions for individual gain; all acts of private revenge, or connivance at such acts.

Offences to the contrary shall be severely punished, and especially so if committed by officers.

12. Whenever feasible, Martial Law is carried out in cases of in-

dividual offenders by Military Courts; but sentences of death shall be executed only with the approval of the chief executive, provided the urgency of the case does not require a speedier execution, and then only with the approval of the chief commander.

13. Military jurisdiction is of two kinds: first, that which is conferred and defined by statute; second, that which is derived from the common law of war. Military offences under the statute law must be tried in the manner therein directed; but military offences which do not come within the statute must be tried and punished under the common law of war. The character of the courts which exercise these jurisdictions depends upon the local laws of each particular country.

In the armies of the United States the first is exercised by courts-martial; while cases which do not come within the "Rules and Articles of War," or the jurisdiction conferred by statute on courts-martial, are tried by military commissions.

14. Military necessity, as understood by modern civilized nations, consists in the necessity of those measures which are indispensable for securing the ends of the war, and which are lawful according to the modern law and usages of war.

15. Military necessity admits of all direct destruction of life or limb of *armed* enemies, and of other persons whose destruction is incidentally *unavoidable* in the armed contests of the war; it allows of the capturing of every armed enemy, and every enemy of importance to the hostile government, or of peculiar danger to the captor; it allows of all destruction of property, and obstruction of the ways and channels of traffic, travel, or communication, and of all withholding of sustenance or means of life from the enemy; of the appropriation of whatever an enemy's country affords necessary for the subsistence and safety of the army, and of such deception as does not involve the breaking of good faith either positively pledged, regarding agreements entered into during the war, or supposed by the modern law of war to exist. Men who take up arms against one another in public war do not cease on this account to be moral beings, responsible to one another, and to God.

16. Military necessity does not admit of cruelty, that is, the infliction of suffering for the sake of suffering or for revenge, nor of maiming or wounding except in fight, nor of torture to extort confessions. It does not admit of the use of poison in any way, nor of the wanton devastation of a district. It admits of deception, but disclaims acts of perfidy; and, in general, military necessity does not include any act of hostility which makes the return to peace unnecessarily difficult.

17. War is not carried on by arms alone. It is lawful to starve the hostile belligerent, armed or unarmed, so that it leads to the speedier subjection of the enemy.

18. When the commander of a besieged place expels the non-combatants, in order to lessen the number of those who consume his stock of provisions, it is lawful, though an extreme measure, to drive them back, so as to hasten on the surrender.

19. Commanders, whenever admissible, inform the enemy of their intention to bombard a place, so that the non-combatants, and especially the women and children, may be removed before the bombardment commences. But it is no infraction of the common law of war to omit thus to inform the enemy. Surprise may be a necessity.

20. Public war is a state of armed hostility between sovereign nations or governments. It is a law and requisite of civilized existence that men live in political, continuous societies, forming organized units, called states or nations, whose constituents bear, enjoy, and suffer, advance and retrograde together, in peace and in war.

21. The citizen or native or a hostile country is thus an enemy, as one of the constituents of the hostile state or nation, and as such is subjected to the hardships of the war.

22. Nevertheless, as civilization has advanced during the last centuries, so has likewise steadily advanced, especially in war on land, the distinction between the private individual belonging to a hostile country and the hostile country itself, with its men in arms. The principle has been more and more acknowledged that the unarmed citizen is to be spared in person, property, and honor as much as the exigencies of war will admit.

23. Private citizens are no longer murdered, enslaved, or carried off to distant parts, and the inoffensive individual is as little disturbed in his private relations as the commander of the hostile troops can afford to grant in the overruling demands of a vigorous war.

24. The almost universal rule in remote times was, and continues to be with barbarous armies, that the private individual of the hostile country is destined to suffer every privation of liberty and protection, and every disruption of family ties. Protection was, and still is with uncivilized people, the exception.

25. In modern regular wars of the Europeans, and their descendants in other portions of the globe, protection of the inoffensive citizen of the hostile country is the rule; privation and disturbance of private relations are the exceptions.

26. Commanding generals may cause the magistrates and civil

officers of the hostile country to take the oath of temporary allegiance or an oath of fidelity to their own victorious government or rulers, and they may expel every one who declines to do so. But whether they do so or not, the people and their civil officers owe strict obedience to them as long as they hold sway over the district or country, at the peril of their lives.

27. The law of war can no more wholly dispense with retaliation than can the law of nations, of which it is a branch. Yet civilized nations acknowledge retaliation as the sternest feature of war. A reckless enemy often leaves to his opponent no other means of securing himself against the repetition of barbarous outrage.

28. Retaliation will, therefore, never be resorted to as a measure of mere revenge, but only as a means of protective retribution, and, moreover, cautiously and unavoidably; that is to say, retaliation shall only be resorted to after careful inquiry into the real occurrence, and the character of the misdeeds that may demand retribution.

Unjust or inconsiderate retaliation removes the belligerents farther and farther from the mitigating rules of a regular war, and by rapid steps leads them nearer to the internecine wars of savages.

29. Modern times are distinguished from earlier ages by the existence, at one and the same time, of many nations and great governments related to one another in close intercourse.

Peace is their normal condition; war is the exception. The ultimate object of all modern war is a renewed state of peace.

The more vigorously wars are pursued, the better it is for humanity. Sharp wars are brief.

30. Ever since the formation and co-existence of modern nations' and ever since wars have become great national wars, war has come to be acknowledged not to be its own end, but the means to obtain great ends of state, or to consist in defence against wrong; and no conventional restriction of the modes adopted to injure the enemy is any longer admitted; but the law of war imposes many limitations and restrictions on principles of justice, faith, and honor.

SECTION II.

Public and Private Property of the Enemy—Protection of Persons, and especially Women; of Religion, the Arts and Sciences—Punishment of Crimes against the Inhabitants of Hostile Countries.

31. A victorious army appropriates all public money, seizes all public movable property until further direction by its government,

and sequesters for its own benefit or that of its government all the revenues of real property belonging to the hostile government or nation. The title to such real property remains in abeyance during military occupation, and until the conquest is made complete.

32. A victorious army, by the martial power inherent in the same, may suspend, change, or abolish, as far as the martial power extends, the relations which arise from the services due, according to the existing laws of the invaded country, from one citizen, subject, or native of the same to another.

The commander of the army must leave it to the ultimate treaty of peace to settle the permanency of this change.

33. It is no longer considered lawful—on the contrary, it is held to be a serious breach of the law of war—to force the subjects of the enemy into the service of the victorious government, except the latter should proclaim, after a fair and complete conquest of the hostile country or district, that it is resolved to keep the country, district, or place permanently as its own, and make it a portion of its own country.

34. As a general rule, the property belonging to churches, to hospitals, or other establishments of an exclusively charitable character, to establishments of education, or foundations for the promotion of knowledge, whether public schools, universities, academies of learning, or observatories, museums of the fine arts, or of a scientific character—such property is not to be considered public property in the sense of paragraph 31; but it may be taxed or used when the public service may require it.

35. Classical works of art, libraries, scientific collections, or precious instruments, such as astronomical telescopes, as well as hospitals, must be secured against all avoidable injury, even when they are contained in fortified places whilst besieged or bombarded.

36. If such works of art, libraries, collections, or instruments belonging to a hostile nation or government, can be removed without injury, the ruler of the conquering state or nation may order them to be seized and removed for the benefit of the said nation. The ultimate ownership is to be settled by the ensuing treaty of peace.

In no case shall they be sold or given away, if captured by the armies of the United States, nor shall they ever be privately appropriated, or wantonly destroyed or injured.

37. The United States acknowledge and protect, in hostile countries occupied by them, religion and morality; strictly private property; the persons of the inhabitants, especially those of women; and the sacredness of domestic relations. Offenses to the contrary shall be rigorously punished.

This rule does not interfere with the right of the victorious invader to tax the people or their property, to levy forced loans, to billet soldiers, or to appropriate property, especially houses, land, boats or ships, and churches, for temporary and military uses.

38. Private property, unless forfeited by crimes or by offenses of the owner, can be seized only by way of military necessity, for the support or other benefit of the army of the United States.

If the owner has not fled, the commanding officer will cause receipts to be given, which may serve the spoliated owner to obtain indemnity.

39. The salaries of civil officers of the hostile government who remain in the invaded territory, and continue the work of their office, and can continue it according to the circumstances arising out of the war—such as judges, administrative or police officers, officers of city or communal governments—are paid from the public revenue of the invaded territory, until the military government has reason wholly or partially to discontinue it. Salaries or incomes connected with purely honorary titles are always stopped.

40. There exists no law or body of authoritative rules of action between hostile armies, except that branch of the law of nature and nations which is called the law and usages of war on land.

41. All municipal law of the ground on which the armies stand, or of the countries to which they belong, is silent and of no effect between armies in the field.

42. Slavery, complicating and confounding the ideas of property (that is of a *thing*), and of personality (that is of *humanity*), exists according to municipal law or local law only. The law of nature and nations has never acknowledged it. The digest of the Roman law enacts the early dictum of the pagan jurist, that "so far as the law of nature is concerned, all men are equal." Fugitives escaping from a country in which they were slaves, villains, or serfs, into another country, have, for centuries past, been held free and acknowledged free by judicial decisions of European countries, even though the municipal law of the country in which the slave had taken refuge acknowledged slavery within its own dominions.

43. Therefore, in a war between the United States and a belligerent which admits of slavery, if a person held in bondage by that belligerent be captured by or come as a fugitive under the protection of the military forces of the United States, such person is immediately entitled to the rights and privileges of a freeman. To return such person into slavery would amount to enslaving a free person, and neither the United States nor any officer under their authority can enslave any human being. Moreover, a person so

made free by the law of war is under the shield of the law of nations, and the former owner or State can have, by the law of postliminy, no belligerent lien or claim of service.

44. All wanton violence committed against persons in the invaded country, all destruction of property not commanded by the authorized officer, all robbery, all pillage or sacking, even after taking a place by main force, all rape, wounding, maiming, or killing of such inhabitants, are prohibited under the penalty of death, or such other severe punishment as may seem adequate for the gravity of the offense.

A soldier, officer or private, in the act of committing such violence, and disobeying a superior ordering him to abstain from it, may be lawfully killed on the spot by such superior.

45. All captures and booty belong, according to the modern law of war, primarily to the government of the captor.

Prize money, whether on sea or land, can now only be claimed under local law.

46. Neither officers nor soldiers are allowed to make use of their position or power in the hostile country for private gain, not even for commercial transactions otherwise legitimate. Offenses to the contrary committed by commissioned officers will be punished with cashiering, or such other punishment as the nature of the offense may require; if by soldiers, they shall be punished according to the nature of the offense.

47. Crimes punishable by all penal codes, such as arson, murder, maiming, assaults, highway robbery, theft, burglary, fraud, forgery, and rape, if committed by an American soldier in a hostile country against its inhabitants, are not only punishable as at home, but in all cases in which death is not inflicted, the severer punishment shall be preferred.

SECTION III.

Deserters—Prisoners of War—Hostages—Booty on the Battle-field.

48. Deserters from the American army, having entered the service of the enemy, suffer death if they fall again into the hands of the United States, whether by capture, or being delivered up to the American army; and if a deserter from the enemy, having taken service in the army of the United States, is captured by the enemy, and punished by them with death or otherwise, it is not a breach against the law and usages of war, requiring redress or retaliation.

49. A prisoner of war is a public enemy armed or attached to the hostile army for active aid, who has fallen into the hands of the captor, either fighting or wounded, on the field or in the hospital, by individual surrender or by capitulation.

All soldiers, of whatever species of arms; all men who belong to the rising *en masse* of the hostile country; all those who are attached to the army for its efficiency and promote directly the object of the war, except such as are hereinafter provided for; all disabled men or officers on the field or elsewhere, if captured; all enemies who have thrown away their arms and ask for quarter, are prisoners of war, and as such exposed to the inconveniences as well as entitled to the privileges of a prisoner of war.

50. Moreover, citizens who accompany an army for whatever purpose, such as sutlers, editors, or reporters of journals, or contractors, if captured, may be made prisoners of war, and be detained as such.

The monarch and members of the hostile reigning family, male or female, the chief, and chief officers of the hostile government, its diplomatic agents, and all persons who are of particular and singular use and benefit to the hostile army or its government, are, if captured on belligerent ground, and if unprovided with a safe conduct granted by the captor's government, prisoners of war.

51. If the people of that portion of an invaded country which is not yet occupied by the enemy, or of the whole country, at the approach of a hostile army, rise under a duly authorized levy, *en masse* to resist the invader, they are now treated as public enemies, and if captured, are prisoners of war.

52. No belligerent has the right to declare that he will treat every captured man in arms of a levy *en masse* as a brigand or bandit.

If, however, the people of a country, or any portion of the same, already occupied by an army, rise against it, they are violators of the laws of war, and are not entitled to their protection.

53. The enemy's chaplains, officers of the medical staff, apothecaries, hospital nurses and servants, if they fall into the hands of the American army, are not prisoners of war, unless the commander has reasons to retain them. In this latter case, or if, at their own desire, they are allowed to remain with their captured companions, they are treated as prisoners of war, and may be exchanged if the commander sees fit.

54. A hostage is a person accepted as a pledge for the fulfilment of an agreement concluded between belligerents during the war, or in consequence of a war. Hostages are rare in the present age.

55. If a hostage is accepted, he is treated like a prisoner of war, according to rank and condition, as circumstances may admit.

56. A prisoner of war is subject to no punishment for being a public enemy, nor is any revenge wreaked upon him by the intentional infliction of any suffering, or disgrace, by cruel imprisonment, want of food, by mutilation, death, or any other barbarity.

57. So soon as a man is armed by a sovereign government, and takes the soldier's oath of fidelity, he is a belligerent; his killing, wounding, or other warlike acts, are no individual crimes or offenses. No belligerent has a right to declare that enemies of a certain class, color, or condition, when properly organized as soldiers, will not be treated by him as public enemies.

58. The law of nations knows of no distinction of color, and if an enemy of the United States should enslave and sell any captured persons of their army, it would be a case for the severest retaliation, if not redressed upon complaint.

The United States cannot retaliate by enslavement; therefore death must be the retaliation for this crime against the law of nations.

59. A prisoner of war remains answerable for his crimes committed against the captor's army or people, committed before he was captured, and for which he has not been punished by his own authorities.

All prisoners of war are liable to the infliction of retaliatory measures.

60. It is against the usage of modern war to resolve, in hatred and revenge, to give no quarter. No body of troops has the right to declare that it will not give, and therefore will not expect, quarter; but a commander is permitted to direct his troops to give no quarter, in great straits, when his own salvation makes it *impossible* to cumber himself with prisoners.

61. Troops that give no quarter have no right to kill enemies already disabled on the ground, or prisoners captured by other troops.

62. All troops of the enemy known or discovered to give no quarter in general, or to any portion of the army, receive none.

63. Troops who fight in the uniform of their enemies, without any plain, striking, and uniform mark of distinction of their own, can expect no quarter.

64. If American troops capture a train containing uniforms of the enemy, and the commander considers it advisable to distribute them for use among his men, some striking mark or sign must be adopted to distinguish the American soldier from the enemy.

65. The use of the enemy's national standard, flag, or other emblem of nationality, for the purpose of deceiving the enemy in battle,

is an act of perfidy by which they lose all claim to the protection of the laws of war.

66. Quarter having been given to an enemy by American troops, under a misapprehension of his true character, he may, nevertheless, be ordered to suffer death if, within three days after the battle, it be discovered that he belongs to a corps which gives no quarter.

67. The law of nations allows every sovereign government to make war upon another sovereign state, and, therefore, admits of no rules or laws different from those of regular warfare, regarding the treatment of prisoners of war, although they may belong to the army of a government which the captor may consider as a wanton and unjust assailant.

68. Modern wars are not internecine wars, in which the killing of the enemy is the object. The destruction of the enemy in modern war, and, indeed, modern war itself, are means to obtain that object of the belligerent which lies beyond the war.

Unnecessary or revengeful destruction of life is not lawful.

69. Outposts, sentinels, or pickets are not to be fired upon, except to drive them in, or when a positive order, special or general, has been issued to that effect.

70. The use of poison in any manner, be it to poison wells, or food, or arms, is wholly excluded from modern warfare. He that uses it puts himself out of the pale of the law and usages of war.

71. Whoever intentionally inflicts additional wounds on an enemy already wholly disabled, or kills such an enemy, or who orders or encourages soldiers to do so, shall suffer death, if duly convicted, whether he belongs to the army of the United States, or is an enemy captured after having committed his misdeed.

72. Money and other valuables on the person of a prisoner, such as watches or jewelry, as well as extra clothing, are regarded by the American army as the private property of the prisoner, and the appropriation of such valuables or money is considered dishonorable, and is prohibited.

Nevertheless, if *large* sums are found upon the persons of prisoners, or in their possession, they shall be taken from them, and the surplus, after providing for their own support, appropriated for the use of the army, under the direction of the commander, unless otherwise ordered by the government. Nor can prisoners claim, as private property, large sums found and captured in their train, although they had been placed in the private luggage of the prisoners.

73. All officers, when captured, must surrender their side-arms to the captor. They may be restored to the prisoner in marked cases, by the commander, to signalize admiration of his distinguished

bravery, or approbation of his humane treatment of prisoners before his capture. The captured officer to whom they may be restored cannot wear them during captivity.

74. A prisoner of war being a public enemy, is the prisoner of the government, and not of the captor. No ransom can be paid by a prisoner of war to his individual captor, or to any officer in command. The government alone releases captives, according to rules prescribed by itself.

75. Prisoners of war are subject to confinement or imprisonment such as may be deemed necessary on account of safety, but they are to be subjected to no other intentional suffering or indignity. The confinement and mode of treating a prisoner may be varied during his captivity according to the demands of safety.

76. Prisoners of war shall be fed upon plain and wholesome food whenever practicable, and treated with humanity.

They may be required to work for the benefit of the captor's government, according to their rank and condition.

77. A prisoner of war who escapes may be shot, or otherwise killed in his flight; but neither death nor any other punishment shall be inflicted upon him simply for his attempt to escape, which the law of war does not consider a crime. Stricter means of security shall be used after an unsuccessful attempt at escape.

If, however, a conspiracy is discovered, the purpose of which is a united or general escape, the conspirators may be rigorously punished, even with death; and capital punishment may also be inflicted upon prisoners of war discovered to have plotted rebellion against the authorities of the captors, whether in union with fellow-prisoners or other persons.

78. If prisoners of war, having given no pledge nor made any promise on their honor, forcibly or otherwise escape, and are captured again in battle, after having rejoined their own army, they shall not be punished for their escape, but shall be treated as simple prisoners of war, although they will be subjected to stricter confinement.

79. Every captured wounded enemy shall be medically treated, according to the ability of the medical staff.

80. Honorable men, when captured, will abstain from giving to the enemy information concerning their own army, and the modern law of war permits no longer the use of any violence against prisoners in order to extort the desired information, or to punish them for having given false information.

SECTION IV.

PARTISANS—ARMED ENEMIES NOT BELONGING TO THE HOSTILE ARMY—SCOUTS—ARMED PROWLERS—WAR-REBELS.

81. Partisans are soldiers armed and wearing the uniform of their army, but belonging to a corps which acts detached from the main body for the purpose of making inroads into the territory occupied by the enemy. If captured, they are entitled to all the privileges of the prisoner of war.

82. Men, or squads of men, who commit hostilities, whether by fighting, or inroads for destruction or plunder, or by raids of any kind, without commission, without being part and portion of the organized hostile army, and without sharing continuously in the war, but who do so with intermitting returns to their homes and avocations, or with the occasional assumption of the semblance of peaceful pursuits, divesting themselves of the character or appearance of soldiers—such men, or squads of men, are not public enemies, and therefore, if captured, are not entitled to the privileges of prisoners of war, but shall be treated summarily as highway robbers or pirates

83 Scouts or single soldiers, if disguised in the dress of the country, or in the uniform of the army hostile to their own, employed in obtaining information, if found within or lurking about the lines of the captor, are treated as spies, and suffer death.

84. Armed prowlers, by whatever names they may be called, or persons of the enemy's territory, who steal within the lines of the hostile army, for the purpose of robbing, killing, or of destroying bridges, roads, or canals, or of robbing or destroying the mail, or of cutting the telegraph wires, are not entitled to the privileges of the prisoner of war.

85. War-rebels are persons within an occupied territory who rise in arms against the occupying or conquering army, or against the authorities established by the same. If captured, they may suffer death, whether they rise singly, in small or large bands, and whether called upon to do so by their own, but expelled, government or not. They are not prisoners of war; nor are they, if discovered and secured before their conspiracy has matured to an actual rising, or to armed violence

SECTION V

SAFE-CONDUCT—SPIES—WAR-TRAITORS—CAPTURED MESSENGERS—ABUSE OF THE FLAG OF TRUCE.

86. All intercourse between the territories occupied by belligerent

is not ratified, even if a certain time for the elapsing between giving notice of cessation and the resumption of hostilities should have been stipulated for.

141. It is incumbent upon the contracting parties of an armistice to stipulate what intercourse of persons or traffic between the inhabitants of the territories occupied by the hostile armies shall be allowed, if any.

If nothing is stipulated, the intercourse remains suspended, as during actual hostilities.

142. An armistice is not a partial or a temporary peace; it is only the suspension of military operations to the extent agreed upon by the parties.

143. When an armistice is concluded between a fortified place and the army besieging it, it is agreed by all the authorities on this subject that the besieger must cease all extension, perfection, or advance of his attacking works, as much so as from attacks by main force.

But as there is a difference of opinion among martial jurists, whether the besieged have the right to repair breaches or to erect new works of defense within the place during an armistice, this point should be determined by express agreement between the parties.

144. So soon as a capitulation is signed, the capitulator has no right to demolish, destroy, or injure the works, arms, stores, or ammunition, in his possession, during the time which elapses between the signing and the execution of the capitulation, unless otherwise stipulated in the same.

145. When an armistice is clearly broken by one of the parties, the other party is released from all obligation to observe it.

146. Prisoners, taken in the act of breaking an armistice, must be treated as prisoners of war, the officer alone being responsible who gives the order for such a violation of an armistice. The highest authority of the belligerent aggrieved may demand redress for the infraction of an armistice.

147. Belligerents sometimes conclude an armistice while their plenipotentiaries are met to discuss the conditions of a treaty of peace; but plenipotentiaries may meet without a preliminary armistice: in the latter case, the war is carried on without any abatement.

SECTION IX.

ASSASSINATION.

148. The law of war does not allow proclaiming either an indi-

vidual belonging to the hostile army, or a citizen, or a subject of the hostile government, an outlaw, who may be slain without trial by any captor, any more than the modern law of peace allows such international outlawry; on the contrary, it abhors such outrage. The sternest retaliation should follow the murder committed in consequence of such proclamation, made by whatever authority. Civilized nations look with horror upon offers of rewards for the assassination of enemies, as relapses into barbarism.

SECTION X.

INSURRECTION—CIVIL WAR—REBELLION.

149. Insurrection is the rising of people in arms against their government, or a portion of it, or against one or more of its laws, or against an officer or officers of the government. It may be confined to mere armed resistance, or it may have greater ends in view.

150. Civil war is war between two or more portions of a country or state, each contending for the mastery of the whole, and each claiming to be the legitimate government. The term is also sometimes applied to war of rebellion, when the rebellious provinces or portions of the State are contiguous to those containing the seat of government.

151. The term *rebellion* is applied to an insurrection of large extent, and is usually a war between the legitimate government of a country and portions or provinces of the same who seek to throw off their allegiance to it, and set up a government of their own.

152. When humanity induces the adoption of the rules of regular war toward rebels, whether the adoption is partial or entire, it does in no way whatever imply a partial or complete acknowledgment of their government, if they have set up one, or of them, as an independent or sovereign power. Neutrals have no right to make the adoption of the rules of war by the assailed government toward rebels the ground of their own acknowledgment of the revolted people as an independent power.

153. Treating captured rebels as prisoners of war, exchanging them, concluding of cartels, capitulations, or other warlike agreements with them; addressing officers of a rebel army by the rank they may have in the same; accepting flags of truce; or, on the other hand, proclaiming martial law in their territory, or levying war-taxes or forced loans, or doing any other act sanctioned or demanded by the law and usages of public war between sovereign belligerents, neither proves nor establishes an acknowledgment of the

rebellious people, or of the government which they may have erected, as a public or sovereign power. Nor does the adoption of the rules of war toward rebels imply an engagement with them extending beyond the limits of these rules. It is victory in the field that ends the strife, and settles the future relations between the contending parties.

154. Treating, in the field, the rebellious enemy according to the law and usages of war, has never prevented the legitimate government from trying the leaders of the rebellion or chief rebels for high treason, and from treating them accordingly, unless they are included in a general amnesty.

155. All enemies in regular war are divided into two general classes; that is to say, into combatants and non combatants, or unarmed citizens of the hostile government.

The military commander of the legitimate government, in a war of rebellion, distinguishes between the loyal citizen in the revolted portion of the country and the disloyal citizen. The disloyal citizens may further be classified into those citizens known to sympathize with the rebellion, without positively aiding it, and those who, without taking up arms, give positive aid and comfort to the rebellious enemy, without being bodily forced thereto.

156. Common justice and plain expediency require that the military commander protect the manifestly loyal citizens, in revolted territories, against the hardships of the war, as much as the common misfortune of all war admits.

The commander will throw the burden of the war, as much as lies within his power, on the disloyal citizens of the revolted portion or province, subjecting them to a stricter police than the non-combatant enemies have to suffer in regular war; and if he deems it appropriate, or if his government demands of him, that every citizen shall, by an oath of allegiance, or by some other manifest act, declare his fidelity to the legitimate government, he may expel, transfer, imprison, or fine the revolted citizens who refuse to pledge themselves anew as citizens obedient to the law, and loyal to the government.

Whether it is expedient to do so, and whether reliance can be placed upon such oath, the commander or his government have the right to decide.

157. Armed or unarmed resistance by citizens of the United States against the lawful movements of their troops, is levying war against the United States, and is therefore treason.

THE LAWS OF WAR ON LAND.

CODE RECOMMENDED BY THE INSTITUTE OF INTERNATIONAL LAW, 1880.

GENERAL PRINCIPLES.

1. The state of war does not admit of acts of violence, save between the armed forces of belligerent states. Individuals who form no part of a belligerent armed force should abstain from such acts.

2. The armed force of a state includes:

1st. The army proper, or permanent military establishment, including the militia and reserve forces.

2d. The national guard, landsturm, free corps, and other bodies which fulfill the three following conditions; *i. e.*,

(*a.*) They must be under the direction of responsible chiefs.

(*b.*) They must have a uniform, or distinguishing mark, or badge, recognizable at a distance, and worn by individuals composing such corps.

(*c.*) They must carry arms openly.

3d. The crews of public armed ships, and other vessels used for warlike purposes.

4th. The inhabitants of non-occupied territory, who, at the approach of the enemy, take arms openly and spontaneously to resist an invader, even if they have not had time to organize.

3. Every belligerent armed force must carry on its military operations in accordance with the laws of war.

The only legitimate end that a state may have in war is to weaken the military strength of the enemy.

4. The laws of war do not recognize in belligerents an unlimited liberty as to the means of injuring the enemy. They are to abstain from all needless severity, as well as from all perfidious, unjust, or tyrannical acts.

5. Agreements made between belligerents during the continuance of war, such as armistices, capitulations, and the like, are to be scrupulously observed and respected.

6. No invaded territory is to be regarded as conquered until the end of the war. Until that time the invader exercises, in such territory, only a *de facto* power, essentially provisional in character.

Application of General Principles.

I. Hostilities.

A. Rules of Conduct with Regard to Individuals.

7. It is forbidden to deal harshly with inoffensive populations.
8. It is forbidden,
   (*a*.) To make use of poison, in any form whatever.
   (*b*.) To make treacherous attempts upon the life of an enemy; as, for example, by keeping assassins in pay, or by feigning to surrender.
   (*c*.) To attack an enemy by concealing the distinctive signs of an armed force.
   (*d*.) To use improperly the national flag, uniform, or other distinctive signs of the enemies; the flag of truce, or the distinctive signs of the Geneva Convention.
9. It is forbidden,
   (*a*.) To employ arms, projectiles, or materials of any kind, calculated to cause needless suffering, or to aggravate wounds—notably projectiles of less weight than four hundred grammes (fourteen ounces avoirdupois), which are explosive, or are charged with fulminating or explosive substances.
   (*b*.) To kill or injure an enemy who has surrendered, or who is disabled; or to declare in advance that quarter will not be given, even by those who do not ask it for themselves.

10. Wounded or sick soldiers shall be collected together and cared for, to whatever nation they may belong.

11. Commanders-in-chief shall have power to deliver, immediately, to the outposts of the enemy, soldiers who have been wounded in an engagement, when circumstances are such as to permit this to be done, and with the consent of both parties. Those who are recognized, after their wounds are healed, as incapable of serving, shall be sent back to their own country. The others may also be sent back, on condition of not again bearing arms during the continuance of the war. Evacuations, together with the persons under whose direction they take place, shall be protected by an absolute neutrality.

12. Persons employed in hospitals and ambulances, comprising the staff for superintendence, medical service, administration, transport of wounded, as well as chaplains, and the duly accredited agents of relief associations, who are authorized to assist the regular sanitary staff, shall participate in the benefit of neutrality while so em-

ployed, and so long as there remain any wounded to bring in or to succor.

13. The persons designated in the preceding article should, even after occupation by the enemy, continue to attend, according to their needs, the sick and wounded in the hospital, or ambulance, to which they are attached.

14. When they request to withdraw, the commander of the occupying troops shall fix the time of departure, which he shall only be allowed to delay, for a short time, in case of military necessity.

15. Suitable arrangements should be made to assure to neutralized persons, who have fallen into the hands of the enemy, the enjoyment of suitable salaries.

16. An arm-badge (brassard) shall be worn by neutralized individuals, but the delivery thereof shall be regulated by military authority.

17. The commanding generals of the belligerent powers should appeal to the humanity of the inhabitants, and should endeavor to induce them to assist the wounded, by pointing out to them the advantages that will result from so doing. They should regard as inviolable those who respond to this appeal.

18. It is forbidden to rob, or mutilate, the bodies of the dead lying on the field of battle.

19. The bodies of the dead should not be buried until they have been carefully examined, and all articles which may serve to fix their identity, such as names, medals, numbers, pocket-books, etc., shall have been secured. The articles thus collected, from the bodies of the enemy's dead should be transmitted to their army or government.

20. Individuals who form a part of the belligerent armed force of a state, if they fall into the hands of the enemy, are to be treated as prisoners of war, in conformity with articles 61 78 of these instructions. The same rule is observed in the case of messengers who carry official dispatches openly; and towards aeronauts charged with observing the operations of an enemy, or with the maintenance of communications between the various parts of an army, or theatre of military operations.

21. Individuals who accompany an army, but who are not a part of the regular armed force of the state, such as correspondents, traders, sutlers, etc., and who fall into the hands of the enemy, may be detained for such length of time only as is warranted by strict military necessity.

22. Spies, captured in the act, cannot demand to be treated as prisoners of war.

23. An individual may not be regarded as a spy, however, who, belonging to the armed force of either belligerent, penetrates, without disguise, into the zone of military operations of the enemy. Nor does the term apply to aeronauts, or to couriers, or messengers, who carry openly, and without concealment, the official dispatches of the enemy.

24. No person, charged with being a spy, shall be punished for that offence, until the fact of his guilt shall have been established before a competent military tribunal.

25. A spy who succeeds in quitting the territory occupied by an enemy, incurs no penalty for his previous offence, should he at any future time fall into the hands of that enemy.

26. The bearer of a flag of truce, who, with proper authority from one belligerent, presents himself to the other, for the purpose of communicating with him, is entitled to complete inviolability of person.

27. He may be accompanied by a drummer or trumpeter, by a color-bearer, and, if need be, by a guide and interpreter, all of whom shall be entitled to a similar inviolability of person.

28. The commander to whom a flag is sent, is not obliged to receive the flag under all circumstances.

29. The commander who receives a flag has a right to take such precautionary measures as will prevent his cause from being injured by the presence of an enemy within his lines.

30 If the bearer of a flag of truce abuse the trust reposed in him, he may be temporarily detained, and, if it be proven that he has taken advantage of his position to abet a treasonable act, he forfeits his character of inviolability.

B. Rules of Conduct with Regard to Things.

31. It is forbidden,

(a) To pillage, even places taken by assault.

(b.) To destroy public or private property, unless such destruction be commanded by urgent military necessity.

(c) To attack, or bombard, open or undefended towns.

32. The commander of an attacking force, save in cases of open assault, shall, before undertaking a bombardment, make due effort to give notice of his intention to the local authorities.

33 In case of bombardment all needful measures shall be taken to spare, if it be possible to do so, buildings devoted to religion and charity, to the arts and sciences, hospitals, and depots of sick and wounded. This on condition, however, that such places be not made use of, directly or indirectly, for purposes of defence.

34. It is the duty of the besieged to designate such buildings by suitable marks or signs, indicated, in advance, to the besieger.

35. Ambulances and military hospitals are recognized as neutral, and, as such, are to be protected by belligerents, so long as any sick or wounded remain therein.

36. The same rule applies to buildings, or parts of buildings, in which the sick or wounded are gathered together, or cared for.

37. The neutrality of hospitals and ambulances ceases if they are guarded by a military force. This does not preclude the presence of an adequate police force.

38. As the equipment of military hospitals remains subject to the laws of war, persons attached to such hospitals cannot, in withdrawing, carry away any articles but such as are their private property. Under the same circumstances, an ambulance shall, on the contrary, retain its equipment.

39. Under the circumstances foreseen in the above paragraphs the term *ambulance* is applied to field hospitals, and other temporary establishments, which follow the troops on the field of battle to receive the sick and wounded.

40. A distinctive and uniform flag is adopted for ambulances, hospitals, and evacuations It bears a red cross on a white ground. It must, on all occasions, be accompanied by the national flag.

II. Occupied Territory.

A. Definition.

41. Territory is regarded as occupied when, as the consequence of its invasion by the enemy's forces, the state from which is has been taken has ceased, in fact, to exercise there its regular authority, and the invading state, alone, finds itself able to maintain order therein. The limits within which this state of affairs exists determine the extent and duration of the occupation.

B. Rules of Conduct with Respect to Persons.

42. It is the duty of the occupying military authority to inform the inhabitants, at the earliest practicable moment, of the powers that he exercises, as well as to define the limits of the occupied territory.

43. The occupying authority should take all due and needful measures to assure order and public tranquillity.

Printed in Dunstable, United Kingdom

91222347R00338